ABELARD

THE SEPULCHRAL CHAPEL & SARCOPHAGUS,
OF ABELARD & ELOISE.

The tomb of Abelard and Heloise, taken from *Picturesque views of the Principal Monuments in the cemetery of Père La Chaise near Paris*, drawn by John Thomas Serre 1825. By permission of the Syndics of Cambridge University Library.

ABELARD

A MEDIEVAL LIFE

M. T. CLANCHY

BLACKWELL
Oxford UK & Cambridge USA

© 1997, 1999 by M. T. Clanchy

BLACKWELL PUBLISHING
350 Main Street, Malden, MA 02148-5020, USA
9600 Garsington Road, Oxford OX4 2DQ, UK
550 Swanston Street, Carlton, Victoria 3053, Australia

The right of M. T. Clanchy to be identified as the Author of this Work has been asserted in accordance with the UK Copyright, Designs, and Patents Act 1988.

First published 1997
First published in paperback 1999

5 2005

Library of Congress Cataloging-in-Publication Data

Clanchy, M. T.
    Abelard : a medieval life / M. T. Clanchy.
       p. cm.
    Includes bibliographical references and index.
    ISBN 0-631-20502-0 (alk. paper) — ISBN 0-631-21444-5 (pbk: alk. paper)
       1. Abelard, Peter, 1079–1142. 2. Theologians—France—Biography.
    3. Civilization, Medieval—12th century. I. Title.
    BX4705.A2C57   1997
    189´4.—dc21
    [B]   97–33340
                                                                     CIP

ISBN-13: 978-0-631-20502-9 (alk. paper) — ISBN-13: 978-0-631-21444-1 (pbk: alk. paper)

A catalogue record for this title is available from the British Library.

Typeset in 10 on 12 pt Sabon
by Pure Tech India Ltd, Pondicherry
Printed and bound in the United Kingdom
by TJ International, Padstow, Cornwall

The publisher's policy is to use permanent paper from mills that operate a sustainable forestry policy, and which has been manufactured from pulp processed using acid-free and elementary chlorine-free practices. Furthermore, the publisher ensures that the text paper and cover board used have met acceptable environmental accreditation standards.

For further information on Blackwell Publishing, visit our website:
www.blackwellpublishing.com

Contents

PART III   RELIGIO – 'RELIGION'

Scholarium nostrorum petitioni, prout possumus
satisfacientes, introductionem conscripsimus.

Abelard, *Theologia*

Dedicated to my students of the Abelard Special Subject Class
at the University of Glasgow
1970–1985

Preface

As the dedication to my former students declares, this is a teacher's book. It is intended as an introduction to the life and times of Abelard and not as an exhaustive account. His works on logic and theology and his writings for Heloise and her nuns are so rich and complex that there will never be an end to discussion of them. As for the enigmas concerning the documentation of Abelard's life, I am convinced (principally by the arguments of Peter Dronke and David Luscombe) that the letters of Abelard and Heloise are not forgeries. This means that Abelard's auto-biographical letter, the 'history of my calamities', is the most important document for any biographer of him. I refer to it repeatedly and I am conscious that sometimes my book is little more than a commentary on it.

Because this is an introductory book, I have not referred either in the notes or in the Further Reading section to all the scholarship on Abelard of the last two or three decades, let alone of the last century. Usually, I refer only to primary sources. (C. J. Mews provides a full bibliography in his 'Peter Abelard', *Authors of the Middle Ages* ed. P. J. Geary, 1995.) I have depended on the editors, translators and authors of various nationalities and academic disciplines, who have contributed so much to the clarification of Abelard's writings in recent years. The work of David Luscombe and his collaborators at the University of Sheffield in sorting out Abelardian manuscripts has been crucial in this respect. I acknowledge with gratitude the publications (over the last 30 years or so) of the following on Abelard: S. Bagge, R. H. Bautier, J. F. Benton, E. Bertola, D. F. Blackwell, C. N. L. Brooke, C. S. F. Burnett, E. M. Buytaert, N. Cappalleti Truci, J. Châtillon, M. L. Colish, G. Constable, M. dal Pra, M. de Gandillac, L. M. de Rijk, P. de Santis, P. Delhaye, P. Dronke, G. R. Evans, D. K. Frank, L. Georgianna, E. Gössmann, L. Grane, T. Gregory, A. Gurevich, N. M. Häring, E. Hicks, M. Huglo, Y. Iwakuma, K. Jacobi, C. S. Jaeger, Sister Jane Patricia, E. Jeaneau,

J. Jolivet, P. H. Jussila, L. Kolmer, H. C. R. Laurie, J. Leclercq, J. Le Goff, E. Little, D. E. Luscombe, J. Marenbon, R. McKeon, M. M. McLaughlin, T. P. McLaughlin, C. J. Mews, J. Miethke, L. Minio-Paluello, A. J. Minnis, J. Monfrin, P. Morin, J. T. Muckle, B. Newman, P. J. Payer, R. Peppermüller, D. W. Robertson Jr, J. M. A. Rubingh-Bosscher, H. Silvestre, B. Smalley, E. R. Smits, R. W. Southern, B. Stock, J. Szöverffy, R. Thomas, N. Y. Tonnerre, M. M. Tweedale, U. Ulivi, D. van den Eynde, C. Vasoli, J. Verger, E. B. Vitz, P. von Moos, C. Waddell, T. G. Waldman, P. G. Walsh, R. E. Weingart, and P. Zerbi.

In 1992–5 I presented the ideas for a number of the chapters to the Earlier Middle Ages seminar at the Institute of Historical Research in London and received very helpful comments. The chapter on Abelard as a knight was presented at the Strawberry Hill conference in 1994 and is published in its conference form in *Medieval Knighthood V* ed. S. Church and R. Harvey (Boydell Press, 1995). For discussion of 'Heloise's education of Abelard' I am grateful to Rhoda Bucknill and to the seminar at Bochum in 1996 organized by Ludolf Kuchenbuch and Hanna Vollrath. For commenting on particular chapters or sections in typescript, I thank John Baldwin, Marjorie Chibnall, Giles Constable, Lindy Grant, John Marenbon, Burcht Pranger and Susan Reynolds. David d'Avray has most generously read nearly the whole book in typescript and suggested improvements. None of these readers is responsible for my opinionated remarks. I have been greatly encouraged by publishers' editors, particularly John Davey (a collaboration of thirty years), Simon King, Carol O'Brien and Stuart Proffitt. The libraries of the University of London's central campus have made my task incomparably easier: notably the Warburg Institute, the Institute of Historical Research, the Senate House Library and University College Library.

The extract from W. H. Auden is reproduced by permission of Faber and Faber and Random House, Inc. The extract from *Murder in the Cathedral* by T. S. Eliot, copyright 1935 by Harcourt Brace & Co. and renewed 1963 by T. S. Eliot, is reproduced by permission of Harcourt Brace & Co., and Faber & Faber Ltd. The picture of the Harrowing of Hell from the Winchester Psalter is reproduced by permission of the British Library (MS Cotton Nero C. IV, fo. 24). For the purposes of this book, it symbolizes the bodily resurrection and salvation of Abelard and Heloise. The drawing of their tomb by J. T. Serres, *Picturesque Views of the Principal Monuments in the Cemetery of Père-Lachaise near Paris* (1825) is reproduced by permission of the Syndics of Cambridge University Library.

During the ten years the book has taken to complete (instead of the two I envisaged) I have been supported in every way by my wife, Joan, and it is to her that I and the readers of this book owe their greatest debt.

M. T. CLANCHY

Institute of Historical Research
University of London

Reprinting has enabled me to make minor corrections. I am grateful to the following for bringing these to my attention: Brenda Cook, William J. Courtenay, Christopher Holdsworth, Donald Logan and Susan Reynolds. I hope to reconsider larger questions (such as the identity of Abelard's father and Abelard's relationship with his son, Astralabe) in a subsequent edition. I should have made clear that all the translations from Latin are my own. In making them, I have benefited in particular from the translation of the letters of Abelard and Heloise by B. Radice and of the letters of St Bernard by B. S. James.

M. T. CLANCHY
November 1998

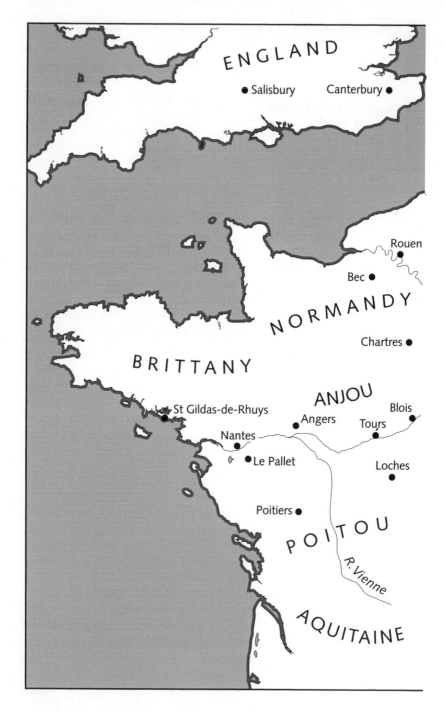

Map 1   France in Abelard's time

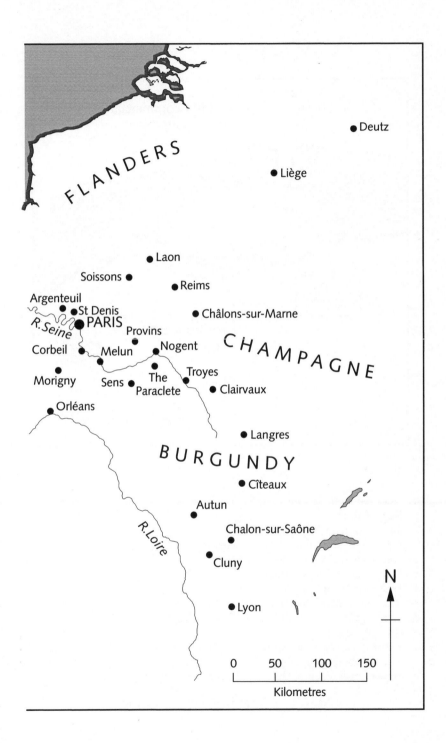

FLANDERS

Deutz

Liège

Laon

Soissons

Reims

Argenteuil

St Denis

R. Seine

PARIS

Châlons-sur-Marne

Provins

CHAMPAGNE

Corbeil

Melun

Nogent

Morigny

Sens

The
Paraclete

Troyes

Clairvaux

Orléans

Langres

BURGUNDY

Cîteaux

Autun

Chalon-sur-Saône

R. Loire

Cluny

Lyon

N

0   50   100   150

Kilometres

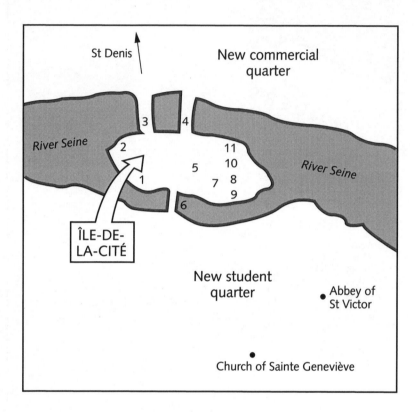

Details of the Île-de-la-Cité

1 Royal palace
2 Tower (Donjon) of Louis VI (1108–37)
3 New Grand-pont (bridge) and Châtelet (fortified gate)
4 Old Grand-pont (demolished by ?1116)
5 Synagogue and Jewish quarter
6 Petit-Pont (rebuilt in stone by ?1120)
7 Remains of Merovingian cathedral of St Stephen
8 Carolingian and later cathedral of Notre-Dame
9 Bishop's palace
10 Cloister (cathedral close) of Notre-Dame (location of Abelard's school and Heloise's home in *c.*1117)
11 New great house and chapel of Stephen de Garlande

Map 2   Paris in Abelard's time

I

The Story of Abelard

Peter Abelard, now forgotten, was once the most famous man in the world. Or so Heloise said: 'What king or philosopher could equal your fame? What kingdom or city or village did not long to see you? Who did not rush to set eyes on you when you appeared in public and crane their necks after you? What married woman, what young girl did not desire you in absence and was not on fire in your presence? What queen, what great and powerful lady did not envy me my joys and my bed?'[1] These questions are translated from Heloise's passionate and accomplished Latin. By the time she wrote them, at least ten years after she had first met Abelard when he was a master and she was his student in Paris, no lady any longer envied Heloise her bed. She was by then an abbess and he an abbot. They were separated by a journey of 350 miles, as she was enclosed in the convent of the Paraclete east of Paris while he was abbot of St Gildas-de-Rhuys on the Atlantic coast of Brittany. To a medieval person this was the world's end; here the boundless Ocean Sea began from which no voyager returned. For Abelard himself, St Gildas meant exile from his beloved Paris and the end of everything he had striven for. Brittany was his homeland, but he had not wished to return there. Like Heloise, he dramatized his predicament: 'There, by the waves of the horrifying Ocean where the last point of land afforded me no further flight, I used to go over and over again in my prayers the words of the Psalmist: "To thee have I cried from the ends of the earth when my heart was in anguish!" ... There is nobody now, I think, who does not know of the overwhelming torment which my heart has suffered day and night.'[2] Like Heloise too, Abelard took it for granted that he was so famous that everybody knew of his misfortunes.

The year was 1132 or a little earlier (Abelard does not give precise dates). He was fifty or more and engaged in writing his autobiography, the 'history of my calamities' as he described it. This is one of the great works of literature of the Middle Ages. Whether it is a factual history is a different matter; autobiographers aim at something more complex than simple truths and Abelard was no exception. Autobiography was rare in the Middle Ages and those who engaged in it were mostly monks more concerned with describing the state of their souls than recording mundane facts. Although Abelard wrote as a monk, ostensibly to show others how to avoid the 'calamities' he had suffered, he was unusual in linking his inner life and feelings with actual events and real people. He could do this because his experience had not been that of a monk isolated from the world, but of a secular cleric involved in the politics of France – and of Paris in particular – for the past thirty years.

What gives zest to Abelard's 'history of calamities' is the way he writes as a great hater as much as a great lover. He presents himself as a complete egoist: everything he does is of the utmost importance and interest, in his own opinion, and everyone he meets – including Heloise – exists only in the light of his own brilliance. Events move fast on a big stage in Abelard's account of his 'calamities', as he is relentlessly pursued by the furies he has brought to life and he only just avoids being lynched as a heretic and imprisoned for treason, to say nothing of other escapades. In the period after the writing of his autobiography, his 'calamities' accelerated as the accusations of heresy and disloyalty were renewed, led this time by St Bernard abbot of Clairvaux. Abelard was now up against the most powerful voice in Christendom. St Bernard spoke out against what he saw as corruption and moral decay in high places, castigating princes, prelates and even the pope himself. When St Bernard warned that Abelard was an acolyte of Antichrist, the cardinals in Rome had to heed him and Abelard was condemned as a heretic in 1140.

But Abelard attracted influential and devoted supporters as much as fanatical opponents and he had a way of popping up again even after the most serious setbacks. He was defended from St Bernard by Peter the Venerable, an equally formidable and eloquent abbot. His brand new abbey church of Cluny in Burgundy was bigger than St Peter's in Rome. The abbot of Cluny was called 'the king' by satirists because he was the overlord of hundreds of monasteries extending from Spain to Germany. Evoking the Old Testament prophets (as he often did), St Bernard likened Peter the Venerable's power to that of the priests of Baal.[3] But not even St Bernard could blow down the walls of Cluny. Once Abelard was safe inside, no one could touch him – neither pope, bishop nor king – without Peter the Venerable's permission. Abelard died as a Cluniac monk (probably in 1142) and to show how wrong the accusations of heresy against him had been, Peter the Venerable assured Heloise that he had been truly 'Christ's philosopher'.[4] Between these extremes of vilification and praise, each reader has to decide for himself which abbot understood Abelard better.

Earlier in his life Abelard had found a more dubious defender and counsellor in another monk, Fulk prior of Deuil. He confirms the romantic effect Abelard had on women, as he describes the ladies of Paris sighing for their tragic 'knight'; but Fulk was more interested in the young men who had flocked to Abelard's school from all over Europe. What follows is abbreviated from Fulk's fulsome prose:

> Rome sent you her pupils to teach; she who had once been mistress of all the arts acknowledged your learning to be greater than hers. No distance over land, no mountain ranges, no deep gorges, no difficult road or danger from robbers, prevented the students from rushing to you. The tempestuous sea did not deter the crowd of young men from England. Once they had heard your name, they came streaming towards you, contemptuous of every danger: Bretons, Angevins, Poitevins, Gascons, Iberians. Normandy and Flanders, the German and the Slav enthused about your genius, to say nothing of the inhabitants of Paris itself and those of the nearest and remotest parts of France who thirsted to be taught by you.[5]

Fulk's style is inflated though his facts are not. Future cardinals came from the papal curia in Rome, and Arnold of Brescia and other clerics made their way from elsewhere in Italy. John of Salisbury was the most distinguished student from England, as Otto of Freising was from Germany. These are only the famous names; most have disappeared without trace or survive in manuscripts which are now anonymous. Books of Abelard's were brought back by his students to the libraries of the new cathedral at Durham, on the northernmost frontier of England, and to Prüfening south of the Danube near Regensburg.[6] These places are nearly 500 miles from Paris, though it was not so much the distance which presented difficulties (Prüfening was only a month's walk from Paris for a fit young man) as the terrain and the human dangers of robbery and murder. Understandably enough, Abelard wrote of this triumphant time: 'I thought myself then to be the only philosopher in the world.'[7]

Otto of Freising thought Abelard so important that he included an account of his career in the introductory book of his history of Frederick Barbarossa, the great German Emperor, although Abelard had had nothing to do with the Empire other than teaching German and Italian students. Following the practice of the best medieval chroniclers and Roman historians, Otto sketched in Abelard's character. He had been 'quite stupid' at anything which was not academic, in Otto's opinion, and he was 'so arrogant and confident of his own genius that he could scarcely descend from the heights of his exalted mind to listen to his masters'.[8] The greatest of these were Anselm of Laon and William of Champeaux, both 'very serious men' whom Abelard could not stand because he enjoyed making jokes. This brings Otto's narrative to the triumphant time when Abelard became the master at the cathedral school of Notre-Dame in Paris (probably in 1114 when he was thirty-five). But there then occurred 'a certain well enough known event when he was not well treated'.[9] By this innuendo Otto referred to the notorious occasion when Abelard had been ambushed within the precinct of Notre-Dame and castrated.

The explanation for this went back a year or more, when Abelard had accepted the hospitality of Fulbert, who was a canon of Notre-Dame like himself and the uncle and guardian of Heloise. Abelard took up residence in Fulbert's house, very close to his school, in exchange for giving Heloise personal tuition. *Quid plura?*, Abelard asks, 'Need I say more?'[10] He abducted Heloise and she gave birth to a son at Abelard's home in Brittany.[11] At Fulbert's insistence, Abelard brought Heloise back to Paris and married her. But Fulbert and his family soon came to believe that he had repudiated the marriage, as Heloise insistently denied that it had taken place and Abelard had then removed her again, this time to the convent where she had been brought up as a girl. To put a wife into a convent was tantamount to divorcing her. Abelard admitted that he had had a religious habit made for Heloise, apart from the veil which signified final vows, and that he had vested her in it himself.[12] From her family's point of view, he had first robbed them of Heloise's virginity in Fulbert's own house and then he had had the effrontery to make her a nun, as if she were still a virgin and not his responsibility. Punishment in personal disputes was the duty of the family. Vengeance and counter-vengeance, the bloodfeud, was the rule and Fulbert persuaded his kinsmen to exact the appropriate penalty and castrate Abelard.

Two of the men responsible were caught and a further penalty was exacted from them: they were blinded as well as being castrated.[13] This put Abelard in mortal danger, as his family in Brittany were incapable of defending him from an escalation of the feud. Nor could he rely on the Chapter of the cathedral of Notre-Dame, as Fulbert was one of its members. So Abelard was 'compelled by confusion and shame, rather than religious devotion, to take cover in a monastery' and he insisted on Heloise taking the veil at the same time.[14] As on other occasions, however, Abelard landed on his feet, as the monastery which took him in was the abbey of St Denis, the mother house of the French kingdom. Later on, he preached a sermon on how monks were spiritual eunuchs; a monastery was therefore an appropriate sanctuary for a castrated fugitive like himself.[15] But a convent was no such haven for Heloise, who had been forced to abandon first her son and then her husband. She insisted to Abelard that she remained absolutely and unconditionally in love with him, spiritually and physically. She had no love left for God. She only became a nun because he had ordered her to do so. 'I would not have had the least hesitation', she wrote, 'in following you to Hell, if that was your command; indeed I would have gone in front.'[16]

Otto of Freising probably knew nothing of Heloise's deeper feelings, as the letters of Abelard and Heloise were not published until the 1270s when Jean de Meun, the author of the Romance of the Rose, translated them into French. Probably Otto's only source of information on the subject was Abelard's love songs (now lost), which were still being sung in the early 1130s when Otto was a student in France.[17] Taking a male point of view, he was mainly interested in how Abelard's castration affected his career. In this light, Otto welcomed it because it had made Abelard into a serious person. At St Denis he 'devoted himself day and night to reading and thinking; from being clever, he became even cleverer, and from being learned he grew doubly learned'.[18] In other words, becoming a monk made Abelard turn his formidable energies to religion and within three years of joining the abbey of St Denis he had produced one of the most original books of his time. He described it as 'a treatise on theology'.[19] Abelard was the first modern 'theologian', in the sense that he was the first teacher to promote the word 'theology' and to use it to mean the reconciliation of human reason with Christian revelation. 'Theology' became Abelard's new mission and his passion. As a young man he had won fame as a master of logic, explaining Aristotle and the structure of language; now, as a monk and a 'religious', he would explain the logic of God and the structure of the Trinity.

Abelard was convinced that Christianity was the most reasonable of all religions and that its truths must be demonstrable by reasoning. Christ was the logos, the epitome of logic. Once Christianity had been proved by the theorems of logic, everyone would accept it, just as they accepted that $2 + 2 = 4$. As 'Christ's philosopher', Abelard was to be the saviour of mankind – once he had found the answers to all the questions. His programme was not novel, although he gave the impression that it was. St Anselm had proceeded in a similar way in the generation before Abelard's with his ontological proof of the existence of God. Because Abelard was 'the only philosopher in the world' and logic had been his profession for the last twenty-five years, he believed that he could easily do better than St Anselm. His admirers shared his confidence. For Peter the Venerable he was 'our Aristotle'.[20] Praise as unstinted was lavished on 'that marvellous work of theology'. But the speaker in this instance was Abelard himself, in the literary persona he had created of a classical Philosopher who debates with a Christian and a Jew about the truth of their beliefs. The Philosopher asks Abelard to judge between the world's religions because 'that marvellous work' is 'the acme of your genius'.[21]

ST BERNARD

Abelard had resorted to puffing his own work probably because it had received such a buffeting at his trial at Soissons in 1121. Again, at the time of his trial at Sens in 1140, St Bernard had taken the name *Theologia*, which Abelard was so proud to have contributed to scientific discourse, and ridiculed it: it was 'stupid-ology', not 'the-ology'.[22] As well as being abusive, St Bernard homed in on Abelard's vanity. 'Tell us, tell us, whatever it is that has been revealed to you and to no one else....[23] I listen to the Prophets and the Apostles; I obey the Gospel, but not the Gospel according to Peter Abelard. Are you writing a new Gospel for us? The Church has no place for a fifth Evangelist.'[24] Bernard described Abelard as 'altogether ambiguous'.[25] How could Abelard have produced such passionate and yet contradictory reactions in the people he met? There is no record of anyone being indifferent to him.

One explanation is that contradiction was Abelard's profession as a logician. He lived for and delighted in contradiction and argument. Medieval logic proceeded through dialectic. Conflicting statements were put alongside each other and a series of logical tests were applied to them: distinguishing between affirmation and negation, genus and species, property and accident, and so on. Contrary to simplistic views of the Middle Ages, the scholastic philosophers and theologians were not naive and uncritical believers in religious faith. Scholastics like Abelard aimed to question everything – and anything – in order to test and demonstrate its validity. They were confident that God had created an ordered and rational universe and that He had made mankind in His own image, as was stated in the Book of Genesis. This meant that the most brilliant individuals of the species mankind, like Aristotle and Abelard, might comprehend the universe by asking questions about it in an orderly way. In the book he called *Sic et Non* ('Yes and No') Abelard collected hundreds of apparently contradictory statements from the Church Fathers for students to sort out. He saw no scandal nor any overwhelming difficulty in the existence of these contradictions, for 'by doubting we come to inquiry and by inquiry we perceive the truth'.[26] Scientific research was as simple as that.

It was in their optimistic confidence in human reason, and not in their rejection of it, that scholastics like Abelard were simplistic. He was no more nor less naive than all the other intellectuals down the centuries who have championed the primacy of reason and believed in progress. In this respect, he was right to claim that he was not an innovator, but a continuator of Christian thought in the mainstream Graeco-Roman tradition. His most distinguished predecessors were those mediators between the ancient and the medieval worlds, St Augustine (who died in 430 AD) and Boethius (who died in 524). These are the authors whom Abelard quotes most frequently and with whose writings he was most familiar. He could build on them with confidence, as they stood as pillars of authority in the Roman Church and in Latin culture throughout the Middle Ages. Nevertheless, as Abelard's title *Sic et Non* made clear, the Church Fathers including Augustine were so rich and profound because they said such different things 'and they even appear to contradict themselves'.[27]

St Bernard's attack on Abelard, which culminated in the council of Sens in 1140, appealed with equal conviction to St Augustine and the Church Fathers. It was absurd, St Bernard argued, to believe that mere 'human ingenuity' could solve everything.[28] 'What is more contrary to reason than to try by reason to transcend reason? And what is more contrary to faith than to refuse to believe anything that reason cannot reach?'[29] In the Old Testament, St Bernard reminded Abelard's opponents, Moses had approached the dark cloud surrounding God's presence all alone, not with a crowd of students.[30] It was indeed true that Abelard had explicitly proposed in *Sic et Non* to provoke students to the maximum effort in seeking out the truth by sharpening their wits on the contradictions in the Church Fathers which he had collected.[31] *Sic et Non* used the most sacred texts and mysteries of the Christian religion as exercises in comprehension. Abelard was exposing mysteries which had been closed and sealed, St Bernard declared. 'The faith of the simple is being ridiculed, God's secrets are being torn out by the guts, questions about the highest things are being recklessly aired.'[32] St Bernard's language, 'torn out by the guts' (*eviscerantur*), could be as strong and explicitly crude as the carvings of monsters and devils on the Romanesque churches built in his time.

Abelard was asking too many questions, St Bernard argued. He was insulting the Church Fathers, who had judged that difficult problems 'are much better quietly buried than solved'.[33] Although St Bernard exaggerated, he was right about the methods of scholasticism. Inevitably, divinity was treated in the schools as an abstract idea for analysis and not as the living presence of God. When St Bernard talked about

sacred mysteries which had been closed and sealed, he was evoking a
sense of the divine which was best expressed not in the clarity of the
schoolmen's logic, but in the half-lit interiors of the great Romanesque
and Gothic churches and in their massive jewel-encrusted liturgical
books, whose illuminated pages were opened only on the altar for the
priests to see. The 'faith of the simple' was preserved as a mystery by
preventing lay people getting too close to the altars or seeing the miraculous shrines of the saints other than in the flickering light of candles.
Even when sunlight was let into churches through stained glass windows, a technique developed on a large scale only in Abelard's lifetime,
the new light did not make everything clear. It was even more ethereal
than candles, as it dimmed and brightened with the seasons and the time
of day, as if God Himself was ringing the changes. This awesome and yet
intimate effect is best experienced today at Chartres cathedral or in the
Sainte Chapelle in Paris, though both these buildings date from after
Aberlard's lifetime.

The feeling of awe and otherness which strikes anyone entering a
great medieval church, particularly if it retains its glass and the organ
is playing or the choir chanting, is something which academic theologians could not replicate. Neither did they wish to. The medieval schoolmen were scientists, who were determined not to be overawed by God
or mystified by anything in His creation. They intended to study divinity
by dissecting it, or tearing it apart by the guts if St Bernard was right.
According to him, Abelard's book *Theologia* depersonalized God's Trinity and this made it a deadly threat to every Christian soul. It must
therefore be destroyed and its perpetrator silenced for ever as a heretic
and a blasphemer. In 1140 the *Theologia* was ceremonially burned
in Rome and 'Peter Abelard, perverse fabricator of dogma and impugner
of the Catholic faith', was sentenced by Pope Innocent II to imprisonment.[34]

Abelard had replied to St Bernard with dignity and reasonableness
that the accusations against him stemmed from malice or ignorance; St
Bernard was misquoting him.[35] His philosophy was certainly more
complex and varied than Bernard had allowed for. He was indeed
mistaken – or malicious – to portray Abelard as a crude rationalist
with no feelings or moral sense. Abelard had addressed problems of
right and wrong at length, not in *Theologia* where they were out of
place, but in his treatise on self-knowledge which he described as *Ethica*
('Ethics'), and in the various exhortatory and didactic works which he
wrote for Heloise and her nuns. Although Abelard's love songs for
Heloise have been lost, many of his hymns survive and these show
that he had not depersonalized God nor ignored the Bible. On the con-

trary, he was at the forefront of the movement in the twelfth century to bring God closer to people by concentrating on the suffering humanity of Christ. *Nostra sunt, Domine* – 'They are ours, O Lord!', Abelard wrote, *nostra sunt crimina* – 'the crimes are ours. Why were You made to suffer tortures for our crimes? Now make our hearts suffer for all of those things, so that our compassion may be worthy of Your forgiveness'.[36] This is as personal and passionate an appeal as John Donne's

> Batter my heart, three person'd God; for, you
> As yet but knocke, breathe, shine, and seeke to mend.[37]

St Bernard and Abelard had many ideas – and ideals – in common. Both were monks, both were reformers, both were extraordinarily clever with words, and both expressed a passionate commitment to Christ crucified. The vehemence of St Bernard's attack on Abelard suggests that he was confronting something like his *alter ego*: he too could have been a great master, fascinating to women and idolized by young men. His attack was so personal – and therefore so effective – because he had convinced himself that Abelard was saying that there was no Redemption; if this were true, his own sacrifice in joining the Cistercian order more than twenty-five years before was worthless. Like a husband and wife who suffer a painful and public divorce, St Bernard and Abelard turned on each other rather unexpectedly and possibly against their better judgement. They were swept along by their supporters and their own rhetoric. Each of them summoned their partisans to the debate between them which was to be held at the council of Sens in 1140.[38] This was not to be a quiet or exclusively clerical meeting but a big show, like a tournament, held in the presence of King Louis VII, Thibaud the count palatine, and numerous other nobility and lay people.[39] In the event Abelard refused, or was unable, to answer St Bernard when he stood before him face to face in the cathedral at Sens. Abelard appealed to Rome and he was never seen in public again; this is when he was protected from the vengeance of St Bernard by Peter the Venerable at Cluny.

HELOISE

Heloise, who was ten or twenty years younger than Abelard, lived until 1163 or 1164, though she insisted that she had died in her heart forty or fifty years earlier: on that fatal day following Abelard's castration, when he had ordered her to become a nun and had personally witnessed her making her final vows sobbing at the altar. 'At the moment of her profession she offered herself to death so that Abelard might live.' Sir Richard Southern (whose words these are) adds: 'Abelard killed Heloise and she willingly made the sacrifice of her life.'[40] He killed her in the sense that he terminated their life together; his castration by itself did not necessarily invalidate their marriage, nor did it prevent them from living together in a spiritual marriage. As Heloise had been so unwilling to enter the religious life, it seems surprising that she won such a golden reputation as a nun, being admired by Peter the Venerable and also by the numerous clerics and lay people who made donations to her convent of the Paraclete. The answer may be that she could play the part in public of the perfect nun precisely because her heart was dead; she was dead to the world, as every religious person should be. Abelard, on the other hand, who retained all his worldly ambitions despite becoming a monk, had a disastrously unstable monastic career, quarrelling with one monastery after another until he returned in the 1130s to his former life as a master in the Paris schools.

In the private correspondence of Abelard and Heloise, as distinct from their public lives in France in the 1130s, their roles as bad monk and good nun are reversed. He repeatedly presents himself as a wise monk, while she insists that her life in the convent is a sham because in her heart she is still his irreligious and physical lover: 'People who call me chaste do not know what a hypocrite I am.'[41] In his self-appointed role as her spiritual counsellor, Abelard distanced himself from her. He becomes patriarchal and patronizing: 'I beg you, sister, do not vex the Father Who is correcting us in so fatherly fashion, but attend to what is written: "For whom the Lord loveth, He chastiseth".'[42] But it was not as a surrogate brother or father that Heloise most wanted Abelard; she wanted him still as her lover. She could not accept that his castration was a loving God's providential chastisement: 'I charge Him always with the utmost cruelty for that injustice. As I oppose His dispensation, I offend Him more by my indignation than by anything I do in mitigation as penance or satisfaction.'[43] Presumably deliberately, for she was very good at Latin, Heloise chose legalistic terms to describe her case against God: 'I charge Him' (arguo) with an 'injustice' (injuria); 'I oppose' (contraria) Him. Overwhelmed by the cruelty of life, Heloise is one of those people who say: 'If God exists, I have no wish to know Him or to be on His side.' If God is good, He may forgive such an attitude; but it was His goodness which Heloise questioned.

Abelard realized that he had to replace her love for him at the least by love for Christ's suffering humanity, if not for God the all-powerful Father Whom Heloise opposed and charged with injustice. Abelard brought before her eyes the image of the crucifixion: 'Are you not moved to tears and remorse by the only begotten son of God in His innocence being scourged, blindfolded, mocked, buffeted, spat upon, crowned with thorns, and finally hanged between thieves on that shameful gallows of the cross?'[44] Heloise replied that her feelings were not within her control. The only sufferings that moved her were those of her beloved Abelard. Henceforward though, she assured him, she would avoid writing about her own feelings; they could conduct instead an impersonal correspondence as monk and nun, just as he wanted.[45] They could at least be penfriends, showing off their erudition, which is how their affair had begun all those years ago.

To start them off, she asked him to tell her about nuns and she wittily pointed out how unsuitable the Rule of St Benedict was for women. Abelard entered into this task with a will, in the hope perhaps that Heloise would change character later on in the correspondence. Throughout the 1130s he worked very hard to convert her, sending her not only the letters in their famous correspondence, but prayers, hymns, sermons, solutions to difficulties raised by Biblical texts, a remarkable disquisition on the origin of nuns, an even longer treatise to serve as a rule for her convent, and finally the confession of faith that he had refused to make to St Bernard. Whether she responded to all, or any, of this by withdrawing her charges against God is unrecorded.

At the beginning of her first letter to Abelard (the first letter, that is, which still exists) Heloise drew attention to her doubts about what she had become and what either of them stood for. How should she address him, now that he was a monk and she a nun? It was different from the old days when they had written many letters to each other as lovers, and different too from the later time when they had been man and wife. Did he remain her 'Lord', or should she now call him 'Father'? (She was writing this when Abelard was abbot of St Gildas and an ordained priest.) Was he still her husband, or should she now call him 'Brother'? (In subsequent letters she refused to respond to his addressing her as 'Sister'.) Did she remain his faithful 'servant' and lady, or was she now his spiritual 'daughter'? In rehearsing these variations on their status in society, Heloise emphasized how in the Church's dispensation names meant the reverse of what they did in real life, a point which would interest Abelard, as the significance of names was his specialism in philosophy. Priests were called 'Father' and yet the Church refused to recognize their children as legitimate. (Heloise herself was perhaps the daughter of such a 'Father'.) Monks and clergy called each other 'Brother' or 'Sister' and yet they shared no kinship. All this could be seen either as the height of hypocrisy and absurdity, or as a way of bringing God's heavenly dispensation to earth.

For Heloise, putting together these diversities of status was her *Sic et Non*, her way of coming to inquiry by doubting. She concluded them with their own names: 'To Abelard from Heloise'.[46] As they had not adopted new names on entering the religious life, here at last was something secure. And yet even these personal names raise doubts about identity. 'Abelard' was not his baptismal name; that was 'Peter', which Heloise never uses. Roscelin, who was Abelard's first teacher of philosophy, knew him only as 'Peter'; though he told him after he had been castrated that he could not call him 'Peter' any more because it was a masculine name. Like Heloise, but more sardonically, Roscelin questioned Abelard's status in society: 'What name should I give you now, if you are neither a cleric nor a layman nor a monk?'[47] The name 'Abelard' was presumably given him at a later date than Roscelin had known him. What it meant is unclear. (The problem is discussed in chapter 9.) Possibly it was intended to have no meaning, and in that case it was another philosophical reference to Abelard's interest in naming. Some of the troubadours adopted performance or stage names, like Abelard's contemporary 'Marcabru'. Perhaps 'Abelard' was a stage name for use in the lecture room. Heloise may always have called him 'Abelard' because it was as 'Abelard' that she had first encountered him, lecturing to awed students in the precinct of Notre-Dame in Paris which was her home.

As for Heloise, a person who had the confidence to oppose God – and to oppose Abelard as well, without forfeiting his support – who was she? Her mother was called Hersindis, but there is no record of who her father was. Possibly both her parents had died when she was a child. Abelard describes her as Fulbert's 'niece' and there is no suggestion that this was a euphemism for illegitimate daughter.[48] Heloise's childhood had not been spent with Fulbert at Notre-Dame, but at the prestigious convent of Argenteuil (now a suburb of Paris). Her presence at Notre-Dame, in the period which Abelard describes as her 'adolescence', seems to be connected with furthering her education beyond what the nuns of Argenteuil could teach her.[49] Even before Abelard taught her, she was reputed to be the most learned lady in France. Fulbert seems to have delighted in her precocity and to have encouraged her to pursue learning for its own sake. Her knowledge of the classical philosophers would not have made her a more attractive match for a lay husband and clerics were no longer permitted female companions, however learned they might be. There is no example from Heloise's time of a learned laywoman being able to lead an independent life; indeed, her own story suggests that it was impossible. She was more like a cleric than a lady, and yet she apparently had had no wish to be a nun or an abbess. Nor could she have stayed in Fulbert's house indefinitely, as pressure mounted in the 1120s and 1130s to expel women from ecclesiastical precincts.

In their elusive identities, as much as in the conduct of their lives, Abelard and Heloise raise all sorts of questions about themselves and the times in which they lived. Roscelin had chided Abelard with the 'unheard of novelty of your life'.[50] It was wrong for a monk or a Christian to do anything new, as he should conform to the way of life of all the others. But was Abelard really so novel? Or did he simply present familiar ideas in new ways? He certainly exaggerated his originality, both in his 'history of calamities' and in his *Theologia* and *Ethica*. Nor was Heloise necessarily so novel, not even in confessing to Abelard that she opposed God. Monks and nuns were meant to confess their innermost thoughts. In the previous generation Otloh of St Emmeram recorded that he had been tempted to doubt 'whether there was any truth in the Holy Scriptures and whether an almighty God exists'.[51] Although Abelard lectured Heloise on the need for faith, he admitted in his *Ethics* that he did not see why innocent children, who had never learned about Christ, should be condemned to eternal death as the consequence of Original Sin. Yet he was prepared to acknowledge that this was 'not absurd', considering the Psalmist's words: 'Thy judgements are a great deep, O Lord.'[52]

Where Heloise differed from Abelard was in her refusal to acknowledge that the judgements of God were too deep to comprehend. When it came to judging what was right and wrong, she had the blasphemous impertinence – or the blind courage – depending on one's point of view, to charge God with injustice and to persist in opposing Him. Whether she thought that God should be on the side of all victims, or only of her beloved Abelard is not clear. Her attitude has more in common with the poets of the *Carmina Burana* than with monks making their confessions. The Archpoet, who was her contemporary, 'seething inwardly with vehement indignation', declares that 'in bitterness I will speak my mind':

> Estuans intrinsecus ira vehementi,
> In amaritudine loquar mee menti.[53]

This is the beginning of his 'Confession', made famous today in the music of Carl Orff, and it is the reverse of a religious confession. The Archpoet claims to be much greedier for sex than for salvation because, like Heloise, he is 'dead in the soul'. Interestingly, though, neither Heloise nor the Archpoet totally disbelieves in the afterlife and neither of them thinks that they will be damned. Heloise says that she will be satisfied with whatever corner of Heaven God allocates to her, while the Archpoet trusts that when he drops dead in a tavern, the angelic choir will joyfully sing 'God be propitious to this drunkard'.[54] Neither Heloise nor the Archpoet are atheists, as they assume that God is going to give them His personal attention.

It may be objected that this is not comparing like with like. Heloise was a real person confiding her innermost thoughts to her real lover, whereas the 'Archpoet' is a pseudonym for a professional entertainer who wrote his 'Confession' for publication. Heloise wrote facts, the Archpoet fiction. But this dividing line is not so clear cut. Every writer produces fiction to the extent that every piece of writing is contrived. In medieval culture this was certainly so, as no writer could casually take up a pen and set down his thoughts. She (as we are talking of Heloise) had either to incise rudimentary notes with a stylus on to a portable writing-tablet, or she had to go to the scriptorium (the special place for doing writing which monasteries provided) and prepare quill-pens, ink and parchment. Medieval writing techniques produced wonderful end-products; illuminated books are among the greatest works of art in the world, but they could not be casually produced. Most authors had to dictate their work to scribes; they did not undertake to write themselves. Letters produced in these circumstances could not be completely con-fidential or personal. No less a person than St Bernard believed that his most trusted secretary, Nicholas of Clairvaux, had sent out misleading letters in his name. Nuns had more modest facilities than monks and it may be that Heloise wrote her own letters. Even so, she would still have had to go to the scriptorium for the final stage of writing up her draft and sealing and addressing the letter.

For a medieval writer the difficulties of getting the text on to parch-ment were relatively simple compared with the initial problem of con-verting one's thoughts into Latin. This required years of training. Because it was nobody's mother tongue and its rules of style and con-struction had been established more than a thousand years earlier, Latin tended to take over anyone who began to write it. To the rhetoric of the classical authors (Virgil, Cicero, Ovid and so on) had been added the even more powerful models of the Latin Bible and the Latin liturgy, with which every monk and nun was in daily contact through chanting and hearing readings. A writer like Heloise was doubly bound, by classical training and liturgical experience, to think in terms of texts when she composed Latin. Although she might have thoughts of her own, Latin demanded that they be expressed in phrases or whole sentences from classical or sacred authors or in learned references to them.

Latin used the same word, *litterae*, to describe three different sorts of 'letters': there were the simple 'letters' of the ABC, the advanced 'letters' of classical literature, and 'letters' in the sense of correspondence. The 'letters' of Heloise and Abelard are not preserved in the form of individual signed missives. They exist only as fair copies in manuscripts dating from 1280 or so; this is a century and a half after they were composed. So it cannot be proved that any letters ever were actually exchanged between Abelard and Heloise, or that they are the authors of the letters in the fair copies. Someone may have forged them in the thirteenth century, or even in the twelfth. But the modern scholars who have argued that the letters are forgeries have not been able to explain satisfactorily who might have forged them or why they should have done so. Abelard's 'history of calamities' contains numerous points of detail, which a forger would have found very difficult to get right, unless he was a contemporary who knew Abelard personally. A number of works of medieval literature, the *Song of Roland* and the *Poem of the Cid* most notably, exist only in copies made later than their original composition. Twelfth-century letters have usually survived only when they have been copied into registers as precedents or models for future generations. The letters of St Bernard and Peter the Venerable are preserved in this form for example; they do not exist as originals.

Books and documents in manuscript were repeatedly renewed and old or worn out copies were discarded; the originals were not often reverently preserved like the first editions of printed books. The earliest existing manuscript of the letters of Abelard and Heloise belonged to the cathedral Chapter of Notre-Dame, who sold it in 1346 to Roberto de Bardi. He was a friend of the poet Petrarch, who also owned (and annotated) a copy of the letters which still exists. This and other information about the manuscripts suggests that the letters of Abelard and Heloise were published in Paris at the end of the thirteenth century, when a renewed interest was being taken in works of romantic love.[55] What we possess today are the publishers' copies and not the master copy from which they were made. Hazarding a guess, the latter was a register (like the letter registers of St Bernard and Peter the Venerable) which had been compiled by Heloise at the convent of the Paraclete, perhaps with Abelard's full knowledge. A century and a half later some interested outsider saw the literary potential of the letters and brought Heloise's register from the Paraclete to a commercial scriptorium in Paris, where multiple copies were made for publication. Judging from the provenance of the earliest extant copies of the letters of Abelard and Heloise, intellectuals and aesthetes in France and Italy appreciated them in a way the nuns of the Paraclete had never done. They revered Abelard and Heloise as the founders of their convent; they did not necessarily want to know that they had written some of the greatest love letters of all time.

The letters of Abelard and Heloise are typical of twelfth-century letters in existing only in fair copies. It is of course true of any fair copy that we cannot be certain that it reproduces the original in every detail. To that extent medieval letters contain elements of fiction. Furthermore, for those trained like Abelard and Heloise in Latin rhetoric, writing anything down made the author adopt a particular literary stance and speak with an artificial voice. An author was obliged to write 'literature' as well as 'letters'. Every piece of writing had to fit a recognized genre; otherwise it would not be effective or even comprehensible. In his 'history of calamities', for example, Abelard spoke as a person who has suffered misfortune. Did he really think his life had been a series of calamities, or was this merely the voice or persona he adopted for this particular work? He explained in its conclusion that he adopted this tone in order to console a friend and fellow monk, though Abelard does not name him and he may not have been a real person. The 'history of calamities' may have been written in the form of a letter to an anonymous friend because fictitious correspondence was a well-understood convention, as the rhetoric of letter-writing (the *ars dictaminis* or 'art of dictation') was taught along with Latin in the classroom.

Writing allows a person to speak with different voices and even to pretend to be someone else. This is what Heloise was announcing in her first letter, when she rehearsed whether she was Abelard's 'servant', or 'daughter', or 'wife' or 'sister'. All societies stereotype people and expect them to perform fixed roles and, conversely, each individual searches for the role which will win him most esteem. Medieval society sometimes stereotyped men into three orders: clergy who pray, knights who fight and peasants who labour. In art it distinguished each order by its appearance: the clergy by their tonsures and vestments, knights by their armour, and peasants by their poverty and uncouthness. Ideally, everyone played these roles to the full and avoided overlapping. The cleric or the monk, who had dedicated his life to Christ, should be humble and poor, and yet he must not be so poor as to be mistaken for a peasant. The knight must be good and strong, without being scrupulous like a cleric or rough like a peasant. These roles inevitably contained contradictory or subversive elements. Although the cleric should be humble, he had also to be conscious of his superior calling as a man of God. The knight was to be a gentleman and yet his business was killing people. The peasant was to be uncouth and yet he too had been created in the image of God and was superior to any animal.

GENERALIZING ABOUT THE MIDDLE AGES

Our assumptions about the Middle Ages derive from these medieval stereotypes, though they are further distorted and removed from reality by the thousand years that separate us. We tend to think either of pious angels on a Christmas card or of barbaric torturers in some castle dungeon. The stereotyped angels (and the Christmas cards) derive from the Victorian Gothic Revival, while we get the reverse image of the Middle Ages as a time of irredeemable barbarity from the humanists of the Italian Renaissance. Of course, there is some truth in these stereotypes. Barbaric things were done in the Middle Ages, not least the castration and persecution of Abelard. But whether Europe was more barbaric in the twelfth century than in the twentieth is very hard to say, partly because of the difference in scale. The crusaders' atrocities in Jerusalem in 1099 were limited in scope, and perhaps also in intention, compared with Auschwitz. Nevertheless, it may be true that medieval anti-Semitism is the foundation of modern anti-Semitism. Abelard is one of the few medieval churchmen who shows any understanding of what the Jews suffered at the hands of Christians. 'We are confined and oppressed, as if the whole world had conspired against us alone. It's a wonder we are allowed to live', he has a Jew say.[56]

Abelard and Heloise did not know that they were 'medieval' and that they would therefore be classified as peculiar and primitive 900 years later. Medieval people did not think their predecessors to be of no importance, as we do. Abelard and Heloise would have been astonished to be told that they had lived in the Dark Ages, when the Latin classics were no longer understood and the Roman Empire had ceased to exist. They would have found this unrecognizable. Abelard's generation invented the word 'modern' and he thought of himself as modern. But he and his fellow 'moderns' in the schools did not aim to destroy the legacy of their predecessors but to surpass it, just as the Romanesque architects surpassed the ancient Romans in the construction of arches and vaults. The abbey of Cluny in its third and final enlargement, which had been begun in the 1080s when Abelard was a little boy and was complete by the time he became a monk there in 1140, was the largest church in Latin Christendom, longer and taller than St Peter's in Rome (this was the basilica built by the Emperor Constantine, not the present church by Michelangelo). In Abelard's time the Roman Emperor *semper Augustus* ('Augustus as always') was still the most important ruler in the West, even though he was elected in Germany and was often opposed by the Papacy. As for the ancient classics, Abelard and Heloise and their fellow writers were living proof that Latin learning flourished. They did not think, as later humanists did, that the only true Latin had been written in ancient Rome and the best they could do was imitate it, as that could only be the death of Latin and the end of Roman power.

Far more damaging for understanding the Middle Ages than the distortions of Renaissance humanists has been the belief in the inevitable march of progress from century to century, as this means that only recent events are considered important and people who lived a long time ago are bypassed as irrelevant. Abelard and Heloise were better off with nineteenth-century Romanticism, which gave them a Gothic Revival tomb at the cemetery of Père-Lachaise among the heroes of France. This became such an object of devotion for American visitors to Paris that one commented: 'The grave of Abelard and Heloise has been more revered, more widely known, more written and sung about and wept over than any other in Christendom, save only that of the Saviour. Go when you will, you will find somebody snuffling over that tomb.'[57] Today their tomb still stands, but it is mostly deserted. Visitors to Père-Lachaise have so many more recent martyrs to remember: the communards of 1870, Oscar Wilde, the dead of two World Wars.

Despite modern priorities, Abelard's story remains significant because he wrote so brilliantly, though not necessarily truthfully, about his own chequered life; and as a philosopher, a theologian and a poet, he commented on life in general. He articulated all sorts of recurrent human dilemmas: about individual integrity, teaching and learning, the mismatch of love and marriage, the effects of intimidation whether mental or physical, the need for solitude, the difference between public and personal religious devotion. Not least he was a jester who knew, as another of his contemporaries wrote, that

> Fas et nefas ambulant pene passu pari.
> Right and wrong they go about cheek by jowl together.[58]

This is Helen Waddell's idiomatic translation from the *Carmina Burana*. A literal translation underlines the point: 'Right and wrong walk along almost perfectly in step.' In other words, they go so close together that one can look like the other. Abelard had shown how right and wrong walk 'almost perfectly in step' in the hundreds of apparently contradictory statements he collected in *Sic et Non*. His fascination with contradiction exposed him to St Bernard's charge that he was altogether ambiguous: a dangerously split personality. *Homo sibi dissimilis est*, St Bernard hissed, 'he is a man dissimilar even from himself'.[59] Another contemporary said he acted more like a jester (*joculator*) than a professor.[60] He was perceived to be an actor because he played so many roles. As a musician and a poet, Abelard was well qualified to be a *joculator* in the sense of a jongleur or minstrel. As for his being a jester in a wider sense, Otto of Freising said he excelled 'in moving men's minds to jokes'.[61] Like a Shakespearean jester, Abelard was also a moralist who naively told unpalatable truths. It was logic that had made him hateful to the world, he concluded in his final confession of faith to Heloise.[62]

The schoolmen believed that harmony would emerge from the tension of opposites (*Sic et Non*) which they created in their disputations. Abelard and Heloise, or Abelard and St Bernard, dispute as if they were irreconcilable opposites and yet they seem to flourish and gain strength from their discord. Abelard's contemporary, the ecclesiastical lawyer, Gratian, called his encyclopedic collection of contradictory rulings from Church councils a 'Concord of Discordant Canons' (*Concordia Discordantium Canonum*). This title evoked medieval ideas about the fundamental harmony which exists in things and which is made manifest in the structures of music, mathematics and the universe itself. To accord with scholastic ways of thinking and to take account of his enemies' strictures that he was a contradictory personality, this study of Abelard aims to bring harmony out of dissonance by focusing on the discordant and dissimilar elements in his life. Medieval society required consistent presentations of the self, whereas he – whether consciously or unconsciously – performed a diversity of roles, clerical and lay, pagan and Christian, rational and emotional.

THE STRUCTURE OF THIS BOOK

This book discusses Abelard's roles one by one in successive chapters ('Literate', 'Master', 'Logician', and so on) in order to build up a composite portrait of him. The sequence of chapters accords very roughly with the chronology of Abelard's life: from his precocious success in the schools (chapters 3–5), through his affair with Heloise (chapters 8–9), to his controversial career as a monk and theologian (chapters 11–13). Two chapters are devoted to his affair with Heloise because this was the turning point of his life, even though the events it comprised were concentrated in not much more than a single year (1117 or 1118). The concluding chapter (14), entitled 'Himself', centres on the Delphic subtitle he chose for his book on ethics: 'Know Thyself'. Overarching the fourteen chapters are the three parts, with their Latin titles, into which the book is divided: *Scientia* ('knowledge' or 'science'),

Experimentum ('experience' or 'experiment') and *Religio* ('religion' or 'monasticism'). These three parts characterize Abelard's successive approaches to life and they function at the same time as an introduction to medieval culture in the period of the twelfth-century Renaissance. In Part I, Abelard expounds the 'science' which the Middle Ages had inherited from classical antiquity. In his native Loire valley he had begun his road to knowledge as a 'Literate' (chapter 3), that is, as a *literatus* and Latinist; then in Paris he had been acknowledged as a 'Master' (chapter 4) of students. He 'who alone knew whatever was known' was a 'master' also in the sense of *magus*. His wisdom and magic comprehended all the knowledge of the ancient Greeks in philosophy and logic (chapter 5), the queen of the sciences.

Contrasting with this theoretical and scholastic knowledge is *Experimentum* (Part II): learning not from books, but from experiencing life in the raw. Theory and fact, reflection and action, contrast – and often conflict – in Abelard's life, as they do in medieval culture as a whole. In his book on ethics, he had argued that actions in themselves are indifferent; only the intention of the actor makes them right or wrong. Abelard 'experimented' with sex and violence. He compared himself to a knight (chapter 7), conducting feuds and mock battles in the schools, and then suddenly he found himself up against Fulbert and Heloise's other kinsmen in a real feud. In castrating Abelard, they took no account of his good intentions, but only of his action in putting Heloise into a convent. Because the Church put such value on celibacy, Abelard's castration had the peculiar effect of converting him to 'religion' (Part III), in the sense that it made him become a monk. Such was the attraction of monasticism in the twelfth century that the adjective *religiosus* (chapter 10) was synonymous with 'monastic', as if there was no religion outside the cloister. Abelard made repeated efforts to be a good monk (chapter 11), but he never could reconcile the exclusiveness of monasticism with his broad vision of theology (chapter 12), in which good pagans worshipped the true God and acknowledged the Trinity. He was not only a failed 'religious', St Bernard taunted, he was a blasphemer and a heretic (chapter 13).

To write a biography of Abelard giving equal weight to each stage of his life is not possible, as we have too little personal information about him, despite his 'history of calamities' and his massive academic works. We have no certain date for his birth or death, no portraits of him at any stage of his life, and none of his writings are explicitly dated or definitely in his own hand. This lack of what a twentieth-century biographer thinks of as essential basic information is not due to deliberate secrecy on Abelard's part, nor to his writings having been censored because he was a heretic, and neither is it accidental. A lack of chronological and biographical information is a characteristic of medieval culture. It is primarily due to more emphasis being put on divine revelation, the life of God as recorded in Holy Scripture, than on the relatively insignificant lives of individual human beings. Without paper or electronic equipment, making any sort of record necessitated writing on parchment. In one way or another all medieval writing was associated with Scripture because that is what 'writing' (*scriptura*) meant. The majesty of medieval writing, particularly in illuminated manuscripts, inhibited authors and scribes from recording much about their own lives, despite producing huge books.

Abelard tells us at the beginning of his 'history of calamities' where he was born (at Le Pallet near Nantes), but he does not say when. Perhaps he did not know, though this is unlikely, as birthdates were significant for devotion to particular saints' days and they were also essential for astrology. A more likely explanation is that Abelard was reluctant to specify the year of his birth because this meant deciding where his loyalties lay. He could have said for example that he had been born in the thirteenth year of the reign of Hoel, duke of Brittany (1079 AD). But, as Abelard was writing his 'history of calamities' at St Gildas in the 1130s when he was miserable in Brittany, he may not have wished to associate his own birth with the duke. An alternative was to say that he had been born in the nineteenth year of the reign of King Philip I of France. But Abelard may have felt that this was presumptuous, as he was not a Frenchman, despite his love of Paris and his ambition to return there. Even more presumptuous would have been to specify the year *Anno Domini* (1079 or whatever it was), as that would have suggested that Abelard's birth had a special place in God's providential plan of Christian salvation. Even he may not have been egoistical enough to claim that. The easiest solution was to give no dates for anything and this is what Abelard does.

Abelard's writings fill a whole volume (no. 178) of Migne's *Patrologiae: Series Latina* comprising about 800,000 words. His *Theologia* in its various versions (Abelard kept revising it over the decades 1120–40) contains more than 200,000 words; *Sic et Non* has 130,000, his sermons 115,000, the commentary on St Paul's Epistle to the Romans 90,000; for Heloise he wrote another 70,000 words. Migne's volume does not include Abelard's writings on logic: one big book, *Dialectica*, survives (though it is not complete) in addition to other commentaries and lectures. It is certain that some works have been lost, like the commentary on the Prophet Ezechiel which Abelard says he wrote in Paris and the love songs which he reminded Heloise were still being sung in the

1130s. As his surviving writings amount to about 1 million words, his total output must have considerably exceeded that.

Once he started writing for publication and posterity, which may not have been until after he became a monk in 1117 or 1118, Abelard must have spent much of his working life in the scriptorium pen in hand, or dictating to a monastic or a hired scribe. Cold, bad light and failing eyesight would have been greater obstacles to his career as a writer than castration. Even more painful (Abelard said) was adverse criticism, which took the extreme form of putting him on trial and burning his books. Writers turn their lives upside down; they make themselves and those they love or hate into a public spectacle. In St Bernard's opinion Abelard turned God into a public spectacle as well. It is because Abelard was such a successful writer that he can still reach us today. His books have survived the vitriol of St Bernard and the bonfires ordered by the pope and the bishops of France, as well as the wear and tear of nine centuries. What Auden wrote in memory of Yeats is an appropriate coda, as it takes one great writer to understand another:

> Time that is intolerant
> Of the brave and innocent,
> And indifferent in a week
> To a beautiful physique,
>
> Worships language and forgives
> Everyone by whom it lives.[63]

Part I

Scientia – 'Knowledge'

The Years 1079–1117

Chronological Table 1079–1117

Gregory VII, pope, 1073–85
Urban II, pope, 1088–99
St Anselm, abbot of Bec, 1078–92, archbishop of Canterbury, 1093–1109
Ivo, bishop of Chartres, 1090–1115
Philip I, king of France, 1060–1108
Louis VI, king of France, 1108–37
William the Conqueror, duke of Normandy 1035–87, king of England 1066–87
Hoel count of Nantes 1050–84, duke of Brittany 1066–84

c.1079	Birth of Abelard at Le Pallet, near Nantes.
1092	Roscelin's trial for heresy at Soissons.
c.1093–*c*.1099	Abelard taught by Roscelin at Loches.
1098	St Anselm of Canterbury dedicates his refutation of Roscelin to Pope Urban II.
c.1100	Abelard taught by William of Champeaux in Paris.
c.1102–*c*.1105	Abelard becomes master at Melun and then at Corbeil.
c.1105–*c*.1108	Abelard returns home 'exhausted from studying'.
1108	Stephen de Garlande reappointed chancellor by Louis VI. Abelard returns to Paris.
c.1108	Abelard challenges William of Champeaux on the question of universals.
c.1112	Abelard challenged in his own school at Mont Sainte Geneviève by St Goswin.
c.1112	Abelard again returns home, when his parents retire into monasteries.
1113	Abelard goes to Laon to be taught divinity by Anselm of Laon.
1113	William of Champeaux becomes bishop of Châlons-sur-Marne.
c.1114	Abelard returns to Paris as master of the cathedral school of Notre-Dame.
c.1117	Rupert of Deutz challenges Anselm of Laon and William of Champeaux.

2

Scientia – 'Knowledge'

Abelard was reputed by his contemporaries to be a scientist: the greatest in the world in the opinion of his admirers, the maddest and most dangerous in the opinion of St Bernard. There was nothing he did not intend to know about, Bernard warned; he pushed his head into the heavens to scrutinize God's secrets.[1] St Paul had taught that 'knowledge puffeth up'. Abelard was a giant of Philistine arrogance, the Goliath of the schools, whom Bernard (like David in the Book of Kings) prayed he could destroy with his single little stone of righteousness.[2] All generations have been fascinated by the idea of an omniscient genius, a Newton or an Einstein, whose intellect comprehends the secrets of the universe. Through the superhuman range of his knowledge and insight, the great scientist commands the powers of heaven and earth. In ascribing this range of abilities to Abelard, St Bernard was wanting his audience to see him as an evil magician, a Dr Faustus who had made a pact with the devil in order to learn forbidden things. 'Let him who has scanned the heavens go down into the depths of Hell,' Bernard prayed, 'and let the works of darkness that he has dared to bring forth be clearly revealed in the light of day.'[3]

The most famous medieval magician was Merlin, whom Geoffrey of Monmouth wrote about as if he were a real historical person. Merlin's prophecies were treated with respect even by such an intellectual and orthodox churchman as John of Salisbury. He dated his arrival in Paris, when he came to study with Abelard, from the death in 1135 of Henry I of England, whom he identified with the 'Lion of Justice' prophesied by Merlin.[4] Merlin's prophecies looked impressive in Geoffrey of Monmouth's version of them, as he had apparently predicted the drowning of Henry I's heir in the White Ship ('the Lion's cubs shall be transformed into salt-water fishes') and the civil war of Stephen's reign ('the island will lie sodden with the tears of the night').[5] Merlin was more specific about the drowning than the civil war because Geoffrey was writing *after* the White Ship disaster in 1120, but before the accession of Stephen in 1135. It was difficult in the twelfth century, even for discriminating scholars like Abelard and John of Salisbury, to check their information, as no two books in manuscript were exactly the same and they were hard to get hold of in the first place. This made any acquisition of knowledge look impressive, even if it were of very doubtful veracity like Geoffrey of Monmouth's history of the kings of Britain. The scarcity of books gave knowledge a rarity value and this inflated the reputation of every village wise woman as well as that of Merlin, the mythical magician, and of Master Abelard, who was reputed the most learned philosopher since Aristotle.

SCIENCE AND MAGIC

The borderline between science and magic – and reality and myth – was very fluid because each dealt in marvels and ancient esoteric knowledge. Each was concerned with invisible forces at work in the world, which experts alone could divine or control. The border between science and religion was equally fluid for much the same reasons, as religion addressed the supernatural and promised life beyond death. The distinction between magic and religion depended on the observer's point of view. 'Magic' was the pejorative term used by religious teachers to describe occult practices, or appeals to the supernatural, which alarmed them or seemed alien to them. Pagans performed 'magic' through charms, incantations and other allegedly demonic practices, whereas Christians practised true religion. Prohibited 'magic' contrasted with prescribed 'sacraments' in Christian theological thinking. The rituals of Baptism and the celebration of the Eucharist (Holy Mass) might look like magic to an unbeliever, when he first confronted a missionary. To the Christian priests themselves, on the other hand, the Church's sacraments and liturgical practices were entirely familiar, orthodox and devoid of superstition. They were not the work of the devil, as witchcraft was, but invocations to the true God to enlist His aid against the demons, who were believed to threaten mankind on every side.

The ecclesiastical authorities of Abelard's time, primarily meaning bishops assembled in their provincial councils and the pope and his cardinals in Rome, were not opposed to knowledge as such, nor had they ever been. On the contrary, they wanted Christians to know as much as they could about their religion. The difference between orthodoxy and heresy depended on the sort of knowledge a Christian aspired to. It should not be the sort that 'puffeth up'; it should not be merely worldly, nor should it make the knower conceited. Heresy was a moral failing, rather than an intellectual one. This is why St Bernard used such irate language against Abelard; his pride in reasoning and logic was, according to Bernard, a usurpation of divine authority and tantamount to blasphemy. Christian 'science' (*scientia*) was enshrined in the Bible and the teachings of the Church Fathers; interpreting these writings was the primary function — and duty — of those who sought knowledge. In fact, though, contrary to Bernard's allegations, Abelard made a massive contribution to Christian knowledge in his *Sic et Non* by providing scholars with texts of the Church Fathers, which were assembled in such a way that they could be systematically analysed point by point to build up an encyclopedic summation (*summa*) of doctrine.

Reliance on the Bible and the Fathers, as the principal sources of knowledge on every conceivable subject, had consequences which give medieval scholasticism its distinctive character. The obscurest prophets of the Old Testament, like Ezechiel (Abelard's first theological work in *c.*1115 was a commentary on Ezechiel), were treated as though every word in them was pregnant with meaning, while the writings of the great Graeco-Roman philosophers were assigned a secondary place in the hierarchy of knowledge. It is true that Plato and Aristotle, and Cicero and Seneca, were generally regarded as giants of wisdom throughout the Middle Ages, but ambivalence about them was unavoidable because they had been pagans. In theory, the most ignorant Christian convert knew more of value than they ever had. Monks secluded in their cloisters understood more than masters debating in the schools, in St Bernard's opinion. In his prosecution of Abelard, Bernard was spurred on by William of St Thierry and other Cistercian religious revivalists to restate in uncompromising terms fundamental Christian misgivings about the moral value of secular learning. Bernard conceded that Abelard might indeed be the cleverest and most learned man in the world, but where had his knowledge come from and where did it lead — to Heaven or Hell?

At the council of Sens in 1140 Bernard accused Abelard of dabbling in the murky waters linking magic, religion and science (though he did not express himself in these modern analytical terms). Abelard had taught (Bernard claimed) that the bread and wine of the Eucharist hang in the air, that demons make suggestions to us through contact with stones or plants, and that the world is an animal and the Holy Spirit is its soul (the concept of the World Soul which derived from Plato).[6] In Bernard's opinion, these accusations proved Abelard was a pagan, though he did not (he said) consider such rubbish worthy of detailed refutation, by comparison with Abelard's credal errors about the Trinity and the

Redemption. Abelard had certainly taught that stones and plants have special properties which linked them with demonic forces, as he says this in his book on ethics. The subject had arisen when he was discussing the psychological question of how bad thoughts and temptations enter our minds. He pointed out, correctly from both an ancient and a modern scientific viewpoint, that some plants and stones contain natural substances ('forces' he calls them) which have 'the capacity to excite or calm our minds'.[7] Speaking as if he were an experimental botanist or pharmacist, Abelard explained that 'those, who diligently know how, can easily do these things'. Where he parts company with modern science is in adding that the forces of nature are harnessed by demons, who incite us through them to sexual desire and 'the other passions of the mind'. Demons do this, Abelard explains, because they are geniuses or 'scientists' (*scientes*), as Isidore had explained in his authoritative *Etymologies*.[8]

This discussion by Abelard of psychological medicine and drug therapy is not as absurd as it looks at first sight. He was trying to reconcile Graeco-Roman natural science with the Christian belief in the existence of demons. Any great church in Abelard's time depicted titanic struggles between demons and angels for the naked and vulnerable souls of mankind. Human possession by demons was authenticated by Christ himself in the New Testament and it was also a favourite subject of Romanesque art. It was entirely orthodox to argue that bad thoughts come into our minds through the suggestions of demons, as the devil was identified with the 'subtle serpent' in the Book of Genesis who had first tempted Adam and Eve. Abelard's accusers may well have objected, however, to his rationalizing and materializing the process of temptation by saying that demons used their knowledge of science to alter our mental state with drugs made from stones or plants. The Church did not deny that miraculous transformations occurred daily in the sacraments, but these should be performed only by those whom it had ordained: that is, by priests in the celebration of the Eucharist and by the minor orders of clergy in the case of exorcisms and other cures of the sick at the shrines of saints.

Whatever reputation Abelard had as a magician probably owed much to his being twice condemned for heresy and to his books being ritually burned 'in a celebrated bonfire' in St Peter's, Rome (or so Geoffrey of Auxerre, St Bernard's secretary, triumphantly reported). Those works that escaped burning 'were long preserved in secret by his disciples', one obituary alleges.[9] Abelard's books had occult qualities. 'It is said', William of St Thierry had told St Bernard, 'that they hate the light and cannot be found even when searched for'.[10] Some of Abelard's notoriety may also have been due to his Breton connections. Like Merlin, he was reputed to come from the Celtic lands at the very edge of the world: from 'the last point of land by the horrifying waves of the Ocean', as Abelard described his situation when abbot of St Gildas.[11] But he was ambivalent about his Breton heritage. He came only from the border, he explained; his birthplace at Le Pallet was south of the river Loire and closer to Aquitaine and Anjou than Celtic Brittany. In his lectures Abelard called the Bretons 'brutes' in order to get a laugh from his students in Paris, and he described the country as 'barbarous' in his 'history of calamities'.[12] Nevertheless, Abelard was considered a Breton by outsiders; this is what made him so clever in their opinion. Brittany produced clerics 'of acute intelligence', Otto of Freising explained.[13]

One obituary confused Abelard's reputation as a Breton with being a 'Briton' and it mistakenly described him as 'English by birth'.[14] This obituarist had probably muddled Abelard up with his contemporary, Adelard of Bath, who was indeed famed as a mathematician. The mistake was easily made, as Adelard (like Abelard) had written about the meaning of universals in philosophy. Without annually printed reference books like Who's Who, it was difficult to check up on confusions of this sort. Medieval scholars had a fund of information about the Bible and the Church Fathers, but very little about their own contemporaries. Even where monasteries kept chronicles, they were often of only local interest and the information in them was usually sparse as well as being unverifiable. This is why Geoffrey of Monmouth's tales of Merlin and King Arthur gained greater credence in Abelard's time than more accurate monastic histories. The grand sweep of Geoffrey's Latin prose looked as impressive to contemporaries as that of the classical Roman historians.

Like Otto of Freising, this obituary considered Abelard of 'inestimable cleverness, unsurpassed memory and superhuman capacity': as well as grammar, dialectic and divinity, he had mastered the subtleties of geometry and arithmetic. It was a commonplace among twelfth-century intellectuals, who were strongly influenced by Pythagorean and Platonic thought, that the numerate arts were the key to understanding the deepest mysteries of the universe because everything was governed by number. As Abelard wrote in *Theologia*:

All order in nature and the symmetry of numbers and ratios are signs and demonstrations of this. Numbers occur in everything and their congruence is the most perfect of all exemplars. This truth is not hidden from those who reflect on the mysteries of philosophy. This is also why arithmetic, which entirely concerns the relations of numbers, is said to be the mother and mistress of the rest of the arts. Upon distinctions of number depend the underlying principles of everything.[15]

Those who understood numbers were masters of their environment and lords of creation. As architect of the universe, God Himself was depicted with a gigantic pair of geometer's dividers. The Romanesque and Gothic churches built in Abelard's time are a monument to numerical theories of harmony, as much as to the numeracy of their craftsmen. Abelard would certainly have seen something of the innovative buildings at Cluny, Laon, St Germain-des-Prés, St Denis and Sens, to name only well-known churches of which portions still stand today. Despite his philosophical interest in numbers, Abelard admitted – perhaps self-deprecatingly – that he was 'completely ignorant' of arithmetical methods.[16] Even so, he certainly had mathematical inclinations, as the syllogisms of formal logic (the 'dialectic' in which he specialized) have affinities with theorems and equations. He may even have made a contribution to the theory of architecture, as he seems to have been the first Biblical interpreter to point out the congruence between the ratios used in the building of Solomon's temple in Jerusalem, as described in the Book of Kings, and Pythagorean musical harmony.[17] Solomon's temple, and the medieval churches which drew inspiration from it, tapped into numerical ratios to create an image of Heaven and evoke its ineffable harmony. This is an illustration of what Abelard meant by numerical symmetry being the 'most perfect of all exemplars'.

MUSIC AND SCIENCE

Abelard could have acquired his mathematical reputation through his success as a musician. His ability to compose and sing was what made him so attractive to women in Heloise's opinion. Some of the liturgical music he composed for Heloise and her nuns at the Paraclete survives, the best known being the hymn 'O Quanta Qualia'. Although Abelard's secular music is lost, the laments he composed on themes from the Old Testament ('Saul and Jonathan', 'Samson' and others less well known) give some idea of how talented he was.[18] Music was one of the 'arts' or skills of the *quadrivium*, the fourfold path to numeracy in the medieval curriculum (the other three were arithmetic, geometry and astronomy). Music had been associated with numeracy since at least the time of Pythagoras. Harmony was fundamental to the ordering of numbers in arithmetic (as Abelard pointed out), to the theorems of geometry, and to the movements of the stars and planets as demonstrated by astronomy. Through the mathematics of its harmonies, music gave assurance that life would continue: the stars would remain on their courses and the seasons rotate from year to year. Medieval philosophy had inherited from the Greeks the belief that the stars are held in place by vast transparent spheres, which sound harmonies as they move round the universe. The fact that people on earth cannot hear this sublime music, nor see these crystal spheres, did not prove that these things did not exist. They were as true as the existence of God. A person of musical talent like Abelard was therefore thought to be endowed with an almost divine power that tapped into the nature of the universe.

Master Hugh of St Victor, Abelard's rival in Paris in the 1130s for the hearts and minds of students, explained that there were three sorts of music: the greatest was the unheard music of the universe, next came the unheard but physically experienced 'music of man' (*musica humana*), and in third place came the various sorts of instrumental music needed by those who were so deaf that they could only hear through their ears.[19] By the 'music of the universe' Hugh meant much more than the harmonies sounded by the crystal spheres, as this related to time as well as space and it described the changing seasons as much as the passage of the stars. By the 'music of man' Hugh meant the harmony which each individual could – and should – feel between the body and the soul; in modern terms, the body's genetic programming and its hormones are its music. Hugh was not aiming to say anything original here, as he was quoting from Boethius's *De Musica* (written in *c*.510 AD) which in its turn reached back a further thousand years to Pythagoras. To this way of thinking, music was the supreme science which concerned the fundamentals of life itself and linked each individual with the universe.

Abelard was indeed multi-talented and remarkably knowledgeable, a musician and poet as well as a philosopher (and a great lover too, according to Heloise); but he was not a scientific genius in the experimental sense, in the way that Roger Bacon aspired to be in the thirteenth century or Leonardo da Vinci was in the fifteenth. The success of experimental science over the past 150 years has altered the meaning of the word 'science' in English, so that today it is confined to natural or physical science rather than including all systems of knowledge. Abelard defined science as the 'comprehension of the truth of the things which are' (*scientia est comprehensio veritatis rerum que sunt*).[20] Today's scientists would not necessarily quarrel with this, but they would want to know how this 'comprehension' was to be achieved.

Medieval science differed from modern not so much in the objective of comprehending the truth, as in its priorities and methods. Whereas modern science prioritizes physical experiments and the application of technology, medieval science concentrated on applying abstract thought to received knowledge. The differences between the medieval and the modern approach need be no more than superficial at the initial level of schooling. Much modern science is not really experimental and much medieval scholarship went beyond received knowledge. Today's science teacher places his pupils in a laboratory instead of a classroom and they go through the motions of doing experiments, though essentially he is teaching received knowledge generated from books. A pupil whose experiment has a different outcome from the one laid down in the textbook will be told that he is mistaken, and not that the originality of the result makes him the intellectual heir of Roger Bacon and Leonardo da Vinci. In fact, the experiments of medieval natural scientists were often as flawed as those of today's beginners because they insisted on finding out everything for themselves and they rejected received knowledge even when it was correct. Bacon maintained that gold was subject to magnetism like iron, and Leonardo thought he knew enough chemistry to reject the traditional way of mixing paints, causing the loss of much of his work to posterity. Experimental science in the Middle Ages stood at the fringes of knowledge, where it was associated with alchemy and magic. It could not point to many practical successes and neither did it look like an intellectual system.

This is why mainstream scholars, like Abelard and Hugh of St Victor, believed that the prime need was not to experiment but to recover – and fully understand – what had been known in the ancient world. They were as conscious of, and respectful towards, the legacy of the past in secular matters as in religious ones. According to Hugh, 'the things by which each person advances in knowledge are principally two, namely reading and meditation, and of these reading (*lectio*) holds the first place'.[21] The student (Hugh continued) must know what books to read, in which order to read them, and how they should be approached. Hugh insisted that his rules applied to secular writings as much as to the scriptures. This had to be so when medieval scholars treated the texts of Plato and Aristotle as the foundation of natural science in the same way as the Bible was the foundation of divine science.

DWARFS AND GIANTS

John of Salisbury recollected how Bernard of Chartres had taught his students that they were dwarfs perched on the shoulders of giants.[22] In Chartres cathedral the stained glass windows show the great prophets of the Old Testament, like Isaiah, carrying on their shoulders smaller figures of Matthew, Mark, Luke and John, the evangelists of the New. From their superior vantage point, the evangelists look out across the cathedral at the triumph of the Christian gospel. Medieval scholars –

including Abelard – were prepared to acknowledge that they were dwarfs by comparison with the giant sages of antiquity; but, by the same token, they were confident that they saw further than their predecessors, simply because they had been born more recently and so they stood higher on the ladder of accumulated knowledge. Intellectuals of Abelard's generation thought that they were in the specially privileged position of being the beneficiaries of both the world's great cultures, the Graeco-Roman and the Judaeo-Christian. (They knew virtually nothing about Africa, India or China and were therefore not concerned about being ignorant of them.)

The parodox of the dwarfs standing on top of the giants implied that even lowly and limited men of Abelard's generation could see further in secular science than Aristotle and Plato, and further in divine science than the evangelists who had written the Gospels. Belief in inevitable progress caused the most optimistic scholars of Abelard's generation to coin a new word to describe themselves: they were 'modern', the far-seeing men of 'now' (modo); they were 'today's men' (hodierni), by contrast with the 'ancient' philosophers and Old Testament prophets. Abelard has an imaginary pagan philosopher demand of the Jews and Christians why there has not been the same progress in religious belief that has taken place in everything else, 'where human understanding increases with the passing of the ages and the succession of time'.[23] The modernizing scientists of the twelfth century had as confident (and as naive) a belief in the inevitability of progress as their counterparts in the twentieth century.

Interpreted in this way, Christianity itself carried a message of progressive improvement. No medieval scholastic could ever totally respect the learning of either the philosophers or the prophets, because they had not known Christ. Plato and Aristotle, Isaiah and Jeremiah, shared the overwhelming misfortune of being born before Christ, a misfortune that consigned them to something close to damnation as well as ultimate intellectual oblivion. One of the sculptures at the western entrance of Chartres cathedral (dating from about the time of Abelard's death in the mid-twelfth century) shows the Incarnation of Christ, with the ancient Greek philosophers seated on either side at the base in the act of writing. They bend over their desks, not looking up from their work, as they cannot recognize Mary and the Christ Child because He represents the true wisdom which they never knew. Similarly, the Jewish past is represented in medieval sculpture by the tragic female figure of Synagogue who is blindfolded. The ambivalent attitude which the 'dwarfs' of Abelard's generation had towards their inheritance from antiquity gave them the confidence or the arrogance (depending on one's point of view) to profit from the giants' mistakes. They proposed to take what suited them from the past and make it their own.

Abelard demonstrated in *Sic et Non* how he and his modern 'dwarfs', his 'tender readers' as he called them, proposed to surpass the works of the giants as far as the Christian heritage was concerned.[24] He assembled, in coherent order under 158 headings, hundreds of quotations from the Church Fathers, particularly from St Augustine and Gregory the Great, in order to highlight and sort out the inconsistencies between them. Abelard was not intending to bring the Church Fathers into disrepute by minutely examining whether they said 'Yes' or 'No' (*Sic et Non*) to his 158 questions. He was confident that the discrepancies in the quotations which he had amassed would readily disappear, once scientific methods of criticism were applied to them through the linguistic arts like logic in which he excelled. Abelard and his 'tender readers' could then climb with confidence on to the gigantic shoulders of the Church Fathers. From this vantage point, master and students would see the Christian religion clearly and whole for the first time.

THE ACQUISITION OF KNOWLEDGE

Abelard's confidence in this programme of study is epitomized by his announcement in the prologue to *Sic et Non* that 'by doubting we come to inquiry and by inquiry we perceive the truth'.[25] Simplistic and even naive as this is as a description of how knowledge is acquired, it was very influential in the medieval schools. A century and more after Abelard, the *Summa Theologiae* of Thomas Aquinas displays the same optimism and the same method. Any question, even on the profoundest points of theology or natural science, is answered in a page or two, and Aquinas addresses them by juxtaposing quotations from authorities. The difference between *Sic et Non* and *Summa Theologiae* is that Aquinas actually answers the questions posed, by discussing the authorities one by one, whereas Abelard left this to future research and his 'tender readers'. The scholastic method allowed its practitioners to save the appearances of the authorities, while putting forward original solutions of their own whenever the sources required further explication, which was extremely often. Abelard's *Theologia*, for example, cites numerous ancient authors, both classical and Biblical, and yet its arguments were so novel that they were stigmatized by William of St Thierry and St Bernard as dangerously heretical.

The weakness of the scholastic method, whether in the hands of Aquinas or Abelard, was that ultimately it could only be as good as the authorities it depended on. Even in Abelard's time it was becoming apparent that some of the ancient sages had not been intellectual giants at all, but faltering human beings. As the prologue to *Sic et Non* pointed out, it was heresy to dissent in any way from what was written in the Old and New Testaments, even though there were errors in them, but the classical philosophers were not so privileged. A century after Abelard, by Roger Bacon's time in the 1250s, the repeated process of 'doubting and coming to inquiry' was revealing that some Graeco-Roman science had not made sense in the first place and so it could never be reconciled with the truth. Reasoning on the basis of false authorities might prove worse than useless. The best way forward, for natural science in particular, was to do what Roger Bacon recommended and try things out by experiment. The danger in the long term for the received system of knowledge in experimental science was that the Bible's account of the Creation in the Book of Genesis might itself start to look dubious.

It was not only later experimental scientists who questioned the validity of the scholastic method. St Bernard took the offensive at its very inception in his attack on Abelard at the council of Sens in 1140. 'Away!', he wrote to the pope, 'away with any idea that the Christian faith should have its limits in the estimates of those academics who doubt everything and know nothing. I go secure in the sentence of the Master of the Gentiles, and I truly know that I shall not be confounded.'[26] Bernard deliberately uses scholastic jargon here in order to undermine it. In place of the hundreds of 'sentences' (the scholastic term for quotations culled from authorities) amassed by Abelard in *Sic et Non*, Bernard declares that he relies on a single 'sentence' of his 'master', St Paul, the Apostle of the Gentiles: 'I know in whom I have believed, and I am certain thereof' (II Timothy, ch. 1, verse 12). Bernard turns on Abelard, as if he were actually present in the room where this letter was being dictated, and reproaches him for his temerity: 'You whisper to me that faith is an "estimate" and you mutter about ambiguity to me, as though nothing were certain.'[27]

Abelard had indeed defined faith in his *Theologia* as an 'estimate' of things which are not apparent.[28] He and St Bernard were operating at cross-purposes here, rather than really disagreeing about fundamentals. By 'faith' Bernard meant 'conviction', a psychological experience deep in the mind. He cited St Augustine: 'Faith is not in the heart of anyone who has it only as a conjecture or an opinion; but it is certain knowledge acclaimed by the conscience.'[29] A person has 'certain knowledge' (*certa scientia*) of something when his 'heart', which is the centre of the emotions, combines with his faculty of knowing ('conscience' –

conscientia) to form a conviction. Abelard's definition of faith as an 'estimate' focused on an earlier stage in the psychological process. Otto of Freising noted that Abelard 'incautiously' mixed in the terminology of natural science with that of theology, and this is what he was doing here.[30] In his treatise on how the mind works (*De Intellectibus*) Abelard had distinguished between 'understanding' (*intellectus*), 'estimating' (*existimatio*) and 'knowing' (*scientia*). A proposition has to be understood first of all, regardless of whether it is true or false. Next comes the process of 'estimating' or assessing whether the concept, now formed in the mind, should be believed. 'If I do not give credence to the concept', Abelard says, 'I believe it is not as I conceive it to be.'[31] Finally, there is the stage of 'knowing', which is the state of 'certitude of mind'.

Given these distinctions, St Bernard was right to say that Abelard's definition of faith as an 'estimate' fell short of knowledge or certainty. Abelard argued that knowledge and faith were different things. He was deliberately putting out a warning against the sort of mindless faith which believes anything. If Christians believed nonsense, they were no better than pagans. Repeatedly in his work Abelard insisted on the priority of understanding over faith and he knew that this was a reversal of St Anselm of Canterbury's rule: 'I believe so that I may understand' (*credo ut intelligam*). St Anselm had intended this as a generalization about the acquisition of any sort of knowledge; the way believing works is not restricted to religious faith. St Anselm's formula points out that only when the mind allows itself to be convinced of something can it begin to explore its meaning. An elementary modern example would be that it is necessary to believe in the North Pole before you can find out how to get there (and even if you do get there, you have to believe your navigational instruments in order to understand that you are there). However, St Anselm's rule also makes sense in reverse. In order to believe, I have first to understand. If I begin by confusing the 'Pole' with a 'pole', I will not attain my objective.

Abelard justified his definition of faith when he recollected in his 'history of calamities' the anti-Anselmian opinions of his students, who had insisted that 'nothing can be believed unless it is first understood and that it was ridiculous for anyone to tell others something which neither he nor those he taught could grasp with the intellect'.[32] Abelard showed he shared his students' views by adding in his *Theologia* that it was 'absolutely ridiculous' for anyone who wants to teach someone something to say that he does not himself understand what he is talking about.[33] This statement reveals Abelard's priorities as a classroom teacher in the Socratic mould, who invites questions and disagreement from his pupils in order to reach the truth, for 'by doubting we come to inquiry'. In the classroom, a belief has to be defined as an 'estimate'. If it were a conviction, it would not be discussable; master and students could then do no more than confess their faith, as if they were in church reciting the creed. For Abelard, faith has to be an 'estimate' because (as he stated in his treatise De Intellectibus) 'everyone who makes an estimate of something necessarily understands what it is he is estimating'.[34]

St Bernard accused Abelard of 'holding God suspect' by refusing to believe anything unless he had first discussed it rationally.[35] This was a good debating point for the prosecution, but it did not answer the classroom teacher's objection that it must be possible to explain to the pupil or would-be believer what it is he should believe. Much the same argument as St Bernard's, in equally emotive language, had been made by St Anselm himself fifty years earlier, when he accused Roscelin of presumptuously placing intellect before faith.[36] Abelard had been involved in this acrimonious and irresolvable debate about faith and reason all his adult life, as he had been Roscelin's student (at an impressionable age in his teens) in the 1090s when the controversy between St Anselm and Roscelin was at its height.

ABELARD AND SCHOLASTICISM

Although St Bernard's accusations against Abelard proved very effective (he was condemned to perpetual silence as a heretic by Pope Innocent II in 1140), it was Abelard rather than Bernard who was in the mainstream of scholastic thought and European science. If Bernard's ideology had triumphed in the long term over Abelard's, the schools would have been closed down and all thinking men would have become monks, as they do in some Buddhist communities. (Whether this would have been a good or bad thing for Europe is a different question. Possibly monasticism might have brought peace and enlightenment in the long term, even though it failed to do this in the Middle Ages.) St Bernard was not opposed to learning as such, but to its misuse. He pointed out that scientia was not the same as sapientia (wisdom) and that many people without schooling, from St Peter downwards, had found favour with God.[37] Bernard argued that experience – his own sort of experience as a monk – was superior to book learning. 'Believe an expert,' he wrote, 'you will find something more in the woods than in books. Woods and stones will teach you what you cannot hear from "masters". Do you think you cannot suck honey from rocks and oil from the hardest stone?'[38] Bernard was making a scriptural and mystical reference here.

He probably had even less knowledge than Abelard of the chemical properties of stones and plants, though some monks were herbalists.

'Why search for the Word among words?', St Bernard demanded in the same context, 'when He is already made flesh right before your eyes?'[39] Bernard means that scholastics like Abelard are not 'modern', as they liked to see themselves; they are centuries out of date. They are still bent over their desks, like the old Greek philosophers sculpted at Chartres, too absorbed in their texts to look up at the light. Among the 'multitude of words' (as Abelard described the mass of texts in *Sic et Non*), the scholastics had failed to notice the arrival of the one true Word, who is Jesus Christ.[40] This is Bernard's meaning. In order to teach about this now ever-present Christ, Hugh of St Victor used diagrams and modelling techniques rather like a modern scientist. Alongside a colour-coded scale drawing of Noah's Ark (the model of salvation through the Church), Hugh depicted the person of Christ 'in visible form, so that you may have a clear exemplar'.[41] Hugh's school of St Victor was immensely successful, and influential on spirituality and art as well as academic subjects, but his approach was not one which commended itself to Abelard. The rivalry between them went back to the origins of the school of St Victor and Abelard's bitter dispute with William of Champeaux in the early 1100s.

In reality Abelard, Hugh of St Victor and St Bernard had a great deal in common. All three of them were theoretically bound by monastic discipline, though none of them lived secluded lives, and they all had the same objective of using their extraordinary talents for words to teach and preach the Christian Word of God. They were all very clever, particularly at argument, and they were all unstoppable writers. They were all, too, considered by their contemporaries to be at the forefront of knowledge and understanding and they all made deliberate appeals to attract the young. Hugh was more conservative than Abelard or Bernard on some matters of doctrine, notably the Redemption, but in other areas he and Bernard were more adventurous than Abelard, for example in what they had to say about relations between the sexes.[42] Needless to say, perhaps, all of them insisted on absolute orthodoxy in religious matters, though they differed in some respects about what was orthodox. Of the three, Abelard is the least easy to read because he does not carry his learning as lightly as Hugh or Bernard. Despite Master Jocelin saying he was more of a jester than a professor, Abelard has much of the pedant in him. He was one of those academics who cannot resist lecturing his audience and citing his authorities verbatim and at length. (This is what made Abelard's works such a rich quarry for later scholastics, particularly Peter Lombard.) Beneath this delight in instruction, the habit of a lifetime in the schools, lay deeper differences between Abelard and Bernard. In answer to his question 'Why search for the Word among words?', Abelard was convinced that the search had to begin with texts. He did not deny that 'Christ alone is the Word of God', but he added:

> This is what the Greeks call the *logos*. Hence St Augustine says in *The Book of Eighty-Three Questions*, chapter 44: '"In the beginning was the Word" [John, ch. 1, verse 1], which in Greek is called *logos*.' Hence also, in accordance with the etymology of this noun, whosoever clings to this true and perfect Word through doctrine and love should truly be called 'logicians' and philosophers. Therefore no discipline ought more truly to be called 'logic' than Christian teaching.[43]

Abelard's arguments here are typically scholastic in content and style. First he insists on referring to the Greek text of St John's Gospel, rather than the Latin Vulgate. As the Greek was not available to him (and he probably knew no Greek anyway), he relies on St Augustine's authority for the meaning of *logos*, and he cites him (as a scholar should) by book title and chapter number. Abelard then turns to etymology, a dubious science in which medieval and Renaissance scholars put too much trust, in order to demonstrate that since 'Christ' means *logos*, 'Christ-ians' must be 'logic-ians' and Christian teaching means logical teaching.

Christians must be logicians, Abelard argued throughout his career, because logic alone makes sense of language. St Bernard and Hugh of St Victor, as much as Abelard, agreed that the word of God had been transmitted to the Church primarily through language and in particular through the Bible. They also all agreed that the Latin Vulgate text of the Bible (as established by St Jerome in 382–400 AD) was authoritative for the Roman Church and that, consequently, all clergy must be instructed in Latin and accept its disciplines. St Bernard might encourage a few carefully chosen monks to search for enlightenment as hermits in the woods, but he was as opposed as anyone else in authority to uninstructed preachers taking to the streets. Everyone, not least Abelard, agreed that there had to be authority and order in teaching.

The scholastic approach to knowledge, which Abelard exemplifies, differed from the monastic approach not so much in its content as in its expectations. When Abelard declares that Christians are logicians, he is confident that there is much to be learned from the Graeco-Roman heritage and that he and his fellow schoolmen will make sense of their world. The idea that there was a 'Twelfth-Century Renaissance', a revival of learning and hope, is now commonplace among historians. Although Abelard never spelt this out in so many words, he would certainly have agreed with its optimism and its emphasis on Plato and

Aristotle. He and his students, his 'tender readers', were dwarfs mounted on the shoulders of giants. From their eminence as 'moderns', they looked forward to the perfection of science. The monks, on the other hand, who competed with the schoolmen for the hearts of the young, had no exalted expectations of the world around them. They were committed to isolating themselves from it and transcending its fallible secular knowledge. The intellectuals among them, most vociferously St Bernard, had good reasons for not following Abelard's academic path. Doubting might not lead to inquiry but only to further doubt. It was Abelard, rather than Bernard, who was the naive believer.

Abelard's castration (in *c*.1118) terminated his secular career in the schools and obliged him to become a monk. He was already close to forty years of age and (as he describes in his 'history of calamities'), try as he would, he could never find monastic tranquillity. He remained a 'master', battling with words, and delighting in his students and his books. In the wake of his castration Fulk prior of Deuil exhorted him, as a brother monk, to give up worldly desires. Purportedly to console him, Fulk recalled his fame. Students had come running to him from all over Europe. They had been 'deeply moved', Fulk wrote, 'by the clarity of his intelligence, the grace of his eloquence, his supreme skill with language and the subtlety of his science'.[44] Fulk summed up Abelard's achievements, as if this were an epitaph for a monk now dead to the world. In fact, Abelard's mind and his magnetism remained very much alive. Over the next twenty years (*c*.1118–*c*.1138), he showed what he understood by being a monk by applying himself to the logic of religion in his *Theologia*. St Bernard almost certainly intended his comment that 'we have in France a new theologian converted from an old master' to be derisive, but it paid Abelard the compliment of acknowledging that his intellectual energy was undaunted.[45]

3
Literate

One of the first things Abelard tells us about himself in his 'history of calamities' is that he was brought up to be literate (instructed in 'letters' is the term he uses), as if this were something unusual or special. Today literacy is a commonplace, the familiar routine of schooling which everyone experiences in one form or another. For Abelard and his contemporaries, reading and writing were much more remote. Books, where they existed at all, were largely confined to churches and writing materials were even less accessible. Traditionally, they were the prerogative of monks, isolated in the *scriptoria*, or writing workshops of their monasteries, cut off from the *laos* – the crowd of ordinary or 'lay' people – by the monastery's stone walls and iron-studded doors. Within the cloister, reading was *lectio divina* – 'divine reading' – by which was meant Bible-study or knowing the 'sacred page' of Scripture. This sort of literacy preferred quality to quantity. The Rule of St Benedict prescribed that once a year at the beginning of Lent each monk was to be given a single book from the library, and he had to read and digest every word of it before returning it the next year.[1]

The 'page' was made doubly sacred by the letters on it being embellished with colours and precious metals. Today these illuminated manuscripts are exhibited in the world's great libraries and can be examined – and wondered at – at leisure. In the Middle Ages no one ordinarily saw them open except the clergy. All that the laity in church glimpsed were the closed books, wrapped in silk and surrounded by candles, being carried in procession from their strongboxes to an altar or lectern for liturgical reading or chanting. Writing had ceased to be commonplace with the passing of the Roman Empire. Latin literacy in the West had been taken over and transformed by monks into something peculiarly precious, most famously in the remote island monasteries of Iona and Lindisfarne, where the Lindisfarne Gospels and other early illuminated manuscripts were made (from about 600 AD onwards). This tradition of writing was therefore 500 years old by Abelard's time and it was still creating fresh forms. Among the most magnificent illuminated manuscripts ever produced are the glossed books of the Bible emanating from the Paris schools in the twelfth century. These incorporate the commentaries, particularly on the Psalms and St Paul's Epistles, of Abelard's colleagues and students like Gilbert de la Porrée and Peter Lombard.[2]

No such lavishly produced manuscripts of Abelard's own works are extant from the twelfth century, nor does any piece of writing survive that is thought to be in his own hand. Like his contemporaries St Bernard and John of Salisbury, Abelard probably preferred to dictate his works to secretaries rather than write them out himself. Academic masters were trained to formulate their Latin aloud and think on their feet. This practice explains why no manuscripts of Abelard are clearly autographs, but other explanations are required for the relative paucity of early manuscripts as such. In 1140 Pope Innocent II ordered Abelard's books to be burned 'wherever they might be found' and many may have been destroyed as a consequence, although some were kept secretly by his followers (one obituary said) and, here and there, the papal order was ignored or not known about.[3]

An early copy of the first book of Abelard's *Theologia* is still kept at Durham cathedral (on the northernmost frontier of England), possibly brought back by a monk on his return from the Paris schools in the 1130s (before Abelard was condemned by Innocent II). As the opinions of Laurence prior of Durham (who died in 1154) are cited along with Abelard's in a manuscript now in Rouen, it is possible that the Durham copy of *Theologia* had originally belonged to Laurence.[4] As distant from Paris in an easterly direction was the abbey of Prüfening (south of the Danube), which possessed the best copy of Abelard's *Ethics* and listed it in its library catalogue in 1165 or earlier (this manuscript is now in Munich).[5] A number of contemporaries recorded that Abelard's students came from all over Latin Christendom and this is what the distribution of his manuscripts attests. Far-flung religious houses, like Durham or Prüfening, were not provincial backwaters. They may have become so later, but in the twelfth century they were at the height of their energies, and their monks travelled huge distances to study or to promote the interests of their houses. Judging from existing manuscripts, Abelard's writings were not nearly as popular in the twelfth century as St Bernard's, but he was wholly exceptional. Considering the pope's ban and Abelard's dubious academic standing in the first place, it is remarkable how many of his works survive, particularly in copies from the four-teenth and fifteenth centuries.

The monks of Durham cathedral (who owned the Lindisfarne Gospels as well as a book of Abelard's *Theologia*) were exhorted in a sermon from Prior Laurence's time to be 'God's writers'. They must guide the pen of memory over the parchment of a pure conscience, which had been scraped by the penknife of divine fear, smoothed by the pumice of heavenly desires, whitened by the chalk of holy thoughts, ruled by the straight will of God, and so on. The preacher ingeniously extended these metaphors to every stage of the writing process.[6] They emphasize how, in ecclesiastical eyes, 'letters' were keys to sacred mysteries. They were not something to be entered into lightly because every literate was potentially a saint or a heretic, as Abelard was to discover through his own life of 'calamities'. By mastering 'letters', the literate gained entry to the world of the spirit and he was well advised to remain there.

GENDER AND LITERACY

The 'sacred page', bright and pure, demanded reverence from its devotees, whether they were monks or schoolmen. In Abelard's time, as much as in the days of St Cuthbert of Lindisfarne, those who were dedicated to literacy were expected to live like monks, celibate and isolated from the imperfections of ordinary life. Abelard reminded Heloise of this ideal when he told her how lucky she was to be a nun and not a housewife. 'How unseemly that those holy hands, which now turn the pages of sacred books, should be degraded by the obscenities of women's business.'[7] Heloise had herself referred to this 'women's business' in her objections to their marriage. She wanted Abelard to be pure and celibate, for 'what harmony can there be between scholars and maid-servants, or between the scriptorium and the nursery?'.[8] By contrast with the 'squalid tasks' (as Heloise described them) of parenting, literacy was a clean and elevated profession, and it had been so ever since the ancient Greek philosophers had given dignity to scholarship. Heloise drew her ideas about the social consequences of scholarship from the examples of Pythagoras, Socrates and Seneca, the Roman Stoic. She urged Abelard not to sink himself in 'obscenities', but to live in honourable simplicity like the ancients, particularly as he was a 'cleric and canon'.[9]

The very existence of Heloise (and she was undoubtedly a real person, even if her letters have fictive elements) demonstrates that women were not as strictly excluded from the clerical order as they were from the priesthood or knighthood. A class distinction applied to literacy. Women might enjoy books, provided they kept their hands clean and avoided the domestic labour of 'women's business'. Great ladies were patrons of literature and by Abelard's time they were beginning to read romances in their private chambers. Theoretically, though, the male elite preferred the lady in her home to be reading prayer-books rather than fairy tales. She should have a chaplain to instruct her; she should say her prayers daily and keep herself chaste for her husband. This was a regular and secluded way of life, which was not unlike that of a nun or an abbess. The Virgin Mary was idealized as the model of such a lady and – because of increasing literacy – she began to be depicted as a pious reader herself: either with her books in her oratory at the moment of the Annunciation, or showing a book to the Child Jesus in her chamber. These are the sort of images that Abelard was evoking when he described the 'holy hands' of Heloise turning the pages of sacred books. Holy hands were clean hands and an oratory was depicted in medieval miniatures as a place of solitary and orderly quiet, with a spotlessly clean floor and neat shelving.

By contrast, 'women's business' was a messy business. Women produced more fluids, Heloise pointed out by citing the authority of Macrobius and Aristotle (and Abelard quoted it back at her).[10] She was conducting a half-teasing debate with him about whether men or women were better suited to the monastic life. The greater wetness of women's bodies meant that they absorbed alcohol better and they expelled its fumes faster through their larger number of orifices. Nuns were therefore less likely to get drunk than monks, Heloise concluded. Nevertheless, like any writer on feminism before the twentieth century, she had to concede that women could not control their bodies as well as men. The mess of 'women's business' was due to the involuntary functions of menstruation, childbirth and breastfeeding. (Tampons, contraceptives and disposable nappies underpin the equal opportunities culture of the twentieth century.) Heloise argued that daily chores and the squalor of domesticity would 'crucify' Abelard if he lived with her.[11] He paid her the compliment (as he often does in their correspondence) of repeating this idea. In one of his sermons he asks: 'What chain is heavier than the marriage bond? What servitude can be graver for a man than not having control over his own body? What life is more onerous than being crucified by the daily cares of a wife and children?'[12]

The dedication to the 'sacred page' that monks enjoyed was made possible in practice only by the elaborate domestic provisions of monasteries, which a self-employed teacher like Abelard could not afford (as Heloise had pointed out to him). It was monastic sanitation, with its drains and running water, which ensured that monks had 'holy hands', just as it was the quiet of the cloister which made concentrated reading possible. Writing demanded even more by way of special provision, as it was possible only in a scriptorium, apart from the temporary notes made on portable writing-tablets or slates. A literate person was in much the same situation as a scientist today. He needed a laboratory with controlled light, heat and humidity to keep the writer and his materials (particularly parchment and inks) in a workable state. To be literate, a person had therefore to be a 'master', not only in the scholastic sense, but also in the sense that a man was 'master' of his house with fetchers and carriers at his beck and call. These are the principal reasons why Heloise, as much as Abelard, thought of literacy as a primarily male profession.

Abelard describes how his father 'had each one of his sons instructed in letters'; nothing is said about Abelard's mother or sisters and the implication is that they were not literate.[13] We know that he had at least one sister, as she was given Abelard's and Heloise's baby boy to bring up – to do the 'women's business' of toilet training and loving – while his parents returned to Paris to attempt to continue their contradictory life as married scholars.[14] The fact that Abelard wanted Heloise and her nuns to be literate (in Greek and Hebrew as well as in Latin) underlines the rule that letters were not ordinarily 'women's business'.[15] When Peter the Venerable, abbot of Cluny, praised Heloise's erudition he thought of it primarily in relation to men. 'At a time when knowledge can scarcely find a foothold not only among the female sex but even among virile minds', Peter wrote, 'you have beaten all women and surpassed almost all men.'[16] Heloise had told Abelard that she disliked praise and did not seek a crown of victory, but Peter could think of literacy only in schoolboy terms of beating others.[17] Her achievement in surpassing 'almost' all men was the ultimate that a woman could attain in his book. He does not seem to have begun to consider whether Heloise might be not only the equal but the superior of 'virile minds' like his own and Abelard's.

In day-to-day reality, as distinct from ideals, as long as clerical celibacy was not rigorously enforced, various women were to be found within church precincts enjoying a dubious status as the wives, mistresses or children of clerical officials. Heloise, whom Abelard met in c.1117 living in the cathedral precinct of Notre-Dame of Paris in the house of Canon Fulbert, next to Abelard's school, is the most famous woman in this category.[18] She had lived there as Fulbert's niece for ten or fifteen years (Fulbert is first named as a canon in 1102). Why could she not continue to reside there as Abelard's wife? The short answer is that Fulbert had initially refused consent to their marriage because Abelard had seduced Heloise. But why had Abelard done this? Why had he not asked his fellow canon, Fulbert, for her hand in marriage in the first place? Heloise's explanation, as we have seen, is that the domestic responsibilities of marriage would have 'crucified' Abelard. Furthermore, as master of the school of Notre-Dame, he was expected to set an example to his students and fellow canons by being exclusively dedicated to his clerical vocation. Canon Fulbert might live with his niece in the cathedral precinct. Canon Stephen de Garlande might build a house there and be the king's chancellor and military commander.[19] But Abelard, as their schoolmaster, must maintain his responsible rank in the clerical militia and not 'lapse into conjugal voluptuousness' (the phrase is the canon lawyer's, Ivo of Chartres).[20]

The moral and intellectual rigour of Abelard's predecessor as master, William of Champeaux, had attracted students to Paris from France and beyond.[21] Abelard had to uphold this position and avoid any sexual scandal, which might cause ecclesiastical patrons of students throughout Christendom to withdraw their funding from Notre-Dame. In the exceptional case of university masters, market forces implemented clerical celibacy with immediate effect. Requiring masters to be celibate was one facet of the disciplining of the clergy as a whole, in accordance with the ideals of 'Gregorian Reform' (the programme associated with Pope Gregory VII, 1073–85). For complex reasons, the application of celibacy to masters was enforced more rigorously in the northern schools (like Paris and Oxford) than in the Italian ones (like Bologna and Salerno), even though they were closer to Rome. In France during Abelard's lifetime, pressure was put on married or otherwise domesticated clergy in the major churches to give up either their benefices and offices or their female households. Ideally, all churches and their clergy, of whatever rank, were to accept monastic discipline. Women, or rather ladies, therefore began to be banned from ecclesiastical precincts. In practice, lower-class women might still be admitted to do the 'women's business' of cleaning or prostitution; but – at least in the northern universities – students, masters and other clerics no longer engaged in intellectual intercourse with women of their own class.

Gregorian Reform proceeded piecemeal and Heloise probably could have continued to reside in Fulbert's house within the precinct of Notre-Dame for a few more years after c.1117 in the role of his niece, if that is what she was (possibly she was his daughter, or the daughter of another cleric). What could not be tolerated was her moving in next door with 'Master' Abelard as his lawful wife and equal in learning. More significant in its consequences for European culture than the castration and persecution of Abelard (the 'calamities' which followed his marriage) was the silencing of Heloise, as that was a prelude to the silencing of academic women as a class for the next eight centuries. 'I have set the bridle of your injunction on the words which issue from my unbounded grief', she acknowledged to Abelard, 'so that at least in writing I may moderate what it is difficult or impossible for me to forestall in speech.'²² She insisted that she would continue to think her own thoughts and to voice them. Neither Abelard nor anyone else in the clerical order had the power to take them from her or make her change them. But she acknowledged that it was no longer appropriate for her to express them in writing. She and Abelard continued to correspond about nuns and other ecclesiastical matters, but she wrote nothing more about her love.

Heloise's silence meant she could no longer record her feelings. This applied to much more than not writing love letters to Abelard, as her feelings were integral to her understanding of classical literature. In her letters to Abelard she had shown him that the writings of the classical philosophers and particularly the Stoics were not just words on the page, to be puzzled over by students, but moral statements made by human beings like himself. After her silencing, Heloise could only ask him 'baby questions' and pretend to be satisfied with his answers.²³ She was probably the last medieval lay woman to be so highly trained in classical 'letters'; a century later even many nuns had stopped learning Latin. It is true that lack of Latin did not mean that medieval women had lost their voice within the privacy of their own homes. Some, too, were among the pioneers of writing in vernacular languages in the later Middle Ages; Marguerite Porete, Julian of Norwich and Christine de Pisan are obvious examples. Nevertheless, until the end of the nineteenth century, women remained excluded from the academic world, with which Heloise had been familiar and in which she had gained such distinction. Although the promise of Heloise's literary career was brutally cut short, she had already demonstrated in the letters to Abelard that survive (which are only a portion of those she wrote) that she was a match for 'virile minds'.

ABELARD'S CHOICE OF LITERACY

Abelard's initiation into literacy had not been of his own choosing, as it was the decision his father made for each of his boys. They probably began instruction in the ABC at the age of seven or even earlier. The difference in Abelard's case was that he enjoyed Latin so much that he continued with it beyond the rudiments which his father and his other brothers acquired. This is when he made his own choice of 'letters', probably at the age of twelve or thirteen, when he would have been big enough either to begin training in earnest as a knight or to go to a more advanced clerical school. Abelard describes his choice in the terms of a love affair:

> Because I was the eldest son and therefore most dear to my father, he saw to it that I was brought up very carefully. And so the further I went in the study of letters the more easily I made progress, and the more ardently I became attached to them. I was seduced into so great a love of them that I abdicated entirely from the court of Mars so that I might be educated in the bosom of Minerva. I therefore made over to my brothers the pomp of military glory, along with the inheritance and privileges of my primogenitors.[24]

As the eldest son of a knight, Abelard could have expected to be head of his family, a landowner of standing in his country, with an inheritance to pass on to his sons and a fortune to make in his lord's wars (assuming he survived). His description of his 'abdication' shows how fateful the decision to be a *literatus* could be, when every *literatus* was potentially a *clericus* and every *clericus* was potentially like a monk. Literally, *clericus* meant 'chosen' or 'elect'. Once he had opted for literacy, Abelard was set apart from the 'lay' members of his family; he became one of God's chosen vessels like the predestined 'elect' of Calvinistic theology.

Abelard's saying he had 'abdicated entirely' from the court of Mars suggests that his choice of a clerical career was irrevocable. Certainly the Church taught that those who were tonsured as clergy should not return to a secular life, even if they were not yet old enough to become priests or be fully professed as monks. Nevertheless, exceptions were made in practice. Abelard's contemporary, Guibert de Nogent, recounts how his widowed mother gave him the option of giving up Latin and training as a knight instead.[25] This was the softer option in Guibert's opinion, as his schoolmaster beat him horribly (his mother had seen the weals on his back). But, Guibert says, he had been dedicated to a clerical career from birth and he had the courage to continue with the agony of learning. (His reward, apart from becoming a brilliant writer like Abelard, was to be offered the confiscated prebend of a married priest.)

Abelard's choice may have been irrevocable only because he could not help himself. He found 'letters' overwhelmingly attractive and even sensual. He had been 'seduced' into the bosom of Minerva, goddess of learning, just as later on he fell in love with Heloise, 'supreme in the abundance of letters'.[26] He makes a suggestive pun about his education: *educarer* means 'I was educated' and 'I was lifted up'.[27] So, when he was still a boy, he was 'lifted up' on to the metaphorical bosom of Minerva. At the end of his life a Latin poem describes him in rather similar terms.

After he had been silenced by St Bernard and his monks (at the council of Sens in 1140), this poem imagines that he metamorphosed into a divine spirit. His bride, Lady Philology (signifying the learned Heloise), searches in vain for her Palatine (Abelard was called 'Palatine' from his birthplace at Le Pallet) whom she had cherished at her bosom.[28]

Abelard's father had therefore got more than he bargained for when he gave his favourite son the gift of letters. There was now a risk that if Abelard's younger brothers failed to survive him and his father, his 'abdication' of his birthright would bring his family's line to an end. This would not only bring dishonour on Abelard himself; it might also involve the surrender of the entire family property to the feudal overlord (probably the count of Nantes). In fact, though, Abelard did not cut all ties with his family. In particular he returned home in c.1113 to oversee the retirement of both his parents into religious houses.[29] His father's retirement must have required the allocation of his knight's fee to one or more of Abelard's brothers and a renegotiation of the rights of primogeniture. Tantalizingly, he says nothing about these mundane details. Although in Abelard's case his family was not eliminated by his choice of a clerical career, it was true even for him that literacy was divisive and potentially dangerous. He describes how he became an exile, 'perambulating' from school to school across the provinces of France.[30] He was the archetypal wandering scholar, hungry for fame and affection.

Abelard describes his father ensuring that his sons were instructed in 'letters' before being trained in 'arms'.[31] This may have been a way of covering their career options, though Abelard suggests that his father was motivated simply by his love of 'letters'. As contrasted here, 'letters' and 'arms' represent alternative ways of life: literacy led to a clerical career with prospects of being a bishop or abbot, and knighthood led to secular honour and lordship. Both were forms of service, subject to discipline and training. Both too were career paths for the ruling class only. The third estate of peasants and manual workers was excluded from 'letters' as much as from 'arms'. Like other clerical writers, Abelard uses the word *rusticus* or 'peasant' as the opposite of *literatus*.[32] 'Illiterate' and 'rustic' were synonyms. A talented individual of obscure family might in exceptional circumstances clamber up the ladder of ecclesiastical preferment (the poet and bishop Marbod of Rennes was of humble parentage, and so possibly was John of Salisbury), but peasants as a class could not.

Abelard and his brothers had the choice of 'letters' or 'arms' only because they had been born into a knightly family. The very idea of a 'career', of shaping and directing one's own life, was necessarily restricted to the ruling class and to the active males among them.

Abelard takes the superior status of his family for granted and he has nothing to say about the peasants they ruled, whereas other clerical commentators were very conscious that their intellectual dedication was made possible only by the physical labour of the poor. Later on in his life, when he tried to be a hermit, Abelard had to acknowledge, with the unjust steward in St Luke's gospel, that 'To dig I am unable and to beg I am ashamed.' He got his students to do the digging.[33] Literacy made a man soft, as Abelard had emphasized when he contrasted the role models of Mars and Minerva.

A cleric was desexed; he became a spiritual eunuch, bent over his desk in the schoolroom, like the figures of the Evangelists portrayed in medieval Gospel books. If he raised his eyes from his text to experience the world around him, as Abelard and many other medieval clerics had the temerity to do, the *laos* – the crowd, the family, the people – might come back into his life with a vengeance. Footloose clerics, enjoying the immunity of ecclesiastical law, were a threat to every man's wife and daughters. When Heloise's kinsmen castrated Abelard, they made clerical celibacy into a reality for him. In theory the Church should have been able to protect him within the precinct of Notre-Dame of Paris and within its artificial extended family, where kinless men were addressed as 'Father' or 'Brother'. After his castration Abelard insisted on addressing Heloise as 'Sister', even though she gently and elegantly reminded him that she was still his 'wife' and his 'unique' one.[34] Often in their correspondence she showed him which of them was the master of the admired rhetorical art of letter-writing (in every sense of 'letters') and of forms of address in particular.[35]

LATIN LETTERS

The disjunction between literacy and family in medieval culture was reinforced by the language in which literacy was expressed. A modern literate usually learns to read in his mother tongue and he or she may learn the elements of reading from his own mother. In Abelard's time learning 'letters' meant learning Latin, which was no longer anybody's mother tongue, right from the stage of reciting the ABC up to reading classical literature.[36] This was harder than learning to read and write a living language for functional purposes. The grammar and vocabulary of Latin was already more than a thousand years old by Abelard's time and its literature was consequently huge and complex, ranging from the ancient classics like Cicero and Virgil, through the Church Fathers like St Augustine and Gregory the Great, to contemporary writers. Abelard's contemporary, the English monk William of Malmesbury, cites over 200 ancient Latin authors in his writings.[37] Although he did not necessarily know all of these at first hand, his citations (from about 400 works in all) are usually accurate and well understood.

Generally, Abelard and his contemporaries write good classical Latin (they do not make mistakes in grammar, constructions or vocabulary), as they were rigorously schooled in the ancient authors. John of Salisbury recalled how Bernard of Chartres, 'the greatest fount of letters in Gaul in modern times' (he died in c.1130), had taught his boys and young men first to imitate the classical authors and then to speak and write prose and verse of their own.[38] What John describes is very similar to the way Latin was taught in the Prussian gymnasiums, French lycées, and English public schools until within living memory, and this is not surprising as the tradition of teaching went back to ancient Rome itself and to its rhetoricians, particularly Quintilian. Although the period in which Abelard lived is now described by historians as the Twelfth-Century Renaissance, this term can be misleading, as he and his colleagues believed they lived in a continuum with the classical past. 'Romanesque' is a better description of their culture than 'Renaissance'. There could be no 'rebirth' of Latin in the twelfth century because it was not yet dead, even though it was no one's mother tongue.

Because Latin was still a living language, masters recommended contemporary authors as models of style as well as ancient ones. When John of Salisbury's pupil, Peter of Blois, gave some advice on teaching Latin, he mentioned Suetonius, Tacitus, Livy and other ancient authors, but in pride of place for elegant prose he put Hildebert of Lavardin, whose letters he had been made to memorize when he was growing up.[39] Hildebert, who was chiefly famed for his elegies on the ruins of ancient Rome, had been bishop of Le Mans and then archbishop of Tours (he died in 1133). Twelfth-century writers did not model themselves exclusively on ancient authors, any more than a twentieth-century dramatist would make a pastiche of Shakespeare. Italian Renaissance scholars of the fourteenth and fifteenth centuries, on the other hand, were much more scrupulous and truly classical in their Latin because, by then, the life had been knocked out of living Latin by the new vernacular literatures. Renaissance scholars saved Latin from extinction at the cost of making it into a museum piece. In Abelard's time this was not yet necessary nor possible, as his contemporaries were among the freshest writers of Latin there have ever been. St Bernard was arguably the most powerful rhetorician since Cicero, Heloise the best letter-writer, and the authors of the *Carmina Burana* the most original poets.

Bernard of Chartres had told his students that they were dwarfs standing on the shoulders of giants.[40] They therefore believed in making progress in 'letters'. The obvious example of a medieval 'improvement' on classical models is the innovation of making Latin verse rhyme, a form of writing in which Abelard excelled. Here are some lines from his lament for Samson, the betrayed strongman of Israel:

> Quid tu, Dalida,
> quid ad hec dicis, impia,
> que fecisti?
> quenam munera
> per tanta tibi scelera
> conquisisti?[41]

(What about you, Dalila? What do you say to this, you betrayer? What have you done? What sort of rewards did you hope to gain by such great wickedness?)

The rhymes look crude and simplistic when printed out on the page, but they give effective emphasis if spoken aloud.

Abelard and his contemporaries excelled in the originality and range of their Latin because it was the only way they knew to give their thoughts lasting shape. In other words, they had not learned any other way to write. They contrasted the 'tenacious letters' of Latin with 'naked and transient' speech.[42] A century after Abelard, vernacular writing had developed sufficiently in France for it to become the primary medium of thought and the best way to record speech. Later still, when Renaissance schoolboys translated from their vernacular literatures into Latin, it was evident that Latin had become redundant as a literary language in its own right, though it survived for centuries where innovation was not desired, particularly in the schoolroom and the Roman Church. Abelard, growing up around 1100, belonged to the last generation in France for whom Latin was not yet a distinct foreign language but simply the 'letters' in which boys like himself learned to read and write. Being literate and knowing Latin meant the same thing for anyone educated in this way. A person described as *literatus* was 'literate' and he was also instructed in Latin 'literature'; these two senses could not be disentangled.

Latin had generally been described as 'letters' because it was the only writing people ordinarily came across. The long-standing exception to this generalization is the British Isles, where other languages (Anglo-Saxon and Celtic) had been written down for centuries. In the late 1120s Abelard became abbot of St Gildas-de-Rhuys in western Brittany, which was an outlier of this Celtic culture (Gildas had been the historian of post-Roman Britain). Abelard says 'the country was barbarous and its language unknown to me', which presumably means that he could neither speak nor write Celtic and that he had no wish to do so.[43] In the course of his life he would have confronted not only writers of Celtic languages but also the pioneers of writing in French and Occitan (the southern French of the troubadours). Though technically born in Brittany, Abelard came from south of the river Loire and his father had probably been a Poitevin. Abelard's contemporary, the troubadour Jaufré Rudel, says that 'we sing in the plain Romance tongue' (en plana lengua romana) which he links with the 'Poitevin people' of Berry, Guienne and Brittany.[44] Abelard's birthplace at Le Pallet is at the axial point of this region: with Brittany to the north, Poitou and Guienne to the south, and Berry to the east (to the west is the estuary of the Loire and the Atlantic Ocean). Abelard may therefore have been brought up to speak the 'plain Romance tongue' of this extended Poitevin region on both sides of the Loire.

Abelard came from the border of the very region where troubadour culture was being developed. If his father was a Poitevin knight, Abelard may have had the option as a youth of going to the court of the first troubadour, William IX count of Poitou and duke of Aquitaine (1086–1127), and learning to sing and fight with him. Instead, as we have seen, he chose to be a scholar. The love songs which he composed for Heloise (they no longer exist) were almost certainly in Latin rather than any form of French. She says that 'even the illiterate' could remember the sweetness of their melodies, which suggests that the words were harder to remember because they were in Latin.[45] Abelard, as a devotee of the classics and a 'cleric and canon' (as Heloise reminded him), may have regarded all vernacular writing as crude, unprofessional and impermanent. He had not given up his birthright for the 'plain Romance tongue' which he knew and (probably) spoke, but for 'letters' in the time-honoured classical and patristic tradition of Cicero and St Augustine. Abelard wanted to be a man of the world; his ambitions were directed towards Paris and Rome, rather than the towns along the Loire which he had known as a boy.

Latin made Abelard renowned as 'the world's prince of studies', as Peter the Venerable called him.[46] This was scarcely an exaggeration, as his students and admirers came from all over Latin Christendom. He was not to know – or he did not have the imagination to see – that the troubadours of his home country were pioneering in their 'plain Romance tongue' the beginnings of one of the world's great literatures. Abelard and the other brilliant Latin writers of his time would have been astonished to learn that they had had misjudged posterity and that the future of literature in Europe lay with the vernacular languages and particularly with something called 'French'. The fact that in the twentieth century somebody might be described as 'literate' even though he knew no Latin at all would have seemed bizarre. And yet Abelard should perhaps have been more aware of what was happening. Within fifty years of his death the most ambitious author in the new French, Chrétien de Troyes, triumphantly declared that 'of the Greeks and Romans no one now says either much or little; there is no more word of them; their bright flame is extinguished. . . . Chivalry and learning has arrived in France; God grant that it remain here.'[47] With the Romans' flame extinguished, their language, Latin, became secondary to French.

THE LATIN CLASSICS

Contrary to Chrétien's boasting, it was not so much that the flame of Latin had suddenly been put out in the twelfth century as that writing in French had at last begun to find patrons. Like the writers of Latin with whom he was in competition, Chrétien was almost certainly a cleric by training. But, because he wrote in French, he looked to patrons from the laity rather than bishops and his fellow clergy. It was to attract the nobility, and ladies in particular, that he claimed that chivalry as well as learning had arrived in France. He was entitled to boast as vernacular writers like himself would soon command the place that Latinists had enjoyed at the courts of kings and princes. When – a generation or more before Chrétien – Abelard had decided to 'stick' (*inhesi* is the word he uses) with Latin, all kinds of considerations may have been in his mind in addition to the reason he gives of being seduced by Minerva.[48] 'Letters', in the form of Latin grammar and rhetoric, had given their devotees splendid careers for over a thousand years and it must have been hard to believe in 1100 that anything could ever supersede them. Although increasing pressure was being put on clerics by Gregorian reformers to make them live like monks, the young Abelard would have seen that bishops and other diocesan officials were still among the richest and most powerful men in the land, just as their pagan predecessors had been when they had governed the Roman Empire.

   The officials of the Church had stepped into the shoes of the ancient imperial civil service and the essential qualification for entry, therefore, remained expertise in Latin, including classical literature. Although Gregorian reformers wanted religious devotion to be the essential prerequisite for ecclesiastical office, this was a harder condition to enforce

than knowledge of Latin, not least because the strictest reformers withdrew entirely from public office and became hermits. At the time of
Abelard's birth the cathedral schools remained the gate through which
all ambitious clerics had to pass and the old classical curriculum
persisted. A successful master could exert a wide influence in the
Church, particularly over a long career when his own pupils began to
be appointed to high office. Masters themselves could expect to be
appointed archdeacons, chancellors or even bishops, like Abelard's master, William of Champeaux. By the same token, masters who became
monks expected to be abbots, like Abelard himself when he was elected
abbot of St Gildas.

In 1096, when Abelard was in his teens and probably studying with
Roscelin at Loches (twenty miles south of Tours), Hildebert of Lavardin
was made bishop of Le Mans and Marbod bishop of the adjoining
diocese of Rennes. Hildebert and Marbod were principally distinguished
as Latin poets, as was Baudri abbot of Bourgueil (30 miles west of
Tours) who became archbishop of Dol in Brittany in 1107. The message
for Abelard in their promotions must have been that in the archdiocese
of Tours, which included the whole of north-western France, it paid an
ambitious cleric to be a Latin poet. Nevertheless, an atmosphere of
scandal surrounded clerical poets because they wrote, like Ovid and
Catullus, of their love for boys and girls. These lascivious poems, of
which hundreds survive from the eleventh and twelfth centuries, were
not necessarily all schoolroom exercises or light fiction, though it is hard
to assess exactly how they should be interpreted. How real, for example,
was the correspondence in verse between Baudri of Bourgueil, probably
writing in the 1080s before he became an abbot, and Lady Constance,
who describes herself as a 'bride of God' (she was probably a nun in the
neighbouring city of Angers)?

Baudri is crudely direct: 'Tu virgo, vir ego' (You virgin, Me man),
while insisting at the same time that they should be chaste: 'let there be
modesty in fact, but fun in the pen'.[49] In this facetious spirit he describes
to Constance how he looks forward to her naked hand touching his
naked page and laying it in her lap, and much more of the same. In
accordance with the rules of rhetoric, she purportedly replies by enlar-
ging on this theme: 'With my hand I have touched your naked songs'; 'I
have put your parchment under my left breast adjoining my heart'; 'the
page you wrote, though lying at my breast, has set my womb on fire'.[50]
Baudri wrote in comparable style to boys as well, as did Marbod of
Rennes, and Hildebert of Lavardin is credited with a poem defending
those Greek gods who loved boys rather than girls.[51] Composing erotic
letters and verse made learning Latin more interesting and the practice

may have become more common, rather than less, in Abelard's time when standards of Latin were improving and reformers' strictures were making actual sexual encounters in the schools harder to achieve.

This is the social context in which Abelard places his first meeting with Heloise at her uncle's house in the cloister of Notre-Dame in *c*.1117. Because of her great fame as a Latinist, Abelard hoped to enjoy 'jocund intercourse' with Heloise, 'as many things can be put in writing more audaciously than they can be said'.[52] They were to be penfriends and have fun, like Lady Constance and Baudri of Bourgueil. When any literary lover of girls and boys achieved a senior appointment in the Church, he could draw attention to his ability as a Latinist once more by publishing a retraction of his youthful indiscretions, as Marbod did after he became bishop of Rennes. He addressed his confession to his fellow poet and bishop, Hildebert of Lavardin.[53] This confession was itself a literary artifice, as Marbod was more concerned to regret the dated style of his early poems than their lascivious content. A talented clerical poet expected to be forgiven his youthful indiscretions and, judging by the careers of Marbod, Hildebert and Baudri, they often were. Abelard's 'history of calamities', which he wrote when he had achieved promotion as abbot of St Gildas, similarly combines admission of his indiscretions with literary display. He must have been surprised when Heloise, instead of offering forgiveness or 'jocund intercourse', responded with literary fireworks of her own, telling him that she was prouder to be his whore than the empress of Rome and that she would willingly have followed him to Hell.[54]

A predilection for the Latin classics is a commonplace of clerical memoirs because it demonstrated the subject's erudition. Even St Bernard was said to have composed 'jesting little songs' in adolescence.[55] Abbot Suger's biographer described how 'he could not forget' the ancient poets because of his tenacious memory and he would sometimes recite twenty or thirty lines of Horace.[56] In Norman England Herbert Losinga, the first bishop of Norwich (1091–1119), used to recite elegiac verses in bed until he decided he was too old for such 'obscenities'.[57] His difficulty was not in remembering them, but in the belated realization that to reach Heaven he must read the Scriptures. The fullest account in Abelard's time of the attraction of Latin poetry comes from Guibert de Nogent, who describes how he found it sexually arousing when he was growing up.[58] He composed indecent and frivolous verses of his own, which he attributed to fictitious authors, and he showed them to no one (he says) apart from a few friends. Guibert's account explains how verses like those allegedly exchanged between Baudri of Bourgueil and Lady Constance might have come into existence. The dubious verses of precocious students found their way into anthologies and thence into the canon of Latin poetry. As Roman love poetry had often been sexually explicit, the medieval schoolmen's 'obscenities' were classical in spirit as well as in diction.

In *Theologia Christiana*, which Abelard wrote in sombre mood shortly after his castration and condemnation as a heretic at Soissons in 1121, he purported to disapprove of all classical literature. He quoted the familiar story of how St Jerome had dreamed that when he was required to identify himself and answered that he was a Christian, the magistrate had told him that he was lying because he was a Ciceronian.[59] In another story, which Abelard quoted in the same context, an angel had snatched away the book which Jerome was reading because it was by Cicero.[60] Making no mention of his own love poetry for Heloise, Abelard condemned poets as a class, along with the 'jesters, acrobats, conjurors and singers of filth' who came into town on the Church's feast-days.[61] 'Why', he demanded, 'are bishops and doctors of the Christian religion not kept apart from poets in the city of God, just as Plato had banned them from the ideal republic?'[62] The short answer was that much of the 'filth' that circulated in Latin verse had been composed or copied out by the bishops and doctors themselves when they were at school. Abelard himself was described by a rival master as a jester (*joculator*), who more often played the fool than the professor (*doctor*).[63]

But this was not Abelard's last word on the classics, as in the final version of *Theologia*, which he composed in the 1130s, he modified his tone. Possibly he had been influenced by his correspondence with Heloise, whose admiration for the ancients was more wholehearted than his own. He again quoted St Jerome's rhetorical question: 'What has Cicero got to do with St Paul?'; but this time he gave an answer.[64] 'No one', Abelard pointed out, 'who knows about holy Scripture is ignorant that spiritual men have made better progress in sacred doctrine by the study of "letters" than by the merits of religion.'[65] St Paul was not a greater apostle than St Peter (Abelard continued) and neither was Augustine a greater saint than Martin; but Paul and Augustine have made larger contributions to the understanding of Christian doctrine because they had been educated in secular literature before their conversion to Christianity and so they had learned how to express themselves. 'I therefore judge', Abelard provocatively concluded, 'that the study of secular letters is especially commended by divine dispensation.'[66]

Secular values and pagan images were bound to persist as long as Latin itself remained a living language. Classical paganism was inextricably intertwined with Christianity because they shared in Latin 'letters' the same vocabulary and range of imagery. In Abelard's lifetime this complex and contorted relationship was most strikingly displayed in Romanesque sculpture, particularly in Poitou and the Languedoc (for example at Aulnay and Moissac and numerous village churches). Centaurs, sea monsters, furies and other mythical creatures of antiquity – some making obscene gestures – stare out from roof corbels and form an interlace around entrance porches and the capitals of pillars, even in the cloisters where monks did their reading. St Bernard famously asked: 'What are filthy apes doing there, and wild lions, and monstrous centaurs, and half-men, and striped tigers...?'[67] They were there, as Bernard knew very well, because the books the monks read in the cloister, particularly the Old Testament, were full of imagery. Noah's ark, Samson and the lion, David and Goliath, Jonah and the whale, and Daniel in the lions' den, matched the power of Greek and Roman mythology. Representing these images three-dimensionally in sculpture was one way of coming to terms with them.

Abelard illustrates another way of dealing with classical myth when he concluded his Confession of Faith to Heloise by exorcizing the monsters faced by Ulysses two thousand years earlier: 'Securely rooted in the Faith, I have no fear of the barking of Scylla, I scorn the whirlpool of Charybdis, I have no dread of the deadly songs of the Sirens.'[68] Raging dogs, spiralling waves and seductive mermaids are frequent subjects of Romanesque art. This was probably Abelard's last public statement, made at the time of the council of Sens in 1140. At last, it seemed, he had laid the terrors and blandishments of the ancient world to rest. But, as so often with Abelard, a hint of ambiguity remains, as Ulysses had overcome these horrors by his own courage and ingenuity and not by faith. Like Ulysses sailing into the west beyond the pillars of Hercules, Abelard was bidding farewell to his long-suffering wife before his last voyage into the unknown.

LADY GRAMMAR

The mythological figure whom Abelard never exorcized was his first love, the goddess Minerva, and her medieval personifications as Lady Grammar or Lady Philology. The latter was characterized in a Latin poem as Abelard's bride.[69] Heloise, 'supreme in the abundance of letters', was a real-life incarnation of these personages. A goddess of letters had no need to be as beautiful as Venus, and Abelard says no more about Heloise's appearance than that she was 'not ugly in the face'.[70]

Lady Grammar was usually depicted as matronly and severe. At the western entrance of Chartres cathedral she is shown (in a sculpture dating from the mid-twelfth century) grasping a huge bunch of birch-rods in her right hand and an open book in her left; at her feet cower two boys, one ready stripped for beating and the other keeping his head down. Lady Grammar was a personage of dubious sexual orientation. 'In one and the same action she is father and mother', the scholastic Alan of Lille explained, 'by her blows she makes up for a father, by her milk she fills the role of a mother.'[71]

Learning Latin was a traumatic rite of passage from the nursery to the male-dominated adult world. Guibert de Nogent recalled how he used to sit by himself in his clerical tunic, 'like a beast' awaiting slaughter, watching the other children playing.[72] Abelard is explicit about the bestial and sadistic element in grammar teaching. When Fulbert hired him as Heloise's master, 'he was giving me total licence to do anything I wanted with her, and also the opportunity to do it even if we did not want to, as I could make her bend with threats and blows if I did not succeed with caresses'.[73] He claims that he hit Heloise as a way to avert suspicion; Fulbert would attribute any screams to the normal process of Latin teaching. Abelard ascribes his violence not to himself but to his 'love and affection', which gave Heloise blows 'surpassing the sweetness of all ointments'.[74] 'No step in love-making was omitted (he continues) and if love could think up anything out of the ordinary, it got added in as well.'[75]

Of Abelard's contemporaries, only St Anselm of Canterbury linked beating with bestiality. His biographer, Eadmer, recorded his views at length as an example of his unusual sensitivity. 'Out of human beings you have nurtured beasts,' Anselm told an abbot who thought there was no alternative to beating boys, 'they have grown up perverted and vicious because they were never nurtured in genuine affection for any-body.'[76] Children were routinely beaten because teaching was envisaged as the reshaping of the fallen human being. Even St Anselm conceded that the growing boy needed shaping when he used the metaphor of applying gold-leaf to metal or parchment: the artificer moulds the leaf and he may strike it gently; what he does not do is shatter it.[77]

Unlike Guibert de Nogent, Abelard says nothing about how he first learned to read, perhaps because he thought it commonplace and he had enjoyed it. His only reference to the subject is in a letter he wrote to Heloise's nuns, where he quoted St Jerome's recommendation to have some toy letters of wood or ivory in the nursery, so that the child could learn their names and put them in order.[78] Abelard's contemporary, Orderic Vitalis, was handed over to a priest to learn the rudiments at the age of five in 1080.[79] But Orderic's father was himself a priest (there were many married priests despite the clerical ideal of celibacy) and he may have appreciated the value of starting young. Some mothers must have wished to prolong infancy to the age of six or even later, as 'letters' meant separation, a master and the birch. Nothing is known about where Abelard and his brothers received their earliest instruction in Latin. Perhaps they went to a local priest, like Orderic, or there may have been a chaplain in the house, as in Guibert de Nogent's case. Much must have depended on the wealth of Abelard's father, which is an unknown quantity. Alternatively, Abelard and his brothers may have had to leave their community of Le Pallet altogether in order to find grammar schooling (probably not the institution of a 'school' as such) in one of the neighbouring towns or churches.

Appropriately enough, learning 'letters' began with the ABC, letter by letter. Each one had to be pronounced individually and given its exact sound in Latin. This was primarily a physical and memorizing exercise, for which the rules had been laid down by Martianus Capella early in the fifth century. (The methods used to teach reading were centuries old and were considered all the better for that.) Martianus had tried to make his work more palatable by entitling it *The Marriage of Philology and Mercury*. This had sexual undertones, as the boy student 'married' Lady Grammar and the other muses of learning. But being told that the letter 'M' is impressed on the lips, that 'N' strikes hard with the tongue on the teeth, or that 'O' is formed with the breath of the rounded mouth, cannot have been much like a wedding celebration, least of all to a child of five or six threatened with a birch as big as himself.[80] Emphasis was put on the correct pronunciation of each letter because the next stage was to form syllables and then apply these rote-learned phonetic rules to reading Latin aloud. Accurate readers of Latin were produced by this method without their having to understand a word of the texts they voiced.

Because he had musical talent, Abelard may have found this kind of listening and repeating by rote very easy. Reading was as closely associated with chanting in school as it was in church. Learning the letters did not even require a book, as the ABC could be written out for each child on a board or slate. In English this device was later known as a 'horn-book' (named from the slice of horn which shielded the text from childish fingers) and in Latin it was an *abecedarium*. Hence elementary pupils were 'ABC boys' (*abecedarii*). Syllables were treated in the same way. Poor Guibert de Nogent had learned to recognize the letters, 'but hardly yet to join them into syllables', when his mother found him a real master, equipped with a whip and pretensions to grammar, instead of the household chaplain.[81] Needless to say, there were no reading books designed for the child. Once the pronunciation of the letters had been mastered, reading began with familiar Latin prayers or the Psalms. This may have been an excellent way of initiating reading, as in a household like Abelard's, prayers (starting with the *Pater Noster*, the 'Our Father') should have been recited daily. Instruction began with prayers because these were the texts most likely to be available and, more importantly, because reading was *lectio divina*. It was a precious skill, which should not be dissipated on such mundane observations as 'the cat sat on the mat'.

The average lay reader, like Abelard's father, was not going to get an opportunity to read very much (books were expensive and even monastic libraries were sparse), so he should only read what was worthwhile. The Psalms had been loved by Christians from the days of the early Church because they formed a rich cycle of prayers, which retained their musicality and resonance in St Jerome's Latin translation. Furthermore, they were chanted daily in the monastic liturgy, which was the model for everyone's worship. Reading, that is enunciating Latin, inevitably merged into worship and chant in the home as much as in school. The main function of reading in a home like Abelard's was prayer. In Le Pallet, or any other village in eleventh-century France, literacy served no useful day-to-day purpose. There were no newspapers, no advertisements coming through the mail, no government forms to be filled in, no public notices, apart from in churches where texts from the Scripture might be written up in capital letters. In short, there was no point in being literate except for religious purposes (which was of course a very powerful motivation in any Christian household).

VOICES AND LETTERS

Abelard commented that 'in monasteries anyone is said to "know letters" who has learned to pronounce them. And yet, as far as comprehension goes, monks who admit that they do not know how to read a given book have something just as closed in front of them as the lay people they choose to call "illiterate".'[82] Many monasteries, according to Abelard, only taught chant, which is 'merely a way of forming words without understanding them' like the bleating of sheep.[83] Hildegard of Bingen's description of how she suddenly (and miraculously in her opinion) came to understand the Latin that she had been chanting as a nun for thirty years confirms Abelard's comments, though it also suggests that monks and nuns might come to comprehend Latin by daily exposure much as a child learns its mother tongue without being taught it.[84] In a different context, Abelard had commended to Heloise's nuns St Jerome's statement that one 'reaches the sense of the words from their sound, and someone who learns to pronounce them will already want to understand them'.[85]

The term St Jerome used for 'words' here is 'voices' (*voces*) because this is how words were thought of before the invention of printing enabled people to see them mass-produced in the pages of books and newspapers. The strong emphasis on speech and rote learning made memory an essential element in medieval literacy. By constant repetition the clergy learned the liturgy by heart. In monastic choirs the demon Tutivillus was believed to collect up sackfuls of dropped syllables from the Psalms to be weighed up at the Last Judgement against those who voiced the texts inaccurately.[86] Monks who failed to say their prayers correctly invalidated them and endangered not only their own souls but their patrons' as well. The most important medieval books, the great illuminated Psalters and Gospel books, were designed to be placed ceremonially on lecterns as expositions of the 'sacred page'; their texts were already known to their readers. Memory skills were valued as highly by scholastic masters, like Abelard, as they were by monks. He is described as having 'an unheard-of memory'.[87] His contemporary and rival, Hugh of St Victor, taught his students how to learn all the Psalms by heart and repeat them in any order.[88] When books were hard to come by and even making notes was difficult (wax, wood and slate are refractory materials to write on), memory was understandably more prized than in modern society. But there was more to it than that.

Speech was thought to be the essence of language and therefore of all understanding. John of Salisbury, who had been Abelard's student, defined 'letters' as 'indicators of voices'.[89] The human voice names things and makes sense of language. (Whether such 'things' are realities, in the sense of universals, is one of the issues which divided 'Nominalist' philosophers from 'Realists' in Abelard's time.) Words which were only written down – and therefore unvoiced – were not felt to be complete, as writing was a means to an end; it was the preservative in which past speech was conveyed to a future hearer. The reader's primary task was therefore to convert the words he saw on the page back into meaningful language by 'voicing' them. This did not necessarily imply that every word had to be read out loud, though a medieval reader would tend to do this as he had been taught that reading began with pronunciation. No medieval person could read without listening. 'The wise and learned letter would perish if man existed with deaf ears', wrote Abelard's contemporary, Bernard Silvestris.[90] A modern analogy is with the reader of a play or musical score, who will want to speak or hum some parts (or listen to the 'voices' of the actors and instruments) in order to comprehend the text.

The attenuated letters on the parchment had to be rejuvenated by the human spirit. Abelard associated his abilities in literacy with his youthful *ingenium* – his 'genius'. 'Through genius', he says at the beginning of the 'history of calamities', 'I grew up with a facility for literary discipline.'[91] This looks at first sight like an example of his conceit, but he is probably referring to the sixth sense which was needed for reconstituting texts. His 'genius' gave him the facility to turn letters back into voices. Because enunciation and memory were highly stressed, the dividing line between literacy and illiteracy is difficult to draw. A really literate person, like Abelard or St Bernard, did little reading or writing. Masters of the 'sacred page' knew the texts by heart and they composed by dictation.

In society as much as in the classroom, a master like Abelard headed a group of people of varying scholastic attainments. In such a group, members can participate in literacy without everyone having to read and write. In the eleventh and twelfth centuries people came together in 'textual communities' (the term is Brian Stock's), focused on the precepts of Scripture and other rules for the conduct of life, which they learned through participation.[92] Examples of such 'textual communities' in Abelard's time are St Bernard's monks, or religious and lay fraternities such as the Paterenes of Milan discussed by Stock. Despite the Bible being a closed book to the laity, the words of the 'sacred page' extended in a variety of ways beyond the little groups of monastic or professional scribes, who penned them, and the *literati* who had the grammar to construe them. Every Latinist voiced the words he read and, explicitly or implicitly, he translated their dead and alien diction into his living vernacular understanding.

Through the Church's daily but regularly changing liturgy of chant and readings, the Latin Scriptures reached everyone who could see and hear, provided they could get to a place of worship. This was probably a crucial limitation on numbers, as great churches like Cluny or St Denis were not numerous, nor necessarily welcoming, and most labourers were not permitted the time to go to them anyway. The ideal of a priest and a church in every village and a chaplain in every manor house was far from realization in the twelfth century, though things were moving in that direction. Abelard's family – exceptional perhaps even among the gentry – with its four educated sons and their pious father, might likewise be seen as a 'textual community'. An understanding of the Latin prayers and the Psalms may have extended beyond the formally literate males to the mother (who became a nun in old age) and the sister (who brought up the son of Abelard and Heloise to be literate), and possibly also to their household servants and their peasants. According to long-standing ecclesiastical law, everyone was meant to know the basic prayers like the *Pater Noster* and to recite the creed in Latin. If Abelard's parents' household were like Guibert de Nogent's, a cycle of prayers would have been said daily.

Like so much in medieval culture – and in Abelard's life – its literacy was a mass of contradictions. It was remote and yet accessible, Christian yet pagan, and dead and alive in its use of Latin. It put extraordinary emphasis on speech and memory and yet it also produced the most elaborate books. Literacy was a male preserve and yet Heloise excelled in it. Grammar was taught through fear, yet many scholastics grew up to adore the classics. However diverse these characteristics might be, they all made literacy interesting and gave it high standing, especially because it was the language of Scripture – the 'sacred page'. To be a *literatus* and a *clericus* was as privileged and promising a calling in medieval society as being a knight, and it was Abelard's chosen destiny.

4

Master

Magister Petrus – 'Master Peter', this is how Peter the Venerable abbot of Cluny describes Abelard in his letter to Heloise telling her of his death.[1] Peter called him 'Master' as a tribute to his 'mastery' (*magisterium*) of knowledge and also as a sign of respect, because 'Master' was the rank he had attained in society. Peter was writing in the 1140s, just when 'Master' was beginning to be prefixed as a title to the names of those who had graduated from the great international schools, as well as describing the masters who taught in them. A satirical poem from later in the twelfth century describes the ambition of Burnell the Ass to make a ten- or twenty-year progress through the schools of Paris and Bologna until he attains the title of 'Master': 'Then "Master" shall precede my name and if anyone fails to make that addition of "Master Burnell", he will be my sworn enemy.'[2] Unfortunately, Burnell meets up with his former 'master' in the old sense of animal driver, who crops his ears and forces him back into servitude and reality.

THE TITLE 'MASTER'

Abelard had fought as long and hard as Burnell the Ass to be recognized as a 'Master' and even St Bernard accorded him the title, though not with consistency or generosity. In some of the letters he wrote to the cardinals of the Roman curia at the time of the council of Sens in 1140 Bernard called Abelard 'Master Peter', while in others he did not.[3] The pattern of use suggests he entitled Abelard 'Master' only when he thought the addressee would be offended if he left it out. The letters of Pope Innocent II of 1140, condemning Abelard as a heretic, accord him no title.[4] By describing him as 'Master', Peter the Venerable was restoring Abelard's public dignity for Heloise, as well as returning his body to her for burial at the Paraclete. In her letters Heloise never addresses

Abelard as 'Master', though she does call him 'Lord'. Neither does she address him as 'Peter'. He is simply 'Abelard', 'her only one', who is 'especially hers'.[5] 'Master Peter' was presumably too impersonal and official a mode of address for Heloise to use herself.

'Master' was a title that was rapidly coming into fashion in the twelfth century, not only in the schools but also among craftsmen like master masons and a variety of officials such as master cooks, master falconers and the Master of the Knights Templar. The usage seems to have originated in the great schools of northern France and then spread to other institutions and forms of mastery. When, for example, William IX of Aquitaine claims for himself 'the name of "undisputed master"' in the art of love-making, he was probably parodying the rivalries of schoolmen like Abelard about who should be accredited a master.[6] The way one sense of 'Master' merged into another is well illustrated by the life of Gilbert of Sempringham, who was born in the 1080s (just a few years after Abelard). Like Abelard, he was the son of a knight and, like Abelard too, he left home to traverse the provinces of France in search of learning 'until he achieved the name and rank (literally the 'grade' – *gradus*) of "Master"'.[7] On returning to his home in Lincoln-shire, he started teaching local boys and also girls. His biographer (who was writing late in the twelfth century, as Gilbert lived to be a hundred) describes him as a 'Master' in three contexts: he was a schoolmaster, he was a graduate of the French schools, and thirdly he was master of his sexual desires; he 'kept himself clean' is how his biographer puts it.

Abelard, too, associated being a master with clean living. There are those, he writes, who 'impudently arrogate to themselves the name of "Master in the Divine Page" even though they live carnally and filthily and do not reform, as if they were throwing the temple of the Holy Spirit wide open to everyone'.[8] Abelard was being wise after the event here, as he wrote this after his castration. When four or five years earlier he had seduced Heloise in Fulbert's house in the precinct of Notre-Dame, he too had been acting carnally and filthily, as he was the cathedral master responsible for teaching the 'divine page' of Scripture. Celibacy was essential to Abelard and Gilbert of Sempringham because they both became the male superiors of groups of religious women. In this capacity Gilbert was formally described as 'Master' of the order of Sempringham.[9] When Peter the Venerable called Abelard 'Master', he may have been thinking of him not only as a scholastic master but also as a 'master' of nuns.

All these diverse meanings of 'Master' coalesced in the person of the supreme master, Jesus Christ. In his *Ethics* Abelard quoted the words of Matthew's Gospel: 'Master, I will follow thee whithersoever thou goest.'[10] To monks in Abelard's time the words 'school' and 'master' evoked their own monastic life rather than anything secular or academic. The Rule of St Benedict opens with the words: 'Hearken to the precepts of the Master' and it exhorts its followers to establish a 'school' of the Lord's service.[11] St Bernard recalled this old Benedictine ideal of a school of religion, when he assured another Cistercian abbot that he was his fellow student 'in the school of piety under Master Jesus'.[12] In Bernard's opinion academic masters, particularly those who taught Scripture like Abelard, had usurped a title and a role that properly belonged to Christ and the religious. Abelard himself was aware of this when he quoted the text 'Neither be ye called masters: for one is your Master, even Christ'.[13] But he did not draw the conclusion that mortals like himself should not be addressed as 'Master'. The most original thinker of the time, St Anselm of Canterbury, registered his doubts about what 'Master' should mean in a typically humble and yet confident form: 'I am called "Master",' he says in one of his prayers, 'though I do not know what being one is.'[14]

By contrast with St Anselm's ready recognition as a master (by the same winning combination of confidence and humility he became abbot of Bec and archbishop of Canterbury), Abelard's struggle to secure recognition was protracted and controversial. His experiences embittered him so much that the account he gives of them in his 'history of calamities' is overtly prejudiced. Those of his contemporaries who were familiar with the people involved would have read between the lines and recognized which parts of Abelard's narrative were most obviously distorted or special pleading. The 'history of calamities' was perhaps intended as a single document in a pamphlet war between rival masters in France but, because the arguments of his opponents have survived in fragments or not at all, Abelard's story has sometimes been treated as if it were an authoritative revelation of the state of learning in the Twelfth-Century Renaissance. The 'history of calamities' may well have been true to Abelard's understanding of his experiences, but that does not mean that it is – or was intended to be – factual in a modern historian's sense. Instead of taking Abelard's narrative in isolation, it is best to start with what can be pieced together from a range of sources not excluding the 'history of calamities'.

The Beginnings of Abelard's Career as a Master

The fullest reconstruction of Abelard's career as a master has been made by R. H. Bautier as part of his study of the development of

Paris, the city which was the focus of Abelard's ambitions throughout his professional life.[15] He deliberately sought out the leading masters of his time. 'First he had Roscelin as a teacher,' says Otto of Freising. Roscelin's importance was that he was 'the first person in our times to introduce Nominalism into logic'.[16] Nominalism was central to Abelard's career as a philosopher and most of his ideas about the application of linguistic theory to Christian doctrine may have come from Roscelin, whose own works do not survive. Otto of Freising did not explain that Roscelin had been charged with heresy at the council of Soissons in 1092, although he had not been banned from teaching and his trial may have enhanced his reputation as a radical thinker. His teaching of Abelard probably began at this time, when he was thirteen or fourteen years old and it continued throughout his teens. 'From boyhood up until youth', Roscelin later reminded him, 'I showed you so much in the name and act of a master.'[17] (There is a Nominalist allusion here to the difference between names and acts.) In the same context Roscelin says that he taught at Loches. It looks as if Abelard's 'perambulation of the provinces' (as he called it) in search of logicians had taken him up the Loire valley, from his birthplace at Le Pallet (near Nantes at the mouth of the Loire) through Anjou until he reached the Touraine and Blois.[18]

The most decisive step in Abelard's early life was when he stopped following the course of the Loire, which would have led him further east to the cathedral school at Orléans, and turned north to the valley of the Seine and the area which he and his contemporaries called 'France' (when Abelard later had to leave Paris and return home, he described himself as being 'remote from France').[19] Just as 'France' was confined in the twelfth century to the Île-de-France, so Paris for Abelard meant the little island in the Seine which harboured the cathedral of Notre-Dame at one end and the Palais Royal at the other. When he recalled how 'At last I reached Paris', he meant that he had finally succeeded in entering this special precinct at the heart of 'France', where he rubbed shoulders with the households of the bishop and the king (unfortunately Abelard says nothing about where his first lodgings were).[20] The Paris school was headed by the formidable master, William of Champeaux, archdeacon and confidant of the king, Philip I. Here Abelard arrived as a stranger, a foreigner indeed, probably around the year 1100 when he was twenty-one. Because Roscelin had been his master, he arrived in Paris with an already compromised reputation, which helps explain why he subsequently distanced himself from Roscelin. Abelard described Paris as being 'already' a powerhouse, where the discipline of logic 'had most especially been accustomed to flourish', and he acknowledged that William of Champeaux was 'outstanding in his mastery in fame and in fact'.[21]

As Abelard had now attained the ultimate ambition of any student of being taught by the best professor at the best institution, one might have thought that he would settle down and seek promotion by winning the good opinion of his seniors. But, to his credit perhaps, this was never Abelard's way. It took him a decade or more to get a secure teaching post (from c.1104 to c.1114) and, once he had got it, he threw it away by seducing Heloise. Abelard repeated this pattern of throwing away hard-won success time and time again. Having been rescued from his affair with Heloise by the abbey of St Denis, the most distinguished monastery in the Paris region, Abelard questioned the authenticity of St Denis himself, the patron of the abbey and of the kingdom of France. Accused of treason, he was protected by Count Thibaud of Champagne and given land by the bishop of Troyes on which to found a monastery of his own (later Heloise's convent of the Paraclete). But this too he abandoned when he became abbot of St Gildas in Brittany (probably between 1125 and 1127), and so his 'calamities' continued for the rest of his life. He attributed their origin to his first arrival in Paris and the 'envy' shown him by his fellow students and their master, William of Champeaux.[22]

To obtain a secure appointment as a master, Abelard needed to be elected to a benefice by the canons of one of the great churches. Beneath this rank there were less formal – and less secure – teaching appointments in other churches or as assistants to masters. The biography of Abelard's contemporary, Odo of Orléans, describes how he won such a reputation for learning when young ('adolescent' is the Latin word) that he was thought 'worthier to have the name of master than pupil'. He secured his first teaching post in Toul and then 'he was called by the canons of Our Lady of Tournai and constituted master of their school'.[23] This was a permanent appointment, which enabled Odo to write books on philosophy and attract students to Tournai from all over western Europe, which was presumably what the canons had hoped for when they had appointed him. Abelard, too, described himself as an 'adolescent' ambitious to have a school of his own.[24] He achieved this first of all at Melun (south of Paris), which he describes as a 'fortress and royal seat'; this was probably in 1102, when he was aged twenty-two or twenty-three.[25]

Abelard makes clear in his 'history of calamities' that he was already involved in some sort of political intrigue, as it was 'potentates of the country' who protected him at Melun from William of Champeaux.[26] As archdeacon, William had ecclesiastical authority over him, as well as having influence at the royal court. It looks as if Abelard countered this by getting the support of Stephen de Garlande, who was another archdeacon of the Paris diocese and belonged to a family that held numerous royal and ecclesiastical offices in France; he became royal chancellor in 1105.[27] He was not much older than Abelard and he lived in an atmosphere of scandal, as he functioned both as a cleric and a knight; but he had the experience and French connections which Abelard lacked. Abelard's story is that he chose (probably in 1104) to move his school from Melun to Corbeil, which was another fortress town further down the Seine, so that he could be nearer Paris and engage in 'more frequent bouts of disputation' with William of Champeaux, whose reputation as a master was on the verge of extinction.[28] In reality, as distinct from Abelard's wisdom after the event, he may have been expelled first from Melun and then from Corbeil by the power of William of Champeaux.

Abelard's explanation of what happened next is personal and scholastic. He was 'compelled to repatriate', that is, to go home to Le Pallet (probably in 1105), because of an illness brought on by excessive studying.[29] He remained 'remote from France for some years'; he probably did not return to Paris until 1108.[30] His breakdown may have been caused by temporary exhaustion, compounded by intimidation by William of Champeaux's followers. He never again seems to have experienced long-term mental breakdown despite the 'calamities' of castration, ·condemnation as a heretic, accusations of treason, death threats at St Gildas, etc. The psychological weakness that he did acknowledge was instability: 'I justly merited the reproach' (he says of a later incident) 'that here was a man who "began to build and was not able to finish".'[31] Many of his books are incomplete and he never settled anywhere for long.

After his breakdown Abelard had to start all over again in Paris. Once more he became William of Champeaux's student and challenged him successfully at least once; Abelard's use of the logical term 'indifferently' is conceded in a report of William's teaching.[32] After various intrigues, Abelard says that he was put 'in charge of the study of dialectic' in the Paris cathedral school by the master who taught there.[33] But in a few days William of Champeaux undermined his position and compelled him once more to retreat to Melun.[34] However, in 1109 William himself withdrew further from the Île-de-la-Cité area of Paris, when his monastic school of St Victor was re-established on the south bank of the Seine outside the city walls. This gave Abelard his opportunity: 'I returned immediately from Melun to Paris, hoping for peace from him henceforward.'[35] As so often, he had underestimated his adversary.

William prevented him from getting any nearer the cathedral school of Notre-Dame than the church of Sainte Geneviève, on the south bank of the Seine outside the city walls. Abelard describes how 'I pitched camp with my students there, as if to besiege the occupier of my place' on the Île-de-la-Cité.[36] This was largely bombast, as the bridges to the island were defended by the real soldiers of the king and the bishop. Abelard is non-committal about the outcome of this struggle; he concludes his account of it with an ambiguous quotation from Ovid saying 'I was not vanquished'.[37]

Whatever it was that really happened in Paris, Abelard was again 'compelled to repatriate'.[38] He says his mother was responsible for this, as she had chosen to retire to a convent, once his father had likewise entered a monastery. (This form of retirement was a way of ensuring that the family property was passed on to the next generation under parental supervision, as well as giving husband and wife the chance to prepare for the next world.) Although Abelard had already surrendered his interest in the property at Le Pallet, confirmation of this was probably required. Unsuccessful clerics like him, who had not yet irrevocably committed themselves to celibacy by becoming priests, might return home unexpectedly like the Prodigal Son and get the fatted calf.

In 1113 Abelard went back to 'France', though not to Paris where he may have been *persona non grata*. He went instead to the cathedral school at Laon, at the north-eastern frontier of the Île-de-France and eighty miles from Paris. He says he went there to 'learn divinity'.[39] Possibly his choice was influenced by his parents retiring to monasteries. The discipline of logic and dialectic, in which he had specialized for the last fifteen years, was a secular subject even though it had applications to the interpretation of Scripture. Studying divinity, on the other hand, led directly to understanding religion (and it might also lead to a bishopric). Once more Abelard, now aged thirty-two or thirty-three, was starting all over again, as he came to Master Anselm of Laon with the status of a student. After more than a decade of humiliation and frustration, a less single-minded person than Abelard might have chosen a school closer to home and settled down as a master in peaceful obscurity by the Loire. But the message of his 'history of calamities' is that he was driven by ambition: he had to be the greatest philosopher in the world, 'for so I rated myself'.[40] (He achieved this status in the opinion of his admirers like Peter the Venerable.) Without the force of this ambition and the sufferings and passions it aroused, posterity would never have heard of Abelard – nor of Heloise either.

THE FOUNDATIONS OF A MASTER'S POWER

At Laon, Abelard adopted the same tactics he had used in Paris. But Master Anselm proved as formidable an adversary as William of Champeaux. John of Salisbury noted that no one attacked Anselm of Laon or his brother Ralph (the school was a double act) with impunity.[41] Anselm's career at Laon had spanned thirty or forty years; he had taught many bishops and abbots of the French and Rhineland churches, as well as others in Italy and Britain. Rupert of Deutz described him as 'more famous than any bishop' and he pointed out that Anselm's power depended on his 'office as much as his standing as a master'.[42] The 'office' which Anselm of Laon exercised was that of dean and chancellor, which meant that he was in charge of the cathedral and the bishop's business. Laon is a small hill city, dominated by its cathedral. When Abelard arrived there in 1113, Anselm was at the apogee of his power. The year before, he had survived a rising by the townspeople against the clergy, in which the bishop, Gaudry, had been killed. Anselm had contributed to pacifying the city and restoring its reputation as a magnet for students. He was so successful that a letter of 1115, to a correspondent in Pisa, describes the crowds of international students in Laon and the urgent need to book lodgings.[43] By this time Anselm was archdeacon, with authority over clergy in the diocese, as well as being dean and chancellor.

Guibert de Nogent, whose abbey was only twenty miles from Laon, repeatedly calls Anselm 'the master' and he gives a number of examples of his political acumen: Anselm had advised against electing Gaudry as bishop in the first place; he had warned Gaudry of the plot to kill him; he had persuaded the townspeople to surrender the bishop's body for burial.[44] Anselm's brilliance and power made Rupert of Deutz call him 'Lucifer'; Rupert thought him a blasphemous innovator.[45] More common was the opinion of his devotees, like Guibert de Nogent or John of Salisbury, that he and his brother Ralph were the brightest lights of France.[46] Rupert had an equally unusual and unfriendly opinion of William of Champeaux, whom he nicknamed the 'High Priest'.[47] His objection to Anselm and William was that they commented on the Scriptures in their teaching and yet they were not monks, but secular clerics who professed the liberal arts and were steeped in ecclesiastical business. In fact, William of Champeaux had become a canon of St Victor in c.1105 in order to lead a more religious life, although he had returned to ecclesiastical business in 1113 when he became bishop of Châlons-sur-Marne.

The careers of William of Champeaux and Anselm of Laon show that masters did not live in ivory towers. They needed the security of fortified churches and they had to be as ready to destroy rivals as knights were in their castles. A master's power rested on the twin foundations of his academic fame, which attracted international students to his city, and his ecclesiastical offices which entitled him to discipline the local clergy. Anselm of Laon was as deeply involved in the politics of France as William of Champeaux because Laon was a royal bishopric. After Bishop Gaudry was killed, King Louis VI invaded the Laon region in order to drive out Thomas de Marle, who was terrorizing the city and had allegedly been responsible for the plot to kill the bishop. (This is described by Guibert de Nogent and also by Louis's biographer, Abbot Suger.) The new bishop of Laon, Hugh dean of Orléans, owed his appointment to Louis VI's chancellor, Stephen de Garlande, who in the process obtained the deanery of Orléans for himself.[48] After only a few months in office, however, Bishop Hugh died at the beginning of 1113.

This is the point at which Abelard arrived in Laon. According to his own account, his intentions were purely academic; he had come to study under the great Master Anselm. But Anselm cannot have seen his arrival in so simple a light. Abelard had been master of the church of Sainte Geneviève, whose dean was Stephen de Garlande, the king's chancellor who had obtained the bishopric of Laon for Hugh dean of Orléans. Abelard may have gone to Laon (a hazardous place to go to in 1113) as Stephen's agent in order to strengthen royal influence there after the murder of Bishop Gaudry and the unexpected death of Stephen's nominee, Bishop Hugh. Anselm must have been suspicious of Abelard even before he opened his mouth and he may have felt as threatened by Stephen de Garlande and his clerical agents as by Thomas de Marle and his knights. Anselm's awe of the king's chancellor is underlined in a story by Peter the Chanter describing how he threw himself at Stephen's feet to intercede for his nephews, who had been imprisoned for Bishop Gaudry's murder. 'That noble and distinguished man' was so impressed by Anselm's humility that 'he descended from his pedestal' and offered not only to release the nephews but to make them knights.[49]

Abelard describes in his 'history of calamities' how he undermined Anselm of Laon's classes by making complaints and failing to attend; he even had the temerity to start giving his own lectures in Anselm's school. As in Paris with William of Champeaux ten years earlier, this aroused Anselm's 'envy' and Abelard was expelled. Abetted by Stephen de Garlande, Abelard's plan may have been to destroy the authority of 'this old man' (as Abelard describes Anselm) and take over the school of Laon himself.[50] As on previous occasions, he had underestimated his adversary. But this time the consequences were not disastrous for Abelard, since he was soon appointed master at Notre-Dame in Paris. Considering the recent opposition to him there, this is remarkable. Possibly Stephen de Garlande exerted influence over Abelard's appointment in order to reward him for his work at Laon, even though its outcome had been unsuccessful for him personally.

Abelard saw his return to Paris as a triumph: 'And so, after a few days, I came back to Paris: to the school which had been destined for me for so long and which had been offered me when I was first expelled (in 1109); I was in peaceful possession there for some years.'[51] These are probably the years between 1114 and 1117. In 1116 his position was further strengthened by the promotion of his supporter, Gilbert the chancellor and archdeacon, to the bishopric of Paris. At the age of thirty-seven or thirty-eight, Abelard was at last at the top of the greasy pole. He could now go back and forth across the bridges on to the Île-de-la-Cité whenever he chose, for he was the bishop's man and the king's chancellor's man. This is the time that Heloise remembered, when every neck craned and every eye strained to see him when he went out in public.[52] He was the first in that line of French intellectuals, extending through Voltaire to Sartre and Foucault, who became fascinating and controversial public figures in Paris. This is the time, too, which Fulk of Deuil recalled, when students came crowding to him from all over France and even from the extremities of Europe.[53]

Although Abelard was as successful as William of Champeaux in attracting students to Paris, he failed to consolidate his position there in the way William had done. If Abelard had become chancellor or archdeacon of Paris in succession to Gilbert in 1116, his position might have been as strong as William's or as Anselm's at Laon. He might then have been able to ride out the furore caused by his seduction of Heloise the next year. Probably, though, he had not had enough time by 1116 to build up personal support in the cathedral chapter of Notre-Dame, as distinct from winning a following among students and street entertainers. One of his purposes in agreeing to teach Heloise and residing in Canon Fulbert's house may have been to ingratiate himself with Fulbert and the other senior members of the cathedral chapter of Paris. If these were the circumstances, seducing Heloise was the most imprudent thing he could have done.

The really successful masters had a head for business and understood that they were executives as much as intellectuals. Obvious examples from Abelard's time are Lanfranc (abbot and archbishop), St Anselm of Canterbury (abbot and archbishop), Ivo of Chartres (prior and bishop), William of Champeaux (prior and bishop) and Anselm of Laon (dean, chancellor and archdeacon). There were no university authorities yet to license masters or control students. Sir Richard Southern has best described this 'short time, broadly corresponding to the first half of the twelfth century, when there was a wide opportunity for individual enterprise and for ruthless competition, which was never again so uncontrolled'.[54] Competition was so strong that masters who did not have their wits about them – in the common sense meaning of 'wits' – might be ousted by rivals. The extreme method of doing this was to accuse a master of heresy, as notoriously happened to Roscelin in 1092, to Abelard himself in 1121 and 1140, and to Gilbert de la Porrée in 1148. Otto of Freising coupled Abelard's case with Gilbert's and remarked that Abelard had lacked common sense because he was a Breton. At 'business' (*negotia*) he was 'quite stupid', despite being so intelligent at the liberal arts, like his fellow Bretons, the brothers Bernard and Thierry who became masters at Chartres.[55]

The reputation of Thierry of Chartres as a master was as brilliant and controversial as Abelard's. He too complained of rumour and envy whispering that he was a magician, a heretic and a corrupter of student morals.[56] Abelard draws a vignette of this fellow spirit in action at his own trial at Soissons in 1121. When it came to the solemn moment of pronouncing sentence, the papal legate allegedly made a theological error and Thierry jeered.[57] When he whispered the correct formulation from the Athanasian Creed, his bishop warned him that he was liable to be prosecuted himself for lese-majesty against papal authority. Nevertheless, according to Abelard, Thierry stood his ground and demanded a retrial. The president of the court, the archbishop of Reims, immediately stood up and declared that no deviant should be heard.[58] So Thierry was silenced and Abelard was condemned without being permitted to defend himself. Deviant masters, like Thierry or Abelard, were a threat to the hierarchical and institutional system of authority, which the Papacy was struggling to put in place, because they claimed to know the truth through their own wits and they could run rings round anyone – apart from St Bernard – who had not had a scholastic training.

THE WRITINGS OF ABELARD'S MASTERS

As has already been suggested, Abelard's account of his masters in his 'history of calamities' is prejudiced and misleading. For a start, he makes no mention of Roscelin, although it is certain that Roscelin taught him. The probable explanation for this omission is that Roscelin had insulted Abelard in a letter he wrote him mocking his castration. There is no way of knowing exactly what Roscelin contributed to Abelard's mental formation, as the only work which is definitely his is this letter to Abelard.[59] But statements attributed to him in the course of controversy by Abelard and St Anselm of Canterbury suggest that he had revived the theological debate about the logical meaning of the Trinity.[60] This was the debate, extending back to St Augustine and Boethius, which Abelard was to pursue in *Theologia*. There is also a text 'On Universals' attributed to a 'Master R'. As it has common features with Abelard's ideas, it may indeed be Roscelin's and, in that case, it suggests that Abelard owed much of his understanding of universals to him.[61]

Like William of Champeaux and Anselm of Laon, Roscelin was not a monk. He was a master of the liberal arts, who had had the temerity to apply classical grammar and logic to Christian doctrine. To a conservative monk like Rupert of Deutz this was blasphemous and dangerous, even if it could not be proved heretical. St Anselm of Canterbury had written a refutation of Roscelin in 1092, and in 1098 he submitted a revised version of this to Pope Urban II, inviting him to censor it. St Anselm of Canterbury insisted that 'everyone should be warned to approach questions about the sacred page with the utmost caution. Those dialecticians of our time – or rather those heretics of dialectic – who think that universal substances are mere words (literally 'the breath of the voice' – *flatum vocis*) should be blown right out of any discussion of spiritual questions.'[62] St Anselm of Canterbury was therefore arguing that Roscelin and his followers were heretical in their interpretation of the liberal arts of dialectic and logic, as well as being religious heretics. The young Abelard was presumably one of these 'heretics of dialectic', as in 1098 he was still in Roscelin's school or just leaving him to go to Paris.

The way Abelard omits Roscelin from his account of his education brings into question the reliability of what he has to say about William of Champeaux and Anselm of Laon. As in Roscelin's case, little or nothing survives of their work in a form they themselves wrote or authorized to be published. Statements attributed to them are extant either in excerpts or in texts of dubious provenance.[63] In this respect Abelard's masters contrast with Abelard himself, as his theological works survive in whole books, despite papal instructions to destroy them following his trial at Sens in 1140. In Roscelin's case accusations of heresy may have proved more effective than in Abelard's in destroying his writings, although it is hard to see why that should have been so. Heresy cannot be the explanation for William of Champeaux and Anselm of Laon leaving so little by way of writings, as they were reputed models of orthodoxy – except by eccentrics like Rupert of Deutz. By contrast with William of Champeaux and Anselm of Laon, their contemporary, St Anselm of Canterbury, ensured that his works (*Monologion, Cur Deus Homo?* and many others) were published and preserved. In his own time St Anselm of Canterbury's reputation as a master did not match that of Anselm of Laon or William of Champeaux's, judging by the number of eulogies of each of them. St Anselm of Canterbury was relatively isolated because he was a monk, first in Normandy and then in England, and he did not seek out students from all over Christendom. The explanation for the better preservation of his works may simply be because he was a monk. As an abbot, he commanded the facilities of a scriptorium and the high regard of his fellow monks, who best knew how to put his ideas into lasting form on parchment. Monks were 'God's writers', who converted 'the bare and transient words of perfunctory speech into the tenacious letters of writing' (as one monk put it).[64]

Secular masters of arts, on the other hand, like Roscelin and Anselm of Laon, came from a different tradition of learning. They descended from the Roman schoolmasters who had taught Latin diction through grammar, rhetoric and dialectic. In John of Salisbury's frequently quoted account of how Bernard of Chartres (Thierry's brother) taught the classical authors, the emphasis throughout is on the students hearing and speaking; 'writing' (*scribendum*) is mentioned only once.[65] Masters lived a more hand-to-mouth existence than monks, even when they had benefices. Many of them had neither the place nor the time to settle down in seclusion and compose fundamental works, like those of St Anselm of Canterbury. They had to prepare their classes for the next day and the day after that, as well as dealing with students' personal and academic problems as they arose. Until the most far-sighted masters had turned their cathedral schools into university institutions – with campus police, endowments, vacations, examinations, teaching assistants, copy shops and libraries – they had few opportunities for writing and fewer still for publishing and preserving what they wrote. By the end of the thirteenth century much of this programme had been achieved in the great universities like Paris, Bologna and Oxford, although the medieval schools always remained hectic places compared with monastic cloisters.

Abelard may have succeeded in preserving more writings than his own masters primarily because he became a monk in the latter part of his career, as a consequence of his castration in c.1118. Thenceforward, like St Anselm of Canterbury, he may be presumed to have had access to a scriptorium and to have become conscious of the need to produce copies of his works. This can be no more than a conjecture, however, as none of Abelard's works are explicitly dated. He may have completed his major book on logic, *Dialectica*, in the 'cell' of the abbey of St Denis, where he taught the liberal arts as well as theology in 1118 and 1119. Within the text of *Dialectica*, he refers to other works which 'we have written', notably something he describes as an introduction to dialectic for beginners.[66] Some of these works may have been produced by Abelard before he became a monk, as he had already been teaching logic for fifteen years or more; but he may not have published them (in the sense of producing multiple copies for circulation) until later on. The first work which he describes publishing is his treatise on the Trinity (which he later described as *Theologia*): 'I had read it publicly and I had already seen to its transcription by many people'.[67] But Abelard's zeal in publishing got him into serious trouble, as this was the reason why the papal legate at his trial for heresy at Soissons in 1121 allowed the prosecution to proceed.

Abelard's experience with his publication and republication of *Theologia* suggests that a master did himself no favours by writing books. During his lifetime, a master's prestige did not depend primarily on his writings, as these could only have a limited circulation when all books were manuscripts. His crucial publications were his oral lectures and the reports which were made of them. Students, young and old, came away from these telling their colleagues that they must go and hear Master Anselm at Laon or Master Abelard in Paris. By contrast with the talkative and frenetic schools, the monastic cloister focused on silence and on forms of writing and reading which were meditative and respectful. When Abelard entered the abbey of St Denis in *c.*1118, he entered into the monastic tradition of writing, which was conservative in every sense, and which could therefore help him to conserve his own works. But in Abelard's case, unlike St Anselm of Canterbury's, writing books brought him great pain because he was incautious about what he wrote. At his prosecutions for heresy in 1121 and 1140, his books were ceremonially burned; but – parodoxically – it was the writing of them which has preserved them for posterity.

These considerations help explain why Anselm of Laon, who never retired to a monastery, may never have succeeded in publishing anything in the form of a book under his own name. His school was too busy and his life too hectic, reaching its highpoint of crisis in 1112 with the murder of the bishop, for which Anselm of Laon's own nephews were imprisoned. Peter the Chanter says Anselm of Laon was never able to complete his commentary on the Bible because 'the canons whose dean he was and many others, used often to hinder him in his work by drawing him into their lawsuits, making much of him in adulation, oppressing the poor whom he was obliged to protect, or badgering him to take part in the business of the chapter'.[68] As Anselm of Laon was the chancellor of the diocese as well as being dean of the cathedral, all these matters were indeed his responsibility. It is possible that he enjoyed holding these offices, or at least he wanted to make sure that no one else held them, as he became archdeacon as well in 1115. Why William of Champeaux published so little is more of a problem, however, as he was a monk (a canon regular) at the abbey of St Victor, probably from 1105 onwards. But St Victor was a new foundation and not a great Benedictine monastery, like St Denis, with an ancient scriptorium and library. William of Champeaux remained a busy master in the Paris schools long after he went to St Victor; possibly he had to do this because St Victor depended on the money he could bring in from students' fees. Abelard's explanation is that William had never intended to stop teaching in the schools; he entered St Victor only to make him look more religious, so that he might be promoted to a bishopric.[69] Among the distractions from writing books that William of Champeaux must have faced in the early days of St Victor was the nuisance of Abelard and his students trying to compete with him in Paris. Only in the next generation, that of Hugh of St Victor, did the house of St Victor achieve the ideal combination of being both a monastery and a school. Hugh's writings on the sacraments and on the liberal arts were much more influential and respected than anything Abelard ever produced. They both died in the 1140s and some obituary writers coupled them together as the twin lights of scholarship in France, although their characters were very different.[70]

For many masters in Abelard's time anthologies survive of what look like excerpts from their lectures. Some of these are no more than a few lines long, while others extend over a page or two. They could have originated either in students' notes or in the masters themselves issuing synopses of their lectures on single sheets for copying. Excerpts ('sentences' was the technical term) bearing the names of William of Champeaux and Anselm of Laon are preserved in the *Liber Pancrisis*, which was probably composed around the time of their deaths (Anselm died in c.1117 and William in 1122) or a decade earlier. This anthology bears the grandiose title *Liber Pancrisis* because, its opening words explain: 'golden sentences are contained here'.[71] *Pan-Chrisis* means 'all-gold' in Greek, as the opening words also explain. (It was fashionable to dignify books with Greek titles, even when their authors knew little Greek; in this spirit Abelard entitled his book *Theologia*.)

What is unusual about the *Liber Pancrisis* is that it intermixes the 'all-gold' sentences of Latin Church Fathers (it names Augustine, Jerome, Ambrose, Gregory the Great, Isidore and Bede) with those of recent masters, as if their opinions were of equal weight. Three 'modern masters' are given pride of place: William of Champeaux, Ivo bishop of Chartres and Anselm of Laon. They were all Abelard's contemporaries and Ivo (he died in 1115) was the only one who had not taught him. He had probably met Ivo, however, as he was as formidable a figure in the French kingdom and in ecclesiastical politics as William of Champeaux. He had been imprisoned by Philip I in 1092 and retaliated by involving himself in the affairs of the bishopric of Paris; all the bishops between 1094 and 1123 were his former pupils.[72] Suger of St Denis attributed the securing of the succession of King Louis VI in 1108 to Ivo.[73] He is given the status of a 'modern master' in the *Liber Pancrisis* because he was the greatest expert on canon law.

The *Liber Pancrisis*'s choice of modern masters is selective, not to say prejudiced. It leaves out Manegold of Lautenbach, who had been called the 'master of the modern masters', and likewise St Anselm of Canterbury.[74] The criterion of selection seems to be that 'modern masters' must be French, in the specific sense of residing in the Île-de-France and being involved in the business of the French kingdom, and this suggests that the *Liber Pancrisis* originated in France. In French students' eyes, Manegold and St Anselm of Canterbury were no longer 'modern': that is, 'men of now' or 'today's men' – *hodierni*. To the young, no pundit is so unfashionable as yesterday's master. By making contemporary French professors into the equals of St Augustine and St Gregory the Great, the *Liber Pancrisis* foreshadows the declaration of Chrétien de Troyes a generation later that the bright lights of the Greeks and Romans are extinguished, now that 'chivalry and learning have arrived in France'.[75] The triumphalist attitude of Chrétien and the *Liber Pancrisis* explains why Abelard was so determined (judging by what he says in his 'history of calamities') to belong to France and to Paris in particular. Only a Frenchman could win a golden reputation and count as an intellectual.

ABELARD'S DEBT TO HIS MASTERS

Various scholars have pointed out that the *Liber Pancrisis* is the precursor of Abelard's *Sic et Non* and of many later scholastic textbooks. The 'sentences' of the masters are arranged in the *Liber Pancrisis* by subject matter and not arbitrarily by author's name. For example the opinions of Anselm of Laon, St Augustine and William of Champeaux are all cited on the definition of the human soul.[76] Abelard's *Sic et Non* is superior to the *Liber Pancrisis* because its arrangement by subjects is more coherent and wide-ranging. He brought the sources together with far greater thoroughness than they had ever been assembled before, as well as introducing the novelty of inviting the reader to compare and contrast the citations. Another difference between the *Sic et Non* and the *Liber Pancrisis* is that Abelard did not include the three 'modern masters' in his anthology, presumably because two of them were the teachers he despised. To construct *Sic et Non* Abelard took an existing structure, that of the *Liber Pancrisis* or something like it, and improved it almost out of recognition. This is typical of his work. Although he described himself as 'light-hearted' (*animo levis*), he approached texts in a remarkably rigorous and orderly way.[77]

Abelard seems to have treated what he had learned from William of Champeaux and Anselm of Laon (and likewise from Roscelin) in much the same way as he treated the *Liber Pancrisis* as a whole. In other words, he took over without acknowledgement his masters' organizing principles, as well as their subjects of research, and pursued them on a grand scale as if they had been entirely his own. Abelard's achievements look so impressive and original today because substantial and complete works of his survive, sometimes in a series of progressively elaborated versions as in *Theologia*, whereas the teachings of his masters on theological questions exist only in reported excerpts. Moreover, it is difficult to disentangle the influence of Anselm of Laon from that of William of Champeaux in Abelard's writings because William had been Anselm of Laon's pupil. Abelard may have absorbed many of Anselm's ideas not at first-hand when he made his abortive visit to Laon in 1113, but intermittently over the previous decade when he had been William's student in Paris.

Although Abelard never acknowledged any intellectual debt to his masters, it must have been considerable. He was not necessarily being a plagiarist in taking so much from them, but a good student. He and his masters were bound to address many of the same questions because these were the central debates of the time. Abelard was not an autodidact attempting to cross a pathless field, but a highly instructed intellect who had spent twenty years (c.1096–c.1114) in and out of the best schools before he became a fully accredited master himself. It was not the custom of medieval writers to acknowledge all their sources anyway, particularly if these were living 'modern' individuals. Abelard shared with William of Champeaux and Anselm of Laon – and above all with St Anselm of Canterbury – a convention of presentation which ostensibly depended as little as possible on the citation of authorities. The 'sentences' of William of Champeaux and Anselm of Laon in the *Liber Pancrisis* sometimes quote Scripture, but only very occasionally is any reference made to the Church Fathers and none whatsoever to modern masters. Like his masters', Abelard's education had been in the liberal arts of a grammar school. His starting point was therefore the Latin classics and Aristotelian logic, and not the 'divine page' of Scripture on which boys in monasteries focused their studies.

The essence of the scholastic method was not to explicate the Scripture line by line, as monks did, but to pose wide-ranging questions and answer them from logical principles as if for the first time. 'Modern' masters, Abelard included, still found it convenient to do Scriptural commentaries, but they used them as a means of raising general questions which they then enlarged on. Abelard used this technique in his commentary on St Paul's Epistle to the Romans and he may have learned it from Anselm of Laon, whose 'question' and 'solution' (on whether Christ's knowledge as God differed from his knowledge as man) in his commentary on the Epistle to the Colossians is recorded in the *Liber Pancrisis*.[78] The most famous scholastic question of Abelard's time had been posed in the 1090s in the title of St Anselm of Canterbury's book *Cur Deus Homo?* ('Why [did] God [become] man?'). This question, though not St Anselm's succinct three-word form of it, may already have been a commonplace at the school of Laon, as the *Liber Pancrisis* records Anselm of Laon's brother Ralph saying that 'it is usual to ask': Why God wished to redeem mankind by becoming incarnate, when this could have been done by any prophet or angel?[79]

Although St Anselm of Canterbury frequently presented his work as if it were the solitary meditation of a monk, he addressed current questions from first principles like a master of arts. He had prefaced *Cur Deus Homo?* with the justification that 'not only the learned (*literati*) but even many lay people (*illiterati*) ask this question and want an explanation for it'.[80] The *Cur Deus Homo?* takes the form of a dialogue between himself and a junior monk, Boso. Investigation by 'interrogation and response' (as St Anselm called it) allowed him to introduce, in Boso's name, questions from the schools and answer them without reference to ecclesiastical authority.[81] He acknowledged the possible unorthodoxy of this: 'it may be that enough should have been said already by the Church Fathers'.[82] 'Nevertheless,' St Anselm persisted, 'for those who ask, I will take care to show what God has deigned to disclose to me about it.' These are the same seemingly naive and personal explanations that Abelard used thirty years later to justify writing *Theologia*. His students 'demanded human and philosophical explanations' and so 'it happened to me that I first applied myself to discussing the foundation of our faith by analogies from human reason'.[83] Like St Anselm of Canterbury, Abelard conceded without demur to his questioners' demands. It was at his students' insistence, and not his own, that he started reasoning; it was just something that 'happened' to him. Like

St Anselm also, Abelard added that God had enabled him to compose his work.[84]

Abelard was not the inventor of the scholastic method, nor was he the pioneer of non-authoritarian thought. Twenty years before *Cur Deus Homo?*, in *Monologion* in the 1070s, St Anselm of Canterbury had announced that his audience demanded that 'nothing whatsoever should be asserted here on the authority of Scripture; everything is to be argued by individual and specific investigation'.[85] By 1100, when Abelard was just beginning his career, St Anselm had won the approval of Pope Urban II for his writings and had thus established a place for pure reasoning in speculative theology. He had achieved this by conceding limits to his procedure of 'faith seeking understanding' and he had shown that he was prepared to police these limits by condemning Roscelin in his letter to Urban II.[86] Abelard did not have to fight for the right to ask questions as such, as 'interrogation and response' was well established in the leading schools. Nor did he have to champion the right of logicians and masters of arts to subject Christian belief to pure reasoning, as St Anselm had established that as a general principle and Anselm of Laon's school had been putting this 'modern' teaching into practice for at least twenty years.

Nevertheless, Abelard did have a special problem because he had been Roscelin's pupil. When he arrived at William of Champeaux's school in Paris in c.1100, Abelard had to demonstrate that he could work within the limits of 'faith seeking understanding' and not go beyond them in the way St Anselm of Canterbury alleged Roscelin had done. Judging from the *Liber Pancrisis*, William of Champeaux did 'modern' teaching in his school just as Anselm of Laon did. Abelard describes in his 'history of calamities' how he soon 'tried to contradict William's "sentences" and to reason against him'.[87] Abelard was particularly proud of making William change his position on the meaning of universals.[88] On the technical point of logic Abelard was doubtless right. What he does not explain is that he was arguing from a Nominalist point of view similar to Roscelin's. William might have been associated with Roscelin's heresy if he agreed with Abelard. This could have engulfed the good name of William's school, as well as Abelard himself. William would not have felt immune from accusation by virtue of being an established master, as Roscelin had been that and Berengar of Tours before him. Accusations of heresy could flare up very suddenly and smoulder on for years (as Abelard too was to find out).

It was not the subject matter of Abelard's researches, nor his method of proceeding by disputation, that made him such a controversial figure from his first appearance in the schools of Paris in c.1100. It was his association with Roscelin and his pride. He later acknowledged that pride and lust had brought his 'calamities' upon him.[89] The *Liber Pancrisis* has a rubric (a heading in red): *Guillelmus de superbia* – 'William of Champeaux on pride'.[90] He had defined pride as the love of one's own excellence: from pride envy is born; from envy detraction, and from detraction comes slander. Perhaps he had had Abelard's attacks on him in mind when he formulated this. St Anselm of Canterbury's formula of 'faith seeking understanding' meant in practice that arbitrary judgements were bandied about as to whether this or that master was in good faith or not. In his 'history of calamities' Abelard accused William of Champeaux and Anselm of Laon of being in bad faith: they were motivated against him by 'envy' of his talents.[91] In return, they 'persecuted' him because they judged him to be Roscelin's student and a troublemaker.

One of the most radical-looking teachings of William of Champeaux and Anselm of Laon was that right and wrong ('sin' in theological terms) are subjective. It is not the nature of the deed which distinguishes them, but the doer's intention. William of Champeaux pointed out that the Church Fathers taught that 'sin is nothing' because it is not God's creation; 'solely the intention, and the will which stems from it, is evil'.[92] Ascribed to Anselm of Laon is the proposition that 'God does not assess the magnitude of a sin by the magnitude of the things done, but its magnitude relates to the intention of the doer'.[93] Abelard pointed out in his book on *Ethics* that God works like this because He can see into people's hearts. Human judges, on the other hand, can only punish people for what they do, not for what they secretly think.[94] Abelard's *Ethics*, which looks so daring and original, was built on the ideas of his masters. Exactly how much he owed to them is impossible to assess, as their works survive only in excerpts whereas his are voluminous.

Certainly, the major theological and philosophical questions that Abelard addressed were those addressed by William of Champeaux and Anselm of Laon, as indicated by the excerpts in the *Liber Pancrisis*: Trinity, Creation, Body and Soul, Conscience, Original Sin, Predestination, Incarnation, Redemption, Baptism, Eucharist. This is not surprising, as these are the questions that the Church Fathers had addressed. It was to have them explained, with the clarity of grammar and logic which the 'modern' masters commanded, that students flocked to the school of Anselm at Laon and William of Champeaux at Paris. Abelard was their heir, even though they refused to recognize the legitimacy of his succession and he acknowledged his debt to them only through the prejudiced account he gave of them in his 'history of calamities'. As importantly, he was Roscelin's heir, even though he had omitted Roscelin from his story altogether. At his first trial for heresy in 1121 at Soissons (the same place where Roscelin had been tried in 1092) Abelard too became a scapegoat for 'faith seeking understanding', while his prosecutors (he said) 'aspired to reign alone' in place of Anselm of Laon and William of Champeaux 'and even to succeed them as their heirs'.[95]

HOW WAS THE TEACHING DONE?

How teaching was done is harder to reconstruct than what was taught because contemporaries took this for granted and the evidence is primarily anecdotal. Did the typical master lecture to a silent and dutiful audience, or did he invite questions and discussion? Looking back from the twelfth century to classical ideals, did he declaim like Cicero or think on his feet like Socrates? The Socratic method stimulates clever students, but it can leave weaker ones confused and the syllabus uncovered. A Ciceronian approach surveys the subject elegantly and comprehensively, but it does not allow for disagreement, nor does it demand the audience's attention. Socratic teaching is erratic and inspirational where Ciceronian is professional and practised. Over the ages most teachers have used both modes: the 'Ciceronian' lecture for surveying a subject and the 'Socratic' seminar for discussion.

The distinction between 'lecture' and 'seminar' fits Abelard's account of the school of Laon. 'One day' (he says in his 'history of calamities') 'we students were joking together after some "collations of sentences".'[96] The Latin collatio literally means a 'bringing together' and hence a 'conference'; a 'bringing together of sentences' was therefore a discussion of prescribed texts, the equivalent of a seminar. (Abelard's 'Dialogue of a Philosopher with a Jew and a Christian' was described as 'collations' because it brought together spokesmen for the different faiths.[97]) Abelard distinguishes the 'collations' at the school of Laon from the formal 'lectures' (lectiones) of Master Anselm, which he despised and deliberately failed to attend.[98] Because he was a dialectician, Abelard was a Socratic teacher by training as much as by temperament: he was the Gallic Socrates, as Peter the Venerable wrote in his epitaph.[99] 'Indignantly', Abelard told the students at Laon 'that it was not my custom to advance through practice, but through intelligence' – ingenium (the Latin word implies innate ability or 'genius').[100] This was also when he told them to come the very next day to the lecture they had challenged him to give (on the prophet Ezechiel, one of the hardest books in the Bible), whereas they had counselled him to take his time as he was inexperienced.[101]

'Practice makes perfect' was too ponderous a rule for Abelard. What was wrong with Anselm of Laon in Abelard's opinion was that 'the old man' owed his great name to 'long use' rather than intelligence.[102] He describes Anselm's teaching methods as the antithesis of Socratic ones: 'anyone who knocked with some question went away more uncertain than he came; he was a marvel in the eyes of an audience but a nobody in the view of questioners; he had a marvellous way with words, but their sense was contemptible and devoid of reason; when he lit a fire, he filled his house with smoke instead of lighting it up'.[103] The *Liber Pancrisis* confirms that Anselm had a marvellous way with words. For example, he explained *Cur Deus Homo?* with dramatic dialogue reminiscent of the contemporary Anglo-French *Play of Adam*:

Man says to God: Get me out of the Devil's power!
But God can answer: You subjected yourself against my command. Get out by yourself, if you can.
So Man says to the Devil: Either have no wish to possess me, or fulfil the promises to me which you cannot fulfil: 'Ye shall be as Gods,' you promised.
To this the Devil can answer: I don't have to fulfil promises to you because you should not have tried to make me give them....[104]

Abelard had an irreverent question (St Bernard described it as 'jeering') to ask about *Cur Deus Homo?*: How could transgressing God's first command in paradise, merely by tasting one apple, be a greater sin than crucifying His son on Calvary?[105] How did killing an innocent person, still worse God, make amends for a symbolic apple? These may have been among the questions with which Abelard tried to knock Anselm off his perch at Laon in 1113. But Anselm may have come across them already, as the *Elucidarius* of Honorius Augustodunensis (who had perhaps been a pupil of St Anselm of Canterbury's) contains the following Socratic dialogue:

Pupil: How great was the sin of eating the apple?
Master: So great that the whole world could not suffice to atone for it.
Pupil: Prove it.

The Master then sets about doing so by demonstrating that Adam committed no less than six crimes in this single action.[106]

Whether real exchanges between masters and students in the classroom were as stark as this imaginary dialogue is hard to know. Certainly, from the time of St Anselm of Canterbury onwards, masters – including teachers of the sacred page of Scripture – were assumed to have an obligation to answer questions and prove things. Abelard in 1113 could certainly have asked Anselm of Laon harder questions than any-body else, since he had been William of Champeaux's most demanding pupil and William had been Anselm's pupil. Furthermore, as already suggested, Anselm may have feared that Abelard was Stephen de Gar-lande's political agent in Laon.[107] Abelard's questions may not have been intended to elicit theological argument but to cause Anselm to lose face, as a first step to destroying him. Only a few years later a pupil of Anselm's, Master Alberic, was undermined at the cathedral school of Reims by Walter of Mortagne, a mature student and an unbeneficed master like Abelard, who attended his classes and then set up a rival school in the city when Alberic proved unable to answer his questions.[108]

Abelard describes how he disconcerted Anselm's students at Laon by claiming that he was really astonished that any 'instruction' (*magisterium*) in divinity was needed at all: in order to understand the commentaries of the Church Fathers, their own writings and the glosses should be sufficient for educated men like themselves.[109] He seems to have been voicing a current talking-point here, which was essentially the old question of whether Holy Scripture needed interpreters. Hugh of St Victor mentions 'triflers', his rival Abelard among them presumably, who said that listen-ing to masters was not necessary as divine utterances were self-explanat-ory.[110] Abelard did have a serious point, however, as his *Sic et Non* is based on the premise that students (his 'tender readers') will be provoked by the seeming contradictions they encounter ('dissonance' is the term he uses) to make greater efforts to ask questions and discover the truth.[111]

The belief that contradictions in the authorities were resolvable went back to St Augustine and it had been enunciated, in much the same terms as Abelard's, by Anselm of Laon. 'The sentences of all the Catholic Fathers are diverse but not adverse,' he had written to an abbot in Liège (perhaps in response to Rupert of Deutz), 'those with experience soon show that harmony comes from dissonance'.[112] Abelard used the 'diverse–adverse' dichotomy in the opening sentence of his prologue to *Sic et Non*.[113] So, this looks like yet another idea which Abelard took from his masters without acknowledgement. But the implications which he drew from the diverse–adverse dichotomy were far-reaching. The prologue to *Sic et Non* proposes that the contradictions in the sources should be resolved not by 'those with experience', as Anselm of Laon had recommended, but by its 'tender readers'. The prologue recom-mends the most inexperienced and ignorant students of Christianity to start making their own inquiries. They should do this without any instruction from a master, as Abelard was confident that their own asking of questions was the first key to wisdom. This was indeed the Socratic method. But where would it lead to in practice? To the truth, or to anarchy and contempt for all authority, as Abelard's (and Socrates's) prosecutors feared?

The *Sic et Non* is a massive 'collation of sentences', a self-generating textbook for seminars, and this is why it was raided for teaching materials by Peter Lombard and the other masters who followed on from Abelard. He had probably put it together when he was at St Denis in 1122, though he may have first conceived the idea for it when he was at Laon in 1113, as Anselm's school (judging by the *Liber Pancrisis*) specialized in 'sentences' and it used Socratic methods of teaching.[114] Anthologies like *Sic et Non* and the *Liber Pancrisis* were invaluable in the schools because students had no access to complete books of the Church Fathers, unless they came from major monastic libraries like Cluny or St Denis. Even when whole volumes were available, they were difficult to follow, as indexes and contents tables could not be standardized in manuscripts. Abelard was one of the first masters to apply a numbering system to his questions, as in his 158 consecutive headings in *Sic et Non*. The numbering could be transferred in identical form from one manuscript to another. Thomas Aquinas perfected this system as a teaching aid a century later with the numbered parts, questions and articles of *Summa Theologiae*.

NOTE-TAKING AND GLOSSES

The hardest thing to work out about classroom teaching in Abelard's time is what sort of notes the students took and how they made them. Rapid note-taking was difficult with quill pens and parchment, and not much easier with styluses and wax tablets. The schools had no purpose-built writing facilities on the scale of monastic scriptoria. As has already been argued, even masters as distinguished as Anselm of Laon may never have succeeded in publishing anything for a variety of reasons: too little time, inadequate facilities, and too little motivation. As a master's fame depended on his students' oral reports of his lectures, books might damage his business. They were hostages to fortune. A master who succeeded in publishing a book of lectures made himself redundant or, worse, got prosecuted for heresy, as happened to Abelard with *Theologia*.

Some writing was of course done. In his account of his time at Laon Abelard describes 'glosses being transcribed'.[115] In this context he distinguishes between his first 'lecture' (*lectio*) on the prophet Ezechiel and the 'glossing' (*glosandum*), which the students urged him to do afterwards 'in accordance with the tenor of my lecture'.[116] Literally 'glossing' meant explaining difficult words. Why did the students urge

Abelard to explain the tenor of the lecture he had just given? John of Salisbury says that Abelard's lectures were remarkably clear, so basic indeed that they could be puerile.[117] Moreover, Abelard had just told the students at Laon that instruction was not necessary in divinity anyway. Nevertheless, he acceded to the students' urging. Those who had missed his first lecture (he says) rushed to the second and the third ones because they were all very keen 'to transcribe the glosses which I had begun on the first day'.[118]

By the middle of the twelfth century 'glosses' generally meant the highly compressed commentaries which crowded the margins of scholastic books. Abelard's student Robert of Melun commented that even 'the "masters of the glosses", for that is the name they have now attained', had difficulty understanding their own systems of abbreviation.[119] The meaning of 'gloss' had therefore extended from explaining individual words to writing masses of abbreviated notes. It is in this latter sense that Abelard uses 'gloss' in his account of the school of Laon. At the time he was composing the 'history of calamities' in c.1132 it must have been a very 'modern' piece of scholastic jargon. When the students urged him to 'gloss' his own lecture, they were asking him to write up authoritative notes with them in what would now be called a 'workshop' session. Detailed notes were not made in the lectures themselves because writing on parchment could be done only in a scriptorium – however makeshift it might be – provided with desks, ink and equipment for cutting and folding parchment (assuming that the parchment itself could be bought ready-made). At lectures master and students concentrated on reading the prescribed text. Depictions of masters teaching generally show them holding open a book, while the students hold similar (usually smaller) books in which they follow the text; writing implements are not shown.

Abelard describes how at his first lecture on Ezechiel he used an *expositor*, meaning an existing commentary, as the basis of his own exposition.[120] His lecture was a commentary on the commentary. The 'gloss' which the students urged him to make would have combined extracts from this *expositor* with the new explanations he had given in the lecture.[121] It is necessary to say 'would have', as Abelard's gloss on Ezechiel does not exist and perhaps he never published it, although he says that when he returned to Paris, 'I set myself to complete the glosses on Ezechiel which I had begun at Laon'.[122] Various hypotheses for failing to publish can be put forward. He was not yet a monk and he may therefore have not yet learned enough about publishing. Or, this may be another instance of his inability to carry tasks through: 'here was a man who began to build and was not able to finish'.[123] Or, his affair with Heloise may have distracted him from the book of Ezechiel altogether.

As far as Anselm of Laon was concerned, it was bad enough that Abelard should have been giving lectures in his school, but worse that he should be writing up glosses, since 'anything mistaken which I wrote there would be attributed to him'.[124] Abelard claims that this was a frivolous objection which arose from Anselm's envy. However, at his trial at Sens twenty-five years later, Abelard took a very different view and insisted on acknowledging his own mistakes but not those which had been misattributed to him.[125] It is known that Anselm of Laon exercised control over the writing done in his school, as a note on a book says: 'Here ends the gloss of Master Gilbert de la Porrée, which he read out in the presence of his master, Anselm, so that he might emend it.'[126] This suggests that Gilbert was being supervised when a student (possibly at the same time as Abelard was at Laon) at something like the glossing sessions which Abelard describes.

The golden 'sentences' of Anselm of Laon and William of Champeaux collected in the *Liber Pancrisis* may be the summaries of their masters' lectures which the students made under their supervision. All a master's 'sentences' came to be thought of as 'glosses' because they referred to the sacred page of Scripture and they emended the existing commentaries and *expositors*. The 'collations of sentences', which Abelard also describes at Laon, then make very good sense as the seminars in which masters followed up their lectures and checked on what was being written down. If the 'sentences' in the *Liber Pancrisis* were written under their masters' supervision, their style is as noteworthy as their content: for example, in Anselm of Laon's use of dramatic dialogue or William of Champeaux's liking for syllogisms. In what appear to be records of lectures rather than seminars by Anselm, he presents his material as a series of arguments linked by replies to hypothetical objectors: 'to whom we say...'; 'someone wanting to contradict this sentence would say...'; 'I readily grant you this...'; 'but show me how...'; 'I don't see...'.[127] The last of these expressions was also a favourite of Abelard's: 'I don't see (*non video*) how, in the case of little children, not believing in Christ can be their fault'; 'I don't see what the point of confession is when God knows everything'.[128]

ABELARD IN THE CLASSROOM

Like Anselm of Laon, Abelard argued with imaginary interlocutors: 'but perhaps you will say...'; 'but I say that if we consider this more carefully...'; 'tell me, whoever you are...'; '"No," you say...'; 'I reply: "Well said!" ...'.[129] He also had to argue with actual interrupters. Like knights errant, disputatious students might appear on the scene and challenge the master to verbal combat in the presence of his class. By this means Walter of Mortagne had almost unseated Alberic of Reims, and Abelard had attempted much the same against William of Champeaux and Anselm of Laon. The life of St Goswin describes how a group of conservative intellectuals (the 'saner' ones is the biographer's description of them) were indignant at the unheard-of novelties in Abelard's 'sentences' and they chose Goswin to go and challenge him. This was probably in 1112, when Abelard had 'pitched camp' with his students at the church of Sainte Geneviève, while he attempted to oust William of Champeaux and return to the Île-de-la-Cité.[130] 'Master Peter Abelard' (the life of St Goswin says) 'used a public school in the cloister of Sainte Geneviève and he had gathered many students around him' there.[131] This cloister (which was demolished in 1807) measured about ninety feet down each of its sides; it cannot have accommodated more than sixty or seventy students under cover and within hearing distance of the master.[132]

What number of students the life of St Goswin meant by 'many' is therefore difficult to estimate. Odo of Orléans, at his school at Tournai in c.1100, is described heading 'a cohort of almost 200 clerks'.[133] His admiring biographer describes how he taught them outside 'in front of the doors of the church'; sometimes he walked to and fro, like the Peripatetics, and sometimes he sat recollected and still like the Stoics.[134] The biographer recalled a summer night, when Odo gave a lesson in astronomy by pointing up at the Milky Way and the Zodiac. Nevertheless, his teaching cannot have been done in the church porch in the winter and neither could 200 students have huddled into it. Similarly, Abelard could not have assembled hundreds of students in the cloister of Sainte Geneviève; even small numbers under cover must have found it miserably cold in the winter. Unfortunately, contemporaries did not think these mundane problems worth explaining to posterity.

Goswin's biographer says he found Abelard in his school 'reading' (legentem), which presumably means 'lecturing', as he was 'inculcating his novelties into his students'.[135] Abelard's lecturing style is graphically described: 'there he was – detonating for his audience astonishing and unprecedented opinions, as if to make a mockery of the ranks of the sane and the wise'.[136] (His mocking style is best seen in his attack on St Anselm of Canterbury and other masters in Theologia Christiana.[137]) As soon as he witnessed Abelard's 'detonations', Goswin got up to speak. Abelard 'turned his savage eyes upon him and threatened him vehemently: "See that you keep quiet and be careful not to disturb the course of my lecture."' But (continues the biographer) Goswin 'had not come there to be quiet and he fiercely persisted'.[138] Abelard paid no attention to the words pouring from Goswin, as he judged it 'undignified that such a puny youth should be answered by so great a professor as himself'.[139] He was judging Goswin only by his fresh face, the biographer explains, and he had failed to notice the intelligent and perspicacious heart within.[140]

The most revealing part of the story then follows. As Goswin had interrupted Abelard's lecture, it was not unreasonable to ask him to be quiet until it was finished. Nevertheless, when he persisted with his protest, the students said that 'they knew the young man well enough and so Abelard must not avoid answering him, as he was a sharp disputant and a great credit to the science'.[141] They added that 'there was no dishonour in undertaking this sort of disputation, whereas it was most dishonourable to go on refusing'. Cornered like a knight in an epic on a point of honour, Abelard had no choice but to face Goswin. So he said to the students: 'Let him speak, if he has anything worth saying.' Goswin's great moment had come. Unfortunately, his biographer never says what the subject of the disputation was; perhaps he had not understood when Goswin explained it. But the biographer does not fail us entirely, as he describes how Goswin conducted the debate: 'assuming that and affirming this, and by his affirmations not wholly contradicting that – for he was by no means ignorant of these subtleties – until the subterfuges of diversion were entirely closed to his opponent and Abelard was at last compelled to assert that he was not being consistent with reason'.[142] A better summary of the rules of disputation could hardly be given.

Whether Goswin ever really did get the better of 'Master Peter Abelard' is impossible to know, as no one else mentions it. Over the years Goswin's memory of how, as a young man, he had dared to dispute with Abelard may have grown in his mind and his biographer enlarged the story further. Certainly it has rhetorical elements, as the protagonists are compared to David and Goliath.[143] A similar problem of wisdom after the event presents itself in Abelard's account of getting the better of William of Champeaux and Anselm of Laon. In his description of Anselm, Abelard has set his readers a puzzle. He is compared first with the barren fig-tree cursed by Christ in Matthew's Gospel, and then with the venerable oak standing dead in the middle of a field of corn described by Lucan: 'There stood the shadow of a noble name.'[144] This gives Abelard the opportunity to say self-righteously: 'So, I did not lie idle in that shadow for long.'[145] For Lucan, the venerable oak was

Pompey and his younger rival, 'never standing still', 'keen and indomitable', was Caesar who 'enjoyed making his way by destruction'.[146]

By quoting Lucan, was Abelard acknowledging that he too enjoyed making his way by destroying others? Certainly this is how he was perceived by St Goswin's biographer, who cited the prophecy 'His hand will be against all men, and all men's hands against him'.[147] (The biographer was writing after Abelard's death, so it was not difficult to cite prophecies.) In his 'history of calamities' Abelard acknowledged that he was an outlaw, forever cursed like Cain.[148] Moreover, he had dealt with William of Champeaux in his 'history of calamities' by the same technique of citing a line from Ovid with an ambiguous context.[149] But these quotations could only carry their full meanings to those who knew their contexts and it cannot be certain that Abelard did know this. Classical authors were frequently cited from anthologies, or from memory where excerpts had been learned at school, as complete books, even of the best-known authors like Virgil and Ovid, were hard to come by. On the other hand, classical enthusiasts in the Twelfth-Century Renaissance set traps for their less knowledgeable readers by citing quotations which were ambiguous or even inventions. John of Salisbury excelled at this and, as Abelard had been the master he most admired, he may have learned the technique from him.[150] Abelard himself was a Latin poet and he had had his education in the Loire valley in the 1090s, the very time when Hildebert of Lavardin, Marbod of Rennes and Baudri of Bourgueil, the most learned Latin poets of the age, were publishing their works and encouraging imitation of the classics.

Compared with John of Salisbury, however, Abelard is sparing in his use of classical quotations and he was primarily a logician rather than a literary writer. But this does not mean that he was not a precocious enough Latin scholar to make the most of the context of the quotations he cites. The first citation he makes from a classical poet in his 'history of calamities' is from Ovid: 'Envy seeks the heights, the winds sweep the mountain tops.'[151] This refers to Envy's resentment of Genius and it gets its real bite against William of Champeaux further on, in the unquoted line: 'Go and rupture yourself, voracious Envy! My name is already great.'[152] In another classical allusion Master Jocelin had warned the young Goswin that Abelard grasped the club of Hercules, which he would not surrender lightly because he had not snatched it easily.[153] Snatching the club from Hercules is a symbolic act, like the myth of killing the priest of Diana at Nemi which introduces Frazer's *Golden Bough*. The successor is legitimated by the trial of strength in which he overcomes his predecessor. The grammarian's birch rod, both symbol and reality from the ancient world, was the medieval master's club of

Hercules. However formidable a master might look, students competing for his place could be confident that in the end his grasp would fail: he would drop dead like that Lucifer (in Rupert of Deutz's opinion), Anselm of Laon; or he would run away to become a bishop like that hypocrite (in Abelard's opinion), William of Champeaux; or he would be disgraced in a heresy trial like Roscelin and his pupil, Abelard.

5

Logician

Logic was the centre of Abelard's intellectual world from his earliest days as a wandering student until the end of his life: from the time, that is, when he describes setting out from home in the 1090s 'armed with dialectical reasonings' until his final admission, in his Confession of Faith to Heloise at the time of the council of Sens in 1140, that 'logic has made me hateful to the world'.[1] Dialectical reasoning, which taught batteries of rules to distinguish valid arguments from false ones, made logic the key to all knowledge in the opinion of its devotees. In the words of St Augustine (700 years earlier), which Abelard quoted with delight because he was the most revered intellectual authority in the Western Church, dialectic was 'the discipline of disciplines' because 'it teaches how to teach and how to learn'.[2] In dialectic, St Augustine continued (with a strong sexual image) 'reason shows her own self: she opens up what she is and what she wants'. Because it depended on clarity and openness, dialectic opposed obscurity and mystification. Augustine went so far as to claim that dialectic 'knows knowing (*scit scire*): it alone not only tries but is able to make people into scientists (*scientes*)'.

In the opinion of Abelard's admirers, he achieved everything in logic and dialectic that Augustine describes. 'This is sufficient for an epitaph', wrote one of them in elegant Latin verse: 'Peter lies here – Abelard – to him alone whatever was knowable was made clear.'[3] St Bernard expressed much the same opinion from a hostile point of view: 'I know not what there is in the heavens above or in the earth beneath which he deigns to know nothing of; he puts his head in the clouds and scrutinizes the high things of God and then he brings back to us unspeakable words which it is not lawful for a man to utter.'[4] To a logician, to whom everything was reasonable and open, there could be no forbidden words or unspeakable mysteries. Very ingeniously, Bernard's competitor for the hearts and minds of his contemporaries, Peter the Venerable abbot of Cluny, combined Abelard's reputation for being all-knowing with Christian humility. In his letter to Heloise telling her of Abelard's death in 1142, Peter the Venerable wrote: 'And so Master Peter has ended his days. He was known for his unique mastery of knowledge throughout almost the whole world and he was famous everywhere as the student of Him who said: "Learn of Me, for I am meek and lowly in heart".'[5] Peter the Venerable paid Abelard the supreme compliment of describing him as Christ's philosopher.

For Abelard and his contemporaries in the schools, logic and dialectic were synonymous, which was revealing in itself. Logic embraced the study of the *logos* (the 'word' in Greek) and hence the whole under-standing of language, at the deepest philosophical level as well as the elementary grammar taught to schoolboys. The Graeco-Roman discip-lines of the *trivium* were all ways of examining language: through its structure in 'grammar', its forms of expression in 'rhetoric', and its meaning in 'dialectic'. The three paths of the *trivium* had theoretically been held in equal esteem in the Graeco-Roman curriculum, whereas in Abelard's time they were treated as a progression in difficulty: starting with elementary Latin ('grammar'), going on to the composition of prose and verse ('rhetoric'), and finally attaining the high point where the structure of language itself was analysed ('dialectic'). Another epi-taph for Abelard describes him as: '*grammaticae fons, rhetoricae pons, ac logicae mons*'.[6] In other words, Abelard had taught each stage of the *trivium*: he had been a 'fount of grammar', a 'bridge of rhetoric' and a 'mountain of logic'. Despite its crudity, this epitaph is revealing in making rhetoric, meaning the composition of Latin, a 'bridge' between the primal source of knowledge in grammar and its apogee in the 'mountain of logic', on which Abelard had stood pre-eminent.

ABELARD AND ARISTOTLE

Abelard was probably not exaggerating his academic reputation when he said in his Confession of Faith to Heloise that his enemies acknowl-edged that 'I am absolutely outstanding in logic'.[7] 'The alternative Aristotle', St Bernard derisively called him.[8] Peter the Venerable answered this jibe as decisively as he had answered Bernard on Abelard's all-knowingness: Abelard was indeed another Aristotle; he was '*noster Aristoteles*', Peter wrote, 'unequalled, unrivalled, among the logicians who ever were'.[9] By '*our* Aristotle' Peter meant 'ours' in France or 'ours' in the West. John of Salisbury confirms this idea. The 'Peripatetic from Le Pallet' (*Peripateticus Palatinus*), as John called Abelard, 'won such distinction in logic over all his contemporaries that it was believed that he alone really understood Aristotle'.[10] As most of Abelard's surviving lectures on logic consist of expositions of a limited part of Aristotle's works, it is not surprising that he acquired a reputation for being like Aristotle, a reputation which he may have done nothing to discourage. When John of Salisbury came to Paris in 1136 to 'sit at Abelard's feet' (his own description), in order to learn the rudiments of logic, he describes gobbling up every word that fell from Abelard's lips and he was very disappointed when Abelard left.[11] By then, Abelard had been lecturing on the rudiments of logic for thirty or forty years. Paradoxically, he was able to bring Aristotle to life for his audiences year after year precisely because he lectured only on a restricted part of Aristotle's writings. This obliged Abelard to think aloud with his students (which is very much the impression Abelard's treatises on logic give) in order to reconstruct the missing bits of Aristotle's reasoning for himself.

In reliving the achievements of Aristotle, Abelard fulfilled his boyhood ambition of being the 'emulator of the Peripatetics' of classical Athens.[12] Medieval scholars understood 'Peripatetic' to mean that the Athenian logicians had wandered from place to place, whereas it had probably meant either that they had walked about while working out their ideas or that the school of Aristotle (from which they took their name) had been situated on a covered walk. Whatever 'Peripatetic' really meant, it had a good Greek sound to it which appealed to Abelard and his students, who did not know classical Greek but were much attracted by it. The fashion for Greek names had been revived in Abelard's time by St Anselm with the publication of his *Monologion* (probably in 1077), which was so called because it was a monologue in the form of a philosophical debate with himself. John of Salisbury entitled his book on life and logic *Metalogicon*, meaning higher logic or super-logic. This is the book in which John calls Abelard '*Peripateticus Palatinus*', which may have been one of his nicknames among his students, with *Palatinus* referring to Abelard's birthplace at Le Pallet. *Peripateticus Palatinus* could also be understood in other ways. Abelard called Aristotle the 'Prince of the Peripatetics' and Abelard was therefore his 'Palatine' or the mayor of his palace.[13] Ranging from the sublime to the ridiculous, 'Peripateticus Palatinus' could equally mean the 'Wanderer from Le Pallet', implying that Abelard was a provincial adventurer chancing his luck in Paris like so many French intellectuals over the centuries.

Abelard was not as interested in finding the lost works of Aristotle as in writing his own; this is what being 'our Aristotle' probably meant to him. John of Salisbury remembered him saying that it would be easy for one of his contemporaries to write a book on logic which would be as good, or better, than those written by the ancients, but it would be impossible or very difficult to get such a book accepted in the schools as an authority.[14] This was because Aristotle had been the prescribed author for the last millennium and a half, through the commentaries put together by Porphyry (a Greek who had died in AD 300) and Boethius (a Roman senator who had been executed in AD 524). The most recent books that Abelard assigned for his logic students were therefore the commentaries by Boethius, which were 600 years old. Even in the most ambitious of his own works on logic, the *Dialectica*, Abelard purported to do no more than summarize the traditional prescribed books. In a prologue he explained that there are only three prescribed authors (Aristotle, Porphyry and Boethius):

> of whose seven books everyone in this art with an education in Latin should be armed. Only two of Aristotle's books are still known to the use of the Latins, namely the *Categories* and the *De Interpretatione*. One book is Porphyry's: that is the one written about the five 'predicables' (genus, species, difference, property and accident); this is an introduction preparatory to the *Categories*. We usually treat Boethius as four books: that is the *De Divisione*, the *De Topicis*, the *De Syllagismo Categorico* and the *De Syllagismo Hypothetico*. The text of my *Dialectica* will include a very full summary of all of these, and it will see the light – so that readers can use it – provided the Creator of our life grants us a little time and Envy relaxes her grip on our works.[15]

This is a revealing statement for a variety of reasons, both academic and personal. The allusion to Envy is similar to the feelings of persecution which Abelard voices in his 'history of calamities'; it could refer to almost any stage in his career.[16] When Abelard says that the three prescribed authors are in seven 'books' (*codices*), it is not clear whether he has actual bound volumes in mind. None of these 'books' was very large and the introductory one, Porphyry, was little more than a pamphlet. Abelard wants everyone to be 'armed' with these because logic is the art of scholastic warfare; like him, his students must set out on their careers 'armed with dialectical reasonings'.[17]

Abelard emphasizes in this passage that he is restricting himself to the two works of Aristotle known in the West in their traditional Latin versions. This statement shows that he was aware that further treatises by Aristotle on logic existed in Greek. Some of this so-called 'New Logic' was beginning to circulate in France in Abelard's lifetime, but it is difficult to know how much use he made of it. 'I remember', he says, 'having seen a certain little book, which was entitled the *Sophistici Elenchi* and was under Aristotle's name, and I diligently read over it.'[18] This 'little book' was Aristotle's treatise on fallacies, which had been translated into Latin by Boethius and lost sight of for centuries. Abelard probably saw this version, rather than the new translation from the Greek by James of Venice which may not have been published until the 1140s. Abelard did not know Greek and, even if he had known enough to deal with the technical terms of logic, his students would not have been able to learn it to that standard and Aristotle would therefore have remained a closed book to them. The achievement of the medieval scholastics was not primarily in translating ancient Greek works, but in creating their own language of logic in Latin. This remained the language of science until the eighteenth century and it has shaped the technical terms of all western European languages. Although they purported to be mere interpreters of traditional authorities, the scholastics of the twelfth century created new structures and forms of understanding, just as the Gothic architects did in the cathedral churches of Laon, Paris and Chartres (the very places which were also the cradles of scholasticism).

Historians sometimes write as if extending Greek learning in the Twelfth-Century Renaissance was simply a matter of importing some new books, which crusaders might bring back in their knapsacks or Mediterranean merchants unload from their ships. But new books were no use unless the masters in the West already knew why they wanted them. Abelard's recollection of the *Sophistici Elenchi* suggests that he was not confident that it was an authentic book of Aristotle's and, even if it were, he was unsure how to fit it into his syllabus of lectures. One master said that Abelard did not understand this book anyway. This may not be true, as he remarks in *Dialectica* that he had written a book on fallacies, though (like a number of Abelard's works) this cannot be traced. Abelard's recollection of the *Sophistici Elenchi* also emphasizes that books were hard to come by. He had seen and read over the *Sophistici Elenchi* but he did not possess a copy. Even if he had possessed one, he might not have assigned it to his students unless other copies were available. Abelard may have stuck to the traditional seven books in his *Dialectica*, because (as John of Salisbury says) he did not wish to make difficulties for his students. The traditional books were already available in ecclesiastical libraries, and as they were familiar – by name at least – to the students' superiors in their cathedrals and monasteries, they might follow up their lectures by studying Porphyry and Boethius in the vacation.

OBJECTIVES IN TEACHING LOGIC

Abelard's expressed purpose in *Dialectica* was to make a complete 'summary' (*summa*) of the seven prescribed books. The scholastics

excelled in making summaries, both because students wanted textbooks
and because producing a *summa* or encyclopedia was appropriate to the
self-image of the all-knowing philosopher. Because logic categorized
knowledge, it was an excellent tool for constructing a *summa* in any
branch of science, including logic itself. At the least, logic taught students how to make headings and sub-headings and list objectives; it was
the medieval equivalent of management training in this respect.
Although medieval logicians claimed to be true philosophers, distinguishing truth from falsehood like the ancient Greeks, they did not
present themselves as sages generating their own wisdom from deep
within the mind. On the contrary, the fundamental thinking had already
been done by Aristotle, Porphyry and Boethius and they could never be
set aside. Logicians started with them, making another commentary on a
commentary on a commentary, much as students of divinity started with
the Church Fathers.

Studying logic was rather like studying law. The master provided
students with an up-to-date summary, which explained the latest thinking on the long-established rules of the statutory authors. Abelard was
very good at this. A glance at the table of contents of his *Dialectica*
shows how closely it sticks in its arrangement to the seven prescribed
books, starting with Porphyry, proceeding to Aristotle's *Categories*, and
culminating with Boethius's works on making syllogisms and distinctions (which derived from Aristotle and Cicero). This way of proceeding
was intelligible as well as being traditional, as it progressed from the
simple to the complex. 'To write logic perfectly', Abelard explained, 'it is
necessary to investigate the nature of simple expressions first of all, then
composite ones, and finally to achieve the end of logic in argumenta-
tion.'[19] Porphyry dealt with 'simple expressions', Aristotle's *Categories*
with 'composite ones', and the books of Boethius discussed different
sorts of arguments.

In the structure and declared purpose of his books on logic (though
not necessarily in their detail), Abelard was much less innovative than in
his works on theology. This is evident even from their titles. *Dialectica* is
simply the traditional name of the art of logic, whereas Abelard's *Theologia* and *Sic et Non* are unusual and provocative titles. 'I must confess',
wrote William of St Thierry to St Bernard, 'that the title *Theologia Petri
Abelardi* made me curious to read the book . . . I hear that there are also
works of his of which the names are *Sic et Non*, *Scito Te Ipsum*, and
some others. I fear that the teachings of these may be as preposterous as
their names are monstrous.'[20] (William thought these titles to be monstrous because they turned Christian doctrine into pagan logic. He and
Bernard purported to want none of Abelard's 'God-logic', nor his equi-

vocal 'Yes and No'.) As well as having novel titles, *Theologia* and *Sic et Non* are arranged in ways which Abelard invented, whereas his writings on logic are primarily presented in the traditional form of commentaries (or 'glosses', as the students called them) on the well-worn Latin translations of Porphyry and Aristotle. *Dialectica* is the only work of Abelard's on logic which is not in the form of a commentary and even it claims to be no more than a *summa* of the prescribed authors. A commentary may be very learned and even innovative, but it cannot address a subject from first principles, as the structure has already been provided by the pre-scribed author. Even after he went over to writing theology, logic remained Abelard's bread-and-butter skill in teaching students. He confesses this in his 'history of calamities' and the poem by Hilary of Orléans, recounting the demands of his students in the 1120s, confirms it.[21] John of Salisbury found Abelard teaching elementary logic in Paris in 1136. By then Abelard must have known Porphyry and Boethius almost off by heart.

Abelard lectured on logic in the same predictable way that other masters taught classical authors like Virgil or Cicero. First of all, the master explained about the book. Generally, medieval students were not introduced to a subject or discipline as such (grammar, for example, or rhetoric), but to whichever was the first of the books traditionally prescribed for it. Abelard exemplifies this practice by starting logic with Porphyry. He begins one of his commentaries with the elementary but reassuring explanation that the Greek title of Porphyry's book, the *Isagoge*, means 'introduction'. Abelard then confirms that he is going to proceed in the conventional way: 'the intention, the matter, the manner of treatment, the utility, and the part of dialectic under which the present science is to be placed will be distinguished briefly'.[22] Porphyry's intention (Abelard continues) is to provide an introduction to the categories of Aristotle. His subject matter is the five 'predicables': genus, species, difference, property and accident. His manner of treatment is to discuss these words one by one and then the five of them together. The utility of Porphyry is in understanding Aristotle's categories, as Boethius pointed out (Abelard adds, appealing once more to precedent). The part of dialectic to which Porphyry's book belongs is that concerned with finding arguments, because 'an argument is derived from the nature of genus and species'. Abelard then sets off for two pages discussing genus and species and categories, presumably losing any of his audience who really were beginners, before recollecting himself and returning to Porphyry's text with the customary formula: 'After these preliminaries, let us take our stand on the letter.'[23] This meant: 'Let us do a word-by-word commentary.'

The first words of Porphyry's book in its Latin translation are *Cum sit necessarium* and so Abelard begins by defining 'necessary', at some length, and concluding that in this context it means 'useful'. 'Construe it thus', he tells his audience, 'it is "necessary", that is, "useful" to know what genus is [*quid genus sit* in the Latin text of Porphyry]'. Instead of directly explaining what 'genus' is, Abelard gets distracted by the word *quid* ('what') preceding it and he loses any beginners in his audience once more by launching into a discussion of 'accident', 'property' and 'substance'. He then fastens on Porphyry's reference to 'Aristotle' and he seems to labour the obvious by explaining that Porphyry means 'Aristotle's treatise'; for 'a book is sometimes designated by the name of its author', as when we say 'Lucan' for example.[24] Possibly Abelard is not labouring the obvious here but addressing two audiences at once: beginners, who will welcome his straightforward explanation of 'Aristotle', and advanced students, who will realize that Abelard is alluding to the problem of naming which concerned him so much as a philosopher. The problem in logic is: what could the name 'Aristotle' signify, once that individual had ceased to exist? In this case, Abelard answers, the name 'Aristotle' means a book by him.

Later on in this commentary on Porphyry, Abelard poses the problem of naming in a more general and memorable form: if there were no longer any roses in the world, the name 'rose' would still have significance for the understanding, even though there would be nothing to name; otherwise, the statement that 'there is no rose' could have no meaning.[25] This scholastic enigma has been immortalized by Umberto Eco in the title of his medieval mystery story *The Name of the Rose*. In the Book of Wisdom (ch. 2, verse 8) the rose is an emblem of the transitoriness of physical beauty and the rose garden is symbolic of carnal love in later medieval literature. The problem of naming the rose may seem no more than a conundrum in a fairy story, or a little puzzle that Abelard has set his students to attract their attention in his lecture. But it is more important than that, as he explains that he has added it as a fourth item to the three questions Boethius had asked about the nature of non-physical beings like God and the soul. We know (if we are Christians) that these can exist without bodies. Can the rose likewise exist without a body? When we say 'there is no rose', we affirm that we understand what a rose is. Does this innate understanding mean that our conceptions have real existence outside our minds?

Following Abelard line-by-line this illustrates the strengths and weaknesses of teaching logic by the commentary method. His student audience at least had something specific and authoritative on which to focus in Porphyry's text, but its presence causes Abelard to introduce technical terms before he has explained them and to get distracted at the same time into expounding insignificant words in the text like 'necessary' and 'what'. Even more distracting, though admittedly intriguing, is his introduction of fundamental questions of being and non-being, like saying 'there is no rose'. John of Salisbury thought a lecturer on Porphyry should not deliberately make difficulties: everywhere he should generate simplicity; 'this, I remember, was the practice of the Palatine Peripatetic'.[26] The commentary of Abelard's cited in the preceding paragraphs may have been written twenty years before John came to sit at his Palatine's feet in Paris in 1136. It is possible that Abelard had considerably simplified his lectures by then. If he had still been making Porphyry difficult in 1136, he might have qualified for inclusion in John's denunciation of those 'senile academics who sift every syllable – indeed every letter – of what has been said and written, doubting everything, always searching but never arriving at knowledge'.[27]

DATING ABELARD'S WRITINGS ON LOGIC

None of Abelard's writings on logic are explicitly dated. In putting them in chronological order, modern scholars have worked on the assumption that he progressed from the simple to the complex.[28] His most elementary commentaries are therefore said to date from the early 1100s, when he was with William of Champeaux in Paris, and the more complicated ones from the 1120s or even later. Certainly, Abelard might have composed treatises on logic at any time in his adult life, as he continued to teach it from c.1100 to c.1140 (when his career was terminated by his trial for heresy at Sens). A commentary on Boethius, which is thought to be very early because it is an unadventurous word-by-word literal exegesis, has the title: 'Of Peter Abelard, the Younger, Palatine, Supreme Peripatetic' (*Petri Abaelardi Junioris Palatini Summi Peripatetici*).[29] Why Abelard is described as 'the Younger' cannot be explained, but the rest of the title is resonant of John of Salisbury's description of Abelard as the 'Palatine Peripatetic'. Furthermore, the style of this commentary accords with John's description of how Abelard simplified things even to the point of being puerile. So this commentary may date from John's time with Abelard in the 1130s, rather than from the 1100s.

Abelard's writings on logic may have developed from the complex to the simple, rather than the other way about. The elementary commentaries do not match Abelard's description in his 'history of calamities' of how he began his career by engaging William of Champeaux in dialectical contests. Abelard set up schools of his own in the neighbouring towns of Melun and Corbeil in order to make more 'importunate and frequent assaults of disputation' on William in Paris.[30] Abelard's elementary commentaries on Porphyry and Boethius cannot be read as 'assaults of disputation' and neither are they 'importunate' in tone. In order to beat William of Champeaux, Abelard had to take up the most complex questions of logic, not elementary points of exposition, and this is what he did when he compelled William to change his position on the significance of individuality.[31] There is nothing of this complexity in Abelard's elementary commentaries and neither do they mention William of Champeaux (as *Dialectica* does, for example, where it calls him 'our master').[32] In the early years of his career in the 1100s Abelard may not have written anything for publication. But if he did so, there is no reason to think it was elementary, as he still had his reputation to make *vis-à-vis* William of Champeaux. Abelard was typical of young academics in making a name for himself by being more subtle than his masters; being a good teacher and simplifying things for students came later.

Thirty years on, in 1136 when John of Salisbury was attracted by his simple style, Abelard could afford to lecture in a straightforward and uncluttered way because he no longer had to impress anybody. He was the 'Supreme Peripatetic', who had won such distinction that he alone was believed to understand Aristotle.[33] John of Salisbury conceded that Abelard was simplistic and some of his opinions were out of date, but this did not deter students, nor John himself, from admiring him. Master Alberic, Abelard's younger competitor in Paris in the 1130s, acted towards him rather as Abelard had behaved towards William of Champeaux; he accused Abelard of not understanding Aristotle's arguments.[34] But Abelard was now big enough to ignore such criticism, however accurate it might be. Although logic was meant to make everything clear, its practitioners never could agree about it, and their disputes were notorious. John of Salisbury's vantage point was that of a disillusioned initiate, who had abandoned academic life in preference for employment with the archbishops of Canterbury. In his opinion, many old logicians – with the honourable exception of Abelard – were 'windbags' (*ventilatores*); they promised great things, but all they produced was equivocation.[35]

Any logician was liable to be called an equivocator, because he specialized in distinguishing between meanings and in that process he created a peculiar language of his own. Porphyry's five 'predicables' – genus, species, difference, property and accident – were only the start of the technical terms. 'We begin with definition', John of Salisbury recollects in a passage reminiscent of the story of the Mock Turtle's education in *Alice in Wonderland*: 'I am taught how to define anything I wish in a few words.' First identify the genus, then aggregate the substantial differences until they are equal to the conversion of the proposition. Remember, though, that the highest and lowest genera cannot be defined by their differences but only by their properties. 'There you are!' John concludes, 'now that I have been instructed in the art of definition, we proceed to division. . . .' After more of the same, John has the temerity to ask his professors for examples to illustrate how their rules operate in practice. They indignantly reply that they are pure philosophers who only acknowledge logic.[36]

Over the millennium and a half which separated the Peripatetics of Athens from the scholastics of twelfth-century Paris, logicians had created not only a private language and canon of prescribed books but a special world of their own. Even if some masters of logic were as difficult as those John of Salisbury described, they introduced students to a secret garden where a rose might be glimpsed when there were no roses. Whether this wonderland was real or illusory was a matter of unending debate. Ancient and medieval logicians were involved in psychology because analysing language necessitated examining the workings of the mind. Like his Greek predecessors, Abelard described how the mind might construct whole cities in the imagination and dream of things which look more perfect and vivid than anything on earth. In an analogy which reached back to Plato (and forward to Jung), Abelard asked whether such visions reflect realities, as a mirror seems to do, or whether they are nothing more than tricks of the light. To search for metaphysical reality in reflections was to move in the direction of religion and mysticism. To argue on the other hand, as Abelard did, that 'the image in the mirror can be truly said to be nothing' but a transient contrast of colour was to be 'scientific' in a modern sense.[37] The modern scientist concentrates his gaze on materially demonstrable knowledge. The mirror image is strictly speaking 'nothing', in Abelard's terms, because it is not a substantial 'thing'. It has a superficial 'fictive quality' and, Abelard adds, 'neither an understanding nor any true essence can be formed from a fictive quality'.

ABELARD AND ROSCELIN

In his writings on logic Abelard was generally careful to keep transcendental comparisons with the attributes of God out of his explanations and examples. This is something he may have learned in his early days as a student in the 1090s when Roscelin was under attack. Although Abelard makes no mention in his 'history of calamities' of his having been taught by Roscelin, Roscelin reminded him in a letter that he had studied under him as his 'master from boyhood up until his youth'.[38] How much of his mental formation Abelard owed to Roscelin is impossible to say; probably a great deal, as many of the questions which Abelard addresses seem also to have been Roscelin's concerns. At one point in *Dialectica* Abelard does acknowledge that Roscelin was his 'master', when he says that Roscelin was 'insane' to argue that no thing is composed of parts.[39] Logic and theology were treated as entirely distinct subjects by Abelard's contemporaries because they were based on different prescribed authors: Aristotle was the principal text for logic and St Augustine for theology.

An exception to the rule that Abelard kept discussion of God out of his work on logic is a passage in his commentary on Porphyry, where the question of God's intellect inevitably arises because the problem of knowledge of the future is under discussion. God's perception of the future, Abelard says, is most sensibly resolved by saying that:

> His substance, which alone is unchanging and simple, is varied by no conceptions of things nor by any other forms. For, although the custom of human speech presumes to speak of the creator in the same way as of creatures, by calling Him provident or intelligent for example, nevertheless nothing in Him should be – or can be – understood as distinct from Him: neither perception nor any other form. Therefore any question about perception is irrelevant so far as God is concerned.[40]

Abelard is spelling out here that God is altogether above the rules of logic and beyond discussion by dialectic. This is not because the logician is forbidden to discuss God, but because he cannot do so, as the nature of God surpasses the logic of the human mind. Because God's nature is sublimely unchanging, Porphyry's predicables and Aristotle's categories have no application to Him. The word Abelard uses for 'irrelevant' in this passage is *supervacuus*: any and every question concerning God is 'completely vacuous' and 'superfluous'.

This insistence that God is not discussable may seem surprising coming from Abelard, who was twice condemned as a heretic for discussing the Trinity and whose writings on theology (as distinct from those on logic) show him on almost every page asking and answering questions about God. Abelard's answer to this was that there was a fundamental difference between applying dialectic to the nature of God Himself, which is impossible and therefore completely vacuous, and applying dialectic to the various statements which human beings over the centuries have made about God. The latter application of dialectic was commendable and very necessary because it helped theologians to clarify what belief in God meant. In his first book on theology, the *Theologia Summi Boni*, in 1119 or 1120 Abelard boasted that his contribution to the subject was to bring the 'sword of dialectic' to bear on human reasoning about God, just as the boy David had used Goliath's own sword to overcome the Philistine.[41] Abelard insisted that he directed this gigantic pagan 'sword of dialectic' not at God, but at wicked and stupid human beings who misrepresented Him. In the first rank of these Philistines he placed his former master Roscelin, whom Abelard described as a pseudo-dialectician and a pseudo-Christian.[42] He hoped to prove his orthodoxy by abusing Roscelin, but this tactic went drastically wrong when Abelard was condemned as a heretic at the council of Soissons in 1121.

LOGICAL TRUTH AND DIVINE TRUTH

'We do not promise to teach *the* truth, which everyone agrees neither we nor any other mortal can know', Abelard says, spelling out his orthodoxy, 'but only a verisimilitude of it which accords with human reason and is not contrary to holy scripture. This we direct against those who boast that they impugn the Faith by human reasonings. . . . What truth is, the Lord knows; but I am the judge of what may be said about what its verisimilitude is and what is most consistent with the philosophical reasonings which we use.'[43] Abelard was the judge of these things, in his own opinion at least, because he was the best logician; teachers of Christian doctrine who have not been trained in dialectic are in no position to discuss philosophical issues. This is the culmination of the section of Abelard's *Theologia*, entitled 'In Praise of Dialectic', which he had opened with the quotations from St Augustine (cited at the beginning of this chapter) on how dialectic is the discipline of disciplines. Abelard was not always so scrupulous, as he was in the passage above, in distinguishing between 'verisimilitude', which was humanly attainable, and 'truth', which was not. He is famed for his confident announcement in *Sic et Non* that 'by doubting we come to inquiry and by inquiry we perceive the truth' (*veritas*).[44] This would not have sounded so impressive if he had said: 'by inquiry we perceive something like the truth' (*quid verisimile*).

Whether the truth really was the truth, or only a verisimilitude of it, raised the same sort of question in logic as the problem of the name of the rose or the reflection in the mirror. How do our perceptions relate to the external world? Which things are realities, and which are figments of the imagination? Christianity taught that the ultimate realities – God, the soul and truth – lay beyond human perceptions. This is why Abelard says he is concerned only with verisimilitude. Nevertheless, this semblance has to approximate to the real truth because logic demands that 'truth is not opposed to truth'.[45] But how close was the resemblance between human rational truth and divine truth? By what path did logic lead to God's truth? Had Plato and Aristotle, through their pursuit of logic, come to understand the truth about God before the birth of Christ? Or, to the contrary, was logic a pagan and deceptive science which Christians should avoid, just as they were enjoined to avoid magic and astrology and other ancient arts? At the least, Abelard could say in defence of logic that all such questions had to be framed in human language and the science of dialectic explained what was valid in language and what was spurious.

In much of his work, particularly in *Theologia*, Abelard assumed that God was as reasonable a being as himself. 'All knowledge (*scientia* – "science") is good,' he declared in *Dialectica*; 'we do not say that mathematics is evil, even though it can be misused by astrologers, and neither should we think dialectic intrinsically evil.[46] It is the science 'to which every distinction of truth or falsehood is subject, as it has the principal command over all philosophy and the regulation of every doctrine'.[47] Abelard made clear that he meant Christian 'doctrine' (*doctrina*) here, and not just 'teaching' in general, as he described how St Ambrose and St Augustine had used dialectic. By 'regulation' Abelard did not mean that dialectic should form Christian doctrine, but that it should and could distinguish between the true and the false – the correct and the mistaken proposition – in the man-made language in which doctrine was necessarily expressed. 'The dialectician examines the truth or falsehood of "construction" (in language), and if someone is doubtful, he should remove the doubt by his arguments. Therefore it is not for dialecticians to be interrogators, but rather to help with proof.'[48]

These claims for dialectic make Abelard sound conservative and constructive. The dialectician is not a doubting Thomas nor some dubious academic; he is a language therapist, whose expertise removes the pain of doubt. But Abelard immediately followed this affirmation by insisting that dialecticians do address themselves to questions:

The investigation of dialecticians is appropriate for those particular questions (*questiones*) – in which the principal business of this art consists – where we may actually establish the truth or falseness of something by arguments. Hence it is clear that [dialectic] is pertinent solely to those statements which contain truth or falsehood. These are the propositions, which we have already mentioned, whose definition as true or false Boethius discusses in his *De Topicis*.[49]

Here again Abelard was being careful and moderate in referring to Boethius's authority, and not his own, in order to decide which statements qualify for dialectical treatment. Nevertheless, Abelard went well beyond these restrictive terms of reference in other parts of *Dialectica* and at one point he even claimed that the dialectician can distinguish truth and falsehood in the Christian Trinity itself. The Trinity's sublime non-sense confronted every medieval logician and rationalist because it insisted that one equals three.

THE LOGIC OF THE TRINITY

Abelard purports to show how dialectic's rules for distinguishing names from realities, or abstraction from substance, can resolve the contradiction of three persons being one:

> Very rightly the Father is believed to be God and the Son and the Holy Spirit, but they are not considered as several gods, since these are three names designating the divine substance. So likewise Tullius is truly said to be a man and so is Cicero and Marcus also is called a man. Yet in no way are Marcus and Tullius and Cicero [different] men, since these are words designating the same substance. Indeed, several things differ from each other only in expression and not in substantial meaning.[50]

This looks like an elementary way of explaining the paradox of the Trinity: there are not three gods but three names for the one God, just as Marcus Tullius Cicero had three names. Abelard uses Aristotle's category of 'substance' to distinguish between words referring to things and those which refer only to names. To anyone familiar with the Christian creed, however, this analogy was obviously fallacious – if not heretical – because in the Trinity the three names ('Father', 'Son' and 'Holy Spirit') designate three persons, whereas the names of Cicero designate a single person. Abelard noted this objection but put it aside, saying that his analogy 'can be sufficient' for his present purpose.

This is the kind of argument that gave logicians, and Abelard in particular, a bad name. Admittedly, an analogy was a verisimilitude, not the truth, and it therefore could not fit all the facts; indeed any human analogy for the Trinity was bound to be imperfect. But in that case, what was the point of logicians constructing analogies which could never really work? The answer is that St Augustine had constructed them and, when Abelard was beginning his career as a logician around 1100, St Anselm had put forward new ones in his attempt to refute Abelard's master, Roscelin. The perfect analogy for the Trinity seemed on the verge of discovery, rather like the discovery of a new drug in modern science, and then the most fundamental problem of Christian theology and belief would have been solved. The successful discoverer would achieve the reputation of a Father of the Church, like St Augustine himself. If the analogy failed, on the other hand, the discoverer might be condemned as a heretic and imprisoned or killed. The stakes were therefore high and Abelard, as the highest player of his time (like Sky Masterson in *Guys and Dolls*), gambled against his soul to solve the mystery of the Trinity, at first tentatively in *Dialectica* and then with more elaboration in *Theologia*.

Abelard finally met his match on this issue, both in power of reasoning and ruthlessness of argument, in St Bernard at the council of Sens in 1140. 'Why put this together with so much labour?', Bernard demanded.[51] 'Why thrust it at us with such an inane multiplicity of words? Why produce it with such a flourish, if it does not effect the purpose for which it is adduced: that is, when the components [of the analogy] do not match up in congruent proportions?' The objection of incongruence between any man-made analogy and the divine mystery of the Trinity was hard to deny. Bernard confronted Abelard as an equal at his own word-games, despite having much less training in logic. Like St Augustine, who recalled in his *Confessions* how he taught himself Aristotle's categories and who could not see why his fellow students found them so hard, Bernard had little difficulty with logic.[52] In his opinion it was trivial, schoolboy stuff. (The word 'trivial', coined from the scholastic *trivium*, was not yet in use, though the idea was already there.) According to Bernard, Abelard had strayed from his elementary school into the man's world of religion; his proper place was in the nursery 'arguing with boys and consorting with women'.[53]

Abelard had had the audacity (Bernard claimed) to conduct his 'rude and green little pupils, just weaned from the breasts of dialectic – and those who can hardly digest, so to speak, the first elements of the Faith – into the mystery of the Trinity, into the holy of holies, into the king's bedchamber, to Him who is shrouded with darkness'.[54] The sexual implications are clear: Abelard, the eunuch from the women's quarters, had treacherously snooped with his silly little boys around his Lord's bedchamber. He had already been castrated physically for seducing Heloise; now he should be castrated mentally for seducing his students. Although logic was a childish game, it could be dangerous in the wrong hands; this was Bernard's argument. Abelard had 'played with the art of dialectic from an early age and now he acts the fool with the sacred scriptures'.[55] The word Bernard uses is *insanit* – literally, 'he raves insanely'. Abelard was like a crazed professor in science fiction, who

has discovered how to destroy the world; he might blow the Bible apart
with dialectic and then nobody would be saved. Even John of Salisbury
associated Abelard with insanity, when he reported Gilbert de la Porrée's
opinion that Abelard had been contaminated by the foolishness of
logicians while trying to combat it.[56] This charge was hard to rebut,
as Abelard had indeed claimed in *Theologia* to use dialectic 'to answer
fools in accordance with their foolishness'.[57]

LOGIC AND ABSURDITY

Answering fools with foolishness was a jester's game (still familiar to
modern audiences in many Shakespearean scenes for instance) and this
delight in word-play stemmed from elementary logic being a commonplace of the school curriculum until the eighteenth century. St Bernard
could very effectively suggest that logic was childish – and even insane –
because it had traditionally been taught in a playful way. There were
good reasons for doing this, as the students were young and jests
engaged their attention and challenged them to refute absurdities. The
practice went back to Aristotle himself, who had used the venerable
figure of Socrates as the logician's random exemplar of 'a man' who may
sit or stand, walk or run, and be white or black (these different states are
all 'accidents' of man). So strong and literal was the Aristotelian tradition that Socrates was still the chief butt of the logician's examples in
Abelard's *Dialectica*, just as he had been in the commentaries of Porphyry and Boethius. What had originally been a private joke of Aristotle's about a near contemporary had been turned by Abelard's time into
a surreal presence in the lecture room. Throughout the medieval logicians' texts, Socrates is made to perform humiliating tricks like an
animal in a circus.

'It is possible for Socrates to be a bishop; it is possible to sit down
standing up'.[58] These are two absurd examples which Abelard gives to
illustrate what logicians call 'counterfactuals'. The latter example is
explained by pointing out that a standing person is capable of sitting
down: that is, it is in the 'nature' (another logician's term) of a person
both to sit and to stand. Abelard explains the former paradox in a
similar way:

When we say 'It is possible for Socrates to be a bishop', even though he
may never be one, this is none the less true, since his nature is not
repugnant to a bishop's. We infer this from other individuals of the same
species, whom we see now actually participating in the property of (being

a) bishop. We conclude that whatever actually happens to one individual can happen to all those of the same species, since they are altogether of the same nature. Whatever substance is common to one (applies) to them all; otherwise they would differ in species, whereas they differ only in accidents.[59]

Abelard's explanation makes sense, provided it is understood that 'Socrates' does not mean the historical Socrates but 'a man' as such. It must be possible for 'a man' to be a bishop because being a bishop is an 'accidental' feature of a man. The fact that the historical Socrates could not have been a bishop is irrelevant because historical events are 'accidents' which do not affect the substance of the species. Abelard may have been aiming to amuse as well as instruct his audience with this example, as many of his students hoped to be bishops, if they survived the schools. This example might even date from 1113, when Abelard's rival and sparring partner in the schools of Paris, William of Champeaux, was promoted bishop of Châlons. In that case, Abelard's example demonstrates how it is possible for any clown, even William of Champeaux, to be a bishop. Abelard had a well-attested reputation as a jester and he could not bear 'those very serious men, Anselm of Laon and William of Champeaux'.[60]

People are absurd, is the subtext of Abelard's Dialectica, though how deliberate or conscious this was on his part is difficult to establish, as absurdity was integral to ancient logic. The rule went back to the Greeks that man is distinguished from the other animals by his laughter. It is the 'property' of man to laugh, Porphyry says, just as it is the 'property' of a horse to neigh.[61] A 'property' is that characteristic of the species which is unique or 'proper' to it. The Latin risibilis ('risible') means both 'capable of laughter' and 'laughable'. So here was an ambiguity which Abelard could exploit in his teaching of logic: 'If anyone is a man, he is risible': 'if anyone is risible, he is a man'; 'if Socrates is a man, man is risible'; 'if he is an animal because he is a man, then he is risible because he is a man and, because he is risible, he is an animal'.[62] For the classical Greeks, man's capacity to laugh was an essential biological fact. For Abelard, who was more of 'a jester (joculator) than a professor (doctor)', it seems to have been a way of commenting obliquely on the human condition.

From a biographical point of view, the most intriguing examples in Abelard's Dialectica are those which look as if they are personal, as well as being potentially subversive or absurd. The example immediately preceding 'if anyone is a man, he is risible' is: 'Peter loves his girl' (Petrus diligit suam puellam).[63] As 'Peter' was Abelard's baptismal name, he is presumably referring to himself and Heloise here and, in that case, he is saying to his student audience: 'We can all laugh because that is the capacity which distinguishes us as men, and I am laughable, even though I am your professor, because love makes fools of us all.' In his 'history of calamities' Abelard recalls that he got bored with lecturing during his affair with Heloise; the examples he gives in *Dialectica* presumably succeeded in stimulating himself and his students.[64] He confirms that he refers to himself as 'Peter' in an earlier example illustrating the meanings of the verb 'to be': 'when we say "I am Peter", we may also mean by this "I am called Peter"'.[65] In other words, we define who we are by telling someone our name. This suggests that names must refer to realities. Roscelin had reacted to Abelard's calling him a pseudo-dialectician by mocking the logic of his castration. He could no longer call himself 'Peter', Roscelin told him, because the genus of this name is masculine and when something degenerates from its gender, it does not signify the previous thing. Names which lose their appropriate significance, Roscelin continued, are considered 'imperfect'; logically Abelard should now call himself 'imperfect Peter'.[66] This line of argument also gave Roscelin an opportunity to make some jokes about 'parts' and 'wholes' in logic and life.

References to Abelard's personal life in his works are rare, as he normally kept a tight rein on himself in the classroom. His conservative credentials were best established by using the long-suffering Socrates, rather than himself, as an example of dilemmas in logic. The personal examples Abelard gives nearly all point to his affair with Heloise. They suggest that he was so preoccupied with this at the time (around 1117) that he could not resist referring to it. In *Dialectica* he described Heloise not only as his *puella* ('girl') but also as his *amica*. She had told him that the name of 'friend' or 'lover' (*amica*) was dearer to her than 'wife'. Abelard gives as examples of the subjunctive in *Dialectica*: 'May my *amica* kiss me!' and 'May my *amica* come quick!'[67] In another instance it is difficult to know whether he had his affair with Heloise in mind explicitly or only at a subconscious level. He was discussing verbs which are ambiguous because they are in the active and the passive voice at the same time (a situation possible in Latin though not in English) and he chose as his examples: *amplector* 'I embrace / I am embraced'; *osculor* 'I kiss / I am kissed'; *criminor* 'I incriminate / I am incriminated'.[68] This series neatly summarized the course of his affair: after the initial embrace came the kissing and then the recriminations. Medieval logic could articulate the ambiguities of real life because it used Latin as its mode of expression, which was a real historical language, and not an artificial construct like modern logicians' formulas.

These linguistic examples, which occur throughout *Dialectica*, illustrate how much of Abelard's work on logic is concerned with explaining the meaning and functions of words and constructions. Because it explained words, logic served as an advanced course in Latin, which overlapped in this respect with the other linguistic arts of the *trivium*, grammar and rhetoric. It was the practical training in categorizing words which made logic such a popular course with students. Those 'who had learnt that there were only fourteen (or was it nineteen?) kinds of valid argument and only nine (or was it ten?) categories of experience, and that every possible statement could be classified on a simple system whose rules even a schoolboy could learn to apply, were ready to extend the same process of analysis to the deadly sins, the cardinal virtues, the gifts of the Holy Spirit, the sacraments, and even to the persons of the Trinity'.[69] Sir Richard Southern, whose words these are, cites a letter from St Anselm in 1103 to a monk at Arras: 'You asked me to recall for you the three modes of pride, of which I spoke to you, because you have forgotten two of them'.[70] St Anselm then reiterates them and elaborates his system of categorizing the sin of pride by describing double modes and triple modes with numerical equivalents. The 'mode' was a term borrowed from logic: monks, like St Anselm's correspondent, who talked about 'modes' must have looked very modern and numerate to their fellows, even if they could not always remember what they were talking about. Logic was the 'management-speak', the latest business-school jargon, of Abelard's time and he was its most famous (or notorious) practitioner.

LOGIC AND CHRISTIAN DOCTRINE

Logicians were ready to transfer their skills to any other kind of business which demanded analytical thought. A good example is the appointment in 1119 of William of Champeaux as the pope's negotiator with the Emperor Henry V to resolve the vexed question of who should appoint bishops and abbots (the Investiture Dispute).[71] Reconciling opposing forms of words by making distinctions was the basic skill of every experienced logician and this was the way the Investiture Dispute was resolved. Even if logicians could not solve problems, they were adept at expressing them in different words in order to save the appearances and give the impression that something had been achieved. Abelard, who was in deep trouble in 1119 (he had been castrated about a year earlier and was already suspected of heresy), may well have viewed his former master's success with jealous dismay. The pursuit of logic had taken

Abelard likewise in the direction of the papal court in 1119 but not, like William of Champeaux, as a prince of the Church; Abelard was due to appear there as a petitioner, unsuccessfully suing the bishop and canons of Paris over their alleged connivance in his castration.[72]

The time around 1119 is also when Abelard began the strategy he pursued for the rest of his life of trying to recover his reputation by applying logic to Christian doctrine, as well as to Aristotelian texts. 'I first' (he says) 'applied myself to discussing the foundation of our faith by analogies from human reason' because his students insisted that 'it was ridiculous for someone to set forth for others what neither he, nor those whom he teaches, can grasp with the intellect.'[73] As the students' favourite professor, Abelard purported to accede to their demands. His success in classical logic had depended on appealing to students, ever since the beginning of his career in the 1100s when he had competed for William of Champeaux's students in the schools of Paris. The surge of student demand would rush him once more to the top, this time as the greatest master of divine logic or 'theology'.

Years later, St Bernard accurately and sarcastically summed up Abelard's approach: 'Our theologian says: "What is the use of setting forth to speak about doctrine, unless what we want to teach can be explained so as to be intelligible?" And so he promises understanding to his hearers, even of those sublime and hallowed things which are lodged deep in the bosom of Holy Faith.'[74] In this image of Bernard's, Abelard is no longer a sly eunuch who has strayed out of the women's room; he is a sexual predator groping in the bosom of Holy Faith. Abelard's contemporary, Master Gilbert of Sempringham, who was renowned for his chastity (and lived to the age of a hundred), dreamt that he put his hand into a girl's bosom and could not get it out.[75] But everything had turned out for the best, as the dream girl was a prefigurement of Holy Church and Gilbert's hand had therefore stuck in the right place. Bernard's clerical audience all knew where Abelard's hand had wandered, and Bernard knew as well that sexual innuendo and sarcasm were more persuasive forms of language than logic because they appealed to the passions. Abelard's voice of reason was no match against Bernard's tone of divine wrath.

Bernard continued his diatribe, again with accuracy, by saying that Abelard 'put degrees in the Trinity, modes in the Majesty, numbers in Eternity'.[76] This was in fact what all theologians did because medieval theology was essentially the application of logic to religious teaching. The instance of St Anselm numbering the modes of pride and doubling and tripling them illustrates this very well, as does Abelard's description of applying 'analogies (*similitudines*) from human reason' to the Faith.

There was nothing new in this. Roman Christianity had been a religion of logic certainly since AD 325, when the Emperor Constantine had presided over the definition of the Nicene creed. Definitions of the profoundest mysteries of the Faith had been recited daily in Christian churches ever since and they could be learned, though not necessarily understood, by anybody. Indeed, the Church enjoined that the creed must be known by everyone; by the thirteenth century (fifty years after Bernard's time) theology had advanced to the point where a person who was incapable of putting degrees in the Trinity, or explaining the mode by which God's Majesty became man, might be examined by the Roman inquisition and burned as a heretic. By then too, all sorts of numbers categorized the eternal verities: seven deadly sins, four cardinal virtues, seven sacraments, and so on.

Pagan Greek logic and Christian scholastic theology were not really opposed to each other, as they shared the same premises. Theology, as Abelard stressed, did not promise to teach God's truth but only its human 'verisimilitude'.[77] Conversely, logic was not immediately self-evident; it too was a doctrinal system which had to be accepted on faith. Aristotle's categories and Porphyry's predicables are as firmly – or as weakly – grounded in human experience as the Trinity and the Incarnation. No one has ever seen a 'genus' and no one can therefore demonstrate how it generates species. The Latin version of Porphyry available to Abelard defined 'genus' as the 'principle of each and every one's generation', which comes close to being a circular definition.[78] Abelard himself said that the 'genus creates species in a material sense (*materialiter*) at the point when the general essence is transferred into the substance of the species'.[79] But he did not explain what this 'general essence' (*generalis essentia*) consisted of materially. Was it a solid or a liquid, was it hot or cold? How and when did its transfer into the species take place? What had the 'substance of the species' (*substantiam speciei*) consisted of before the transfer? Essence and substance, like genus and species, were logicians' technical terms. Probably, Abelard did not intend them to be treated literally in a material sense, like the terms of modern natural science. Neither by training nor by temperament was he equipped to examine anything physically or numerately, as Roger Bacon claimed to do with his experimental science a century later. Abelard was interested in the congruence of numbers in the Platonic philosophical tradition, but he was not a mathematician.[80]

Common linguistic concepts are explicable if we assume that all our intellects are linked into some single 'principle of each and every one's generation'. In *Dialectica* (and more fully in *Theologia*) Abelard discussed whether the World Soul, which animated all beings in what he described as the 'Platonic faith', was similar to the Holy Spirit in the Christian faith. The World Soul stems from the divine mind, the *nous*, much as the Holy Spirit proceeds from God the Son in the Trinity.[81] This idea attracted Abelard because it suggested that all human beings, by their nature as rational animals who shared in the divine mind, were capable of the same thoughts. Among the accusations brought against him at the council of Sens in 1140 was that he had taught that the Holy Spirit is the World Soul. Abelard had proved himself a heathen by sweating to make Plato a Christian was how St Bernard put it.[82]

Powerful and cogent as they are, Bernard's attacks on Abelard should not be seen as the only orthodox view about logic. Bernard's purpose was to put the case for the prosecution and he exaggerated the threat which Abelard posed. St Anselm of Canterbury, William of Champeaux and Abelard himself had not resorted to logic in some desperate and ill-judged attempt to defend Christianity from its critics. Rather, they believed they had found in classical logic a delightful and God-given tool, which helped explain Christian revelation. Logic aided teaching and, as St Anselm had shown, intellectual cogitation led to prayerful meditation on the meaning of God. It was not logic as such that Bernard attacked, but Abelard's allegedly inappropriate use of it. Whereas St Anselm had been been humble and worshipful in his contemplation of the logic of God, Abelard's tone was arrogant and irreverent to the point of being blasphemous. This was what Bernard alleged and it was difficult to refute.

In his Confession of Faith to Heloise, quoted at the start of this chapter, Abelard acknowledged that logic had made him hateful to the world. He purported to acknowledge also – after a lifetime of arguing for and about logic – that he was willing to surrender. If he had to choose between logic and St Paul, he chose St Paul: 'I do not wish, I do not wish (he repeated), to be such a philosopher as to reject Paul; I do not wish to be such an Aristotle as to be shut out from Christ'.[83] This declaration is not as forthright as it looks. The subjunctive mood of the verbs to 'reject' (*recalcitrem*) and to 'shut out' (*secludar*) have a hypothetical implication. Abelard had devoted the fourth part of *Dialectica* to hypothetical statements, single and multiple, simple and composite, and many other varieties. He was not finally admitting that philosophy was indeed opposed to St Paul and that Aristotle did exclude Christ. Gilson pointed out that Abelard was still secure in his conscience: he 'is not yet convinced that he is wrong. His persecutors have not yet got him to admit the errors they reproach him with. The tired old warrior feels that he has not yet spoken his final word'.[84] Abelard's Confession of Faith reiterates what he had always argued: that he never had wished to be any kind of untruthful philosopher or pseudo-Aristotle. On the contrary, he was the real thing: 'Christ's philosopher' and 'our Aristotle', as Peter the Venerable described him.[85]

Abelard's argument was that logic alone made sense of Christian doctrine because all doctrine had to be expressed for us, as human beings, through the structures of language, and logic alone made sense of language. It was nonsensical to teach or preach anything that could not be grasped with the intellect. Abelard was typical of scholastic intellectuals in seeing Christianity not as a mysterious cult, but as a rational code of rules. Its lifeblood was logic, and not the visual and tactile attractions upon which the great Romanesque pilgrimage churches of Abelard's day depended. Logic was a science which had to be painstakingly learned in the schools; it could not be miraculously acquired in a day, like a cure at a saint's shrine. Of course Plato and Aristotle could not be made into Christians, but they had shared in – and supremely articulated – the faculty of reason which distinguished man from all the other animals, and which distinguished in particular educated men from the ignorant herd. The force of Abelard's argument was demonstrated by the way St Bernard and the pope and all Abelard's opponents tried to refute him through reasoned language, through (that is) the Latin of Cicero and the terminology of ancient Greek philosophy, because the Roman church had based its authority on a logically defined creed since at least the time of the Emperor Constantine.

There is no unequivocal evidence that Abelard ever surrendered the claim he had made in the first version of his *Theologia* in 1119 or 1120 that he, as the master of logic, should be the judge of that 'verisimilitude' of the truth, which is all we can know on earth.[86] He acknowledged logic had limitations, though they were not the limitations recognized by St Bernard. Logic did not deal with physical nature, nor with ultimate realities. 'The Supreme Architect', Abelard wrote in *Dialectica*, 'has committed the making of language (literally the "imposition of voices" – *vocum impositionem*) to us, but He has reserved the nature of things to His own disposition'.[87] What Abelard refused to acknowledge was that his own contemporaries, whom he knew personally and whose judgement he questioned, most notably William of Champeaux and St Bernard, had authority to silence him. They were no builders of the truth, commissioned by the Supreme Architect, but 'twisted twisters' or 'perverse perverters' as he calls his accusers in his Confession of Faith to Heloise.[88] As far as the making of language was concerned, Abelard was entitled to make his voice heard because he was the supreme logician. Even his enemies acknowledged that, he said.[89]

Part II

Experimentum – 'Experience'

The Years 1117–18

Chronological Table 1117-18

Paschal II, pope, 1099–1118
Gilbert, bishop of Paris, 1116–23
Adam, abbot of St Denis, 1099–1122
Louis VI, king of France, 1108–37
William IX, count of Poitou and duke of Aquitaine, 1086–1127
Alan IV, count of Nantes and duke of Brittany, 1084–1112
Conan III, count of Nantes and Duke of Brittany, 1112–48

c.1117	Abelard lodges in the house of Fulbert, canon of Notre-Dame in Paris.
c.1117	Abelard seduces Heloise, Fulbert's niece.
c.1118	Abelard abducts Heloise to his home at Le Pallet, where she bears them a son, Astralabe.
c.1118	Heloise and Abelard are married in Paris in the presence of Fulbert and witnesses.
c.1118	Heloise swears that she is not married.
c.1118	Abelard sends Heloise to the convent of Argenteuil and vests her as a nun, apart from the veil.
c.1118	Abelard is castrated by Fulbert's kinsmen.
c.1118	Abelard orders Heloise to take the veil at Argenteuil.
c.1118	Abelard becomes a monk of St Denis.

6

Experimentum – 'Experience'

Experimentum in Latin meant proof from actual experience or experiment, often physical experience, as opposed to purely theoretical demonstration by logic. The dialectical method so loved by Abelard proceeded by stringing together a series of hypothetical statements snatched from the air: 'All men are animals, Socrates is a man...' and so on. Frequently, conditional clauses and negatives were introduced which made the logic look even more speculative and bizarre: 'If Socrates is neither rational nor irrational, he is not an animal...'.[1] At its extreme, *experimentum* rejected this sort of logic as nonsensical theorizing. In natural science, valid proof comes from experience and not from reasoning: to know that fire burns and that it hurts, a man should put his hand in it. This is the deliberately provocative contention of Roger Bacon, writing a century and more after Abelard. Bacon saw himself as a solitary crusader, battling against scholastic theorizing which had been overemphasized since Abelard's time, or even since Aristotle's.

There was no disagreement among scholastics about the need for proof and questioning, 'for by doubting we come to inquiry and by inquiry we perceive the truth', as Abelard had confidently announced in the prologue to *Sic et Non*.[2] The difference arose over what constitutes a proper 'inquiry'. The word Abelard uses is *inquisitionem*, meaning verbal interrogation of the authoritative works of the Church Fathers, which he had reduced to quotations and juxtaposed on an encyclopedic scale in *Sic et Non*. Through minutely dissecting and comparing the sayings of St Augustine, Pope Gregory the Great, St Jerome, and many others, we come to perceive the truth. This sort of application of logic to language was classically Greek and Abelard appropriately cites Aristotle in his support.

Equally ancient and Greek, and in a long tradition of mysticism as much as empiricism, was the contrary argument from experience. Roger

Bacon maintains that by the experience which the man has in getting his hand burned, 'the mind is assured and it rests in the full light of truth; therefore, reasoning (*argumentum*) does not suffice, but experience does'.[3] Experience concerns the facts of life. It comes from outside us, beyond our immediate comprehension, and it suddenly illuminates the mind like turning on a light. Therefore, *experimentum* is more effective than reasoning because it touches the feelings of the whole being, instead of being locked up in the intellect or hidden in books. 'Examples often go further than words in stirring or soothing human feelings.'[4] This is the opening sentence of Abelard's 'history of calamities' and it shows that he understood the psychological and philosophical case for *experimentum* well enough, although in his books and lectures on logic and theology he repeatedly maintained that dialectic is the principal basis of science.

Abelard's 'History of Calamities'

'I have decided', Abelard continues, 'to write about the experiences (*experimentis*) of my calamities.'[5] The paradox in this, which Abelard may well have been aware of, is that writing down his experiences converted them also into mere words. For the anonymous friend whom Abelard purports to address, his *experimenta* served as 'examples' only in the sense that a medieval preacher told exemplary anecdotes to point the moral of a sermon; neither Abelard's words nor a preacher's *exempla* were evident facts. For Abelard himself, on the other hand, the process of writing about his experiences was a way of making contact with his feelings, whether 'stirring or soothing', and a way too, perhaps, of acknowledging that 'reasoning does not suffice'. He wrote his 'history of calamities' when he was about fifty years of age, when he had been a monk for more than a decade. It is common in middle age for a person to want to look back over his life, which is now beyond recovery but not yet beyond recall, and monks had a special reason to do this because they were dedicated to perfecting themselves through prayer and contemplation.

Abelard's story of his experiences fits loosely within an accepted genre of monastic writing. A generation before Abelard, Otloh of St Emmeram (in Regensburg) had written a 'letter to a friend' offering examples for spiritual consolation; but the examples he gives are biblical not personal, although in another work he did write of his own temptations.[6] Abelard's contemporary, Guibert abbot of Nogent, wrote a fascinating account of his childhood, framed in the form of a confession and appeal to God, in imitation of St Augustine's *Confessions*. When he reaches the events of adulthood, however, Guibert becomes less introspective and more anecdotal like a chronicler or preacher. Suger abbot of St Denis, Abelard's rival who drove Heloise out of the convent of Argenteuil, wrote – explicitly for the memory of posterity – an account of his material achievements: in building work and in amassing treasure for his abbey. Abelard's story is more coherent than Guibert's and more personal than Suger's because it is structured around the events of his life and Abelard integrates what he feels about them within his narrative.

Recording reminiscences was not confined to monks nor even to clerics. The fragment of an autobiography by Fulk IV count of Anjou, written at some time between 1096 and his death in 1109, is a reminder that every landowner had to be able to give an account of himself, particularly if he had come by his possessions illegally (Fulk had deposed and imprisoned his elder brother in 1067). Like Abelard, he begins forthrightly with the Latin 'Ego' – 'I, Fulk count of Anjou....'[7] He then sets down the names of his ancestors and a bald account, much more summary than Suger's, of how he and they had come into possession of their lands and fortresses, as if listing them all somehow provided him with deeds of title. Fulk set down his family history to justify his conquest of Anjou (his 'honour' he called it), much as William the Conqueror had Domesday Book made in 1086 to justify the Normans' title to England. Unlike Abelard or Guibert de Nogent, Fulk makes no reference to his inner feelings about his life; he probably thought that public confessions were best left to monks. Even when complete, his autobiography probably amounted to no more than an inventory or *aide-mémoire* to hand on to his heirs. Even humble families must have had some memory of this sort to pass on from one generation to the next by word of mouth; Fulk was unusual in putting his in writing.

Without some explanatory enlargement, Fulk's summary account of his life could not have acted as a guide to conduct. Even if it is true that 'reasoning does not suffice', Bacon's alternative that 'experience does' is simplistic. Personal experience by itself can tell us only about isolated fragments of the past, whereas every individual – as much as every philosopher – needs coherent rules to apply to the future. As a dedicated Christian monk, believing that God has a plan for the world and every one of its creatures, Abelard had to see a providential pattern in the events of his life, even in the grotesque experiences of being castrated and then mentally assaulted by being made to burn his own book as a heretic. Through these horrors, Abelard purports to see his bodily lust cured and his mental pride humbled, and this enables him to conclude his 'history of calamities' with the 'Thy will be done' of the Lord's

Prayer. 'Let us then take heart from these proofs and examples', he assures his reader, 'and bear them the more confidently the more they happen to be undeserved.'[8] Unlike St Augustine and Guibert de Nogent, who bemoan their sins and beg God's forgiveness, Abelard puts less emphasis on his own wrongdoing and more on the catalogue of wrongs allegedly done to him.

As moral advice, Abelard's story lacks complete conviction, because he is too interested in the incidental particulars of his life, his *experimenta*, and in the reflection of his own brilliance. His opponents are invariably seen as rivals, who envy his talents and who are driven by jealousy to persecute him. Instead of concentrating on recording personal failings and spiritual warnings, as a contemplative writer should, Abelard packs his sentences with material information, rather as Abbot Suger packs his with details of his building works and jewels. This is why Abelard and Suger prove such precious historical sources, whatever shortcomings their works have as religious tracts. Abelard sets the tone of his story from the beginning:

> I originate from a certain town (or fortress) constructed on the border of Brittany, which is properly called by the name *Palatium* (Le Pallet), eight miles – I believe – in an easterly direction from the city of Nantes.[9]

The cautious 'I believe' (*credo*) and the insistence on the correct name of his birthplace alerts the reader that Abelard is an academic and possibly a pedant. Proper names were his speciality as a philosopher and belief was his concern as a theologian. The reader may feel that Abelard has been so conditioned by his philosophical training to see difficulties in even the most straightforward statement that he is incapable of saying anything simply. But this is to underestimate the difficulties of autobiography. The events of a person's life are hard to recall with chronological or factual accuracy, because the memory reworks them continually. Abelard holds on to as many facts as he can. Because of the suspicion of forgery, his 'history of calamities' has been subjected to repeated checks against known historical facts and it comes well out of such tests.

Monks meant something special by experience. When St Bernard exhorted his hearers to turn their attention inwards and 'read in the book of experience', he was referring not to their experience of daily life at the abbey of Clairvaux in the 1130s, which should have been entirely uniform and uneventful (for that was the purpose of the monastic rule), but to their individual mystical experience. Bernard asked whether any of his monks had received the intimate experience and privilege of a kiss from the mouth of Christ.[10] Bernard's question made sense within the context of his monks' search for divine perfection. Because it embodied supernatural power, the knowledge gained by the experience of Christ's kiss overrode both an intellectual's book-learning and Bacon's experimental science. Although Abelard was a monk when he wrote his 'history of calamities' and although he presents himself as Christ-like in his sufferings, he makes no claim to mystical experience or supernatural enlightenment. The kisses Abelard describes experiencing were those of Heloise; the fire he had come closest to was not that of the divine spirit, but the executioner's when his book was burned at Soissons. At heart, Abelard always remained an intellectual. It was a flash of self-knowledge at the end of his life, when he acknowledged that 'logic has made me hateful to the world'.[11]

THE LITERATURE OF EXPERIENCE

By reviewing his experiences in the light of providence, Abelard was compelled to give them a literary form. Any writing in Latin tended to turn into literature. Furthermore, Abelard was very much a 'writer' in the modern sense of a professional self-publicist who makes anything, however personal or shameful, into a literary happening. He perhaps wrote for his son Astralabe, whom he can scarcely have known, an elaborate poem of advice; he certainly wrote a huge amount for Heloise; how much of it was intended for immediate publication, as well as for posterity, is hard to establish. In his 'history of calamities' he seems to have been writing for himself and for posterity, as much as for the anonymous friend. Abelard cannot help creating a literary persona to be the hero of his 'history' because this is what the genre of personal recollection demanded.

This persona is both factual and fictitious, like the persona Dante creates in the *Vita Nuova* who links together literary recollections to form a compelling narrative. 'I think no one could read it or hear it dry-eyed,' was Heloise's immediate reaction to the 'history of calamities'.[12] She was so moved because Abelard's story does not culminate in an exemplary and happy ending, as a moral tale should. He finishes his 'history' in the middle. Like Dante, Abelard has lost his way *nel mezzo del cammin di nostra vita* – 'in the midst of the course of life'.[13] There is something desperate in Abelard's concluding his 'history' with 'Thy will be done', as his difficulties at the time of writing (in about 1132) were totally unresolved. He had failed to keep order even in his own abbey of St Gildas in Brittany and was in danger of being killed by his own monks. If these were imaginary fears, which is possible, he was in equal danger of going insane and that was worse. Abelard records that he had been insane ten years earlier, immediately after the burning of his book, and he had perhaps had breakdowns before that when he had to withdraw from the schools and go back to his parental home.[14]

St Bernard reviewed the salient points of Abelard's experience more starkly than he could do himself: 'We have in France one Peter Abelard, a monk without a rule, a prelate without responsibility, an abbot without discipline, who argues with boys and consorts with women.'[15] In Bernard's view, Abelard had not been chastened by his calamities: 'He had long been silent; but while he kept silence in Brittany, he conceived sorrow, and now in France he has brought forth iniquity.'[16] A monk should rejoice in his salvation; sorrow was a sign of worry and of not having a clear conscience. This is why Bernard links Abelard's sorrow with bringing forth iniquity. Bernard is referring here to the seventh Psalm and he would have expected his audience to supply for themselves the next verses: 'He hath opened a pit and dug it: and he is fallen into the hole he made; his sorrow shall be turned on his own head.' Here was another succinct account of Abelard's career. He may indeed have 'conceived sorrow' in writing his 'history of calamities' because the stance of providential repentance, which he was obliged to adopt in it, prevented him from acknowledging that he had enjoyed his early life and was pleased with what he had done.

Did recollecting his experiences make Abelard repent his sins, or merely regret the past? Was he really convinced that loving Heloise and writing his book of theology were sins? In his influential commentary on the Book of Job, Pope Gregory the Great says: 'There are some people who confess their faults with loud voices, and yet they still speak joyfully of the things they lament.'[17] This is much what Abelard does in his 'history of calamities'. He takes pride, for example, in the love songs he had written for Heloise, which were still widely sung, and even greater pride in his book of theology which had been burned as heretical at Soissons. If Abelard had really groaned over his sins, as Pope Gregory describes the true penitent doing, he would have been ashamed of the success of his songs and he would not have renamed his book *Christian Theology* shortly after it was burned, nor would he have reissued it in an enlarged edition, including a supplement ridiculing the authorities who had caused his condemnation at Soissons.[18] As an example of human courage, Abelard's resilience and repeated refusal to acknowledge he was in the wrong looks admirable, but it does not suggest repentance of the sort the clergy demanded. Heloise quotes Pope Gregory's words, when she reminds Abelard that she does not repent of their love affair, even if he does. 'When I should be groaning over what I have done, I can only sigh over what I have lost.' Outsiders might not detect the difference between a groan and a sigh, but she and Abelard could – and so too could St Bernard and the other 'pseudo-apostles' (as Heloise called them) who lay in wait.[19]

WILLIAM IX OF AQUITAINE AND JOY

The most striking self-examination from Abelard's time came not from a monk or a professional religious at all but from a poet and a prince, the troubadour William IX count of Poitou and duke of Aquitaine. Like Abelard, he was a self-conscious author, who created a literary persona through his songs. Purportedly facing exile or even death, William IX – 'in great fear and great peril' – confronts his sadness through song. (This may have been when he was wounded at the battle of Taillebourg, which probably occurred around 1120. In that case William IX was aged about fifty, like Abelard at the time of writing the 'history of calamities'.) William IX acknowledges in his song that he must give up his old way of life and, 'since it pleases God, so be it and I beseech Him to keep me with Him'. He neither groans over his sins as recommended by Pope Gregory, nor confesses with pride like Abelard, nor does he sigh for what has been lost like Heloise. William IX simply recalls the joy he has had in his life: 'I have belonged to prowess and to joy, but now we part from each other... I pray all my friends that at my death they come and do me great honour; for I have had joy and delight, far and near, and in my home.'[20]

This is not at all what the clergy and reforming monks like St Bernard wanted to hear a man announce on his deathbed, particularly not a prince of this world like William IX of Aquitaine. In his song, William IX does not even acknowledge that 'chivalry and pride' and sensual furs (the 'vair' and the 'gris') are sinful and worldly; he simply takes leave of them with dignity. A man like this, in conventional clerical opinion, should have been howling for mercy at the mouth of Hell. Instead of which, William IX speaks in his song to Jesus 'on his throne' as one prince to another, and he has the temerity to pray to Him 'in romance' (in Occitan French) as well as in the clerical language of Latin. According to the English monk, William of Malmesbury, William IX had assaulted bishops, built a brothel in the form of a convent near Niort, and behaved as if he believed that everything was governed by chance.[21] In his reputed irreligion, William IX may have voiced the opinions of many people of all social classes. This is why the clergy were so vociferous in their condemnation of unbelief.

By comparison with William IX's song, Abelard's 'history of calamities' comes close to denying the integrity of his experiences. He purports to confess that his prowess in scholarship was no more than overbearing pride and that his joy in Heloise was lust, and yet he finishes up confused and directionless. He cannot say with William IX that he has had honour and joy among his friends and in his home. The 'history of calamities' names many of Abelard's enemies but none of his friends other than the forbidden 'girl-friend' (*amica*), Heloise. Possibly Abelard did not have friends so much as partisans and admirers among his students and juniors. As for a home, Abelard says that after quarrelling with the monks of St Gildas, 'I can find nowhere to rest or even to live; I am a vagabond and a fugitive, going everywhere marked as if by the curse of Cain.'[22] Friendless and homeless, the tragic hero of Abelard's 'history of calamities' has reached the point of despair, while the real Peter Abelard – somehow or other – was at that very time preparing to return to Paris and win over a new generation of student admirers, headed by John of Salisbury (who came to Paris in 1136).

Abelard stemmed from the same cultural milieu as William IX, though on a more modest scale. Although Abelard had been born in the county of Nantes and therefore in Brittany, his birthplace was south of the Loire and bordered on Poitou. His father was a Poitevin and he was literate and a knight, like William IX. Abelard, too, had a reputation as a jester and a doubter. As the eldest son and heir, he might have been a knight and a poet, rejoicing in love and war in Aquitaine like William IX. Strife and passion are powerful elements in the account Abelard gives of his clerical career in the schools before he became a monk and a moralist. 'You, cleric and canon,' Heloise teasingly reproved him, 'is this what you should be doing? Will you not shamelessly sink for ever in these obscenities? If you do not care about the prerogative of a cleric, at least defend the dignity of a philosopher.'[23] Belatedly Abelard did so, when he justified himself in his 'history of calamities'.

The Intellectual and Ethics

Through the motif of *experimentum*, the chapters which follow look at Abelard's life and feelings beyond the clerical orbit which he had willingly entered, and beyond its demanding roles which he could not sustain. Otto of Freising suggests that Abelard's difficulties ran so deep because they had been programmed into him from birth, as Brittany is 'a country fertile in clerics of acute intelligence and application to the arts, but quite stupid in any other business'.[24] Otto's comment reinforces the characterization of Abelard as an intellectual, who found books and theories easier to understand than people and actions.

In his book on ethics Abelard had argued that actions in themselves are indifferent; only the intention of the actor makes them right or wrong. This is an intellectual's point of view, making thinking more important than doing. 'For God does not think of which things get done, but of the state of mind in which they are done. . . . Often in fact the same thing may be done by different people, justly in the one case and wickedly in the other.'[25] The chilling example Abelard gives is of a good hangman, who hangs a criminal out of zeal for justice, and a bad one who does so in pursuance of his own vendetta. Abelard acknowledges, however, that his emphasis on intentionality is idealistic, 'for people do not judge by what is hidden but by what is evident; they are concerned not so much with the guilt of the accused as with the thing done'.[26] This explains why human judges, who cannot possess God's moral omniscience, punish wrongdoing rather than sin.

Abelard's actual experience of life may have led him to this theoretical point of view, which was very unusual at the time and which Heloise shared. As he saw it, his intentions had been good, even though their outcomes were calamitous. His intention in marrying Heloise, for example, was generous and loving, but its outcome had been her confinement in a convent and his castration. Likewise his intention in writing about the Trinity was to explain it properly; but his judges, being human, foolishly read his book as heresy and made him burn it.

Although a cleric and an academic, Abelard was never content to be a cloistered thinker. He deliberately climbed up on to the stage, first to act out verbal duels with rival masters of dialectic and then to engage in sex and violence. Thereby he won the immortal love of Heloise and the adulation of some of his students. At terrible cost to himself, through the mental and physical attacks made upon him, he demonstrated that *experimentum* does matter and that good intentions are not sufficient. Roger Bacon recommended putting your hand into the fire to experience the true meaning of proof. Closer to Abelard's time and place another moralist, the troubadour Marcabru, warned: love acts like the spark which catches the soot in the chimney; '*Escoutatz*! Listen! – a man who is devoured by fire does not know which way to run.'[27] Abelard kept running for the rest of his life.

7

Knight

Abelard was the eldest son of a knight, but he chose to give up this birthright in order to be a scholar.[1] Nevertheless, he retained throughout his life all the belligerence of a knight. He was 'an extremely bellicose man, accustomed to winning', says the biographer of Abelard's challenger in the schools, St Goswin.[2] In his 'history of calamities' Abelard describes his scholastic controversies with rival masters as 'wars' governed by chance: 'Fortune gave success in these wars to our men [meaning Abelard's students], and especially to me.'[3] Abelard uses military metaphors like 'I pitched camp' and 'I laid siege' not just for literary effect, but because he was involved in something very close to warfare. In order to be a master in the schools of Paris, he had to take sides in the feuds and actual fighting surrounding the French royal court, which was struggling to establish itself in the early 1100s. The king's strategy was to augment the prestige and revenues of the crown by intervening to protect Church property and ecclesiastics against the lay nobility, and in this process even a junior cleric like Abelard might be of service.

Connection with the court may originally have given Abelard his nickname of *Palatinus*. A *palatinus* was a man at the palace, a courtier who did the king's business. Abelard was the *palatinus* from Le Pallet (*Palatium*); the ironical pun contrasts his high status as a *palatinus* with his small-town origins at Le Pallet. John of Salisbury called Abelard *Peripateticus Palatinus*.[4] This was another ironical pun, as a *palatinus* should have been housed in a palace and not living as a peripatetic, wandering the streets. Abelard described himself as an 'emulator of the Peripatetics', which was a learned reference to the name of the followers of Aristotle. Abelard also meant by this that he had wandered from place to place, in pursuit of philosophy, until he reached Paris.[5] He was a typical wandering scholar. Nor was arrival in Paris the end of his journeying, as he remained on the move: first following the royal court to Melun and elsewhere in the early 1100s, then (in 1113) going to Laon and back to Paris, and in 1121 he had had to flee from the king's anger to Count Thibaud of Champagne at Provins. Not far from there, in the woods, Abelard founded his ideal community of the Paraclete. Thibaud's patronage may be another reason why Abelard was nicknamed *Palatinus*, as Thibaud was the premier count of France, the Count 'Palatine' or master of the palace.[6]

There is an element in Abelard's journeying of the knights errant in romances, who wander through the forest in quest of treasure or enlightenment; but there is an element equally of the stipendiary knights, who move from one lord to another in pursuit of better pay. Abelard was too proud to be anyone's retainer for long, even when he had attained his goal of Paris and shared the Île-de-la-Cité with the king of France. As well as being a courtier, Abelard had a reputation for courtliness, in the romantic sense of being a love-object for ladies. 'What married woman, what young girl', Heloise asks, 'did not desire you in absence and was not on fire in your presence?'[7] Fulk of Deuil, in his mocking letter of advice to Abelard, describes something similar. When his women friends learned that Abelard had been castrated, they wept and wailed 'for you, their knight, as if each one of them had lost a husband or lover in battle'.[8] This is one of the earliest instances of the medieval stereotype of damsels mourning for their knight. Fulk's description also suggests the popular literary theme of a debate between the respective merits of a knight and a cleric as lovers; the cleric is preferred by some ladies to his warrior counterpart because he is better educated and better mannered. In reality, according to Abelard's own account at least, he had worked so long at his books that he had had no time to frequent the society of ladies, and he had therefore known little of these affairs before he met Heloise.

JESTER AND TROUBADOUR

Even though Abelard claimed he was 'held back from the society of gentlewomen by the assiduity of my studies and I did not have much contact with lay people', he had a reputation as an entertaining and sociable person before he met Heloise.[9] As was the practice of lecturers in logic, he enlivened and illustrated his arguments with jokes: 'Socrates is an ass'; 'it is possible for Socrates to be a bishop'; 'Peter loves his girl'.[10] He presented himself as the fat and jolly Master 'Abelard': 'this name has been allocated to me so that something of my substance may be referred to through it'.[11] 'Abelard' may have been his nickname in the lecture room: a stage name, like the names some of the troubadours adopted.[12] Otto of Freising confirms that when Abelard was a master in Paris, he excelled not only in philosophy, but 'in moving men's minds to jokes'.[13] This was why he could not bear his masters, 'those very serious men' (as Otto calls them), Anselm of Laon and William of Champeaux.[14] Abelard himself recounts how, when he was at Anselm's school at Laon (in 1113), 'we students joked together'.[15]

A year or two before Abelard went to Laon, Master Jocelin had warned the young St Goswin that Abelard was a 'jester' (*joculator*) rather than a 'professor' (*doctor*).[16] 'I was light-hearted,' Abelard explains at the beginning of his 'history of calamities'.[17] The Latin *animo levis* can also be translated as 'volatile', or even 'capricious'.[18] In this, Abelárd was like his contemporary, the Archpoet:

> I am of one element, levity my matter,
> Like enough a withered leaf for the winds to scatter.[19]

In reacting against the seriousness of his masters, Abelard was also agreeing with the Archpoet:

> Never yet could I endure soberness and sadness,
> Jests I love, and sweeter than honey find I gladness.[20]

Abelard explains that it was 'the nature of my country [literally my "land" or "soil" – *terra*] and ancestry' which made him 'light-hearted'.[21] Otto of Freising enlarges on this idea that a particular terrain produces a certain sort of person, much as it produces specific crops. He explains, for the benefit of his German readers, that 'this Peter had his origin in a part of France, which is now called Brittany by the inhabitants. This country is fertile in clerics of acute intelligence concerned with the arts.'[22] Abelard was typical of them, being 'dedicated from an early age to the study of literature and other trifles'.[23] In his own account of his origins, however, Abelard is careful to explain that he came from the borderland, 'at the entrance to Brittany', a refinement which Otto of Freising may not have appreciated because he was a foreigner.[24]

The land which made Abelard 'light-hearted' was not Atlantic or Celtic Brittany, therefore, but the southerly borders of the river Loire, where his birthplace at Le Pallet is situated. From there, routes led inland to Anjou and the heart of France, or south to Poitou and Aquitaine, the land of the troubadours and Occitan culture. Le Pallet (as already suggested in chapter 3) is situated at the axial point of the area where the troubadour, Jaufré Rudel, says 'we sing in the plain Romance tongue'.[25] Furthermore, a reliable chronicler, Richard of Poitiers, says Abelard's father was a Poitevin.[26] So, the 'country and ancestry', which made Abelard 'light-hearted', was the very territory and culture which formed the troubadours. Like other knights from the south, Abelard's father had been educated in 'letters' and he saw to it that all his sons got a similar education.[27] Although Abelard specialized in the arts of the trivium (Latin grammar, rhetoric and logic), he also acquired a knowledge of music and he was famed for his love songs for Heloise. These were probably in Latin, though they could have been in a mixture of Latin and French, like the poem about Abelard by Hilary of Orléans. Heloise says the sweetness of their melodies kept her name on everyone's lips, and made women especially sigh with desire, because 'even the illiterate' could remember the tunes.[28]

Abelard makes the interesting comment about his love songs that 'a lot of them are still repeated and sung in many regions, particularly by those whom that manner of life amuses'.[29] In 'that manner of life' Abelard contrasts the irresponsible ways of the wandering minstrels or 'jongleurs' with the scholars at his lectures, who wanted him to return to the serious work of philosophy. Abelard's words also suggest that some of his songs entered the jongleur repertory, and in that case they could be concealed among the numerous anonymous pieces recorded in the *Carmina Burana*. Abelard was not the mysterious Archpoet, who sought his patrons in Germany, though the youthful Abelard shared with the Archpoet a bitter-sweet attitude to life, as well as great originality in versification. Abelard's secular image was so strong that he retained his reputation as a courtier and lady's man long after he had been castrated and become a monk. He was not the Archpoet, but he may have been the original lord of misrule, 'Bishop Golias', who gave his name to the 'Goliardic' poetry of the *Carmina Burana*.[30] (The argument is that St Bernard's comparison of Abelard with Goliath – *Golias* in Latin – was taken up by Abelard's student followers, who were proud to call themselves 'Gol-iardi' in honour of their persecuted master, as they were the 'Abel-iardi'.)

The only musical compositions of Abelard's surviving today are liturgical pieces, notably his hymn 'O Quanta Qualia' and his sequences or laments *(planctus)* on Old Testament themes.[31] His lost secular music, the melodies on the lips of the illiterate, were presumably as bold and original as his surviving liturgical pieces. Although his love songs for Heloise were composed in Paris for a primarily metropolitan French audience, they may have drawn on the vernacular styles and instruments of the land from which Abelard originated, where 'we sing in the plain Romance tongue'. As a musician and poet, he had the potential to be a *joculator*, in the sense of a professional 'jongleur', as well as using these talents for the amusement of himself and his friends. 'We know', Heloise teased him, 'that the other philosophers were not at all successful' at this.[32] This was not strictly accurate, as ancient Greek philosophers studied music. What Heloise meant was that Pythagoras and Plato had not used music 'as a game' or 'recreation', as Abelard did.[33] He adds in his 'history of calamities' that he had hoped to have 'jocund intercourse' with Heloise by sending her letters, as it was easier to say audacious things through messengers.[34]

After his castration, Abelard turned his back on his past and he condemned poets as a class, along with 'jesters and other singers of filth'.[35] This showed a proper monastic frame of mind, which was most eloquently championed by St Bernard in his book *On the Degrees of Humility and Pride*. The first three steps on the road to pride in St Bernard's analysis are: 'curiosity', 'light-heartedness' (*levitas animi*) and 'inappropriate mirth'. These lead to the fourth step, which is 'boasting'.[36] St Bernard wrote this in the 1120s, the very time when Abelard became a monk. Bernard could have learned all about Abelard's insubordinate ways from his bishop and patron, William of Champeaux, the master whom Abelard had ridiculed. Bernard describes the monk who suffers from 'light-heartedness' as having 'hilarity in his face and vanity in his gait; he is prone to joking and is always ready with a laugh'. Such a man cannot control his raucous 'guffaws' (*cachinnos*).[37] Years later, in his attack on Abelard at the council of Sens, Bernard warned against Abelard's jeering blasphemies: 'Listen to his guffaws!' (*Audite cachinnos*).[38]

In being reputed a scoffer, who 'turned everything into a joke and made his listeners distend themselves with guffawing', Abelard was like the first troubadour, William IX of Aquitaine.[39] The clergy had to be serious because they knew humanity was in serious difficulties and this was no laughing matter. 'Among lay people a joke is a joke', St Bernard wrote, 'whereas in the mouth of a priest it is blasphemy'; it is disgusting to be moved to guffaws, but even worse to make other people laugh.[40] Joy, in the way William IX and the troubadours understood it, was inimical to true religion. 'In great fear and peril', William IX had confronted his sadness through song and not by running to the priests. Abelard could join him in his lament: 'I have been joyful and lighthearted; but Our Lord does not wish this any more; now I can suffer the burden no longer, so close have I come to the end.'[41] Or, as Abelard himself wrote in his lament for Samson, the mutilated strongman of Israel: 'From jests to seriousness (*a jocis ad seria*) the long-excited mind is brought.'[42]

THE IMAGE OF THE KNIGHT

The serious business of the knight was fighting in his lord's wars and William IX's lament had probably been occasioned by his being wounded in battle. When Fulk of Deuil described women mourning for Abelard, their 'knight', that was likewise in the context of his having been wounded (by being castrated).[43] The word Fulk uses for 'knight' is *miles*, which in classical Latin had usually meant nothing more than a foot-soldier. By the 1130s, however, when Abelard was writing his 'history of calamities', the Roman foot-soldier was completing his long metamorphosis into the medieval knight. In military terms the chief difference between the Roman *miles* and the medieval one was that the knight was no longer one of the rank and file; he had grown in stature to become an officer, mounted on horseback. It is easier to describe than explain why the noble personage of the knight came to embody the ideals of western Christian society and of numerous individuals within it, male and female, from the eleventh century (or even earlier) until the sixteenth. Abelard already registers some of this idealism when he describes how his father: *militari cingulo insigniretur.*[44] One translator renders this: 'he girded on himself the soldier's belt'; another has 'he donned the uniform of a soldier'; and a third simply says 'he was a soldier'.[45]

All these translations give the wrong impression of what Abelard had in mind because they fail to distinguish between an ordinary soldier and a knight, who was an officer and a gentleman. The verb *insigniretur* cannot mean 'girded on himself' or 'donned', as it is in the passive. Literally it means 'insignia-ed'; in other words, Abelard is explaining that his father 'was distinguished by insignia'. The insignia in question was the 'military belt' (*militari cingulo*), meaning the knight's sword-belt.[46] The verb is passive because a knight did not confer this insignia on himself. Arms and armour were granted to young men by their seniors in ceremonial inaugurations, which went back centuries into the past, back indeed to the fall of the Roman Empire when the Germanic warriors had conquered the Romans. Among these warriors were the Franks, who gave their name to France.

The sword (and hence the sword-belt) was one of the insignia of knighthood because it epitomized power. 'Gird thy sword upon thy thigh, O thou most mighty', says the Psalmist.[47] Since at least the tenth century, swords had been ceremonially blessed in church as God's instruments against evildoers. In the *Song of Roland* (which is contemporary with Abelard in its present form) the dying Roland addresses his sword, Durendal, by name. He recalls how long the two of them have been together, ever since Charlemagne (who had received this special sword from an angel) girded it on him. With his beautiful Durendal, so fair and bright in the sun's rays, Roland claims to have conquered nearly all the lands of Europe (which he names one after another, as far as Scotland and Ireland).[48] It would shame France if Durendal fell into the hands of the pagans, and so Roland tries to break it. But the sword is too strong for him, both in its hammered steel and in its magic, as its hilt is stuffed with St Peter's tooth and other choice relics. The *Song of Roland* evoked the mythical past of the Frankish warriors and their present destiny as God's own knights of France. By saying his father was distinguished by the 'military belt', Abelard was therefore evoking a whole range of ideas about knighthood which were circulating at the time.

The way Abelard describes the insignia of the 'military belt' suggests his father had undergone some sort of knighting ceremony. What form this took, and when and where it happened, can only be conjectured. The Bayeux Tapestry shows Duke William of Normandy ceremonially conferring arms on Harold (the future king of England) on the battle-field, immediately after they had defeated the Bretons in 1064. Abelard's father could have been one of the Breton knights fighting the Normans on this occasion. He may have been knighted on a battlefield on a day more auspicious for the Bretons than this. Alternatively, arms may have been conferred upon him at the time of his coming of age, or of his marriage, either by the count of Poitou (who was also duke of Aqui-taine) or by the count of Nantes (who was also duke of Brittany). The county of Poitou is where Abelard's father probably came from and the county of Nantes is where he married into.

Abelard provides no details about his father's career as a knight, except that he ended it by becoming a monk. There are other instances of knights doing this. Entering a monastery on retirement made good sense in material terms, even if the monastery required a large payment or gift on entry, as the entrant was assured of nursing and support in old age. In spiritual terms the benefits might be even higher, as the ex-knight hoped to say enough prayers in his remaining years to make amends for the wrongdoing of his former life; if he got in early, he might even have time to pray for someone else as well. In this context of 'conversion to the monastic profession', Abelard gives the name of his father as 'Beren-gar', without clarifying whether this was his father's name in religion or his familial name.[49] In the charters of the Nantes region in the second half of the eleventh century, the only person named from Le Pallet is 'Daniel de Palatio', who appears in two documents.[50] In one, dating from c.1084, he witnesses a gift confirmed by Duke Alan of Brittany and his brother, Count Matthew of Nantes. Daniel's name precedes that of 'Geoffrey the Norman, Warin the Seneschal and the rest of the laymen from Nantes', as distinct from the 'Bretons' in the witness list. In the other document, dating from c.1096, a grant by Daniel is confirmed by Count Matthew of Nantes.

Both these documents suggest that Daniel was the lord of Le Pallet and a follower of the count of Nantes. He identified with Nantes and the border-lands south of the Loire, rather than with Celtic Brittany. Abelard's mother was presumably Daniel's daughter and heiress. She married Berengar, who was a Poitevin, perhaps shortly before the birth of Abelard in c.1079.[51] As the eldest son of Berengar and the grandson of Daniel, Abelard stood to inherit the lordship of Le Pallet in due course. He explains that this is what he had to give up when he chose to be a cleric: 'I made over to my brothers the pomp of military glory, along with the inheritance and privileges of my primogenitors'.[52] Abelard does not enlarge on what the legal and military 'privileges of my primogenitors' were, but they must have amounted to something. His mention of 'primogenitors' suggests that the family prop-erty at Le Pallet was conserved as a unit by restricting inheritance to the eldest son. Primogeniture was primarily in the interests of the greater lords, who wanted their knightly tenants to have sufficient property to maintain their superior status at their own expense.

Abelard probably had three younger brothers.[53] One of them, Dago-bert, encouraged Abelard to write *Dialectica*, reminding him that it was intended for the instruction of his nephews.[54] Dagobert may have been either a learned knight, or a cleric who made no secret of having a family. It may not only have been for learning's sake that Abelard's father had all his sons educated in 'letters'. Inheritance by primogeniture meant that families had to keep their options open in case the eldest son died childless.[55] A younger brother with male heirs of his own needed to be ready to step into his shoes, if the inheritance was to be kept in the family. Clerical marriage allowed for this. Because they were literate and therefore qualified as clerics, those of Abelard's brothers who were excluded from inheriting by primogeniture could acquire ecclesiastical benefices. Dagobert was perhaps such a cleric. Supposing he was the third son, he and his male heirs stood to inherit Le Pallet, if the second brother died childless and Abelard persisted with his clerical career.

Clerics taking over knightly inheritances in emergencies is one expla-nation for the phenomenon of literate knights, which twelfth-century commentators remark on.[56] If Dagobert had inherited Le Pallet, he would have been a knight who was so highly educated in the liberal arts that he could understand Abelard's *Dialectica*. Furthermore, his sons were destined for similar knowledge. A cleric could revert to a knightly status, provided he had remained in minor orders and not advanced too far up the clerical ladder. Opinions varied as to which step was irrevocable. This helps explain Abelard's conduct as the eldest son. He fell in love with the scholastic life and surrendered the birthright of his 'primogenitors' and yet he did not proceed to study divinity until twenty years later, when he went to Anselm of Laon in 1113. Significantly, this was immediately after he had gone home to Le Pallet to settle the business of his parents retiring into religious houses, at which point they had presumably surrendered their property to the next of Abelard's brothers in seniority. Abelard took a significant step up the clerical ladder when he was appointed master of the school of Notre-Dame in Paris in c.1114. In this capacity Heloise describes him as 'cleric and canon'.[57] At this stage Abelard still had the option of resigning. He only irrevocably became a cleric when he was castrated and entered the abbey of St Denis as a monk in c.1118.

Without more specific information, it is difficult to speculate about what sort of knight Abelard's father was. Whether rich or poor, he presumably conformed in some degree to the stereotype of the lordly man riding out to war. The Middle Ages idealized their knights and nineteenth-century romantics, Pre-Raphaelite painters as much as Tennysonian poets, compounded this. The image of the knight was decisively taking shape during Abelard's lifetime, when knights galloping on their chargers, with swords drawn and heraldic shields displayed, begin to make their appearance on their seals. Most appropriately William the Conqueror's is the earliest-known seal of this kind, and the Bayeux Tapestry is the first large-scale depiction of knights in battle.[58] Every image or description, whether medieval or modern, presents too idealistic a picture of the knight when compared with the realities of warfare. This is as it should be, as the purpose of the idealistic image was to counterbalance the reality of what knights did.

> You are 'the best of cut-throats': do not start;
> The phrase is Shakespeare's, and not misapplied:
> War's a brain-spattering, windpipe-slitting art.[59]

Byron's reminder to the duke of Wellington is as applicable to the combat of the Middle Ages as it is to fighting Napoleon. The man on horseback, the medieval knight, stood up in his stirrups above the foot-soldiers and did his 'brain-spattering' from this vantage point, until his horse was hit by an arrow and threw him, or he confronted an enemy knight ready to strike with a couched lance.[60]

ABELARD'S ATTITUDE TO WAR

Clerics were not meant to resort to arms, but this did not make them pacifists. On the contrary, they urged the knights on and justified their wars. When Roland kills dozens of pagans, Archbishop Turpin congratulates him on being a valorous knight (*chevaler* in Old French) and not a worthless monk who can only say prayers all day.[61] In the Bayeux Tapestry, Bishop Odo of Bayeux is depicted at the battle of Hastings performing much the same role as Archbishop Turpin in the *Song of Roland*. Holding a big stick, instead of a sword, Odo 'comforts the boys'.[62] This has a double meaning. Odo wields a stick in deference probably to the papal decree of 1046 prohibiting priests from bearing arms; a stick did not count as 'arms' because it did not necessarily draw blood. Odo's stick is also the symbol of the medieval schoolmaster, who has to beat Latin grammar into his boys. By this token, Odo 'comforts the boys' in the battle line by reminding them of the grammar of discipline. In this way, as in many others, the ideologies and practices of clerics and knights linked up.

Even closer to Abelard's time and place is Abbot Suger's account of the wars of his hero, Louis VI of France (1108–37). He describes, for example, Louis's knights in 1109 'piously cutting up the impious by mutilating their members (that is, blinding and castrating them) and most delightfully disembowelling the others'.[63] By the 'divine hand' (and therefore not really by the knights themselves) both the living and the dead were thrown out of the castle windows at La Roche Guyon on to the lancepoints below. The heart of the principal defender, 'swollen with deceit and iniquity', was paraded on a stake and the knights floated mutilated corpses down the Seine on hurdles as a warning to the king's enemies in Normandy. Suger's description of disembowelling being 'most delightful' or 'sweet' (*dulcissime*) may suggest that clerical supervisors of military operations, like himself, took more pleasure in their atrocities than the knights who did them. But his *dulcissime* is comparable also with the Easter poem by the troubadour knight, Bertran de Born (later in the twelfth century), extolling the delights of the spring, when the birds sing in the woodland and the killing season begins: 'I tell you there is no such pleasure in eating, or drinking, or sleeping, as when I hear riderless horses whinnying in the shade and cries of "Help! Help!".'[64]

In his best-known hymn, 'O Quanta Qualia', Abelard says:

Vera Jerusalem est illa civitas,
Cujus pax jugis est summa jocunditas.[65]

(The true Jerusalem is that city,
Whose surpassing peace is the highest joy.)

At first sight, this looks like a pacifist rejoinder to militaristic clerics, like Suger, and in particular to the crusaders' atrocities at the capture of Jerusalem in 1099, which occurred when Abelard was at the impressionable age of twenty. This interpretation is almost certainly mistaken, however. Abelard is evoking here the Augustinian commonplace that 'the true Jerusalem' is not an earthly city, but that heavenly city whose peace we shall experience in the next world. According to St Augustine's *City of God*, it is not possible for Christians to achieve peace on earth and it is presumptuous of governments to think they can do so; the Romans tried it and conspicuously failed. Life is bound to be a kind of 'hell on earth' (Augustine's description) because of Adam's fall and original sin; the only language fallen humanity understands is the force wielded by schoolmasters, soldiers and executioners.[66]

Abelard was influenced by St Augustine more than any other Father of the Church and it is in Augustine's spirit that he addresses the ethics of killing in *Sic et Non*. Under the heading 'That it is lawful to kill people, and not so', Abelard assembled seventeen quotations.[67] Eleven of these come from Augustine and all seventeen of them justify killing by soldiers or executioners because they are lawful officers of government. Likewise under the heading 'That it is not lawful for Christians to kill anyone for any cause, and the opposite', Abelard assembled six quotations, all from Augustine, and all saying in various ways that it *is* lawful for Christians to kill, where necessity makes war or punishment essential.[68] By not supplying any unequivocal quotations on the pacifist side, Abelard made a nonsense of his claim to marshal quotations for and against each of the propositions in his headings. But a number of the sections of *Sic et Non* are like this and Abelard was probably not being deliberately anti-pacifist. He and his researchers would have had difficulty finding uncompromisingly pacifist pronouncements in the writings of the Latin Church Fathers from which *Sic et Non* was compiled. The quotations in *Sic et Non* comprise work in progress; they were not intended to be Abelard's last word on the subject.

In the Christian tradition, particularly in its Roman shape after the conversion of the Emperor Constantine, the pacifist precepts in the Gospels (which are a tiny part of the Bible as a whole) were understood to justify the use of force by peacekeepers, both against individuals (in the form of punishments) and rival communities (in the form of war). Once the emperor was a Christian, the Gospel could no longer be associated with anarchism or a pacifist millennium. Perfectionist precepts were understood to apply to the next world only. St Augustine's view of a 'hell on earth' is vindicated by medieval archaeology. The massive stone castles and fortified towns and the iron strength of doors and windows, even in churches, show that strangers were not trusted. The true Jerusalem could be built on earth, if at all, only within a monastery. The peace of the cloister can still be experienced in the ruins of medieval monasteries across Europe (and in The Cloisters in New York). Modern visitors do not always realize, however, that this enclosed peace depended on the monastery's external defences and on the internal disposition of the monks themselves. The Rule of St Bene-dict did indeed offer peace to a select few in monasteries, but only through a lifetime of personal discipline reinforced by stone walls.

According to Abelard's account in his 'history of calamities', he brought peace and justice to none of the communities he joined. He had to leave school after school and monastery after monastery. Worst of all, he disrupted the peace of the cloister of Notre-Dame in Paris, the place he had most wanted to be, by pursuing a bloodfeud with his fellow canon, Fulbert, over which of them should possess Heloise. In this dispute Abelard says nothing about the Gospel's precepts of turning the other cheek or not judging others. In retaliation for his castration, two of the perpetrators were blinded as well as being castrated and (according to Fulk of Deuil) Abelard did not think that even this was sufficient.[69] He does not tell us whether the two survived being blinded, which was much more dangerous than being castrated, nor how they got a living afterwards, even though one of them had been his servant. Nor does Heloise, when she discusses the injustice of Abelard's castration, make any comment about the punishment of the perpetrators.[70] In short, according to his own account, Abelard showed neither compas-sion nor forgiveness. Fulk of Deuil reminded him that he was now a monk: 'it is no longer permissible for you to take revenge'.[71]

SCHOLASTIC WARFARE

Abelard's persistent belligerence is explicit in his description in his 'history of calamities' of his wars in the schools.[72] Scholastic life might involve all the stratagems and excitement of the knightly life without the bloodshed. The price of failure in these clerical battles could be severe when it took the form, as Abelard found out, of public humiliation – or worse – at heresy trials. In one episode he describes William of Cham-peaux as if he were a general, returning to Paris 'to deliver from my siege his knight, whom he had abandoned'.[73] As well as being master of the

schools when Abelard first came to Paris in *c*.1100, William of Champeaux was an archdeacon and a royal counsellor, who was 'almost the
first with the king'.[74] Abelard never achieved such eminence as this in
France, much as he may have wished it.

In order to compete with William, Abelard had to find a patron at
court and R. H. Bautier has plausibly argued that he soon attached
himself to Stephen de Garlande, who became royal chancellor in
1105.[75] For the rest of his life, Abelard was involved with Stephen and
hence with the intrigues of the French royal court. Abelard's career in
Paris waxed and waned with Stephen's fortunes. Stephen and his exten-
sive family (he was one of five brothers, all of them royal officers at one
time or another) aimed to dominate the king and place their nominees in
influential positions, both ecclesiastical and secular.[76] In 1120 Stephen
became the seneschal, which meant that he was the king's high steward
and commander of the royal army; he was reputed to be the most powerful man in France. Abelard acknowledged that Stephen was instrumental
in 1122 in settling his dispute with the abbey of St Denis and getting this
ratified by the king and council.[77] Where a more worldly-wise man than
Abelard would have benefited from Stephen's elevation to get himself
elevated likewise, at court or in the Church, Abelard found himself
having to use Stephen merely to get out of a tight hole.

The disadvantage of getting Stephen de Garlande's help was that it
compounded Abelard's reputation for being a warmonger, rather than a
peaceful monk. Stephen was an ecclesiastical pluralist, as well as being
the king's seneschal. 'I ask you', St Bernard demanded of Abbot Suger,
'what sort of monster is this?'[78] Bernard called Stephen a 'very bad
smell' and added that he would have made much more offensive
remarks, if Stephen were not reputed to be a friend of Suger's.[79] Bernard
claimed that it was scandalous for Stephen to wear armour one day and
ecclesiastical vestments the next, or to sound the battle trumpet one day
and holy words the next. To this, Abbot Suger and Stephen himself
would presumably have replied that the seneschal of France fought
only for righteousness in defence of Holy Church against the king's
enemies (just as Archbishop Turpin had fought for Charlemagne).
Holy war was the most venerable tradition of the French; that is why
Suger described it as 'most sweet'. Abelard, however, who had ambitions
to be a reformer himself, must have found Bernard's strictures harder to
rebut, as Stephen lived as a knight and a layman on the wealth that came
to him from his numerous ecclesiastical benefices. Corrupt clerics at the
court of the king of France, like Stephen, were associated with intimidation and fraud as well as bribery, whereas Abelard claimed to be a
scholar and an idealist who was above worldly intrigue.

Abelard's association with Stephen de Garlande may have been the origin of St Bernard's opinion that 'he has nothing of the monk about him except the name and the habit'.[80] By the time of Abelard's prosecution at the council of Sens in 1140, Bernard had magnified Abelard's reputation for belligerence to gigantic proportions: 'Goliath advances, mighty in bearing, girt all round in his fine accoutrements of war and preceded by his armour-bearer, Arnold of Brescia.'[81] Bernard admitted that all this had to be seen with the eye of faith, rather than in reality, as Abelard and Arnold dressed and lived like monks and cleverly concealed that they came from Satan. Bernard was able to convince the pope and many influential clergy that Abelard was vicious and that he had been 'a man of war from his youth' because there was some truth in this.[82] They would have recognized here a reference to Saul's warning to David that he was but a boy, whereas Goliath had been a warrior from his youth.[83] They would not have thought the scriptural parallel weakened the truth of Bernard's words, or that he was being presumptuous in comparing himself to David. On the contrary, history repeated itself and evil remained the same, whatever its modern guise. Abelard himself had used the David and Goliath parallel, when he claimed in *Theologia* to be 'poor little David' battling against 'the immense and swollen Goliath' of false dialectic.[84]

'When all have fled before him', St Bernard told the pope in 1140, Abelard (who is Goliath) 'calls me out, the least of all, to single combat.'[85] Similarly the biographer of St Goswin describes his challenge to Abelard in c.1112 as 'not much less than the battle between the saintly David and the spurious Philistine'.[86] The single combat of David and Goliath is often depicted in Romanesque art, most powerfully on a capital at Vézelay, a church which Bernard knew and which dates from his time.[87] Trial by battle was the customary way of resolving disputes among the knightly class and Bernard's acceptance of the call to single combat against Abelard may have appealed to chivalric values as much as Biblical precedent. Although Ivo of Chartres and other lawyers reiterated an earlier papal ruling that the precedent of David and Goliath did not sanction trial by combat, the use of the David and Goliath story by ecclesiastics as diverse as Abelard, St Bernard and St Goswin's biographer shows how attractive the idea still was.[88] It was as powerful an image for clerics as for knights because it showed an ill-equipped youth triumphing over an experienced warrior.

One of the themes of the chivalrous life, in both literature and historical fact, is the young man challenging a senior and forcing him to stand down. Sons confronted their fathers, demanding their inheritances, and young knights forcibly supplanted older ones. Abelard's military rhetoric in his 'history of calamities' concerns the same theme of a young man challenging his seniors: first William of Champeaux (on numerous occasions between 1100 and 1110) and then Anselm of Laon in 1113, whom Abelard disparages as 'this old man, who owed his reputation more to long use than intelligence'.[89] In 1117 Rupert of Deutz travelled from the Rhineland to engage William of Champeaux and Anselm of Laon in what he described as 'a most powerful battle of disputation'.[90] Like St Goswin, he saw himself as a 'youth' challenging a senior, although he was forty-two. According to Rupert's account, that 'Lucifer' Anselm dropped dead at his approach to Laon, and the 'High Priest' William of Champeaux 'with whom I had a sharp conflict' did not survive the year (William actually died in 1122).[91]

The clergy's delight in verbal fights and military rhetoric compensated for their lack of physical weapons. Just as knights routinely committed physical atrocities, clerics considered gross verbal abuse permissible – and indeed admirable – if it were done in the good cause of defending themselves or the Church. St Bernard was the greatest exponent of verbal abuse in Abelard's time, as well as being the author of the most eloquent meditations and sermons. He used his eloquence deliberately as a weapon, in response to what he saw as the deadly weapons being aimed at God's servants. When he accused the archdeacon of Paris of murder in 1133, Bernard described him as having 'teeth which are spears and arrows and a tongue which is a sharp sword'.[92] This murder concerned Abelard indirectly because the victim was the prior of St Victor (the school founded by William of Champeaux) and Stephen de Garlande was suspected of being implicated in it (the murder had been done close to his castle). At an unknown date around 1133, Abelard returned from the abbey of St Gildas in Brittany to his school at Mont Sainte Geneviève in Paris under the protection of its dean, Stephen de Garlande. Abelard was therefore associated with a suspected murderer of the head of a neighbouring school. It says much for his resilience that he could successfully return to teaching in Paris in the 1130s, despite having been a condemned heretic, a fugitive monk and a traitor to France (over the St Denis affair), as well as still being the dependant of Stephen de Garlande.

Despite his aggressive rhetoric, Abelard may have been disgusted by violence in reality. Certainly he admits to being alarmed by his monks at St Gildas who, he believed, had repeatedly intimidated him and tried to poison him.[93] The murder of the prior of St Victor must have been equally alarming, whoever was responsible for it, because it showed that the schoolmen had no protection beyond their own walls. In being associated with Stephen de Garlande in the Paris of the 1130s,

Abelard had moved from the rhetoric of violence dangerously close to its reality, but he probably had no choice in this as he needed a protector. He cannot have forgotten that it was within the precinct of Notre-Dame of Paris that he had been castrated and betrayed. He was writing his 'history of calamities' in transit, as it were, between the violence of St Gildas and the violence of Paris. Possibly the purpose of his 'history' was to win sympathy in Paris and to rebut any suggestion that he was a man of violence himself. One of its messages is that, although wrong and violence has repeatedly been done to Abelard, he remains Christ-like and long-suffering.

In this light, the military rhetoric at the beginning of the 'history' may not be all that it appears to be. Abelard concludes his account of his struggle with William of Champeaux with some lines of verse: 'To tell the outcome of this fight, I was not vanquished by that wight.'[94] This is a quotation from Ovid and, significantly, it does not say that Abelard won. In Ovid's text, as Abelard points out, these words are said by the Homeric hero, Ajax. Ovid recounts that Ajax was a braggart, who was driven mad and killed himself when he lost his contest with Ulysses. Abelard's text therefore tells those of his readers who knew classical mythology that he, like Ajax, was a desperate braggart. He only pretended to have won his contest with William of Champeaux, as William's reputation was unimpaired. The event which followed on Abelard's being 'not vanquished' by William was his withdrawal home to Brittany and, when he returned, it was not to Paris but to Laon and no longer as a master but as a student. Abelard implies that he voluntarily chose this humble role, but it is as likely that his failure to vanquish William of Champeaux made it impossible for him to return to Paris as a master in 1113.

COURTLINESS

The obverse of the violent braggart was the courtly knight, the love-object of ladies. Because of the fame of his love affair with Heloise, Abelard retained a reputation for courtliness throughout his life. Their love was still being widely sung about, he boasted, in the 1130s when he was an abbot and she an abbess.[95] He explains that he seduced her because 'I believed I could do it very easily, as I was then such a big name and so outstanding in grace of youth and form that I feared repulse from no woman whatsoever, whom I might dignify with my love'.[96] In the history of the ideal of the courtly lover, the key word here is 'grace'. Abelard was described by one contemporary, Hugh Métel, as having great 'elegance of manners', which led Helen Waddell to say he had 'the graces of a *grand seigneur*'.[97] This may not be too fanciful, as an anecdote by the preacher and master, Odo of Cheriton, recalled Abelard's fine clothes, fine horse and retinue of servants.[98] Odo was writing about a century later. Even if his testimony is unreliable, it is significant that it was Abelard's fine style which was remembered in oral tradition, rather than any clerical virtues. His 'grace' was likewise a characteristic to which Heloise alluded, when she reminded him that what had made him especially attractive to women was his singing.[99] Abelard's talents in music, combined with his origin in the west, made him comparable to Tristan, just as Heloise's compulsive and illicit love made her like Iseult. The romance of Tristan and Iseult was taking shape in the lifetimes of Abelard and Heloise and it is possible that their own tragic story contributed to its interest for twelfth-century audiences.[100]

The nickname of *Palatinus* may be associated with Abelard's image as a courtly lover and entertainer, as much as with the concept of the *palatinus* as a man of business at court. Walter Map (writing later in the twelfth century) combines both meanings in observing that when *palatini* finish their tiresome official business, they descend from the palace for recreation and pleasantries.[101] Abelard was good at pleasantries, as Otto of Freising observed.[102] Even at the end of Abelard's life, after his trial for heresy at Sens in 1140, he was still being seen as a courtly 'palatine'. An allegorical poem (perhaps composed in 1141) imagines the learned lass, Lady Philology, searching in vain in the court of heaven for her 'palatine', 'whose spirit showed itself totally divine'.[103] As Heloise was famed for her learning and Abelard was called *Palatinus*, Lady Philology very plausibly doubles up as Heloise in this context. The Lady 'asks why he has crept away, like an exile, he whom she had cherished at her breasts and bosom?'

Lady Philology receives the answer that the *Cucullatus populi Primas cucullati* has silenced the great seer. The Latin *cucullatus*, literally meaning 'cowled', was a colloquial word for a monk. Possibly it had a comic or sexual implication because of the prefix *cucu-*; Fulk of Deuil had addressed Abelard as *cucullato* after his castration.[104] The 'cowled Primate' of the 'cowled people' can only be St Bernard who, at the request of other monks like William of St Thierry, had headed the prosecution of Abelard at Sens. By 1140 Abelard had himself been a monk for more than twenty years and yet he is presented in this poem as the courtly *Palatinus* and not as a *cucullatus*. He and Heloise were therefore persistently remembered in their romantic guises: he as the divinely talented courtier and seer, and she as the epitome of learning and sensuality. Such extravagant praise and emotion was a rhetorical reaction to the equally extravagant vilification to which Abelard had been subjected by St Bernard. Another defender of Abelard, his young student, Berengar, wrote with similar extravagant passion, when he compared Abelard's trial with that of Christ and St Bernard with the high priest, Caiaphas.[105]

The use of *palatinus* to mean 'courtier' was an innovation of twelfth-century Latin. Abelard was at the height of fashion in this as in so much else. Palaces were growing more complex as centres of administration and more impressive as centres of culture. The palace became the focus of life and ceremonial for the ambitious knight, much as the cathedral was for the cleric. 'What king, what court, what palace?', Abelard's hymn 'O Quanta Qualia' asks, can express the joy of the kingdom of heaven?[106] Even where parts of Romanesque palaces survive, as in the Tower of London, scarcely anything remains of the interior decoration. The great exception to this is Roger II of Sicily's palace at Palermo with its superb mosaics. One very full description does exist of the interior of a palatial room in France in the 1100s, but it is difficult to know how factual it is. This is Baudri of Bourgueil's account, in over 1000 lines of Latin verse, of the fixtures and fittings in the bedchamber of Adela, countess of Blois, a daughter of William the Conqueror.[107] Her room was hung with tapestries, which had been specially made for her, showing stories from the Old Testament and classical mythology, and above her bed was a scene of the battle of Hastings (to emphasize that miraculous victories were not just a thing of the past). On the ceiling was a planetarium, painted in silver and gold, and the floor matched this with a map in mosaic of the earth and the seas. There was much more besides.

The biographer of St Goswin calls Abelard *rhinoceros indomitus* and this description sums up his knightly qualities. The reference is to Pope Gregory the Great's commentary on the Book of Job, where he describes the rhinoceros as being 'altogether indomitable in its nature'.[108] Abelard himself quoted this passage in a sermon.[109] The rhinoceros is an allegory of pride: since the earliest days of the Church, it has flirted with heresy and rampaged over the field of voluptuousness. It was too proud to stand with the ox and the ass at the Christmas crib. But, Pope Gregory continues (as does Abelard in his sermon), a rhinoceros can be tamed miraculously: not by military force, but by the lure of a virgin. When she shows her breast, the rhinoceros loses all his belligerence and nuzzles up to her.[110] To twelfth-century readers this *rhinoceros* was familiar in the shape of the unicorn in the Bestiary, the popular handbook of zoology and folklore. The unicorn is distinguished by its grace and agility from the real African rhinoceros, which no one in northern Europe had seen or would have thought more or less mythical than the unicorn. The Bestiary says the unicorn is so sharp that none of the ranks of angels can understand him and the cleverest devil cannot find him out.[111]

In being dangerous, graceful and very clever, the unicorn's reputation was like Abelard's and he, like the unicorn, had been lured by a virgin. There is also a parallel here with the *palatinus*, as the Bestiary describes how the unicorn springs up into the virgin's bosom 'and she warms the animal and nourishes him and takes him up into the palace of kings'.[112] This is close to the description of Lady Philology, after Abelard's trial at Sens, searching for her 'palatine', whom she had cherished at her breast. The image of Abelard as a courtly knight, loved eternally by his lady, was as idealized and removed from real life as the myth of the unicorn. In the eyes of many he was a eunuch and a heretic. His trial at Sens in 1140 had not made him into a 'palatine', but an outcast; he was not a noble knight, but a monk on the run. Nevertheless, Abelard's partisans persisted in seeing him as courtly and glamorous because, in their opinion, he had never been honourably defeated at Sens. He lived on in the minds of his partisans as a courtly fighter. For Berengar or for John of Salisbury, their memory of their master was larger than life. The most extravagant praise of all came from the most powerful of Abelard's supporters, Peter the Venerable, abbot of Cluny. His epitaph recalls Abelard's fame as a fighter on the battlefield of learning.[113] Peter promotes Abelard in rank from 'palatine' to world-famous 'prince'. Whereas Abelard had used the ambiguous words of Ajax to describe how he had not been vanquished, Peter's epitaph is unequivocal in having him 'vanquish everything by force of reason'.

Knighthood was so creative an ideal because it attracted opposites: courtliness and violence, humility and pride, peace and war. The literature of knighthood, particularly in the Arthurian romances which were beginning to take shape in Abelard's last years, shows individuals confronting the profoundest dilemmas of free will and sexual passion. The divisions which medieval society imposed between cleric and lay, celibate and married, monks and knights, could not be hermetically sealed. Abelard, and probably many other people in his time, cut across these divisions in a variety of ways. He was indeed a monk and a 'cleric and canon'; but it also made sense to call him 'knight' and 'palatine' or even *rhinoceros indomitus*.

8

Lover

According to his 'history of calamities' Abelard had two great loves in his life and he aspired to a third. In his youth he had been 'seduced by so great a love' of letters that he gave up his birthright as a knight 'to be educated in the bosom of Minerva', goddess of learning.[1] Then, in his late thirties, he was 'totally enflamed with love for this adolescent girl', Heloise.[2] Finally, after his castration and conversion to monasticism, he aspired to a broader and supposedly higher Christian love. In this spirit he addressed the unknown recipient of his 'history of calamities' as 'dearly beloved brother in Christ and closest companion of our religious conversion'.[3] He tried addressing Heloise too as 'his dearly beloved sister in Christ', now that she was a nun, but she responded with: 'To her only one after Christ from his only one in Christ'.[4] When Abelard persisted in lecturing her on loving Christ instead of him, she responded the second time with uncompromising clarity and economy of words: 'To him especially from her alone.'[5] In effect, she was saying to Abelard: 'Leave Christ out of our love.'

HELOISE'S ONLY LOVE

This verbal sparring brings out the profoundest differences between Abelard and Heloise. When he had first met her as a student in Paris, he had looked forward to 'jocund intercourse' with her as a penfriend.[6] In their subsequent correspondence (some fifteen years later) he got more than he bargained for, both in keeping up with her dazzling wit and in answering the disconcerting questions which she raised. Whereas he was endeavouring to be a good monk and to climb the ladder of spiritual perfection, she remained at the bottom, fixated on the memory of him as he used to be when he was her lover. Although this had been fifteen years ago, it was as fresh as yesterday to her because her emotional life had come to an abrupt end on the day she became a nun on Abelard's orders. In spirit Abelard killed Heloise, as Sir Richard Southern has pointed out.[7] Her years of dutiful life as a nun counted for nothing because Abelard remained her 'only one' (*unicus*), as she kept reminding him.[8] In classical Latin *unicus* meant 'unique individual', which was certainly how Heloise regarded Abelard, and it had two additional meanings in medieval Latin which she may have been aware of: it meant 'entire' and also 'unmarried' or unlinked to anyone else. In repeatedly calling Abelard *unicus*, Heloise was insisting that not only was he absolutely special, he was also – to her – still the complete and free person he had been before their disastrous marriage, which she had done her best to prevent.

By addressing him 'especially' (*specialiter*) in her next letter, Heloise was again stressing his uniqueness and also making a philosophical allusion for his benefit as a specialist in the Categories of Aristotle: he was the *species* or the whole category, of which she was no more than a constituent unit.[9] It was because she was part of Abelard's very being, literally 'his singularly' (*sua singulariter*), that her mind remained fixated on him. She would readily have gone to Hell with him, for 'my mind was not with me but with you'.[10] Her state of mind, her passionate feelings, were beyond her control. She could not change them overnight, even at his behest. Here there was an understandable contradiction: she was ready to obey every command of Abelard's except his command to terminate their love. She had already destroyed herself, she would not destroy him – or even her ideal of him. She would not see her prince turn into a frog. This fairy-tale allusion is not made by Heloise and yet it is appropriate, as the psychological state she describes is like that of being bewitched.

In pointed contrast to Heloise, Abelard always claimed to be in control of his destiny and to act deliberately, even when he acted wrongly or imprudently. As a male and Heloise's senior, as well as being her appointed teacher, he saw himself as her master in every sense. He must therefore be the initiator of their love and the director of its course. As he describes it in his 'history of calamities', his love story had begun not with Heloise but with his own seduction as a youth by Minerva. In medieval literature she is portrayed as a severe mistress, similar to the allegorical personifications of learning, Lady Grammar and Lady Philology, and identified too with Pallas Athene who had sprung fully armed from the head of Zeus without sexual intercourse. Fortified with these intellectual arms, Abelard says, he had sprung into action, as if he too were a classical Athenian, and so he had made himself the 'emulator of the Peripatetics'.[11] When he first met Heloise,

twenty or so years into the career that made him famous as the 'emulator' of Socrates and Aristotle, Abelard recollected her as 'not ugly in
the face' but 'supreme in abundance of letters'.[12] Her initial attraction
for him may therefore have been as a personification of the goddess of
learning, with whom he had already long been in love.

Abelard's negative description of Heloise as 'not ugly' (literally 'not
the lowest' – *non infima*) suggests that he had not been strongly
attracted to her physically. Fulbert, her uncle, would never have allowed
Abelard anywhere near her, if he had given the least indication of being
physically attracted. Fulbert and the other canons of Notre-Dame presumably thought that this newly appointed member of their community,
Master Abelard, was a cold fish, who was in love with the ancient
Greeks and with his own success. Abelard's story is that, although he
had no sexual experience, he set out to seduce Heloise and to deceive
Fulbert and his friends from the start. This is possible, as Abelard did
have a fatal tendency to act against his own best interests. More probably, perhaps, and this is no more than a conjecture, Abelard may
initially have agreed to live in Fulbert's house and teach Heloise as a
way of ingratiating himself with Fulbert and his fellow canons of Notre-
Dame, who were now his colleagues in Paris. As the most recent arrival
in the precinct, Abelard had not yet been allocated a house of his own
and Fulbert's was 'right next to my school'.[13] This convenient and
mutually advantageous arrangement went disastrously wrong, however,
as Abelard's plans so often did, because he had not allowed for his own
feelings and he took no account of other people's. St Bernard later jibed:
'there is nothing he does not know about in heaven or earth, except his
own self'.[14]

When challenged by Heloise to say whether he had ever really loved
her or cared about her, Abelard had no hesitation in answering: 'I
gratified in you my wretched desires and this was all that I loved.'[15] In
assessing these devastating words it is essential to remember that they,
like everything else he says about Heloise, were written fifteen years or
so after the event. The trauma of castration may have disgusted him
with sexuality and distorted his memories. What he had thought about
their love when he had first touched Heloise, or when she had first
touched him, is not on record, though it was once, as she says that he
had inundated her with letters 'when long ago you used to seek me out
for shameful pleasures'.[16] She does not say anything further about these
earlier letters of his and she may not have kept them. For us today they
must – frustratingly – remain a closed book, despite various letters
between girls and their masters being attributed to Heloise and
Abelard.[17]

THE LOVE OF MONK AND NUN

Abelard also had a particular purpose in telling Heloise that his love had only been lust, as he was now a monk and she a nun. They must both love God and not each other. This was the only way Abelard could respond to her insistence that she was still his 'only one' and that God was cruel and unjust to have allowed him to be castrated.[18] Not only was it embarrassing for Abelard as abbot of St Gildas to have a nun swearing undying love to him and complaining about God, it was also unrealistic of Heloise to persist with this line, as she too was an abbess. His castration was an irreversible fact and so were the monastic vows which they had both taken. Neither ecclesiastical law nor the opinion of lay society would allow either of them to renege on these undertakings. Even if Heloise's fate was widely felt to be ill-deserved, it would be even harder for her than for Abelard to abandon monasticism because her chastity continued to require physical protection, whereas his was already assured.

It was also a fact that in 1129, ten or more years after entering the convent of Argenteuil and when she was its prioress, Heloise and some other nuns had been expelled for notorious immorality.[19] Whatever the truth of this was, this expulsion had been authorized by the papal legate, the bishops of the region and the king of France himself. Abelard had rescued her by setting her up as abbess of his own monastery of the Paraclete. Neither of them could afford to incur further scandal and ecclesiastical odium. The convent of the Paraclete was dangerously close to St Bernard's abbey of Clairvaux and miles away from Abelard at St Gildas. St Bernard did indeed come and nose round the Paraclete, but Heloise succeeded in flattering him (she told him he was like an angel) and she warned Abelard that he was asking awkward questions.[20]

As well as needing to stop up Heloise's flow of emotions and recriminations, Abelard retained enough affection for her to want to convince her that her life in the convent need not be one of negative and hopeless suffering on his behalf; it could and should consist of positive joy in their new-found love for Christ. Christ the Redeemer merited her sympathy, Abelard did not. Long ago she had fallen in love with a fallible human being; surely now she could fall in love with Christ, Who really was divine and Whose bride she had become when she took her vows as a nun. To convince her of this, Abelard composed a prayer for them both, which is as dazzling a piece of Latin rhetoric as anything Heloise achieved. It was framed to make her accept that what had happened to them was just and providential. If she could accept this now, they would both have their reward hereafter. If she refused, she would exclude Abelard, whom she claimed to love beyond measure, as well as herself. 'Thou hast joined us and Thou hast parted us, O Lord, when and in what manner it pleased Thee,' Abelard's prayer concludes. 'Now, O Lord, what thou hast mercifully begun, most mercifully fulfil, and those whom Thou hast parted from each other for a time on earth unite entirely to Thyself in Heaven.'[21] With this pious hope, Abelard bid farewell to Heloise, reminding her once more that she was the bride of Christ and that she must live as such.[22]

Abelard's pious farewell succeeded in silencing Heloise to the extent that she recorded nothing more about her love for him. She maintained contact at a formal level by allowing him to act in some respects as her religious superior, and he demonstrated his continuing concern for her by providing her and her sisters of the Paraclete with numerous texts.[23] Abelard was the greatest provider of devotional literature for nuns in the twelfth century. Considering all the work which he had put into his own monastic development, as well as the 70,000 words he wrote for Heloise as a nun, it was ungenerous and mischievous of St Bernard at the time of Abelard's prosecution for heresy in 1140 to say that there was nothing of the monk about him except the name and the habit.[24] Nevertheless, St Bernard probably knew that this characterization would strike a chord with his audience, as not even many of Abelard's friends thought of him as a monk. The Latin poem *Metamorphosis Goliae*, which reacted to Abelard's prosecution, cast him in the role of an adversary of the monks. It imagined him in the company of the great authors of ancient Rome: Ovid, Propertius, Tibullus, Cicero, Catullus, Pliny and Apuleius, each of whom has brought his lady to a heavenly feast of learning. However, the bride of Abelard cannot find her 'palatine' in this company because 'the cowled primate of the cowled people' has silenced him.[25] In other words, Abelard's controversy with St Bernard was interpreted by this poet as a struggle between classical humanists led by their courtly 'palatine' and obscurantist monks headed by their self-appointed 'primate'.

The most significant part of *Metamorphosis Goliae* is the emphasis the poet puts on Abelard's bride. After twenty years or more of being a nun, Heloise is still pictured searching for her lover, whom she envisages in his secular guise as a 'palatine'. Nor does *Metamorphosis Goliae* cast her in the role of silence and submission which Abelard was demanding of her as a nun. She does not 'learn in silence with all subjection', as St Paul said every Christian woman must.[26] On the contrary, Abelard's bride is still the Heloise he first met in Paris, that famous lady of pagan learning, who had the knowledge to speak face to face with the authors of ancient Rome. To his bride, Abelard remains 'totally divine' and she recalls the old days when she had 'cherished him at her breasts and bosom'.[27] This description of the bride suggests that the poet of *Metamorphosis Goliae* was familiar with Heloise's insistence in her letters to Abelard that he was her 'only one' and that she was still physically in love with him. 'The lovers' pleasures which we explored together', she wrote to him, 'have been so sweet to me that they cannot displease me and scarcely have they faded from my memory. Wherever I turn they are always before my eyes, bringing with them desires and imaginings which will not even let me sleep.'[28] Even if God has 'cured' Abelard by his providential castration, she remains unchanged. Indeed her 'experiences of the most joyful of pleasures are even more inflamed'.[29]

In telling Abelard how much she enjoyed sexual intercourse, Heloise was not refusing to be ashamed of what he and the Church called 'lust'. She was saying only that she could not feel ashamed yet, since God had not 'cured' her in the way He had cauterized Abelard. But Heloise had presumably foreseen that Abelard would be incapable of responding to these admissions, as he could not renew physical intercourse with her and neither could he change her mind. Ungenerously perhaps, she used his castration as a way of humiliating him and she remained dominant in their relationship henceforward. Unless and until Heloise experienced her own mental castration – and there is no record that she ever did so – she would continue to have sexual fantasies and accuse God of being unjust and cruel. Whether her failure to record her repentance from 'lust' makes Heloise a better or a worse person can only be a matter of opinion. The Catholic priest J. T. Muckle, who edited her letters in 1953, was shocked that Abelard failed to remonstrate with her about 'such impassioned and sinful protestations of love'.[30] Muckle brought Heloise into line with conventional orthodoxy on the conduct of nuns by arguing, on the flimsiest of evidence, that the 'extravagant and sinful' parts of her letters were forgeries.

Knowledge of Abelard and Heloise at the Time

In response to these and other allegations of forgery, various scholars in the 1970s and 1980s have shown how the letters' contents accord with other writings of the time. Helen Laurie has argued that Chrétien de Troyes, the originator of French romantic writing, possessed a copy of the letters, which he might have obtained in the Troyes region where the convent of the Paraclete is situated.[31] Christopher Brooke has suggested that ladies mixed freely with the highly educated clerics in cathedral closes and this is the environment which produced Heloise.[32] Most importantly, Peter Dronke has described the context of medieval women's writing and he has edited difficult and fragmentary Latin texts concerning Abelard and Heloise.[33] One poem about Abelard's castration is aware of the argument in Heloise's letters that she bears no guilt for what happened because she gave no consent. Another poem associates Abelard's seduction of Heloise with his mother becoming a nun, which is correct chronologically and may also be correct psychologically. In this poet's opinion, Abelard did not deserve to be called a lover, as he was cruel to Heloise, whereas she did for him 'whatever love can fulfil' and obeyed him even to the point of taking the veil on his orders and thus accepting his desertion. The existence of these two poems suggests that the affair of Abelard and Heloise was discussed in clerical circles and that it continued to be discussed even after her entry into the convent.

There is no proof that the letters of Abelard and Heloise were published before Jean de Meun issued them in French in the 1270s.[34] How, then, did these earlier authors know how Heloise felt? They need not have known about the letters of Abelard and Heloise in the form in which we have them today. The knowledge of contemporaries about Abelard and Heloise did not need to come exclusively from complete texts but from hearsay of various sorts, including vernacular French gossip and fragmentary Latin poems like those edited by Dronke. In literary circles Heloise was the most famous woman in France, as a number of sources attest, and Abelard was the most famous – or notorious – master in Christendom. Everybody knew what they had done, Roscelin said, 'from Dan even to Beersheba'.[35] Their doings, separately and together, continued to be of interest for the rest of their lives. Heloise said there was nothing personal or private about the poor opinion which 'everybody' had of Abelard's neglect of her since she had become a nun. This was not merely a conjecture of hers, it was common knowledge. 'I only wish it were' just my opinion, she told Abelard.[36] By 'everybody', of course, Roscelin and Heloise meant the chattering classes in France and not every peasant in Christendom. Even so, this suggests that her continuing expectations from Abelard were 'common' knowledge, as she says.

Heloise's interest in what 'everybody' was saying also suggests that she participated in this gossip. Although Abelard was cut off from the mainstream of communication when he withdrew from metropolitan France to St Gildas in c.1125, Heloise was never geographically or socially isolated, either as prioress of Argenteuil or as abbess of the

Paraclete. Argenteuil was only half a day's journey from the centre of Paris. Although the foundation site of the Paraclete was described as a wilderness by both Abelard and Heloise, this was only meant figuratively, as it was less than five miles from Nogent-sur-Seine, which was on the main road and water route from Troyes to Paris and convenient for the fairs of Champagne, the biggest market in France.[37] In being near a main road the convent of the Paraclete was typical of medieval hermitages and holy places, which depended on having numerous visitors for funds and psychological support. Monasteries were centres of communication and monks were the principal purveyors of news. St Bernard's system of messengers and letter writers at Clairvaux was matched by Peter the Venerable at Cluny. As a female, Heloise was expected to be more modest in her pronouncements, and nuns did not have the network of resources of the Cistercian and Cluniac orders. Even so, she was not sworn to silence and once she became a prioress and then an abbess, she could go where she liked and speak to whom she chose. Heads of religious houses lived apart from the inmates and they had no superiors.

As prioress of Argenteuil, an ancient and royal convent, and then as abbess of the successful new foundation of the Paraclete, Heloise had reached the pinnacle of independence for a woman. Some of the talk about her continuing love for Abelard may have emanated from Heloise herself, either from things she said or from the controversy surrounding her. She came to the Paraclete with a bad reputation, however ill deserved, as she had been expelled from Argenteuil. Her regime as prioress of Argenteuil had possibly been lax, as the convent was familiar to her from childhood and she was inexperienced. When she pleaded her innocence, Abelard reminded her that he had once made love to her in the refectory at Argenteuil. He was ashamed of this, particularly because the place was dedicated to the Virgin Mary, whereas she told him that 'not only what we did, but the times and places where we did it are so fixed in my mind that I act everything out there with you again'.[38]

Abelard describes in his 'history of calamities' how people gossiped about his setting up Heloise as abbess of the Paraclete, whatever he or she did. At first he ignored her and the locals said he was mean. But when he started visiting her, they said that he was still the slave of sexuality and he could not bear to be without his beloved.[39] Even after he had gone away and Heloise had assured him that she would write nothing more to him about her passion, he could not be sure that she was going to take being a nun seriously. She could tease him just as well by writing to him as her religious director as her lover. She asked him to advise her on how an abbess should behave. Should she fraternize with guests? Should men sit at her table as well as women? What if they got drunk or – worse – lecherous? This reminded her of some lines of Ovid, 'the teacher of lust and wickedness' she told Abelard (as if he did not know), in his *Art of Love*. She quoted six lines; either she knew them off by heart or she had a copy of the *Art of Love* in the convent. The *Art of Love* was one of the classical texts used in schools to teach Latin and so there may have been a copy in the convent, as Abelard wanted the nuns' Latin improved. Thoughts of lecherous men in the convent lead Heloise on to the wiles of women. It might be worse to have only women at the abbess's table, she surmises, as a woman most readily passes on 'the foulness of a corrupted mind' to another woman.[40]

At this statement Abelard had reason to be a bit alarmed. She had repeatedly told him how 'foul and corrupted' her mind was; she thought of sexual intercourse even during Mass – and she was not ashamed or sorry about it.[41] She had also spelt out to him that although she would not *write* anything more to him about her passion, it was 'not so much difficult as impossible' to temper her speech. 'I cannot hold my tongue,' she confessed.[42] Heloise and the other 'foul-minded' women at the abbess's table may have exchanged sexual confidences. This is not to suggest that she retailed scandal about Abelard or anybody else. But she may have been over-ready to talk about her own sexual feelings and to discuss unchaste classical literature like the *Art of Love*. This would not have disconcerted prelates with a traditional classical education as advanced as hers, like Baudri of Bourgueil, Hildebert of Lavardin or Marbod of Rennes.[43] Neither would it have alarmed advanced church-men like St Bernard and William of St Thierry, who devoted thousands of words to preaching and writing about love and sexuality. But Heloise may have scandalized local clergy, and even more local lay people, who were not used to theorizing about sex in public with Cistercian abbots or bishops famed for their Ovidian verses.

Above all, Heloise may have scandalized Abelard himself, as he was now perhaps disgusted by sexuality. His reaction to the letter in which she quoted the *Art of Love* was to tell her to keep quiet. He had an opportunity to do this, as she had asked him to give her a rule for her nuns; so he could riposte that the main rule was silence.[44] In Abelard's scheme 'silence' replaces 'obedience' as one of the three monastic virtues. Nuns who were silent would automatically be obedient, as they could not answer back. Silence, he added, had to be studied; we have to want and intend to be silent.[45] In response to Heloise not being able to hold her tongue, he cited the Epistle of St James: the tongue is so powerful that it can cause a forest fire and so venomous that it can kill.[46] Women's tongues were even worse than men's, and this gave

Abelard an opportunity to add the testimony of St Paul's Epistle to Timothy on how women have to learn from men in dutiful silence.[47]

This patriarchal stance may either have amused Heloise or infuriated her, coming as it did from the man who had learned so much from her. (No further writings of Heloise survive, so her reactions can only be guessed at.) Abelard summed up his rule for her nuns by telling her: 'We must tame the tongue by continual silence and most especially in these times and places: in the oratory, the cloister, the dormitory, the refectory, in all food preparation and in the kitchen; above all, silence should be observed by everybody from the time of Compline [in the evening] onwards.'[48] Heloise does not seem to have paid much attention to this, as the statutes of the Paraclete enjoin silence only when books are being read in the refectory and after Compline.[49] Furthermore, where Abelard had substituted 'silence' for 'obedience', the statutes restored the three traditional monastic virtues of poverty, chastity and obedience without mentioning silence.

PETER THE VENERABLE'S VISION OF LOVE

As Heloise could not − or would not − hold her tongue, she may have gone on talking about her passionate feelings for Abelard for years after their exchange of letters. Her persistence may have been known, and respected even, in elite clerical circles. This would explain the remarkable way in which Peter the Venerable reported Abelard's death to her. As abbot of Cluny, he had a duty to inform her, and he admits that he had been tardy in getting round to it, that her former husband and religious benefactor had died in a Cluniac house, fortified by the rites of Holy Church. A letter of condolence from abbot to abbess was all that was required. Instead, Peter wrote Heloise a long and personal letter, 'consciously and daringly' (in Dronke's judgement) describing her relationship with Abelard in erotic and sexual terms.[50] It was becoming common for high-thinking clerics to use strong terms of endearment when writing to each other, not least to compensate for the physical and emotional distance that separated them in reality. But Peter seems to have gone further than this. He told Heloise that the Lord God was now 'cherishing' Abelard 'in His bosom in your place as another you'.[51] In case she might jump to the conclusion that this meant that God had taken Abelard away from her, Peter further assured her that 'He is reserving him for you': at the Last Trumpet and the bodily Resurrection 'he will be restored to you by His grace'.

As a nun, Heloise had become a bride of Christ and this is how Abelard had described her, however reluctant she may have been to acknowledge it. Peter the Venerable seems aware of her reluctance and so he suggests that at the bodily Resurrection, Christ will restore Abelard to her. The theology of this is 'baffling indeed', to use Gilson's words, and yet (he argues) it is appropriate in the circumstances.[52] Peter presented Heloise with a vision of God which she could hardly reject, however despairing and rebellious she may have felt, particularly at the news that Abelard was dead. After his castration he had repeatedly made the mistake of telling her to accept God's love instead of his. With greater understanding and subtlety, Peter promised that loving God would most surely lead her back to Abelard. She had told Abelard that she would have followed him to Hell, indeed she would have gone in front.[53] Your Abelard is now in Heaven, Peter assures her, so you should prepare to follow him there and then the two of you will live happily ever after. Although Heloise had told Abelard that she did not seek a crown of victory and that she would be satisfied with whatever corner of Heaven God allocated to her, Peter realized that she would not want to go to Heaven at all unless Abelard was to be there giving all his attention to her.[54] Defiantly she claimed no crown for herself, but she would certainly insist that Abelard should have one and that she should share it as his long-suffering lover and wife. Peter understood that he was dealing with a prima donna.

Peter did not meet Heloise until after Abelard's death and neither had he corresponded with her previously. But he told her that he had been following her career ever since he was young, when he had heard about her extraordinary dedication to classical literature and philosophy.[55] (This was when she was still 'in the world', before she had met Abelard and before Peter was abbot of Cluny; he was prior of Vézelay from 1115 or 1116 and this may be the period he refers to.) Peter's interest in Abelard, on the other hand, may have been much more recent. Peter had been a monk since boyhood in his native Burgundy and there is no evidence that he attended the schools of Paris as a young man, when he might have got to know Abelard. Possibly Peter had never met Abelard until he gave him asylum at Cluny after the council of Sens in 1140. Then Peter was completely won over by him, as he makes clear in his letter to Heloise. He had an additional reason for defending Abelard, which was that Peter, like Abelard himself, had been slandered by St Bernard, not only across France but at the papal curia in Rome. This had been in 1139, only a year before Abelard's condemnation, when St Bernard had succeeded in getting Peter's Cluniac candidate removed from the bishopric of Langres.[56]

Peter's vision of Abelard and Heloise embracing in Heaven has affinities with the defence of Abelard in the allegorical poem *Metamorphosis Goliae*, even though it evokes pagan mythology. As already discussed, this poem contrasts Abelard, the courtly 'palatine', with the monks and their 'cowled primate', St Bernard.[57] The palatine's bride vainly searches in the palace of the gods for her beloved and she is told that her 'wanderer' has been silenced by the cowled primate.[58] Peter may have been aware of this poem when he wrote to Heloise, as it concerns what happened to Abelard after the council of Sens and it celebrates Heloise's undying love for him. If Peter did know of the poem, one of his intentions would have been to assure Heloise that she and Abelard had friends among the 'cowled people' and that he, Peter abbot of Cluny, was the true primate of the monks and not St Bernard. Most importantly, Peter assured Heloise that she need search for her beloved 'wanderer' no longer, as he had found a secure haven, first at Cluny and then in the true Heaven, which is better than the imagined palace of the ancient gods.

Why Peter went so far to placate Heloise nevertheless remains something of a mystery. He compared her with the Amazons and the heroic ladies of the Old Testament, and he told her he had loved her for a long time.[59] Furthermore, he came in person to the convent of the Paraclete to deliver Abelard's body to her for burial. His extravagant praise of her may have originated in his concern to carry out Abelard's last wishes to the full, even if belatedly. Now that Abelard was dead, Peter took his place as her spiritual father. He wrote as if he were in love with her himself: 'I have saved a place especially for you in the innermost recesses of my heart', he told her.[60] But monks tended to say things like that. It was all part of the rhetoric of spiritual friendship. St Bernard was the greatest practitioner of this sort of writing. To the Countess Ermengard, who was an aristocratic nun like Heloise, he began: 'I wish I could find words to express what I feel towards you.... Search your heart and you will find mine there too.'[61] He cannot have known the countess well, though he had consecrated her as a nun.

Sophisticated abbots like St Bernard and Peter the Venerable wrote intimately to women they did not know well because monks were literary exponents of love as much as the troubadours. Loving God and living with Him in daily intimacy was not a matter of having a warm feeling of well-being in choir on some enchanted evening, but of maintaining a real and sustained relationship with a being Who could not be seen or experienced in the ordinary way. Love therefore needed analysis and St Bernard provided a brilliant exposition of it in his eighty-six sermons on the Song of Songs. In learning how to love God, monks had to begin with their own feelings and the sexuality of their bodies. The Song of Songs was such an important text because it provided them with a sexual vocabulary sanctioned by Scripture. Citing its opening line and identifying Christ with the Bridegroom of the Song of Songs, St Bernard asked his monks which of them could say from his heart that Christ had kissed him 'with the kiss of His mouth'.[62] When he considered the reactions of the Bride, St Bernard described the ideal of selfless or pure love in what would later be thought of as romantic terms:

> Pure love is not mercenary; it draws no strength from hope and neither is it weakened by any mistrust. This is the love that is felt by the Bride; for all that she is, is only love. The very being of the Bride, and her one hope, consists in love. In this she abounds and with this the Bridegroom is content. He seeks nothing else and she has nothing else to give. It is for this that she is the Bride and he is the Bridegroom.[63]

DIVINE LOVE AND HUMAN LOVE

A non-believer in God or in romance, then or now, might respond that mystical monks like St Bernard and Peter the Venerable dealt in nothing more than pious fictions, even if they were able to construct mighty edifices from them. The Song of Songs is a pagan poem, not a Christian revelation. The idealized love which St Bernard ascribed to the Bride did not exist, except in his fond imaginings. His and Peter the Venerable's expressions of affection are not what they seem. Their extravagantly intimate letters were intended to compensate for their physical and emotional isolation from their correspondents. Peter the Venerable effusively thanked Heloise for his 'fleeting or stolen visit' to her, which (he said) had seemed so much more to him than 'a single passing night'.[64] But she described his visit more soberly: he had celebrated Mass 'as our abbot and lord' and then he had preached to the nuns in Chapter.[65] Heloise presumably never saw him out of his liturgical vestments or unaccompanied by his retinue. He was after all the greatest prelate in Europe apart from the pope. As for St Bernard and the Countess Ermengard, Dom Jean Leclercq, a twentieth-century monk and the editor of his letters, comments that the purpose of his rhetoric was to get Ermengard 'really believing in his affection. Once this had been assured, everything essential was done, and physical presence mattered little.'[66] Those with true faith did not require the physical presence either of God or St Bernard.

For these monks, pure love was a wholly metaphysical ideal, which was not to be confused with human sexuality, even though they both used erotic language. Woe betide any monk or nun who confused divine or spiritual friendship with human love between the sexes. This was made clear by another distinguished Cistercian abbot, St Ailred of Rievaulx, who described with some approval how a nun of Watton (in Yorkshire) had been made to castrate her lover in the presence of the other nuns, and his bleeding testicles were then pushed into her mouth as a symbolic revenge for the violation of her chastity.[67] Like the nun of Watton, Heloise felt that she had been responsible for the castration of her lover. Although she insisted that Abelard had been castrated without her consent or even her knowledge (as she was enclosed in the convent of Argenteuil), she admitted that she could not avoid blame, as the act had been done by her family to avenge her honour: 'Why was I ever born to be the cause of such a crime?', she lamented.[68] 'Even if my conscience is clear through innocence, for no consent of mine makes me guilty of this crime, too many sins preceded it to allow me to be wholly free from guilt.'[69]

Dilemmas of this sort are the subject of Abelard's treatise on ethics, which Heloise may have inspired through her relentless analysis of her own misery. What were largely theoretical questions of moral philosophy for Abelard were desperate realities for her. She felt that through no fault of her own she had done an irretrievable wrong and because she could not put it right, she had no way of winning forgiveness. To Abelard she expressed this as a paradox: 'Although I am very guilty, I am very innocent, as you know.'[70] She had undoubtedly done evil and yet she had only intended good. In apportioning blame 'it is not the doing of a thing, but the intention of the doer which makes the crime; justice takes account not of what things are done, but of the state of mind (*animo*) in which they are done'.[71]

Heloise's understanding of her 'state of mind' is the foundation of her complex stance towards Abelard. The Latin *animus* means 'mind' not so much in the sense of the 'intellect' directing the brain, as of the 'spirit' or the 'heart' which is the metaphorical core of the feelings. For Heloise the *animus* is the 'consciousness' which activates the body through the feelings and also the 'conscience' which tells her what is right and wrong. When explaining to Abelard how she is both guilty and innocent, she added: 'What my state of mind towards you has always been, you alone who have experienced it can judge.'[72] And she reinforced this by saying that 'if my mind is not with you, it is nowhere; truly without you, it can be nothing at all'.[73] In other words, she had given her heart to Abelard. But this was not a romantic notion so much as a psychological description of her inability to change her mind. Abelard was more than willing to give her 'mind' back to her and he implored her to turn her heart to Christ, her Heavenly Bridegroom. She did not need to refuse outright, as she could simply repeat that her *animus* was beyond her control: 'Nothing is less within our power than the heart; we are compelled to obey it much more than we can command it.'[74]

The priority which Heloise gives to her feelings, her state of mind, explains the mercurial changes of tone and mood in her letters to Abelard. They frequently come close to contradicting themselves and yet it is this tension which gives them the power and resonance of a stretched drum. She began by contradicting her own rule that her mind was not within her power to control. She told Abelard that 'immediately at your command I changed my habit (when she was veiled as a nun) as well as my mind (*animus*), so that I might show you to be the only possessor of my body as well as my mind'.[75] If she had 'immediately' changed her mind when he had commanded her to become a nun at the time of his castration, why could she not change it again when he implored her fifteen years later to love Christ instead of him? She had been more than willing to follow him to Hell, why could she not find it in her heart to follow him to Heaven? What Heloise meant by saying that she had changed her mind when she became a nun is unfathomable, as on her own admission she only changed her external appearance. Nor did being vested as a nun demonstrate that Abelard was the 'only possessor' of her body. On the contrary, the public ceremony of vesting, conducted in Heloise's case by the bishop of Paris himself, made her the bride of Christ in Heaven and the ward on earth of the convent of Argenteuil. In law this terminated Abelard's possession of her body as her husband, though it is true that he was assured by her becoming a nun that no other man could lawfully possess her. She became a nun at Abelard's command in order not to add insult to his injury by being compelled by her family to marry someone else.

It was a paradox, as Heloise pointed out, that love drove her to such 'insanity' that she gave up what she most desired without hope of recovery.[76] Castration had deprived her of Abelard's sexual power, it need not have deprived her of his presence and it certainly should not have deprived her of his affection. She explained her becoming a nun in terms of her pure love for Abelard: 'God knows I never sought anything in you except yourself: *te pure* – simply you – I coveted nothing of yours. I looked for no marriage bond and no dowry. Above all, as you know for yourself, I studied to fulfil not my own pleasures and desires but yours.'[77] Like St Bernard's ideal in the Song of Songs, 'the very being of the Bride, and her one hope, consists in love; in this she abounds and with this the Bridegroom is content'.[78] But Abelard was not content with the self-sacrifice of his bride. Heloise reproached him for the

inaccurate account he had given of her feelings in his 'history of calamities': 'You kept silent about most of my reasons for preferring love to
wedlock and freedom to chains; I invoke God as my witness' that if the
Emperor Augustus had offered to marry me and confer the whole world
on me for ever, 'it would seem dearer and more honourable to me to be
called your mistress than his empress'.[79]

This piece of bravado reinforced Heloise's having just told Abelard
that 'although the name of "wife" may seem holy and true, the word
"girl-friend" (*amica*) has for me always been rather pleasanter or, if you
are not too shocked, "concubine" or "whore"'.[80] This last word *scor-
tum*, meaning a 'skin' or a 'rent-boy', in the sense of a prostitute of
either sex, was perhaps intended to bring Abelard up with a start and
make him see how he had treated Heloise. Surely, one might protest, she
cannot have been serious, as she would never have wanted to be Abelard's 'whore' because a whore's love is the opposite of pure. But the key
to her statement is her saying that she preferred 'to be called', or 'to be
spoken of' (*dici*), as a mistress or whore. She had no intention of really
being Abelard's whore, as she loved him inordinately. In order to
demonstrate the purity of this love, she was prepared to humiliate
herself utterly.[81]

Heloise was describing real events here, as she did indeed pretend that
she was Abelard's mistress when she was in fact his wife. In order to
keep their marriage secret and protect Abelard's clerical reputation, she
solemnly swore that they were not married, even though Fulbert's family
and friends had witnessed the ceremony in the church.[82] In denying the
truth of the marriage sacrament, Heloise was denying the validity of the
oath she had made before God as well as wrongly accusing her family of
telling lies. In revenge for this insulting repudiation of the marriage,
Fulbert's family castrated Abelard. It is not known why they did not
attack Heloise also. She may have been too well protected in the convent
of Argenteuil, or Fulbert may have said that she was not to be touched
as she had only done what Abelard had told her to do. An additional
reason for her being 'immediately' vested as a nun at Argenteuil, may
have been that if she came out of the convent, her family would take
revenge on her for cursing them and calling them liars.

ABELARD'S DEBT TO HELOISE

While Heloise insisted that she loved Abelard purely and simply for
himself, as if she were St Bernard's ideal of the Bride in the Song of
Songs, she kept repeating at the same time that he had incurred a debt to

her. 'Remember, I beseech you, what I have done and pay attention to how much you owe me,' her first letter concludes. 'Ponder your own lack of justice, if when I deserve more you pay out less – or rather, nothing at all.... Ponder, I beseech you, what you owe me. Pay attention to what I claim.'[83] This is the vocabulary of a money-lender rather than a lover. It makes clear that Heloise did want her pound of flesh from Abelard, even though she said that it was only a small thing she was asking and less than her due.[84] She had first brought up the subject of his debt to her in the context of his 'history of calamities'. She was hurt that Abelard had written to this anonymous correspondent but not to her. 'You discharged your debt of friendship and comradeship to this "friend and colleague" and yet you are obligated to us by a debt which is so much greater that it requires no arguments nor witnesses for its proof.'[85] Here again Heloise was using the legalistic language of money-lending. She told Abelard that his gift to her of the convent of the Paraclete put him in her debt. To forestall his answering that on the contrary it was she who owed something to him for rescuing her from Argenteuil, she added: 'And, apart from anything else, think how great the debt is by which you are obligated to me in particular.'[86]

How did Heloise reconcile her ideal of pure love for Abelard with her insistence on his being 'obligated' to her? A partial answer is that she had spoken about pure love in the context of the time before they were married. Their marriage, which Abelard had wanted and she had opposed, brought their pure love for each other to an end, as its purity was replaced by legal constraints. He had quoted in his 'history of calamities' how she had wanted to preserve a love that was free and which was therefore not to be 'constrained by any force of a nuptial bond'.[87] Once she was married, however, it was not illogical of her to insist on her legal rights. In particular she needed to scotch any suggestion that their marriage had been brought to an end either by Abelard's castration or by their entry into religion. In a sermon to monks Abelard had spoken contemptuously of 'the bond of the conjugal tie', which suggests that he did not consider himself to be married any longer.[88] Heloise, on the other hand, was arguing at much the same time: 'You must know that you are bound to me by an obligation which is all the greater for the close bond of the nuptial sacrament.'[89]

By this argument Abelard had become 'bound' to Heloise as a consequence of their marriage. But in the same sentence she modified this by adding: 'And you are always all the more liable to me, as is obvious to everyone, for the unbounded love with which I have embraced you.'[90] Her 'unbounded love' had created obligations exceeding even the bonds of marriage. The word Heloise used for 'liable' is *obnoxius*, which is stronger than 'obligated' (*obligatus*). An *obnoxius* debtor is rendered 'submissive' or even 'crippled' by his debt. Heloise's love had indeed 'crippled' Abelard. But her point is that his castration compounded his debt to her because it made *her* grief so much greater. 'You alone are the cause of my grief, you alone can console me.... It is you alone who owe me so very much, and most especially now.'[91] Abelard got over the psychological effects of his castration by accepting it as God's providential way of liberating his spirit; physically it had scarcely even hurt, he said.[92] Heloise could not get over it so readily because it had destroyed her faith in the goodness of God. This is what she kept stressing: 'For if I truthfully admit to the sickness of my most wretched soul (*animus*), I find no penitence in it with which I can appease God, as I charge Him always with the utmost cruelty for that injustice.'[93]

Abelard's castration had wounded Heloise's soul because she felt it was her fault. Henceforward she suffered what she describes as an 'interior disease': her heart or 'mind' (*animus*) was out of touch with her body.[94] 'If only my aching heart were as ready to obey as the hand is that writes this,' she told Abelard.[95] He described her trauma at the time of his castration in his 'history of calamities'. 'Weeping and sobbing', she nevertheless made her public exit in style by quoting the passage from Lucan where Cornelia blames herself for Pompey's defeat at Pharsalia: 'O greatest of husbands, I am unworthy of your bed! Did Fortune have power even over one as great as you? Why did I so wrongly marry you and bring you to disaster? Now accept the penalty which I am ready to pay.'[96] Abelard says Heloise cried out these words in everyone's presence, as 'she rushed forward to the altar' to receive her nun's veil from the bishop of Paris.[97] If these really were the circumstances, the bishop should have suspended the proceedings, not because Heloise had quoted a pagan poet instead of a Christian prayer, but rather because she was evidently in no state of mind to make her final vows. Like the nun of Watton, Heloise was sacrificed on the altar of clerical purity *pour encourager les autres*.

What did Heloise mean by comparing herself with Cornelia? Lucan's *Pharsalia* was a familiar work in the Latin curriculum and so in this case one may assume that Abelard and the rest of Heloise's clerical audience knew the context. Pompey has arrived home from the battle so exhausted and dirty that Cornelia faints at the sight of him. Had Heloise fainted at the sight of Abelard after his castration? Cornelia wants to die and she asks Pompey to scatter her limbs on the sea to bring him victory by appeasing the gods. Had Heloise too wanted to die? In that case, receiving the nun's veil signified the death of her spirit; this was her sacrifice. Cornelia wears her mourning veil, when 'clasping her sorrow' she lies inert in the bow of the ship carrying her away.[98] At least ten years after Heloise's histrionic performance, Abelard replied by pointing out that she had omitted an essential part of Cornelia's story. When she faints and weeps, Pompey rebukes her for despairing, as he is still alive even if his fortune is gone. 'That is what you loved', Pompey says, 'and that is what you are weeping for.'[99]

Was this also true of Heloise? Despite her protestations of pure love, had she really cared about Abelard's fame rather than him? Certainly this is a prominent theme in her first letter: 'What king or philosopher could equal your fame? . . . What great lady did not envy me my joys and my bed?'[100] Heloise could not bear to see Abelard humiliated and the joys of her bed removed because this destroyed her reputation as a great woman of the world. She recalled her former success: 'How could Fortune ever set any great or noble woman above me or make her my equal, and then as irrevocably cast me down dejected by grief? What glory Fortune brought me in you, what ruin she brought upon me in you!'[101] These sentiments do suggest that Heloise had been in love with Abelard's 'fortune'. Because her 'ruin' was not physical but mental, and because its focus was Abelard and not her, she could find no way of dealing with it. Her only hope was that he could raise her up somehow, but how could he? What had he now got to give her? Even if he agreed that she was entitled to her due from him, they could not return to living as man and wife; indeed they never had wanted to live as man and wife. Apart from the disability of castration, they had both taken irrevocable monastic vows.

In the light of these considerations, Abelard's repeated answers to Heloise, telling her to pray for them both and to love Christ rather than him, were not necessarily uncaring. Other than suicide or running away together, neither of them had any alternatives. The tone which Abelard adopted was severe because he matched Heloise's imperatives with ones of his own. When reminding her of Pompey's warning to Cornelia, he says: 'Pay attention to this, I beg you, and blush for shame. . . . Accept, sister, accept, I beseech you, with patience what has so mercifully happened to us. This is a father's rod, not a persecutor's sword.'[102] Although Abelard persisted in calling her 'sister', Heloise had at least persuaded him that their marriage still existed and he turned this to their spiritual advantage by arguing that the law of marriage made them now one in Christ. 'Whatever is yours cannot, I consider, be other than mine.'[103] Because he had become a monk, Abelard argued, Heloise had him now as her 'servant, whereas previously you looked on me as your lord. I am joined to you more by love now, since it is spiritual, than when I subjected you by fear.'[104] But he was describing the metaphysical love of a monk or a nun for God, which was far removed from the realities of ordinary human intercourse. As Heloise could not accept the goodness of God, she could not share in His love.

Heloise's attitude might be interpreted as that of a Stoic rather than a Christian. Lucan and Seneca are among her favourite authors. Her most shocking remark was not her repetition that God was cruel, but her hope that the end for Abelard and herself should be sudden. She quoted Lucan's *Pharsalia* in this context: 'The poet prays to God, saying "Whatever you prepare for us, make it sudden; the minds of men should be blind to the future".'[105] This is a deliberate challenge to the idea of divine providence in which Abelard had put his trust. A Christian hoped to die at peace fortified by the rites of the Church, as Peter the Venerable described Abelard dying, and not suddenly without any opportunity for repentance. Monks made their great liturgical round of daily prayers to ensure the salvation of themselves and their benefactors after death. If Heloise did not look forward to a holy death for herself or for Abelard, she was in no state to lead her nuns in their prayers at the convent of the Paraclete. She was a hypocrite, as she told Abelard.[106]

Although Heloise made accusations against God and acted in bad faith, she nevertheless expected to go to Heaven, as she told Abelard that she would be satisfied with whatever corner of it God allocated to her.[107] Does her confidence in some sort of salvation in Heaven mean that she did not think of herself as a pagan or a Stoic? Not necessarily, since she may have believed that good pagans deserved to be saved and so they would be by a just God. When she wrote that Lucan 'prays to God', she probably meant this literally. Although he was a Stoic, Lucan knew God and God knew him. 'In every people', Heloise argued, 'whether pagan, Jewish or Christian, some men have always stood out for their faith or the probity of their morals.'[108] The pagan philosophers were not called sages or lovers of wisdom because they were clever, but because they were outstandingly good in moral terms.[109] On this point Heloise quoted St Augustine, whose *City of God* served its medieval readers as an introduction to the ancient world.[110] St Augustine's purpose had been to show that even the greatest pagan philosophers, the Platonists, were not as good as Christians, whereas Heloise used the information he supplied to argue that Christianity did not have a monopoly of wisdom and that the best pagans had been as good as Christians. The Greek and Roman philosophers whom Heloise quoted to Abelard as examples were Pythagoras, Socrates, Cicero and Seneca.[111]

HELOISE'S INFLUENCE ON ABELARD'S WRITING

Heloise's championship of the pagan philosophers is the earliest piece of thought we now have from her, as it forms part of the argument which she used to oppose (without success) Abelard's marrying her. He recorded her arguments in his 'history of calamities', though Heloise complained that he had kept silent about most of them.[112] In his works on theology and ethics, which all postdate his marriage to Heloise, Abelard took up the idea that the pagan philosophers were as good as Christians and he provocatively went further by arguing that they had even known about the Trinity. This is why, at the time of the council of Sens in 1140, St Bernard accused Abelard of 'sweating to make Plato a Christian'.[113] Twenty or twenty-five years earlier, on the other hand, at the time of Abelard's marriage to Heloise, he may have known much less about ancient philosophy and classical literature than she did. From boyhood he had specialized in logic. This meant that he knew a great deal about this technical aspect of Aristotle's teaching, but not necessarily very much about his encyclopedic works as a whole, nor about Stoicism and subsequent Greek and Roman moral philosophy and humanistic writing.

In other words, it may have been Heloise who gave Abelard's writing its distinctive character. She may have shown him that the canon of classical literature embodied an ideal of how to live, rather than merely being 'letters' learned at school. As an already accomplished stylist, she may also have demonstrated to him, through her earliest letters (which are no longer extant), how writing Latin prose could be individually distinctive while remaining classical.[114] At the time of his marriage Abelard was 'studying to complete' his commentary on the prophet Ezechiel, which he had begun at Laon, and he may have published some of his lectures on logic.[115] Like his own masters, William of Champeaux and Anselm of Laon, his success up to that point had depended primarily on the reputation of his oral teaching. Because of her training in literature, Heloise may have inspired Abelard to become a writer, with something really grand to leave to posterity, as well as being a brilliant talker and teacher.

'Without the sobering effect of his castration and the influence of the mature Heloise, Abelard might have remained a relatively obscure figure, known chiefly as a great and influential master in the schools. Some of his voluminous writings were composed especially for Heloise after she had become abbess of the Paraclete. Although it is risky to speculate concerning historical alternatives, it seems possible that Abelard might not have written very much at all, aside from treatises for the immediate use of his students, without her steadying influence and the availability of the Paraclete as a repository for books. We should be willing to accord Heloise some credit for nourishing Abelard's literary ambitions and encouraging the production of his works'.[116] This is the hypothesis of the literary critic and medievalist D. W. Robertson Jr. Had it not been for Abelard's affair with Heloise, we might know as little now about him as we do about those once equally famous masters William of Champeaux and Anselm of Laon. His love for her transformed Abelard's life and transcended his 'history of calamities'. (Her pervasive influence on his ideas is discussed in chapter 12, below, which looks at Abelard as a 'Theologian'.)

Critics will never all agree about the influence Abelard and Heloise had on each other because so much depends on speculation about their innermost thoughts. Once it is acknowledged that Heloise was highly trained in literature, her own role grows even more complex. The character who develops line by line in her love letters is extraordinarily powerful and thought-provoking. But she is not necessarily the real Heloise, whatever that might mean, as the most striking feature of the character in the letters is that she is a self-conscious writer. She is a 'writer' in the modern sense of creative author and also in the sense of a stylist and rhetorician, who has been instructed in – and delights in performing variations on – the most advanced manoeuvres in Latin composition. She is steeped in Latin literature, both in the modes of expression of its classical authors and in their subject matter, particularly their discussions of exemplary heroes and heroines. So familiar is this classical world to Heloise that she sees nothing absurd in comparing herself with the empress of Augustus Caesar, nor with Cornelia, the wife of Pompey the Great. For her, these noble Romans are living presences and an inspiration even though they were pagans.

After they separated, Abelard and Heloise sublimated their love for each other in opposing ways. He directed his passion as well as his mind towards analysing the example of Christ, Whose suffering on the cross 'has so bound us to Himself in love' (in Abelard's words) that 'we will not fear to endure all things for His sake'.[117] Because Heloise would not – or could not – accept the justice of Abelard's castration, she could not turn to Christ for solace. She took her stand instead, with Cornelia and the Roman Stoics, on self-sacrifice and the ultimate resort of despair. Whether this was only a literary posture on her part, or whether it was a deeply-held moral conviction, is for each reader of her letters to decide. Certainly the Heloise of the love letters speaks with the voice of a pagan proudly confronting adverse Fortune, rather than that of a Christian humbly acknowledging God's grace. 'Many people say her letters show insanity', commented their first publisher, Jean de Meun, 'but she wrote marvellously.'[118]

A lawbook from Abelard's time noted how 'we proffer respect and love only to those whom we cannot do without'.[119] This is what makes love the foundation of the family and of society, and hence of religion. The Heloise of the love letters might be able to do without God, but never without Abelard. He, on the other hand, could get on without her, but never without his conception of Christ's love. He had marginalized her by writing his 'history of calamities' for the comfort of a stranger, and he had even had the insensitivity to recount their story to this stranger as if she could not speak for herself. 'Neither reverence for God, nor love for us, nor the example of the Church Fathers', she chided him, 'made you try to comfort me, even though I was wavering and exhausted by prolonged grieving.'[120] In her earliest and most difficult years as a nun, she maintained, he had offered her nothing, 'whether present or absent, not a word of consolation nor a letter'.[121]

Her repeated reproaches at last found their mark, when Abelard responded in the 1130s by sending her his hymns, sermons, and other writings for the convent of the Paraclete. For Heloise as a private person, however, as distinct from in her official role as abbess of the Paraclete, all this may have been too little too late. Abelard's letters and songs now concerned their would-be exemplary lives as abbot and abbess and not the actual love they had known. It may be significant that, although he kept writing to her, no letters of acknowledgement or gratitude on her part are extant. Possibly she deliberately failed to respond, so as to show him what it was like to receive 'not a word of consolation nor a letter'; or she may not have considered what she wrote in this regard worth keeping.[122]

When it came to the bitter end, to Abelard's last recorded communication with her at the time of the council of Sens in 1140, he concluded his confession of faith not with the orthodox 'Amen' ('So be it') of the Creed, but with a classical coda which seems blasphemous in this context. In Gilson's words, 'the impenitent humanist is unwilling to conclude his solemn profession of faith, written during the hours of trial, without mobilizing once more the Sirens of the Aeneid'.[123] Abelard assured Heloise that, fortified by faith, he had no fear of Scylla and Charybdis nor even of the Sirens.[124] In making this declaration, he may have been aiming to exorcize these ancient pagan monsters along with his own fears.[125] Or, as Gilson suggests, this may have been a literary reference to the Aeneid (and back to the Odyssey), which Heloise would appreciate. Abelard may also have had a deeper purpose in concluding his profession of faith with Ulysses. By evoking a classical hero, he may have been paying Heloise the final compliment of assuring her that his pagan courage in adversity was equal to her own. He was still her Ulysses, defiantly voyaging into the unknown; and she remained his Penelope, forever weaving and unweaving their shroud.

9

Man

At the time of his seduction of Heloise, Abelard described himself as 'pre-eminent in grace of youth and form', whereas she was an 'adolescent'. The year was probably 1117.[1] He was then in his late thirties and she was younger, though not perhaps much younger. In using the terms 'youth' and 'adolescent' he was evoking the commonplace of the Seven Ages of Man. Beginning as an 'infant', the individual progresses to 'boyhood' or 'girlhood', and then advances through 'adolescence' and 'youth' to the maturity of 'manhood'. After that, in Shakespeare's words, 'the sixth age shifts into the lean and slipper'd pantaloon' of old age, and finally there is 'decrepitude' – 'sans teeth, sans eyes, sans taste, sans everything'. These stages of life do not have exact numerical equivalents in terms of years; the early stages occur a decade or so later than modern usage is accustomed to. Thus Abelard had described himself as an 'adolescent' when he took charge of his first school at Melun in c.1102 or c.1103, even though he was at least twenty-two or twenty-three.[2] So he was not necessarily being vain in describing himself as a 'youth' when he first met Heloise. Indeed, she told him he was 'adolescent' at this stage of his life. Many women envied her, she remembered, and she understood this: 'For what perfection of mind or body did not adorn your adolescence?'[3]

Abelard's description of Heloise as an 'adolescent' does not mean she was a teenage bride, as her biographers have assumed. She may have been in her twenties (as Abelard was when he went to Melun), or even close to thirty. He says that at the time they met, the fame of her learning 'had made her most renowned in the whole kingdom' of France. Peter the Venerable confirms this: 'I had not yet fully gone beyond the bounds of adolescence, nor had I yet passed into youthful years, when the fame of your name first reached me. I used to hear at that time of the woman who, although not yet disentangled from the bonds of the world, devoted the highest zeal to literary science.'[4] It can be inferred from this that Heloise was older than Peter: he was an 'adolescent' reaching 'youth', when she was a 'woman'. As he was born in 1092 or 1094, she had presumably been born around 1090 or earlier. She can hardly have been a teenager in 1117, as it would have taken her some time, years perhaps, to acquire (in the face of male prejudice) the scholarly renown which Abelard and Peter describe.

Because it is a stage on man's journey, each of the Seven Ages characterizes an approach to life rather than an exact period of years. This is why Heloise could describe Abelard as 'adolescent' when she first met him; she was 'adolescent' and so his character should match hers. 'Adolescence' and 'youth' were the springtime of life, the season of blossoming and joy; though, by the same token, they were also a time of intemperance and folly by contrast with the mature wisdom of manhood and old age. Abelard's contemporary, William IX of Aquitaine, tells his companions: 'I will make a fitting verse, and there will be more folly in it than sense, and it will be all mixed up with love and joy and youth.'[5] Whatever age Abelard and Heloise were when they first met, they too were 'all mixed up with love and joy and youth'.

YOUTH AND PHYSIQUE

As a cleric of many years' standing and master of the school of Notre-Dame in Paris, Abelard should have left 'youth' behind him. By courting Heloise, he was making a sudden and belated bid for a place in the sun. Many of the lyrics in the *Carmina Burana* address the theme of the transitoriness of life and give a freshness to this cliché. They also give us some idea of what the lost love songs which Abelard wrote for Heloise may have been like; indeed, poems of Abelard's may be included anonymously in the *Carmina Burana*, as they circulated widely. This is the beginning of 'Obmittamus studia' in Helen Waddell's translation:

> Let's away with study, folly's sweet.
> Treasure all the pleasure of our youth:
> Time enough for age to think of Truth.[6]

For the first and only time in his life Abelard had deliberately taken a mental holiday from the schools: 'it was utterly tedious for me to go to the school and equally tiresome to remain there and keep up studying in the daytime when my nights were sleepless with love-making. As my interest and concentration flagged, my lectures lacked all inspiration and became repetitive.'[7]

In his description of the pre-eminence of his 'youth', Abelard emphasized his physical beauty, his 'grace of form', and Heloise did likewise.[8]
This is something of a problem, as there are no precise accounts of
Abelard's physique. When the remains of Abelard and Heloise were
brought from the convent of the Paraclete to Paris in 1792 during the
French Revolution, the bones of both of them were described as 'big'
and Abelard was said to be of 'great stature'.[9] Not only is this description vague, it is also unreliable, as the last abbess of the Paraclete,
Charlotte de Roucy, had told an inquirer in 1787 that the bones of
Abelard were almost totally reduced to dust, apart from the skull
which was indeed very big.[10] Heloise's bones were better preserved,
the abbess had added, and her skull was also big with remarkably
white teeth. Nothing has been done, then or since, to measure the
skeletons of Abelard and Heloise or to assess their age of death by
dental examination. But as the bones were repeatedly handled as curi-
osities and they were not interred in the cemetery of Père-Lachaise until
1817, it is doubtful whether anything authentic survives.

Medieval descriptions of people's appearance are notoriously unreliable and this applies to both Abelard and Heloise. For her, we only have
Abelard's ambiguous statement that 'she was not the worst in the
face'.[11] What contemporary descriptions there are of Abelard suggest
that he was indeed a big man; possibly, even, he was fat. The only
contemporary explanation given for the name 'Abelard' is that it
meant 'licker of lard'; he was a 'full dog' who enjoyed eating the fat.[12]
Twice in *Dialectica* Abelard used his own name to demonstrate points of
logic. To illustrate the Nominalist argument that words and names are
arbitrary constructs, which nevertheless take on meanings of their own,
he says: 'This name "Abelard" has been allocated to me so that something of my substance may be referred to through it.'[13] Possibly he was
joking here about how his name indicated his physical substantialness,
as well as signifying his 'substance' in terms of logic. His second example also illustrates a Nominalist argument. The arbitrariness of language
is shown by the way we may attach more than one meaning to a
particular word. Abelard gives Latin deponent verbs as an illustration,
as they can be understood either actively or passively in accordance with
the context. The three verbs he takes as examples may have had a
subconscious significance for him (as already suggested in chapter 5).
They are: 'I embrace/I am embraced'; 'I kiss/I am kissed'; 'I incrim-
inate/I am incriminated'.[14] To illustrate Boethius's point that this class
of ambiguous words must nevertheless refer to a single logical 'substance' in each case, Abelard adds: 'and so I think "Abelard" still suits
only me'.[15] This may be another joke about his bulky 'substance' and it

may refer also to the aftermath of his castration, if he is suggesting that he is 'still' the essential 'Abelard', even though he has lost his manhood by being 'incriminated'.

Opposed to this bulky image of Abelard are those who argue that he was unusually small. They discount the archaeological evidence of the bones, which cannot now be scientifically examined nor proved to be the remains of Abelard and Heloise in the first place. A. M. Landgraf identified Abelard with the master whom students nicknamed 'tiny' (*magistrellus*) or the 'little master'.[16] In *Theologia* Abelard describes himself as 'little David' facing Goliath.[17] When St Goswin went to confront Abelard in his own classroom, his biographer allegedly described Abelard as 'of slim build and no great stature'.[18] But more probably the biographer was referring to Goswin here and likening his boyish physique to that of David confronting Goliath.[19] This is supported by Goswin's biographer explicitly identifying Abelard with Goliath. St Bernard, too, compared Abelard with Goliath.[20] The much-used David and Goliath allusion may throw no light on the physique of the medieval protagonists. If Abelard were small, it might have been all the more effective for his opponents to call him 'Goliath' to make him look ridiculous.

Goswin's biographer also described Abelard as a *rhinoceros* because he was so wild and fierce.[21] Even this does not prove that he was big and heavy, however, as the biographer may have been envisaging not the lumbering African rhinoceros but the small and graceful unicorn of the medieval Bestiaries. Abelard's description of his 'grace of youth and form' are not necessarily incompatible with his being heavy or ugly in the opinion of other people, or in other circumstances, as his purpose was to idealize his appearance at the critical moment when he first met Heloise. Goswin's biographer likened Abelard also to Proteus, the Homeric sea-god who repeatedly changes shape to avoid answering questions, and St Bernard said he was 'dissimilar even from himself'.[22] If he seemed so varied to eyewitnesses and contemporaries, admittedly prejudiced ones, it is not going to be easy to agree on his physical appearance 900 years later. A plausible imaginary portrait was constructed by his first and best biographer, Charles de Rémusat, in 1845: 'He was a man of expansive appearance, with a lively, proud expression and noble demeanour, whose beauty still preserved some of the *éclat* of his youth.'[23]

After the stage of 'youth' in the Seven Ages of Man comes 'manhood' (*virilitas*), the high point of achievement and authority, when a man should be 'adorned with powers' (*viribus*) and be a '*vir*' also in the sense of husband and head of a family.[24] (In Latin *vir* meant both 'man' and 'husband'.) As Abelard was a cleric, the equivalent of 'manhood' for him should have been attaining a tenured office in the Church, which he had indeed achieved when he was appointed master of the Paris school at the time he met Heloise. Furthermore, he had also just displayed his manly maturity towards his family in Brittany by settling their affairs when his parents retired to monasteries.[25] Castration deprived Abelard of his 'manhood' in every sense, not only physically but also socially and culturally within the framework of the Seven Ages of Man. It meant that he had proceeded suddenly and catastrophically from the Fourth Age of 'youth' to the Sixth Age of 'old age'. Fulk of Deuil mischievously imagined Abelard saying to himself: 'The characteristic of manhood usually lasts a man into his age. But my cheeks are already bare, with only wisps of hair to adorn them, my glorious complexion has withered into wrinkles, and an unfamiliar pallor distorts my face.'[26] On the other hand, in the opinion of Otto of Freising at least, Abelard did come into his productive maturity as a consequence of his castration, as it made him become a monk and concentrate on serious writing.[27]

The apparent changeableness of Abelard's physique, expressed over time through the Seven Ages of Man and over the diversity of contemporary opinion through allusions to the Bible and mythology, raises philosophical questions about what man is. How does the individual retain the same identity, 'the *genus* of man' as Fulk of Deuil put it, throughout his Seven Ages? How can he change and yet remain the same? Can a person become somebody else, or even something else, as people frequently do in ancient mythology? Is St Goswin's biographer's comparison of Abelard with a rhinoceros and the sea-god Proteus merely a literary conceit, or does it show that medieval people believed in mythology and magic? Where is the dividing line between mythology and religion, or magic and science, and who is to draw it: priests or scientists? Such questions were of professional as much as personal interest to Abelard, as he aspired to be the new Aristotle.

ADAM AND EVE

The medieval reader's starting point in questions of science was the Bible and the Book of Genesis in particular. This gave him an exalted opinion of man's place in the world, as God is described giving Adam dominion over the earth and all its creatures. Like other would-be scientists, Abelard wrote a commentary on the Six Days of Creation as recounted in Genesis. As was often done in such commentaries, he pointed out the congruences between the Six Days of Creation and the Six Ages of the

World described by medieval chroniclers: 'infancy' from Adam to Noah; 'childhood' from the Flood to Abraham; 'adolescence' from God's covenant with Abraham to King David; 'youth' during the captivity of God's people in Babylon; 'old age' up to the coming of Christ. In this chronological scheme the years of grace *Anno Domini* are the final age of 'decrepitude', when mankind awaits the world's end and the Last Judgement.[28] Like many medieval Christians, Abelard felt that these Last Days were imminent. Writing *Theologia Christiana* shortly after his condemnation at Soissons in 1121, he identified his prosecutors with the blasphemers who will precede Antichrist and, with batteries of Scriptural quotations, he warned his readers to prepare for the worst.[29] Abelard was also being profoundly pessimistic in his commentary on the Creation in equating the Fourth Age of 'youth' with the Jewish captivity in Babylon, as that associated his sexuality with bondage and Heloise with the whore of Babylon. He had made the Six Ages of the World congruent with the Seven Ages of Man by coalescing 'youth' and 'manhood'. 'Youth' for Abelard was 'the virile age' of lust.[30]

On the other hand, the Six Days of Creation could equally well be interpreted in an optimistic way. The purpose of equating the Ages of the World with the Ages of Man was to show how God had made man as a microcosm of the world. As the crowning achievement of Creation, mankind as a species has a destiny across time and space, while each individual has a personal destiny within his allotted life-span. No more optimistic or sublime view of mankind is conceivable than the vision which Hildegard of Bingen recorded and had painted in *c.*1163, about twenty years after Abelard's death. She saw a man – naked and beautiful, but without genitals – standing calmly at the centre of the primal cosmos, with his arms extended towards its swirling waters, winds, fires and precious metals. A miniature of Hildegard herself is depicted in a corner of this vision, clothed from head to foot in her nun's habit, as she earnestly labours to note all this on her writing tablets. She has just witnessed the creative force of life explaining to her that:

> I am Reason who bears the breeze of the sounding word, through which every creature is made. And I breathe into all these things, so that none of them is mortal in its generation. I am life, whole and entire – not sparking from flints, nor bursting from branches, nor rooted in male virility. For everything vital is rooted in me, as Reason is the root from which the sounding word blooms in the world.[31]

So it was not to shield convent sensibilities that Hildegard's ideal of man was depicted without genitals, but to show that there is more to life than male virility, a lesson that Abelard was made to learn by his castration.

As a logician, he might have applauded, too, Hildegard's description of Reason creating everything through the breath of the 'sounding word', that is, by voicing the names of things, a concept which emphasized that nothing can exist without the language describing it. Hildegard's vision of words making things 'bloom' was a metaphor which could unite Nominalists and Realists.

Abelard's commentary on the Six Days of Creation agreed with Hildegard, too, that 'the human spirit is stronger in power by its very nature than all the others' and 'only it is capable of reason and wisdom and participating in divine love'.[32] The doctrine that man is essentially different from, and superior to, all the other creatures because he alone possesses the power of reason formed the common foundation of Judaism, Christianity and Islam. Abelard explored some of this common heritage in his imagined dialogue between a Christian and a Jew, and in *Theologia* he emphasized that this doctrine was also a commonplace of classical Greek philosophy. Because man is made in the image of God, Abelard argued, the three divine persons of the Trinity encapsulate the distinguishing characteristics of man, who 'is said to be made like the Father because of the power which he has over the rest of the creatures, and he imitates the Son through reason and the Holy Spirit through the goodness of the innocence which he afterwards lost by his fault'.[33] The first two of these points (that man has authority over all other creatures and that he alone is distinguished by reason) continue to be the justification of claims to exploit nature to man's advantage. To that extent, the Book of Genesis remains the foundation of science.

Unlike today's scientists, however, medieval thinkers were most concerned about the third point: that man has fallen from his original state of innocence through his own fault. Every medieval person knew that this 'fault' was Adam and Eve's eating the forbidden apple in the Garden of Eden, and that Eve had tasted it first. Heloise likened herself to Eve in the fatal effect she had had on Abelard: 'The first woman immediately lured the man out of paradise, and she who had been created by God as his helpmate became the instrument of his utter downfall.'[34] Belief in the Fall brought at least one benefit, however, as it enabled mankind to seem good and bad at the same time, which made better sense of everyday experience than seeing human nature either as perfect or as the embodiment of evil. The fate of Adam and Eve also emphasized the moral dimension of man's nature. Unlike the other creatures, Adam had choices to make and he bore responsibility for his actions. He was the lord of all creation on earth and yet a single wrong choice had exposed his nakedness and vulnerability. The Romanesque artists of Abelard's time excelled in depicting Adam and Eve as pathetic figures, clutching their fig leaves to their unlovely anatomies, as they stagger out of paradise, stunned by the severity of God's sentence.

Did fallen man have the same exalted status as Adam and Eve had been given when they were first placed in the Garden of Eden? Did man remain God-like in his ability to reason, or had he shown himself to be an ass? None of the other animals, over whom he claimed to have power of life and death, had made such a humiliating mistake or suffered such a penalty. Adam had been easily misled by a woman, who had been deceived in her turn by a soft-talking serpent. So, Adam and Eve had not even been the cleverest creatures in the garden. The absurdity of man is a theme which Abelard seems to allude to in his *Dialectica*. He had included himself and Heloise in this category by associating the personal admission that 'Peter loves his girl' with the ancient logician's proposition that 'if anyone is a man, he is risible'.[35] Traditionally the Greek logicians had demonstrated the absurdity of man by making Socrates, the best and wisest of men, the butt of their most ridiculous hypothetical propositions. Abelard joined in this old game with a will. He altered the textbook example of 'Socrates is white' to 'Socrates is asinine'. This gave him an opportunity to perform variations on such propositions as 'if Socrates is asinine, some man is asinine', or 'every man is asinine', and 'if Socrates is an animal and that animal is an ass, Socrates is asinine'.[36]

The man who is transformed into an ass, which was a motif as old as the Greeks and Romans, must still have had enough power in it to make Abelard's student audience laugh uneasily, just as it made Shakespeare's audience laugh in *A Midsummer Night's Dream*. Among the multitude of sculptures on the church from Abelard's time at Aulnay is a priest vested for Holy Mass, but with an ass's head, reading from a Gospel Book which is held ceremonially open for him by another ass.[37] This scene forms part of a carnival of fifty or so creatures, real and imaginary, on the tympanum above the south door. They evoke classical and barbarian mythology as well as actual animals of the medieval forest: stag, wolf, boar, eagle and owl. As in other Romanesque carvings, sexual symbolism is explicit: a centaur exhibits his genitals frontally, a mermaid grasps her erect tail, a tonsured naked man is raped by a dog-headed monster. How such images should be understood is a debatable question, however; possibly they were intended to have multiple meanings. Do they demonstrate the persistence of paganism and folklore in medieval Christianity? Or, to the contrary, do they show how the Church authorities confined paganism to the margins: to the exteriors of churches rather than the interiors, and to high places rather than accessible ones? Some grotesque imagery may be a comment by the local priests and clergy on the superstitions and gross sexual habits of their lay flocks. Or, one group of clergy may criticize another; the asinine priest at Aulnay could be a comment on the ignorance of the local clergy by the Cluniac monks who controlled this church.

Whatever its meaning, whether pagan or Christian, most of this imagery worked on the premise that there is a hierarchy of creatures in the world, and that man stands at the top of it, despite the Fall and all the wrongs he does. Where there seems to have been lingering doubt, even among some clergy, was whether the dividing line between man and all the other creatures could be drawn as sharply as it was in the Book of Genesis. Were creatures which bridged that line, like centaurs and mermaids, all mythical? Could not the spirit of one creature enter another? Certainly the New Testament sanctioned belief in people and animals being possessed by demons, even though Christianity opposed the transmigration of souls. In medieval art demons were nearly always represented in animal form, as toads or bats for instance. Satan himself usually stands upright, like a human being, but with hooves and a tail. Intellectuals like Abelard argued that such representations should be understood symbolically; they did not depict physical realities because 'Hell' is a mystical way of describing punishment.[38] Whether symbols or realities, the way demons were represented as animals indicates the mixture of apprehension and disgust in which animals were held. They were the old enemy. At best they were seen as slaves 'destined by nature' (in St Bernard's words) 'to alleviate the needs of man'.[39] At worst they were condemned as physical and moral dangers to man. Any animal that accidentally caused a human death was killed. In the Church's penitentials, which list penalties for different sins, copulating with a variety of mainly domestic animals is prominent. From such miscegenation sprang the monsters of Romanesque art.

The oldest of man's animal enemies was the serpent, which had caused the Fall in the Garden of Eden. According to the Book of Genesis, God cursed it and condemned it to crawl on the earth as the most lowly and despicable of creatures. St Bernard evoked this commonplace of the hierarchy of creation when he warned Cardinal Guy of Castello to curb his affection for Abelard, lest his love for him grow 'earthy, animal and diabolical'.[40] At Autun cathedral Gislebertus, the Michelangelo of Romanesque art, created an image of Eve which brings together many of these diverse ideas about man's place in the world. Gislebertus's Eve, which is contemporary with Heloise, is a powerful visualization of her description of the first woman 'luring' man out of paradise.[41] The word Heloise used is *captivavit* – literally, Eve 'captivated' or 'ensnared' Adam. Gislebertus shows Eve prone at ground level, partly concealed by foliage but temptingly revealed in her nakedness. Like the serpent, whose message she is bringing to Adam, she is sinuous and languid. But she does not crawl like the serpent, and neither is she ugly like a personification of lust. Enticing and tender, she seems to be almost floating or swimming towards Adam. Her sexuality and fertility are emphasized rather than concealed by the stylized plant, culminating in seed-pods, which rises over her genitalia. Her right hand is cupped to her mouth to whisper to Adam, or even to sing to him like a Siren. With her left, she lightly plucks the fatal apple.

Gislebertus's Eve is beautiful and unashamed of her nakedness because she is shown immediately before the Fall, unlike the commoner Romanesque image of Adam and Eve being expelled from paradise. It was the Fall that perverted men's and women's bodies and made the naked female into the symbol of lust and the male into the laughable animal with the jerking penis. The classic analysis of the Fall was St Augustine's, who argued that once Adam had lost control of himself by sinning, this was passed down the generations in man's inability to control his sexuality.[42] Because of the Fall, a man cannot direct his penis entirely through will-power, as he may have an erection involuntarily or not at all. This is why he has to hide it under his clothes. Even married people are ashamed of the sex act and find a private place to do it. St Augustine's teaching, which can look prurient or comic when crudely summarized in this way, was so influential because he interpreted man's sexual failings as proof of the whole gamut of sinfulness which came with the Fall. In Peter Brown's words, 'sexual dreams and sexual temptations betrayed the tread of far heavier beasts within the soul – anger, greed, avarice and vainglory'.[43]

Abelard's account in his 'history of calamities' of his own fall from grace exemplifies St Augustine's teaching. He says his success as master of the Paris school enervated the vigour of his mind. 'And so, when I was labouring totally in pride and lechery, divine grace provided me with a remedy for each of these diseases, though not ones of my choosing: first for my lechery by depriving me of the parts of the body with which I practised it, and then for my pride by humiliating me by the burning of my book' (at the council of Soissons in 1121).[44] Abelard describes pride and lechery as 'diseases' because this is what sins were in Augustinian terms. They were sicknesses of the soul, to which man had been made prone by Adam's original sin. Like Adam in the Garden of Eden, Abelard had put his desire for gratification and his own mistaken opinion before God's commandments. Like Adam too, he had suffered terrible retribution which he painfully learned to accept as the just judgement of God, indeed as a way of teaching him.

Like mankind as a whole, Abelard was therefore ready for redemption. This is why he laboured to show in his commentary on St Paul's Epistle to the Romans that redemption meant Christ's supreme demonstration of love and humility in His life and death on earth. Christ's unique example gave fallen man the strength to overcome pride and lechery and 'endure all things for His sake'.[45] True love, as distinct from Abelard's initial sensual love for Heloise, was engendered by pain and sacrifice. Biblical teaching and his own theological thinking therefore enabled Abelard to interpret his affair with Heloise in heroic terms. He was not a dirty old man who had seduced a student committed to his care, but a saint making his pilgrimage to self-knowledge by the steep path of experience. He had no hesitation in comparing himself with Christ. Quoting St John's Gospel, Abelard told the 'friend' to whom he addressed his 'history of calamities': 'If they have persecuted me, they will also persecute you.'[46]

ABELARD'S ACCOUNT OF HIS MARRIAGE

Historians who have made use of Abelard's 'history of calamities' have generally assumed that its account of his marriage is reliable and unprejudiced. He does indeed tell his 'friend' and correspondent that he wants him to know the true story of this event 'in accordance with fact rather than hearsay'.[47] But the crucial word here is 'hearsay'. Abelard explains that people were still gossiping about him and Heloise and saying he was a slave to lust, even though he had been castrated for fifteen years.[48] The reason for the persistence of such talk was that at the time he was writing the 'history of calamities' (in c.1132) Abelard was desperate to give up his post as abbot of St Gildas, because he was terrified of his monks, and coincidentally he was helping Heloise establish her nuns at the Paraclete after their expulsion from Argenteuil in 1129. As Abelard actually left St Gildas and visited Heloise in person at the Paraclete (a journey of 350 miles), he must have looked at this time very like the disorderly monk 'consorting with women' whom St Bernard satirized.[49]

Whether he went back to the Paraclete, or whether he re-established himself as a master at Paris (the outcome which in fact occurred), Abelard needed to demonstrate in his 'history of calamities' that he had acted correctly and honourably as far as his marriage was concerned. He could afford to reveal his failures as a conventional monk, as he was about to leave St Gildas and traditional monasticism. He could not admit, on the other hand, that his opponents were right in describing him as a corrupter of youth, as that would make him unfit to continue as a master. In his account of the beginning of his affair with Heloise, Abelard was therefore at pains to show that Fulbert was in the wrong, or at the least that he acted selfishly and naively, whereas Abelard was a man of the world. Representing, or misrepresenting, Fulbert was made easier by c.1132 because he was dead or retired; he is last recorded at Notre-Dame in 1124.[50] Abelard could not deny the many aspects of the affair which were still public knowledge. But he could explain in his own way those things which had been known only to himself and Fulbert. The most sensitive of these was the precise nature of the marriage contract which they had negotiated. Not even Heloise had first-hand knowledge of this, as she had been held hostage at Abelard's home in Brittany when he dealt with Fulbert in Paris.

'If he were to kill me', Abelard explained, 'or to debilitate my body in any way, he had to fear the most dreadful thing – that his most beloved niece would be made to suffer for it in my country.'[51] By this sentence Abelard made clear that he had conducted a bloodfeud or private war against Fulbert. There might be nothing dishonourable in this, provided the feud was conducted in accordance with the customary laws of war. In war, taking hostages is a prudent step which ensures that violence by the other side is reciprocated. If Fulbert's men were to 'debilitate' Abelard, for example by castrating or blinding him, the people of his 'country' (literally his 'fatherland' – *patria*) at Le Pallet might respond by aborting Heloise's child and blinding her. The word Abelard used for Heloise being made to 'suffer for it' is *plecteretur*, a Roman legal term meaning 'punished by due process'. Heloise might have been duly punished, 'member for member' and 'an eye for an eye', because reciprocity of terror was the logic of the bloodfeud as of any war. Taking reprisals against non-combatants has proved an effective tactic in war in the twentieth century as much as the twelfth.

Abelard describes how he played a waiting game with Fulbert who was in a state of 'immoderate anxiety'.[52] 'Then at last I had a meeting with the man and I vehemently accused myself of the highest treason.'[53] He was guilty of treason because he had betrayed Fulbert's trust in his own house. Abelard uses the same word 'treason' (*proditio*) later on to describe the crime of his servant, who had let Fulbert's men into the private room of his house to castrate him.[54] The servant had taken a bribe (Abelard says) and so when he was caught, he was blinded and castrated. Blinding and castrating was imposed for non-sexual offences, like that of Abelard's servant, as a mitigation of the death penalty. In sexual offences it was thought appropriate on the 'member for member' principle: the man's eyes had given him sight of the maiden and his testicles had induced the hot lust. Abelard was liable for blinding and castrating at the very least, as he had multiplied his offences. First he had 'corrupted' (literally 'broken into') a virgin, which was an irreversible crime as her 'member' could not be restored. He had betrayed Fulbert's hospitality, moreover, by doing this in his home. Fulbert had discovered them like Mars and Venus, naked and clasped together.[55] The reference is to the way Venus's aggrieved husband, Vulcan, made chains of such fine metal that they ensnared Mars and Venus and made a public spectacle of them. Henceforward, Abelard and Heloise, like Mars and Venus, were held together by invisible chains of shame and passion.

Most seriously of all, Abelard had betrayed Fulbert's trust a second time by abducting Heloise when she got pregnant: 'I secretly snatched her away from her uncle's house and sent her without delay into my country.'[56] Abduction, implying the use of force and deception, was tantamount to rape. It was Abelard's most serious crime, but it was also his best move, as it enabled him to use Heloise as a hostage. In coming to terms with Fulbert, Abelard would have been in a weak position otherwise, as he had no kin-group in Paris to match the men he describes as Fulbert's 'people' (suorum) or his 'blood-relatives and kinsmen' (consanguinei et affines).[57] There is some circumstantial evidence that Fulbert belonged to the Montmorency family, and in that case he could call on the support of one of the most powerful clans in France.[58] If Abelard were caught and taken to the castle of Montmorency, a little way down the Seine between St Denis and Argenteuil, the chances of anyone rescuing him were remote, even though he was a canon of Notre-Dame. If the Montmorency family castrated him, that might have been considered perfectly proper. If he died, the bishop of Paris might have written a letter urging the king to punish the perpetrators, but that is probably as far as the matter would have gone. The biography of Louis VI by Suger of St Denis is a yearly catalogue of the king's attempts to avenge violence done to churchmen. Abelard, a junior cleric and known troublemaker, might not have been given high priority. Furthermore, according to Suger, Burchard of Montmorency was an ally of Louis VI at this time.[59]

Nevertheless, Abelard held a trump card as long as his family had Heloise in their power. Le Pallet was far enough away from Paris for him to give the impression that he too came from a noble family in his native country. No Frenchman could reach Heloise there, not even a Montmorency. Perhaps this is when Abelard began to give himself grandiose airs as a Palatinus, a lord with influential friends back home. The Bretons had a reputation for primitive violence, which must have worked in Abelard's favour on this occasion. Once this precarious balance of fear was in place, Abelard engaged with Fulbert in the process which a later lawbook calls 'redeeming the members'.[60] Despite their being forfeit, a man could save his eyes and testicles provided the girl and her family agreed. Lawbooks contrasted the bad old days, when both men and women lost their lives in virginity cases, with their own day's enlightenment when even the lesser penalties of blinding and castrating were negotiable.

Abelard describes 'supplicating' Fulbert, which literally means getting down on his hands and knees, and 'promising him whatever sort of amends he might think fit'.[61] Abelard needed to make generous concessions because his advantage lasted only as long as Heloise remained in the power of his family. This is why he 'vehemently accused' himself of treason, though he also pleaded extenuating circumstances. 'Since the beginning of the human race', he reminded Fulbert, 'women have brought the noblest men to ruin.'[62] As so often, Abelard blamed someone else for his 'calamities'. This time it was the fault of Adam and Eve and of the 'force of love'.[63] At this point Abelard's story intersects with the stuff of the earliest romances, those Breton tales of forbidden love – heavy with sex, violence and betrayal – like Tristan and Iseult or Lancelot and Guinevere. In Breton folk-myth the reputation of Abelard and Heloise for learning turned them into a sinister couple who brew potions and do magic.[64]

Having eloquently begged Fulbert's forgiveness, Abelard came to the essence of the business: 'I offered to make him satisfaction by joining to me in matrimony her whom I had corrupted.'[65] Abelard says this was 'more than he could have hoped for'.[66] But would Fulbert have said the same? If he had been a Montmorency, or if he intended to cash in on Heloise's education by getting her appointed an abbess, he might have thought that Abelard was not good enough to marry her. On the other hand, Heloise herself later commented to Abelard: 'You made satisfaction for me more than amply by humiliating yourself and thereby you raised me and all my kin up to your level.'[67] This suggests that Heloise and Fulbert may not have been Abelard's social equals. But that, too, is hard to believe, as canons of great churches like Notre-Dame were generally drawn from the nobility. Possibly Heloise was not referring to the social standing of her 'kin' but to their moral and spiritual standing. By his Christlike generosity in humiliating himself before Fulbert, Abelard had exalted them all, and yet Fulbert had responded as meanly as ever by betraying the trust Abelard put in him.

In emphasizing that Fulbert betrayed Abelard, Heloise was reiterating his main point in the account of the marriage in his 'history of calamities'. There Fulbert and his 'people' are described 'entering into an agreement' about the marriage which they reinforced with pledges of good faith and kisses of peace.[68] Like Judas kissing Christ, Fulbert did this (Abelard alleges) 'the more easily to betray me'.[69] In other words, Fulbert intended to get Heloise back home to Paris and then renege on the agreement and take his revenge. Heloise had warned that Fulbert would never be placated by any sort of satisfaction, 'as later became evident' (Abelard adds).[70] Was he right to think that Fulbert had set out from the start to trick him? As the eventual outcome was that Abelard was castrated by Fulbert's men, it is understandable that he should have thought that Fulbert had intended this all along. The extent of his bitterness is shown by his appealing to Rome against the leniency shown to Fulbert, who had been punished only by the confiscation of his property.[71] But Abelard's failure to pursue this appeal and the restoration of Fulbert to his canonry at Notre-Dame (probably in 1119) suggests that the bishop and canons of Paris did not consider that he had committed such a heinous offence. There had been repeated provocation and many extenuating circumstances.

THE SECRECY OF THE MARRIAGE

Abelard does not conceal that the apparent generosity of his offer to Fulbert had been modified by his stipulation that the marriage 'be done secretly, so that I should not incur damage to my reputation'.[72] Lawyers dislike secret conditions in agreements. The most respected lawyer of Abelard's day was Ivo bishop of Chartres. He was especially influential in Paris because the bishops Galo (1104–16) and Gilbert (1116–23) were his protégés and he had played a large part in putting Louis VI on the throne in 1108. He was famed particularly for his views on marriage because he had objected to Philip I making a bigamous marriage in 1092. Both of Ivo's main works, the Decretum and the Panormia, cite authorities for it being unlawful to marry in secret.[73] The illegality of such a marriage meant that it incurred penalties; it did not mean that it was invalid de facto. The secret marriage of a bigamist was of course invalid, whereas the exchange of vows of a couple in good faith was not. Writing of marriage as a sacrament, Abelard's fellow master in Paris in the 1130s, Hugh of St Victor, insisted that 'whether such an agreement has been made publicly or secretly, it is judged a perfect sacrament of matrimony'.[74] However, secret marriages gave rise to so many disputes that Gratian concluded that forbidden unions should be invalid as well as illegal.[75] But Gratian's Decretum was not published until the 1140s. What mattered to Abelard in c.1117 was the opinions of Ivo of Chartres.

Secret marriages are particularly disliked in societies which depend on marriage alliances to transfer property, as they look like conspiracies to defraud. The secrecy which Abelard stipulated was certainly meant to defraud somebody: if not Fulbert, then his bishop and fellow canons of Notre-Dame, or the students who were sent to him from churches all over Europe because of the fame of his austerity as much as his brilliance. It was his 'reputation for continence' that had persuaded Fulbert to take him into his house in the first place.[76] This was the 'reputation' (*fama*) which Abelard could not afford to 'damage'. The opposite of good 'fame' was infamy, which carried severe ecclesiastical penalties. According to Ivo of Chartres, an infamous person could not proceed in court as a reliable witness and neither could he hold an ecclesiastical office.[77] This put Abelard's mastership of the schools of Notre-Dame in jeopardy. He stood to lose his career and the work of the last twenty years.

There was also the question of whether it was lawful for a man to marry his concubine, which is what Heloise had become. Later on Abelard included Ivo of Chartres's opinion on this question in his *Sic et Non* under the rubric: 'That nobody is allowed to take in marriage the woman he has fornicated with, and the contrary'.[78] The objections here were similar to those against secret marriages; a man might conspire to fornicate with an heiress and thereby defraud her parents and the lawful suitor of their property prospects. However, St Augustine had thought it permissible to marry one's concubine (though he had not married his own) and this led Ivo of Chartres to conclude that much depended on whether the law should be interpreted strictly or whether mercy should be shown in individual cases. The fact that Abelard was marrying his concubine and that Heloise was not a virgin cast shadows over his projected wedding, but these were probably not strong enough reasons for trying to make it secret.

Much more serious was that, in the diocese of Paris itself only a few years earlier, Ivo of Chartres had ruled that a canon who married should lose his benefice, even though the marriage was valid.[79] By 'lapsing from continence into conjugal voluptuousness', Ivo argued, the canon had descended from a superior to an inferior rank in the clerical militia. The clerical order had been instituted for the service of God and it was financed by the laity solely on that basis. 'Manifestly', he concluded, 'a married cleric is a violator of the canonical institution' as he gets something for nothing. Ivo's use of 'manifestly' suggests that he was pushing his argument further than the precedents warranted. Nevertheless, his opinion accorded in general with that of ecclesiastical reformers and idealists of the previous fifty years and, in particular, with the prohibition issued by the council of Beauvais in 1114.[80] At the council of Reims in 1119, a year or two after Abelard's marriage, similar legislation was issued. Conducting his fight with Fulbert in Paris in c.1117, Abelard found himself in a very sensitive time and place as far as the sexual relations of the clergy were concerned.

In reaching a decision on Abelard, the bishop of Paris and the canons of Notre-Dame had various choices. They were not bound to follow the advice of Ivo of Chartres. Among the most senior canons was the archdeacon, Stephen de Garlande, who had been castigated by Ivo of Chartres in 1101 as an adulterer and excommunicate and yet was still in place; he may also have been Abelard's patron.[81] As Stephen was Louis VI's chancellor and his brother was the royal seneschal, he was among the most powerful men in France. His prominent place – and permanence – in the chapter of Notre-Dame took visible shape in the magnificent house and chapel he built himself on the northern side of the cloister. If Archdeacon Stephen de Garlande chose not to know officially that Abelard was married, then no such marriage had taken place as far as one ecclesiastical authority was concerned.

Like the secular life of Stephen de Garlande, Abelard's marriage could be an official secret and a private reality at the same time, even within the cloister of Notre-Dame where Abelard, Heloise and Fulbert were proposing to live at close quarters once more. Outsiders like Ivo of Chartres (and St Bernard in the 1120s) might repeat that Stephen was a disgrace to the clerical order, but his colleagues in Paris continued to turn a blind eye. It was safer that way. When in 1133 a new bishop commissioned Thomas prior of St Victor to investigate the archdeacons of Paris, he came too close to Stephen de Garlande's castle at Gournay-sur-Marne and was murdered.[82] He died in the arms of the bishop of Paris under Stephen's castle walls. Nobody was successfully prosecuted. But the fact that Stephen might get away with murder did not mean that Abelard's offence of abducting a fellow canon's daughter was equally privileged. Being Stephen's protégé, if that is what he was, did not save him from Fulbert's revenge. On the night of the castration, Abelard had no bodyguard; he was protected only by the servant who allegedly betrayed him.[83] Perhaps, however, Stephen's knights lent a hand after the castration in blinding and castrating Abelard's servant and the man of Fulbert's who was caught.

The fact was that the marriage could be kept secret only if Fulbert and Abelard co-operated over every detail of the plan. First of all, Heloise had to continue living with Fulbert, as if she were still his ward, and he had to allow Abelard to make conjugal visits, even though it was the sight of them together that had driven him almost insane in the first place. Since then, however, he and Abelard had exchanged the kiss of peace and sworn eternal friendship. There was just a chance, therefore, that they could make the secrecy of the marriage work. Some clergy, like the Norman bishops and canons in England, kept wives and concubines officially secret for years.[84] But they were in a stronger position than Abelard, as they were themselves the enforcers of the law, whereas he was not even an archdeacon. The secrecy of the marriage was a humiliation for everyone concerned, especially for Fulbert who got no public redress for the dishonour he had suffered. All he had achieved by his agreement with Abelard was the return of Heloise to his house. Some of his family, if not Fulbert himself, may have thought this was insultingly little.

With each month and year that passed, keeping the marriage secret would grow more difficult and also more necessary, if Abelard was to maintain his reputation as an austere and celibate master. In France ecclesiastical reformers were becoming more vociferous and influential, notably St Bernard who came into full voice in the 1120s. Further children might be born to Heloise and Abelard, who would have to be smuggled out of the cloister and adopted, like the unfortunate Astralabe who remained at Le Pallet. Pressure might be put on Heloise by her family or by admirers to marry someone else and she would find it difficult to explain why she could not. Over time, too, one or other of the canons of Notre-Dame might break ranks and reveal the secret. Senior ones, who remembered Abelard harassing William of Champeaux or who agreed with St Goswin that he was a mere jester, would be delighted to see him expelled. Unlike Stephen de Garlande, he was not an essential member of their community, as he was not a royal officer nor a commander of knights. He was not a Parisian nor even a Frenchman, but a Breton adventurer who deserved to be judged infamous.

Abelard may have exaggerated the secrecy of his marriage in order to put the blame on Fulbert for disclosing it. He insists that he and Heloise 'returned to Paris secretly', leaving their 'poor little one' in the care of his sister at Le Pallet.[85] The Île-de-la-Cité, moated round by the Seine, could scarcely be approached secretly, least of all by Abelard, who was allegedly so famous. Heloise had been away from Paris for six months or more. Her return would give rise to speculation and gossip and she might have difficulty concealing her distress. She had been threatened with violence, compelled to leave her little baby as a hostage in Brittany, and now she was expected to start living with her uncle again as if nothing had happened. Abelard describes how he and Heloise celebrated a night's 'secret vigil of prayer in a certain church' on the eve of the wedding.[86] Keeping this vigil shows how seriously they took the religious side of the marriage. As far as secrecy was concerned, however, the vigil cannot have been prudent, as its celebration required lit candles and chanting.

The 'certain church' where the wedding took place has never been identified, to the disappointment of visitors to Paris over the centuries. It is just possible that Abelard and Heloise were married in Stephen de Garlande's new chapel, if this were complete by c.1118, as it had the advantage of adjoining the cloister of Notre-Dame and being relatively private. In his 'history of calamities' Abelard does not describe a clandestine ceremony, as he needed to emphasize that the wedding complied with canon law. It was celebrated 'at dawn', to accord with the rule that weddings must take place in daylight, and 'we were joined by the nuptial blessing in the presence of her uncle and certain friends of ours and his'.[87] The presence of these witnesses for both parties likewise complied with canon law, and Abelard's mention of the nuptial blessing shows that the ceremony was conducted by a priest. In all essentials, their marriage accorded with the legal and sacramental requirements of the Church at the time.[88] It was the events following the wedding which were so peculiar.

MARRIAGE AS DIVORCE

The biggest secret about the marriage of Abelard and Heloise was that it was effectively a divorce. He describes how they separated as soon as they came out of the church 'and we did not see each other any more except very occasionally and secretly, concealing to the uttermost what we had done'.[89] The unforgivable thing they had done was to get married. For a cleric, marrying was a more serious offence than fornicating because marriage was irreversible and provable. It was a formal commitment to repeated acts of sexual gratification, even though these were limited by numerous ecclesiastical prohibitions concerning the times, postures and states of mind and body appropriate to sexual intercourse.[90] In the eyes of the clergy, the sexual element in marriage was something gross, which they had dedicated themselves to overcoming. This is why Ivo of Chartres had called the married state 'conjugal voluptuousness' in his letter to the bishop of Paris.[91] Marriage was demeaning to the 'clerical militia' because they were the elite corps in the daily fight against 'voluptuousness' and all the worldly evils it comprised.

As Ivo's letter had been written to the bishop of Paris perhaps only a year or two earlier, Heloise may have had his words in mind when she reminded Abelard that he, as a 'cleric and canon', should rise above 'filthy voluptuousness' and not 'shamelessly and irrevocably get immersed in these obscenities'.[92] The keyword here is 'irrevocably'. Occasional visits to her, just for a quick dip as it were, were preferable to the total immersion involved in marriage. In this world turned upside down, Heloise was right to insist that it was more honourable for her to be called Abelard's mistress or 'girl-friend' (*amica*) than his wife.[93] The dishonour of her marriage was soon demonstrated. Fulbert and his household began to publicize it, contrary to the promise they had made (Abelard says), because they could not bear the ignominy of their situation.[94] Instead of rescuing her family and friends from their humiliation by admitting that she had married Abelard, and that Fulbert and others had witnessed this, Heloise denied she was married. She 'cursed and swore that it was a total falsehood'.[95] Fulbert was 'vehemently aroused'.[96] By insulting her family with these blatant lies, Heloise was in danger of being driven from her home. This forced Abelard to come out into the open and take charge of her.

'I sent her', he says, 'to an abbey of nuns near Paris called Argenteuil, where she had been brought up and educated when she was a little girl'.[97] The word Abelard uses for 'I sent' is *transmisi*, literally 'I transmitted' her, which is the same word he had used to describe his earlier abduction of her, when he had 'transmitted' her to his family in Brittany as the first move in his feud with Fulbert.[98] This time, though, Abelard was acting with greater legality, provided he made it clear he was Heloise's husband and was therefore entitled to remove her from her family home. She confirms that it was at his 'command' that she went to Argenteuil, 'and thus we were separated from each other, so that you might study more in the schools and I have more freedom to devote to prayer and meditation on sacred books'.[99] Although Abelard had been entitled to 'command' Heloise to leave Fulbert's house, he may have been exceeding the powers of a husband in making her enter a convent, as that was tantamount to terminating their marriage. Strictly speaking, Argenteuil should have refused to accept Heloise if she were not coming in of her own free will. A couple might separate by mutual consent when they both elected to enter religious houses, as Abelard's parents had done on their retirement, but this was not what he was doing. He can have had no intention of entering a monastery at this time, as that would have endangered his career in the schools. It was also questionable whether he could, one-sidedly, terminate the marriage contract which he had so recently and formally entered into with Fulbert.

In one respect, as Heloise pointed out to Abelard, their lives did accord with the monastic rule, as their separation meant that they were 'as holy as they were chaste'.[100] But he spoiled her idyllic picture by reminding her how he had made love to her in the nuns' refectory at Argenteuil.[101] What was he doing in the convent in the first place? His recollection of being in the refectory, and having nowhere else to go (he adds), suggests that he may have been allowed to visit Heloise, provided he kept to the public parts of the convent. (She shows in her later questions to Abelard about proper monastic conduct that men might sit at an abbess's table, even though there was the risk of their getting drunk or lecherous).[102] She may have been permitted visitors at Argenteuil because her status was not that of a fully-fledged nun but of an associate; *conversans* is the term which both Abelard and Heloise use.[103] A 'conversant' shared in the life of the convent without being either a full nun or a novice. As a 'conversant' Heloise wore a nun's habit, apart from the veil which signified final vows.

When Fulbert and his family heard about this, Abelard admits they thought he had tricked them and that he merely wanted to find an easy way out for himself by making Heloise a nun.[104] As he acknowledged that 'I had the religious habit fitted for her and I put it on her', this was the obvious conclusion to draw, as investing a person with a uniform signified a rite of passage from one status in society to another.[105] In their subsequent correspondence neither Abelard nor Heloise offer any other explanation for this. Before considering Fulbert's extreme response of castrating Abelard, it is worth asking why he objected to Heloise being a nun. Entering a convent was the best solution for her, provided she did it of her own free will and Abelard could be persuaded to follow suit. (These conditions had not yet been met.) In returning to Argenteuil, Heloise was settling back into her childhood home. She could not have remained in Fulbert's house at Notre-Dame indefinitely, as he too might be subject to the mounting pressure to expel all women from ecclesiastical precincts. Her precocious education had prepared Heloise for no other role than being a nun.[106] The days were gone when an ambitious cleric like Abelard could live with a woman as his social and intellectual equal, although he might still have a mistress on the side (as Heloise pointed out).

Does this mean that Abelard and Heloise had no other way out? Or, could they have got married with Fulbert's assent and lived openly as man and wife? Almost certainly they could have done so, provided Abelard resigned his office as master at Notre-Dame. He might readily have found other honourable employment, either in Paris or elsewhere. If he was Stephen de Garlande's protégé, he might have got a job at the royal court or been found a benefice in some part of France where the rules of celibacy were less demanding. Stephen was notorious for dealing in rich benefices. If Abelard had been a royal officer, he would have been on a faster career track for a bishopric than by struggling in the schools of Notre-Dame. Alternatively, he might have found a benefice in Brittany or Poitou through his own family connections. Later on, a canonry was found at Nantes for Astralabe (Abelard and Heloise's son), even though he was disqualified from ecclesiastical office by being the child of a cleric.[107] Even without an ecclesiastical benefice at all, Abelard could have turned to schoolmastering, as he had done at the beginning of his career, when William of Champeaux had driven him out of Paris. In a secluded provincial school Heloise might have assisted with the teaching, when child-bearing and domestic circumstances permitted, much as Master Manegold of Lautenbach's daughters are said to have assisted him.[108]

In reality, speculations of this sort are vacuous because Abelard did not consider himself an ordinary person, who should take whatever employment was available to support his wife and child. 'I thought myself to be the only philosopher in the world,' is how he describes his state of mind at this time.[109] He had no mundane ambitions for benefices or money, but he did expect everyone to acknowledge the uniqueness of his genius. This was the personage whom Heloise fell in love with. She believed in his role of superman as much as he did. 'What king or philosopher could equal your fame?', she rhetorically demanded.[110] He was her emperor and she would be his handmaiden, or even his whore. Their relationship had not begun as a partnership of equals and it had little prospect of developing into cosy domesticity.

This is the significance of Heloise's recorded objections to the marriage, which look extravagant and perverse unless they are seen in the light of their shared obsession with Abelard's standing in the world. 'Nature', she told him, 'had created him for everybody' and so he must not subject himself to one woman; to do so would be gross moral turpitude.[111] The great sages of the ancient world, Pythagoras and Socrates, Cicero and Seneca, had lived and died for their philosophy. Scepticism or Stoicism had not been part-time occupations, but utterly absorbing and lonely vocations. This is why these sages had quarrelled with their wives or divorced them. Domesticity had degraded Socrates and it would 'crucify' Abelard, Heloise warned him.[112] If he did not care about his own rank as a cleric, he should at least uphold the dignity of a philosopher.[113] Even if reverence towards God was to be despised, his love of honour should at least restrain his shamelessness.[114] Marriage could not bring them any closer, nor could it deepen their love. At best, it would separate and humiliate them; at worst, it would destroy them. Because this prediction came true, Abelard believed Heloise had prophetic powers, whereas she seems simply to have been following through the consequences of his thinking that he was superior to the ordinary conventions of human society.[115]

If Abelard thought so highly of himself, why did he insist on getting married? Perhaps he was frightened into it by Fulbert and his kinsmen. The explanation he gave later to Heloise was that 'I wanted to keep you for myself for ever, as I loved you inordinately'.[116] Had they not been held by the bond of marriage, he explained, she might 'easily' have been enticed by sexual delights elsewhere or persuaded by her family to leave him.[117] He persisted in telling her this even after she had chided him for his lack of faith in her.[118] She might always fail him, he seems to have thought, because she was a woman and weaker by nature. 'Woman has been created for catastrophe,' he wrote in his lament for Samson, 'she invariably brings the greatest ruin on strong men.'[119] Dalila had drained Samson, a 'noble champion' like Abelard, of his strength and manhood. This lament may have been written 'first and foremost for Heloise', though how she was expected to interpret it is a controversial question.[120] As she had expressed an equally low view of womankind, Abelard may have been echoing her or even parodying her. The tone of such statements is difficult to gauge, as they belong to a genre of anti-feminist writings going back for centuries.[121]

After he had become a monk, Abelard made attacks on marriage which likewise accord with centuries of anti-feminist writing. He told some monks in a sermon that no chain was heavier than the marriage bond because it takes away a man's power even over his body.[122] 'We learn from earlier testimonies and the experiences of lapses', he wrote in *Theologia Christiana*, 'how great are the obstacles, the burdens, and the dangers in which marriage abounds'.[123] This statement is significant because it can be dated to a few years after his castration and his reference to 'experiences' may mean that he was thinking of his own case. Abelard's attacks on marriage suggest that he thought castration had released him from its 'chains'. No importunate wife could make demands on his body because it had been irrevocably deprived of its virile power. When he came to write his 'history of calamities' (about a decade after *Theologia Christiana*), he described Heloise as: 'our sister in Christ rather than wife'.[124]

Christopher Brooke has argued that when Abelard made Heloise become a nun, he was insisting that 'their union be dissolved spiritually as well as carnally, by both partners entering religion'.[125] This may well have been what was in Abelard's mind, though he must also have been aware that they remained married in terms of ecclesiastical law, as separation did not dissolve marriage and neither did impotence after consummation. This is why Heloise insisted, fifteen years later when they exchanged the letters which follow on from his 'history of calamities', that he should pay his debts to her in accordance with the 'close bond of the nuptial sacrament', and he reciprocated by acknowledging that 'God has bound us together by the indissoluble law of the nuptial sacrament'.[126] They were spiritually united, though physically set apart, like all couples who separated in order to lead a monastic life. This is what Abelard's own parents had done on their retirement. He argued that his spiritual marriage with Heloise, the bride of Christ (which is what she became on being a nun), raised their love to a higher plane; whether her silence means that she agreed with him is impossible to know. A contemporary poem comments that it was right for his mother to take the veil because she was old, whereas he had forced Heloise into the convent and abandoned her there.[127]

Castration as Reconciliation

Abelard's castration had as paradoxical consequences for him and Heloise as their marriage had done. The marriage had inevitably brought about their immediate separation. The castration, on the other hand, brought them closer together, first in adversity and then in spiritual love. At least, this was his interpretation of events, even if she did not share it. He addressed his last recorded statement, his Confession of Faith, not to St Bernard and the prelates at the council of Sens in 1140 who were demanding it, but to Heloise: 'once dear to me in the world, now dearest in Christ'.[128] 'In the world', as he had confessed to her in previous letters, he had been violent and exploitative: 'because you were weaker by nature, I often drove you to consent with threats and whippings, as I was so strongly coupled to you by burning lust and obscenity'.[129] This may be exaggerated, as he was writing with remorse long after his castration, and it is also conceivable that she had liked it that way. He adds that he habitually hit her, when he had been her tutor, in order 'to avert suspicion'.[130] This may well be so, as corporal punishment was integral to medieval education. But, if he continued beating her after he was married, he put himself in danger. If she returned to Fulbert's house from a clandestine conjugal visit and showed signs of bruising, she could not defend herself with the argument that a husband, as much as a schoolmaster, was entitled to administer corporal punishment, as she denied that Abelard was her husband. His violence towards her may have been a contributory cause of Fulbert's family's infliction of violence on him.

The immediate cause of the castration was presumably the one that Abelard gives in his 'history of calamities': that Fulbert and his family thought he was going to get out of his marriage by making Heloise a nun.[131] Even Abelard admitted that his castration was not an act of mindless violence, but a punishment. Where he differed from Fulbert's family was in thinking the penalty excessive. 'They punished me', he says, 'with the cruellest and most shameful revenge.'[132] This was an exaggeration, as he describes in his next sentence how two of his attackers suffered an even crueller punishment, as they were blinded as well as being castrated.[133] One of these was Abelard's servant who had betrayed him and might therefore be appropriately punished for treason, but the other was presumably a kinsman of Fulbert's who was doing no more than his familial duty in being in the castration party. Not surprisingly, Heloise agreed with Abelard that his punishment had been excessive:

The penalty you suffered would have been sufficient for men caught in flagrant adultery. What others deserve for adultery, you incurred through a marriage which you were confident had made satisfaction for all previous wrongs. What adulterous women bring upon their paramours, your own wife brought upon you.[134]

In one way Heloise was being naive, as she was not taking account of the wrongs they had both done to her family *since* their marriage: she by denying that it had taken place and he by abducting her to Argenteuil. Nevertheless, her point of view is endorsed by an anonymous Latin poem, which compares the castration of Abelard with that of another distinguished Breton, Matthew the Consul, son of the duke of Brittany. He was 'justly punished' for adultery, the poem says, whereas Abelard's castration was a 'supreme betrayal'.[135] Only Abelard's wife, the poem adds, 'is free of guilt, for there was no consent on her part to make her culpable'.[136] This last comment, which rebuts Heloise's reproaches of herself, suggests that the poet was a schoolman familiar with the arguments of Abelard's *Ethics* that there can be no sin without consent to the deed. This need not mean, however, that the poet had read anything of Abelard's, as gossip was rife and his predecessor in the Paris schools, William of Champeaux, had likewise taught that sin is not a thing in itself.[137] The poet's aim may have been to reassure his audience, in the immediate aftermath of the castration, that Heloise had not been a party to it despite being a member of Fulbert's family. This is why she described herself as 'very guilty and very innocent' at one and the same time.[138]

It is significant that Heloise and the poet agree that castration is a lawful punishment, but that it should not apply to Abelard because he is not an adulterer. No lawbooks survive from northern France from this period to clarify what was lawful practice in sexual cases. But there is enough anecdotal evidence to leave no doubt that the prosecution of such cases was the jealously-guarded prerogative of the aggrieved family, rather than of any public authority, and that this meant resort to blood-feud and private war. There is a lawbook from England, the *Laws of Henry I*, which is contemporary with Abelard's castration and which has connections with France, as it was probably written by a Norman. Its chapter on the rules for conducting feuds throws some light on Abelard's case. A man is entitled to fight (i.e. to use force), the author says, against anyone he finds with his wife, daughter, sister or mother within closed doors or under the same bedcover.[139] It was when Fulbert discovered Abelard and Heloise clasped together 'like Mars and Venus' that Abelard had taken flight and abducted Heloise.[140] But the *Laws of Henry I* strictly limit the aggrieved man's rights of retaliation: he has to have discovered and warned the fornicator three times before proceeding; he has to have seen the couple's genitalia actually joined in sexual intercourse; and even then, castration is prescribed only for persistent offenders.

The limitations described in the *Laws of Henry I*, combined with Heloise's and the poet's comments, suggest that many contemporaries thought Abelard's castration was an excessive punishment. This accords with his description of the news of it giving rise to 'the utmost consternation', a reaction that is corroborated by Fulk of Deuil, who describes the bishop of Paris trying to adjudicate among the 'multitude of canons and clerics', while the citizens worry that the spilling of blood has violated the good name of the Cité.[141] Fulk agreed too that the castration itself had been an act of deception, rather than a lawful move in a bloodfeud, and here again he corroborates Abelard (and Heloise). 'You had surrendered your members to rest and sleep,' Fulk reminded him, 'you were intending no harm to anyone, when suddenly impious hands with fatal steel showed no hesitation in liberally shedding your innocent blood.'[142] But Fulk did not agree with Abelard that Fulbert had been treated too leniently. He pointed out that even though Fulbert denied the castration had been done by him, the bishop and canons of Notre-Dame had expelled him and confiscated all his goods and possessions.[143] 'So don't go calling the bishop and canons your destroyers and the spillers of your blood', Fulk warned Abelard, 'as they intended justice. They have done as much as they could, both on your account and their own.'[144] The records of Notre-Dame confirm that leniency was shown to Fulbert, as his canonry had been restored by 1 April 1119, when he witnesses a charter.[145] His expulsion had lasted no more than a year or two.

Fulbert's denial of responsibility deprived the castration of any legality which it might have had, as he was the offended party who had duly sworn with his kinsmen to exact punishment.[146] His denial of his own oath left the men who had done the castration with no legal defence. But it saved Fulbert's canonry and possessions. They would almost certainly have been forfeit, if he had admitted to plotting a bloodfeud against a fellow canon within the precinct of Notre-Dame. Fulk confirms that 'some of the men' (Abelard says 'two') who did the castration were blinded and castrated, but neither writer says who carried this out.[147] At a guess, it was done by the knights of Stephen de Garlande, who was the dean of Notre-Dame, as well as perhaps being Abelard's patron. How the alarm was raised so quickly, and why some of Fulbert's men failed to get away is not known.

Fulbert was technically correct to say that the castration had not been 'done by him', as he had presumably not wielded the knife in person and he may not even have been present. Exactly what happened can only be conjectured. The castrating party may have been hidden by Fulbert in his house in the precinct of Notre-Dame until well after dark, when they received a signal from Abelard's servant that his master was asleep. The party is unlikely to have consisted of a 'gang of roughs' or 'thugs', as recent historians have suggested.[148] If Fulbert was a member of the Montmorency clan, he should have been able to call on the best professional help. Even if he were not, he had to ensure that Abelard was not killed in the process, as that would certainly have put Fulbert's canonry – and perhaps even his life – in danger. (Clerics were not supposed to shed blood whatever the circumstances, though the presence of Stephen de Garlande as archdeacon and dean at Notre-Dame made a nonsense of that rule in Paris.) A drawing of a judicial castration in a thirteenth-century lawbook from Toulouse shows a knight pulling a man's tunic over his head, while a civilian (possibly a surgeon) stands behind him. With additional knights standing guard on each side, the civilian draws the man's scrotum tight with a cord (to stem the bleeding) while he cuts the testicles out with a knife.[149] This was presumably the professional way to perform a castration. A cruder way is described by Guibert de Nogent, who alleges that in the rebellion at Laon in 1112 Thomas of Marle hung prisoners up by their testicles.[150]

Abelard's castration seems to have been done with surgical care. It was so 'short and sudden', he says, that 'I felt almost no pain'.[151] His servant may have secretly given him some sort of soporific drug, as

Abelard adds that he was 'weighed down by sleep'. As a canon of Notre-Dame, Fulbert had access to the best surgical and pharmaceutical services in France, and he need not have revealed what he was intending, as he might have wanted to assist a wounded knight or some other sick person.[152] In addition to an anaesthetic, it looks as if antiseptic measures were taken, as Abelard says the wound did not afflict or debilitate him nearly as much as the fractured neckbone he suffered later when he fell from his horse.[153] Even on the morning after the castration, he remembered being 'hurt much more by the commiserations of my students than by the pain of the wound', and he felt himself blushing with shame rather than bleeding from the cut.[154]

Abelard's comments are of course subjective and their purpose in his 'history of calamities' is to demonstrate that physical pain is as nothing, compared with the mental agony of being condemned as a heretic (at Soissons in 1121) or persecuted by his own monks (at St Gildas ten years later).[155] Even so, his admission that the castration was not physically painful confirms that it was an exaggeration to call it the 'cruellest' penalty.[156] Four or five years earlier in 1113, when he had been at Laon doing his best to undermine Master Anselm, Abelard might have been taken prisoner by Thomas of Marle and subjected to far greater cruelties, particularly if he were thought to be an agent of Stephen de Garlande.[157] Abelard exaggerated because he was recalling such strong and conflicting emotions. He remembered all sorts of thoughts coming to his mind at the time of the castration: yesterday he had been at the height of his glory, today he was utterly destroyed; by God's judgement he had been justly struck down in the very part of his body which had offended; there was even some justice in Fulbert's treachery, as he was simply paying him back for the way Abelard had treated him; with what glee his rivals would gloat over the manifest appropriateness of his castration![158] There was also the certainty that his family would get to hear of it in Brittany and his 'singular infamy would be the talk of the whole world'.[159] 'What way out was there now?', Abelard desperately asked himself.[160]

It seems to have been Gilbert, the bishop of Paris, who found a way out for Abelard. In Fulk of Deuil's words, he did what he could 'to make room for justice'.[161] This meant making compromises and not insisting on the letter of the law. On the one hand, the bishop supported Abelard by blessing the veil which symbolized Heloise's final vows at Argenteuil. This was improper, if not illegal, as she had not made her vows of her own free will and neither had she completed a novitiate (though she was a 'conversant').[162] On the other hand, to compensate Fulbert for the loss of his beloved niece, the bishop punished him relatively lightly, and this leniency may also have recognized the provocation he had suffered and his denial of responsibility for the castration itself. (Fulbert's aim in the castration may have been to dissolve the marriage and then compel Heloise to leave Argenteuil and return home. But Abelard, aided by the bishop of Paris, outmanoeuvred him by making her take the veil.) As for Abelard himself, he was got out of sight by making him a monk of St Denis. He should have no reason to feel humiliated there, as it was one of the most distinguished abbeys in France. It was also close enough to Paris for him to keep in touch with the schools, and close too to Argenteuil, if he were concerned about Heloise. Whether Abbot Adam and the monks of St Denis wished to take Abelard in is a different matter, however. Perhaps they believed that castration had chastened him, or they may have succumbed to the pressures of Bishop Gilbert and Abelard's other Parisian supporters. He always had friends in high places.

Castration did not subdue Abelard for long. First of all, he tried (without success) to sue the bishop and canons of Paris in the papal curia at Rome for showing leniency towards Fulbert.[163] Then Abelard began 'frequently and vehemently' telling the monks of St Denis how lax and scandalous they were, and in particular how Abbot Adam's pre-eminence was only matched by the infamy of his life.[164] Roscelin (admittedly an enemy) gives a very different account of how Adam, the 'wisest' of abbots, out of pity for Abelard and in consideration for his weakness, dispensed him from the rigour of the monastic rule.[165] What was really going on at St Denis is impossible to establish. The significant point is that Abelard's account shows that he entered into monastic life with the same competitive and critical spirit he had shown in the schools: his fellow monks were fools, or worse, and their abbot was a scoundrel. Just as he had thought himself to be 'the only philosopher in the world' when he headed the Paris schools, so now he was the only true monk.[166] As his 'calamities' gathered pace, his egotism swelled to sustain him. In 1118, as he rapidly recovered his self-esteem by telling his benefactors at St Denis that they were all in the wrong, his worst 'calamities' were only a few years away. The furies were hunting him down. Satan allowed him no rest, Abelard thought; his torments came from within and without: from the fears churning up inside him and from the strife that incessantly surrounded him.[167]

Part III

Religio – 'Religion'

The Years 1118–42

CHRONOLOGICAL TABLE 1118–42

Innocent II, pope, 1130–43
Anacletus II, antipope, 1130–8
Cono of Praeneste, papal legate, 1111–22
Geoffrey de Lèves, bishop of Chartres, 1116–49
Peter the Venerable, abbot of Cluny, 1122–56
St Bernard, abbot of Clairvaux, 1115–53
Suger, abbot of St Denis, 1122–51
Louis VI, king of France, 1108–37
Louis VII, king of France, 1137–80
Thibaud, count palatine, count of Blois and Chartres 1107–52, count of Champagne 1107–1152, count of Troyes 1125–52
Conan III, count of Nantes and duke of Brittany, 1112–48

c.1119	Abelard resumes teaching at a cell of the abbey of St Denis, perhaps close to Paris.
c.1120	He complains to Gilbert bishop of Paris about Roscelin.
1121	Abelard's *Theologia* condemned at Soissons.
1121	He insults St Denis and flees to Count Thibaud at Provins.
1122	Stephen de Garlande makes peace between Abelard and Suger of St Denis.
c.1122	Near Troyes, Abelard founds the hermitage which he subsequently dedicates to the Paraclete.
c.1125–*c*.1127	He goes back to Brittany as abbot of St Gildas.
1129	Heloise and her nuns expelled from Argenteuil by Suger of St Denis. Abelard returns to Champagne and gives them his hermitage of the Paraclete.
1130	Papal schism: double election of Innocent II and Anacletus II.
1131	Abelard at Morigny with Pope Innocent II and St Bernard.
1131	Innocent II takes Heloise and her nuns under papal protection.
c.1132	A papal legate (?Geoffrey bishop of Chartres) goes to Brittany to discipline the monks of St Gildas.
c.1133	The monks again try to kill Abelard. He returns to Paris as a master at Mont Sainte Geneviève.
1136	John of Salisbury is taught logic by Abelard at Mont Sainte Geneviève.
c.1139	Arnold of Brescia joins Abelard as a master at the church of St Hilary on Mont Sainte Geneviève.
1140	Abelard accused of heresy by St Bernard at the council of Sens. Appeals to Rome.

1140   Abelard sentenced by Pope Innocent II to perpetual silence as a
            heretic.
1140   Abelard protected by Peter the Venerable at Cluny.
c.1142   Abelard dies at the Cluniac house of St Marcel near Chalon-
            sur-Saône.

10

Religio – 'Religion'

The most precise date in Abelard's life concerns his religion. The chronicle of Morigny abbey describes how on 20 January 1131 he was present when Pope Innocent II, with eleven cardinals and many other prelates in his entourage, consecrated 'the altar in front of the crucifix' in the abbey church.[1] The chronicle devotes more words of praise to Abelard than to anyone else in that distinguished congregation, though St Bernard comes a close second, as he is described as 'the most famous preacher of the divine word that there was in France at that time'.[2] Abelard is praised as a monk and abbot and also as 'that religious (*religiosus*) man' and 'most excellent director of schools, to which the learned men from almost the whole of the Latin world came flocking'.[3] One might think that Abelard had supplied his own 'press-release' to the Morigny chronicler, which got copied down verbatim. This is possible, as Abelard is not shy about singing his own praises elsewhere in his works, and Thomas, the abbot of Morigny, was a schoolman himself who claimed to be Abelard's very special friend.[4]

In 1131 Abelard needed all the praise and friendship he could muster, as his purpose in seeking out the pope at Morigny was to get help against his monks at St Gildas, who he believed were trying to poison him. In this he was successful, as Geoffrey bishop of Chartres (who had been the preacher at the ceremony at Morigny) was sent to Brittany as a papal legate and he exacted pledges of good behaviour from Abelard's monks.[5] In the event this turned out to be worse than useless, as Abelard says the remaining monks tried to cut his throat.[6] This is when he left St Gildas for good (perhaps by the end of 1132). The gap between the rhetoric of the Papacy's claim to be the greatest ruler on earth and the reality of its ineffectiveness on the ground was often exposed like this, and yet people kept flocking to it for justice and protection. Heloise, too, sought its favours and got a bull from Innocent II placing her nuns and all their endowments under the protection of the Apostolic See.[7]

This was dated 28 November 1131. As papal bulls might take months to ratify, Heloise's document may have first been asked for at Morigny on 20 January when Abelard was present. The fact that the chronicler makes no mention of her presence at Morigny does not mean that she was not there, as he lists the congregation in hierarchical order. Just as women had no part in the ceremonial procession into the abbey to consecrate the altar, so they have no record in its chronicle.

Entries in monastic chronicles tend to be like this one from Morigny. They are very precise and detailed about points of religious ceremonial which now seem of little importance, while being partial or silent about matters of social or political history. But this is to misunderstand the purpose of chronicles. For the monks of Morigny the consecration of their altar by the pope was a much more important matter to record than whether Heloise had been present in the abbey church as well as 'that religious man', Master Abelard. The chronicler may have thought that the less said about Heloise the better, as it was less than two years since she had been expelled from Argenteuil for notorious immorality (whatever the rights and wrongs of that may have been) by the papal legate, Cardinal Matthew of Albano, and the bishops of the Paris region, including Geoffrey of Chartres who was present at Morigny, as was the cardinal of Albano.[8]

THE PAPAL SCHISM OF 1130

From the modern historian's point of view, the Morigny chronicle is silent about a more important fact than the presence or absence of Heloise, and that is that Innocent II was not necessarily the rightful pope. He was travelling round France in 1131 doing his best to be agreeable to religious houses as modest as Morigny because his rival, Pope Anacletus II, had driven him out of Rome. The cardinals, whose sonorous Roman titles ('Cardinal Deacon of St Maria Novella' and so on) are so lovingly recorded by the Morigny chronicler, were replicated in Rome itself by another set.[9] The double election had taken place on 14 February 1130. So, Innocent II was still in the thick of his struggle for recognition, when he came to Morigny (south of Paris, near Étampes) on 20 January 1131. The week before, he had won the support of Henry I of England and Normandy, who pledged obedience to him at Chartres, and shortly before that of Louis VI of France.[10] Until he had established himself, Innocent II and his cardinals needed to be helpful to people even with reputations as dubious as Abelard and Heloise. This was a change from the time of the formidable Calixtus II (1119–24), when Fulk of

Deuil had advised Abelard that he did not stand a hope of winning his prosecution against Fulbert and the canons of Notre-Dame in the Roman curia: 'Have you never heard of the avarice and filth of the Romans? Who could ever satisfy with money the gaping hole of such harlots?'[11]

Innocent II's most crucial supporter was St Bernard, even though he was neither a bishop nor a king. He was more than the 'most famous preacher in France', as the Morigny chronicle described him, because the force of his personality impacted on everyone with whom he came into contact and he seems to have been as effective through his letters as he was in person.[12] A letter from St Bernard literally put the fear of God into its recipient. His style is well illustrated by his letter in 1131 to Hildebert of Lavardin (the great Latin poet), who was archbishop of Tours and was being slow to recognize Innocent II. 'I will speak to you in the words of the prophet,' St Bernard begins, 'those who are of God have freely joined with Innocent, the Lord's anointed, and he who stands over against him is of Antichrist.'[13] After a battery of Biblical warnings about the abomination of desolation, Shimei in his wrath, Achitophel the false counsellor, and bowing the knee to Baal, St Bernard turns his charm (which could be as effective as his threats) on Hildebert, who was his senior in age as much as in status:

And so, Father, your decision is eagerly awaited, late though it may be, descending 'like rain upon the mown grass'. We do not blame your slowness. For, at the Annunciation, Mary did not reply to the angel's salutation immediately, before she had thought over what sort of salutation it might be.[14]

St Bernard and Innocent II grew to depend on each other. His success in winning supporters for the pope convinced him that he spoke for God. And, as Innocent II's power as pope began to extend over Christendom, St Bernard too came to believe that his voice should be heeded everywhere and that he had no earthly superior.

At Morigny in 1131 Abelard could not have been expected to see the relevance of all this to himself. He could not know that he was in the presence of the men who would destroy him nine years later at the council of Sens: St Bernard himself, Henry archbishop of Sens (who was the pope's chaplain at Morigny), Geoffrey bishop of Chartres (the preacher at Morigny), and Innocent II and Cardinal Haimeric the chancellor (both back in Rome by 1140) who sentenced Abelard as a heretic. Hardest to foresee would have been the volte-face made by Thomas, the abbot of Morigny, as he wrote the principal defence of St Bernard against Abelard. In 1140 it was St Bernard whom Thomas described as the 'most religious' (*religiosissimum*) man and 'the most learned' (*litteratissimum*), whereas Abelard was 'stupid'.[15] Thomas was probably responsible for prompting St Bernard to ridicule the title of Abelard's *Theologia* by calling it *Stultilogia* – 'Stupidology'.[16] This jibe reached Abelard, as he repeated it to his supporters when appealing for their help against St Bernard.[17]

In 1140 Thomas argued that Abelard had grown too proud, whereas in 1131 his reputation had needed building up after a decade of disasters. A favourable notice in the Morigny chronicle might have been some help to him, as chroniclers exchanged and passed on their news. Abelard's life as a monk had been as calamitous as his career as a master. After quarrelling with his abbey of St Denis, the first version of his *Theologia* had been burned at the council of Soissons in 1121; then in 1122 he had been accused of treason and forced to flee from St Denis (for a second time) to the king of France's rival, Thibaud count of Champagne; in c.1125 he had abandoned his own foundation of the Paraclete and disappointed his new patrons, Count Thibaud and Hatto bishop of Troyes. (Both of them would be present at the council of Sens in 1140.) Falling back on his Breton family connections, Abelard had been appointed abbot of St Gildas, one of the most distinguished and ancient Celtic monasteries. He was no more successful here than in his previous monastic establishments. When the expulsion of Heloise from Argenteuil in 1129 gave him a pretext for returning to Champagne, he did so. But his gift of his own foundation of the Paraclete to Heloise had given rise to renewed gossip, instead of praise of Abelard for his generosity, because he insisted on associating with her and her nuns instead of returning to his own monks at St Gildas. This extraordinary tale, told by Abelard against himself in his 'history of calamities', could not make him a model of 'religious' stability in the monastic sense.

When Abelard appeared at Morigny in 1131, he purported to be returning to St Gildas and this is why he asked for a papal legate to discipline his monks. But it is also significant that the Morigny chronicler described him as the 'most excellent director of schools', as if he were preparing the ground for Abelard's return to France as a master rather than a monk. If he were to attract students from the great churches of France and beyond, as he had done when he had been a master in Paris, his moral reputation would need to be of the highest. Abelard may have blackened the name of the monks of St Gildas in order to exonerate himself from the charge that he himself was a runaway monk and a womanizer, who was unfit to be in charge of anybody. It was also debatable whether any monk, even one with an impeccable reputation, should be a professional teacher. Ten years earlier, Roscelin had reminded Abelard of St Jerome's words that the job of a monk was to weep, for his own sins and the sins of mankind.[18] St Benedict had indeed founded 'a school of the Lord's service', but it was not a school of this world.[19]

THE PROFESSION OF RELIGION

When the Morigny chronicler described Abelard as *religiosus*, he meant that he was a monk rather than a religious person in a modern sense. No lay person could be described as *religiosus*, however devout he or she might be, and within the clergy a distinction was made between seculars and monks. The secular (literally the 'worldly') clergy were the Church's ministers, ranging from the minor orders of porters and acolytes through the major orders of deacons and priests up to the bishops and arch-bishops. The monks, who aimed to be other-worldly and dedicated to pure prayer, were reputed to be the only truly 'religious' people among either clergy or laity. Their monasteries, large and small, which were growing at an unprecedented rate in Abelard's lifetime, were the best evidence of the respect in which monks were held by the lay aristocracy, who endowed them with their lands and supplied them with recruits from their own families. In 1135 the Norman monk, Orderic Vitalis, observed that 'although evil abounds in the world, the devotion of the faithful in religion grows even more abundantly; in the Lord's field a great crop stands high. Everywhere, in the mountain pastures and in the plains, monasteries are being built and swarms of cowled people are spreading over the world.'[20]

Although Abelard had not become a monk voluntarily, he cham-pioned 'religion' in its strict monastic sense with the same enthusiasm as he had previously championed scholasticism. His objection to the abbey of St Denis, where he had found his first monastic home, was that the life there was too 'secular'.[21] In a sermon addressed to 'his beloved brothers and fellow monks' (probably at St Gildas in 1127), Abelard voiced the traditional view that those who withdraw from the world to weep and pray are the only true 'religious':

> 'Monk' or 'hermit' is the name of religion itself, whereas 'bishop' or 'cleric' is the word for an office or a duty more than for a vocation.... In God's Church the laborious occupation of the clergy and the bishops is in no way equal to the quiet of monastic contemplation, at least as far as the quantity of merit is concerned rather than ecclesiastical rank. This is why

we frequently see not only clerics but even bishops descend to the humility of monks in order to amend their lives. The Church, on the other hand, does not usually have the presumption to involve monks in the offices of the clergy, with the exception of the supreme rank of priest, and even that is not without some detriment to religion.... The usage of the Church attests how greatly monks exceed clerics in merits when, in the invocations in the litany, we all say: 'All holy monks and hermits, pray for us!' No one would presume to say: 'All holy clerics, bishops and canons, pray for us!', because these are not names for people pre-eminent in the sanctity of their lives.[22]

This is a typical piece of Abelard's bravado, making debating points to justify his own situation. As sharply on the lookout for rivals in the religious life as in the schools, he has St Norbert in his sights in this sermon. He was too similar to Abelard to be tolerated, as he was a canon who had formed in 1121 a group of hermit preachers, originally including women as well as men, on land at Prémontré (about eighty miles north of the Paraclete) given him by the bishop of Laon. Abelard describes Norbert as 'bloated with the false name of "religion"' and he ridicules him for trying to raise people from the dead in his evangelizing sessions.[23]

When Abelard says that no one would invoke bishops or canons to pray for them, he was probably referring in particular to St Norbert's order of Premonstratensian Canons, and the debate which had been going for the last thirty years and more about whether canons were as good as monks. In a letter to St Norbert from Rome in 1124 both the future rival popes, Anacletus II and Innocent II, commended him for renewing the life of the primitive Church and of the Apostles themselves through his Premonstratensian Canons. The canonical life, the cardinals assured him, 'is to be considered no less meritorious than preserving the flourishing religion of the monks'.[24] The cardinals were citing the well-known and authoritative pronouncement of Urban II in 1092 that monks and canons had both originated in the earliest days of the Church and they both had apostolic authority.[25] By arguing that only monks and hermits were really religious, Abelard was expressing a point of view which may have appealed to the conservative monks of St Gildas, but which was contrary to the ideals of reformers. It was out of character for Abelard to be on the conservative side of an argument and yet he often found himself in conflict with monastic reformers, most notably St Bernard. In the case of the Premonstratensian Canons, Abelard was perhaps blinded by jealousy because St Norbert had won approval in Rome, whereas he had failed to win compensation for his castration in the Roman curia and had then been condemned as a heretic by a court headed by a papal legate.

The Papacy's purpose in insisting that canons were as good as monks was to reform the secular clergy as a whole and re-inspire all those ministers of the sacraments, whose work Abelard purported to despise as 'laborious' and second-rate. The first of a series of councils in Rome had ruled in 1059 that all clergy should live in communities, sharing their property like the Apostles in the New Testament.[26] These papal initiatives had had some success in northern Italy and the Rhone valley by 1100 and they were becoming increasingly influential in northern Europe at the time Abelard became a canon in *c*.1114. Both St Norbert and he were canons of unreformed communities: Norbert at the church of St Victor in Xanten (in Lorraine) and Abelard at Notre-Dame in Paris. Their attitudes to clerical reform profoundly differed. By marrying Heloise clandestinely while remaining a canon of Notre-Dame, Abelard showed his indifference to the papal decrees, as married clergy were the greatest institutional obstacle to reform. Norbert, on the other hand, tried to get his fellow canons at Xanten to lead a communal life without personal property and, when he failed, he resigned his benefices and became a wandering preacher. This was in 1115, probably shortly before Abelard became involved with Heloise.

St Norbert's action at Xanten was like that of William of Champeaux, who had resigned his benefices at Notre-Dame and withdrawn to the church of St Victor in *c*.1105. Because they could not persuade their colleagues to reform themselves in accordance with the papal decrees, William and Norbert made a clean break, so that they could start again with new groups of canons of their own. Both were very successful with their new foundations: William with the School of St Victor and Norbert with his Premonstratensian Canons. Neither William nor Norbert chose to become monks of the traditional sort, though Norbert was repeatedly invited to, because they wanted to reach out to people; William taught students free of charge from all over western Europe and Norbert preached in the market-places of Flanders and the Rhineland. As well as being evangelists, canons claimed to be as good as monks in being bound by a rule, since the word 'canon' itself meant 'rule' and they were therefore 'regulars' and professionals. Canons bridged the divide between secular clergy and monks. Instead of despising the seculars, as Abelard does in his sermon, a contemporary canon from Liège concludes that if they live as they should, in common and without excess, then 'they will rightly be called "canons", that is, "regulars"'.[27]

The reformed ideal of the canonical life is the context of Heloise's appeal to Abelard, immediately before their marriage, to put aside self-gratification and the 'obscenities' of sexual intercourse and live up to his 'profession of religion': 'What is it you should be doing, you who are a cleric and a canon?'[28] This is part of her argument that Abelard should stand by his ideals and not make compromises for her sake. He must continue to be the austere sage and distinguished canon of Notre-Dame, whom she had first fallen in love with. Being Heloise, she takes the ideal of the austere holy man back beyond the early Church and the Apostles to the classical philosophers of Greece and Rome. Quoting Seneca's insistence that philosophy is an all-absorbing pursuit, she argues that 'those who are most truly to be called monks among us today' endure privation for the love of God, just as the noble pagans of antiquity lived for their philosophy.[29] 'Among us', she repeats, 'those are truly monks (*monachi*) who imitate either the common life of the Apostles or the earlier solitary life of John the Baptist.'[30] Canons and hermits, in other words, are the truest monks. Heloise reaches this conclusion by understanding the soleness, which *monachus* literally means, to refer to the single-minded dedication of an austere life. Every people, she argues, whether pagan, Jewish or Christian has its holy men dedicated to austerity.[31]

Although Abelard subsequently incorporated Heloise's insights about the pagan philosophers being like Christians into his *Theologia*, she seems to have sensed at the time of their marriage that he was not ready to absorb her ideas about canons being dedicated holy men. 'If you do not care', she continues, 'about the prerogative of a cleric, at least defend the dignity of a philosopher.'[32] In referring to clerical prerogative, she may have had Ivo of Chartres's recent ruling in mind that the marriage of a canon is dishonourable and incurs demotion in the ranks of the clerical militia.[33] In reality, because Abelard was determined to marry Heloise and risk the consequences, he could aspire neither to Ivo's ideal of an elite clerical officer nor to Heloise's model classical philosopher. Would Abelard have been on the idealists' side, if reform had not been complicated for him by his passion for Heloise? Perhaps not, as he records only contempt for canons who reform. In addition to his attack on St Norbert, there are his disparaging remarks about William of Champeaux's departure for St Victor. Abelard attributes William's 'conversion to the order of regular clerics' to his desire to be thought more religious, so that he would be promoted to a bishopric or abbacy.[34] Possibly he was jealous of William's success in his religious career, as Abelard too was a secular canon who converted to a 'regular' life (when he entered the abbey of St Denis following his castration), and he too was promoted (to the abbacy of St Gildas). The difference between them was that Abelard took these steps out of desperation, not choice, and every step in his official religious career was disastrous.

Abelard's animosity towards William of Champeaux may have had consequences as profound for his religious career as it had had in the schools. When William was promoted to the bishopric of Châlons-sur-Marne, he became the patron and mentor of St Bernard in his earliest days as abbot of Clairvaux (beginning in 1115). It may well have been from William that St Bernard first heard anything about Abelard, and it was presumably not complimentary. Abelard's feud with William also meant that at the time of his castration he could not seek asylum at the abbey of St Victor, even though this would probably have suited him better than St Denis because it was dedicated to scholarship. Hugh of St Victor, the abbey's greatest scholar, joined at about this time. Years later, because he and Abelard died at about the same time, they were seen as the 'two lights of the Latins in France'.[35] But they had never in fact co-operated with each other as far as is known.

WHAT WAS ABELARD'S RELIGION?

There is no simple answer to this question. If there was one, Abelard's prosecutors or his defenders at his trials for heresy would have found it. St Bernard said he was 'altogether ambiguous'.[36] There is, for example, a contrast, though not necessarily a contradiction, between the emotional commitment of his hymns and the detached tone of his academic works, even when they deal with the same subject. His Good Friday hymn to Christ crucified ('They are ours, O Lord, the crimes are ours'), or his appeals to Heloise to love Christ and not him, contrast with the apparent indifference with which he declares in his *Ethics* that: 'If someone asks whether the persecutors of the martyrs or of Christ sinned in doing what they believed was pleasing to God...we cannot say that they have sinned in this'.[37] Abelard's opponents said he had no business to be raising hypothetical questions ('If someone asks...'), or foisting his own opinions on his readers under cover of such phrases as 'we cannot say' or 'it seems to us'.

In his *Ethics* Abelard was conducting a philosophical discussion, as if with students in the classroom, explaining pros and cons and drawing out difficulties from apparently simple statements. At his trial at Sens, on the other hand, his prosecutors reduced his complex arguments to single articles of faith. His discussion of whether Christ's crucifiers incurred guilt thus became a single accusatory statement: that it is heretical to maintain that those 'who crucified Christ in ignorance did not sin'.[38] Whether this was heretical, and whether Abelard had raised this question in bad faith as a blasphemer or conscientiously as a teacher, depended on how the words were understood. 'Very often', he had pointed out in his prologue to *Sic et Non*, 'the same words have different meanings, when one and the same word has been used to express now one meaning, now another. For, each one of us abounds in his own words, just as he does in his own sense of them.'[39] Each individual is locked into his own vocabulary and his own sense of himself. Abelard had probably first reached this existentialist conclusion through his study of logic, which made him see how fluid language is.

When he turned to religious thought, Abelard applied the same rules to it as to the language of logic. Each individual must begin by 'knowing himself' – *Scito te ipsum* – as the title of his book on *Ethics* announced. And he began it with the controversial words: 'We call morals vices and virtues of the mind.'[40] This could mean that moral standards do not exist and that right and wrong are figments of the imagination, a tenable position for a philosopher, but not for a master teaching the next generation of teachers in Christian Europe. In some passages in his *Ethics* Abelard looks like an existentialist like Kierkegaard, or even like an atheist. But this is to misunderstand him. Any thinker who used the language of Graeco-Roman philosophy to explain the meaning of the Bible, which is what Abelard was doing, was bound to look like a sceptic sometimes. In fact, the fundamental points he was making were not original, nor were they intended to be. They had been made by his masters, William of Champeaux and Anselm of Laon, and – as they all knew very well – they derived from the infinitely rich writings of St Augustine, who at the end of the Roman Empire had addressed all the main problems of Christian doctrine.

Although St Bernard suggested the contrary, Abelard never asserted that everything was relative or that everything was uncertain. His often-quoted epigram 'By doubting we come to inquiry and by inquiry we perceive the truth' enshrines his confidence in the existence of truth, not doubt.[41] At neither of his trials for heresy was Abelard asking for toleration for personal or eccentric opinions of his own. On the contrary, he maintained that he knew the truth and everybody else must acknowledge it, starting with his judges and accusers. Those who were against him, he thought, were temporarily blinded by malice or ignorance; they would come to the truth one day, just as he had. So confident was he of his rectitude that he likened his teachings to Christ's. In his 'history of calamities' he applied the Gospel texts to himself. At his trial at Soissons in 1121 the clergy and people say: 'Here he is speaking openly and no one utters a word against him'.[42] Abelard used this same reference to St John's Gospel in his manifesto at Sens in 1140, insisting he had always 'spoken openly'.[43] His student defender, Berengar, compared Abelard's prosecutors at Sens with Christ's:

> Then gathered the chief priests and the Pharisees a council, and said, 'What do we?' for this man doeth many miracles. If we let him thus alone, all men will believe on him. And one of them, named Abbot Bernard, being the high priest of that council, prophesied saying: 'It is expedient for us that one man should die for the people, and that the whole nation perish not'. Then from that day forth they took counsel together for to condemn him.[44]

Berengar may have written this pastiche of St John's Gospel with Abelard's full knowledge, as it accompanied his personal Confession of Faith to Heloise. It was not necessarily blasphemous to compare one's own life with Christ's, as every Christian was an imitator of Christ. Nor was it wrong to adapt the Scripture to a rhetorical purpose, as St Bernard did this repeatedly. The combination of a classical training and familiarity with the Biblical texts made this hard to avoid. The morality of the text depended on the author's intention. Berengar spoiled his case by claiming later on that he had only attacked St Bernard in a fit of youthful exuberance: 'Anything personal I said about the man of God is to be read as a joke and not seriously.'[45]

The danger for Abelard in Berengar's exuberant defence of him was that it might be said that he had learned to make jokes about the Scripture from Abelard himself. One of the bishops, Jocelin of Soissons, who was a signatory in 1140 to the letter to the pope condemning Abelard, had warned St Goswin years before that Abelard acted more like a jester than a professor.[46] 'Listen to his jeering,' St Bernard warned at the time of the council of Sens.[47] He quoted Abelard's *Commentary on St Paul's Epistle to the Romans*, where Adam and Eve's original sin is described as 'tasting one apple'.[48] If this sin was so big that it could be expiated only by Christ's death, Abelard asked, what expiation will be required for the crime of murdering Christ?[49] Crucifying the Son of God was surely a bigger sin than tasting an apple in a garden. That sounded to St Bernard like the voice of a scoffer. Those who sympathized with Abelard, his former students in particular, might have explained (with Otto of Freising) that he excelled at jokes, or (with John of Salisbury) that he liked to stimulate his students with childish things rather than being obscure like a serious philosopher.[50] These were the signs of a brilliant teacher perhaps, but also of a controversial one. Because of his 'incautious' (Otto of Freising's word) way of expressing himself, Abelard had given hostages to any accuser who questioned his good faith.[51]

Berengar appealed to St Bernard to let Abelard 'be a Christian with you; and, if you will, he will be a Catholic with you; and, if you will not, he will be a Catholic none the less, as God is common and not private'.[52] This sounds like sense, but it would not have mollified St Bernard's supporters. Abelard had indeed argued in *Theologia* that knowledge of God is common to everybody, whether pagan or Christian: 'reason educates each single person naturally about God'.[53] But this philosophical ideal of a non-exclusive God was one of the points at issue in Abelard's prosecution. In St Bernard's opinion, his determination to make Plato a Christian proved Abelard a pagan.[54] 'He prefers the inventions of the philosophers and his own novelties to the doctrine and faith of the Catholic Fathers', he told the pope.[55] Contrary to Berengar, the Catholic Church was on St Bernard's side and he was vindicated by Innocent II's bull condemning Abelard in 1140. It begins by insisting that the unity of the Catholic faith depends on papal authority which derives from St Peter, the prince of the Apostles, and therefore from God.[56] Abelard was condemned because he was judged to have endangered Catholic unity in this sense.

What was Abelard's religion? 'Pernicious doctrines and other perverse teachings contrary to the Catholic faith' is Innocent II's authoritative answer in the bull of 1140.[57] Yet even this is elusive, as Peter the Venerable assured Heloise that Abelard was restored 'to apostolic grace by letters and my labour'.[58] This may have followed the reconciliation which Peter says he arranged between Abelard and St Bernard.[59] If Abelard survived into the pontificate of Celestine II, who was consecrated on 26 September 1143, Peter the Venerable may have had little difficulty getting favourable letters, as in his previous persona as Cardinal Guy of Castello the new pope had great affection for Abelard, according to St Bernard at least.[60] On his death in 1144 Celestine II left his copies of *Theologia* and *Sic et Non* to his church of Città di Castello.[61] This is remarkable, as Innocent II had ordered Abelard's 'erroneous books' to be burned wherever they were found.[62] *Theologia* and *Sic et Non* were Abelard's biggest books and they would have been difficult to conceal. Guy of Castello presumably did not think them to be erroneous. The fact that a senior cardinal held on to Abelard's books in Rome itself, and that he was elected pope two days after Innocent II's death, shows how the Papacy was not a monolithic power. Like other autocracies, it was soft at the centre and this was its salvation.

In his account of his struggle with William of Champeaux thirty years earlier, Abelard had cited the Homeric hero, Ajax, to demonstrate that 'I was not vanquished'.[63] As Ajax had killed himself with his own sword, the reader is left wondering what message Abelard wished to convey. Was annihilation in 'non-defeat' the best that he could report, once he stopped boasting and faced realities? Was his career in 'religion' as disastrous a 'non-defeat' as his career in the schools? Single-handed, he had taken on the greatest powers in western Christendom (not to mention the allegedly homicidal monks of St Gildas): Cardinal Cono of Praeneste and his prosecutors at Soissons in 1121; Abbot Suger of St Denis and the French monarchy in 1122; and finally St Bernard and all the forces of the Papacy in the 1130s. Each time Abelard had had to retreat and yet he could say with justice: 'I was not vanquished.' He owed his final, last-minute rescue to Peter the Venerable, who may have saved Abelard's life as well as his reputation. If he had gone on to Rome to make his appeal, he might have been lynched before he got there, or even burned, as Arnold of Brescia was later.[64] St Bernard said there was nothing to choose between Abelard and Arnold; indeed Abelard was worse because he was the leader of the forces against the pope.[65]

For Peter the Venerable, on the other hand, Abelard was close to being a saint: 'I speak of the man' (he wrote to Heloise) 'who will often and always be named with honour, Christ's servant and true philosopher, Master Peter, whom divine providence brought to Cluny in the last years of his life.'[66] St Bernard and Peter the Venerable were the two most powerful churchmen in western Christendom. A middle way between their contrary opinions of Abelard may not exist. They are a conundrum as complex as any he set his students in *Sic et Non*. Certainly Abelard saw his life and sufferings as a witness to his Christian faith and, equally certainly, he believed that whatever he thought was right. Whether this makes him a saint or a heretic, or neither, or both, depends on what 'saint' and 'heretic' are understood to mean in the context of Abelard's life.

Monk

Although Abelard admitted that it was the confusion and shame of his castration that drove him into a monastery, his change of career should not have disadvantaged him either materially or spiritually.[1] As the monastery he had entered was the abbey of St Denis, with its close connections with Paris and the French monarchy, his prospects remained good. Monks were among the most admired and influential men in medieval society. Or rather, abbots were. They usually had no superiors and spent much of their time outside their monasteries, spreading God's word to the rich and powerful who were their patrons and protectors. Most abbots came from the aristocratic class themselves. In the 1120s and 1130s the most prominent abbots of this sort were Suger of St Denis (abbot from 1122 to 1151), St Bernard of Clairvaux (abbot from 1115 to 1153) and Peter the Venerable of Cluny (abbot from 1122 to 1156). Despite being involved in business of every sort, particularly in key appointments in the Church from the Papacy downwards, each of these abbots kept their religious ideals in view: Suger rebuilt and refurbished his abbey church and described how he did it in a book; St Bernard produced his inspirational sermons and treatises for his monks at Clairvaux; and Peter the Venerable restored the authority and dignity of the abbey of Cluny. Even so, St Bernard described the dilemma of them all when he confessed to a Carthusian (the strictest sort of monk) that he was a monster, being neither cleric nor layman: 'I retain the habit of a monk, but I long ago abandoned the life.'[2]

Abbots could not afford to stay peacefully in their monasteries, if they were to keep their houses going. New benefactors had continually to be found, old acquisitions had to be revived and, in the twelfth century in particular, rival groups of monks or canons had to be prevented from winning recruits or funds. Above all, monasteries had to demonstrate to their patrons and benefactors that the prayers they offered for them were being duly performed: year in and year out, day and night, in the manner best pleasing to God. This is why such huge sums were spent at Cluny and St Denis on building and decorating the abbey church. The patrons saw value for money in the massed stone and the gold and silver, and Suger assured them in his book that all these precious things delighted God as well. Although the Cistercians purported to despise such ostentation, they too built on a monumental scale and created a distinctive aesthetic of their own in their proto-Gothic abbeys like Fontenay. The monastic life was a paradox. Monks withdrew from the 'world' and lived in austerity in order to make prayers that were pure for themselves and their patrons, but they had to ensure at the same time that their efforts were not lost sight of.

The patron's demand for continual prayer is best illustrated by an anecdote about St Hugh, a Carthusian monk in the generation after Abelard. When Henry II of England was caught in a storm at night in the English Channel, he revealed his thoughts: 'If my Carthusian Hugh were awake now and was either saying his own prayers, or was out of bed celebrating the divine office with his brethren in due solemnity, God would not forget me for so long.'[3] The king then regretted his lack of confidence in Hugh and he began to pray: 'O God, whom Hugh serves so truly, have mercy and clemency on us through his intervention and merits.' This worked wonders, as the storm ceased immediately. The point about this anecdote – and about monasticism as a whole – was that it was viewed by the lay aristocracy as a system of delegation or substitution, something every lord and retainer was familiar with. A monk was delegated to pray on his patron's behalf, just as a knight was delegated to fight. Sir Richard Southern comments that 'monks could be relied upon to perform their service of substitution for ever'.[4] This was true of the greatest monasteries, like Cluny or St Denis, but not of lesser ones whose endowments might fail, or – worse – whose monks might fail through negligence to perform their unending round of prayer.

Henry II had been worried that St Hugh might not have been at prayer, as the storm was in the middle of the night, and in that case the king's ship would have sunk under the weight of his sins. Providentially, however, the merits and prayers of 'my Carthusian Hugh' were there to counterbalance the king's wickedness and calm the storm. 'Henceforth', Hugh's biographer comments, 'the king's veneration for the man of God was total.' Southern emphasizes how monks were workmen who performed a service, the *opus Dei* (literally the 'work of God'), through the cycle of prayers prescribed in the daily liturgy. Monastic reformers who accused other monks, the Cluniacs for example, of not keeping to the Rule of St Benedict could have devastating effects, as they threatened the validity of the 'work of God' done in church. Disaffected patrons might then transfer their loyalties to St Bernard and his Cistercians or some other vociferous reformer. The rivalry between Peter the Venerable and St Bernard kept reasserting itself because they were both Burgundian aristocrats competing in the same territory for the same hearts and minds.

In becoming a monk, Abelard was not therefore entering a haven of tranquillity, but an arena of competing abbots and demanding patrons. This was especially so in France in the 1120s, when new orders of monks and canons were proliferating in France: Augustinians, Carthusians, Cistercians, Premonstratensians, and many smaller local groups. In holding his own in such an environment, Abelard already had two decades of experience of struggles in the schools, when he had had to win royal and local support and see off rivals, not always successfully. Becoming a monk presented him with a great opportunity, comparable with becoming a master. If he succeeded in becoming an abbot of the standing of Peter the Venerable or St Bernard, he could reward his friends and family with ecclesiastical benefices and win back the wealth and prestige he had sacrificed by going to the schools in the first place. Abbots were lords of lands and men; they commanded networks of influence far exceeding those of masters in the schools. Abelard did indeed succeed in becoming an abbot of a first-class historic abbey, at St Gildas in c.1125 or later, but this proved an unmitigated disaster. This is where he wrote his 'history of calamities'.

It was Heloise who saved Abelard's monastic reputation by inviting him – in response to his 'history of calamities' and the letters that followed – to write a rule and numerous other works, most notably his hymns, for her nuns at the Paraclete.[5] She knew he could write brilliantly about anything he turned his hand to, even if he was incapable of looking after himself or her and her nuns. These writings reveal Abelard's areas of competence and incompetence. The rule, which Heloise requested he institute at the Paraclete, looks worse than useless as a working document, as it is too long and discursive. It seems to have been tacitly ignored for practical purposes by Heloise and her nuns. 'Not one document from the Paraclete cartulary or from any other contemporary source refers explicitly or implicitly to the rule of Abelard.'[6] Nevertheless, it is impressive as a moralizing and learned treatise (it contains nearly 400 quotations) on what sort of rules there should be in monasteries. Abelard's essay on the origin of nuns, which Heloise requested along with the rule, is an excellent piece of historical research, drawing on the Old and New Testaments, the Church Fathers and Latin literature, in order to demonstrate the 'dignity of women' (Abelard's words) in ancient religion.[7] Abelard's works for the Paraclete are the most substantial body of writing done by any monastic founder of the twelfth century and they are likewise the most substantial writings on women's place in Christianity. By personally returning Abelard's body to Heloise for burial at the Paraclete, Peter the Venerable acknowledged Abelard's achievement at the Paraclete, even though he told her only of Abelard's exemplary life at Cluny.

MONKS AND CASTRATION

On becoming a monk, Abelard's immediate priority was to restore the reputation for austerity which he had forfeited when his affair with Heloise became known. He had to make the best of his castration, as he was well aware of the Old Testament texts stating that God held eunuchs in abomination.[8] No one would want Abelard to pray for them, let alone teach them or be their abbot, if he was an abomination before the Lord. His sermons and letters as a monk suggest that he went about restoring his reputation with undiminished energy. This is the context in which he extolled the vocation of monks over clerics and canons, and denigrated a suspected competitor in St Norbert.[9] Abelard answered objectors to his being castrated by reminding them of the Prophet Isaiah and St Matthew's Gospel, where eunuchs who keep the Lord's sabbaths and those who are eunuchs for the kingdom of Heaven's sake are commended.[10] The implication is that because he is a monk, Abelard is such a holy eunuch. He exhorted the monks to whom he was preaching to preserve their own monastic sons (that is, the younger monks) in continence by castrating them 'spiritually'.[11] He may have won some sympathy in his audience for this, as every monk needed to be castrated in spirit.

The biography of the Carthusian, St Hugh, which has already been cited, describes how such a spiritual castration might be achieved. In a vision Hugh saw his groin being cut open and something like red-hot coals being wrenched out of it, which were thrown away in disgust. The 'doctor' then withdrew and Hugh was 'cured in both body and spirit'.[12] Closer to Abelard's experience is a miracle story concerning the master (scholasticus) at Beverley Minster, whose scholarly discipline grew tepid when he became obsessed with a girl. In answer to his prayers, St John of Beverley restored him to his profession by rendering him impotent.[13] Abelard described his castration as a 'remedy for disease' and he assured Heloise that 'divine grace had cleansed me, rather than deprived me; for what else did it do than remove the dirty and disgusting parts in order to conserve the purity of cleanliness?'[14] Heloise herself had prompted this diagnosis, as she had congratulated him on having found 'a most faithful doctor': 'by curing you of those urges, a single wound in your body has healed many wounds in your soul'.[15]

Castration in adulthood does not necessarily cause impotence, and yet it is evident from their writings that Abelard and his contemporaries believed it did. It may have been the trauma that made Abelard impotent, rather than the actual removal of his testicles. In that case, he too had been 'spiritually' or psychologically castrated. The dream which rendered St Hugh impotent was so vivid that he saw the hand first holding the knife and then throwing his burning testicles far away from his monk's cell.[16] Abelard may have seen nothing so distressing as this at his castration, if his head was covered in the way shown in the Toulouse lawbook, and he says he felt almost nothing.[17] It was the shame which appalled him, not the physical act. By becoming a monk he overcame this shame by joining with his brethren, who were dedicated to achieving castration for the kingdom of Heaven's sake.

'You are a monk,' Fulk prior of Deuil reminded Abelard, and he teasingly addressed him as *cucullato*, 'a cowled man' or a cuckold.[18] Monks should be proud to accept humiliation and sexual disparagement at the hands of the world. 'You need to return to yourself,' Fulk advised him.[19] Now that the raging fire has been extinguished, you must take a firm grip on your mind, which has wandered through so many and such sweet insanities of lust. Now (Fulk continues) 'you will be able to be free to understand all the paths and causes of reason, whereas those who are in the grip of sexual desire's numerous incitements perceive little or nothing'.[20] This was the ideal of celibacy to which every monk aspired. St Anselm of Canterbury described how God had created man as a rational being; before the Fall, Adam had not been driven by 'bestial and irrational voluptuousness' but by human and rational values.[21] St Anselm saw sexual desire as 'the one evil above all other evils', which had been with him since childhood and through all the stages of his life, and which had left his soul weak, destitute and empty.[22] He had experienced no spiritual castration like St Hugh. For the castrated Abelard, then, there was promise that his liberated soul would achieve even greater intellectual feats than his former self, or than St Anselm. Arguably this did occur, as Abelard's extant writings (with the possible exception of his works on logic) date from after his castration.

The tone of Fulk of Deuil is difficult to gauge; his advice purports to be given in good faith by one monk to another and yet it is double-edged. Abelard would certainly have agreed that castration had liberated him, as he compared himself with Origen, the Church Father who was thought to have castrated himself: 'God's mercy has been kinder to me than to him, for he is believed to have acted improvidently and incurred not a little blame, whereas it happened to me through no fault of mine, so that God might make me ready and free for similar work.'²³ The implication of 'similar work' is that Abelard is destined to become a prolific and inspired Christian writer like Origen. Fulk seems aware of this ambition, as he warns Abelard against taking Origen as a role model: 'Origen's great wisdom is everywhere extolled and praised – apart, that is, from certain errors which he failed to correct. According to St Jerome, he blamed these on Ambrose, his pupil, who published them in an unauthorized edition before they were ready to see the light of day.'²⁴ Perhaps Fulk had already heard rumours of Abelard's controversial proposal to write a book called *Theologia*, although he had been expelled from Anselm of Laon's school of divinity. When Fulk rehearses the social benefits Abelard will experience from castration, it is difficult to believe he is being serious or well-intentioned:

> You ought also to consider it a great advantage that no one will be suspicious of you. You will be received much more warmly as a house-guest, as the man with a wife will no longer fear violence from you, nor the risk of being beaten up in his bed. With the utmost decorum you will pass inviolate through phalanxes of well-furnished married women. As for the choruses of splendid virgins in the flower of youth, who often excite even impotent old men into a frenzy of helpless lust, you will be wonderfully safe and sinless, as you have nothing to fear from their approaches and wiles. In future you will certainly avoid the secret recesses of sodomites.... From the remnants of your experience of such things you will know what I am talking about much better than I can explain in words.²⁵

As Peter Dronke comments, Fulk treats Abelard's castration as the stuff of a farce or medieval fabliau: 'the cock of the roost has been caponised'.²⁶ It has been conjectured that Fulk wrote as a partisan of Fulbert's family deliberately to discredit Abelard.²⁷ Ridicule was the most effective response to Abelard's self-righteous justification of his castration.

Impotence invites ridicule; it is this which makes Fulk of Deuil's tone so variable and difficult to gauge. What did he wish to imply by appearing so worldly wise about women? Was he speaking from experience? Or, had he been reading misogynist books? Did he think his own celibacy, his monastic choice of voluntary impotence, any less a cause for ridicule than Abelard's? He was a *cucullatus* as much as Abelard. Monks were potential figures of fun because the celibate ideal became absurd if everyone took it up. Monks were entirely dependent for recruitment on the laity whom they purported to despise. They could not really separate themselves from the rest of humanity, as they had no way of reproducing themselves asexually. To argue (as Abelard did) that the testicles were 'the vilest members', as if they were not a proper part of his body, was wishful thinking, even if this commonplace belief helped him to accept his own castration.[28] When in his *Ethics* Abelard was speaking generally and not about his own case, he took a more rational line: because sexual feelings are natural bodily functions, 'it is clear that no natural pleasure of the flesh should be attributed to sin, nor should it be considered a fault for us to take pleasure in it'.[29] But Abelard knew this to be a daring opinion, contrary to conventional Christian teaching.[30]

The principal authority in this matter was St Augustine, who had identified the Fall with Adam and Eve's sexuality.[31] Guilt is inherited through the genitals themselves, which pass down Original Sin like a sexually-transmitted disease. St Augustine reinforced the psychological link between bodily revulsion and guilt. It was in this spirit that Abelard called his testicles vile; in his case they manifestly had brought disaster upon him. In his despondency, he would doubtless have agreed with St Anselm that sexual desire was the greatest of all evils.[32] A modern liberal might protest at what looks like excessive prudery: 'Is war not a greater evil?'; 'Or torture?'; 'Or cruelty to children?'; 'Why were medieval monks so obsessed with sex?' St Augustine would have had little difficulty answering objections of this sort. Yes, he had certainly been concerned with sexuality; but this was not from prudery; it is because sexual desire is the root cause of other sins. Freud, the Marquis de Sade, and modern psychiatrists would concur with St Augustine about the overwhelming power of desire, though they formulate their ideas differently. (This agreement among such disparate people is partly due to modern psychiatry itself stemming from Biblical and classical writing, as did St Augustine's own intellectual development.)

If sexuality is the root of other evils, it makes sense to aim to root out evil by eliminating sexuality. This is the endeavour to which medieval monks were dedicated. They wounded their bodies in order to preserve their souls: as Heloise pointed out to Abelard, the single wound of his castration healed many wounds in his soul.[33] This ascetic endeavour proved recurrently attractive over the whole medieval millennium (AD 500–1500), and monasticism reached its high point in attracting recruits in western Europe in Abelard's lifetime. As so often, he was in touch with his times. The biographer of St Hugh has him say that his spiritual castration will liberate him 'from the law of sin and death which is in my members'.[34] In physical terms, of course, no one can overcome death or the demands of their bodies, and the monks knew this. Monasticism was indeed absurd as a recipe for everybody. It responded, like all religions, to aspirations for peace and security which transcended ordinary life, but which were no less powerful for that. In the words of Abelard's hymn 'O Quanta Qualia' (as translated by Helen Waddell):

> There, all vexation ended and from all grieving free,
> We sing the song of Sion in deep security.

> (Illic, molestiis finitis omnibus,
> Securi cantica Sion cantabimus.)[35]

He was not writing of any place in this world, not even of a monastery, but of the heavenly Jerusalem.

MONKS AS TEACHERS

When Abelard joined the abbey of St Denis immediately after his castration, he describes some of the monks as well as his own friends appealing to him to continue as a teacher: 'As I had been liberated from the temptations of the flesh and the tumults of daily life, I should devote myself to the study of learning and truly become God's philosopher rather than the world's.'[36] The aspiration of uniting the Greek ideal of the philosopher with the dedication of the monk reached back to St Jerome, whom Abelard makes into a model for the conduct of his own life in his 'history of calamities'. Heloise, too, had appealed to Abelard, immediately before their marriage, to give up 'voluptuousness' and be a philosopher-monk like the Stoic sages of antiquity.[37] The picture Otto of Freising draws of Abelard at St Denis confirms his dedication to philosophy, in the broad sense of gaining wisdom. He became even more learned, Otto says, as he 'concentrated on reading and thinking day and night'.[38]

Abelard's mastery of the works of the Latin Church Fathers, which he demonstrates in *Sic et Non*, may have been laid when he started studying in the library at St Denis.[39] Possibly this was the first time he had ever had unlimited access to a great library, as none of the schools in which he had taught (including Notre-Dame in Paris) would have possessed such a rich stock of books. It may likewise have been at St Denis (as already suggested in chapter 4) that Abelard first met the organized writing facilities of a scriptorium.[40] He could now give permanence to his thoughts, either by dictating them to a scribe or by doing the writing himself. The scriptorium served much the same purpose for him as a laboratory does for a scientist. The making of *Sic et Non* needed the combined resources of a great library, a well-provided scriptorium and a team of assistants as readers and copyists. The 2000 or more quotations from the Church Fathers used in *Sic et Non* had to be extracted from a variety of books and then reassembled in their appropriate places in accordance with Abelard's plan. Now that he was a monastic 'philosopher', in command of books and word-processing facilities, Abelard could aspire to write like the great Christian scholars he admired so much, St Augustine, St Jerome and the Venerable Bede (whom he describes having read 'by chance one day' in the library at St Denis).[41]

But was this what Abelard should have been doing as a monk? Medieval monks are remembered now for their illuminated books and their learning; from St Jerome's time in the fourth century through Bede's in the eighth up to St Anselm's in the eleventh monastic scholars had made learning a central concern of monasteries. Nevertheless, reformers of Abelard's generation questioned whether monks should be involved in scholarship, just as they questioned everything which detracted from the severity of monastic life. Most extreme was the contention of St Bernard that there was more to be found in the woods than in books: 'woods and stones will teach you what you cannot hear from "masters".'[42] But St Bernard did not reject book-learning as such, only its misuse. Medieval Christianity, with its roots in the Bible and the writings of the Church Fathers, was not an animistic religion of the 'woods and stones'. St Bernard's point was that the masters in the schools (like Abelard in his previous persona as master at Notre-Dame) grew conceited, instead of heeding the words of Ecclesiastes that 'in much wisdom is much grief'. 'I will not ask', St Bernard says to his monks, 'which looks the more useful and necessary for salvation: he who is puffed up or he who grieves.'[43] This is the sort of argument that entitled Roscelin to warn Abelard, when he was first at St Denis, that the role of a monk was to weep and not to teach.[44] Much the same objections were marshalled by Hugh of St Victor a few years later:

> If you are a monk, what are you doing in the crowd? If you love silence, why do you delight in spending your time with debaters? You ought always to be taken up with fasting and weeping. Are you searching for what it means to be a philosopher? The simplicity of the monk is his philosophy. 'But I want to teach others,' you say. It is not your job to teach, but to wail.[45]

Hugh wrote this in his *Didascalicon*, which is an introduction to the curriculum of the liberal arts. He may have had Abelard's ambition to be a monk-philosopher in mind in this passage. In that case his words serve as a rejoinder to Abelard's attacks on William of Champeaux, the founder of the school of St Victor, and on canons generally.[46] Hugh's point is that Abelard should cease being a teacher because he has chosen to become a monk of the traditional sort at St Denis. He should therefore live up to the ancient monastic ideals of prayer, fasting and seclusion. Hugh and his fellow canons of St Victor, on the other hand, have a duty to teach because this is what they have dedicated themselves to do as canons regular. Reformed canons may teach, unreformed monks may not, sums up this point of view.

Like St Bernard, Hugh emphasizes that it is how knowledge is approached which is important. The study of Scripture should not be made into an 'occupation' or a 'business' because that leads to pride and vainglory.[47] In *Sic et Non* Abelard could certainly be said to have made scriptural study into a 'business', as it systematically lists contradictions and discrepancies in the most fundamental Christian beliefs, starting with the concept of faith itself. *Sic et Non* is a university textbook, entirely unsuited to pastoral or liturgical use, and therefore not the right sort of book for a monk to be writing. A monastic book should be an act of worship, in its contents as much as in its illuminated lettering. Hugh of St Victor's *Didascalicon* is written in this worshipful mode, even though it concerns the secular curriculum of the arts, and he concludes it with a prayer for enlightenment.[48] Abelard's *Theologia*, on the other hand, is written in a debating style and he was not modest about its merits, describing it as the acme of his genius.[49] Monastic humility is difficult to detect in any of Abelard's works, even in his 'history of calamities' which was intended to exemplify it. Perhaps this is to Abelard's credit, as humility so easily becomes hypocrisy.

Abelard gives his own account of the controversy about his teaching. His story is that Abbot Adam and the monks of St Denis wanted rid of him because he criticized their scandalous lives.[50] So he was allowed to withdraw to a 'cell' of the abbey, where he conducted a school in his usual way.[51] Otto of Freising confirms this: 'after some time he was released from obedience to his abbot and came out in public, taking on once more the office of teacher'.[52] Abelard does not specify where this 'cell' was which he turned into a school. It has been conjectured that it was in Paris itself or very close to it, and in that case Abelard could have recruited many of the students he had before.[53] He says 'the Lord seemed to have conferred on me the grace to interpret the Scriptures no less than secular literature, and so my school began to increase in both fields and all the rest rapidly diminished'.[54] Paris fits this description very well, as it is known to have had a number of competing schools.

On the other hand, Abelard explains later on that he took refuge in the territory of Thibaud, count of Champagne, because 'I had previously stayed there in a cell'.[55] He adds that he had a close friendship from 'previously' with the prior of some monks from Troyes (also in Champagne).[56] The 'cell' of St Denis in which Abelard had his school may therefore have been in Champagne rather than Paris. John Benton surmised that it was in the Nogent area (where Abelard subsequently founded his monastery of the Paraclete). St Denis possessed property in Nogent itself, together with a priory, a church and a grange in separate locations nearby.[57] Any of these might have formed the 'cell' of Abelard's school. Nogent-sur-Seine was strategically placed at the heart of the fairs of Champagne, with roads running east–west between Paris and Troyes and north–south between Reims and Sens. In this area it is possible to believe Abelard that 'so great a crowd of students came flowing in that the place was not sufficient for lodgings nor the land for food supplies'.[58]

Roscelin's letter to Abelard concerns this phase of his life. He confirms that Abelard had crowds of students: 'a multitude of barbarians from all over the place', Roscelin calls them, to whom he taught 'trifles', that is, secular subjects like logic and Latin grammar.[59] He accuses Abelard of having ceased to be a monk, though he still wore a monastic habit.[60] As Abelard describes himself teaching 'in the usual way', it looks as if he was functioning as a master very much as he had done before his castration. Roscelin gives further details which are intriguing, though impossible to confirm. He accuses Abelard of making money out of his teaching and sending it to his 'whore'.[61] (Roscelin presumably means Heloise, who was by then Abelard's wife and a nun of Argenteuil.) Roscelin adds: 'I have heard your fellow monks saying that when you returned to the monastery recently, you brought back the money you had got together, as the price of the lies you teach, so as to send it to that whore.'[62] What the monks of St Denis were saying may have been true, but it was not necessarily discreditable to Abelard. He was remitting his receipts back to his abbey, just as every monk who had charge of an outlying cell should do. Nor was it necessarily improper for him to remit money to Heloise, if he continued to be held responsible for her maintenance because he had vested her as a nun. The abbey of St Denis had a long-term interest in bringing Argenteuil under its control; making Heloise its dependant was a step in that direction.

In another intriguing detail Roscelin accuses Abelard of lasciviously using a seal with a man's and a woman's head on it.[63] The fact that Abelard had a seal at all as a monk suggests that he was a trusted agent of the abbey of St Denis. The two heads on it may have represented the companions of St Denis, Sts Rusticus and Eleutherius or some other pair of saints. If the seal was a reused classical intaglio, representing Castor and Pollux for example, Roscelin might well have mistaken the antique headdresses as those of a man and a woman. (Abbot Suger's description of the treasures of St Denis, written about twenty years later, shows antique gems being adapted to a variety of uses.) All in all, these fragments of evidence suggest that within a year or two of his castration Abelard had re-established himself as the master of a great school, this time with the backing of the abbey of St Denis. He had quarrelled with Abbot Adam and the monks when he lived in the abbey; but now that he headed a cell and remitted them money, they were presumably happy enough to have him as one of their provosts. Successful managers of a monastery's outlying properties were on a career ladder which led to their being appointed abbots and priors themselves. Thus Suger describes the success he had, ten or fifteen years before he became abbot of St Denis in 1122, first at Berneval (near Dieppe) and then at Toury (near Chartres) as a provost of the abbey.[64]

Success in Abelard's 'history of calamities' is usually the prelude to the next disaster. Because his enemies failed to prevent him being a master as well as a monk, they accused him of heresy at the council of Soissons in 1121. (The trial is discussed in chapter 13.) The consequence of the trial was that monastic discipline was enforced on Abelard, and this could have terminated his independence. He was first placed under house arrest at the abbey of St Médard in Soissons in charge of the claustral prior, St Goswin. Abelard says he was well treated at St Médard, though St Goswin's biographer explains that the monastery specialized in dealing with recalcitrant monks and that Abelard had been sentenced to silence.[65] St Goswin is described having various verbal tussles with the 'untamed rhinoceros' and he even threatened to have Abelard flogged.[66] The disparity between these two accounts may be due either to Abelard wishing to forget the humiliations he had suffered at St Médard, or to St Goswin exaggerating in retrospect his triumphing over Abelard.

Whatever it was that occurred at St Médard, Abelard's stay there was brief ('some days', he says), as the papal legate who had overseen his trial at Soissons released him and sent him back to his own monastery of St Denis.[67] But this was no happy homecoming for Abelard, as it meant going back to the abbot and monks with whom he had quarrelled and who had previously put him out of their monastery. So Abelard was back where he had started: no longer running a cell and heading a school, but a rank-and-file monk of St Denis with little prospect of promotion or release, as he was a condemned heretic sentenced to silence. His reaction was characteristically bold: he insulted the memory of St Denis himself and escaped in the night to the count of Champagne.

ABELARD'S FLIGHT FROM ST DENIS

Abelard describes what occurred as an unfortunate misunderstanding. He had been reading Bede's commentary on the Acts of the Apostles and came across his statement that Dionysius the Areopagite was bishop of Corinth.[68] This seemed to flatly contradict the claim of the monks of St Denis that he had been bishop of Athens (before being martyred in Gaul and becoming their patron saint). Whether Dionysius the Areopagite was bishop of Corinth or of Athens may seem no more than a minor and obscure point of Church history. But Abelard realized that his discovery gave him an opportunity to taunt his fellow monks. 'Just as a joke', he recollects in his 'history of calamities', 'I showed some of the brothers who were standing round this testimony of Bede.'[69] Abelard's description of this event incidentally shows how generous the authorities at St Denis had been towards him on his return from his house arrest at St Médard and condemnation at Soissons. He was allowed to browse in the library once again, and apparently to take books out of it, if he 'showed' his fellow monks this passage in Bede. (The books may have been kept in coffers along passages, or adjoining the cloister, and not on shelves in a special building as in a modern library.) The monks were 'extremely indignant' and told Abelard that Bede was a most mendacious writer, as they had the superior testimony of their former abbot Hilduin, who had investigated the matter in Greece itself and had removed all doubts in his authoritative life of St Denis. Abelard replied that he preferred the authority of Bede, whose writings were respected throughout the Latin Church, to that of Hilduin.[70]

Abelard was venturing into historical research, a field of study that was new to him, and into the particularly thorny area of the authenticity of saints' lives. Hilduin, who had been abbot of St Denis from 814 to 840, had given the patron saint of the abbey great prestige by conflating three different holy men named Dionysius or Denis: the martyred bishop of Paris in *c.*250; Dionysius the Areopagite, who had been converted by St Paul himself and reputedly became the first bishop of Athens; and thirdly the mystical writer now known as Pseudo-Dionysius, who had lived in *c.*500, probably in Syria. It is impossible to establish how much Abelard knew about the fabrication of history and the forgery of documents which had gone on at St Denis from Hilduin's time onwards.

Certainly he underestimated the ingenuity of Hilduin's arguments and he may never have realized that Hilduin had mixed up Greek and Latin sources extending over a 500-year period. As Abelard did not know Greek, he was in no position to push his researches very far, even if the monks allowed him to. At the initial stage of making his little joke, Abelard does not seem to have known that he was not making an original discovery at all, as Hilduin himself had questioned Bede's statement.[71] Dionysius bishop of Corinth had lived in the second century and even Hilduin had not wanted this irrelevance muddying the waters.

At a later stage in the controversy Abelard wrote Abbot Adam and the monks of St Denis a conciliatory letter, where he cited other authors and showed he had given the matter further thought. He concluded in scholastic fashion: 'As a solution of all these points, we therefore propose that this is a summary (*summa*): we should concede that either Bede made a mistake, or he presented us with the opinion of someone else, or there were two bishops of Corinth called Dionysius.'[72] Although these concessions were no help to Abelard in the short term, they show that his understanding of textual criticism had advanced beyond simply insisting that Bede was a greater authority than Hilduin. Abelard laid down similar principles for dealing with textual difficulties in the prologue to *Sic et Non*: 'We must be very careful not to be deceived by a false attribution of authorship or by a corrupt text, when our attention is drawn to seemingly contradictory or untrue statements among the words of the saints.'[73] In this context he went even further and said that if anything in the writings of the saints seems at odds with the truth, we should admit that we do not understand it.[74] In his letter to Abbot Adam, Abelard had not been prepared to go as far as admitting his own ignorance. His stance is that of a master coming forward with a solution or *summa*, and not that of a monk begging forgiveness from his superiors.

The significance of the parallels between Abelard's letter to Abbot Adam and the prologue to *Sic et Non* is that it gives us a date for when he worked out the ideas for *Sic et Non*.[75] Abbot Adam died in 1122 and Abelard's controversy about St Denis occurred after his condemnation at Soissons in 1121, so he must have written his letter in 1121–2. He was not original in noticing that there were discrepancies in the writings of the Church Fathers, and even in the Scriptures, as St Augustine had laid down rules for resolving such problems and Abelard's master, Anselm of Laon, had discussed the differences between diverse and adverse authorities.[76] Abelard may have first come across these problems at Anselm's school at Laon, when he began his commentary on Ezechiel (which is not extant and may never have been finished).[77] Where *Sic et Non* is extraordinary is in providing no solutions to the hundreds of problems in the writings of the Church Fathers to which it draws attention. No one before Abelard had shown in such detail the range and number of questions that needed answering in Christian apologetics.

Probably Abelard did not take *Sic et Non* further in 1122 because he had too many other pressing concerns. He was determined to rewrite the book, which he had been made to burn at Soissons, and he gave it a new and more grandiose title: 'Christian Theology' (*Theologia Christiana*). Proving the logic, or the 'theology' as he called it, of the Trinity was a more important project for Abelard than resolving whether St Denis had been bishop of Athens or of Corinth. Abelard's exasperation with historical research is shown by his saying to his fellow monks that 'it did not matter much whether St Denis was the Areopagite or someone from somewhere else, as long as he had won such a bright crown with God'.[78] This remark infuriated the monks even more than his joking about what he had found in Bede. They immediately went to Abbot Adam (Abelard says) and laid a charge against him.[79] He was told that he would be dispatched to the king, 'so that he might take vengeance on me, as one who had made off with his crown and the glory of his kingdom'.[80] In other words, Abelard was charged with treason. His former 'calamities' of being castrated and condemned as a heretic paled in comparison with the vengeance which might be taken on him as a traitor to the kingdom of France. In the *Song of Roland* the villain, Ganelon, was torn limb from limb for this.

Why did Abelard's remarks about St Denis produce such strong reactions? A short answer is provided by the *Song of Roland*. (The song is contemporary with Abelard in its written form and it shows what an audience of French knights might think important.) In order to show the Saracens' determination to conquer France, the song describes Margariz of Seville assuring the other Saracen leaders that 'we will soon be taking our rest in the borough of St Denis'.[81] This represents the heart of France. Likewise when Roland is dying, exhausted and betrayed but still in possession of his sword Durendal, he describes the protective relics enclosed in its hilt: a piece of the Virgin's robe, St Peter's tooth, St Basil's blood 'and some hairs of my lord St Denis'.[82] He is Roland's lord because Roland fights for Christendom and for France. St Denis embodies everything that Roland and the French knights stand for. He is the apostle of France, who died heroically (like Roland himself) as a martyr. And he still lives through the miracles he performs at the abbey of St Denis, where he and his holy companions rest in the vaults with the kings of France. This is why the *Song of Roland*'s Saracens make the abbey of St Denis their objective.

These beliefs were still very much alive: Abbot Suger in 1124 (less than three years after Abelard's letter to his predecessor, Abbot Adam) displayed the relics of St Denis and his holy companions on the high altar of the abbey and conferred a battle standard on Louis VI. The king took it up 'as if from his lord' (St Denis) and he summoned all the forces of France to follow him.[83] This invocation of St Denis worked marvellously, according to Suger at least, as the princes and lords mustered their armies from all over France in a show of force against the German emperor. Throughout the whole period of this triumphant war (Suger says) the silver caskets containing the relics of St Denis and his companions remained on display above the high altar.[84] The monks conducted their office of worship day and night, surrounded by devout people and religious women, all praying for the victory of the French army. By these means Louis VI was assured, like Henry II in the storm in the English Channel, that his monks were performing their service of intercession for him without risk of intermission.

So, when Abelard questioned the history of St Denis, he was challenging something fundamental to French culture and politics. Suger could not have asserted the power of St Denis so effectively in 1124, if it had not had a long history behind it (the *Song of Roland* is one indication among many). Abelard, as an intellectual, might say that it did not matter whether it was St Denis or someone else who was in the silver casket, but the correct identity was crucial to the monks and their clients. The real knights of France, as much as the legendary Roland, risked their lives for 'my lord St Denis' and they had to be sure that his monks had him safe in their abbey. They may have been so indignant against Abelard because they understood better than he did how fragile the artifice of St Denis was. This does not mean that they connived at the fabrications of Hilduin and his successors. But the monks knew that the sacred texts of their patron saint demanded faith from his followers, just like the texts of the Scriptures. For St Denis's devotees, his authenticity was proved by the way he worked for them: as long as miracles happened at his shrine, he was obviously true. The documentary evidence was secondary.

Many of the most ancient monasteries were keepers of shrines like St Denis. If Abelard thought this of only secondary importance, he should have joined one of the new orders, like the Cistercians or the Carthusians, whose members carried no historical baggage and possessed no relics. The diversity of the Church's religious houses and orders gave recruits a wide choice. It looks as if Abelard had wanted to benefit from the fame and wealth of St Denis without playing his part in promoting the cult. Even worse, he had made a joke about the identity of St Denis.

These are the sort of reasons why the monks believed he had betrayed his abbey and betrayed France. Perhaps his being a Breton had contributed to the latter accusation. However, it does have to be pointed out that only Abelard in his 'history of calamities' says he was accused of treason. Suger in his life of Louis VI makes no mention of this incident at all.

As on other occasions, Abelard had supporters as well as opponents in this conflict. He escaped from St Denis at night with the help of some of the monks and 'some of our disciples', by which he probably meant his students.[85] At a guess, the monks knew how to get him out of the abbey and his students met him at the gate and rode away with him into the night. He was over forty years old and not very capable presumably of scrambling over high walls. (We know he could ride because he tells us that he fractured a neckbone, when he fell from a horse about ten years later.[86]) Perhaps we should see him making his escape weighed down by books and notes. His letter to Abbot Adam contains references which he had probably found at St Denis and took with him. If he was already collecting materials for *Sic et Non*, he presumably took these with him as well. Then there were his books for teaching logic (he may have completed *Dialectica* by 1121) and whatever remained of his *Theologia* after he had been made to burn it at Soissons. Abelard says nothing about how he got access to his own writings, let alone those of other authors, in the 1120s and 1130s when his 'calamities' caused him to flit from place to place and his enemies repeatedly tried to silence him. This makes the range and precision of his learning, especially in *Sic et Non* and *Theologia*, all the more impressive.

Abelard's escape from St Denis made him a fugitive monk in legal terms, liable to excommunication together with anybody who protected him. Yet he describes having no difficulty getting protection from Count Thibaud of Champagne and taking up residence in his fortress town of Provins (which is still dominated today by Caesar's Tower, the castle keep dating from Abelard's lifetime or earlier). He says he was known to the count 'just a little' and 'he sympathized entirely with me in my hardships of which he had heard'.[87] Count Thibaud may have helped Abelard for political reasons, as he was frequently at odds with the king of France. Nevertheless, he was also a loyal Frenchman and a benefactor of numerous monasteries, including St Denis and St Bernard's Clairvaux. Why such a great prince helped Abelard, who was a fugitive monk and a heretic, remains something of a mystery.

Count Thibaud continued to support Abelard even when Abbot Adam of St Denis, who made a visit to Provins, threatened Abelard with excommunication.[88] The Rule of St Benedict specified that a monk was to be reconciled from excommunication by ritual humiliation: lying prostrate at the feet of everyone coming out of choir, until the abbot judged that satisfaction had been made.[89] It is difficult to imagine Abelard in this posture. Fortunately for him, Abbot Adam died a few days later (on 19 February 1122) and, after Suger was elected (on 12 March), Abelard had a meeting with him.[90] He does not say where this meeting took place. Possibly it was in Paris, as Abelard adds that he got 'friends' of his to intervene with the king and council.[91] A deal was negotiated by Stephen de Garlande, the seneschal, who was probably the most influential of Abelard's 'friends' at court.[92] As with modern footballers, the concern was that Abelard should not transfer to a rival. Although he had a controversial record, his talent was undeniable. So the abbey of St Denis dropped their threat of excommunication, on condition that Abelard withdrew to a place of solitude and did not subject himself to any other abbey. This was 'agreed and confirmed', he says, 'in the presence of the king and his men'.[93] He had become as important – or unimportant – to the government of France as a castle or a fief. This time, his opponents must have hoped, they had seen the last of him, as he could not make trouble for others in a place of solitude.

THE HERMITAGE OF THE PARACLETE

As a consequence of the agreement with the abbey of St Denis, Abelard became a hermit whether he liked it or not. As always, he was in keeping with fashion, as hermitages were springing up across France and Christendom. 'It seemed as if the whole world would be turned into a hermitage,' St Peter Damian had said.[94] 'Solitude' did not necessarily mean living in the wilderness, though that is how Abelard started, as many hermits lived alongside churches or in groups with separate cells. The anchorite or anchoress was a Christlike figure. Even more than a monk, he or she could be seen to possess nothing and to live in austerity. By being people's spiritual counsellors, and sometimes soothsayers as well, hermits might be very influential despite their isolation. Some of the most famous ones followed the example of St John the Baptist and attracted crowds of people into the wilderness, or they went from place to place preaching repentance. St Norbert established his order of hermit-preachers at Prémontré in 1121, less than a hundred miles from where Abelard was to have his hermitage in 1122. Perhaps because he was jealous of Norbert's success, Abelard called him a hypocrite.[95] On the other hand, he expressed approval for the other hermit-preacher with whom he had much in common, Robert of Arbrissel, who was a Breton and a former master. Because he converted women and lived an unsettled life, he was a figure of scandal in some quarters. It is in this context, defending him against Roscelin in c.1120, that Abelard called Robert 'an outstanding proclaimer of Christ'.[96]

Hermits were freer than monks to act as the spirit moved them; indeed following the spirit was the rationale of being a hermit. 'No one should be disturbed if a certain diversity is apparent in this order', a contemporary comments, 'as each one of them organizes his life differently.'[97] As much as a desire for peace and quiet, this diversity probably attracted Abelard after his experience of traditional monasticism at St Denis. In reality, however, no hermit was entirely liberated from the world or from authority, as he depended on his patrons for the physical means of survival and he also needed ecclesiastical approval. Without the latter, people might think him no better than a beggar or a madman. The examples of John the Baptist and Christ Himself showed hermits ran high risks criticizing society as if they stood outside it. Hermits needed approval and recognition as much as anybody, indeed more than anybody else as they lived alone. This explains the paradox that the hermitage itself needed to be accessible to the public. Many hermitages were located by main roads or rivers. Reaching them might require a walk through a wood, or up a hill, but nothing strenuous enough to discourage patrons from visiting. In the twelfth century as much as in the twentieth, the hermitage was a symbol of rural peace for visitors from the town.

Abelard's hermitage of the Paraclete is typical in these respects. It was less than five miles from Nogent-sur-Seine, in the middle of the fairs of Champagne area, one of the fastest-growing regions of France. It was also close to the village of Quincey and alongside the river Ardusson or Arduzon, though that was not navigable by anything better than a flat-bottomed punt. The original endowment from Milo lord of Nogent probably included cultivated fields, garden plots and reed-beds, as well as the areas of marsh and woodland which were considered a wilderness.[98] Within twenty-five years of its foundation, the Paraclete owned so much property that a map makes it look as if it had colonized the whole area around the Seine between Troyes and Provins.[99] Of course this was not so, as there were many other lords engaged like the owners of the Paraclete in making woodland and marsh economically productive. From a landlord's point of view, monastic foundations were a way of planting population and increasing revenue. Such activities explain why the county of Troyes, to which the lordship of Nogent-sur-Seine was subject, emerges from obscurity for the first time in Abelard's lifetime under Count Hugh I (1097–1125) and then under Count Thibaud of Champagne himself (1125–52).[100]

Abelard describes coming to a 'wilderness' (*solitudo*), where 'I first of all built an oratory of reeds and straw'. Here he could chant with the Psalmist: 'Lo, I have gone off flying away, and I abode in the wilderness.'[101] To emphasize his solitude, he quotes in his 'history of calamities' a passage from St Jerome describing how ancient Greek philosophers abandoned the civilization of cities for the desert.[102] In reality, however, the site of Abelard's hermitage had little in common with the severity of a desert. Its situation was more like that of the 'suburban gardens' which St Jerome describes philosophers abandoning, with their 'water meadows and leafy trees, twittering birds, clear springs and murmuring brooks'.[103] (St Jerome's point is that all these amenities distract the concentration.[104]) Later on, Heloise, too, stressed the savageness of the site:

> Everything here is your creation. This wilderness, ranged only by wild beasts and brigands, had known no human habitation nor dwelling. In the very lairs of wild beasts and lurking-places of robbers, where the name of God was never heard, you erected a divine tabernacle.[105]

But she was not describing something she had seen, as she did not arrive until 1129, six or seven years after Abelard's occupation of the site, by which time stone buildings had been constructed and land had been cleared and drained.[106] Her reference to 'wild beasts and brigands' is a commonplace of descriptions of the medieval forest.[107] Certainly, though, there would have been some impressive animals in the woods, such as deer and boar. When Abelard says he built the first oratory himself, this should perhaps be taken literally, as he explains later that he was compelled to give up manual labour because he had to earn money for his nascent community by teaching.[108] In the vicinity of the river Ardusson building materials of wood and reeds were ready to hand. Abelard had presumably not wielded an axe since he was a young man, twenty or thirty years earlier. He makes no mention of himself or his helpers having any accidents.

Abelard makes clear that even at the start he was not entirely on his own. He was accompanied at first by 'a certain clerk' and then, 'when the students found out where I was, they began to come running from all sides'.[109] They built themselves 'little tabernacles' and lived on wild herbs and coarse bread (the fact that they had bread at all shows they remained linked to the agricultural economy).[110] 'Such were our disciples', Abelard proudly continues, 'who erected their huts by the river

Ardusson and looked more like hermits than students.'[111] The speed with which the students had arrived in this supposedly remote place may be explained by its closeness to Nogent-sur-Seine and the trade routes of Champagne. Furthermore, Abelard says that the place was already known to him.[112] It is possible (as has already been suggested) that he had run a very successful school near Nogent-sur-Seine in the previous year, when he was still under the authority of the abbey of St Denis.[113] In that case, some of these students may have been delighted to return.

Abelard admits that the primitive and heroic life, which he describes his students leading, did not last long, and he too had to come to terms with reality. And so he declares (with the unjust steward in the Gospel parable): 'To dig I was unable and to beg I was ashamed'.[114] With this admission, Abelard's flirtation with manual labour and rural self-sufficiency came to an end. 'I went back to the skill which I knew; unbearable poverty compelled me to run a school.'[115] He made this excuse presumably to forestall critics saying that monks should not be teaching, particularly not a monk who had undertaken to be a hermit. He made a new arrangement with the students whereby they took charge of the domestic arrangements, including food, clothing and the management of land and buildings, so that he remained free to study.[116] He does not say which of his students had the skills of a domestic and estates bursar.

Only one student of Abelard's can be identified from this time, but he gives us a fascinating glimpse of the school. This is Hilary of Orléans (also known as Hilary the Englishman), a distinguished Latin poet of the *Carmina Burana* sort. One poem of his describes a disciplinary crisis at the school.[117] A servant had reported to Abelard some unspecified misbehaviour by the students and he reacted by ordering them all to leave and go and find lodgings in the nearby village of Quincey. 'And so, Hilary, why are you hesitating? Why have you not gone to live in the village?' To which he answers that the days are short, the journey is long and he is overweight. Each verse concludes with a refrain in Old French (*tort a vers nos li mestre* – 'the master has done us wrong') reminding us that this was the language students used in their leisure time and when they really wanted to express their feelings. By adding a French chorus to his Latin elegiacs Hilary may have intended to tease Abelard, who probably insisted on students using Latin at all times because his school was supposed to be a monastery as much as a place of learning.

Hilary's poem confirms Abelard's description of students flocking into his school. He reminds Abelard that 'we are the many who have come together from different places to where the fount of logic was most copious'. But he also reminds Abelard that the students will all depart if they are denied what they want. Hilary concludes with an appeal to the 'master' to relent. Perhaps Abelard did so; we have no way of knowing whether this was a major or a minor incident. The information has only been preserved because it is integral to an admired piece of Latin writing. What the poem does show, however, is that at the time Hilary was writing, Abelard's school was no longer organized as a co-operative. There are servants who report to Abelard and he replies by messenger. He seems a remote and formidable figure: a 'hard master' Hilary calls him. The poem also suggests that the students came to Abelard to learn logic and not theology. Logic is the only subject of study that is mentioned in the poem and it is mentioned three times to stress its importance. Certainly, this is the teaching that Hilary wanted from Abelard. If he was primarily teaching logic and the students did as they pleased, Abelard no longer had a hermitage at the Paraclete but an ordinary secular school. Hilary concedes, though, that Abelard was still trying to lead a monastic life; that is why he said the students must withdraw to Quincey and come in only by the day.

ABELARD'S ACHIEVEMENTS AT THE HERMITAGE

In his 'history of calamities' Abelard gives the impression that he achieved very little during his time at the Paraclete. His 'rivals' kept backbiting and, in addition to that, Hilary's poem suggests that his students misbehaved.[118] On the other hand, Abelard completed *Theologia Christiana* at this time, which was a considerable achievement, though he makes no mention of it in his 'history of calamities'. *Theologia Christiana* is an enlargement and revision of *Theologia 'Summi Boni'*, the book he had been made to burn at his trial at Soissons. By describing his *Theologia* as *Christiana*, Abelard was insisting that it was a Christian and orthodox study. One portion of *Theologia Christiana* does confirm, however, that Abelard was acutely conscious of his 'rivals' and their accusations. He departs from the academic tone he usually adopts to give Apocalyptic warnings: these are the last days before the coming of Antichrist and 'anyone who persists in attacking me' must be blind to the general conflagration which is about to take place.[119] In this context Abelard ridicules several of his fellow masters, never by name but making clear whom he means, including Alberic of Reims who had been his prosecutor at Soissons.[120] Hatred and fear may actually have stimulated Abelard to write, rather than deterring him. Certainly, this is what his 'history of calamities' suggests.

An assessment of how much Abelard achieved at the Paraclete partly depends on how long he spent there, and opinions differ about that. He may not have settled down until 1123 and he may have left for St Gildas in 1125.[121] In that case, he was only at the Paraclete for two or three years. Alternatively, he may have got there shortly after Suger became abbot of St Denis on 12 March 1122 and he may not have left until 1127. He is first named as abbot of St Gildas in a charter dated 15 March 1128 (or possibly 1129).[122] In that case, he could have spent five or six years at the Paraclete. Constant Mews ascribes a substantial part of his writings to his time at the Paraclete: *Theologia Christiana*, *Sic et Non*, the *Tractatus de Intellectibus*, a set of glosses on Porphyry's introduction to logic, the *Soliloquium* (a dialogue with himself between 'Peter' and 'Abelard'), the *Collationes* (Platonic dialogues between a philosopher and a Jew, and a philosopher and a Christian), and possibly also a work on Grammar and another on Rhetoric.[123] Although the *Soliloquium* comprises only a few pages and the Grammar and Rhetoric no longer exist, the others are substantial works, particularly *Sic et Non*. One reason for ascribing so much of Abelard's writing to this period is that it is difficult to see when else he could have done it: conditions at St Gildas were presumably not so favourable and neither were they perhaps when he returned to Paris.

If Abelard wrote so much at the Paraclete, he must have had an all-weather scriptorium and a library. Perhaps (as has already been suggested) he brought a substantial body of notes with him from St Denis. He cannot have done much reading or writing in the hut of reeds and straw, which he describes building first of all. The hut's novelty may have worn off within a few days. An intellectual like Abelard, who had spent his whole professional life debating with opponents, would have found a daily round of personal meditation and repetitive prayer very difficult at first. Fortunately for him, or perhaps by design, the students arrived and brought his experiment as a hermit to an end, and he could return to being a master and a writer. If Abelard was going to produce books with regularity, he needed a substantial room with windows and a fireplace to study and write in. A scriptorium may have been among the first stone buildings which he describes constructing. One advantage of the site of the Paraclete being a 'wilderness' was that there must have been plenty of firewood in the early years and waterways to transport it to Abelard's door. He would not have found himself in the situation of his contemporary, the monastic chronicler Orderic Vitalis of St Evroul in Normandy, who considered it too cold to write in the cloister in winter.[124]

Abelard devotes considerable space in his 'history of calamities' to defending his decision to change the dedication of his hermitage from 'the Trinity' as a whole to God's particular manifestation as 'the Paraclete' or consoler. He explains that this was an afterthought, intended as a thank-offering for the consolation he had received there.[125] (This in itself suggests that there had been times when Abelard had found life in his hermitage very satisfying.) As he makes no mention of the Paraclete's role as 'consoler' in *Theologia Christiana*, he may not have taken an interest in this idea until 1123 or later.[126] It was attractive because the word 'Paraclete' was Greek and looked learned (like his book titles *Theologia* and *Ethica*) and also because the Church Father who had defined the Paraclete as 'consoler' was Origen, the 'greatest Christian philosopher' in Abelard's opinion.[127] (He was interested in Origen because he was believed to have castrated himself for chastity's sake.) For Abelard, the dedication to the Paraclete had the merit of being original and challenging, as there were no precedents for it in the Latin Church. He defended it by referring to Christ's promise: 'And I will pray the Father, and another Paraclete He will give unto you, that He may abide with you for ever'.[128]

So what could be wrong, Abelard argued, with his dedication to the Paraclete, when altars were dedicated to the Trinity as a whole and also to aspects of the life of the Son, such as the Holy Cross and the Holy Sepulchre? He had not made his dedication to a single person of the Trinity, the Holy Spirit (as some believed), but to divine consolation as such. He provocatively concluded: 'Even if I had done that, it would not have been against reason, although it is unknown to custom.'[129] With this remark, he was returning to the questions about the Trinity which had been raised at his trial at Soissons. When he had said to Alberic of Reims 'I will show you the reason for this, if you like,' Alberic had replied: 'We take no account of human reason or your sense of these things, but only of the words of authority.'[130] Abelard raises this issue again in the first chapter of *Sic et Non*, which is headed: 'That faith is built up by human reason, and the contrary.'[131] Alberic, in Abelard's opinion, favoured 'the contrary'. We know from *Theologia Christiana* that Abelard was trying to get his own back on Alberic at this time. Dedicating his oratory to the Paraclete was one way of reasserting his own ideas about the Trinity and drawing attention to himself. His fame (he says) was spreading throughout the whole world, although his body remained hidden.[132]

There is complication about all this, however, as Abelard says he had first of all dedicated his oratory to the Trinity as such, whereas it is more likely that the first dedication had been to St Denis.[133] The reason for thinking this is that the oldest part of the site, later called 'the little monastery' (*le petit moustier*), was dedicated to St Denis. The nuns of the Paraclete specially honoured St Denis and Abelard wrote two hymns for them in praise of the saint.[134] In his 'history of calamities' Abelard was probably not trying to conceal that the original dedication had been to St Denis, but to emphasize that his personal dedication had been to the Trinity. The dedication to St Denis may have been one of the conditions which Abbot Suger had insisted on when he allowed Abelard to withdraw to a hermitage. Abelard acknowledged the continuing authority of St Denis at his hermitage by calling Suger 'our abbot' when he got permission to leave to go to St Gildas and again when he made over the site to Heloise.[135]

'NEW APOSTLES'

Abelard says his dedication of his oratory to the Paraclete stirred up more formidable adversaries against him than his previous rivals. These were two 'new apostles', who boasted that they had revived the life of canons regular and of monks respectively.[136] St Norbert and St Bernard are most probably meant by this veiled reference.[137] Referring to people without naming them was an admired rhetorical art, which Cicero recommends, and which Abelard uses elsewhere.[138] Almost certainly he was being ironical (another rhetorical art) in describing his adversaries as 'apostles'. Heloise went further and called them 'pseudo-apostles'.[139] St Norbert and St Bernard would indeed have been thought of as modern apostles, as they were very successful preachers as well as being leaders of the reforming movement in the religious orders, which was considered an apostolic mission by the papacy.[140]

Abelard attacked St Norbert in a sermon at about this time and so it is not surprising to find him attacked here as a 'new apostle'.[141] St Bernard is more of a problem, as there is no evidence of animosity between Bernard and Abelard as early as the 1120s. In the 1130s, on the other hand, Abelard wrote St Bernard a letter which fits the context of a 'new apostle' very well. Addressing Bernard and the Cistercian order as a whole, Abelard says: 'You who are newly arisen, as it were, and who greatly rejoice in novelty have instituted by your novel decrees a divine office for use among you which departs from the long-established and permanent custom of all clergy and all monks.'[142] This is not the only time in his monastic life that Abelard adopted the stance of a defender of traditional values against innovators. In the sermon in which he attacked St Norbert he also took a conservative stance, arguing that monks, rather than canons or bishops, were the only really religious people.

As Abelard admits that he was lying low at the Paraclete at this time, his information about his detractors came only from hearsay; it depended, that is, on other detractors among his students or visitors. He says he lost even his best friends in this period because everyone was too frightened to speak out.[143] St Bernard published his 'Apologia' around this time (in 1127). This is an attack on the Cistercians' rivals, the Cluniacs, although it does not refer to them by name. In his state of extreme anxiety Abelard may have heard about the 'Apologia' and jumped to the conclusion that Bernard was attacking him, as the 'Apologia' begins by warning against monks who are too proud and whose poverty is insincere.[144] Abelard may also have been suspicious of the 'Apologia' because it was produced in collaboration with William of St Thierry. Later on, the combination of William and Bernard brought about Abelard's trial for heresy at Sens in 1140; this alliance may have had its origins in 1121, at Abelard's first trial at Soissons, when William of St Thierry had been present with the papal legate.[145] By moving from the Paris area to Nogent-sur-Seine, Abelard had placed himself within range of St Bernard, whose abbey of Clairvaux was only fifty miles away. Territorially, the hermitage of the Paraclete was in competition with neighbouring Cistercian houses for recruits, and they shared the same patron in Thibaud count of Champagne.

Abelard says he got so worried that he thought any meeting of ecclesiastics which took place had been convened to condemn him.[146] In the light of what had happened at Soissons in 1121, this was not an unreasonable fear and – looking to his future condemnation at Sens in 1140 – it was positively prescient, as was his concern about the role of St Bernard as a slanderer. (At the same time as being fearful and resentful, Abelard was inviting trouble, as he made clear by dedicating his oratory to the 'Paraclete' and calling his *Theologia* 'Christian'.) He makes the interesting remark that he became so desperate that he was ready 'to go over to the pagans beyond the bounds of Christendom and live there quietly among Christ's enemies as a Christian by paying whatever tribute was required'.[147] The pagans he had in mind were probably the Muslims of Spain, who tolerated Christian communities. He says he thought they would be well disposed to him because he was accused of not being a Christian.[148]

Unlike Peter the Venerable, who became interested in Islam because of the Cluniac houses in Spain and who had the Koran translated into Latin, Abelard's knowledge of Islam seems to have been superficial. He shows a profound concern with non-Christian beliefs: in *Theologia* with the ancient Greeks and in his *Commentary on St Paul's Epistle to the Romans* with the Jews, but he has nothing comparable to say about Islam. This lack of interest is confirmed by Abelard's dialogues or *Collationes*: there is one between a classical philosopher and a Jew, and another between a philosopher and a Christian, but none with a Muslim. Abelard's purpose in mentioning the pagans in his 'history of calamities' was rhetorical. His reference to the bounds of Christendom emphasized that the abbey of St Gildas was the back of beyond and that he came there as an exile from civilization. The monks were far more savage than infidels, Abelard says.[149] He had been driven west 'by the envy of the French', just as St Jerome had been driven east by the Romans.[150] (This is not exactly what Jerome had said, but Abelard turned it to his purpose.[151])

THE ABBEY OF ST GILDAS

The abbey of St Gildas-de-Rhuys was an appropriate place for an exile, as Gildas himself (who lived in the sixth century) was believed to have landed up in Brittany by fleeing south from his native Strathclyde. Dedications of churches to St Gildas and his family can be plotted on a routeway from Anglesey through Wales and then across the Cornish and Breton peninsulas.[152] Like Abelard, Gildas had been a Latin rhetorician, whose book *On the Ruin of Britain* is still read by all students of the Dark Ages. His relics had journeyed again, when they had been taken inland to Berry in the wake of the Viking invasions. His shrine and abbey, generously endowed by the duchess of Brittany, had been re-established a century before Abelard's arrival on its original site. Facing on to the Atlantic by the Pointe du Grand Mont, this dramatic seascape was a typical resting place for a Celtic saint. It was one of the holiest places in Brittany; the golden reliquaries (dating in their present form from the fourteenth century and later) survive to this day.

It is difficult to assess how much Abelard knew or cared about the history of St Gildas. When he had been at St Denis, he had infuriated the monks by saying that it did not matter who St Denis was, as long as he had won favour with God.[153] Like St Denis, the abbey of St Gildas was a pilgrimage centre and this gave Abelard the same sort of opportunity as Abbot Suger to develop the saint's cult. But Abelard shows no interest in shrines; his writings focus on the central Christological issues of the Trinity and Redemption. The fine Romanesque church at St Gildas was built after Abelard's time. Nevertheless, he did write a hymn to Gildas, which shows he was enthusiastic about him for a while at least.[154] It begins by focusing on the sanctuary lamp, placed above the lights of the candelabrum, reflecting the life and spirit of the saint. Abelard is probably describing here a multi-branched candlestick, perhaps many feet high (like the one at the shrine of St Cuthbert at Durham), whose light glints around the gilded and jewelled reliquary of the saint. The hymn then shifts its gaze from the interior of the church to the sea, where the light of Hesperus, the evening star, guides seafarers back 'to the homeland': to 'Brittany circled by the Ocean'. The hymn concludes with praise of Gildas as a warrior saint (like St Denis), who protects the Breton people in battle and leads them to glory.

Already in this hymn, however, there is a hint of Abelard's distaste for his 'homeland'. He describes Brittany as 'barren' and the Ocean as 'immense'. In his 'history of calamities' the descriptions are stronger: the Ocean is 'horrifying' and 'the country is barbarous'.[155] Compared with Champagne (where Abelard was coming from), Brittany is infertile agriculturally and the Atlantic certainly is different from the little river Ardusson. In addition to barbarism, Abelard complained that the language was 'unknown to me'.[156] This presumably means that he could neither read nor speak Celtic. His hymn makes no acknowledgement of Gildas as a Celtic saint. The whole message of Abelard's 'history of calamities' is that he was a provincial boy who wanted to succeed in Paris. He had returned to his 'homeland' only because 'the envy of the French' had driven him there. The expectations of his monks were at cross-purposes with his own. They had presumably hoped for an abbot who would understand them, because he was a Breton, but who could defend them in the wider world because he knew France. Abelard on his side probably had no knowledge of Celtic Brittany (he was careful to explain that he came from the southernmost border) and he was desperate to be accepted as a Frenchman.[157]

We first catch sight of Abelard as abbot of St Gildas in March 1128 or 1129, not in his own abbey but at Nantes in the company of the count, Conan III, who was also duke of Brittany, and various bishops, including the Latin poet Hildebert of Lavardin who was archbishop of Tours.[158] This was the exalted and cosmopolitan company which Abelard was now entitled to keep as an abbot. His abbey of St Gildas was not as remote as he suggested, as it was only a hundred miles from Nantes and the journey could be done without a sea-crossing. He describes visiting the count in Nantes on another occasion, as if it was a common practice.[159] But Abelard's life as a busy abbot required hard riding and he describes another day when he fell from his horse and injured himself.[160] He becomes visible once more in January 1131, again not at St Gildas but in central France at Morigny (250 miles inland). This time he was with the pope and St Bernard and many other prelates.[161] But Abelard had not travelled so far to win favours for his monks. He had come, on the contrary, to get papal help in prosecuting them; Geoffrey bishop of Chartres was duly sent to St Gildas as papal legate.[162]

Knowingly or not, Abelard acted at St Gildas as an agent of French centralism against the separatist aspirations of Celtic Brittany. There was a political struggle going on, in the wake of the Norman Conquest, between Henry I of England and Louis VI of France for the loyalty of Brittany. At the time Abelard became abbot of St Gildas, French interests seemed to be winning, as Conan III had demonstrated his allegiance to Louis VI by answering the great summonses to war in 1122 and 1124.[163] Sending the bishop of Chartres to St Gildas was one among many small actions which reinforced French as much as papal power in Brittany, as Chartres was a royal bishopric. Conan III's strategy as duke was to invoke French authority against his local rivals. This may be why he had agreed to Abelard's election as abbot in the first place. The little that is known of Abelard's activities at St Gildas shows him to have been a partisan of Conan III and this fits in with his family origins in the French-speaking part of the county of Nantes. Astralabe, the son of Abelard and Heloise, subsequently became a canon of Nantes cathedral.[164]

Abelard attributes his 'calamities' at St Gildas not to his political circumstances, but to his altruism in reforming an undisciplined community. The monks plotted to kill him (he says) just as had happened to St Benedict himself.[165] Abelard may have exaggerated these threats, as he was desperate to justify his desertion of his abbey and he had to explain his failure to himself as much as to others. The tone of his 'history of calamities' reaches a climax of self-pity when he describes his precarious situation at St Gildas. Mary M. McLaughlin has suggested in her article on 'Abelard as Autobiographer' that he became mentally deranged: 'It was during his years of exile in this abbey that he endured the most serious and prolonged crisis of his mature life, falling more and more deeply into the depression whose symptoms, culminating in an obsessive fear of physical injury and death, he described in his *story of calamities*'.[166] As Abelard repeatedly thought the monks were trying to poison him, it is possible that his fears were delusions, though depression in its clinical sense is difficult to diagnose from a person's words alone.[167]

Against the hypothesis that Abelard was depressed and deluded at St Gildas is the possibility that he really did face death threats. He certainly was in a barbarous country, in the sense that Brittany was in a state of turmoil. It was probably true, as he reports, that Geoffrey bishop of Chartres had little success in enforcing papal authority at St Gildas. In the solemn presence of Conan III and an assembly of bishops, Geoffrey exacted promises from some of the monks that they would leave.[168] But the response of those who remained was to try and cut Abelard's throat.[169] Telling evidence in support of his fears is Conan III's declaration in 1126 that he was incapable of protecting the abbey of Redon (in southern Brittany like St Gildas), since he could not control his own knights who 'infested' it. Because of 'the accumulated perfidy of the Bretons', the duke admitted, he could not guard it in the way he should and he had therefore handed it over to the pope for protection.[170] The monks of Redon may have written these documents themselves in order to justify severing relations with the duke. Even so, it shows in what contempt they held him. If a Breton abbot could not expect protection from his duke, he had no recourse but to local strongmen. Abelard was an outsider, who had the intelligence to see his own powerlessness: 'Since the entire barbarous population of the land was equally lawless and out of control, I had no one to whom I could go for help.'[171]

Patron of Heloise and her Nuns

Abelard had got to help himself and he did this by helping Heloise. In 1129 Abbot Suger of St Denis gained possession of the convent of Argenteuil, of which Heloise was prioress. The nuns were accused of notorious immorality, a charge endorsed by the papal legate, local prelates and the king himself.[172] There is no way today of deciding the rights and wrongs of this. Suger was a very powerful man in France. But it may have been true that Heloise was unable to keep order at Argenteuil, just as Abelard could not control his monks at St Gildas. He makes no mention of the charge of immorality in his 'history of calamities'. His version is simply that 'it happened that our abbot of St Denis somehow or other acquired the convent of Argenteuil, as an ancient right pertaining to his monastery, and he violently expelled the nuns'.[173] Abelard's description of Suger as 'our abbot' is significant, as it acknowledges the authority of St Denis over Abelard's oratory of the Paraclete, which is attested by its ancient connections with St Denis.[174] Abelard's gift of his oratory to Heloise must have required 'our abbot's' permission. This was a mutually beneficial arrangement, which made Suger look less violent and which gave Abelard a new role as a patron of nuns.

He is explicit about the expulsion of Heloise giving him an excuse for leaving St Gildas: 'I realized that an opportunity had been presented to me by the Lord for providing for our oratory and so I went back there.'[175] This was in 1129 or 1130. He says he 'invited' Heloise and her nuns to come and he gave them everything he possessed there. His gift was confirmed by the local bishop and by Pope Innocent II himself.[176] The pope's letter was issued at Auxerre on 28 November 1131, when he was making the rounds of France winning support against the Antipope Anacletus II in Rome. Since Abelard mentions this papal grant with some pride, he may have personally started the process of petitioning for it when he was with the pope at Morigny in January 1131.[177]

Abelard's movements during these years are impossible to pin down precisely. Because he was criticized for not doing enough for Heloise and her nuns, he says he 'took to returning to them more often' and he decided 'to watch over them in person'.[178] As the monks of St Gildas were persecuting him relentlessly, he explains, 'I kept running back' to the nuns as to a haven in a storm.[179] If he 'ran back' from St Gildas often, he must have spent weeks or months travelling. The distance between St Gildas and the Paraclete is about 350 miles and the journey in one direction would have taken three or four weeks, allowing for rests (Abelard was over fifty years of age), mishaps (like the time when he was thrown from his horse) and attacks from brigands (who were posted to look out for him).[180] It is therefore likely that after Heloise's expulsion from Argenteuil in 1129, Abelard spent little time at the abbey of St Gildas itself. When he was there, he says he withdrew from the community and lived apart in some 'little cells'.[181] These structures may have survived from the original Celtic monastery, like the monks' individual beehive huts on Great Skelling off the Atlantic coast of Ireland.[182] Abelard may have played at being a hermit, as he had done at the Paraclete, in such 'little cells' in the summer. But in winter he seems to have been either at Nantes, ostensibly on the abbey's business, or he went on one expedition or another to central France, to 'watch over' Heloise and the nuns.[183]

Looking after his nuns justified Abelard in travelling around to win support for them. He reports his critics saying that the least he could do was to preach for them.[184] A fund-raising sermon survives in which he pleads for 'this new and still tender plantation'; later on, Heloise enlarged on this ideal of a sacred 'plantation'.[185] All this travel necessitated staying overnight in monasteries and prelates' houses across France, which gave him an opportunity to explain his version of events. Like St Bernard, Abelard could make a greater reputation for himself as a reformer by preaching and attacking others than by residing in his own monastery. Successful fund-raising depended on a reputation for sanctity and, judging by St Bernard's case, that needed widespread and noisy publicity. Abelard's success at this is shown by the Morigny chronicler in 1131 eulogizing him as *religiosus*.[186] Even in Brittany he had a reputation as 'a monk of marvellous abstinence', despite his failure at St Gildas.[187] It was in his interest to describe his own monks in lurid terms and to frighten Heloise with their threats. 'If the Lord shall deliver me into the hands of my enemies, wherever my body may lie, whether buried or unburied, I beg you to have it brought to your cemetery,' he enjoined her.[188] She responded by at least purporting to take these threats seriously: 'Spare her at least, who is yours alone, from words of his sort.'[189]

Abelard was obliged to return to St Gildas, whether he liked it or not, because he had been all too successful in his travelling diplomacy in 1131. A papal legate was sent to St Gildas at his request.[190] His 'history of calamities' concludes at this dramatic point, with the legate's mission having failed and Abelard escaping once more from his murderous monks. 'Every day' at St Gildas, he says, he sees the sword of Damocles suspended over his head.[191] His 'history of calamities' was addressed to a fellow monk, described as his 'dearly beloved brother in Christ and closest companion', though Abelard does not name this individual and he has never been identified.[192] The concluding episodes of the 'history of calamities' suggest that Abelard had written it to justify his abandoning St Gildas altogether. Certainly this is what happened, as he is next found teaching in Paris. Probably he arrived there shortly after 1132.[193]

HELOISE'S OPPOSITION TO ABELARD'S PATRONAGE

Although Abelard's 'history of calamities' may have helped him escape from St Gildas, it grievously offended Heloise because he had written about her to a stranger, as if she had no feelings of her own.

> You wrote your friend a long letter of consolation, purportedly about his troubles though in fact about your own. Even if you were intending your diligent recollections for his comfort, you have hugely added to our desolation. While you may have wished to heal his wounds, you have inflicted new wounds on us as well as reopening old ones. Heal the wounds, I beseech you, which you have yourself inflicted.[194]

With these words Heloise took the initiative in her correspondence with Abelard. They set the tone – relentlessly demanding and occasionally scornful – for what follows. 'Remember what you owe me!' is her constant theme.[195] The imperative followed by 'I beseech you' – *obsecro* – reaches a climax of recrimination at the end of her letter: 'Attend, I beseech you!'; 'Do it, I beseech you!'; 'Remember, I beseech you!'; 'Give, I beseech you!'; 'Consider, I beseech you!'.[196] Heloise was the master of Latin 'letters' in every sense and she used her superiority to point out to

Abelard that he had offended against the rules of letter-writing by producing a letter of consolation, which was self-centred instead of considering the troubles of his friend. Much more seriously, he had crassly offended 'us', meaning Heloise as an individual and as head of her community of nuns. It never seems to have occurred to Abelard that addressing his 'history of calamities' to a friend, instead of to her, would arouse her anger. He may even have sent her a copy by special messenger.[197]

Heloise expressed no gratitude to Abelard for rescuing her from Argenteuil and giving her the convent of the Paraclete. His action was simply another cause for reproach. It left him even more deeply obligated to her, she argued.[198] She could interpret his generosity in this way because she claimed to have had no control over her life since she became a nun. She had had to subject herself blindly to Abelard's will: first he had made her be a nun at Argenteuil and now he was making her prioress of the Paraclete. 'Up to now', she insisted, 'I believed I deserved a great deal from you, since I have done everything for you, and now especially am I persevering in total obedience to you.'[199] Whereas Abelard says he 'invited' Heloise to the Paraclete, she interpreted his call as another test of obedience.[200] He had made no gift, in her opinion, only a further demand on her long-suffering self. 'You disburse nothing at all,' she told him.[201] She reached this conclusion by discounting everything he had given her as worthless.

She demonstrated this argument in its most devastating form by reproaching Abelard with not writing to her, nor even speaking to her: 'Tell me one thing, if you can. Why after our entry into religion, which you alone decreed, have I come to be so neglected and forgotten that I am neither heartened by a word from you when you are present, nor consoled by a letter in your absence?'[202] He admitted in his reply that he had not written her any word of comfort or advice, but this was not out of lack of concern for her: it was because he thought she was doing very well as a nun.[203] He made no comment about her charge that he did not speak to her when they met: on such occasions, presumably, as when he had made over the convent of the Paraclete to her, or when he visited her there subsequently. He remembered these visits as happy havens in a storm.[204] She, meanwhile, was silently raging because he said nothing encouraging to her. They could not have been further apart in their perceptions of what had taken place. Whereas he thought keeping his distance showed his prudent concern to protect her from slander, she was convinced that he did not care about her any more.[205]

When Abelard says he decided to 'watch over' Heloise and her nuns, the literal terms he uses are: 'to invigilate them with his bodily presence'.[206] This suggests that he may have been thinking about transforming himself from being abbot of St Gildas to being the male superior of the nuns.[207] Peter the Venerable, Robert of Arbrissel, St Norbert and even some Cistercians had nuns under their jurisdiction because women were not considered able to cope for themselves. In his 'history of calamities' Abelard objects to abbesses being placed over women in the way abbots are over men, and he objects even more to 'disturbing the natural order' by allowing abbesses and nuns to lord it over clergy and laymen.[208] He underlines his disapproval of women being in superior social positions by quoting the Roman satirist Juvenal: 'Nothing is more intolerable than a rich woman.'[209] This quotation immediately precedes Abelard's declaration that: 'After pondering often what I should do and how best to provide for the sisters, I made up my mind to take care of them and watch over them in person, so that they would revere me the more and I could provide better for their needs.'[210]

By prefacing with a line from Juvenal his decision to 'watch over' and 'provide for' Heloise and her nuns, Abelard was indicating the spirit in which he intended to deal with them. He was tapping into the anti-feminist rhetoric taught in the schools. Much admired in Abelard's time were the writings of Marbod bishop of Rennes (1096–1123) in this genre. He has been described as a misogynist and a homosexual; he was certainly a satirist in the Roman tradition.[211] The antipathy to women which he voiced was shared by many clergy. Nor was it mere literary licence or schoolroom humour which such writing expressed, as anti-feminism was explicit in the medieval interpretation of the story of Adam and Eve. Marbod showed he was serious by writing in his capacity as a local bishop to Robert of Arbrissel, warning him against having women in his ministry. 'Sin began with a woman and it is through her that we all die,' Marbod warned, 'without doubt you cannot long remain chaste if you dwell among women.'[212]

Such a warning applied equally to Abelard, whom St Bernard accused of being 'an abbot without discipline, who argues with boys and consorts with women'.[213] Bernard used the diminutive *muliercula* here, meaning 'little woman' and implying that Heloise and her nuns were silly little women or low immoral women.[214] Abelard had defended Robert of Arbrissel as 'an outstanding proclaimer of Christ' and he also defended himself by citing St Augustine's observation that 'women were such inseparable companions of the Lord Jesus Christ and His apostles that they accompanied them even when they went out to preach'.[215] But at the same time Abelard conceded Marbod's argument that it was hard to remain chaste in women's company, by extolling the special merits of eunuchs as their protectors.[216] Abelard was under such pressure from his detractors that he seems to have clutched at any argument that came to hand. Furthermore, at the time he wrote his 'history of calamities', he probably shared the conventional anti-feminist views of his monastic and scholastic colleagues. As a monk he had preached against marriage and importunate wives, and in his lament for Samson he agreed with the familiar argument used by Marbod that Eve causes death: 'she hands on the cup of death to everyone'.[217]

How deep the anti-feminist prejudices were which Abelard voiced when he quoted Juvenal depends partly on whether he expected his readers to know the context of the single line he cited. Juvenal satirized the rich woman as part of an attack on the 'intolerable' vanities of women. Immediately preceding the rich woman is his attack on the clever woman, 'who insists on keeping to the rules of correct diction and who is a classicist quoting verses at me which I don't know'.[218] Judging from her letters, Heloise was just such a classicist and stickler for correct style. Did Abelard intend to cut her intellectual pretensions down to size by 'watching over' her at the Paraclete? He would have every justification in doing so, within the patriarchal terms he lays down, as nuns were meant to be humble and abbesses in particular should be subordinate to men. If Abelard was harbouring such ambitions at the time he wrote his 'history of calamities', he had forgotten how formidable Heloise was. He may have hoped that her fourteen or fifteen years as a nun had taught her humility. But, as he had had (according to her) no discussions with her during all these years, he had no way of knowing what she thought.

There has been debate about whether the letters of Abelard and Heloise record a progression, which culminates in Heloise's conversion from her irreligious and insubordinate opinions to being a good nun. Although no conversion is spelt out in her letters, some critics have argued that it is there implicitly.[219] What has attracted much less attention, though it is explicit in the letters, is Abelard's conversion from anti-feminism in response to Heloise. From being conventionally patronizing and satirical in his 'history of calamities', he becomes the champion of women's religious equality in his essay on the origin of nuns. 'He could hardly have gone to greater lengths', as Mary M. McLaughlin has observed, 'in his quest for arguments, testimonies and examples that would exalt and dignify both the sex and the vocation of religious women.'[220] As if to make amends for quoting Juvenal's disparagement of women, he repeatedly insists on their dignity.[221] He even gives a new slant to Adam and Eve by arguing that 'the creation of woman surpasses that of man in dignity, since she was created within paradise and he outside it'.[222] The idea that Adam had not been created in paradise was debatable, as Abelard showed in *Sic et Non*.[223] But it allowed him to draw the delightfully novel conclusion that paradise is women's 'native land'.[224]

Once Abelard got hold of a novel idea he tended to pick it up and run with it wherever it led, regardless of maintaining consistency with his previous statements. In this adventurous spirit he attributed ecclesiastical authority to women in his essay on the origin of nuns, despite having declared this to be disturbing and intolerable in his 'history of calamities'. In pursuit of women's dignity, Abelard put forward interpretations of the New Testament which were rarely advanced at the time. He starts with the truism that Christ, as the embodiment of justice, came to redeem both sexes alike. This commonplace bore repeating, as it was undermined by anti-feminist rhetoric and much more seriously by the growing demands of the celibate clergy to exclude women altogether from ecclesiastical precincts. Abelard turned to the evidence of the Gospels and argued that Christ had included both sexes in 'the true monkhood' of His apostolic mission; 'authority is therefore given to women equally with men in this profession'.[225] This meant that nuns, as much as male clergy, have their origin and entitlement in the New Testament itself. 'There', says Abelard, 'we read of a community' (he uses the word *conventum* – a 'convent') 'of holy women renouncing all worldly property and possessing only Christ.'[226] He was referring to the women, 'truly nuns' (Abelard adds), who were Christ's devoted followers in the Gospels.[227]

The most prominent of these women was Mary Magdalene. Abelard interprets her anointing of Christ as a sacrament which 'consecrated Him as king and priest and thus made Him corporally "Christ", that is, the anointed one'.[228] What greater dignity could women have than sanctifying Christ Himself for His mission?, Abelard demands.[229] The events of Christ's resurrection reinforced Mary Magdalene's special status because she and the holy women were the first to meet Him. Abelard concludes that they 'were constituted as if they were female apostles (*apostolas*) above the male apostles'.[230] In a sermon Abelard took up the theme, which was familiar from the litany of the saints, that Mary Magdalene was 'the apostle of the apostles'. He gave this honorific title a more substantial and legal significance by adding that she was 'the (female) legate (*legata*) of the (male) legates'.[231] In other words, Mary Magdalene was superior to any of the legates sent out from the papal curia in Rome.

These ideas would not necessarily have pleased Heloise, despite their feminist slant. Abelard was evidently thinking in terms of an ecclesiastical hierarchy and profession set apart from the mass of Christians. He was arguing for some select women, nuns as a profession and Heloise herself as a 'deaconess' (a title Abelard derived from the early Church), being accorded special dignity and included in the clerical elite.[232] She had argued in the other direction: women's experience of indignity, of not being treated as an elite, brought the need for elites itself into question. Why should there be specially designated 'religious' orders, set apart by their rules and privileges? 'Would that our religion could rise to this height', Heloise argued, 'that it fulfil the Gospel and not go beyond it, lest we attempt to be something more than Christians.'[233] She was not alone in her time in arguing that the Gospel was all that Christians required. Where she differed from ecclesiastical reformers was in concluding from this that the laity too were religious. 'It should be considered a great thing if we could equal religious lay people,' she asserted.[234] This was a contradiction in terms, as only monks were described as *religiosi* in everyday usage. But she pointed out that in the Old Testament 'the religion of lay people' had not been so devalued: Abraham, David and Job had all been laymen.[235]

Abelard did not follow Heloise down this fundamentalist road, probably because he was too attached to his own standing as a monk and *religiosus*; he had preached a sermon on the theme that 'monk' is the name of religion itself.[236] In his rule for the nuns he sticks to the idea that nuns and monks both have a profession authorized by the Church and they should co-operate with each other. He proposed pairs of monasteries alongside each other, one male and one female.[237] This was an old idea which was being redeveloped in Abelard's time in various forms: the convent of Marcigny with the Virgin Mary as its abbess and the abbot of Cluny as its earthly superior; St Norbert's establishment of nuns alongside his monks at Prémontré in the 1120s; Robert of Arbrissel's establishment (twenty years before Norbert) of his men and women followers at Fontevrault; even the Cistercians had nunneries associated with some of their houses at first.[238] Contemporary with Abelard in England, Gilbert of Sempringham, another master educated in the French schools, was establishing linked communities of men and women, many of them poor and unemployed in origin.[239] As so often, Abelard was in the height of fashion, while at the same time being controversial, as double monasteries readily gave rise to scandal. This was why he had objected in his 'history of calamities' to abbesses having authority.[240] But when he came to write his rule for the nuns, which Heloise had herself requested, he could no longer deny the legitimacy of female authority, as he had already argued that the holy women of the New Testament had been superior to the male apostles.

Abelard calls the male head of his proposed double monastery the 'provost' and the female head the 'deaconess'. The provost is to 'preside' over both monks and nuns.[241] But his authority over the nuns is enigmatic. Abelard says he should act like the steward in a queen's palace, obeying his lady immediately concerning all necessities, but not hearing if she asks for anything harmful.[242] This is a patriarchal role, which assumes that men know best even when a lady is theoretically in charge. On the other hand, Abelard also gives real authority to the deaconess: 'We decree that the monks shall presume to do nothing against the will of the deaconess, but they shall carry out everything at her bidding and everyone, men and women alike, shall make profession to her and promise obedience.'[243] So it is the deaconess and not the provost who receives the obedience due to a traditional Benedictine abbot. By comparing the provost to a great lady's steward, Abelard has made the relationship between him and the deaconess into a courtly one: he obeys his lady's every command (literally 'on the nod'), while at the same time exercising discretion on her behalf. 'He never enters into the secrets of the bedchamber unless he is bidden,' Abelard says.[244]

HELOISE'S RESPONSE TO ABELARD'S WRITINGS FOR HER CONVENT

The preceding paragraphs are no more than a sample of Abelard's extant writings for Heloise and her nuns, which run to 70,000 words or more. In addition to the essay on the origin of nuns and the rule, she requested and received texts (all composed specially for the convent) of sermons, hymns, answers to theological questions, and a commentary on the opening of the Book of Genesis. The hymns and sermons form part of a project to provide the nuns with appropriate texts for every feast day of the year, a customized liturgy of their own.[245] 'I can think of no other monastic foundation of those times of numerous new beginnings that was accompanied by so much new writing by a single friend or patron,' comments David Luscombe in his assessment of the place of monasticism in the lives of Abelard and Heloise.[246] Letters are extant from her asking for these texts, but there are none thanking him or commenting on all his work. Judging from her letter accompanying the theological questions, she was still in no mood to show gratitude: 'remember what it is you owe us'; 'make no delay in paying your debt'.[247] He reciprocated her lack of consideration for him by persisting in making his answers impersonal, even when he was asked whether it is ever sinful to do what one is commanded by one's lord. Obtusely, he interpreted this as a question about forced sexual intercourse within marriage, one of the few problems in life that Heloise and her nuns no longer had to face.[248]

Heloise's silence in the face of all Abelard's writings for her and her nuns leaves a chasm in our knowledge that cannot be bridged.[249] Letters from her may have been lost because, in his peripatetic life, he could not match the facilities she had for keeping an archive in the convent. Just as plausibly, however, she may have stopped writing to him: she may have been overwhelmed by the reality of her unacknowledged debt to him; or she may have continued to feel that however much he did for her, it amounted to 'nothing at all' (to quote her own words).[250] His long letter comprising his rule for the nuns seems to have been ignored.[251] This is remarkable, as she claimed to follow his commands without question. Perhaps she did not consider the rule comprised 'commands' so much as advice. He had indeed described it as 'a sort of (*quasi*) rule for your calling'.[252] Nevertheless, she had explicitly asked him to 'institute a rule for us and direct that it be written down'.[253] When she received it, she should have 'persevered in total obedience' (again to quote her own words) to do whatever it said.[254]

Abelard's proposed double monastery, headed by a provost and a deaconess, is the best example of how his rule was ignored. Heloise is never called 'deaconess' in the convent's charters; she is 'prioress' or 'abbess'.[255] Nor is any male superior ever referred to. Possibly, and this is no more than a conjecture, Heloise feared that a male superior might bring the convent to an end. Abelard might have been tolerable as her 'provost', but on his death (which he frequently warned her of) male authority at the Paraclete would have reverted to the abbey of St Denis as the original patron. She and her nuns might then have been expelled by 'our abbot' Suger for a second time.[256] Abelard's musings about a male superior acting as tactfully as a steward in a queen's chamber were naive. Heloise rightly identified her 'religion' with that of lay people. Her lay benefactors, whose relatives were in the convent, were committed to protecting the nuns' interests, whereas monks were always on the lookout for more property and generally they treated women, other than their mothers and sisters, as alien beings. From her experience at Argenteuil, Heloise may have concluded that monks were the enemy – and that included Abelard, who thought a powerful abbess was contrary to the natural order.[257]

Because he had been her teacher, Abelard could not see Heloise as an independent person, even though she had converted him to arguing for the equality of women in religion at a theoretical level. Peter the Venerable understood her aspirations better, when he likened her to Penthesilea queen of the Amazons and Deborah the champion of Israel.[258] When

Abelard sent Heloise the sermons he had specially composed, he concluded with his usual greeting to her: 'once dear to me in the world, now
dearest in Christ'.[259] But on this occasion he enlarged on what he meant
by adding: 'once in the flesh my wife; now in the spirit my sister and in
profession of sacred purpose my consort'. This defined his role as a
monk and his relationship with her, as he saw it in the aftermath of his
failure at St Gildas in the 1130s (fifteen years or more after his castration). He was echoing ideas from the correspondence which had followed his 'history of calamities'. She had called his foundation of the
Paraclete 'this new plantation in sacred purpose'.[260] He had described
her as 'his inseparable companion', even though they were physically
separated, and he had declared that their love was the better for being
spiritual.[261] Their joint dedication to the religious life (he had argued)
put their marriage on a higher plane: 'For we are one in Christ, one flesh
by the law of matrimony'.[262]

The paradox of Abelard and Heloise being one flesh, even though he
was castrated and they were living apart as monk and nun, is best
explained by his rival in the schools of Paris, Hugh of St Victor. He
argued that the essence of marriage is not sexual intercourse in itself, but
the bond of companionship and love that stems from it. Two people
become one flesh and thence they become one mind. The Bride and
Bridegroom in the Song of Songs, who encapsulate love and prefigure
the Church's relationship with Christ, are destined to become one soul:
'Henceforth and forever, each shall be to the other as a same self in all
sincere love, all careful solicitude. ... Each shall assist the other as being
one's own self in every good and evil tiding, the companion and partner
of consolation, proving united in trial and tribulation. ... In this way
they shall dwell in the peace of a holy society and the communion of a
sweet repose, so that it is no longer the one who lives, but the other. ...
Such are the good things of marriage and the happiness of the chaste
society of those who love each other.'[263] Something like Hugh's vision
was probably shared by Abelard in his ideal of Heloise as his 'consort' in
'sacred purpose'.

One of Heloise's biographers, Elizabeth Hamilton, concludes from
Abelard's words that 'a relationship that is acceptable to him has been
established between Heloise and himself'.[264] True enough for Abelard,
but was this relationship as acceptable to her? The frustration of Heloise's silence has led her biographers into wishful thinking. Her principal
biographer, Enid McLeod, argues that Abelard's words show a 'rare
expansiveness' and they suggest 'a sudden uprush of tender memories
in his heart as he wrote them, [which] may well have consoled Heloise
as she read them for any lack in those that had gone before'.[265] This

tortuous sentence shows McLeod's difficulties in being factual where evidence is lacking. Maybe Heloise was consoled, or maybe she reacted with the scorn she voiced in her earlier letters because their 'tender memories' were not the same. Each reader must make her own guess about what Heloise's silence signifies.

ABELARD'S ACHIEVEMENTS AS A MONK

Abelard's achievements as a monk, like his scholastic achievements, take the form of writings rather than actions. His monastic career was as disjointed and 'calamitous' as his career as a master. He ran away from St Denis, the mother house of the French kingdom, which had twice given him asylum. Then he abandoned the hermitage of the Paraclete, which he himself had founded, and then did the same at the abbey of St Gildas, which had honoured him by making him an abbot in his own country of Brittany. After returning to 'watch over' Heloise and her nuns at the Paraclete, he abandoned that idea too and reappeared as a master in Paris shortly after 1132. At least he still wore a monastic habit, as St Bernard later taunted him with 'having nothing of the monk about him except the name and the habit'.[266] With this reference to 'the name', St Bernard hoped perhaps that the Nominalists among Abelard's students would conclude that he was no monk in reality.

In Abelard's defence it can be said that monasticism, as much as scholasticism, was in a state of creative chaos in the early twelfth century. Reformers competing for funds and influence broke down traditional controls; inevitably there were failures as well as successes. St Norbert, Robert of Arbrissel, even Peter the Venerable and St Bernard, were involved in potential scandals centring on recruitment and discipline. Abelard entered the monastic mêlée with the same self-righteous over-confidence with which he had confronted William of Champeaux and Anselm of Laon. What is remarkable about his monastic career, like his scholastic career, is his resilience and the way repeated failure did not destroy his reputation. He failed at St Denis and rehabilitated himself at the Paraclete, much as he had failed in Paris in his struggles with William of Champeaux and yet became master at Notre-Dame ten years later (only to fall on his face again by seducing Heloise). Even when he was conspicuously failing at St Gildas (after failing at the Paraclete), the Morigny chronicle in 1131 described him as *religiosus*.

Monasteries had been rooted in the esteem of their localities and they flourished as havens of stability and community in a savage environment. Reformers, whether they were St Bernard or Abelard, inevitably destabilized these traditional strengths and ran the risk of destabilizing themselves as well. Abelard was typical of monastic innovators in not spending much time in the cloister himself. His monastic reputation is as contradictory as any other aspect of his career. Against the description of him as *religiosus* has to be set the fact that it was not only his opponents who thought there was 'nothing of the monk about him', but some of his admirers as well. His trial at Sens in 1140 was seen as a struggle between St Bernard, 'the cowled primate of the cowled people', and Abelard, the courtly 'palatine' whose spiritual home was with his bride in the company of the pagan authors of ancient Rome.[267]

Peter the Venerable made the final attempt to rehabilitate Abelard's monastic reputation, initially by giving him asylum at Cluny after his trial at Sens and ultimately by writing his epitaph and his letter of condolence to Heloise. In the epitaph Peter got round the difficulty of describing Abelard's unstable monastic career (between joining St Denis in *c*.1118 and abandoning St Gildas in *c*.1132) by ignoring it completely. Only when he was professed at Cluny in 1140 did Abelard 'cross over to the true philosophy of Christ'.[268] Peter was entitled to say that Abelard had found his salvation at Cluny, as he had died as a Cluniac monk. What Peter did not mention was that Abelard had been under house arrest at Cluny, as the pope had ordered his imprisonment in a religious house and Peter had negotiated a settlement whereby Abelard was allowed to end his days under Cluny's authority.[269] (He had similarly been put under house arrest at the abbey of St Médard following his trial at Soissons in 1121).[270]

To Heloise, Peter described Abelard's exemplary conduct at Cluny: 'his holy, humble and devoted life among us'.[271] Abelard had not required a distinctively sumptuous habit and neither had he asked for special food.[272] (These details confirm St Bernard's attack on the petty luxuries which Cluniac monks enjoyed.) Abelard condemned everything (Peter continued) except what was really necessary.[273] This is entirely credible, as Abelard seems to have been indifferent to material comforts and his first action on entering the abbey of St Denis, when he first became a monk, had been to criticize the laxity of his fellows. In his rule for Heloise's nuns he had said that 'whatever we possess that goes beyond necessity, we possess as plunder and we are the cause of the death of as many of the poor as we could have supported with it'.[274] What was 'really necessary' was a matter of opinion. In his rule Abelard had prescribed 'one silver chalice for the altar', but he then added: 'or even more if necessary'.[275] To service the great church of Cluny required revenues in gold and silver from much of western Europe. Abelard's rule makes clear that in the monastic economy God's poor (the monks and nuns) and their altars take priority over the real poor at the abbey gates. The work of monks and nuns is 'God's work' (*opus Dei*), not social work.

If Abelard had not been tired and old and under house arrest and if he had still been writing his 'history of calamities', he might have denounced Peter the Venerable and his hosts at Cluny as roundly as he had denounced the monks of St Denis and St Gildas. Peter's description of Abelard's exemplary life at Cluny may not have been the whole truth about how he behaved, as the purpose of his letter was to break the news to Heloise of Abelard's death. He had not remained in the monastery at Cluny itself, just as he had not stayed long in the company of his hosts at St Denis and St Gildas. Peter's explanation of this to Heloise is that he had sent Abelard to a dependent priory at Chalon-sur-Saône for health reasons, as it had a milder climate (Cluny itself is up in the hills). Here Abelard recovered enough to 'renew his former studies', though he never returned to Cluny.[276] Peter was by inclination a peacemaker. He may have decided that keeping Abelard away from Cluny was the best way of avoiding trouble. Alternatively, and just as plausibly, Abelard gave Peter no trouble because he really was very ill. A medical professor, Dr Jeannin, has argued that Abelard was dying of brain cancer and the first manifestation of this was his refusal to speak in his own defence at his trial at Sens in 1140.[277] Jeannin compares the trial to a boxing match: the reigning champion, Abelard, entered the ring but the fight had to be stopped in the first round, much to the disappointment of the challenger, St Bernard.

Although we cannot know what Abelard thought of Peter the Venerable and Cluny, there is little doubt of Peter's admiration for him. Peter had indeed saved him from St Bernard and imprisonment or worse in Rome, and he had exerted all his diplomatic skills to give this 'sparrow' (as he described Abelard to the pope) a home.[278] Peter's actions look like pure compassion, as he had nothing to gain from further alienating St Bernard (they were already in dispute over the bishopric of Langres), nor from challenging the pope's judgement in such a serious matter as heresy. Although Peter was theoretically the most powerful abbot in Christendom, with hundreds of monasteries owing him obedience, even he could not necessarily afford to use the power of Cluny to help an individual as controversial as Abelard. Yet this is what Peter did, and with success. The trouble he took is clearly demonstrated by his coming in person to return Abelard's body to Heloise at the Paraclete.[279] Peter could have insisted that Abelard remain interred at the priory at Chalon-sur-Saône where he had died. He was in law a Cluniac monk and that took precedence over any prior relationship with Heloise. In order to return Abelard's body to Heloise, Peter had to commit the dubiously lawful act of bringing it to Heloise in secret; he came in person presumably because he could not trust anyone else to do this.[280] The monks at Chalon-sur-Saône may have hoped to promote a cult of Abelard, particularly after Peter himself had described him virtually as a saint in his letter to Heloise and in his epitaph.

By returning Abelard's body to Heloise, Peter was also belatedly acknowledging that the convent of the Paraclete and not Cluny was Abelard's principal monastic achievement and his spiritual home. He was, in Heloise's words, 'after God the sole founder of this place, the sole builder of this oratory'.[281] Abelard's posthumous return to the Paraclete meant that in death, if not in life, his view of Heloise as 'once in the flesh my wife, now in the spirit my sister and in profession of sacred purpose my consort' was vindicated.[282] As monk and nun they were united, as they had never been as man and wife. When Heloise died in c.1164, she was buried in his grave. As early as 1207 the story is recorded that when the body of Heloise was placed in Abelard's tomb, he raised his arms and embraced her.[283] Something like this had been predicted by Peter the Venerable, who had assured Heloise that God cherished Abelard 'in His bosom in your place as another you' and that at the resurrection 'he will be restored to you'.[284]

12

Theologian

St Bernard repeatedly called Abelard 'our theologian', which he did not intend as a compliment.[1] He called Abelard a theologian because of his book *Theologia*. Abelard's explanation of the name was that 'I entitled it *Theologia* because the Lord granted me its composition'.[2] It was God's work in every sense: 'that glorious work of your theology' as Heloise called it.[3] St Bernard went to the other extreme and called it 'stupidology'.[4] All this emphasizes that Bernard and Abelard both thought 'theologian' and 'theology' to be novel terms. The conventional word for the intellectual study of God was 'divinity'. In his 'history of calamities' Abelard recalls how he went to study 'divinity' with Anselm of Laon, 'the greatest authority in this subject'.[5] The word Abelard uses for 'subject' is *lectio*, meaning 'reading'. The 'reading of the divine books' of the Scriptures was the way a conventional student of divinity proceeded.[6] A theologian, on the other hand, proceeded by reasoning from first principles.

'Theology' was a word of Greek origin and St Bernard insinuated that there was something pagan and suspect about it because a theologian aspires to make sense of God. He warned that Abelard promised his hearers understanding 'even of those sublime and hallowed things which are lodged deep in the bosom of the Holy Faith'.[7] Bernard exaggerated the dangers and unusualness of what theologians did, and Abelard too was claiming to be more novel than he really was. He was not the inventor of theology, though he was its most conspicuous promoter. Honorius Augustodunensis had described his 'Elucidarius', his elucidatory survey of the Church's teaching, as a 'summary of the whole of theology' (*summa totius theologie*).[8] This work emanated from the circle of St Anselm, archbishop of Canterbury, in 1100 or earlier. It was appropriate that the word 'theology' should have been reintroduced into academic discourse in St Anselm's circle, as he had discussed the existence of a supreme being from first principles in his

Greek-titled book *Monologion* (published in *c.*1078). Abelard's contemporary in Paris, Hugh of St Victor, was perfectly familiar with the word 'theology' and knew it to be Greek. He defined it as 'discourse concerning the divine, for *theos* means God and *logos* means discourse or reasoning'.[9]

Abelard first wrote about theology when he was a monk at St Denis and he may have come across the term when searching the works of Abbot Hilduin for information about the identity of St Denis, as Hilduin had given the title *De Theologia Mystica* to his translation of Pseudo-Denis the Areopagite.[10] Another possibility is the contemporary suggestion of Thomas of Morigny that Abelard was inspired by the ninth-century philosopher, John Scotus Erigena, who had likewise translated Pseudo-Denis from the Greek.[11] In fact, though, Abelard need not have looked further than books which were familiar to every medieval intellectual to find 'theology' defined: namely, in St Augustine's *City of God*, Boethius's commentary on Porphyry and Isidore's *Etymologies*.[12] The formative influences in Abelard's understanding of what theology was, as distinct from the novelty of using the word as a book title, were presumably those of his own masters, William of Champeaux and Anselm of Laon, though Abelard had refused to acknowledge his debt to them in his 'history of calamities'. As we have seen in chapter 4, their teachings were anthologized in the *Liber Pancrisis*, the 'All-Gold Book', and – more important to students at the time – they were heard viva voce in lectures and then developed by the next generation of masters in Paris, who included Abelard himself and Hugh of St Victor.[13]

Although Anselm of Laon and his brother Ralph wrote nothing called *Theologia* (as far as we know), John of Salisbury was right to describe them as 'theologians', as they explained the Scriptures in rational terms.[14] This sort of theology attracted students and their ecclesiastical patrons because its objectives were pastoral. Anselm of Laon and his fellow masters equipped trainee clergy with an organized conspectus of Christian doctrine and law, which they could take back home with them and develop for themselves. Because they had been trained in discussion and reasoning (the *logos* of 'theology'), these clergy potentially had a more dynamic approach to Christian teaching than traditional choir monks, whose expertise lay in chanting excerpts from Scripture in the daily round of the Church's liturgy. Over the past six or seven centuries liturgical prayer – and the impressive ceremonial that went with it – had proved a most effective way of voicing the Church's message. The risk with theology, which St Bernard repeatedly emphasized in his attacks on Abelard, was that arguing and reasoning about the Christian faith, as distinct from discoursing reverently upon it (as Bernard did) and acting it out through the liturgy, might explain it away altogether. Abelard does not seem to have appreciated this, despite being the composer of superb hymns for the liturgical year for Heloise's convent of the Paraclete. His deliberate preference for a training in dialectic (which he describes in his 'history of calamities') may have sharpened the intellectual side of his genius at the expense of the emotional and affective side.

THE DEVELOPMENT OF ABELARD'S THEOLOGIA

The explanation which Abelard gave in his 'history of calamities' for writing a 'treatise of theology' in the first place (while teaching as a monk of St Denis, before his condemnation at Soissons in 1121) was that students wanted rational explanations: 'they were demanding things that could be made intelligible rather than mere words; in fact, they said the enunciation of words was pointless if understanding did not follow, for nothing can be believed unless it is first understood'.[15] The latter statement was a reversal of St Anselm of Canterbury's rule that 'Unless you believe, you shall not understand.'[16] Through his students, Abelard was therefore challenging the Anselmian tradition of respectful inquiry through faith. In the same passage Abelard reports his students saying that this was 'ridiculous'.[17] He persisted with this controversial way of justifying his *Theologia* right up to the end, despite the book's condemnation at Soissons and its being threatened again from many sides in the long lead-up to the council of Sens in 1140.

In the prologue to *Theologia Scholarium* (the final version of the *Theologia* written in the 1130s) Abelard's opening words are: *Scholarium nostrorum petitioni* – 'at the request of our students'.[18] For them, he says, he has 'put together a kind of summary (*summa*) of sacred learning as a sort of introduction to holy Scripture'.[19] The modesty of this statement belies what follows. The students claim to be delighted with what they have read of Abelard on philosophy and secular literature, and so they think he should now turn his attention to the 'divine page' of Scripture. My intelligence (or 'genius' – *ingenium*), Abelard reports, 'will much more easily penetrate the meaning of the divine page and the reasons for our holy faith than exhaust the abyss of the wells of philosophy'.[20] In other words, in the opinion of Abelard's students – and presumably it was his opinion likewise – theology was much easier than philosophy. The students are also confident that his intellect is sufficient to resolve all controversies, as 'I have been brought up from the cradle, as it were, in the study of philosophy and especially of dialectic, which is seen as the mistress of all reasoning'.[21]

Abelard's irrepressible vanity was an easy target for the controversialist, Walter of Mortagne, who read this passage and wrote to Abelard asking whether it was true that 'some of your students, who proudly extol your wisdom and subtlety far and wide, declare among other things that you have so thoroughly explored the deepest mysteries of the Trinity, that you understand it perfectly and completely'.[22] The doctrine of the Trinity was indeed the principal subject of Abelard's *Theologia* and he claimed in his 'history of calamities' that his book 'seemed to answer all questions alike on this subject'.[23] 'Since these questions looked the most difficult of all', Abelard continued, 'it was generally agreed that the great importance of the problems was matched by the subtlety of my solution of them.'[24] He knew this to be special pleading, however, as he explained in his next sentence that this was the occasion when his enemies organized the council of Soissons against him and got his book ceremonially burned.

Abelard insisted on the greatness of *Theologia* precisely because it had been so savagely condemned. His reaction to the condemnation was to start writing a second edition. He had evidently saved a copy from the fire, as he reproduced whole passages from the first edition. Constant Mews has pointed out that the edition burned at Soissons was probably not originally entitled *Theologia*, but *De Trinitate* ('Concerning the Trinity'). When Abelard came to revise it for the second edition, he substituted the word 'theologian' for 'divine' in a number of passages and he deliberately gave the book the title *Theologia Christiana*.[25] The new title signified that the book concerned Christian reasoning about God and that it was neither pagan nor heretical. Henceforward, the title *Theologia* constituted part of Abelard's campaign to be rehabilitated and properly understood. His book was Christian because he was 'Christ's philosopher', as Peter the Venerable called him.[26] 'I have now undertaken', Abelard explained, 'to transfer myself wholly to God and leave the world behind. I originally began studying to make money, but now I am converting this to the winning of souls, so that I too can go and labour in the Lord's vineyard even though it is around the eleventh hour.'[27] As a late convert to theology, Abelard became its uncompromising champion, even to the point of enduring prosecution and humiliation.

Despite being twice consigned to the flames (at Soissons in 1121 and at Rome, following the council of Sens, in 1140), the various versions of Abelard's *Theologia* have now been reconstituted. The task was completed in 1987 with Constant Mews's revised editions of *Theologia Summi Boni*, the treatise on the Trinity condemned at Soissons, and *Theologia Scholarium*, the final version condemned at Sens. Abelard has made more difficulties for his modern editors than the bonfires of his persecutors, as he kept altering the text (understandably enough, as it was repeatedly criticized) and inserting new sections. Before the era of printed books with their fixed texts, it is harder to tell what constitutes a deliberate change in a manuscript and whether a particular change was made by the author. No manuscripts of Abelard's have been identified which can be proved to be autographs or even authorized copies. Nevertheless, we can be reasonably sure that we now have the texts of *Theologia* much as Abelard developed them over the twenty years 1120–40. No one at the time, including Abelard, can have had the access to them which is now available through consistently numbered lines and computerized indexes.

Of the three main versions of Abelard's *Theologia*, the first one (the treatise on the Trinity condemned at Soissons) is the most elegantly constructed, as its three 'books' are of approximately equal length and they are clearly articulated by function. The second version, *Theologia Christiana*, is nearly three times as long, because it reacts to the condemnation at Soissons, and it consists of five 'books'. Abelard devoted space to heaping abuse on his colleagues, in order to show that he was cleverer than them, and to ridiculing Alberic of Reims whom he held responsible for his prosecution at Soissons. The tone of some passages is more like that of lectures to students than a fully-considered treatise. The fifth book has been described as 'confused in the presentation of its ideas as well as incomplete'.[28] This is very understandable, as Abelard was recovering from being accused in 1122 of treason to St Denis, on top of his condemnation for heresy in 1121; at the same time he was trying to make a new life for himself as a hermit. Furthermore, disjuncture and attenuation can be indicators in Abelard's work of originality, as they are by-products of his thinking fast and discursively.

In the third version, *Theologia Scholarium*, composed in the 1130s, Abelard completely reorganized the beginning of the work to make it more orthodox and coherent and he also modified the abusive passages. Nevertheless, *Theologia Scholarium* looks unfinished, as it ends with a battery of questions about the meaning of the Redemption, the subject of Abelard's most original thoughts in the 1130s.[29] He was always sensitive to intellectual fashions and he had concluded his first treatise on the Trinity similarly with what he described as 'the very latest question' (*novissima questio*).[30] It would have been characteristic of him to conclude his most ambitious work, *Theologia Scholarium*, likewise with questions instead of answers. Alternatively, the work's abrupt ending may simply be due to Abelard having had no opportunity to finish it, once St Bernard and the prosecutors at Sens required answers to their mass of accusations.

Abelard has been criticized for not leaving as a model for his successors a complete work of systematic theology of his own. 'He was one of those academics constitutionally incapable of finishing anything he started.'[31] Possibly so, but this modern judgement does not allow for the atmosphere of persecution in which Abelard worked. Academics in the liberal democracies of North America and Europe are not accustomed to having their books burned and their characters systematically vilified by their superiors. Even in method, it was not necessarily a weakness of Abelard's to leave questions unanswered. The neat summaries or 'sentences' of his famous successor, Peter Lombard, conceal all sorts of difficulties. Abelard raised questions which he could not answer because he wrote as a teacher and an intellectual almost at the moment of formulating his thoughts. This accounts for the informal tone of portions of *Theologia*: 'But you say to me: "I don't care about the names, but I insist on the truthfulness of the sense...." To which I answer: "To be sure, of course, you can indeed make sense of it...."'[32] Through this dialectical method Abelard lived in perpetual hope of coming up with the answers, even to the paradoxes of the Trinity and the Redemption and even when his books were burned. Later scholastics, as Sir Richard Southern has argued, experienced a loss of hope.[33] The optimism of the twelfth century evaporated, once it began to be realized that there was more to science than reading the Bible and explicating it through logic.

THE CHOICE OF THE TRINITY AS THE SUBJECT OF THEOLOGIA

Abelard's expertise in logic was applicable to any doctrine or text of Christianity which required linguistic analysis. He could have applied it just as well to the Eucharist as to the Trinity and he had applied it first of all, when he was at the school of Laon, to explaining the prophecies of Ezechiel, another work of Abelard's which is lost and perhaps was never finished.[34] (In this case Heloise and castration had intervened.) In choosing the Trinity for his first treatise of theology, as distinct from doing a Biblical commentary as in his work on Ezechiel, Abelard was treading on dangerous ground. This was the subject which had got his master, Roscelin, accused of heresy in the 1090s. St Anselm of Canterbury had dedicated his refutation of Roscelin to Pope Urban II in 1098 in order to draw a line under the subject. This was the first time such a direct appeal to papal authority in the refutation of a heretic had been made and it stood as a warning and a precedent.[35] With papal backing,

St Anselm told presumptuous questioners of the 'sacred page' – and contemporary dialecticians in particular – to proceed with the utmost caution.[36]

Caution had never been Abelard's way. He sought no papal authorization for his treatise and, furthermore, he devoted the whole of his second 'book' to arguing that dialectic was the key to understanding the Trinity. He concluded the final 'book' with his *credo*: 'I believe no one can fully understand these things unless they have stayed up at night studying philosophy, and dialectic most of all.'[37] Abelard's aim seems to have been to distance himself from Roscelin by producing a treatise of his own on the Trinity. The risk with this was that he would be further identified with Roscelin, whose pupil he had been, and embroiled in the same insoluble problems. (Abelard's trial at Soissons, which was the consequence of his miscalculating this risk, is discussed in chapter 13.) The delightfully lucid opening lines of the treatise on the Trinity were all that any prosecutor needed to accuse Abelard of heresy:

> Christ the Lord, who is the wisdom of God incarnate, has diligently distinguished the perfection of the highest good, which is God, by describing it with three names.... He called the divine substance 'the Father', 'the Son' and 'the Holy Spirit' for three causes. He called it 'the Father' in accordance with that unique power of His majesty which is omnipotence, by which He can effect whatever He wills as nothing is able to resist Him. The same divine substance He said is 'the Son' in accordance with the distinction of His own wisdom, by which He can truly judge and discern all things so that nothing can lie hidden by which He is deceived. He likewise called that substance 'the Holy Spirit' in accordance with the grace of His goodness.... This therefore is how God is three persons, that is, 'the Father', 'the Son' and 'the Holy Spirit'. And so we may say the divine substance is powerful, wise and good; indeed, it even is power itself, wisdom itself and goodness itself.[38]

To start by describing Christ 'diligently distinguishing' names, as if He were a master expounding logic, accorded with how Abelard understood Christ as the *logos*, but it exposed him to the charge of reducing the three persons to 'empty names instead of distinct realities' (in the words of Otto of Freising).[39] This suspicion was compounded when Abelard allocated to each of the three persons differing qualities: power, wisdom and goodness respectively. This was not expressly warranted by any of the creeds of the Christian Church and it appeared to depend on his say-so: 'And so we may say (*dicamus*).' In fact he seems to have got the germ of this idea from his own master, William of Champeaux, but he was not going to admit that.[40] Abelard's use of 'we may say' or 'it seems to us' was a commonplace of the lecture-room; but it was ambiguous in tone, as it could indicate either modesty or an ex-cathedra ruling by the master. Interpreting it maliciously in the latter sense, St Bernard teased that the Church had no place for Abelard as a fifth Evangelist.[41]

Abelard's association of power with God the Father caused the most trouble, as it contrasted with the Athanasian creed's declaration that 'the Father is almighty, the Son is almighty and the Holy Spirit is almighty'.[42] (This was why Abelard was made to recite the Athanasian creed at his condemnation at Soissons.[43]) Was he implying that the power of the Son differed from, or was less than, that of the Father? In *Theologia Scholarium* Abelard described divine wisdom as being 'something (*aliquid*) of divine omnipotence' and 'hence divine wisdom is a certain (*quedam*) divine power'.[44] The words 'something of' and 'a certain' suggested that divine wisdom (which Abelard associated with the Son) was less than the omnipotence of the Father. To make one of the persons of the Trinity unequal to another was heresy. Abelard claimed he was not being correctly understood and that words signify different things in different contexts.[45] But going any distance down that road brought the whole enterprise of theology as a definitive science into doubt.

Abelard had put forward his threefold description of God as power, wisdom and goodness as a means to an end. He wanted to prove that everyone, whether Christian or not, knew God was power, wisdom and goodness and hence they knew about the Trinity: 'reason educates each single person naturally about God'.[46] Abelard demonstrated this, to his own satisfaction at least, by citing authorities: first from the Old Testament and then from the Greek and Roman philosophers. His method was crude and literal. Thus Moses, whom medieval scholars believed to be the author of the Book of Genesis, knew of the Trinity because he used a plural form for 'God'.[47] Or, Isaiah recorded the angels around God's throne saying: 'Holy, holy, holy is the Lord of hosts.'[48] This was familiar to everybody from the *Sanctus* chant in the Mass and its three-fold repetition proclaimed the Trinity. Among the Greek and Roman philosophers Abelard cited Hermes Trismegistus, a conflation of the Egyptian and Greek gods of knowledge, who had allegedly written about a son of god; also Cicero had acknowledged there was only one god.[49] Abelard derived his scant information about the ancient philosophers largely from St Augustine.[50] The only philosophical idea from the ancient world treated in any detail in *Theologia* is Plato's World Soul.[51] Abelard was not the first Christian intellectual to see parallels between it and the Holy Spirit which vivifies Christians.

Towards the end of 'Book One' of his treatise on the Trinity (the first version of *Theologia*), Abelard summed up these arguments as follows: 'Since therefore the Lord has announced the tenor of the Catholic faith to the Jews by the prophets and to the Gentiles by outstanding philosophers and seers, Jews as well as Gentiles are given no excuse for not hearing of the salvation of the soul, which is the foundation of the faith, as they have these teachers in everything.'[52] Abelard was certainly eccentric, if not heretical, in arguing that the Greeks and Romans had known of the Catholic faith and of salvation, though the question of whether the Jewish prophets had been saved was quite often considered. What he meant by 'the Catholic faith' in this context is ambiguous. 'Catholic' means universal: according to Abelard, the faith of pagans was 'Catholic' because reason educates everyone. To the Roman Church, on the other hand, 'the Catholic faith' meant the belief system over which it claimed a universal jurisdiction. At the time of Abelard's trial at Sens in 1140 his defender, Berengar, said Abelard was Catholic whether St Bernard liked it or not. But Bernard had already answered this by telling the pope that the inventions of the pagan philosophers and Abelard's novelties were at odds with the doctrine and faith of the Catholic Fathers of the Church.[53]

At the conclusion of 'Book Three' of the first version of *Theologia*, Abelard produced a statement more to St Bernard's liking. Having just declared that 'reason educates each single person naturally about God', Abelard added a disclaimer. He pointed out that St Augustine said this applied 'only to what pertains to the divinity of the Word and not to the mystery of the Incarnation, in which it is certain that the whole sum of human salvation consists and without which all the rest is believed in vain'.[54] Abelard repeated this disclaimer in the subsequent versions of *Theologia*, even though it had the potential to undermine his whole endeavour.[55] If the ancient prophets and philosophers knew nothing about the Incarnation, then they lacked the essence of Christianity. Whereas Abelard had concluded in 'Book One' that Jews and Gentiles alike had been told of the soul's salvation and the Catholic faith, he concluded in 'Book Three' that their knowledge was insufficient.

The Fate of the Unbaptized

Abelard confronted this difficulty in another form in his *Ethics* and again veered in different directions, although his statements are phrased so as not to be inconsistent. On one page he wrote: 'I do not see how in the case of little children, or those to whom Christianity has not been announced, infidelity should be ascribed to fault.'[56] And yet a few pages earlier he had said: 'It is not absurd that some people undergo bodily punishments which they have not deserved, as is evident with little children who die without the grace of baptism and are condemned to an eternal as well as a bodily death.'[57] Many innocents are crushed (he continued), as it is sufficient for damnation to be ignorant of Christ. 'For, of them the Truth says: "He that believeth not is condemned already".'[58] In his commentary on St Paul's Epistle to the Romans Abelard shifted his ground again and said that any good person will be given an opportunity by God to come to know Him. 'And so we say anyone is already a just person through faith and love even before baptism.'[59] Abelard concluded this discussion by declaring love to be the essential ingredient, not the sacraments of the Church: 'Let this be sufficient for us concerning our justification, and the justification of everyone else as well, that it consists in love being interposed among us – and that is before the sacraments are taken up. This is why the prophet declares: "In whatever hour a sinner grieves, he shall be saved".'[60]

In the light of these diverse opinions of Abelard's it is no surprise to find that whether 'the punishment of unbaptized little children is much milder than the rest of the punishments of the damned' is the final question he addressed in *Sic et Non*.[61] Again he reached no convincing conclusion, and neither in this case did he assemble much material. The authorities he ranged against each other begin with St Augustine, who said this surely must be so, as little children have been drawn into no other sin than Adam's original one. But St John Chrysostom and St Ambrose appeared to argue the opposite, though – as quite often in *Sic et Non* – the statements cited throw little light on the matter in hand, as Chrysostom and Ambrose were discussing the fate of the wicked in general without mentioning children.

In discussing the fate of unbaptized children Abelard was addressing a question of popular concern. The preacher and heretical leader, Henry of Le Mans, was reported in the early 1130s to be teaching that it was unjust to condemn children for the sins of other people, particularly when Jesus had said 'Suffer the little children to come unto Me'.[62] In response, Henry's opponent had likened original sin to a disease in sheep or plants, which infects every animal and leaf. Henry was advised to 'stop worrying about how and why children bear original sin. If you do not understand it, believe it none the less, so that you may understand and not be misled by insoluble questions.' (This was St Anselm's rule, which Abelard's students thought ridiculous.[63]) Henry was also given a warning which applied to speculative theologians in general: 'Don't stand around asking a man how he fell into a pit, unless you know some means of getting him out.'[64] Abelard had no means of extricating his readers from the pitfalls he led them into. Instead of resolving the questions he raised in Sic et Non, for example, the best he had to offer was the naive hope that 'by doubting we come to inquiry and by inquiry we perceive the truth'.[65]

Abelard was reputed the greatest logician of his age. Why then did he make inconsistent and ambiguous statements in his theological writings? One answer is because everybody else did. He demonstrated this in Sic et Non with unprecedented thoroughness. There seemed to be no tenet of Christian belief which was not challenged by one statement or another in the Church Fathers dug up by Abelard or his researchers. Such inconsistencies were not necessarily due to faulty texts or elementary misunderstandings, as Abelard had argued in his prologue to Sic et Non. Their roots went much deeper because theologians addressed the most fundamental and controversial questions in human experience and all these questions were interconnected. Explaining one thing satisfactorily in accordance with reason or common sense might bring some other part of the structure of doctrine into doubt. If, for example, a theologian devised a formula of words which acknowledged the good lives of the unbaptized and allowed them to be saved on their merits (and Abelard devised many such formulas for the Greek philosophers), that might make the Redemption by Christ's death on the cross seem unnecessary. This in its turn was morally repugnant. Even when a theologian succeeded in devising a formula which was satisfactory in logic, it had to accord equally well with the teachings of the Church as expressed in the Bible, the creeds and the voluminous writings of the Church Fathers.

Abelard got into difficulties with his theology because he underestimated the magnitude of the task. It is revealing that he has his students say he will find it much easier than philosophy.[66] Also, it was a mistake on his part to conceive theological thinking as a purely intellectual process, an exercise in dialectic for which he was superbly qualified. He was soon to discover that theologians deal with questions which touch people's feelings and deeply-held beliefs, rather than the abstract ideas which he had been used to discussing in his lectures on logic. This was why unorthodox ideas in theology were treated as heresy, a criminal offence, whereas deviation in logic simply caused disputes between rival masters. The difference between medieval theologians and logicians is most obvious in their use of examples. Theologians cited texts from the Bible or the Church Fathers, which were already sanctified and authoritative, whereas logicians constructed hypothetical cases of their own. Thus Abelard had argued in Dialectica that 'it is possible for Socrates to be a bishop'.[67] The use of absurd examples like this confirmed St Bernard in his opinion that logic was a childish game and that Abelard played the fool.[68]

CHRIST AND SOCRATES

Whereas theologians treated Christ and the other persons in their texts with reverential awe, logicians made Socrates, the pagan equivalent of Christ, the butt of their jokes. He served as the random exemplar of a man. In one among many instances in *Dialectica* Abelard performed variations on the proposition: 'if Socrates is asinine, some man is asinine'.[69] Logicians had traditionally and unthinkingly treated Socrates disrespectfully because they were not concerned with historical realities nor with people's feelings. Socrates was just a convenient name. He was not the man who had lived and died heroically in ancient Athens. It was offensive and misleading, both to the Greek past and to the Christian present, to argue that he could be a bishop. In *Theologia* Abelard can be seen to have completely changed his attitude to Socrates. He is placed at the conclusion of the first book as the philosopher who most consummately demonstrates that the noble Greeks and Romans led lives of the highest virtue, even though they were pagans. 'Socrates bravely persisted in the correction of the wicked even unto death', Abelard writes, 'as he was made to suffer for the truth by the very people whose vices he had constantly been attacking.'[70] Abelard supported this with a long quotation from St Augustine's *City of God*, which described the execution of Socrates and how he had believed that only those who led disciplined lives should aspire to understand the supreme good which is God.[71]

The idea that the pagan philosophers had been called sages because they were outstandingly good in moral terms, and not just because they were clever, had been put to Abelard by Heloise in her arguments against their marriage. She had cited the same book of St Augustine's *City of God* that Abelard used in *Theologia* in his eulogy of Socrates.[72] It has already been suggested (in chapter 8) that, at the time they met, Heloise had more understanding of the historical realities of ancient philosophy than Abelard. He seems to have been a typical logician, who treated Socrates as a classroom joke (judging from *Dialectica*), whereas she was famed throughout France for her classical learning.[73] As she was probably in her twenties, or even close to thirty, she may have been studying the ancient world intensively for the past ten or fifteen years. As Barbara Newman has argued, 'Heloise came to Abelard with not only her mind but her imagination already well stocked.'[74] For her, the classical heroes and sages were living presences; like the prophets and saints, they brought messages from the past for our guidance today. She demonstrated this most dramatically by crying out, in front of the altar when she took her final vows to become a nun, Cornelia's lament from Lucan, the Roman Stoic poet.[75]

At the time of their marriage Heloise had told Abelard that if he did not care about the privileges of a cleric, 'he should at least defend the dignity of a philosopher' and 'remember Socrates'.[76] This is what he did in *Theologia* when he argued that the ancient philosophers had known of the doctrine of the Trinity. In Abelard's *Soliloquium* (a dialogue between his persona as 'Peter' and his persona as 'Abelard') 'Peter' says the pagan philosophers 'expounded the whole sum (*summa*) of faith in the Trinity more thoroughly in many ways than the prophets'.[77] This cues 'Abelard' to answer that Christians are indeed philosophers, and logicians in particular, because the *logos* has been revealed to them. Abelard's enthusiasm for this idea is taken to its ultimate point in *Theologia Christiana* where he says: 'We find the way of life of the pagan philosophers, as much as their teaching, expresses evangelical and apostolic perfection very strongly indeed; they differ from the Christian religion in nothing or very little.'[78]

More than a century ago R. L. Poole pointed out that Platonism was 'the vogue of the day' in Abelard's time; 'more intrepid views than his were promulgated without risk by a multitude of less conspicuous masters'. It was Abelard's determination to win fame by publicizing his views that got him into trouble, together with his indiscriminate enthusiasm for whatever novelty he took up: in this case his 'joyful recognition of a world of divine teaching of old' outside the Bible.[79] The moral nobility of the ancient philosophers was new to Abelard only because he had spent his formative years studying logic. It was not new to the hundreds of students of grammar and rhetoric, whose teachers gave them introductions to the prescribed books of the classical authors (Virgil, Lucan, Cicero and many others). Although such introductions – or 'access to the authors' as they were called – were often elementary, they were none the less informative about each author's purpose in writing and his historical context. Through this access, an imaginative student like Heloise could build up a plausible idea of the best of intellectual life in ancient Greece and Rome.

Because the pagan classics were being prescribed primarily to monks and clerics, the teachers of the 'authors' struggled to make the best of them by emphasizing their moral aspects. Even Ovid's books on love were made acceptable to ecclesiastical scruples by emphasizing that they had an ethical purpose, provided they were understood in the right way.[80] In this form, as moralizing treatises, the classical literary corpus was passed down from manuscript to manuscript across the medieval millennium, and this literary and moral curriculum was the direct predecessor of that of the humanists of the Italian Renaissance. In the twelfth century, as in the Italian Renaissance, there was a gulf in aspirations and values between the literary specialists or humanists, on the one hand, and on the other, the logicians who considered themselves to be scientists. In these terms, at the time of their first meeting, Heloise was a humanist and Abelard was a scientist. Fulbert's purpose in sending her to him for tuition was presumably so that she might become even more learned by advancing from literature to logic, which was considered the queen of the sciences.

Abelard was confident he would have little difficulty understanding theology because he thought it was like logic, whereas it actually had as much in common with the classicist's training in explicating literary texts. To medieval teachers the Bible presented itself as a set of books in Latin, like the books of the classical authors. The same method of 'access to the authors' was applied to both. Abelard had at least some knowledge of commenting on books, as he had been to the school of Laon (where Anselm was an expert on Biblical commentary) and Abelard was working on his own commentary on Ezechiel at the time he met Heloise.[81] As this commentary no longer exists and perhaps was never finished, we cannot know what it contained nor whether it already showed an appreciation of the Greek and Roman philosophers. The surviving fragments of Anselm of Laon's teachings demonstrate that he, like Abelard, discussed the fate of the unbaptized and whether 'the ancient fathers', who had lived before the coming of Christ, would be saved.[82] But he did not discuss the question Abelard addressed in *Theologia* of whether the philosophers had known of the Trinity.

HELOISE'S CONTRIBUTION TO ABELARD'S THEOLOGY

Heloise's contribution to Abelard's theological thought would not have been in specific pieces of knowledge or know-how, as no one had anything to teach Abelard in his opinion, and neither were her ideas uniquely hers; indeed some were commonplaces of teachers of the classics. What she contributed was her imaginative understanding of the classics and, in particular, her passionate feelings about the pagan sages. She actually cared about the moral standing of Socrates or the Stoics and this is what she conveyed to Abelard, so that he too insisted in

Theologia (even at the price of coming close to contradicting himself) that they were as good as Christians. At the level of feelings, as much as of imagination, Heloise seems to have set the agenda which Abelard addressed in his theological writings. Both of them may have participated in this at an unconscious level, which nevertheless linked their own searing feelings of guilt to wider religious hopes of divine love and redemption.

Abelard's theological writings look like personal statements, which stem from his developing relationship with Heloise over two decades (the years *c.*1119–*c.*1139), as well as being public and formal contributions to Christian thought. Seen in this light, *Theologia* aimed to redeem the pagan philosophers, even going to the point of arguing that they were good Catholics, because Abelard wanted Heloise to be a good Catholic. Similarly his *Ethics* has a personal purpose: if sin depended on the intention of the doer, then it would follow that neither he nor Heloise were sinful. In his *Commentary on St Paul's Epistle to the Romans*, Abelard came to describe Christ's suffering and love in a new way because he was concerned about his own redemption. He had tried in his correspondence with Heloise to persuade her to join him in love and pity for the suffering Christ, and it seems to have been in this context that he first developed his ideas about redemption.[83] In none of these instances does Abelard spell out, as a modern author might do in a dedication or preface, that Heloise was his inspiration. Even so, this is more than an arbitrary hypothesis, as she can be shown to have expressed these ideas before he did.

The hypothesis that Heloise set Abelard's agenda in theology helps explain why he addressed his final confession of faith to her, and not to his prosecutors at Sens and in Rome who were demanding it. In this document he did not restrict himself to an intellectual *credo* spelling out the principal doctrines of the Catholic faith. He also made an emotional appeal: 'I do not wish, I do not wish (the Latin *nolo* was repeated for emphasis) to be shut out from Christ.... I embrace Him with the arms of faith in the virginal flesh taken up from the Paraclete.' In embracing Christ, Abelard was also embracing Heloise, as the document addressed her as: 'now dearest in Christ'. Her dearness to him contrasted with the odium his devotion to philosophy had brought upon him: 'logic has made me hateful to the world'.[84] For Abelard, the intellectual *par excellence*, this acknowledgement that theoretical study concerned people's feelings was an admission indeed.

Abelard worked out his ideas about ethics and the meaning of sin later than his ideas about the Trinity and the pagan philosophers. The latter were expressed in the various editions of *Theologia*, principally between *c.*1119 and *c.*1135, whereas his *Ethics* was probably not written until the year before his trial at Sens in 1140 and it was never completed.[85] In the first version of *Theologia* when Abelard is discussing the theoretical problem of what knowing something means, he gives as an example: 'no one sins by knowing the sin, but by committing it'.[86] This shows familiarity with a question he would pursue in his *Ethics* twenty years later, but he did not take it further in *Theologia*. Again, it may have been Heloise who inspired him to look harder at moral philosophy. She combined philosophical thinking with her own passionate feelings about their marriage and its outcome. In her first extant letter to him (in response to his 'history of calamities' in *c.*1132) she told him she was both 'very guilty and very innocent' (*nocens/innocens*), since 'it is not the doing of a thing but the intention of the doer which makes the crime'.[87] This is a fundamental premise of Abelard's *Ethics* and nothing he says there expresses the problem more succinctly than Heloise's paradox *nocens/innocens*.

As with the argument about the virtuous lives of the classical philosophers, she was not the first medieval thinker to emphasize the importance of intention in the meaning of sin, as this idea was accessible through St Augustine. Anselm of Laon is recorded making a statement similar to Heloise's, and William of Champeaux said 'sin is nothing'; evil-doing depends upon the individual's intention.[88] For both Heloise and Abelard it may have been William who first introduced them to the philosophical paradoxes of sin and guilt, as he had been Abelard's master as well as the colleague in the precinct of Notre-Dame of Heloise's guardian, Fulbert. William had left Notre-Dame in *c.*1105 to become a canon regular at St Victor. By then Heloise was probably fifteen and she may already have been set by Fulbert on her precocious programme of study. 'The more he loved her', Abelard says, 'the more determinedly he had done everything he could to advance her in the study of the science of learning.'[89] Possibly, and this is no more than a hypothesis, Fulbert had inveigled William of Champeaux into giving her special tuition, just as he later inveigled Abelard.

Heloise displayed her education in moral philosophy to greatest effect in the forty-two questions she set Abelard to answer in the 1130s. In her accompanying letter, she presented them as 'baby questions' (*questiunculas*), which the nuns were sending their teacher like daughters to a father.[90] Many of them concern textual and interpretative difficulties in the Old and New Testaments, which slowed down the nuns' reading of the Scriptures, Heloise explained. It is striking, though, that about half of them have larger implications concerning the meaning of sin, judgement and the enforcement of the law; in other words, the subject matter of Abelard's *Ethics*. The answers he gives to the forty-two questions are mostly brief. An exception is the last question, which is unique in not citing a Biblical text from which it purportedly arises. It asks 'whether anyone can sin in something that he does by permission of, or even at the command of, their lord'.[91] At a personal level, this was the dilemma Heloise had set out in her letters to Abelard; she had obeyed him in everything, right or wrong, and this was why she was both guilty and innocent. At a general level, the question was the same one which Abelard was to pose in dramatic form in his *Ethics*: did the soldiers who crucified Christ commit a sin, when they obeyed orders and did what they believed was pleasing to God?[92]

In his reply to Heloise and her nuns, Abelard answered the question in a peculiar way, addressing neither the personal nor the general aspect of it. Instead, he interpreted it as a question about the lawfulness of sexual intercourse within marriage: had the Lord, in the sense of the Lord God, ordained it? Abelard answered this at length, with many citations of authorities, as if he were addressing a question in his *Sic et Non*.[93] Perhaps he had failed to see what Heloise was getting at, or he saw this only too clearly and he had no wish to get involved in personal acrimony.[94] When he did come to address questions of individual responsibility in his *Ethics* (probably five or six years later, in *c*.1139), he presented his arguments as if they were all his own original thoughts. This makes *Ethics* read very well, as it is not cluttered with citations from authorities, though it conceals Abelard's debt to his masters (including Heloise) and above all to St Augustine. As in *Theologia*, Abelard stated his arguments in provocative forms which look contradictory, though they are not formally so.

His discussion of the culpability of the soldiers who crucified Christ is the clearest example of this. He begins with the rule that an 'action' (*operatio*) is neither good nor bad in itself; it proceeds from a good or bad intention.[95] So, we cannot say that the persecutors of Christ sinned in what they did, as they did not know Him.[96] But this argument conflicted with Scripture. St Luke's Gospel says Christ prayed for his crucifiers: 'Father, forgive them, for they know not what they do.'[97] Why did they need forgiveness, if they had not sinned? Abelard answers that people may be lawfully punished for making mistakes, even when they are not at fault. Christ asked forgiveness for His persecutors, lest they be punished for having made the mistake of failing to recognize Him.[98] This allows Abelard to backtrack on saying that the crucifiers of Christ did not sin. They sinned 'through an action' (*per operationem*), he concludes, 'even though they would have sinned more gravely' if they had spared Christ against their consciences.[99]

Abelard justifies going against his own rule that actions are neither good nor bad by arguing that in colloquial speech we may say someone has sinned through an action. In such an instance we are using the word 'sin' not in its 'proper' (*proprie*) sense, but 'broadly' (*large*).[100] This is comparable with the way he had backtracked in *Theologia Summi Boni* as to whether the Greek and Roman philosophers had known of the Catholic faith.[101] If theologians were going to mix up the broad terms of colloquial speech with their own proper language, then all sorts of ambiguities might arise, which exposed Abelard personally to accusations of incompetence – or worse – and which undermined theology's status as an exact science useful to the Church in clarifying its teaching.

The ambiguities in Abelard's *Ethics*, like those in *Theologia*, provided his prosecutors with plenty of material. Seven of the nineteen indictments of heresy against him at the council of Sens in 1140 concerned the meaning of sin. (This may partly be because *Ethics* was quite a short book, which had been written recently and which was more accessible to his prosecutors than others.) He was indicted on his alleged statements about free will, original sin, the crucifiers of Christ, priests' powers to forgive sins, the value of good or bad works, the power of the devil, and finally (in what Abelard called 'the latest charge') for teaching 'that neither action nor will nor desire, nor the pleasure which drives it, is a sin; nor should we wish to extinguish it'.[102] Although Abelard said this was entirely alien to his statements or writings, this final indictment was a summary of the opening section of his *Ethics*.[103] As so often, Abelard and his prosecutors were at cross-purposes. He had indeed argued that we should not wish to extinguish physical desires, such as eating or copulating, because these are necessary bodily functions which cannot be performed without pleasure.[104] His prosecutors, on the other hand, either maliciously or carelessly, suggested he was arguing that we should not want to extinguish sin.

Provocative as some statements are in *Ethics*, and prominent as they are in the list of indictments, St Bernard did not comment on them in his prosecution of Abelard; or rather, he did not cite them in his long letter to the pope, which is the best evidence we have about what St Bernard focused on. He included the indictments from *Ethics* among the 'stupidities' to which he had no time to respond.[105] He concentrated his attack on three 'graver' matters: the Trinity, the meaning of faith and the Redemption. On all three subjects Abelard differed in important respects from the theology of St Anselm of Canterbury, though St Bernard's purpose was not so much to defend St Anselm as to focus on the 'graver' issues. He showed he had St Anselm's work in mind, however, by using his ontological proof of the existence of God as part of the case against Abelard.[106]

THE LEGACY OF ST ANSELM

Abelard called St Anselm 'that magnificent doctor of the Church', but he also repeatedly attacked his theology.[107] He did this most explicitly in *Theologia Christiana*, when he named St Anselm and suggested his analogy of the Trinity was a great support to heresy (this is the analogy of the course of the river Nile).[108] St Bernard retaliated (though again probably not deliberately in defence of St Anselm) by ridiculing Abelard's analogy of a seal, which he had created as an improvement on St Anselm's watercourse.[109] It was not difficult to make any physical analogy of the Trinity (comparing it to water in St Anselm's case or wax in Abelard's) look absurd, as the Trinity is such an abstract concept. But there was a long tradition in theological writing of attempting to show what the Trinity meant by likening it to everyday things. In Abelard's time the use of seals was becoming increasingly common in northern France. He himself had possessed a seal with a man and a woman's head on it, according to Roscelin.[110] In using a seal as an analogy, Abelard was therefore taking an example that was technologically modern and it also neatly illustrated the difference between matter and form: the brass, of which the seal matrix is made, is distinct from the image or form which is engraved on it. By impressing the matrix on the melted wax, the act of sealing completes what Abelard sees as a threefold or trinity-like process.[111]

This was ingenious, but it was as vulnerable as any other analogy of the Trinity, not least because the seal begins as something in brass and ends up as something in wax. Abelard's first version of the analogy in *Theologia Christiana* (ten years earlier in *c*.1123) had concentrated on the image in the sealing wax and not on the brass matrix. With typical self-confidence, he assured his readers 'that if we apply the reasoning of this analogy to divine generation, it is easy to assign everything to its place and defend what we believe'.[112] He assigned God the Father to the wax and God the Son to the image impressed on the wax.[113] But he had difficulty finding a third element in the analogy to stand for the Holy Spirit and this is why he introduced the brass matrix and the act of sealing into the revised version of the analogy, even though this exposed new inconsistencies. Abelard's careless confidence in the earlier analogy, until he had spotted its weaknesses, shows how readily he exposed himself to criticism.

St Bernard explicitly defended a position of St Anselm's in his attack on Abelard's definition of faith as an 'estimate', as he accused Abelard of reversing the rule 'Unless you believe, you shall not understand'.[114] (This subject has already been discussed in chapter 2 at pages 35–7 above) St Bernard and Abelard, and St Anselm and Abelard, were at cross-purposes here, as they were using 'understand' and 'estimate' to describe different stages in getting to know something. A proposition has to be understood (that is, it has to make some sort of sense), before an estimate can be made of whether to believe it.[115] In his dialogue between a Christian and a Philosopher, Abelard has the latter say that blind faith will just as readily believe in an idol of wood or stone as in the true God. The Christian agrees with this: 'Certainly, no one who is sensible forbids our faith being investigated and discussed rationally, nor can it be assented to unless the things in doubt are assented to on some rational premise.'[116] Opinions will always vary about whether St Bernard was a 'sensible' (*discretus*) person, when he was in full rhetorical pursuit of a quarry like Abelard.

Abelard's most conspicuous departure from St Anselm's theology concerned the meaning of the Redemption and this is also the subject to which St Bernard devoted his most vituperative language in the prosecution of Abelard.[117] Sir Richard Southern has argued that 'Abelard's view stands as a protest against all the essential elements in Anselm's thought' on the subject.[118] The meaning of the Redemption had been debated without reaching agreement for the previous fifty years, ever since the subject had been opened up by St Anselm's *Cur Deus Homo?* ('Why did God become man?') in the 1090s. By Abelard's time St Anselm was no longer central to the debate, as he had been dead since 1109 and he left no school of followers. Judging from the *Liber Pancrisis*, Anselm of Laon and William of Champeaux had discussed the Redemption in detail. As Abelard had been taught by both of them, he most probably derived his knowledge of the subject from them. By the 1130s, when he began to write about the Redemption, his own masters were dead. The rival whom Abelard may have had in his sights in *c*.1133, when he returned to Paris, was Hugh of St Victor whose *De Sacramentis* expressed the traditional doctrine of the Redemption with clarity.[119]

THE MEANING OF REDEMPTION

Christ's work in redeeming mankind had traditionally been explained by analogy with a lord who releases slaves from bondage. Because of his original sin, man had been enslaved by the devil and Christ redeemed him by paying the price or ransom due for his release. In the slave-owning society of the Roman Empire, where Christians had been among the slaves, this analogy had worked well because of its realism, and it still worked in the twelfth century when numerous peasants remained bonded to their lords. At the council of Sens in 1140 the indictment against Abelard was expressed in the traditional terms of the bondage analogy: he was alleged to have denied that Christ became flesh 'in order to liberate us from the yoke of the devil'.[120] Everyone would have seen oxen yoked to carts or ploughs, even if yoked and chained slaves were becoming a rarer sight in France, now that Viking and barbarian raids were a thing of the past. An essential point in the analogy of the yoke was that enslavement was not a total injustice. It was a legal status and the devil had a necessary task to perform in setting man to work and punishing him. Unless man served the bondage that was his due, he could not pay his debt and earn redemption.

This is why Hugh of St Victor and other commentators likened Christian redemption to a lawsuit. For Hugh it was a 'case' (*causa*) involving three parties: man, God and the devil, each with their due claims.[121] (Out of presenting the doctrine in this way came the great liturgical plays, which dramatize the plight of Adam and Eve and give the devil a voice as if he were a person.[122]) Man has deprived the Lord God of His service (Hugh says) by going over to the devil, who in his turn has reneged on his agreement with man. But man can get no redress because he is powerless to bring the devil into court. God, who might act as man's patron and advocate, has refused to take up the case because He is still angry about Adam and Eve's defiance of Him. So, man has a dual task: he must placate his patron and then, with God as his advocate, sue the devil. God at last relents and sends His son, Christ, to earth. He placates God's anger by being born as a man, and then He proceeds against the devil on man's behalf by paying the price with His own blood. Having won the case, Christ obtains a judgement against the devil, which He executes in person by presenting Himself at the devil's residence and demanding the release of his prisoners. This is the powerful image of the Harrowing of Hell in Romanesque art: a triumphant Christ forces open the mouth of Hell with His knightly lance and the righteous people come pouring out, headed by Adam and Eve.[123]

Vivid as Hugh of St Victor's description is, it really throws more light on medieval methods of litigation than on the doctrine of the Redemption. It blithely ignores the objections which St Anselm had made forty or fifty years earlier in *Cur Deus Homo?* to this sort of legalistic thinking. Hugh treats the devil as if he has rights. His power over man can be terminated only by Christ paying the due price for man's release. At the same time Hugh portrays God like an angry and capricious man. The arbitrary anger of a medieval lord might be placated only by money or blood, but God should have a higher sense of justice. These are the sort of difficulties which Abelard raised in his short, but radical, treatment of the Redemption in his *Commentary on St Paul's Epistle to the Romans*.[124] As in his other theological books, he presents his questions as if he has just thought of them, without reference to the contributions of St Anselm or his own masters. Even his most sardonic question (How could man's tasting of a single apple be a greater sin than crucifying the Son of God?) had been asked before.[125]

The point Abelard wanted to make with his disconcerting questions was that the Redemption was not about justice or law; it was about love. In Hugh's analogy of the lawsuit there is no mention either of God's love for man, nor of man's love for God. A medieval lawsuit might be settled by a 'loveday', when the parties were brought into an amicable agreement by arbitration. A later medieval writer describes the Redemption as a 'loveday' between God and mankind with Mary as umpire.[126] But the structure of Hugh's analogy did not allow for this, as it would mean having Christ make a compromise with the devil, instead of winning His case and obtaining an execution of judgement. Like St Anselm, Abelard pointed out that the analogy of paying a ransom was invalid, as the payment was due not to the devil, who held man captive, but to God. How could blood money be due to God? 'How cruel and iniquitous it looks for someone to demand the blood of an innocent person as the price of anything, or that he should take pleasure in any way at the killing of an innocent man, least of all that God should have found the death of His Son so acceptable that He should have been reconciled to the whole world by it.'[127] Abelard presented a similar paradox at the end of *Theologia Scholarium*, the final version of *Theologia*: 'How should the death of Christ be wanted by us, or His suffering be desirable, unless there was good even in an entirely innocent person being killed by wicked ones?'[128]

The significance of this question in *Theologia Scholarium* is that Abelard makes no attempt to answer it. It is one of a battery of questions with which he concludes – or fails to conclude – *Theologia*. This suggests that his questions on the Redemption were among the last pieces of work he did. In *Theologia Scholarium* they are appended to the end of the book and in the *Commentary on St Paul's Epistle to the Romans* they are interpolated into the commentary by using the device: 'At this point a very big question intrudes itself, namely: what may this Redemption of ours by the death of Christ be?'[129] (Pausing like this to ask questions is a technique Abelard used quite often in this comment-ary.[130]) Unlike *Theologia Scholarium*, Abelard answers the questions he poses in his *Commentary*, though he does so cursorily and he abruptly concludes: 'Now, as befits brevity of exposition, this seems to us suffi-cient and succinct concerning the manner of our Redemption. Whatever is lacking in perfection here, we reserve for our treatises on "Tropolo-giae".'[131] This amounts to an admission that Abelard's answers were not altogether satisfactory and no treatise called 'Tropologiae' now exists, though it may have done once.

If Abelard first asked his radical questions about the doctrine of the Redemption only at the end of his career, shortly before his trial at Sens in 1140, his earlier statements fall into place. He had preached a number of sermons when he was a monk for Palm Sunday and Holy Week, in which he expressed the conventional argument that Christ had won a glorious victory over the devil.[132] In his letter to Heloise in c.1132 he accepted that Christ had paid blood money: 'He bought you not with His goods but with Himself. He bought and redeemed you with His own blood. See what a great right He has in you and how precious you appear.'[133] This argument may have been the more offensive to Heloise because Abelard was insisting at the same time that Christ had bought her as His bride, whereas she was opposed to mercenary marriages: 'I preferred love to marriage and liberty to chains.'[134] The Latin word for 'marriage' which she used here, *conjugium*, literally meant 'co-yoking' and this may be why she associated marriage with the bondage of chains. Abelard's desperate wish to get Heloise to join him in accepting Redemption in Christ may have been the catalyst which set him thinking about the traditional doctrine and to reject, as she rejected, the buying and selling of love.

The conclusion which Abelard finally came up with in his *Comment-ary* is that 'our Redemption through Christ's suffering is that supreme love in us which, as well as liberating us from the servitude of sin, confers on us true freedom as children of God, so that we do everything out of His love rather than from fear. For, He has shown us such grace that no greater can be found.'[135] The germ of this idea is in Abelard's letter to Heloise of c.1132, where he appealed to her to open her heart to the suffering of Christ and love Him rather than Abelard, who had subjected her by fear: 'In Him, I beseech you, not in me, should be all your devotion, all your compassion, all your remorse.'[136] Sir Richard Southern has argued that Abelard's reinterpretation of the Redemption 'contains one of the great new ideas of the twelfth century: it asserted that the Incarnation was efficacious, not in satisfying the just claims of God or the devil, but in teaching by example the law of love. It left out the whole idea of compensation to God for human sin, and threw the whole emphasis of the Incarnation on its capacity to revive man's love for God.'[137]

Abelard's conclusion is indeed remarkable for what it so succinctly leaves out. But it was not as original as he makes it look in his *Commentary*, as St Anselm had shown how Christ had given mankind an example of righteousness and William of Champeaux is reported saying that Christ 'has also brought us a greater grace, since we are to love Him who has so loved us'.[138] There is something in William's words of Abelard's emphasis on redemption as a psychological transformation within each individual, which engenders love within us, as William adds that human 'reason is illuminated' by the coming of Christ. St Bernard may also have been an influence on Abelard, as he was telling his monks in the 1130s that Christ's humanity is best explained as an example which teaches mankind how to love. (Bernard, like Abelard, may have been influenced by William of Champeaux, as he was Bernard's mentor in his formative years at Clairvaux.) Bernard recommended everyone at prayer to keep in their mind's eye an image of Christ at some stage of His human life: at His nativity, for example, or teaching, or dying. This image binds the soul with the love of the virtues. Like Abelard, Bernard gave his own explanation for this:

> I think this was the principal reason why the invisible God wished to be seen in the flesh and to live with men as a man. It was so that He might first draw all the affections of carnal men towards the saving love of His humanity, as they were not able to love in any other way, and then to raise them gradually to a spiritual love.[139]

Although Abelard's language is more academic than Bernard's, they both emphasize that Christ came to show us how to love. The mental image-making recommended by Bernard had its visible counterpart in the powerful but tender crucifixion figures in Romanesque and early Gothic art. Abelard and Bernard were voicing perceptions and feelings which touched everybody and reached out beyond the confines of their schools and cloisters. This was what theology in the service of the Church and Christian society was meant to be about. But the writings of Abelard and Bernard show equally strongly that theology engendered hatred and sectarianism because it entitled every theologian to insist that his way was God's way and the only way. Those who disagreed were not just opponents in an academic debate, they were potential heretics.

13

Heretic

Abelard was tried for heresy twice: at the council of Soissons in 1121 and the council of Sens in 1140. He was also from boyhood the student of Roscelin, who had been tried for heresy at Soissons in 1092. So Abelard was associated with heresy throughout his career. This was very unusual, as masters were rarely formally tried for heresy, even if they were accused of it occasionally by rivals. It was equally uncommon for other clergy or lay people to be accused of heresy. From time to time a successful preacher became prominent, like Tanchelm of Antwerp and Henry of Le Mans in the second decade of the twelfth century, who allegedly deceived the populace by fomenting heresy and sedition; but they rarely found a following for long and sometimes they were not even arrested. Larger and more threatening groups of heretics, notably the Cathars, only emerged later in the twelfth century.

Because outbreaks of heresy were sporadic and diverse, the authorities were confused about how to deal with them. This helps explain how Abelard could survive two trials, on the same main charge concerning the Trinity, and how he could make a successful (though very controversial) career in the schools. He was much admired by respected and conservative clerics, like Peter the Venerable and John of Salisbury, despite having been the pupil of Roscelin, who had likewise been repeatedly accused of heresy concerning the Trinity. Elementary questions of procedure in dealing with accusations of heresy had not been resolved. Should the accused be given a hearing? Or was his offence so bad that his blasphemies must not be heard? (Abelard was not given a hearing at Soissons in 1121 and the pope condemned him in 1140 without a hearing.) How was heresy to be proved? By cross-examination of the accused? But what if he were, like Abelard, a better debater than his judges? If, as a result of the trial, the accused agreed to abjure his errors (as Roscelin had done), should he be released as a true penitent? Once he ceased being excommunicate and anathema, what was to stop him fomenting heresy all over again? St Bernard in 1140 compared Abelard to the seven-headed beast of the Book of Revelation: 'one head, a single heresy of his was cut off at Soissons; but now seven greater ones have grown up in its place'.[1]

Guibert de Nogent gives an account of a trial at Soissons in 1114, seven years before Abelard's own, which illustrates these dilemmas.[2] Two local peasants had allegedly been spreading all sorts of heresies: they denied the sacraments of infant baptism, the eucharist and marriage and they indulged in orgies and ritual infanticides including cannibalism. Guibert admits that when the men were examined by the bishop, they gave most Christian answers and when Guibert himself examined them further, they kept repeating: 'We believe everything you say.' No witnesses would come forward to corroborate the accusations. But Guibert knew the men were artfully concealing their wickedness and so he sent them to the ordeal of water. This involved blessing a deep vat of water and throwing the accused person into it, trussed and bound. If he floated, the holy water was deemed to have rejected him and he was therefore guilty. If he sank, he was innocent and he survived, provided he was pulled out in time. (Like the other ordeals, this one was designed to terrify the accused into making a confession or an accusation against someone else, rather than undertaking the ordeal.) In the case described by Guibert the accused peasants floated 'like sticks' and so they were imprisoned, while he and his colleagues went off to Beauvais (a journey of three or four days) to consult about what they should do next. In their absence the problem was resolved for them, as the people of Soissons broke into the prison and burned the heretics. 'God's people', concludes Guibert, 'had shown a righteous zeal against them.'

THE LYNCHING OF HERETICS

Guibert's solution of 'God's people' lynching the heretics was an ominous precedent for Abelard. At his trial at Soissons in 1121 he describes how he and his little group of students were nearly stoned by the people, who had been told by his prosecutors that he taught and wrote that there were three gods.[3] Lynching was no imaginary fear on Abelard's part, as a letter of Ivo bishop of Chartres had justified the stoning of heretics in the case of Roscelin.[4] This letter reproves Roscelin for persisting with his heresy, even after he had abjured it at the council of Soissons in 1092. Ivo describes how Roscelin has been stripped and robbed, but he excuses this violence as 'the just wisdom of God correcting you'. He warns Roscelin that should he come to Chartres, 'some of our citizens might hold you to be odious and suspect me as well. Having heard of your name and former conduct, they might suddenly – as is their custom – start stones flying and smother you under a hail of them.' He follows this overt threat by advising Roscelin to recant, as 'Mother Church corrects you with maternal piety'.

Ivo of Chartres was the leading canon lawyer of his day. His opinions were enshrined in the *Liber Pancrisis*, the 'All-Gold Book', and in later books of ecclesiastical law. His view that people who lynched heretics were doing God's work was evidently shared by Guibert de Nogent, with his reference to 'God's people', and also perhaps by St Anselm of Canterbury, who said Roscelin had recanted only because he feared being killed 'by the people'.[5] Abelard corroborates that Roscelin was nearly killed in England in 1093.[6] The ever-present threat of lynching helps explain why Abelard submitted at Soissons in 1121 to casting his own book into the fire and being imprisoned at the abbey of St Médard within the city. An accused heretic needed a safe place to run to, and monasteries provided this with their stone walls and fortified gates. After Abelard's trial at Sens in 1140, Peter the Venerable provided such a haven on a grand scale at Cluny. St Bernard's biographer, Geoffrey of Auxerre, maintained that Abelard had had nothing to fear at Sens and he would have been given a fair hearing. But in the light of previous lynchings, Otto of Freising's testimony is more credible; he says Abelard refused to answer at Sens and appealed to Rome because he feared a 'rising of the people'.[7]

The threat of lynching puts into sharp perspective St Bernard's inflammatory letters to the pope and cardinals in the aftermath of Abelard's appeal to Rome in 1140, particularly because St Bernard insisted that Abelard was in alliance in Italy with the revolutionary, Arnold of Brescia. They have joined forces against the Lord and His anointed (meaning the pope), Bernard said.[8] Like Guibert de Nogent and the alleged heretics in Soissons, Bernard faced the difficulty that the external evidence did not support him. He admitted that Abelard and Arnold looked like models of piety and angels of light, despite being instruments of Satan in reality. Bernard's words could justify Abelard's lynching. He had written to the pope to say: 'Should not the mouth that speaks such things be shattered with cudgels, rather than rebutted with reasons? Does not he whose hand is against all men deservedly provoke all men's hands against him?'[9] The phraseology is Biblical, but the words 'deservedly provoke' were Bernard's own. His Biblical allusions can either be interpreted figuratively and, in that case, he may not have been literally recommending everyone to smash Abelard's face in. Or, to the contrary, Bernard's citations from the Bible reinforced the lynch law already sanctioned by Ivo of Chartres and Guibert de Nogent. Bernard was Abelard's prosecutor, not his judge, and this is why he used such strong language. Abelard appealed to him to show Christian charity: a Christian should not take up a reproach against his neighbour.[10] But Bernard, as prosecutor, did not acknowledge Abelard to be his neighbour, since heretics were excluded from Christian society. They provoked the same reactions as terrorists in modern society; they 'deservedly' got hurt because they attacked the innocent.

Paradoxically, it may have been because of the overt prejudice and intimidation of heresy trials that the accused person might find sympathizers, who protected him even to the extent of encouraging him to carry on much as before. This had been Roscelin's experience and Abelard's also. A distinction should be made in this respect between masters like Roscelin and Abelard, who came from the same social milieu as their prosecutors, and peasants like those whom Guibert de Nogent sentenced to the ordeal, who were despised and feared by the clergy as illiterate and insubordinate rustics. Masters also stood a better chance of a fair hearing because they had students to support them. The young men served as bodyguards and the older ones could exercise influence with the judges. At the council of Sens in 1140 Abelard summoned his supporters to his aid against St Bernard, rather like a lord summoning his knights.[11] The inflammatory tone of St Bernard's letters is partly accounted for by his belief that there were cardinals at Rome who sympathized with Abelard. Certainly Cardinal Guy of Castello possessed copies of *Theologia* and *Sic et Non*, and he did not surrender them when the pope ordered Abelard's books to be burned in 1140.[12]

Because the circle of masters was relatively small and interlinked, the prosecutors themselves were often associates of the accused. At Soissons in 1121 Abelard's accusers were his former colleagues at the school of Laon, Alberic and Lotulf. Similarly, in Roscelin's case in 1092 St Anselm acknowledged he was a friend of his, though later on he kept quiet about this.[13] William of St Thierry, the initiator of Abelard's prosecution in 1140, said: 'I have loved him and I wish to love him.'[14] Outsiders, to whom the substantive issues of defining the Trinity or the Redemption were obscure, might see in the prosecution of a master nothing more than a quarrel among friends or colleagues. This is how Peter the Venerable interpreted Abelard's trial at Sens. Despite all St Bernard's rhetoric and the solemn sentence of the pope condemning Abelard, Peter sent the pope the surprising news that Bernard and Abelard had agreed 'to put their previous quarrels peacefully to sleep'.[15] So in Peter's view Abelard had been involved in 'quarrels', not heresies, which were best resolved by agreement, not cursings and burnings. We have no knowledge of how the pope reacted to Peter's news, nor is there any evidence – other than Peter's copy of the letter he sent the pope – that this agreement took place. But Peter is generally a reliable source and Bernard made a compromise of a similar sort after his prosecution of Gilbert de la Porrée in 1148.[16]

ABELARD AND ROSCELIN

The ambivalent ways in which Abelard was treated are matched by Roscelin's experience and also by the case of Berengar of Tours in the preceding century. He had been examined by Pope Leo IX in 1050, by the papal legate Hildebrand (the future Gregory VII) in 1054, by Pope Nicholas II and Cardinal Humbert in 1059 and then again by Gregory VII in 1078. Gregory rehabilitated Berenger in 1079 and he died in a hermitage near Tours in 1088.[17] Despite his numerous trials, Berengar may never have actually been excommunicated. The same applies to Roscelin, who reminded Abelard that he had never been formally condemned: 'I never was a heretic. When you belch and throw up verbal vomit, saying I am infamous and that I was condemned in the council [of Soissons], I will prove by the testimony of the churches where I was born, nurtured and educated that this filthy libel is utterly false.'[18] Roscelin's language illustrates, incidentally, that St Bernard was not alone in being inflammatory. The defence of God and righteousness justified strong language. Roscelin's denial is the more remarkable, considering that St Anselm had argued that such a faithless blasphemer should not even be given a hearing: 'Let him remain anathema as long as he persists in this obstinacy, for he is not a Christian at all.'[19] St Anselm thought Roscelin continued to be a heretic and this is why he sent his refutation of him to Pope Urban II in *c.*1095.

This is the very time when Abelard was probably a student of Roscelin's. Why would Abelard have become the pupil of a master with such a dubious reputation? There is no good answer to this question. Even if Roscelin had not been formally condemned at Soissons in 1092, he had been accused of persisting in his heresy after he had abjured it, not only by St Anselm but also by Ivo of Chartres. In other words, Roscelin had been accused of being a relapsed heretic by the greatest theologian and the greatest lawyer of the day. The seriousness of this offence explains why Ivo approved of Roscelin being stoned, if he visited Chartres and it also explains why St Anselm expelled him from England in *c.*1093 and then invoked papal assistance against him.[20] Roscelin describes being Abelard's master 'for a long time' and 'from boyhood up until youth'.[21] Otto of Freising confirms that Roscelin had been Abelard's first teacher.[22] Although Abelard made no mention of Roscelin in his 'history of calamities', he says in *Dialectica*, in an aside at one point: 'This was, I remember, the insane opinion of our master, Roscelin.'[23] So Abelard confirms that he had been Roscelin's pupil and his insulting language shows why Roscelin retaliated with more of the same. Exchanging insults was an admired part of clerical Latin rhetoric; its greatest practitioner in Abelard's time was St Bernard.

Roscelin says he taught Abelard at Loches and Tours.[24] This makes sense, as their paths could have crossed when Abelard was making his 'perambulation of the provinces' (as he called it) up the valley of the Loire from west to east.[25] The Touraine (the region of Tours) was in the process of being taken over by Fulk le Réchin, count of Anjou. Roscelin's finding a haven there after he had been expelled from the kingdoms of France and England also makes sense, as Fulk was the rival of both kings. The Touraine was a buffer region, situated at the southernmost point of the French royal demesne around Orléans and the southernmost point of the Anglo-Norman lordship in Maine. Roscelin was a foreigner in Touraine and Anjou, as he originated from north of Paris at Compiègne and then he had been in Normandy (perhaps at Bayeux) when he got to know St Anselm, while Anselm was prior or abbot of Bec. This makes Abelard's association with Roscelin all the odder, as he too was a foreigner in the Touraine, as he was a Breton, though admittedly a Breton from south of the Loire. If Abelard was ambitious to get to Paris and be acknowledged a true Frenchman, he was imprudent to linger in the Angevin lands with an exile from France.

How long was Abelard with Roscelin as his pupil? This question is crucial for assessing the extent of Roscelin's influence on him. Abelard was born in *c*.1079 and Roscelin did not return from England until *c*.1093, when Abelard was about fourteen. He presumably did not start with Roscelin before then.[26] How long Roscelin meant by 'from boyhood up until youth' and 'a long time' is unclear. This could be any span of years between 1093 and 1100, when Abelard is thought to have arrived in Paris. A twelfth-century source says Abelard got bored with Roscelin, who ordered him to attend his lectures for a year.[27] This source does not explain why Roscelin had the authority to do this, nor how long Abelard had spent with him already. As the years 1093–1100 are when Roscelin was considered a relapsed heretic by St Anselm and Ivo of Chartres, the question repeats itself: why had Abelard chosen such a disreputable master?

One possibility is that in 1093 Abelard and his patrons, including his father, perhaps had no great ambitions for him. They did not envisage him going to Paris and being the greatest philosopher in the world. The city of Tours was metropolitan compared with Abelard's native Le Pallet, or even with Nantes, and in 1093 the newly-arrived Roscelin may have seemed the most distinguished master in the area. He had taught in France, Normandy and England (he may have been one of the first masters at Oxford).²⁸ He insisted he had never been a heretic. He also claimed (though the date is unclear) that he had been welcomed in Rome. At some stage, too, he had been appointed a canon of Besançon in Burgundy.²⁹ Here was a scholar of international standing. Furthermore, he had very strict views on the celibacy of the clergy.³⁰ This made him suitable as a moral tutor for the young Abelard and also the right sort of person to appoint as a master and canon in a great church, as he would not be trying to pass his benefice on to his sons.

The pattern of Roscelin's career looks much like Abelard's own. Both were accused of heresy more than once. In each case there was doubt about what had actually happened at the trial. Both were accused of much the same heresy of applying secular logic to the Trinity. Both were accused by the most powerful religious thinker of the day, who in each case turned to the pope for support: St Anselm appealed to Urban II in *c*.1095 and St Bernard to Innocent II in 1140. Both were expelled from the kingdom of France: Roscelin after the council of Soissons in 1092 and Abelard after insulting St Denis in 1122. Both readily found asylum in other regions of France: Roscelin in the Touraine and Abelard in Champagne under Count Thibaud; Abelard was also given asylum in Burgundy by Peter the Venerable after his second trial in 1140. Both Roscelin and Abelard presented themselves as champions of celibacy and reformers of ecclesiastical discipline, which helped to give them a good reputation in some quarters. Both repeatedly denied they had ever been heretics and pointed to the churches and supporters who had given them benefices. Both claimed to have friends in Rome. And most importantly, both were controversial teachers of logic, who repeatedly succeeded in attracting new students even after they had been tried for heresy.

Roscelin claimed that his influence on Abelard had been immense: 'I showed you so many things and so much.'³¹ Unlike the sentences of Anselm of Laon and William of Champeaux, Roscelin's teachings were not enshrined in any 'All-Gold Book' (*Liber Pancrisis*) and neither are there any writings which are undoubtedly his, other than his letter of *c*.1120 attacking Abelard. (There is a little treatise 'On universals according to Master R.', which may be a report of Roscelin's teaching.³²) So, it is not possible to say exactly what Abelard learned from his master. But as we know that Abelard made no acknowledgement of his sources when he took up ideas of Anselm of Laon and William of Champeaux, the probability is that he was as deeply – or more deeply – indebted to Roscelin, particularly in logic and the application of logic to theological problems. When Abelard arrived in Paris in c.1100 and soon began challenging William of Champeaux, he was successful not only because of his genius (as he describes in his 'history of calamities') but also perhaps because of his training by Roscelin. As importantly, Roscelin may also have passed on to Abelard some of his prejudices, particularly against St Anselm and Ivo of Chartres. What Abelard does not seem to have learned from Roscelin was any sense of caution in discussing matters of doctrine, despite having seen how Roscelin was treated. As Abelard fell out with Roscelin, he probably thought Roscelin deserved persecution whereas he, Abelard, did not.

It is not known when Abelard and Roscelin quarrelled. There is nothing explicit until their letters complaining of each other in c.1120, though the earlier mention of Abelard getting bored with Roscelin may indicate a previous rift.[33] In c.1120 Abelard wrote to the bishop of Paris, complaining that Roscelin had been saying there were heresies in his treatise on the Trinity; this is presumably the whole or a part of the first version of *Theologia*.[34] Abelard requested the bishop to summon a council to decide on this issue by disciplining either Roscelin or Abelard. (Abelard used a similar tactic in the run-up to the council of Sens in 1140, when he requested the archbishop of Sens to summon St Bernard to answer his complaints.[35]) Abelard devoted most of his letter to the bishop of Paris to presenting himself as the champion of orthodoxy and to slandering Roscelin by making allegations about his former life. Abelard's tactics had the reverse effect to the one intended, as it was he and not Roscelin who was put on trial. Abelard gives an account of this in his 'history of calamities', but he makes no mention of Roscelin at all and neither does he explain why the trial was held at Soissons instead of in the diocese of Paris, as he had requested. He attributes his trial entirely to the machinations of his former colleagues from the school of Laon, Alberic of Reims and Lotulf of Novara.[36]

THE POWER OF THE PAPACY

What Abelard does emphasize is that his trial at Soissons in 1121 was held in the presence of the papal legate in France, Cardinal Cono of Praeneste.[37] This former Swabian canon regular was the most senior and formidable of all the papal legates. On his own initiative he had excommunicated the Emperor Henry V in 1111 and again in 1114–15. He was reported to have been chosen by Pope Gelasius II as his successor in 1119, but the French party had preferred Guy bishop of Vienne, who became Calixtus II. Cono of Praeneste stood above the various parties in the papal curia, partly because his speciality was international diplomacy. He favoured neither the French, nor the Germans (though he was one), nor the Roman noble families of whom the Pierleoni were the most important. He would have had no compunction in disciplining Abelard if that were called for, nor in releasing him if that was the appropriate thing to do. As papal legate, Cono's authority overrode that of the bishop of Paris and he could have summoned Abelard to Soissons or anywhere else in the area of France where he exercised jurisdiction. (This was approximately the area in which the Capetian kings had influence over the Church and it excluded Aquitaine, Burgundy and Normandy.) Abelard's account of Cono in his 'history of calamities' does its best to undermine the legate's authority by suggesting that he was 'less learned than was required' and that the assembly at Soissons was merely 'some conventicle' masquerading as a council.[38] Otto of Freising, on the other hand, described it as 'a provincial synod assembled under the presidency of a legate of the Roman see' and this is probably correct.[39]

Abelard's trial may have been held in Soissons, instead of Paris, because Bishop Gilbert considered the dispute between Roscelin and Abelard too serious a matter to be adjudicated in his diocese and he had therefore remitted it to the papal legate. It may have been Roscelin's name which alarmed Bishop Gilbert more than Abelard's, as St Anselm's refutation of Roscelin had been adjudged 'of the very greatest authority' by Pope Urban II and Anselm had insisted in it that anyone responding to theological error should seek papal advice and correction.[40] On these grounds Bishop Gilbert may have left the examination of Abelard's *Theologia* to the council which the papal legate, Cono, was convening at Soissons. The 'repeated insinuations' of Alberic and Lotulf, which Abelard makes so much of in his 'history of calamities', may have been crucial at this point in persuading the legate to put Abelard's book on the agenda of the council.[41]

In 1120 or 1121 Abelard may have moved his school from the region of St Denis and the diocese of Paris to Nogent-sur-Seine in the archdiocese of Reims.[42] In that case, the archbishop had metropolitan authority to summon Abelard to Soissons, even without the papal legate, as Soissons was a bishopric within the province of Reims. Abelard adds that Alberic and Lotulf were concerned that they would lose power over him, if his case was removed outside the diocese and remitted to his own abbey of St Denis.[43] This tends to confirm that Abelard was resident at the time within the jurisdiction of Reims. If Abelard had taken up residence there, he was indeed in enemy territory. Not only were Alberic and Lotulf masters in Reims, there was also his former master, William of Champeaux, who was bishop of Châlons. He may have exercised considerable influence at Abelard's trial at Soissons, though this is not mentioned in Abelard's 'history of calamities'. Abelard may have been as reluctant to discuss William of Champeaux in this context as Roscelin, as he found it too painful to acknowledge that his earliest masters, whom he had grown to hate and despise, had got the better of him even in their old age. He was happy enough to name Alberic of Reims in his 'history of calamities', as he claims to have made a fool of Alberic at the council of Soissons and he ridiculed him afterwards in *Theologia Christiana*.[44]

William of Champeaux had been Abelard's most formidable opponent for more than a decade in Paris, until he departed to become bishop of Châlons in 1113. He had not departed from ecclesiastical politics, however. He was well known to the papal legate, Cono of Praeneste, because they had been colleagues in conducting negotiations with Henry I of England and the Emperor Henry V in Germany in 1120 and 1121. So, at the time of Abelard's trial at Soissons, his former master had not disappeared into oblivion, as Abelard's 'history of calamities' implies. On the contrary, William of Champeaux had been transformed into an international statesman, who was the special confidant of the pope.[45] William was also the patron of St Bernard and it was believed that he had saved Bernard's life in c.1116. Although Bernard was probably absent from Abelard's trial at Soissons, his ally, William of St Thierry, was almost certainly present, as he witnessed a charter there along with the legate, Cono, and Geoffrey bishop of Chartres.[46] Nineteen years later, William of St Thierry became the initiator of Abelard's prosecution at the council of Sens, when he wrote a warning letter, which he addressed jointly to Geoffrey bishop of Chartres and St Bernard. When he told them that Abelard was 'again teaching novelties and writing novelties', he knew they would understand what he meant by 'again'.[47]

William of St Thierry had addressed himself to Geoffrey bishop of Chartres because he was a papal legate in France. Separated by nineteen years, Abelard's trials for heresy in 1121 and 1140 come at a critical period in the history of the Papacy's assertion of jurisdiction over local churches. Controlling trials for heresy was the apex of a wider surveillance of justice. By the thirteenth century the lynchings and ordeals of Guibert de Nogent's day had been replaced, for better or worse, by prescribed procedures for examining heretics under papal commissioners. (These procedures are now known as 'the Inquisition'; though

in fact the Papacy, like any judicial authority using Roman law, conducted all sorts of 'inquisitions'.) The discordant elements in Abelard's
trials indicate faltering steps in the Papacy's attempts to work out new
procedures. What was already clear in Abelard's day, though it was still
novel, was the supervision by papal legates, who acted as the pope's eyes
and ears in the localities. Their authority overrode that of provincial
churches and even of bishops and archbishops. In appointing a legate in
Aquitaine in 1108, Pope Paschal II had explained his purpose to the
local archbishops:

> To lighten your task, so that you have someone near you to whom you can
> bring requests and difficulties, we delegate our own authority for the
> duration of our pontificate to our dearly beloved brother, Gerard of
> Angoulême. For the honour of God and the salvation of your souls,
> faithfully obey him as our vicar and the vicar of the Apostles in your
> lands…Do not disdain, beloved brothers, to hold synods with him when
> they are needed for the good of the Church. For this purpose we grant him
> the power to convoke synods in our place.[48]

When Abelard asserted that the council of Soissons was a mere 'conventicle' and when he questioned the authority of the legate, Cono, he
may have been appealing to the older view that synods were gatherings
of the local ecclesiastical community where decisions were reached
collectively. They should not be overawed by the dictates of a legate,
exercising the plenitude of papal and apostolic power. (When the argument went the other way for Abelard at the council of Sens in 1140, he
appealed to the Roman curia from the collective decision of the council,
whilst Henry archbishop of Sens and his fellow bishops claimed his
appeal was uncanonical.[49])

As part of its new assertion of authority, the Papacy was changing its
system of international alliances. Instead of the German emperor as its
principal protector, it was looking to France, but this was splitting the
cardinals into factions in Rome itself. The new pope elected in 1119,
Calixtus II, who was a Burgundian and not an Italian, hoped to resolve
this problem by coming to an accord with the German emperor, and
this was achieved by the Concordat of Worms in 1122. It was in pursuit
of this agreement that the pope had appointed Abelard's former
master, William of Champeaux, to apply his skills in logic to finding
forms of words acceptable to all parties. One of his assistants in these
negotiations was the cardinal deacon of St Angelo, Gregory Papereschi.[50] He became Innocent II (1130–43), the pope who condemned
Abelard without waiting for his appeal following the council of Sens in
1140. At the time of Abelard's trial at Soissons in 1121, William of

Champeaux may have told the future pope what he knew of Abelard as a troublemaker: from his student days with Roscelin and through the decade and more (c.1100–13) when Abelard and William had competed in Paris.

Pope Calixtus II was an uncle of the queen of France and an overt ally of the king. In the words of Suger of St Denis: 'he strenuously disposed the rights of the Church with the love and service of King Louis and the noble queen, Adelaide'.[51] The legate, Cono of Praeneste, was also influential with Louis VI and he had presided at Senlis in 1120, when the king had taken oaths of fealty from his barons to his four-year-old son and heir, Philip.[52] Any increase in French royal influence should have been good news for Abelard, as his patron is thought to have been Stephen de Garlande, who was at the height of his power in 1121, since he combined the offices of chancellor and seneschal.[53] He should have been able to assist Abelard at least in his dealings with Bishop Gilbert of Paris, but there is no evidence that he did so. By quarrelling with Abbot Adam of St Denis in c.1119–c.1120 and crossing over into the jurisdiction of the archbishop of Reims and the count of Champagne (if that is what he had done), Abelard may have lost royal support and found himself, at the time he was summoned to the council of Soissons, without a patron to protect him. In this context it is significant that he had no bodyguard, other than a few students, when he arrived in Soissons and this is how he was nearly stoned.[54]

At a provincial synod held in the presence of a legate, like that at Soissons in 1121, the power of the Papacy was itself on trial because it was still novel. Cono of Praeneste had to steer the assembly towards decisions which preserved – and preferably reinforced – the newly reclaimed authority of the Holy See. This was likely to involve some sort of compromise. Abelard's trials inevitably, therefore, had a political dimension, as they affected the delicate balance of power between the Papacy and a variety of interest groups in France. At the council of Sens in 1140 St Bernard certainly exaggerated Abelard's political importance, particularly his alliance with Arnold of Brescia, in order to get a conviction. On the other hand, Peter the Venerable's claim was equally tendentious that Abelard's case only concerned 'quarrels' between him and St Bernard.[55] Henry archbishop of Sens's letter to the pope described how 'throughout almost the whole of France, in towns, villages and castles disputes are carried on about the Holy Trinity and what God is, not only within the schools but also at crossroads and public places by boys and simple foolish people, as well as by the learned and students'.[56] Whether there really was such a surge of interest in theology is impossible to prove either way. It is likely, though, that this is what the

French bishops believed, and they saw such conduct as a threat to orthodoxy rather than an advance in education.

Ultimately, as in any show trial, decisions in Abelard's case were not going to be reached by meticulous and neutral examinations of his books or of himself. Judgement depended on whether he was perceived to be a threat to the Church and to public order in France and Italy. In his account of his trial at Soissons Abelard describes how he was expecting his treatise on the Trinity to be read by the legate himself. So he handed it to Cono of Praeneste as soon as he arrived in town 'for him to examine and judge on'.[57] Abelard was shocked when the legate would not look at it and ordered him to take it directly to the archbishop of Reims, so that Abelard's prosecutors could examine it.[58] From his own viewpoint, the legate acted prudently in refusing to express an opinion about the contents of Abelard's book. In his delicate position of representing papal authority at a provincial synod, the legate was not going to override the local archbishop unless he had to, and neither could he afford to be seen to make any sort of theological mistake if he examined the book. Abelard describes how later on in the trial Master Thierry of Chartres jeered, when the legate was imprudent enough to mention doctrine.[59] Cono had been a legate long enough to know that he should exercise the Papacy's powers as rarely as possible, as he had no physical force with which to back them up. The plenitude of papal power depended entirely on the consent of believers.

An academic heresy trial was the medieval equivalent of a trial for financial fraud. A fair decision in such a complex matter was close to impossible because unequivocal proof was so hard to obtain. Abelard describes how the legate, Cono, tried to reach a compromise at Soissons, whereby Abelard would be sent back to his own abbey of St Denis and a meeting of experts would be convened there to consider his treatise.[60] (This was very similar to what Abelard had proposed to the bishop of Paris in the first place.[61]) When Abelard's prosecutors heard this, they realized the case might be postponed indefinitely. So Alberic and Lotulf 'came running to the legate and got him to change his decision – against his better judgement – and to condemn the book without any inquiry and to burn it immediately in the sight of everyone'.[62] They achieved this volte-face by bringing a previous papal decision to the legate's attention. They told him 'it ought to be enough for the book's condemnation' that Abelard had presumed to read it in public and have copies made, although it had been commended by the authority of neither the Roman pontiff nor the Church.[63] Failing to have a book approved might be a disciplinary offence, though there was no established system for censoring books at this time, but it was hardly heresy. How could

burning Abelard's book, without even examining it, be justified in canon
law in these circumstances?

As Abelard says this is what did occur and as his account is confirmed
by Otto of Freising, there must have been some special circumstance
operating here.[64] A fact which Abelard fails to mention in his 'history of
calamities' is that his book had been written against Roscelin, or so he
had claimed in his letter to the bishop of Paris.[65] It was therefore in a
class of its own, as far as canon law was concerned, because St Anselm
had already written a refutation of Roscelin and in it he had won Pope
Urban II's approval for the principle that any such work should be
submitted to the pope for censorship.[66] Abelard had not done this and
neither had he heeded St Anselm's warning in the same context that 'no
Christian ought to dispute about something which the Catholic Church
believes with its heart and confesses with its mouth'; in other words,
discussion of articles of the creed was not admissible.[67]

By reopening the debate about Roscelin's heresy and disputing about
the meaning of the Trinity, without getting papal approval, Abelard had
shown presumptuous disobedience to the Holy See. Here at last was an
issue which the papal legate, Cono, could and must address. Abelard's
book should be burned without even examining it because it reopened a
matter of Christian belief that was already closed. Abelard says he was
made 'an example of for the future benefit of the Christian faith, so that
similar presumption in many others would be forestalled'.[68] In his *Ethics*
he had discussed exemplary punishments of this sort: 'Quite frequently
punishment is reasonably inflicted on someone, even though no fault has
preceded it.'[69] In his own case, however, he did not think this treatment
either reasonable or just.

HERESY IS PRIDE

Disobedience was tantamount to heresy because heresy was not a matter
of making a mistake or being ignorant about some detail of Christian
doctrine, as anyone might do that in all innocence. Heresy meant
obstinately and publicly persisting with a wrong belief after its error
had been pointed out. 'It is solely pertinacity in resisting the doctrine of
the Church which makes a heretic,' Peter the Venerable wrote.[70] A
heretic chose to be heretical, or at least that was the theory. Abelard
cited the classic definition from Isidore's *Etymologies*: 'Heresy comes
from the Greek word for "choice"'; and Abelard glossed it by adding:
'So no one becomes a heretic unless his estimate of his own self-esteem
exceeds other people's.'[71] Essentially, therefore, heresy was intellectual

pride. In the book he was made to burn at Soissons Abelard had insisted on this:

> For it is not ignorance that makes a heretic, but pride. It is when, for example, someone wants – for novelty's sake – to make a name for himself and he boasts in putting forward something unusual, which he then tries to defend against all comers in order to look superior to everyone, or at least not inferior.... Professors of dialectic very easily fall into this trap because they think they are so strongly armed with reasons that they are free to defend or attack whatever they like. Their arrogance is so great that nothing is thought beyond comprehension, or incapable of explanation, by their petty reasonings.[72]

Abelard repeated this in *Theologia Christiana* and reinforced it with some texts from St Augustine. He added that professors of dialectic are 'contemptuous of all authorities and boast that they alone should be believed in'.[73] This is like claiming to see in the dark, Abelard says, and St Augustine had castigated such conceit. In the final edition, *Theologia Scholarium*, Abelard put the rule that 'it is not ignorance that makes a heretic but pride' in his preface in order to give it even greater prominence.[74] He also assured his readers that 'if by any chance I do fall into error, I will defend nothing out of contentiousness, nor will I be presumptuous through conceit, and thus I shall not incur the charge of heresy'.[75]

These disclaimers in *Theologia Scholarium* directly follow on from Abelard's remarks about how easily his genius will penetrate the meaning of Scripture and how his intellect is sufficient to resolve all controversies in theology because he is the most experienced dialectician.[76] He evidently saw no contradiction between his dispassionate (in his opinion) reporting of his own abilities and his strictures against presumption and pride in others. He could not be proud because he really was superior to everybody else. Furthermore, he acknowledged that he had been proud once and he had grievously suffered for it. No one could mistake him now for one of the professors of dialectic he described, though it was true that he had once thought himself 'the only philosopher in the world' and an emulator of the Peripatetics 'armed with reasons'.[77] He had been cured of these delusions by the public humiliation of being made to burn his book at Soissons in 1121.[78]

The rule that heresy did not mean making mistakes, so much as arrogantly persisting with them, cut both ways as far as the accused was concerned. It was not just what he said or wrote that was on trial, but his interior disposition for good or evil. A disposition is impossible to prove or disprove by legal process because it is locked in the accused person's mind and he may not even know it himself. Abelard had pointed this out in his *Ethics*: people have to judge by what is 'manifest, not by what is hidden'.[79] Judges address 'the effect of an action', not interior guilt. Only God can consider the state of mind in which something is done because only He is capable of examining our intentions and apportioning blame in a true trial.[80] By this standard no one should be judged for anything they do and Abelard reminded St Bernard of the Gospel injunction: 'Judge not that ye be not judged, condemn not that ye be not condemned.'[81] Abelard did not live by this injunction himself, any more than St Bernard did. Abelard had been as ready as anyone to vilify Roscelin and to join in the chorus of condemnation against the radical preachers, Tanchelm of Antwerp and Peter de Bruys.[82] Like St Bernard, Abelard demonstrated his own righteousness by attacking others. Both of them justified this by claiming to be champions of the faith. The difference between them was that St Bernard was much more successful at it.

It was because heresy was close to blasphemy, and yet was so difficult to prove in law, that lynching was connived at, or even approved of (as we have seen in the opinions of Guibert de Nogent and Ivo of Chartres).[83] Tanchelm of Antwerp and Peter de Bruys were lynched, in 1115 and c.1132 respectively, and Abelard was threatened with lynching at both Soissons and Sens.[84] St Bernard vilified Abelard and used language which could justify his lynching ('Does not he deservedly provoke all men's hands against him?') because frightening the accused was an essential part of any successful prosecution.[85] Bernard and his assistants had already culled numerous allegedly heretical statements from Abelard's writings. These had finally been reduced to the nineteen summary indictments, of which Abelard stood accused at the council of Sens and which were transmitted to the pope.[86] They were evidence that Abelard had made grave errors, but they were not in themselves proof that he was a heretic. They only became proof when, and if, the accused pertinaciously defended them. Abelard claimed that the nineteen indictments misrepresented his writings, which they frequently did; but he had no way of defending himself without being exposed to further accusations of presumption and pride, which compounded his guilt in the eyes of his prosecutors.[87]

Because heresy was proven by pride, the trial procedure focused on reducing the accused to an abject state of humiliation which could pass for repentance. The last thing the prosecutors wanted was any discussion of theology on the day of the trial, as that might put its outcome in doubt and reduce its value as a warning to others. At both Soissons and Sens the rules were framed to prevent Abelard using his debating skills.

This seemed right to his prosecutors, as they could only prove him a heretic by overriding his power of reasoning, not by engaging with it. Abelard describes how Alberic and Lotulf protested at Soissons when Geoffrey bishop of Chartres proposed that Abelard should have a free hearing: 'Fine advice that is, to bid us contend with the ready tongue of a man whose arguments and sophistries could triumph over the whole world.'[88] As Abelard wrote this himself, he may have exaggerated their belief in his ability, but the remark is echoed by St Bernard's objection before the trial at Sens that he was but a child in scholastic warfare, whereas Abelard was habituated to it from boyhood.[89] The point is that heretics might give very plausible and Christian answers, even though they were creatures of Satan, as Guibert de Nogent had discovered at Soissons in 1114. The trial procedure had to have some way of overcoming the heretic's obstinate belief in his own righteousness.

PROVING HERESY

Nobody but a madman readily admits to a crime, least of all to a crime located inside his head for which the penalty is physical violence in one form or another. Heresy is what George Orwell called 'thought crime' in *Nineteen Eighty-Four*. The authorities can see it, even when the accused denies it. Gaolers and prosecutors down the ages have known the way to get an admission from a prisoner is to reduce him to a state of confusion by combining threats of violence with promises of remission for cooperative behaviour. Abelard says his humiliation at Soissons was much worse than his castration because it affected his good name and not just his body.[90] He describes how Geoffrey bishop of Chartres (who had already called for a free hearing) assured him that the papal legate would release him after a few days of token imprisonment.[91] Geoffrey 'consoled' Abelard so that he pleaded guilty and surrendered to what he later described as 'manifest violence'.[92] As the 'nice policeman', Geoffrey ensured that Abelard put on a good show at the trial and made no trouble for his prosecutors. Abelard accordingly put his 'memorable book' into the fire with his own hand.[93] In addition to Geoffrey's promises, Abelard may have had in mind 'God's people' of Soissons, who had already tried to stone him and who had burned the heretics in 1114, once the ecclesiastics absented themselves.[94] Paradoxically, without his prosecutors, Abelard might have been a dead man at Soissons.

Abelard's breaking point at Soissons did not come when he was burning his book, as he was prepared for that and he had another copy anyway (from which he soon produced the enlarged edition, *Theologia Christiana*).[95] As he had been accused of having many copies of the book transcribed, burning one was no more than a symbol of good faith.[96] As far as is known, no order was given at the council of Soissons in 1121 to burn Abelard's books 'wherever they might be found', like the order given by Pope Innocent II in 1140.[97] It was the next stage of his trial at Soissons which proved traumatic for Abelard. In the full council the archbishop of Reims asked his reconciled 'brother' to make a declaration of faith.[98] So Abelard stood up, confident and unbowed, 'to declare and expound my faith and express in my own words what I felt'.[99] But his prosecutors were not going to let him give a lecture or, worse, a rousing sermon, just when everything was going so well. They told him it was only necessary to recite the Athanasian creed, 'something any schoolboy could do'.[100] (The Athanasian creed was chosen, rather than the Apostles' creed, because it enlarged on the doctrine of the Trinity.) To compound his shame, Abelard was given a copy of the text, as if he was ignorant of it. This was the detail which broke him: 'I read it out as best I could through my tears choked with sobs.'[101]

Psychologically, Abelard was beaten at last. With his abject confession, the show trial was complete. He was taken off 'as if condemned and convicted' to the abbey of St Médard in Soissons.[102] On the short journey he could be fairly sure that, in return for his co-operation, his ecclesiastical gaolers would protect him from lynching. After some days he was released, as Geoffrey bishop of Chartres had promised, and returned to his own abbey of St Denis.[103] But the pain of these days at St Médard should not be underestimated. Abelard describes himself being in despair and 'insane'.[104] This is confirmed by the biography of St Goswin, his gaoler at St Médard, which says Abelard was 'delirious' and 'savaging himself'.[105] This is the psychological state any prosecutor wants to produce, where a prisoner subjected to cruelty blames himself in retrospect for surrendering to it. Nevertheless, Abelard came out of this self-destructive phase, apparently unscathed, and later on in his 'history of calamities' he turned his scorn on his prosecutors and their supporters: Cono of Praeneste, Alberic and Lotulf, William of Champeaux, and Anselm of Laon whose intellectual heirs Alberic and Lotulf claimed to be. Abelard has had the last laugh, as we today depend on his account of these events. He had the best of reasons to be a great hater and a great egoist. He showed he was completely restored to his former self, the daring and triumphant iconoclast, when he insulted the monks of St Denis and their patron saint and escaped with impunity to Champagne.

At Abelard's trial at Sens in 1140 similar patterns can be discerned to his trial at Soissons nineteen years earlier, although the documentation is so different in scale and character that comparisons cannot be exact.[106] For the course of Abelard's trial at Soissons there are only two sources: a few lines by Otto of Freising and Abelard's own account (some 200 lines) in his 'history of calamities'. For his trial at Sens, on the other hand, there are narratives from different points of view: by Geoffrey of Auxerre (a partisan of St Bernard), Berengar of Poitiers (a partisan of Abelard) and Otto of Freising (a concerned neutral). The archbishops of Sens and of Reims also sent accounts of the trial to Pope Innocent II in order to justify their conduct of the proceedings. Although Abelard himself wrote no narrative of his trial at Sens comparable with his description of the council of Soissons in his 'history of calamities', his replies to St Bernard have survived in the form of three manifestos. These comprise: an incomplete 'Apologia' answering the theological accusations point by point; a more general 'Confession' addressed to all churchmen; and thirdly, the 'Confession of Faith to Heloise' which Berengar published on Abelard's behalf. The titles 'Apologia' and 'Confession' may mislead, as these manifestos are not admissions of guilt by Abelard but robust defences of his position. In all three of them he accuses St Bernard of perverting justice.

From St Bernard's side a comparable amount survives. The substance of his case against Abelard is extant in the draft of a long letter (no. 190) to the pope. This is supplemented by numerous shorter letters to members of the papal curia, urging them to condemn Abelard in Rome. His trial at Sens had been set in motion by St Bernard's colleague, the Cistercian abbot, William of St Thierry. His letter to St Bernard survives, as do various lists of the heresies of which Abelard was accused and lengthy treatises refuting them by William of St Thierry himself and Abelard's renegade friend, Thomas of Morigny. All this material makes Abelard's prosecution at Sens the best-documented heresy trial of the twelfth century, although this does not mean that there is agreement about what occurred. St Bernard's letters against Abelard also stand as brilliant literary creations in their own right and they were appreciated as such in the twelfth century. He was the Church's Cicero, a prosecutor and advocate of extraordinary verbal power and ingenuity. Walter Map recalled being at dinner with Archbishop Thomas Becket and two Cistercian abbots in c.1163, when one of St Bernard's letters against Abelard was being read aloud at table.[107] This gave rise to discussion of St Bernard's character; Walter's own opinion was that he was a hypocrite and that Abelard had been more heretical in logic than theology.

ABELARD'S TRIAL AT SENS

Abelard's trial at Sens in June 1140 was intended to be another show trial, like the one at Soissons in 1121. This time, though, it went wrong for his prosecutors. Abelard refused to answer and he was allowed to appeal immediately to Rome, even though his case had not been heard or judged. The large congregation, which had assembled in and around the cathedral of Sens, must have been very disappointed. They had been attracted by the show of saints' relics, which had been promised, as well as by the prospect of seeing St Bernard confront Abelard.[108] (In the twelfth century saints' relics were not usually on permanent display; they were brought out on special occasions which made their veneration the more intense.) Among the congregation were many laymen, including King Louis VII himself, Thibaud count of Champagne (the patron of both Bernard and Abelard), William II count of Nevers and 'innumerable other nobles and people'.[109] On the clerical side were all the bishops of the archdiocese of Sens, most of the bishops of the archdiocese of Reims and 'many religious and wise abbots, reinforced by learned clerics'.[110] This description by Henry archbishop of Sens is confirmed by St Bernard, who adds that 'the masters of the schools from the cities' were present.[111] This is the earliest reference to the expert opinion of masters being on hand at a heresy trial. Finally, Bernard and Abelard took their stand 'face to face as adversaries in the presence of everyone'.[112]

As prosecutor, St Bernard opened the proceedings by holding up a copy of Abelard's *Theologia* and 'he pointed out propositions from the same book, which he had noticed to be absurd or even plainly heretical'.[113] Abelard was given the option either of denying that these were his writings or, if he admitted they were his, he had either to prove their validity or undertake to correct his errors. The procedure at the trial, as described here by Henry archbishop of Sens, looks admirably fair. St Bernard confirms that he opened the trial by producing 'certain propositions' extracted from Abelard's books.[114] But this procedure was not as straightforward as it looked because the 'propositions' (*capitula*) were not verbatim extracts from Abelard's works, but summaries made by St Bernard and his assistants. They had been through Abelard's theological writings and reduced them to a single page, consisting of nineteen allegedly heretical 'propositions' or headings. The Latin word *capitula*, literally meaning 'little headings', makes clear what the 'propositions' were. They constituted the charges of which Abelard stood accused at Sens.

From a forensic point of view, the prosecution was right to frame summary charges in this way. Even nineteen 'propositions' proved too many. In his letter to the pope St Bernard concentrated on three or four, saying it would need volumes to answer them all.[115] The judges, who were the whole body of prelates assembled at Sens, could not be expected to have read through the thousands of words which Abelard had written in his *Theologia* and other works, even if they could understand them. Without printed copies, they could not be provided with identical and authentic versions of these works anyway. St Bernard and his assistants had had considerable difficulty getting hold of Abelard's books. 'I hear there are other little works of his, called *Scito Te Ipsum* and *Sic et Non*,' William of St Thierry had written to St Bernard, 'but they hate the light, as they say, and cannot be found even when searched for.'[116] In manuscript culture every copy of a book was different and even St Bernard could not be sure he was reading Abelard's authentic works. Abelard complained that Bernard had depended on a 'Book of Sentences' of his: 'I learned this not without the greatest astonishment, as nowhere will any book written by me be found which is called *Sentences*.'[117] Nevertheless, he was not telling the whole truth here, as this 'Book of Sentences' does contain Abelard's authentic opinions and it was accepted practice for a master's teachings to be circulated among students in this way.[118]

Before the prosecution could charge Abelard with heresy, it had to establish that the nineteen 'propositions' were indeed heretical. Otherwise, the judges might rule that Abelard had no case to answer. St Bernard could not settle this point much in advance of the council, as its members came from numerous cities and churches in France and arrived in Sens at different times. He overcame this difficulty by grasping the opportunity provided by the prelates assembling for dinner on the eve of the council. He took them through the nineteen charges and got them to condemn them one by one. In theory this was not a rehearsal for the next day's trial, and neither was it a condemnation of Abelard himself. The judges were simply agreeing to the validity of the charges and confirming that they were heretical. The eve of the council was not the ideal occasion to approve the charges, as the prelates were harassed and the time was too short; but St Bernard had no choice when council members came from such a wide area. Any legal process has to operate within constraints of time and place and St Bernard might be thought to have done the best he could in the circumstances.

Although St Bernard's conduct in pre-empting the judges can be defended as a procedural necessity, the fact is that even Henry archbishop of Sens failed to distinguish clearly between condemning the charges and condemning Abelard's teachings. In his letter to the pope describing the eve of the council, the archbishop explained that 'we condemned the statements of that man's depraved dogma because they had infected many people and the contagion had penetrated into their innermost hearts'.[119] The metaphor of heresy as disease justified the prelates in dealing with Abelard as a public health emergency requiring immediate and drastic action. The archbishop gave further details of how St Bernard got the charges declared heretical in advance of the trial: 'they were repeatedly read out and re-read in public audience and proved most convincingly to be not only false but heretical by the most truthful reasons, as well as by the authorities cited from St Augustine and other holy Fathers'.[120]

Abelard's student partisan, Berengar, gave a less decorous account of these proceedings.[121] After dinner Abelard's book was brought out and a cleric, animated by hatred and the worse for drink, read out the charges in a raucous voice. The prelates laughed and jeered and banged their feet, before growing somnolent as the effects of food and drink took their toll. As the reader went through the charges, he kept asking the assembled company: 'Do you condemn this?' The prelates were meant to answer in unison in Latin: 'We do condemn it' (*Damnamus*); but some of them were so befuddled that they could only mumble (in a mixture of Latin and French): ...*namus* – 'we are drowning', as they struggled to keep their heads above water in this whirlpool of theological speculation. Berengar's account is deliberately satirical, but this does not necessarily make it untruthful. He may have been an eyewitness, if he was one of the students of Abelard who had answered his master's call to come to Sens to support him. Berengar's description of the prelates being asked to repeat *Damnamus* accords with John of Salisbury's account of St Bernard taking the prelates through the charges before the trial of Gilbert de la Porrée in 1148 at the council of Reims. John adds that the cardinals in Rome remembered how St Bernard had attacked Abelard 'by a similar stratagem'.[122]

Although St Bernard succeeded in persuading the judges to agree to the charges in advance of the trial, he never matched this by getting Abelard's acknowledgement that they were accurate representations of his thought. Attempts were made in this direction, both by Bernard and Thomas of Morigny, but they ended in recriminations.[123] Abelard maintained that the charges were a travesty of his work, 'put forward either through malice or ignorance'; they proved that St Bernard was a liar.[124] Independently of each other in 1969, Edward Little and David Luscombe went through all nineteen of the charges and showed how their accuracy varied: those from Abelard's *Ethics*, for example, are more accurate than those concerning the Trinity.[125] Abelard absolutely denied the first charge: 'That the Father is full power, the Son some power, the Holy Spirit no power.'[126] This had been extrapolated from the passages in *Theologia* where he had ascribed omnipotence particularly to the Father, which suggested (though Abelard denied this) that the Son and the Holy Spirit had less power.[127] He replied: 'I abhor and detest these words, which are not so much human as diabolical; as is entirely just, I condemn them along with their author. If anyone were to find these words in my writings, I would confess myself to be not only a heretic but an arch-heretic.'[128]

Abelard knew he had to do more than show that the list of charges failed to quote him word-for-word. Addressing St Bernard directly, he wrote: 'In fact, you depart as much from my words as from their sense. You are laboriously arguing with your own inventions, rather than with statements of mine.'[129] Bernard was the heretic, not Abelard, because he misrepresented Scripture like the devil himself.[130] (Abelard was taking advantage here of the ambiguity of the Latin word *scripturae*, which describes both Holy Writ and any author's 'writings'.) He had challenged St Bernard before the trial to produce written evidence to convict him of heresy.[131] 'If you cannot do this and if you invent such great wrongs about your neighbour, it is you yourself who are confounded.'[132] But Abelard realized that St Bernard might get the better of him none the less, because he would maintain that he understood the essence of Abelard's heresy and that went far beyond debates about words. 'Perhaps you will say', Abelard concedes, 'that although these are not the actual words I have written or put forward, I have insinuated the same meaning into them despite the words being different. In that case, I wish you would express *my* meaning in them, so as not to pervert it with words. If that were done, nothing would remain of your calumny in the debate.'[133] Abelard saw that St Bernard's bias (his 'calumny') had been built into the charges against him and this would make it almost impossible to convince the judges of his innocence.

The Role of St Bernard

St Bernard constantly kept in view that it was pride and bad character that proved heresy, not verbal failings. 'Peter Abelard', he maintained, 'proves by his life, by his behaviour and by his books, which are now exposed to the light of day, that he is a persecutor of the Catholic faith and an enemy of Christ's cross. He looks like a monk on the outside, but inside he is a heretic.'[134] St Bernard gave priority to Abelard's 'life' and 'behaviour', rather than to his books, because it was the 'inside' that mattered most and that he could see best. Viewed from within Abelard's depraved mind, the nineteen charges were no more than preliminary agenda for the prosecution. Whether Abelard denied them or admitted them, it was his whole character – and its secret recesses in particular – that proved his heresy. St Bernard's plan for the trial seems to have been to get the charges agreed by the judges in advance, so that complex theological questions would not be raised during the trial itself. Then, on the day of the trial, he would attack Abelard personally with such overwhelming force and cogency that the members of the council would condemn him out of hand. With luck, Abelard might himself break down and confess, as he had done at Soissons, and theological debate would be entirely avoided.

The style of St Bernard's attack can be gauged from almost any page of his draft letter (no. 190) to the pope. Again and again, he stressed Abelard's pride and his refusal to acknowledge authority, whether human or divine: 'I know not what there is in the heavens above or in the earth beneath which he deigns to know nothing of'; 'Tell us what it is that has been revealed to you and to no one else'; 'By his scoffs and insinuations this son of perdition is trying to make vain mankind's redemption'; 'Thus he concludes the mass of calumnies and reproaches, which he belches out against God so impiously and with such ignorance'.[135] Most revealing in this draft letter are the passages where St Bernard addresses Abelard as if he were actually present before him, instead of describing him in the third person: 'Tell us what it is that has been revealed to *you*...'; 'Are *you* writing a new Gospel for us?'; '*You* cannot give thanks with the redeemed because *you* have not been redeemed'.[136] In the presence of the mass of people in Sens cathedral, headed by the king and the archbishops, Abelard would not have been able to respond to this battery of invective by appealing to St Bernard and his judges to address the verbal details of the charges against him, still less to let him speak freely and accord him equal respect with his prosecutor. It is not as if St Bernard's letter no. 190 is a farrago of nonsense. On the contrary, its theological points are closely argued and they are pushed home by well-informed venomous abuse and simulated anger, so that Bernard's hearers will want to lynch Abelard there and then because he is in league with the devil and a threat to them all.

On the day of the trial, St Bernard was deprived of the opportunity of making his verbal onslaught on Abelard and this is why he sent it off to the pope instead. He was outmanoeuvred by Abelard's appealing directly to Rome. The trial may have lasted no more than a few minutes. St Bernard describes how 'when the charges began to be read out,

Abelard refused to listen and walked out. He appealed from the judges he himself had chosen, which we do not think was permissible.'[137] Abelard could walk out with impunity because he did not face St Bernard alone; he had his supporters to protect him.[138] Nevertheless, this does not explain why the council allowed Abelard's appeal so readily. How could he appeal against a case that had not yet been heard? The archbishop of Sens agreed with St Bernard that the appeal 'seemed less than canonical' and the archbishop of Reims concurred: Abelard had appealed 'from the place and the judge that he himself had chosen'.[139] This was true, as it was Abelard who had petitioned the archbishop of Sens to hear his case at the council against St Bernard's alleged slanders.[140] The archbishop had accordingly summoned him to answer Abelard; this was a lawsuit for which St Bernard complained he was unprepared and unprotected.[141] Both Bernard and Abelard sent out letters, calling on their supporters to be at Sens on 2 June to support them in this contest.[142]

If the two archbishops, who spoke for all the bishops at the council, had good reasons for objecting to Abelard's appeal, who was it who persuaded the council to call an immediate halt to the proceedings and disappoint all the people assembled in the cathedral, headed by the king of France? Answers can only be hypothetical. The most plausible is that Geoffrey bishop of Chartres, who was a papal legate, may have intervened to protect Abelard, much as he had done at Soissons in 1121.[143] Geoffrey may have judged that Abelard was in no fit state to plead. The eyewitnesses all agree that he seemed bewildered.[144] On this point his defender, Berengar, is at one with his opponents: Abelard was 'taken aback' at being driven into a corner by Bernard. The archbishop of Sens's report describes how 'he seemed to lose confidence' and Bernard's biographer, Geoffrey of Auxerre, says Abelard explained afterwards that 'at that moment his memory became very confused, his reason blacked out and his interior sense forsook him'. He may either have been reacting to the stress of the occasion, or showing early signs of brain cancer (as Dr Jeannin has argued).[145] By 1140 he was sixty years old and he cannot have been as mentally agile as formerly.

Abelard's refusal (or failure) to answer his accusers may have had a deeper cause – and a deeper significance – than panic or illness. His silence was itself a way of making a plea. Berengar compared his trial with that of Christ's and Abelard too likened himself to Christ, when he insisted that he had always 'spoken openly'.[146] One of his sermons praises the 'incomparable fortitude' of Christ in refusing to answer Pontius Pilate, and in another he highlights Susanna's refusal (in the Book of Daniel) to answer the false accusations of the elders: 'In silence she awaited the sentence of condemnation; she kept silent towards her human accusers and spoke only to God by her weeping'.[147] She had 'cried out with a loud voice' to God and He heard her and saved her through the intervention of Daniel. Likewise at Sens, Abelard's silence 'cried out with a loud voice' for justice and God saved him through the intervention of Peter the Venerable.

St Bernard would not necessarily have had it all his own way in Rome. His Victorian biographer, J. C. Morison, wryly comments: 'Pope Innocent owed so much to Bernard that he could hardly fail to dislike him.'[148] William of St Thierry had warned that Abelard's opinions 'are even said to have the greatest authority in the Roman curia'. He thinks himself quite safe, Bernard complained, because 'he boasts he has disciples among the cardinals and clerks of the curia; he is defended in his errors, past and present, by the very people whose condemnation he ought to fear'.[149] Bernard was referring to two officials in particular: Guy of Castello (the future Pope Celestine II) and Hyacinth Boboni (the future Celestine III). Shortly before the council of Sens, Guy came on a mission to France and he had also been with Abelard at Morigny in 1131.[150] He was certainly a supporter of Abelard's, as he possessed copies of *Theologia* and *Sic et Non* which he did not surrender when Innocent II ordered Abelard's books to be burned.[151] Guy's election as pope in 1143, in immediate succession to Innocent II, emphasizes the depth of the divisions in the papal curia. It was probably Guy who made Hyacinth Boboni a cardinal in 1144, even though he had been a leader of the Roman clergy who had persistently supported the Antipope Anacletus II.[152] Bernard knew of these Roman factions at first hand, as he had been involved in restoring Innocent II's authority in northern Italy in the early 1130s. Despite Bernard's efforts, the papal schism had persisted until the Lateran council of 1139, when the Antipope Victor IV (the successor of Anacletus II) resigned. Abelard's trial at Sens in 1140 therefore came at a politically sensitive time. Bernard wanted people to see Abelard's unequivocal condemnation in Rome as a demonstration of the strength of the restored Papacy.

St Bernard's argument that Abelard headed an international conspiracy, which was bent on destroying ecclesiastical authority, gained credence from Arnold of Brescia's presence in Paris with Abelard on Mont Sainte Geneviève. Arnold had been expelled from Italy by Innocent II for leading a communal rebellion against his bishop in Brescia. John of Salisbury links him with Hyacinth Boboni and suggests that the two of them had come to France in order to ally themselves with Abelard: Arnold became the revolutionary leader of poor students in Paris and Hyacinth 'studiously fostered' Abelard's cause against St Bernard.[153]

Bernard confirms that Hyacinth had shown him much ill will, though (Bernard adds) he was not able to achieve his nefarious purposes.[154] Over a long life Hyacinth became eminently respectable (he died as pope in 1198), whereas Arnold persisted as a revolutionary and was burned in Rome in c.1155 for forming a republic opposed to both pope and emperor. Arnold had been one of Abelard's students and Hyacinth may have been likewise.[155] At the time of Abelard's trial in 1140 Hyacinth held high office in the church of St John Lateran, where another canon (Adam) had been accused of heresy because he was a student of Abelard's.[156]

Taken together, these fragments of information confirm St Bernard's fears that Abelard had disciples in Rome. Bernard could not be certain which faction would have the upper hand in the curia when Abelard arrived there to make his appeal. The death of the pope or of a cardinal might change the situation at any moment and Bernard's long involvement with Innocent II had made him enemies, as well as friends, in Rome. Nearer home, Bernard could not even be confident of the support of the president at Abelard's trial, Henry archbishop of Sens. At short notice (Bernard complained) and at Abelard's request, he had formally summoned Bernard to the trial.[157] Henry may have acted in this unfriendly way because Bernard had written him an insulting letter three or four years earlier, accusing him of perverting the course of justice. 'In everything your own sweet will is law,' Bernard scolded him, 'you think only of power and not at all of the fear of God. . . . Do you really think that the whole world is as devoid of justice as you seem to be?'[158] In the light of Bernard's strictures, one might conclude that he should have questioned Henry's suitability to be the presiding judge at Abelard's trial.

DOUBTS ABOUT ST BERNARD'S RHETORIC

The most recent editor of St Bernard's works, Jean Leclercq, a monk like Bernard himself, draws attention to the problems posed by the rhetoric of his letters. Discussing his aggressiveness in particular, Leclercq asks: 'Where is reality for Bernard? . . . Was he fooled by a sometimes blinding passion? Or was he the victim of his facility for handling invective? Where, in this correspondence, does sincerity end and literature begin?'[159] Leclercq concludes that Bernard 'is so full of contrasts that it becomes confusing'.[160] Such contrasts are evident in Bernard's treatment of Abelard. When William of St Thierry first complained to him of Abelard's heresies (probably in March 1140) Bernard was cautious. He refused to be disturbed during Lent and he told William he knew scarcely anything about these things. 'As you know very well', Bernard added, 'I am not in the habit of trusting much in my own judgement, and especially not in such a big matter as this.'[161]

Even when Bernard was persuaded to proceed against Abelard, he started off with caution and legal propriety. He met Abelard, first in private and then in the presence of witnesses, and admonished him 'in a friendly and informal way' (according to Henry archbishop of Sens's report) to amend his books.[162] Geoffrey of Auxerre says Abelard promised to alter everything in accordance with Bernard's wishes, but later on (probably in April or May 1140) he was persuaded by his supporters to use his superior powers in debate to seek a contest with Bernard.[163] This is when Bernard changed tack from being fraternal counsellor to public prosecutor. Recalling this, Abelard refers to him ironically as 'our friend' and addresses him as 'Brother prosecutor, Bernard'.[164] Berengar (Abelard's pugnacious student) challenged Bernard to say whether he was motivated by disinterested love in correcting Abelard, or by a desire for personal revenge.[165] The latter would have been understandable, as Abelard's appeal to Rome put Bernard in a tight spot. He could not afford to lose, as he might then be thought guilty of slandering Abelard and of perverting the course of justice himself. Bernard's reaction was to dispatch his battery of venomous letters to the pope and cardinals in Rome.

In showering Abelard with verbal abuse, Bernard was using the method which had brought him success in many previous – and even more dubious – disputes. At least in Abelard's case he understood what the issues were and knew his opponent personally, even though he depended very much on the advice of William of St Thierry and Thomas of Morigny. In the Latin rhetorical tradition sharp words were much admired. The clergy could not fight like knights, but (Bernard wrote) 'the teeth are spears and arrows, and the tongue is a sharp sword'.[166] Shortly before his attack on Abelard, he had scored a remarkable victory against Peter the Venerable by getting a Cistercian appointed bishop of Langres. (Situated between Clairvaux and Cluny, Langres stood in the middle of Cistercian and Cluniac spheres of influence in Burgundy.) Bernard succeeded in getting his own prior of Clairvaux appointed bishop, despite the Cluniac candidate having already been elected with the approval of the king of France and the archbishop of Lyons. As in Abelard's case, Bernard sent off exaggerated and venomous letters to Innocent II and the cardinals in Rome. He described the Cluniac candidate as a monster and Peter the Venerable as an enemy of God.[167] At Langres, Bernard claimed, Christ was being made to suffer once more at the hands of wicked men.[168]

Jean Leclercq warns the modern reader of Bernard's letters against being tempted to judge him.[169] Because he frequently took the role of prosecutor, the reader's response is either to jump to the accused's defence or to answer Bernard with more invective. Peter the Venerable's reply to him in the Langres case is a model of how to avoid these pitfalls (as is his brilliantly understated defence of Abelard in his letter to Innocent II following the council of Sens). In spite of provocation, Peter remained dignified, firm and apparently charitable. As lord abbot of Cluny, he could afford to be magnanimous towards Bernard and his upstart Cistercians. Peter wrote:

> Your holiness should not think I am defending a monk of ours because I want him promoted to a bishopric. It is no novel nor surprising thing for our monks to become bishops; we are used to them being bishops, archbishops, patriarchs and even popes of the Roman and apostolic Church. Why is it improper for a wise and learned Cluniac monk to be elected bishop of Langres? I am not at all surprised that evil reports should displease a good man like yourself. But attention should have been given to whether they were true. That should have been looked into before these matters were brought before the tribunals of judges and the thrones of pontiffs. To give credence to such manifest enemies is not the action of a good man. You should put more trust in people at home than in strangers and rely on those you know, not on vicious slanderers.[170]

Peter was right; but the significant point is that Bernard succeeded in getting his way at Langres, as he did likewise in Abelard's case and in many others. Bernard persisted in repeating slanders and exaggerating insults because he found it worked, not least in the papal curia. The closest he ever came to making an apology was to Peter the Venerable in 1149, when he had again insulted him. Bernard was too busy (he explained) to supervise his secretaries: 'When they fail to grasp my meaning fully, they sharpen their pens beyond measure; I cannot look over the things I have told them to write.'[171] As a special concession to Peter, however, Bernard promised to check his letters to him in future.

Bernard's description of his methods explains why his letters against Abelard, or any other opponent, contain such excesses. He did not dictate them word-for-word, and neither did he check the finished writings. His secretaries, like Nicholas of Clairvaux and Geoffrey of Auxerre, were his partisans and they took Bernardine invective even further than he might have wished. When he was pressed to apologize by Peter the Venerable, Bernard blamed the messenger, who was Nicholas of Clairvaux in this instance. Nicholas's first mission for Bernard may have been to write and deliver the letters against Abelard to the

Roman curia in 1140.[172] He had instructions to tell the pope and the chancellor of the curia viva voce everything he had seen and heard; he would give better explanations than Bernard's letters could do by themselves.[173] The letters which Nicholas delivered in Rome were therefore intended as an hors-d'oeuvre; they stimulated their recipients while they settled down to hear the messenger. Scarcely any medieval letter was delivered to its addressee without a messenger to give it personal credence.

The letters of St Bernard which we possess today are the copies which his secretaries compiled at Clairvaux. They are not the originals, as dispatched to Rome in Abelard's case, since Innocent II's archive no longer exists, even if he ever formed one. So, the letters we have may be no more than drafts; in most cases, there is no proof that they ever reached their recipients, though the inference is that they did. Even the letters as dispatched did not necessarily express Bernard's own words, nor did they contain the most important part of the business, as that was delivered viva voce. If Nicholas of Clairvaux was Bernard's messenger to Rome in Abelard's case, the unreliability of the business is compounded, as Bernard later accused him of being a liar and a cheat, worse than Arnold of Brescia.[174] (In fact Nicholas went on to a successful career with Henry the Liberal, count of Champagne.)

ABELARD'S CONDEMNATION IN ROME

Whatever their excesses, St Bernard's letters to the pope and cardinals achieved their object, as Abelard was solemnly condemned before he could reach Rome. Innocent II's letters of condemnation are dated 16 July. To exonerate the pope from the charge of acting hastily, it has been suggested that the year concerned is 1141 rather than 1140.[175] But this raises further chronological difficulties and 1140 is more likely.[176] In that case, the pope condemned Abelard six weeks after the council of Sens, and within two weeks or so of receiving the official report of the proceedings from the archbishop of Sens. Berengar contrasted Abelard's treatment with that of St Paul. Whereas the Roman governor had readily allowed Paul's appeal to Caesar, the governor at Sens (St Bernard) had answered Abelard: 'Hast thou appealed unto Caesar? Unto Caesar shalt thou *not* go.'[177] 'Immediately', Berengar continues, 'letters of condemnation flew from the Roman see throughout the French Church.' Abelard was condemned 'in his absence, without a hearing and unconvicted'. With their eyes shut, his judges pressed on with the business as if they knew what they were doing and 'suddenly they shot the poisoned edict from their evil bow'.[178] Berengar's facts were probably right. Where he differed from Abelard's opponents was in thinking the papal edict unjust.

Immediate action was justified by the archbishop of Sens's report that Abelard's heresy was a 'contagion'.[179] Those clerics and canon lawyers who approved the lynching of heretics would not have considered it unjust to deal summarily with Abelard.[180] He was manifestly a heretic and his clever subterfuge in appealing to Rome should not be tolerated. 'How could this Peter [Abelard]', Geoffrey of Auxerre demanded, 'find a refuge at the see of Peter, when his faith was so very different from Peter's?'[181] John of Salisbury says Abelard 'had no access to the apostolic see'.[182] As he wrote his memoirs of the papal curia as an insider who had worked there, John may have been retailing an official view. Abelard had indeed appealed to Rome, but his appeal was inadmissible; this is why he was condemned without a further hearing.

Innocent II's condemnation of Abelard came in the form of two letters (both dated 16 July): one imposed perpetual silence on him as a heretic and excommunicated his followers, while the other ordered him and Arnold of Brescia to be 'shut up separately in places of religion and their erroneous books to be burned wherever they might be found'.[183] The first letter is a grandiloquent justification of the pope's authority over heresy and Abelard's guilt, intended to be read out in public, while the other is the concise and confidential instruction which executed the pope's sentence. Arnold of Brescia was named along with Abelard only in the confidential letter. The pope's inclusion of Arnold shows he accepted St Bernard's argument that he and Abelard headed an international conspiracy against the Church. In fact, neither of them was immediately arrested. As for the burning of books, Arnold was not the author of anything now known; so this instruction concerned Abelard only. How extensively it was obeyed is impossible to know. Geoffrey of Auxerre says the pope conducted 'a celebrated bonfire in the church of St Peter's'; but we also know that even in Rome Cardinal Guy of Castello held on to his copies of *Theologia* and *Sic et Non*.[184]

In his public letter the pope made clear that he was not acting arbitrarily or without advice. However unworthily (he declared) he occupied the throne of St Peter, upon which the unity of the Catholic Church manifestly depended.[185] This letter is the first one to state in a matter of heresy that the pope has taken advice, 'communicated by our brethren, the bishops and cardinals'.[186] This formula was probably intended to include the French bishops who had condemned Abelard's errors at Sens, as well as the cardinal bishops in Rome. Essentially, what the Roman curia was doing was confirming the decision of the council of Sens. The pope acknowledged receipt of the nineteen 'propositions' (*capitula*) and his letter condemned them 'along with their author and all the perverse teachings of this Peter' (Abelard).[187] The archbishop of Sens's report to the pope had been careful to distinguish between condemning Abelard's errors and deferring to Rome any sentence on his person.[188]

On receipt of the archbishop's report, the pope seems to have pronounced sentence almost immediately. Heresy was contagious and the archbishop said theological discussion was rife in France. In response, the pope cited a decree from 452 of the Byzantine emperor Marcian that 'no cleric, or knight – or anybody else whatsoever – should attempt to discuss the Christian faith in public'.[189] This prohibition had the potential to close down the nascent universities of Europe. The pope's letter then jumped seven centuries 'to these last days and perilous times, when evils multiply in the pernicious doctrines of Peter Abelard'.[190] Two decades earlier, in the aftermath of the council of Soissons, Abelard himself had issued exactly these apocalyptic warnings against Alberic of Reims and his other rivals in the schools.[191] Now it was he who was stigmatized – with comparable exaggeration – as the precursor of Antichrist in 'these last days'. It cannot be emphasized too strongly that Abelard approved of the prosecution of heretics as much as the pope or St Bernard did. The difference between them was that Abelard always thought his own opinions were the height of orthodoxy and his opponents were therefore deluded or malicious. When Peter the Venerable called him 'Christ's philosopher', he was endorsing Abelard's own high opinion of himself.[192]

The Role of Peter the Venerable

The reasons for Peter's intervention in Abelard's case are impossible to unravel entirely. There is so little information to go on, apart from Peter's own letters, which are as difficult to interpret as St Bernard's, though for different reasons. Whereas Bernard's literary style excelled at exaggeration and malice, Peter used the equally deceptive rhetoric of understatement and charm. He probably entered the fray in 1140 because Bernard had been authorized by the pope's confidential letter to arrest Abelard. Bernard might use one of the Cistercian houses in France to confine him in a 'place of religion'. Abelard could not reach Rome without coming in range of the Cistercians, particularly in Burgundy, where he would be beyond the protection of the French crown. We have no information about the size or makeup of Abelard's bodyguard as he made his way towards Rome. His student champions, like Berengar, may have slipped away when they realized the dangers they faced, and Abelard's former strongman and patron, Stephen de Garlande, had been dismissed from the chancellorship when Louis VI died in 1137. Without protection, Abelard risked arrest or lynching.

'Master Peter, well known, I think, to your Holiness, passed by Cluny recently on his way from France. We asked him where he was going.'[193] These are the opening words of Peter the Venerable's letter to the pope. They imply that he knew nothing about Abelard's trial at Sens and his appeal to Rome. For Peter the Venerable, Abelard was not a felon on the run; he was the distinguished 'Master Peter', who had dropped in for a chat because he happened to be passing. Peter the Venerable reported Abelard's answer in similar simplistic style, again without mentioning either Sens or St Bernard: 'He replied that he was oppressed by the vexations of certain individuals, who were calling him a heretic – a name he absolutely abhorred – and he has appealed to the Holy See and wants to seek refuge there.' Peter the Venerable told the pope he had commended Abelard's plan and assured him that 'apostolic justice never failed anyone'. This optimism stretches credulity, as the Roman curia was notorious for corruption and apostolic justice had recently failed Peter himself, in the case of the bishopric of Langres, due to 'the vexations of certain individuals'. Peter did not name St Bernard, perhaps because he wanted to ensure that 'the force of the floods of Langres' (as he described them) did not drown all charitable feelings between them.[194]

Moreover, Peter the Venerable was a Ciceronian.[195] Not naming someone (*denominatio*) was a rhetorical device which drew attention to the person concerned by arousing the reader's curiosity. Who are the 'certain individuals' who had so abhorrently called Abelard a heretic? The pope knew only too well, of course, and so did Peter the Venerable himself. As abbot of Cluny, he headed a network of information-gathering which extended across hundreds of Cluniac houses. Furthermore, Abelard's trial had been played out to a large audience. Although the Burgundian prelates had not been summoned to the council of Sens (they were in the jurisdiction of Lyons), their neighbour, the count of Nevers, had been present.[196] If St Bernard's messenger to Rome was Nicholas of Clairvaux, Peter the Venerable would have been exceptionally well informed about Abelard's case, as Nicholas liked to ingratiate himself with the great and he was Peter's 'most dear son' and confidant.[197] If Nicholas passed through Cluny on his way to Rome, Peter would not even have needed to ask him to open the letters he carried, as St Bernard had instructed him to report everything he had seen and heard viva voce. His role *vis-à-vis* Bernard and Peter can either be seen pejoratively as that of a double agent or positively as that of a mediator: he was 'my Nicholas, who is also yours' (as he described himself, when writing in Bernard's name to Peter).[198]

Peter the Venerable's device in his letter to the pope of not admitting to any knowledge of the council of Sens enabled him to portray Abelard's 'vexations' as nothing more than personal disputes. These had been resolved (Peter informed the pope) by Abelard's going to Clairvaux: he and Bernard 'had agreed to put their previous quarrels peacefully to sleep'.[199] Peter's metaphor of 'putting to sleep' sidestepped the juridical problems raised by Bernard's prosecution of Abelard and the latter's appeal to Rome. No Cistercian chronicler or document refers to this agreement between Bernard and Abelard.[200] It may never have been put in writing, since it was a bond of trust between two fellow monks and abbots. Writing many years later (perhaps as late as 1170) of the trial of Gilbert de la Porrée, who had been prosecuted by Bernard in a similar way to Abelard, John of Salisbury surmised: 'I think he [Gilbert] no longer disagrees with the views of the abbot [St Bernard] and the other saints, for they all now see the truth they searched for.'[201] They were all saints together in heaven and saw God face-to-face in John of Salisbury's optimistic opinion. His optimism applied equally to Abelard, whom John discusses in the context of Gilbert de la Porrée's prosecution by Bernard.

When in *c.*1180 one of the cardinals in Rome inquired of Geoffrey of Auxerre what he knew about Abelard's condemnation, Geoffrey told him of the 'celebrated bonfire' in St Peter's and he also offered to send the cardinal copies of St Bernard's letters against Abelard. He added that he was trying to put together a little book of Abelard's errors. 'I think this should suffice for your inquiry', Geoffrey concluded, 'and you will understand how and why he was condemned.'[202] He said nothing about any reconciliation between Bernard and Abelard. Likewise in his biographical work on Bernard, Geoffrey rounded off his chapter on Abelard with the rhetorical question already quoted: 'How could this Peter find a refuge at the see of Peter, when his faith was so very different from Peter's?'[203] Either Geoffrey was deliberately concealing what he knew, or Bernard may have kept so quiet about the agreement that it soon got forgotten. The third possibility, that there never had been such an agreement and that Peter the Venerable misled the pope, is less likely.

'We should add', Peter continued in his letter, 'that we advised him [Abelard] to curb anything he had said or written which might be offensive to Catholic ears and to remove it from his books, and so he did this.'[204] The job was as easy as that, according to Peter. A manu-script at Balliol College, Oxford, records changes in some sentences in *Theologia* which Abelard may have made at Cluny.[205] They do not alter its underlying thrust, in Constant Mews's opinion, and they might not have satisfied St Bernard, or Abelard's other opponents either. Peter the Venerable's advice accorded with Abelard's own view of how he might amend his work: 'it is appropriate for me to willingly correct my own mistakes, if that is what they are, and equally to rebut the charges which have been wrongly objected against me'.[206] He alone was entitled to judge the orthodoxy of his work because only he appreciated the full significance of his theology.[207] To argue this, in Abelard's opinion, was not to reveal obdurate pride but to state the obvious. St Bernard and his excerptors, on the other hand, with their nineteen 'propositions', had produced malicious heresies which were not Abelard's. Abelard had shown a similar approach to amending his work after the first edition of *Theologia* had been burned at Soissons in 1121. Out of the ashes he produced the enlarged version, *Theologia Christiana*. What Abelard saw as constructive improvements to his work, his enemies – and especially those 'pseudo-apostles', St Bernard and St Norbert – had interpreted as more heresies.[208]

How much new writing Abelard did at Cluny is unclear. Otto of Freising says he produced some of his polemic against St Bernard there.[209] Possibly this was so; replying to Bernard's nineteen 'proposi-tions' is what Abelard would have understood as curbing anything offensive to Catholic ears. Whether Abelard did much writing at Cluny depends primarily on what view we take of his state of health there and what latitude Peter the Venerable allowed him. He described Abelard's monastic life at Cluny as exemplary: 'his reading was contin-uous, his prayer assiduous, his silence perpetual'.[210] Significantly per-haps, Peter says nothing about him writing. Perpetual silence was the punishment which Innocent II had imposed on Abelard.[211] Peter may have been deliberately making his description of Abelard's life accord with the papal sentence. Abelard's good behaviour at Cluny was out of character. If he had been his old self and in vigorous health, he would presumably have denounced his hosts at Cluny for corruption and laxness, just as he had denounced the monks of St Denis and St Gildas. Peter may have removed him to the priory of Chalon-sur-Saône as a preventive measure, for disciplinary as much as health reasons. There, Peter says, 'he renewed his former studies, as far as his ill health allowed, and he was always bent over his books'.[212] Abelard could go through the motions of producing new writing, and that kept him quiet and out of harm's way.

Peter the Venerable's purported ignorance of the council of Sens and of Abelard's appeal to Rome enabled him to interpret to Abelard's advantage the pope's instruction to confine him in a religious house. There was no need to arrest him, Peter assured the pope, because 'on our advice – or much rather, we believe, by divine inspiration – he has chosen a perpetual mansion for himself in your Cluny'.[213] Peter's advice saved Abelard's dignity and the pope's as well. Abelard was already secured in the pope's prison of Cluny with Peter as his gaoler. It was 'your Cluny' because the abbey was dedicated to St Peter and papal power. Peter the Venerable welcomed Abelard to his new home 'with delight' because a monastery was a 'joyous prison' (this is how Peter described the Cluniac convent of Marcigny to Heloise).[214] Having explained Abelard's 'choice' of Cluny to the pope with firmness and tact, Peter reached his peroration:

> And therefore I, as one of your people, beg you, your devoted monastery of Cluny begs you, and he [Abelard] begs you, on his own behalf and through us, and through your faithful sons who bring this letter, and through these very words which he has asked me to write: deign to command that he may spend the remaining days of his life and old age, which perhaps are not many, in your Cluny, so that no one has the power to expel or remove him from this home which the sparrow has found, from this nest in which the turtle-dove rejoices. For the honour in which you hold all good men and because you too have loved him, guard him with the shield of apostolic protection.[215]

In other words, the pope should cancel his letter entitling St Bernard and the archbishops of Sens and Reims to arrest Abelard. As Bernard had just beaten Peter the Venerable in the dispute over Langres, he might win this time too, even though Cluny was an inviolable fortress. This is why Peter had to use all the forces of Latin composition at his command.

How Peter's letter was received in Rome is not recorded. The pope had perhaps heard Abelard described as a rhinoceros and certainly as the dragon of the Book of Revelation, 'that old serpent, which is the Devil and Satan'.[216] Reducing him to the size and disposition of a sparrow or a turtle-dove was perhaps taking the rhetoric of understatement too far. Abelard had met Innocent II at Morigny in 1131.[217] Did the pope agree that he too had loved him? However, according to Peter the Venerable, Innocent II responded favourably and Abelard was restored 'to apostolic grace by letters and my labour'.[218] Unlike the Cistercian chroniclers, William Godell (who became a Cluniac and used material from Sens) confirms that Abelard 'confessed himself a son of the Catholic Church and finished his life affirming this in fraternal peace'.[219]

These testimonies have led historians to conclude that Innocent II lifted the sentence on Abelard, although 'the document rescinding this verdict, referred to by Peter the Venerable, has not survived'.[220] But was Peter referring to a papal 'document'? His phrase 'by letters and my labour' is ambiguous, perhaps deliberately so. Did he mean the pope's letters or his own? Abelard could be absolved from the penalty of excommunication without any sort of document. All that was required was for a papal legate to come to Cluny, satisfy himself of Abelard's contrition, and absolve him in accordance with the sacrament of penance.

Abelard's restoration to 'apostolic grace' need not mean that the sentence handed down by Innocent II in his public letter was rescinded, or that St Bernard had to acknowledge he had been in the wrong. Abelard had been forgiven as a person, but his heresies remained condemned. The pope had damned them from the throne of St Peter 'by authority of the sacred canons'. The lack of further documentation suggests that the forgiveness of Abelard, like the agreement with St Bernard from which it stemmed, was not formally recorded. This would explain why the Cistercian chroniclers, and even John of Salisbury in the papal curia, said nothing about it. When Abelard died, Heloise was concerned about the lack of an official declaration of his forgiveness. Peter the Venerable had promised her a sealed certificate, to hang on Abelard's tomb, declaring his sins absolved.[221] But he delayed sending it, until she reminded him. The document he finally produced declares: 'I, Peter abbot of Cluny, who received Peter Abelard as a monk, by authority of almighty God and all the saints, in virtue of my office, absolve him from all his sins.'[222] As an abbot, Peter was responsible *ex officio* for the salvation of his monks.[223]

The magnificent epitaph, which Peter wrote for Abelard, contains the same idea that he owed his salvation to being a Cluniac monk.[224] Epitaphs like this were composed for the obituary roll, which a messenger took from monastery to monastery when a great man died, so that each house might compete in writing complimentary Latin verses. In this context Peter the Venerable abandoned the rhetoric of understatement and praised Abelard to the skies. He had been the French Socrates, the western Plato and 'our Aristotle'. Without equal or superior, he had been the world's acknowledged prince of learning: 'such was Abelard' – *Abaelardus erat*. But this was far from being the end of the story, since he had then crossed over from the world to Christ's true philosophy, when he was professed a monk of Cluny. 'There he well fulfilled the last things of a long life and – on the eleventh day before the beginning of May – gave hope of being numbered among the good philosophers.' Peter the Venerable does not include the year of Abelard's death in his

epitaph because everyone would have known that. It was probably
1142. A manuscript from the Paraclete, which has been lost since the
dissolution of the convent at the French Revolution, recorded that
Abelard died at the age of sixty-three.[225] This is also recorded on the
inscription of 1701 by the abbess of the Paraclete, Catherine de la
Rochefoucauld, which is now on the tomb of Abelard and Heloise at
Père-Lachaise cemetery.

14

Himself

And later is worse, when men will not hate you
Enough to defame or to execrate you,
But pondering the qualities that you lacked
Will only try to find the historical fact.
When men shall declare that there was no mystery
About this man who played a certain part in history.

T. S. Eliot, *Murder in the Cathedral*

'Abelard is neither a giant of thought, nor an author of the second-rank. His is a lively but limited mind, both helped and hindered by his character and historical circumstances.'[1] Thus a historian of philosophy, Jean Jolivet, epitomizes modern assessments of Abelard. Historians aim to put things in perspective, even when that requires differing from the opinions of people at the time. Jolivet's description of Abelard's 'limited mind' (*un esprit limité*) is obviously at odds with Peter the Venerable's eulogy and Abelard's admission that 'I thought myself to be the only philosopher in the world'.[2] Abelard's intellectual stature has been diminished by twentieth-century historians because they are reacting against eighteenth-and nineteenth-century portrayals of him as a romantic hero, who stood out against the allegedly dark forces of the medieval Church. Michael Haren's survey of *Medieval Thought* (first published in 1985) confirms the current orthodoxy for English-speaking students:

> The controversies and censures which punctuated Abelard's life for long misled historians in their assessment of his work. Modern scholarship has discredited the portrayal of him as a sceptic and freethinker and has restored him to his rightful place as a theologian of serious purpose in the dialectical mould.[3]

Such revisionism leaves little room for Master Jocelin's warning that Abelard was a jester, rather than a professor, or for St Bernard's diatribes at the council of Sens.[4] Abelard could have been a jester and, like Kierkegaard, a theologian of serious purpose. 'I am playful', St Bernard said, 'so that I may be serious.'[5]

Haren's assessment echoes that of David Knowles in *The Evolution of Medieval Thought* (first published in 1962), which in its turn cited Étienne Gilson's judgement that 'the legend of Abelard the freethinker has now become an exhibit of the historical curiosity-shop'.[6] 'Of a truth', Knowles continues, 'Abelard was never a rebel against the authority of the Church, and never a rationalist in the modern sense. He never persisted in teaching what had been censured.' St Bernard would surely have disagreed with every word of this. Abelard *was* a rebel, like Arnold of Brescia, and he made 'human ingenuity usurp everything, leaving nothing to faith'.[7] He *was* a sceptic: one of those 'academics who doubt everything and know nothing'.[8] He certainly 'persisted in teaching what had been censured', as he reproduced whole passages from the book condemned at Soissons in the second edition, which he had the temerity to entitle *Theologia Christiana*.[9] Bernard's claim was that one head of Abelard's had been cut off at Soissons and so he had grown seven more, like the hydra.[10] Knowles's argument is that Abelard may have made errors, but he was not heretical because he had 'the root of the matter' in him.[11] This is Knowles's personal opinion. It was not the opinion of St Bernard, nor of Pope Innocent II and his cardinals, who condemned Abelard as a heretic as uncompromisingly as anyone has ever been judged by the canon law of the Church.

The modern tendency to play down the controversial and radical aspects of Abelard was taken to its ultimate point by John Benton in 1972, when he argued that Abelard's 'history of calamities' was a forgery. 'We can strike from the historical record', Benton concluded, 'the image of Abelard as a calculating seducer or as an arrogant and ungrateful student, who could dismiss Anselm of Laon as a sterile and obfuscating teacher years after the death of that great scholar.'[12] But these aspects of Abelard's conduct are not recorded only in his 'history of calamities'. Concerning the seduction of Heloise, Roscelin told Abelard: 'You taught her to fornicate, you are the filthiest violator of virginal purity.'[13] Fulk of Deuil said: 'You plunged without cease into the whirlpool of fornication.'[14] These allegations are not necessarily true, but they cannot be struck from the historical record. Fulk of Deuil also described Abelard's arrogance: 'Inanely exalting yourself over almost everybody, you thought even the saints inferior to you.'[15] That Abelard disparaged Anselm of Laon is confirmed by Otto of Freising: Abelard 'was so arrogant that he would scarcely demean himself to descend from the heights of his own mind to listen to his masters.... He did not long endure those very serious men, Anselm of Laon and William of Champeaux.'[16] Abelard's disrespectful attitude to other masters is also attested in *Theologia Christiana*, where he ridicules one master after another, starting with St Anselm of Canterbury.[17]

In response to Benton and other revisionists, Peter Dronke called for beginning 'afresh, from medieval assumptions and medieval attitudes for which we have concrete evidence', and not from modern preconceptions.[18] Discussing Roscelin, Fulk of Deuil and many other twelfth-century testimonies about Abelard, Dronke concluded that 'the majority of contemporaries of whom we have evidence, and the generations immediately following, were convinced of the uniqueness and stature of Abelard's and Heloise's love, and regarded their tragedy with wonderment and compassion'.[19] Exactly so, friends and enemies alike recognized Abelard and Heloise to be special. Neither Peter the Venerable nor St Bernard thought Abelard a second-rate or a limited mind. In Bernard's opinion, he was so dangerous because he was so intelligent and clearly focused: 'He proves himself a heretic not so much by his error, as by his pertinacious defence of error. He is a man who goes beyond due measure, making void the virtue of Christ's cross by the cleverness of his words.'[20]

In parallel with his diminishment by modern academics, Abelard's reputation has declined in popular esteem, mainly in the last thirty years or so. In 1780 almost all foreigners who came to France – and especially the English – were said to 'consider it a duty to visit the Paraclete, where they contemplate with a tearful eye the sorrowful tomb of these fatal victims of love and vengeance'.[21] When Abelard and Heloise were reinterred in Père-Lachaise cemetery in Paris after the French Revolution, their grave remained a magnet for tourists: 'Go when you will, you will find somebody snuffling over that tomb.'[22] The heyday of Abelard's fame in the English-speaking world came in the inter-war years 1919–39.[23] In 1921 the novelist George Moore published his *Heloise and Abelard*, and in 1925 C. K. Scott Moncrieff, the translator of Proust, produced a translation of the letters of Abelard and Heloise. Helen Waddell's novel of 1933, *Peter Abelard*, was greeted as a masterpiece and became a best-seller. As the author of *The Wandering Scholars* (1927) and *Medieval Latin Lyrics* (1929), she was the best-known medieval scholar in the English-speaking world. In 1938 two attractive and authoritative books, Étienne Gilson's *Héloïse et Abélard* and Enid McLeod's biography, *Héloïse*, reinforced both general and scholarly interest.

Abelard and Heloise were still being celebrated in 1956, when Ella Fitzgerald recorded Cole Porter's song, 'Just One of Those Things'. Porter had placed Abelard and Heloise in the company of Dorothy Parker, Christopher Columbus, and Romeo and Juliet as free spirits, who acknowledged that their love had been 'great fun, but it was just one of those things'.[24] The song assumes listeners know the story of Abelard and Heloise and will appreciate the irony of such lines as:

> If we'd thought a bit of the end of it
> When we started painting the town,
> We'd have been aware that our love affair
> Was too hot not to cool down.

Porter's song had been written in the 1930s and his reference to Abelard and Heloise may already have been incomprehensible to some listeners by 1956. Forty years on, in 1996, most listeners to 'Just One of Those Things' probably know nothing about Abelard and Heloise. Helen Waddell's novel is out of print and the tomb at Père-Lachaise attracts few tourists. Heloise's reputation has suffered more than Abelard's from Benton's allegations of forgery, as her only extant writings are her letters. The second edition of McLeod's biography of her came out in 1971, just before Benton's allegations in 1972, and this may explain why there was no reprint.

Benton had addressed his allegations to experts in order to start a scholarly debate. At this level he certainly stimulated intensive research into Abelardian texts, but the effect on the wider reading public has not been so beneficial. Once the authenticity of Abelard's 'history of calamities' and Heloise's letters was brought into doubt among experts, the safest response for non-specialists was to say as little as possible about them until the problem had been resolved. In *The Oxford Illustrated History of Medieval Europe*, for example, which was first published in 1988, the editor, George Holmes, wrote in his preface: 'We study the past because it is interesting in the present. Abelard and St Francis would not attract us if we could not to some extent share their hopes and fears.'[25] Holmes grew up in the 1940s and 1950s, when Abelard was still a familiar name among educated people. His remark assumes that Abelard's 'history of calamities' is authentic, as he expressed his hopes and fears nowhere else. But Holmes's younger contributors to *The Oxford Illustrated History* are warier of the Benton debate than he is. In the book itself Abelard is mentioned only once, in a discussion of university masters, and Heloise not at all. In Norman Davies's magisterial *History of Europe* (1996) Abelard's contemporaries find a place (Adelard of Bath, St Anselm of Canterbury, the Archpoet, Gratian, Guibert de Nogent, Otto of Freising), but Abelard and Heloise do not.[26]

The time has come to restore the former fame of Abelard and Heloise among the reading public. Their accounts of themselves are outstanding documents of humanity, however they are interpreted. Both Abelard and Heloise should emerge from scrutiny in the coming years with their reputations enhanced. Aaron Gurevich has rightly made Abelard central to his study of *The Origins of European Individualism* (1995). John Marenbon's *The Philosophy of Peter Abelard* (1997) argues that the view of him epitomized by Jolivet is too negative. Barbara Newman's purpose explains itself in her title 'Authority, Authenticity and the Repression of Heloise' (1992). If, as Newman argues, Heloise 'came to Abelard with not only her mind but her imagination already well stocked', and if she was already nearer thirty years of age than twenty, her influence on Abelard may have been immense, not least because she engaged his emotions as well as his intellect.[27] Having learned so much from his masters, including Heloise, Abelard applied his dialectically trained intelligence (the *ingenium* or 'genius' he describes at the beginning of his 'history of calamities') to assembling and focusing the agenda in which the scholastic philosophers excelled down to Aquinas in the thirteenth century.[28] Just when all this began to look old-fashioned after 1300, Abelard's fame set off on a new trajectory as an inspiration to the Renaissance humanists. Petrarch's annotated copy of the 'history of calamities' still exists; alongside Abelard's description of how he had nearly broken his neck in a fall from a horse, Petrarch wrote: 'and me at night'.[29]

In his posthumous career, as much as in his lifetime, Abelard has proved a survivor, popping up again with new supporters just when he seemed beaten. It is true that many of his works are incomplete and they promise more than they deliver, just as it is true that his provocative discussions of Christian doctrine understandably gave rise to accusations of heresy and blasphemy. 'I have said many things in many schools,' Abelard boasted.[30] Over a lifetime of scholarship he produced at least a million words of text, either by dictation or by writing himself, and – like St Bernard – he does not seem to have checked very much of it. Attitudes to writing were not the same in manuscript culture as in print culture. No handwritten text was completely stable and busy authors did not aim at producing a final and unalterable version. No one book was exactly the same as any other, and all books were hard to come by. Abelard's *Theologia* and his *Sic et Non* probably existed only in a dozen or so copies in his lifetime. They are much more accessible to scholars now than they were to William of St Thierry or St Bernard. For most of his contemporaries, what Abelard said was more significant than what he wrote. Everyone agreed he was an extraordinary teacher, 'overcoming everything by force of reason and skill in speech'.[31] But now that his spoken words (those 'voiced breaths' – *flatus vocis*, as the Nominalists called them) are irrecoverable, we can approach him only through his writings.

Abelard's writings combine clarity and lightness with doggedness and solidity. He was as great an amasser of information as he was an expositor; in manuscript culture it was a considerable achievement in itself to obtain information and vouch for its accuracy. His *Dialectica* and *Sic et Non* reveal this combination of qualities best. Using a few elementary and apparently obvious principles, both books address and organize a mass of intractable material. The encyclopedic scale of *Sic et Non* was unprecedented, though it would later be far exceeded by Aquinas's *Summa Theologiae*. Abelard was so much the master of his material that he could demonstrate to his contemporaries how little they really knew or understood, even about the most familiar teachings of Aristotelian logic or the Church Fathers. This was not something his conservative colleagues wished to be reminded of. Nor was Abelard simply being negative, as St Bernard alleged. He provided his followers with a constructive formula for proceeding further – 'by doubting we come to inquiry and by inquiry we perceive the truth'.[32] Of course this was naively optimistic and simplistic, but these are good qualities in a teacher. As John of Salisbury observed, Abelard followed St Augustine's precept and 'dedicated himself to explaining things'.[33] His refusal to be pompous was integral to his teaching; 'he preferred' (John said) 'to instruct and stimulate his students through elementary points, rather than to be obscure like a grave philosopher'.[34] This was where Abelard differed from 'those very serious men, Anselm of Laon and William of Champeaux'.[35] But there was a price to pay for this and John admitted that some of Abelard's explanations seemed puerile.

'KNOW THYSELF'

For Abelard personally, the price of being such a stimulating and successful teacher was very heavy indeed: madness, castration, despair and public humiliation in his two trials for heresy. *Sibi dissimilis est*, St Bernard hissed: Abelard was dissimilar even from himself.[36] St Goswin's biographer describes how when Abelard was handed over to him to be disciplined following the council of Soissons, 'that rhinoceros' was delirious and was 'savaging himself'.[37] Abelard was one of those people 'whose infallible instinct leads straight to dangerous questions and provoking replies; he is an adventurer of the mind' (this is the conclusion of Étienne Gilson).[38] Goswin's biographer compared Abelard to Proteus, the sea-god in the Odyssey, who knows all things and changes his shape at will.[39] Abelard was so clever, so 'various in genius' (as Peter the Venerable wrote in his epitaph), that he would not be stereotyped and adopt a fixed role through life, as society normally requires.[40] 'He is neither in order, nor of an order' (St Bernard again).[41] 'If you are neither a cleric nor a layman nor a monk, what should I call you?', Roscelin mocked.[42] An anachronistic answer to Roscelin is to say Abelard fitted none of these roles because they were too restrictive. In modern terms he fulfils the role of 'writer' or 'artist', a genius who is an exception to all rules and is considered *sui generis* by the public, whose patronage he seeks and upon whose protection – or at least tolerance – he depends. The writer-artist is a deliberate individualist and commentators on Abelard have argued that this is what he was. Mary M. McLaughlin concludes her study of 'Abelard as Autobiographer':

> At the center of his 'Story of Calamities', at once its author and its subject, stands the autonomous individual who carries his world within, who faces constantly the private decisions and dilemmas, as well as the struggles with his environment, that force him repeatedly to define himself anew, the individual who by choice and action shapes himself.[43]

'Know thyself', *Scito te ipsum*, is the title Abelard gave his book on ethics. It was the counsel of the Delphic oracle and a fashionable maxim among intellectuals of Abelard's time because it was classically Greek and yet it contained a message for Christians. Hugh of St Victor began his *Didascalicon* with it: 'On the tripod of Apollo is written "Know thyself".'[44] Hugh interpreted this in Platonic terms to mean that man should seek within himself the perfect good, which is God. This was not a recipe for eccentric individualism, as everyone should find the same image of God within himself. Although Abelard used 'Know thyself' as a book title, he never enlarged on what he meant by it and this allowed St Bernard to explain it for him: 'It were better for him to know himself in accordance with the title of his book; he should not exceed his measure, but get to know sobriety.'[45] Here was another Greek idea, that of the mean or balance which gives equilibrium. Abelard was unbalanced, in Bernard's opinion, because he was a braggart and a jester, whose playing about with dialectic in his youth led him on to playing the fool with holy Scripture in his dotage.[46] Although Bernard justified playfulness as a path to seriousness in his own case, he thought Abelard's little games had gone too far and had ended in insanity.[47]

In one work Abelard presents himself as a split personality, when he does an imaginary dialogue between 'Peter' and 'Abelard': 'the same self spoke to the same'.[48] But this *Soliloquium*, which was modelled on St Augustine's, is not an examination of Abelard's own self at all. It is a theoretical discussion, like his other works in dialogue form, concerning the meaning of the name of Christ. Nowhere in Abelard's works does he discuss any difficulties he had in knowing himself. Nor did he interpret his 'history of calamities' as an Odyssey, in which 'struggles with his environment force him repeatedly to define himself anew'.[49] As he saw it, the 'calamities under which I laboured, almost since I left my cradle' had always been the same.[50] They were caused not by tensions within himself, but by 'them', those old plotters who were always doing him down. Abelard found comfort in quoting Christ's words: 'They have persecuted me and they will persecute you. If the world hate you, ye know that it hated me before it hated you.'[51]

This comparison with Christ, which is one of a number Abelard makes, shows that – implicitly and perhaps unconsciously – he defined himself in terms of role models.[52] Every Christian should be an imitator of Christ and so there is nothing so special about Abelard's likening himself to Christ. But Abelard also saw himself in other roles. In his 'history of calamities' he compared himself with Ajax, the courageous suicide, and with St Jerome, who was allegedly driven out of Rome.[53] In his Confession of Faith to Heloise he declares he does not wish to play the role of Aristotle (*nolo sic esse Aristoteles*), if that is to exclude him from Christ.[54] He seems conscious here of his reputation as 'our Aristotle', as Peter the Venerable called him.[55] In the final portion of the Confession of Faith Abelard adopts another role: 'I have no fear of the barking of Scylla, I scorn the whirlpool of Charybdis.'[56] Here he speaks in the persona of Ulysses, the most famous of all adventurers. This is a literary allusion of an obvious kind and it emphasizes how statements in Latin tend to be studded with such allusions, whether from the pagan classics or the Bible, because Latin was learned as a tissue of quotations.[57] Every writer of 'letters' had to create a literary persona to be the vehicle of his thoughts because classical Latin was a man-made language and not a mother tongue. The art of rhetoric taught Latinists to speak with different voices to accord with the genre of the work, and Abelard adds to this the advice of St Augustine that a teacher should tailor what he says to whatever his hearers can most readily understand.[58] (This is the feature of Abelard's style which John of Salisbury noted.[59])

In Abelard's prose a different tone can readily be detected distinguishing lectures from sermons, and both of these from letters in the sense of correspondence. Within each genre he adapts his style to the business in hand. In *Dialectica* he occasionally lightens his lectures with jokes, as the subject matter is secular, whereas in *Theologia* his tone is serious and sometimes admonitory. The zest in Abelard's writings comes from his transgressing the particular tone which his readers expect; when, for example, he introduces jokes into his theology. 'He cannot restrain his laughter; listen to his jeering,' was St Bernard's purportedly scandalized reaction.[60] Abelard's letters display a similar variety of tones: from formal reflection (in the letter to a friend, recounting his 'history of calamities'), to the argumentative (in a letter to St Bernard), to something more placatory when addressing Abbot Adam of St Denis or Gilbert bishop of Paris. In Abelard's letters to Heloise he had difficulty finding a role acceptable to her; he could no longer be her physical lover, but how convincing was he as her father in religion or as her dutiful husband? As a creator of dialogues (between a philosopher and a Jew, a philosopher and a Christian, and between 'Peter' and 'Abelard'), Abelard was very conscious of speaking with different voices. 'Yes and No' (*Sic et Non*) was an appropriate title for the resulting cacophony. 'One and the same word has been used to express now one meaning, now another. For, each one of us abounds in his own words, just as he does in his own sense of them.'[61]

Opinions will always vary about how far it is possible to produce concord from such discord. Given that we only have Abelard's writings to go on, can we reach beyond his diverse voices and literary personae to the autonomous individual who produced them? Those who have judged him, whether they were St Bernard in the twelfth century or historians in the twentieth, have been confident they understood him. But in *Sic et Non* Abelard questioned such claims: 'Who does not see how rash it is to judge someone else's intelligence and sense of himself, since our hearts and thoughts are open only to God? Forbidding such presumption in us, He said: "Judge not and ye shall not be judged".'[62] The interiority of sin is the core of Abelard's book on ethics and the reason why he entitled it 'Know thyself'. 'Judge not' is likewise the text with which he concluded his plea to St Bernard at the time of the council of Sens.[63] But this plea for Christian charity reveals another contradiction in Abelard. 'Judge not' is not the rule which he had applied when attacking Roscelin, William of Champeaux, Anselm of Laon, Fulbert, Cono of Praeneste, Alberic of Reims, St Norbert, St Anselm, St Bernard and many others over a lifetime of public strife. Should not Abelard be judged in the way he judged others? On the other hand, his inconsistencies make it harder to reach any single judgement about him. Even the forthrightness of St Bernard's condemnation is a paradox, as he maintained that Abelard was 'totally ambiguous'.[64]

Abelard's life story is extraordinary, even by medieval standards of what was ordinary. It is easy to see why critics wanted to make it more manageable by eliminating substantial portions of it as forgeries. He roused strong and unexpected reactions in people. Peter the Venerable's wholehearted support for him is as surprising as St Bernard's uncompromising condemnation, considering that all three of them (Abelard, Peter and Bernard) were radical and reforming abbots committed to Christian regeneration. Contemporaries agreed that Abelard was proud, but it was this exalted sense of self-esteem which sustained him throughout his 'calamities'. He was indomitable – *rhinoceros indomitus* – the unicorn whom only a virgin can tame: 'she warms him and nourishes him and takes him up into the palace of kings'.[65] He was her palatine, the *Peripateticus Palatinus*, the wandering scholar from Le Pallet, who described his thwarted ambitions so powerfully in his 'history of calamities'.[66] In this life, as Abelard wrote in his hymn 'O Quanta Qualia', our part is to stand up for ourselves (literally, to 'erect the mind') and to make for our spiritual home with total confidence, whatever the circumstances:

> Nostrum est interim mentem erigere
> Et totis patriam votis appetere.[67]

Then at last, after long exile in Babylon, we shall reach the true Jerusalem:

> Et ad Jerusalem a Babylonia
> Post longa regredi tandem exsilia.

Abelard was 'without equal, without superior', Peter the Venerable wrote in his epitaph.[68] He inspired admiration in Peter, in John of Salisbury, in Berengar of Poitiers, in Guy of Castello and many others whose names are not recorded; but he could not tolerate an equal or a superior – except Heloise. She should have the last word: 'I conclude a long letter with a brief ending – *Vale, unice*.[69] 'Farewell, unique one.'

Who's Who

Abelard (c.1079–c.1142)

Born at Le Pallet, near Nantes. Taught by Roscelin at Loches c.1093–c.1099. Arrived in Paris c.1100 and taught by William of Champeaux. Master at Melun and then at Corbeil c.1102–c.1105. Returned home c.1105–c.1108. Came back to Paris c.1108 and challenged William of Champeaux on universals. Abelard was challenged in his turn, at his school at Mont Sainte Geneviève, by St Goswin c.1112. Returned home a second time, when his parents retired to monasteries. Went to Laon to study divinity with Anselm of Laon 1113. Returned to Paris c.1114 as master of the school of Notre-Dame. Lodged in the house of Fulbert, canon of Notre-Dame and uncle of Heloise c.1117. Married Heloise, following the birth of their son, Astralabe, c.1118. Became a monk at St Denis, following his castration by Fulbert's kinsmen c.1118. Withdrew from the abbey of St Denis to a 'cell' (unnamed) to teach and write c.1119–c.1120. Complained of Roscelin to Gilbert bishop of Paris, c.1120. Condemned for heresy at the council of Soissons for publishing *Theologia* 1121. Held under house arrest by St Goswin at St Médard in Soissons and then returned to St Denis. Questioned the authenticity of St Denis and fled to the protection of Count Thibaud of Champagne at Provins 1121. Peace made between Abelard and Suger, abbot of St Denis, by Stephen de Garlande 1122. Founded the hermitage of the Trinity near Nogent-sur-Seine c.1122, which he later dedicated to the Paraclete. Left the hermitage to be abbot of St Gildas-de-Rhuys in Brittany c.1125–c.1127. Gave the hermitage to Heloise and her nuns, when they were expelled from Argenteuil by Suger of St Denis 1129. Returned to Paris as master at Mont Sainte Geneviève c.1133. Joined by Arnold of Brescia at the church of St Hilary at Mont Sainte Geneviève c.1139. Accused of heresy by St Bernard at the council of Sens 1140. Appealed to Rome. Condemned as a heretic by Innocent II 1140. Protected by Peter the Venerable, abbot of Cluny. Died at the Cluniac house of St Marcel near Chalon-sur-Saône c.1142.

Adam, Abbot of St Denis (abbot 1099–1122)

Protected Abelard by allowing him to become a monk of St Denis after his castration c.1118. Described by Abelard as 'evil living and notorious for depravity'. When Abelard attacked his way of life, Adam permitted him to withdraw from St Denis to a 'cell' where he might teach and write c.1119–c.1120. Abelard returned to the abbey of St Denis after his condemnation at the council of Soissons 1121. When Abelard fled from the abbey after questioning the authenticity of St Denis, Adam aimed to prosecute him as a fugitive monk. He wrote Adam a partially conciliatory letter of explanation. A settlement was reached between Abelard and the abbey of St Denis after Adam's death (19 February 1122).

Alberic of Reims   (c.1085–1141)

Abelard's prosecutor at the council of Soissons 1121. Student of Anselm of Laon; responsible, according to Abelard, for his expulsion from Laon in 1113. The most arrogant master in France, in Abelard's opinion. Master at Reims 1118–36. Archdeacon of Reims 1131–36. Archbishop of Bourges 1136–41.

Anselm of Laon   (c.1055–c.1117)

Described by Abelard as 'this old man who owed his reputation more to long use than to intelligence or memory'. Expelled Abelard from his school at Laon 1113. Master at Laon, with his brother Ralph, from c.1090 (or earlier) until his death. Dean and chancellor of Laon from c.1109; archdeacon from 1115. Named, with Ivo of Chartres and William of Champeaux, as one of the three 'modern masters' in the *Liber Pancrisis* c.1120.

Anselm, St   (1033–1109)

Described by Abelard as 'that magnificent doctor of the Church' c.1119, though he repeatedly attacked St Anselm's ideas, most explicitly in *Theologia Christiana* c.1122. St Anselm became a monk at Bec in Normandy 1059. Author of *Monologion* and *Proslogion* 1075–8. Abbot of Bec 1078–92. Opposed Abelard's master, Roscelin, 1092–8. Archbishop of Canterbury from 1093. Author of *Cur Deus Homo?* 1095–8. In exile at Lyons and Rome 1097–1100. Got Pope Urban II's approval in 1098 for his final refutation of Roscelin ('On the Incarnation of the Word').

Arnold of Brescia   (died c.1155)

Described as Abelard's 'armour-bearer' by St Bernard. Condemned as a heretic, along with Abelard, by Pope Innocent II 1140. Former student of Abelard (according to Otto of Freising). An abbot of reformed canons at Brescia, he was expelled from Italy in 1139 for supporting the city commune against the bishop. Joined Abelard as a master at the church of St Hilary on Mont Sainte Geneviève 1139–40. He denounced St Bernard and was expelled from France by Louis VII 1141–2. Reconciled to the Roman church by Pope Eugenius III 1143. Leader of the Roman republican movement against the pope and the emperor c.1145–c.1155. Captured and burned in Rome by authority of the Emperor Frederick Barbarossa and Pope Adrian IV.

Astralabe   (born c.1118)

Son of Heloise and Abelard. Brought up by Abelard's sister in Brittany. Heloise asked Peter the Venerable to find him a prebend c.1144. A canon at Nantes cathedral was called 'Astralabe' c.1150. An 'Astralabe' was abbot of Hauterive in Fribourg 1162–5. The necrology of the Paraclete names him as: 'Peter Astralabe son of our Master Peter'. Abelard says in his 'history of calamities' that Heloise named him 'Astralabe'. A Latin poem of advice to Astralabe is attributed to Abelard.

Berengar   (died after 1113)

Father of Abelard. Of knightly status. Retired to a monastery c.1113.

Berengar of Poitiers   (born c.1120)

Passionate defender of Abelard, 'my teacher', in a letter to St Bernard, satirizing him and the events of the council of Sens 1140. Publisher of Abelard's 'Confession of Faith to Heloise' c.1140. In a subsequent letter to William bishop of Mende (died 1150), Berengar said his attack on St Bernard 'should be read as a joke and not seriously'.

Bernard, St   (c.1090–1153)

Abelard's prosecutor at the council of Sens 1140. Burgundian aristocrat. Became a monk at Cîteaux 1112. Abbot of Clairvaux 1115–53. Aided in the early years at Clairvaux by Abelard's former master, William of Champeaux, bishop of Châlons. Secured the victory of Innocent II in the papal schism 1130–5. Persuaded to prosecute Abelard by William of St Thierry c.1140. Achieved success in this by his letters to Rome, following the council of Sens. According to Peter the Venerable, Abelard made peace with St Bernard through the mediation of Rainald abbot of Cîteaux c.1140.

Cono of Praeneste (Palestrina)   (died 1122)

Papal legate at Abelard's trial at the council of Soissons 1121. Described by Abelard as 'less learned than was necessary'. Cardinal bishop of Palestrina since c.1108. The most experienced diplomat and papal legate of his time, involved in missions to Louis VI of France, Henry I of England and the Emperor Henry V. Refused the papacy in 1119.

Fulbert   (died ?1127)

Uncle and guardian of Heloise. First named as a canon of Notre-Dame of Paris in 1102 (last named in 1126). Responsible for the castration of Abelard, though he denied doing the deed itself (according to Fulk of Deuil). Punished by expulsion and the confiscation of his goods. Restored to his canonry by 1 April 1119 (see ch. 9, n. 145). According to Fulk of Deuil, Abelard appealed to Rome against the leniency of Fulbert's sentence. There is no definite information about his family origins; possibly he was a Montmorency.

Fulk of Deuil

Wrote to Abelard *c.*1118 to congratulate him on his castration. Prior of Deuil, a neighbouring monastery to Abelard at St Denis and Heloise at Argenteuil. Fulk may have written in the interests of the Montmorency, the patrons of Deuil, or of the bishop and canons of Notre-Dame of Paris. Despite its facetiousness and malice, Fulk's letter to Abelard is packed with unique information.

Geoffrey de Lèves, Bishop of Chartres   (bishop 1116–49)

According to Abelard, Geoffrey spoke in his favour at the council of Soissons 1121. Counsellor of Count Thibaud of Chartres, who was Abelard's patron for a while. Approved Suger of St Denis's expulsion of Heloise from Argenteuil 1129. Thought to be the legate of Innocent II, who attempted to make peace between Abelard and the monks of St Gildas *c.*1131. Along with St Bernard and other French prelates, supported Innocent II at the council of Pisa 1135. William of St Thierry addressed his letter, accusing Abelard of heresy, jointly to Geoffrey (as papal legate) and to St Bernard *c.*1140. Signatory of the letter of the archbishop of Sens declaring Abelard guilty of heresy 1140.

Geoffrey of Auxerre   (*c.*1120–*c.*1188)

St Bernard's partisan and biographer. A 'disciple' of Abelard, who was converted to Cistercian monasticism by St Bernard's sermon to the students of Paris *c.*1140. One of St Bernard's secretaries from 1145. Abbot of Clairvaux 1162–5. In his letter to Cardinal Albinus *c.*1180, Geoffrey described the burning of Abelard's books in St Peter's, Rome, by order of Innocent II in 1140. Denied that Abelard was ever reconciled with Rome: 'How could this Peter find a refuge at the see of Peter, when his faith was so very different from Peter's?'

Gilbert, Bishop of Paris   (bishop 1116–23)

Putative patron of Abelard. Chancellor of the chapter of Notre-Dame of Paris 1107–8. Archdeacon of Paris 1112–16. As bishop in *c.*1118, he blessed the veil which made Heloise a nun of Argenteuil. Abelard appealed to Rome, without success, against his leniency towards Fulbert following Abelard's castration. In *c.*1120 Abelard asked Gilbert to convene an assembly to consider Roscelin's alleged heretical slanders against him. Gilbert's response is not known, but the council of Soissons followed in 1121.

Goswin, St   (*c.*1086–1165)

Prior of St Médard in Soissons 1121. Held Abelard under house arrest there after his condemnation at the council of Soissons. Goswin's biography describes Abelard as an untamed 'unicorn' (*rhinoceros*). Goswin had challenged Abelard in his own school at Mont Sainte Geneviève *c.*1112. Abbot of Anchin 1130–65.

Guy of Castello   (died 1144)

Suspected by St Bernard of being a defender of Abelard at the Roman curia 1140. Possessed copies of Abelard's *Theologia* and *Sic et Non*. The first official of the Roman curia to be entitled 'Master'. Cardinal of St Maria in Via Lata from 1127. Present at Morigny with Abelard 1131. On a papal mission in France *c*.1140. Elected pope as Celestine II 1143.

Heloise   (*c*.1090–*c*.1164)

Wife of Abelard and mother of Astralabe. Daughter of Hersindis. Father unknown. Niece and ward of Fulbert, canon of Notre-Dame. Educated at the convent of Argenteuil and the cathedral of Notre-Dame. Married *c*.1118. Ordered by Abelard to take the veil at Argenteuil when he was castrated *c*.1118. Prioress *c*.1123. Expelled from Argenteuil by Suger of St Denis 1129. Abelard gave her his hermitage of the Paraclete for a new convent, of which she was prioress and then abbess. Innocent II took her and her nuns under papal protection 1131. Peter the Venerable, abbot of Cluny, returned Abelard's body to her at the Paraclete in person *c*.1144.

Hugh of St Victor   (*c*.1096–1141)

Coupled with Abelard in some monastic obituaries as 'the two lights of the Latins in France'. Prior and master of the school of St Victor 1133–41. Canon of St Victor from *c*.1115 or later. Spiritual successor of William of Champeaux, founder of the school. Prolific and original author and teacher. In his *Didascalicon* (*c*.1127) Abelard was perhaps the target of Hugh's remarks about arrogant self-taught students and monks who persisted in teaching in the schools.

Hyacinth Boboni   (*c*.1100–98)

Official of the papal curia and supporter of Abelard. He may have been in Paris with Abelard and Arnold of Brescia at the time of the council of Sens 1140. St Bernard complained of him to Innocent II. His support for Abelard is confirmed by John of Salisbury. He had been an adherent of Innocent's rival, the Antipope Anacletus II. He came from the Roman family of Boboni-Orsini. Witnessed papal documents from 1121. Prior of subdeacons at St John Lateran. Promoted cardinal, probably by Celestine II, 1144. Headed numerous legations, particularly to France. Elected pope as Celestine III 1191–8.

Innocent II   (pope 1130–43)

Condemned Abelard before he reached Rome to appeal against his trial at Sens 1140. Gregory Papereschi (a Roman family), promoted cardinal 1116. With Abelard's former master, William of Champeaux, negotiated the Concordat of Worms 1122. Double election in Rome of Innocent II and Anacletus II in 1130. Innocent II fled to France, where he won the support of St Bernard,

Geoffrey bishop of Chartres and King Louis VI. Abelard was present when he dedicated the abbey church of Morigny 1131. Returned to Italy 1132 and secured his position in the north at the council of Pisa 1135. Reasserted papal authority over the whole Roman Church at the second Lateran Council 1139 (following Anacletus II's death 1138). St Bernard portrayed Abelard to him as a supporter of the antipope and a threat to all ecclesiastical authority.

Ivo of Chartres, St (c.1040–1115)

Threatened Abelard's master, Roscelin, with stoning at Chartres c.1093 and attacked his putative patron, Stephen de Garlande, 1101. Canon lawyer and moralist, particularly influential in Paris and therefore indirectly on Abelard's career. Bishop of Chartres 1090–1115. Galo and Gilbert, bishops of Paris 1104–23, were his protégés. Ivo's *Decretum* and *Panormia* 1094–5 discussed clerical status and other matters which would bear on Abelard's marriage to Heloise 20 years later. Named as one of the three 'modern masters' in the *Liber Pancrisis* c.1120, together with Abelard's enemies, William of Champeaux and Anselm of Laon.

Jocelin, Bishop of Soissons (bishop 1126–52)

Warned St Goswin that Abelard 'acted more often like a jester than a professor' c.1112. Taught logic at Bourges. Archdeacon of Bourges and then of Soissons c.1115. Bishop of Soissons from 1126. Ally of Suger of St Denis and St Bernard. Signatory of Abelard's condemnation at Sens 1140.

John of Salisbury (c.1115–80)

Described Abelard as 'a lucid teacher, admired by everybody'. John was his student in logic at Mont Sainte Geneviève 1136. His *Metalogicon* 1159 includes memoirs of his student days. Secretary of Thomas Becket 1162–70. Bishop of Chartres 1176–80.

Norbert, St (c.1080–1134)

Described by Abelard as being 'bloated with the false name of religion'. Reformer and preacher, founder of the Premonstratensian Canons 1121. Probably rightly identified in the 'history of calamities' with the 'new apostle', who had revived 'the life of the canons regular' and who allegedly slandered Abelard in the mid-1120s. Appointed archbishop of Magdeburg 1126, he returned to mainstream ecclesiastical politics when he accompanied the Emperor Lothar II to Italy 1132. He was imperial chancellor of Italy at the time of his death.

Otto of Freising (c.1110–58)

Included a memoir of Abelard in his *Deeds of the Emperor Frederick* [*Barbarossa*] 1152–60. Presumed to have been a student of Abelard's in Paris c.1133. Bishop of Freising 1137–58.

Peter the Venerable   (c.1092–1156)

Abelard's protector after his condemnation at the council of Sens 1140. Abbot of Cluny 1122–56. In dispute with St Bernard over the merits of the Cistercian and Cluniac orders c.1128. Consecration of the completed abbey church at Cluny by Innocent II 1130. In dispute with St Bernard over whether a Cistercian or a Cluniac should be bishop of Langres 1138–9. Attended Innocent II's Lateran Council 1139. Professed Abelard as a monk of Cluny after his condemnation by Innocent II 1140. Negotiated a reconciliation between St Bernard and Abelard and got Abelard readmitted to 'apostolic grace' in Rome c.1140. Told Heloise of Abelard's death and of his admiration for her since his adolescence. Brought Abelard's body to her for burial c.1144. Wrote Abelard's epitaph. Attempted a settlement with St Bernard of current disputes between Cistercians and Cluniacs 1144. St Bernard apologized to Peter the Venerable for his acrimonious language about him (but not about Abelard) 1149.

Roscelin of Compiègne   (c.1050–c.1125)

Claimed to have taught Abelard 'for a long time': 'from boyhood up until youth' (in the period c.1093–c.1099). Abelard makes no mention of him in his 'history of calamities'. Otto of Freising says he introduced Nominalism into logic and was Abelard's first teacher. Accused of tritheism at the council of Soissons 1092. Expelled from France 1092 and from England c.1093. St Anselm wrote 'On the Incarnation of the Word' against him c.1093–c.1095. Threatened with stoning and accused of being a relapsed heretic by Ivo of Chartres. Roscelin claimed he was well received in Rome (? in the pontificate of Paschal II 1099–1118). He was a canon of Besançon, as well as of Loches and Tours where he taught Abelard. Abelard repudiated him and asked Gilbert bishop of Paris to convene an assembly to judge between them c.1120. Roscelin's only definite extant work is his letter attacking Abelard c.1120.

Stephen de Garlande   (c.1070–c.1148)

Putative patron of Abelard. One of five brothers, all connected with the king's court. Described by Hildebert of Lavardin as 'first among the courtiers', by the Morigny chronicler as 'second only to the king', and by St Bernard as 'a bad smell' because he acted simultaneously as a cleric and a knight. Built a great house and chapel on the northern side of the cloister of Notre-Dame. Canon of Notre-Dame when Abelard first arrived in Paris c.1100. Nominated by Philip I to the bishopric of Beauvais 1101; but Ivo of Chartres successfully objected to Rome that he was an adulterer, an excommunicate and an illiterate layman. Archdeacon of Notre-Dame 1104. Chancellor of Philip I 1105–6. Chancellor of Louis VI 1108. Dean of the abbey of Sainte Geneviève (Abelard's school) from 1111. Acquired the deanery of Orléans by promoting Dean Hugh to the bishopric of Laon, when Abelard went to study in Laon 1113. Seneschal (high steward) of Louis VI 1120. Negotiated on Abelard's behalf with Suger abbot of St Denis 1122. Dismissed from all his royal offices 1127. Restored as chancellor c.1133, the time when Abelard probably returned to Paris from Brittany. Fell from power on the death of Louis VI 1137. Retired to the abbey of St Victor c.1140. Stephen's fall from royal favour and his joining the rival school of St Victor may have facilitated Abelard's removal from Paris and prosecution at the council of Sens 1140.

Suger, Abbot of St Denis   (c.1081–1151)

In dispute with Abelard and Heloise in the 1120s. A monk of St Denis since childhood c.1090, though educated outside the abbey. Abbot from 1122. Negotiated with Stephen de Garlande a compromise on Abelard's status as a monk of St Denis 1122. Reclaimed the convent of Argenteuil for St Denis, expelling Heloise and her nuns 1129. Adviser of Louis VI, whose biography he wrote, and also of Louis VII. Does not seem to have been involved in Abelard's trial at Sens 1140; this is the time when he was rebuilding the abbey church of St Denis, as described in his book of 1145.

Thibaud, Count of Champagne   (died 1152)

Holder of many titles. Generally styled 'Count of Champagne' because he primarily resided there. Count of Blois and Chartres 1107–52. Count of Champagne, Provins and Meaux. Count of Troyes from 1125. Elder brother of Stephen king of England 1135–54. Frequently at war with the kings of France. In 1121 Abelard fled to Thibaud's fortress at Provins, when he was accused of disparaging St Denis and the French crown. Abelard remained in Thibaud's lands until he went to Brittany c.1125–c.1127. As count of Champagne, Thibaud confirmed gifts to Heloise at the Paraclete in the 1130s and 1140s. Seignorial patron of St Bernard as well as of Abelard. Present at Abelard's trial at the council of Sens 1140.

Thierry of Chartres   (died after 1156)

Identified with the Master Thierry who, according to Abelard, jeered at the papal legate at his trial at Soissons 1121. Brother of Bernard of Chartres and a Breton like Abelard, according to Otto of Freising. Chancellor of Chartres in the 1140s. Famed for his erudition in the Liberal Arts.

Thomas of Morigny   (c.1080–c.1145)

May have been responsible for drawing up the charges (the 'heads of heresies') for Abelard's trial at the council of Sens 1140. Likewise credited with producing for St Bernard a rejoinder to Abelard's *Apologia*: 'With his *Apologia* he has made the *Theologia* worse, adding new errors to the old ones'. Abbot of Morigny 1110–39. Received Abelard there 1131; claimed to have been 'in the closest friendship' with him. Expelled from Morigny by the archbishop of Sens as a consequence of its dispute with Notre-Dame of Étampes 1139. Given asylum in Paris at the priory of St Martin-des-Champs 1140. Transferred his allegiance to St Bernard, perhaps in the hope of being reinstated as abbot of

Morigny. Withdrew/expelled from St Martin-des-Champs 1144. Died at Colombes c.1145.

Walter of Mortagne (c.1100-74)

Logician. His letter to Abelard in the 1130s preceded William of St Thierry and St Bernard in questioning Abelard's writings on the Trinity and the meaning of sin. Described Abelard as 'of sufficiently wide reading, but not so adequate in solving questions'. Student of Anselm of Laon. Set up a school in Reims in competition with Alberic of Reims c.1120. Bishop of Laon 1155-74.

William of Champeaux (c.1070-1122)

Abelard's master and rival in Paris c.1100-1113. Student of Anselm of Laon. Royal counsellor. Archdeacon of Paris and canon of Notre-Dame. Left Notre-Dame to found a community of regular canons and a school at the abbey of St Victor, adjoining Paris, c.1105. Abelard claimed to have successfully challenged him there on the question of universals c.1108. Left Paris to be bishop of Châlons-sur-Marne 1113. Patron of St Bernard in his pioneering days at Clairvaux 1115-20. Negotiator of the Concordat of Worms on behalf of the Papacy 1120-2 (see Innocent II above). As founder of the school of St Victor, patron of St Bernard and agent of the Papacy, William's influence long outlived him and may have animated Abelard's prosecutors at Soissons and Sens. Named, with Anselm of Laon and Ivo of Chartres, as one of the three 'modern masters' in the *Liber Pancrisis* c.1120.

William of St Thierry (c.1075-1148)

Initiated Abelard's prosecution at the council of Sens in 1140 by sending Geoffrey bishop of Chartres and St Bernard a list of heretical statements, allegedly collected from Abelard's works. Born in Liège. Monk of St Niçaise in Reims c.1095. Biographer of St Bernard, with whom he began his friendship c.1119. Abbot of St Thierry near Reims 1121-c.1135. Probably present at Abelard's trial at Soissons, as he witnessed a document along with Cono of Praeneste at Soissons 1121. St Bernard addressed his *Apologia* against the Cluniacs to him c.1127. Resigned his abbacy to become a Cistercian monk at Signy 1135-48. Wrote a *Disputation* against Abelard, as well as his accusatory letter to St Bernard, c.1140. Claimed that 'I too loved him'. Wrote on many of the same subjects as Abelard: faith, God's love, monastic ideals, redemption, self-knowledge, St Paul's Epistle to the Romans, the Trinity. Followed his success against Abelard by writing against 'The Errors of William of Conches' c.1141.

Abbreviations Used in the Notes

Biblical references are to the Latin 'Vulgate' *Biblia Sacra*, Vatican edition (1592).

Berengar of Poitiers
'Apologia' ed. R. M. Thomson, in *Mediaeval Studies* 42 (1980), pp. 111–33.

Buytaert CCCM
E. M. Buytaert ed., *Petri Abaelardi Opera Theologica*, Corpus Christianorum Continuatio Mediaevalis, vols 11 and 12 (1969).

Checklist
J. Barrow, C. S. F. Burnett, D. E. Luscombe, 'A Checklist of the MSS Containing the Writings of Abelard and Heloise and Other Associated Works', *Revue d'Histoire des Textes* 14–15 (1984–5), pp. 183–302.

'Cluny conference'
Pierre Abélard – Pierre le Vénérable ed. R. Louis, J. Jolivet, J. Châtillon (1975).

Confession of Faith to Heloise
Ed. C. S. F. Burnett, in *Mittellateinisches Jahrbuch* 21 (1986), pp. 152–3.

Confessio 'Universis'
Ed. C. S. F. Burnett, in *Mediaeval Studies* 48 (1986), pp. 111–38.

Dialectica
Ed. L. M. de Rijk, 2nd edn (1970).

Dialogue
Dialogus inter Philosophum, Judaeum et Christianum ed. R. Thomas (1970).

Dronke, *Philosophy*
P. Dronke, ed., *A History of Twelfth-Century Western Philosophy* (1988).

Dronke, *Testimonies*	P. Dronke, *Abelard and Heloise in Medieval Testimonies* (1976).
Dronke, *Women Writers*	P. Dronke, *Women Writers of the Middle Ages* (1984).
Epitaph	Peter the Venerable's epitaph for Abelard, ed. C. J. Mews and C. S. F. Burnett, in *Studia Monastica* 27 (1985), p. 65.
Ethics	*Peter Abelard's 'Ethics'* ed. D. E. Luscombe (1971).
Fulk of Deuil	Letter to Abelard, ed. V. Cousin, in *Opera Petri Abaelardi* (1859), vol. 1, pp. 703–7.
Gilson, *Heloise and Abelard*	É. Gilson, *Heloise and Abelard* trans. L. K. Shook (1953).
Goswin	*Vita Gosuini*, extracts reprinted by M. Bouquet ed. *Recueil des historiens de la France* 14 (1806), pp. 442–6.
Guibert de Nogent	*Autobiographie* ed. E. R. Labande (1981).
Heloise i, ii	Heloise's first two letters, ed. J. Monfrin in *Historia Calamitatum*, pp. 111–24.
Heloise iii	Heloise's third letter, ed. J. T. Muckle, in *Mediaeval Studies* 17 (1955), pp. 241–53.
Historia Calamitatum	Ed. J. Monfrin, 4th edn (1978).
Hymns	Ed. J. Szoverffy (1975).
John of Salisbury	*Metalogicon* ed. J. B. Hall (1991).
Letter ed. Klibansky	Abelard to Bernard of Clairvaux, in *Medieval and Renaissance Studies* 5 (1961), pp. 6–7.
Letter ed. McLaughlin	Abelard's 'Rule for Religious Women', ed. T. P. McLaughlin, in *Mediaeval Studies* 18 (1956), pp. 241–92.
Letters ed. Muckle	Letters of Abelard to Heloise, ed. J. T. Muckle, in *Mediaeval Studies* 15 (1953), pp. 73–7, 82–94; and 17 (1955), pp. 240–81.

Letters ed. Smits

Peter Abelard, Letters IX–XIV, ed. E. R. Smits (1983).

Luscombe, *School*

D. E. Luscombe, *The School of Peter Abelard* (1969).

Luscombe (1979)

D. E. Luscombe, *Peter Abelard* Historical Association (1979).

Luscombe (1988)

'From Paris to the Paraclete', *Proceedings of the British Academy* 74 (1988), pp. 247–83.

Marenbon, 'A Life'

J. Marenbon, *The Philosophy of Peter Abelard* (1997), ch. 1.

McLeod, *Heloise*

E. McLeod, *Heloise, a Biography* 2nd edn (1971).

Mews CCCM

E. M. Buytaert and C. J. Mews eds, *Petri Abaelardi Opera Theologica*, Corpus Christianorum Continuatio Mediaevalis, vol. 13 (1987).

Mews, 'Lists of Heresies'

C. J. Mews, 'The Lists of Heresies Imputed to Peter Abelard', *Revue Bénédictine* 95 (1985), pp. 73–110.

Mews, 'On Dating'

C. J. Mews, 'On Dating the Works of Peter Abelard', *Archives d'Histoire Doctrinale et Littéraire du Moyen Age* 52 (1985), pp. 73–134.

Mews (1995)

'Peter Abelard', *Authors of the Middle Ages* ed. P. J. Geary, vol. 2, no. 5 (1995).

Migne, *PL*

Patrologiae: Series Latina ed. J. P. Migne, vols 1–217 (1843–73).

Migne, *PL* 178

'Petri Abaelardi Opera Omnia', *Patrologiae: Series Latina* ed. J. P. Migne, vol. 178 (1855).

'Nantes conference'

Abélard en son temps ed. J. Jolivet (1982).

Otto of Freising

Gesta Frederici ed. F. J. Schmale (1965).

Peter the Venerable

The Letters of Peter the Venerable ed. G. Constable (1967), 2 vols.

Roscelin

Letter to Abelard, ed. J. Reiners, in *Der Nominalismus in der Frühscholastik* (1910), pp. 63–80.

St Bernard	*Sancti Bernardi Opera*, ed. J. Leclercq, C. H. Talbot, H. Rochais (1957–77), 8 vols.
Sic et Non	Ed. B. B. Boyer and R. McKeon (1976).
Soliloquium	Ed. C. S. F. Burnett, in *Studi Medievali* 25 (1984), pp. 857–94.
Suger, *Louis VI*	*Vie de Louis VI le gros*, ed. H. Waquet (1929).
'Trier conference'	*Trierer Theologische Studien* 38 (1980), ed. R. Thomas.
William of St Thierry	Letter to St Bernard, ed. J. Leclercq, in *Revue Bénédictine* 79 (1969), pp. 377–8.

Notes

CHAPTER 1: THE STORY OF ABELARD

1 Heloise i, p. 115, lines 186–93. The best concise account of Abelard's life is: Marenbon, 'A Life', pp. 7–35.

2 *Historia Calamitatum*, lines 1249–58 (citing Psalm 60, verse 3); 'de calamitatum mearum hystoria', lines 1561–2.

3 J. Leclercq, 'The Monastic Crisis', in N. Hunt ed. *Cluniac Monasticism* (1971), p. 220. St Bernard, letter 166, vol. 7, p. 377, line 12.

4 Peter the Venerable, letter 115, p. 306, line 24.

5 Fulk of Deuil, pp. 703–4.

6 See ch. 3, nn. 4–5 below.

7 *Historia Calamitatum*, lines 254–5.

8 Otto of Freising, p. 224, lines 24–8.

9 Otto of Freising, p. 226, lines 6–7.

10 *Historia Calamitatum*, line 332.

11 *Historia Calamitatum*, lines 395–9.

12 *Historia Calamitatum*, lines 576–8. Marenbon, 'A Life', p. 15, n. 32.

13 *Historia Calamitatum*, lines 588–9.

14 *Historia Calamitatum*, lines 623–9.

15 Sermon no. 33, Migne, *PL* 178, col. 583b.

16 Heloise i, p. 116, lines 247–8.

17 *Historia Calamitatum*, lines 356–7. Heloise i, p. 117, lines 270–1.

18 Otto of Freising, p. 226, lines 8–9.

19 *Historia Calamitatum*, line 693.

20 Epitaph, p. 65.

21 *Dialogue*, pp. 42–3, lines 50–1, 45.

22 St Bernard, letter 190, vol. 8, p. 24, lines 24–5.

23 St Bernard, letter 190, vol. 8, p. 27, line 3.

24 St Bernard, letter 190, vol. 8, p. 27, lines 10–12.

25 St Bernard, letter 193, vol. 8, p. 44, line 18.

26 *Sic et Non*, p. 103, lines 338–9.

27 *Sic et Non*, p. 89, line 2.

28   St Bernard, letter 188, vol. 8, p. 11, line 7.
29   St Bernard, letter 190, vol. 8, p. 18, lines 4–6.
30   St Bernard, letter 332, vol. 8, p. 271, lines 12–14.
31   *Sic et Non*, p. 103, lines 332–3.
32   St Bernard, letter 188, vol. 8, p. 11, line 3.
33   St Bernard, letter 188, vol. 8, p. 11, line 4.
34   Innocent II, ed. J. Leclercq, in *Revue Bénédictine*, 79 (1969), p. 379; and see ch. 2, n. 9; ch. 13, n. 184 below.
35   Confessio 'Universis', p. 138, lines 6–7.
36   Hymns, no. 44, p. 109.
37   Donne, 'Holy Sonnets', no. 14.
38   St Bernard, letter 187. Letter ed. Klibansky.
39   Otto of Freising, p. 228, lines 2–4.
40   R. W. Southern, *Medieval Humanism* (1970), p. 94.
41   Heloise ii, p. 122, line 221.
42   Letters ed. Muckle, p. 91, lines 1–3.
43   Heloise ii, p. 121, lines 170–3; and see ch. 8, n. 108 below.
44   Letters ed. Muckle, p. 91, lines 10–14.
45   Heloise iii, pp. 241–2.
46   Heloise i, p. 111, lines 2–3.
47   Roscelin, p. 80, lines 8–11; and see ch. 4, n. 66 below.
48   *Historia Calamitatum*, line 281.
49   *Historia Calamitatum*, line 280.
50   Roscelin, p. 78, line 1.
51   Otloh, Migne, *PL* 146, col. 32b.
52   *Ethics*, p. 66, lines 16–19; p. 62, lines 1–5; p. 64, line 23; Psalm 36, verse 6.
53   Archpoet, verse 1, in H. Waddell, *Medieval Latin Lyrics* 4th edn (1933), p. 182.
54   Heloise ii, p. 124, lines 286–7. Archpoet, verse 12.
55   For the MSS, see Monfrin in *Historia Calamitatum*, pp. 8ff. and C. J. Mews, 'La bibliothèque du Paraclet', *Studia Monastica* 27 (1985), pp. 44–5. See also R. W. Southern, 'The Letters of Abelard and Heloise', *Medieval Humanism* (1970), pp. 103–4. Recent and reliable discussions of the forgery question are: Mews (1995), pp. 20–6, and J. Marenbon, 'The Letters of Abelard and Heloise', in *The Philosophy of Peter Abelard* (1997), pp. 82–93.
56   *Dialogue*, p. 51.
57   D. W. Robertson, *Abelard and Heloise* (1972), pp. 216–17. E. McLeod, *Heloise* (1938), p. 242.
58   Waddell, *Medieval Latin Lyrics*, p. 200.
59   St Bernard, letter 193, vol. 8, p. 44, line 17.
60   Goswin, p. 442e.
61   Otto of Freising, p. 226, lines 6–7.
62   Confession of Faith to Heloise, p. 152; and ch. 5, n. 1 below.
63   W. H. Auden, *Selected Poems* ed. E. Mandelson (1979), p. 82.

CHAPTER 2: *SCIENTIA* – 'KNOWLEDGE'

1   See ch. 5, n. 4 below.
2   I Corinthians, ch. 8, verse 1. For Goliath see ch. 7, nn. 81–3 below.
3   St Bernard, letter 188, vol. 8, p. 11, line 22 – p. 12, line 1.
4   John of Salisbury, book 2, ch. 10, p. 70, lines 5–6.
5   *The 'Historia Regum Britannie' of Geoffrey of Monmouth*, ed. N. Wright
    (1985), p. 75, no. 11 (Lion of Justice), p. 76, no. 12 (the Lion's cubs, tears
    of the night), trans. L. Thorpe, *History of the Kings of Britain* (1966),
    p. 174.
6   St Bernard, letter 190, vol. 8, p. 26, lines 1–8.
7   *Ethics*, p. 38, lines 2–3.
8   *Etymologiae* book 8, ch. 11, ed. Lindsay (1911), part 15.
9   See ch. 13, n. 184 below; and Luscombe, *School*, pp. 2–3 (citing Alberic of
    Tre Fontane).
10 See ch. 13, n. 116 below.
11 See ch. 1, n. 2 above.
12 See ch. 7, n. 24 below. *Dialectica*, p. 128, lines 28–32. *Historia Calamita-*
    tum, line 1244; and see ch. 11, n. 155 below.
13 See ch. 7, n. 22 below.
14 Ed. C. J. Mews, in *Traditio* 44 (1988), pp. 172–3.
15 *Theologia Scholarium*, Mews CCCM, pp. 373–4, lines 1569–77.
16 *Dialectica*, p. 59. Mews, in *Traditio* 24 (1988), p. 182.
17 O. von Simson, *The Gothic Cathedral* 2nd edn (1962), pp. 37–8.
18 M. Huglo, 'Abélard, poète et musicien', *Cahiers de civilisation médiévale*
    22 (1979), p. 355. For Abelard's songs, see ch. 7, n. 28 below. To the
    bibliography on Abelard's music provided by Mews (1995), pp. 66–72,
    86–7, add: F. Laurenzi, *Le poesie ritmiche di Pietro Abelardo* (1991).
19 *Didascalicon* ed. C. H. Buttimer (1939), book 2, ch. 12, p. 32.
20 *Theologia Summi Boni*, Mews CCCM, p. 117, lines 78–9.
21 *Didascalicon* prologue, p. 2, lines 9–11.
22 John of Salisbury, book 3, ch. 4, p. 116, lines 47–8.
23 Clanchy, 'Moderni', *Speculum* 50 (1975), p. 672. *Dialogue*, p. 45.
24 *Sic et Non*, p. 103, line 332.
25 *Sic et Non*, p. 103, lines 338–9.
26 St Bernard, letter 190, vol. 8, p. 25, lines 15–17.
27 St Bernard, letter 190, vol. 8, p. 25, lines 12–13.
28 *Theologia Scholarium*, Mews CCCM, p. 318, line 5.
29 St Bernard, letter 190, vol. 8, p. 25, lines 13–15.
30 Otto of Freising, p. 226, line 12.
31 *Tractatus de Intellectibus* ed. L. U. Ulivi (1976), p. 108, lines 34–5.
32 *Historia Calamitatum*, lines 698–700; and see ch. 5, n. 73 and ch. 12,
    nn. 15–17, 114–16 below.
33 *Theologia Scholarium*, Mews CCCM, p. 436, book 2, lines 907–8.

34 *Tractatus de Intellectibus* p. 108, lines 35–6.
35 St Bernard, letter 338, vol. 8, p. 278, lines 1–2.
36 *St Anselmi Opera* ed. F. S. Schmitt (1946), vol. 2, pp. 6–8.
37 St Bernard, sermons on Canticles, no. 36, vol. 2, pp. 3–4.
38 St Bernard, letter 106, vol. 7, pp. 266–7.
39 St Bernard, letter 106, vol. 7, p. 266, lines 4–6.
40 *Sic et Non*, p. 89, line 1.
41 *De Arca Noe Morali*, book 1, ch. 2, cited by B. Smalley, *The Study of the Bible in the Middle Ages* 2nd edn (1952), p. 96. P. Sicard, *Hugues de St Victor* (1991), colour plate 6.
42 See ch. 12, n. 121 below; and J. Leclercq, *Monks on Marriage* (1982).
43 *Soliloquium*, p. 889.
44 Fulk of Deuil, p. 704; and see ch. 1, n. 5 above.
45 St Bernard, letter 190, vol. 8, p. 17, line 17.

CHAPTER 3: LITERATE

1   *Rule of St Benedict* c.48.
2   C. F. R. de Hamel, *A History of Illuminated MSS* (1986), chs 3 and 4. M. T. Gibson, *The Bible in the Latin West* (1993), plates 14 and 17.
3   See ch. 2, n. 9 above, and ch. 13, n. 183 below.
4   Luscombe, *School*, p. 91.
5   *Ethics*, p. xliii.
6   Clanchy, *From Memory to Written Record* 2nd edn (1993), p. 117.
7   Letters ed. Muckle, p. 90.
8   *Historia Calamitatum*, lines 469–70.
9   *Historia Calamitatum*, line 530; and see ch. 6, n. 23 and ch. 10, n. 28 below.
10 Letters ed. Muckle, p. 246; Letter ed. McLaughlin, p. 272.
11 *Historia Calamitatum*, lines 478–9.
12 Sermon no. 33. Migne, *PL* 178, col. 582d.
13 *Historia Calamitatum*, line 16.
14 *Historia Calamitatum*, line 559.
15 Letters ed. Smits, no. 9, p. 221, lines 48–55.
16 Peter the Venerable, letter 115, vol. 1, pp. 303–4; and see ch. 9, n. 4 below.
17 Heloise, ii, p. 123, line 261 – p. 124, line 288.
18 *Historia Calamitatum*, lines 305–6, and see C. N. L. Brooke, *The Medieval Idea of Marriage* (1989), chs 3, 4.
19 For Stephen de Garlande, see ch. 9, n. 81 below.
20 See ch. 9, n. 79 below.
21 R. W. Southern, *Scholastic Humanism and the Unification of Europe*, vol. 1: *Foundations* (1995), p. 202.
22 Heloise iii, p. 241.
23 See ch. 12, n. 90 below.
24 *Historia Calamitatum*, lines 19–25; and see ch. 7, n. 52 below.

25 Guibert de Nogent, book 1, ch. 6, p. 18; and see ch. 7, n. 56 below.
26 *Historia Calamitatum*, lines 285–6.
27 *Historia Calamitatum*, lines 24–5.
28 See ch. 7, n. 103 below.
29 *Historia Calamitatum*, lines 155–8.
30 *Historia Calamitatum*, lines 28–9.
31 *Historia Calamitatum*, lines 16–17.
32 *Dialogue*, p. 45, line 121.
33 See ch. 11, n. 114 below.
34 Heloise i, p. 111, line 2; ii, p. 117, line 1.
35 See ch. 8, nn. 4–9 below.
36 S. Reynolds, *Medieval Reading: Grammar, Rhetoric and the Classical Text* (1996).
37 R. Thomson, *William of Malmesbury* (1987), p. 7.
38 John of Salisbury, book 1, ch. 24, p. 52, lines 48–9.
39 Letter 101, Migne, *PL* 207, col. 312. H. O. Taylor, *The Mediaeval Mind* 4th edn (1925), vol. 2, p. 160.
40 See ch. 2, n. 22 above.
41 P. Dronke, *Poetic Individuality* 2nd edn (1986), p. 122.
42 D. L. Douie and D. H. Farmer eds, *Magna Vita S. Hugonis* (1961), p. 1.
43 See ch. 11, nn. 155, 156 below.
44 P. Bec, *Nouvelle anthologie de la lyrique occitane* 2nd edn (1972), p. 179; and see ch. 7, nn. 25, 26 below.
45 Heloise i, p. 115, line 202; and see ch. 7, n. 28 below.
46 Epitaph, p. 65.
47 E. R. Curtius, *European Literature and the Latin Middle Ages* (1953), p. 385.
48 *Historia Calamitatum*, line 21; and see nn. 24, 27 above.
49 *Oeuvres poétiques* ed. P. Abrahams (1926), p. 339. F. J. E. Raby, *History of Secular Latin Poetry* 2nd edn (1957), vol. i, p. 343.
50 *Oeuvres poétiques*, p. 344. Dronke, *Women Writers*, p. 88.
51 J. Boswell, *Christianity, Social Tolerance and Homosexuality* (1980), p. 237.
52 *Historia Calamitatum*, lines 298–9.
53 Raby, *History of Secular Latin Poetry*, vol. i, p. 334.
54 Heloise i, p. 114, lines 157–61; p. 116, lines 247–8.
55 Berengar of Poitiers, p. 111, line 9.
56 Migne, *PL* 186, col. 1195c–d.
57 F. Barlow, *The English Church 1066–1154* (1979), p. 242.
58 Guibert de Nogent, book 1, ch. 17, pp. 134–8.
59 *Theologia Christiana* Buytaert CCCM, p. 188, line 1878.
60 *Theologia Christiana* Buytaert CCCM, pp. 188–9, lines 1884–7.
61 *Theologia Christiana* Buytaert CCCM, p. 192, line 1972.
62 *Theologia Christiana* Buytaert CCCM, p. 192, lines 1968–70.
63 See ch. 7, n. 16 below.
64 *Theologia Scholarium* Mews CCCM, p. 418, lines 355–7. *Theologia Christiana* Buytaert CCCM, p. 188, lines 1870–2.

65 *Theologia Scholarium* Mews CCCM, p. 422, lines 471–3.
66 *Theologia Scholarium* Mews CCCM, p. 422, lines 480–1.
67 St Bernard, 'Apologia', ch. 12, para. 29, vol. 3, p. 106, lines 16–17.
68 Confession of Faith to Heloise, p. 153; and see ch. 8, nn. 123–4 and ch. 14, n. 56 below.
69 Dronke, *Testimonies*, p. 36; and see ch. 7, n. 103 below.
70 *Historia Calamitatum*, lines 285–6; and see n. 26 above.
71 *Anti-Claudianus* book ii, lines 403–4, ed. R. Bossuat (1955), p. 84.
72 Guibert de Nogent, book 1, ch. 5, p. 30.
73 *Historia Calamitatum*, lines 326–9.
74 *Historia Calamitatum*, lines 339–42.
75 *Historia Calamitatum*, lines 342–4.
76 Eadmer, *Life of St Anselm*, ch. 32, ed. R. W. Southern (1962), pp. 37–8.
77 Eadmer, p. 38.
78 Letters ed. Smits, no. 9, p. 219, lines 19–20.
79 Orderic Vitalis, book 5, ed. M. Chibnall (1968–80), pp. 6–9.
80 Martianus Capella, ch. 261, ed. A. Dick (1925), p. 96, lines 4–6.
81 Guibert de Nogent, book 1, ch. 4, p. 26.
82 Letter ed. McLaughlin, p. 289.
83 Letter ed. McLaughlin, p. 287.
84 *Scivias* (Corpus Christianorum 1978), p. 4, lines 30–5.
85 Letters ed. Smits, no. 9, p. 224, lines 123–5.
86 Clanchy, *From Memory* 2nd edn (1993), p. 187.
87 Mews in *Traditio* 44 (1988) p. 172, line 3 of citation.
88 Clanchy, *From Memory* 2nd edn (1993), p. 178.
89 John of Salisbury, book 1, ch. 13, p. 32, line 24. For an alternative translation, see S. Reynolds, *Medieval Reading* (1996), p. 8.
90 *Cosmographia* ch. 14, ed. Dronke, p. 152, lines 78–9.
91 *Historia Calamitatum*, lines 12–13.
92 B. Stock, *The Implications of Literacy* (1983), part ii.

CHAPTER 4: MASTER

1   Peter the Venerable, letter 115, pp. 306, 307; letter 168, p. 401.
2   N. Wireker, *Speculum Stultorum* (1960), lines 1205–9.
3   St Bernard, letter nos 192, 193, 330, 334, 338 call Abelard 'Magister', whereas letter nos 331, 332, 333, 335 do not.
4   For these letters of Innocent II, see ch. 13, n. 183 below.
5   Heloise i, p. 111, lines 2–3; ii, p. 117, line 275; iii, p. 241. See also ch. 1, n. 46 above and ch. 8, nn. 5, 8 below.
6   L. T. Topsfield, *Troubadours and Love* (1975), p. 16.
7   R. Foreville and G. Keir, *The Book of St Gilbert* (1987), p. 14.
8   *Theologia Christiana* Buytaert CCCM, p. 207, lines 380–5.
9   C. R. Cheney, *Texts and Studies* (1973), pp. 46–7.
10 *Ethics*, p. 64. Matthew, ch. 8, verse 19.

11 *Rule of St Benedict*, prologue.
12 St Bernard, letter 106, vol. 8, p. 266, lines 15–16.
13 *Theologia Christiana* Buytaert CCCM, p. 148, lines 552–4. Matthew, ch. 23, verse 10.
14 Prayer no. 17, *St Anselmi Opera* ed. F. S. Schmitt (1946), vol. 3, p. 68, line 14.
15 R. H. Bautier, in 'Nantes conference', pp. 53–77. See also Luscombe (1988), pp. 249–52; Mews (1995), pp. 11–12; Marenbon, 'A life', pp. 11–13.
16 Otto of Freising, p. 224, lines 28–9.
17 Roscelin, p. 63, line 4; and see ch. 13, nn. 21, 26, 31 below.
18 *Historia Calamitatum*, lines 28–9; and see ch. 13, n. 25 below.
19 *Historia Calamitatum*, line 68.
20 *Historia Calamitatum*, line 31.
21 *Historia Calamitatum*, lines 31–4.
22 *Historia Calamitatum*, lines 38–44.
23 Migne, *PL* 180, col. 41. M. B. Pranger, in *The European Dimension of St Anselm's Thinking* ed. J. Zumr and V. Herold (1993), pp. 164–5.
24 *Historia Calamitatum*, line 46.
25 *Historia Calamitatum*, lines 48–9.
26 *Historia Calamitatum*, line 54. Bautier, in 'Nantes conference', pp. 61–2. Luscombe (1988), p. 250.
27 See also ch. 7, nn. 75–80 below.
28 *Historia Calamitatum*, lines 64–5, 60–1.
29 *Historia Calamitatum*, lines 66–7.
30 *Historia Calamitatum*, lines 68–70.
31 *Historia Calamitatum*, lines 1290–1. Luke, ch. 14, verse 30.
32 *Historia Calamitatum*, line 91. O. Lottin, *Psychologie et morale* (1942), vol. 5, p. 192, lines 114, 116.
33 *Historia Calamitatum*, lines 108–9.
34 *Historia Calamitatum*, lines 117–18.
35 *Historia Calamitatum*, lines 127–8.
36 *Historia Calamitatum*, lines 130–2. See also ch. 7, n. 73 below.
37 *Historia Calamitatum*, line 152; and see ch. 7, n. 94 below.
38 *Historia Calamitatum*, line 156. See also ch. 3, n. 29 above and ch. 7, nn. 55, 56 below.
39 *Historia Calamitatum*, line 159; and see ch. 12, n. 5 below.
40 *Historia Calamitatum*, line 255.
41 John of Salisbury, book 1, ch. 5, p. 21, lines 33–4.
42 Migne, *PL* 170, cols 482–3. M. D. Chenu, *Nature, Man and Society* (1968), p. 270, n. 1.
43 R. W. Southern, 'The Schools', in *Renaissance and Renewal* ed. R. L. Benson and G. Constable (1982), p. 116, n. 6.
44 Guibert de Nogent, book 3, ch. 4, pp. 284–90; ch. 7, p. 334; ch. 10, p. 356.
45 Migne, *PL* 170, col. 437. J. H. Van Engen, *Rupert of Deutz* (1983), p. 194.
46 Guibert de Nogent, book 3, ch. 4, p. 284. John of Salisbury, book 1, ch. 5, p. 21, line 31.

47   See n. 45 above.

48   Guibert de Nogent, book 3, ch. 11; ch. 14, p. 394 (dean of Orléans). Suger, *Louis VI*, ch. 24, pp. 176–8.

49   J. W. Baldwin, *Masters, Princes and Merchants* (1970), vol. 1, pp. 151–2; vol. 2, p. 105, nn. 7, 11.

50   *Historia Calamitatum*, lines 222–3.

51   *Historia Calamitatum*, lines 241–3.

52   Heloise i, p. 115, lines 188–90.

53   Fulk of Deuil, p. 704.

54   R. W. Southern, 'The Schools', in *Renaissance and Renewal* ed. R. L. Benson and G. Constable (1982), p. 115.

55   Otto of Freising, p. 224, lines 24–5.

56   Dronke, *Philosophy*, pp. 362–3.

57   *Historia Calamitatum*, line 878.

58   *Historia Calamitatum*, lines 891, 895.

59   See n. 17 above.

60   E. H. W. Kluge, 'Roscelin', *Journal of the History of Philosophy* 14 (1976), pp. 405–7. For 'New Light on Roscelin', see also C. J. Mews, in *Vivarium* 30 (1992), pp. 5–37.

61   J. Marenbon, *Early Medieval Philosophy* (1983), pp. 134–5. Y. Iwakuma attributes a commentary on Porphyry to Roscelin, in *Traditio* 47 (1992), pp. 58–60.

62   *St Anselmi Opera* ed. Schmitt, vol. 2, pp. 9–10.

63   For writings attributed to William of Champeaux, see Marenbon, 'A Life', p. 9, n. 12. See also the *Liber Pancrisis*, n. 71 below.

64   See ch 3, n. 6 above; and Clanchy, *From Memory to Written Record* 2nd edn (1993), p. 145, n. 1.

65   John of Salisbury, book 1, ch. 24, p. 53, line 67.

66   See ch. 11, nn. 51–7 below for this 'cell' of St Denis. Mews CCCM, p. 20, dates *Dialectica* to 1117–1119. Mews (1995), p. 52, lists Abelard's references in *Dialectica* to his having already written an introduction for beginners.

67   *Historia Calamitatum*, lines 850–3; and see ch. 13, n. 63 below.

68   B. Smalley, *The Study of the Bible* 2nd edn (1952), p. 50.

69   *Historia Calamitatum*, lines 75–6. On the beginnings of the school of St Victor, see J. P. Willesme, in 'Nantes conference', pp. 95–105, and R. H. Bautier, in *L'Abbaye parisienne de St Victor* ed. J. Longère (1991), pp. 23–52.

70   Luscombe, *School*, p. 9, n. 6.

71   F. Bliemetzrieder, in *Recherches de théologie ancienne et médiévale* 1 (1929), p. 436.

72   R. H. Bautier, in 'Nantes conference', pp. 59–62.

73   Suger, *Louis VI*, ch. 14, pp. 84–6.

74   For Manegold, see: B. Smalley, *The Study of the Bible* 2nd edn (1952), p. 48; R. W. Southern, 'The Schools', in *Renaissance and Renewal* ed. R. L. Benson and G. Constable (1982), p. 124, n. 26.

75 See ch. 3, n. 47 above.
76 F. Bliemetzrieder, in *Recherches de théologie ancienne et médiévale* 1 (1929), pp. 453–4.
77 *Historia Calamitatum*, line 12.
78 O. Lottin, *Psychologie et morale* (1942), vol. 5, p. 114.
79 Lottin, *Psychologie et morale*, vol. 5, p. 185. R. W. Southern, *St Anselm* (1990), p. 205, n. 9.
80 *St Anselmi Opera* ed. Schmitt, vol. 2, p. 48, lines 5–6. Southern, *St Anselm* (1990), p. 197.
81 *St Anselmi Opera*, vol. 2, p. 48, lines 11–12.
82 *St Anselmi Opera*, vol. 2, p. 48, lines 9–11.
83 *Historia Calamitatum*, lines 693–5, 691–2; see also ch. 5, n. 73 and ch. 12, n. 15 below.
84 See ch. 12, n. 2 below.
85 *St Anselmi Opera* ed. Schmitt, vol. 1, p. 7, lines 7–9. R. W. Southern, *St Anselm* (1990), p. 118.
86 Southern, *St Anselm*, pp. 126, 134–5; and see n. 62 above.
87 *Historia Calamitatum*, lines 36–7.
88 *Historia Calamitatum*, lines 81–100; and see n. 32 above.
89 *Historia Calamitatum*, lines 262–3.
90 O. Lottin, *Psychologie et morale* (1942), vol. 5, pp. 222–3.
91 *Historia Calamitatum*, lines 44, 223.
92 Lottin, *Psychologie et morale*, vol. 5, p. 221, no. 277, lines 12–13.
93 Lottin, *Psychologie et morale*, vol. 5, p. 137. Luscombe, *School*, p. 176, n. 1.
94 *Ethics*, p. 40.
95 *Historia Calamitatum*, lines 712–13.
96 *Historia Calamitatum*, lines 186–8.
97 *Dialogue* trans. P. J. Payer (1979), p. 6, n. 12.
98 *Historia Calamitatum*, lines 181–4.
99 Epitaph, p. 65.
100 *Historia Calamitatum*, lines 207–9.
101 *Historia Calamitatum*, lines 204–7.
102 *Historia Calamitatum*, lines 164–5.
103 *Historia Calamitatum*, lines 166–71.
104 Lottin, *Psychologie et morale* (1942), vol. 5, p. 46, no. 48, lines 18–23. L. R. Muir, *Adam* Leeds Philosophical & Literary Society 13 (1970), pp. 155–204.
105 St Bernard, letter 190, vol. 8, p. 35, line 1. Buytaert CCCM, vol. 11, p. 116, lines 210–14.
106 R. W. Southern, *St Anselm* (1990), pp. 379–80.
107 See nn. 48–50 above.
108 R. W. Southern, 'The Schools', in *Renaissance and Renewal* ed. R. L. Benson and G. Constable (1982), pp. 117–18. J. R. Williams, in *Traditio* 20 (1964), pp. 98–100.

109 *Historia Calamitatum*, lines 192–5.
110 *Didascalicon* book 3, ch. 13, ed. C. H. Buttimer (1939), pp. 63–4.
111 *Sic et Non*, p. 103, lines 332, 331; and see ch. 2, n. 24 above.
112 O. Lottin, *Psychologie et morale* (1942), vol. 5, p. 176.
113 *Sic et Non*, p. 89, line 2.
114 See ch. 11, n. 75 below.
115 *Historia Calamitatum*, line 219.
116 *Historia Calamitatum*, lines 215–17.
117 John of Salisbury, book 3, ch. 1, p. 103, line 5.
118 *Historia Calamitatum*, lines 219–20.
119 C. J. Mews, in *Exemplaria* 2 (1990), p. 498, n. 54.
120 *Historia Calamitatum*, lines 200, 204.
121 B. Smalley, *The Gospels in the Schools* (1985), pp. 7, 65.
122 *Historia Calamitatum*, lines 244–5.
123 See n. 31 above.
124 *Historia Calamitatum*, lines 234–6.
125 Confessio 'Universis', p. 133, lines 16–19.
126 Smalley, *The Gospels in the Schools*, p. 7.
127 O. Lottin, *Psychologie et morale*, vol. 5, pp. 44–5, no. 47, lines 35–50.
128 *Ethics*, p. 66, lines 16–18; p. 98, lines 6–8.
129 *Ethics*, p. 6, lines 11, 18–19, 28, 31, 32–33; and see ch. 12, n. 32 below.
130 Goswin, p. 442d. See also n. 36 above.
131 Goswin, p. 442d.
132 M. Veillard-Troïekouroff, in 'Cluny conference', pp. 745–61, and in 'Nantes conference', p. 86.
133 Migne, *PL* 180, col. 43a. See also n. 23 above.
134 Migne, *PL* 180, col. 41b.
135 Goswin, p. 443b.
136 Goswin, p. 443a.
137 Clanchy, in *Journal of Ecclesiastical History* 41 (1990), pp. 5ff.
138 Goswin, p. 443b.
139 Goswin, p. 443c.
140 Goswin, p. 443b–c.
141 Goswin, p. 443c.
142 Goswin, p. 443c.
143 See ch. 7, n. 89 below.
144 *Historia Calamitatum*, lines 175–9.
145 *Historia Calamitatum*, lines 180–1.
146 Lucan, *Pharsalia*, book 1, lines 145–6, 150.
147 Goswin, p. 442d, citing Genesis, ch. 16, verse 12.
148 *Historia Calamitatum*, line 1491.
149 See n. 37 above.
150 J. Martin, 'John of Salisbury as a Classical Scholar', in *The World of John of Salisbury* ed. M. Wilks (1984), pp. 179–201.
151 *Historia Calamitatum*, line 121. Ovid, *Remedia Amoris*, line 369.

152 Ovid, *Remedia Amoris*, line 389.
153 Goswin, pp. 442–3. Macrobius, book 5, ch. 3, line 16.

Chapter 5: Logician

1 *Historia Calamitatum*, line 25. Confession of Faith to Heloise, p. 152. Abelard's writings on logic are set out and discussed by Mews (1995), pp. 26–31, 52–4, and J. Marenbon, *The Philosophy of Peter Abelard* (1997), ch. 2, pp. 36–53.

2 *Theologia Summi Boni* Mews CCCM, p. 115, lines 38–41. E. R. Smits brings together all Abelard's citations of this passage from St Augustine: Letters ed. Smits, no. xiii, p. 272, lines 24–7 and footnote.

3 Migne, *PL* 178, col. 103d. Epitaph no. 442, Checklist, p. 293. For a more enigmatic translation, see A. Gurevich, *The Origins of European Individualism* (1995), p. 143.

4 St Bernard, letter 190, vol. 8, pp. 17–18.

5 Peter the Venerable, letter 115, p. 307. Matthew, ch. 11, verse 29.

6 Migne, *PL* 178, col. 105a. Epitaph no. 448, Checklist, p. 295.

7 Confession of Faith to Heloise, p. 152.

8 St Bernard, letter 190, vol. 8, p. 22, line 7.

9 Epitaph, p. 65.

10 John of Salisbury, book 1, ch. 5, p. 20, lines 13–14.

11 John of Salisbury, book 2, ch. 10, p. 70, lines 6–7.

12 *Historia Calamitatum*, line 30.

13 *Dialectica*, pp. 88, 145, 152, 432. On the meaning of *palatinus* see also ch. 7, nn. 101–3 below.

14 John of Salisbury, book 3, ch. 4, p. 116, lines 35–9.

15 *Dialectica*, p. 146, lines 10–20. J. Marenbon surveys 'Medieval Latin Commentaries and Glosses on Aristotelian Logical Texts, before 1150 AD', in C. S. F. Burnett ed., *Glosses and Commentaries on Aristotelian Logical Texts* (1992), pp. 77–127.

16 *Historia Calamitatum*, lines 41–4, 1239.

17 See n. 1 above.

18 *Dialectica*, p. xvii.

19 *Dialectica*, p. xxiv.

20 William of St Thierry, ed. Leclercq, in *Revue Bénédictine* 79 (1969), p. 377, lines 27–8; p. 378, lines 71–4; and see ch. 13, n. 116 below.

21 *Historia Calamitatum*, lines 668–79; and see ch. 11, n. 117 below.

22 *Logica Ingredientibus*, ed. B. Geyer (1919–27), p. 2, lines 18–20.

23 *Logica Ingredientibus*, p. 3, lines 22–3, p. 4, line 17.

24 *Logica Ingredientibus*, p. 4, lines 34–5, p. 5, lines 1–2, 6–8.

25 *Logica Ingredientibus*, p. 30, lines 3–4; cf. p. 8, lines 19–21.

26 John of Salisbury, book 3, ch. 1, p. 103, line 5.

27 John of Salisbury, book 2, ch. 7, p. 66, lines 10–13.

28 D. E. Luscombe, 'Peter Abelard', in Dronke, *Philosophy*, pp. 280–2. Mews (1995), pp. 27–30, 52–4. J. Marenbon, *The Philosophy of Peter Abelard* (1997), pp. 38–9.
29 *Scritti de Logica* ed. M. Dal Pra, 2nd edn (1969), p. 155.
30 *Historia Calamitatum*, lines 64–5.
31 *Historia Calamitatum*, lines 85–91.
32 *Dialectica*, p. xxi.
33 See n. 10 above.
34 *Dialectica*, p. xvii, n. 4.
35 John of Salisbury, book 2, ch. 7, p. 66, line 26.
36 John of Salisbury, book 2, ch. 6, p. 64, lines 23–4; p. 65, lines 63–5.
37 *Logica Ingredientibus*, p. 21, lines 14–17.
38 Roscelin, p. 63, lines 3–4.
39 *Dialectica*, pp. 554–5; and see ch. 13, n. 23 below.
40 *Logica Ingredientibus*, p. 27, lines 9–15.
41 *Theologia Summi Boni* Mews CCCM, p. 122, line 224.
42 Letters ed. Smits, no. 14, p. 280, line 41; and see ch. 13, nn. 34–6, 65–7 below.
43 *Theologia Summi Boni*, p. 123, lines 232–6, 243–6.
44 *Sic et Non*, p. 103, lines 338–9.
45 *Dialectica*, p. 469, line 17.
46 *Dialectica*, p. 469, lines 20, 25–8.
47 *Dialectica*, p. 470, lines 4–7.
48 *Dialectica*, p. 153, lines 1–5.
49 *Dialectica*, p. 153, lines 24–31.
50 *Dialectica*, p. 470, lines 18–24.
51 St Bernard, letter 190, vol. 8, p. 23, lines 10–13.
52 St Augustine, *Confessions*, book 4, ch. 16, para. 28.
53 St Bernard, letter 332, vol. 8, p. 271, lines 9–11.
54 St Bernard, letter 331, vol. 8, pp. 269–70, lines 16–18.
55 St Bernard, letter 190, vol. 8, p. 17, lines 17–18.
56 John of Salisbury, book 1, ch. 5, p. 20, lines 1–3, 13–16.
57 *Theologia Summi Boni*, p. 122, line 220.
58 *Dialectica*, p. 191, lines 15–16; p. 361, lines 27, 34. J. Marenbon, 'Abelard's Concept of Possibility', *Historia Philosophiae Medii Aevi* ed. B. Mojsisch and O. Pluta (1991), pp. 597–601.
59 *Dialectica*, p. 193, lines 34–7; p. 194, lines 1–5.
60 See ch. 1, nn. 8, 60, 61 above; and ch. 7, nn. 9–21 below.
61 'Porphyrii Isagoge: Translatio Boethii', ed. L. Minio-Paluello, in *Aristoteles Latinus*, vol. 1, part 6 (1966), p. 20, lines 2–6.
62 *Dialectica*, p. 319, lines 12, 17; p. 350, line 37; p. 311, lines 35–6.
63 *Dialectica*, p. 319, line 6.
64 *Historia Calamitatum*, lines 347–54.
65 *Dialectica*, p. 131, lines 8–9.
66 Roscelin, p. 80, line 19.

67 *Historia Calamitatum*, lines 547-8. *Dialectica*, p. 151, line 15; p. 152, line 21. P. Bourgain, in 'Nantes conference', p. 227.
68 *Dialectica*, p. 566, line 23; and see ch. 9, n. 14 below.
69 R. W. Southern, *The Making of the Middle Ages* (1953), p. 181.
70 R. W. Southern, *St Anselm* (1990), pp. 393-4.
71 S. E. Chodorow, 'Ecclesiastical Politics and the Ending of the Investiture Contest', *Speculum* 46 (1971), pp. 629-32.
72 Fulk of Deuil, p. 706.
73 *Historia Calamitatum*, lines 690-4; and see ch. 2, n. 32 above.
74 St Bernard, letter 190, vol. 8, p. 18, lines 16-19.
75 R. Foreville and G. Kerr, *The Book of St Gilbert* (1987), pp. 16-18,
76 St Bernard, letter 190, vol. 8, p. 18, lines 19-20.
77 See n. 43 above.
78 'Porphyrii Isagoge: Translatio Boethii', ed. L. Minio-Paluello, in *Aristoteles Latinus*, vol. 1, part 6 (1966), p. 6, lines 8-9.
79 *Dialectica*, p. 576, lines 29-30.
80 See ch. 2, nn. 15-17 above.
81 *Dialectica*, p. 558, line 36.
82 Luscombe, *School*, pp. 123-7. St Bernard, letter 190, vol. 8, p. 26, line 6.
83 Confession of Faith to Heloise, p. 152.
84 Gilson, *Heloise and Abelard*, p. 109.
85 See n. 5 above; and Epitaph, p. 65.
86 See n. 43 above.
87 *Dialectica*, p. 576, lines 35-7.
88 Confession of Faith to Heloise, p. 152.
89 Confession of Faith to Heloise, p. 152.

CHAPTER 6: EXPERIMENTUM – 'EXPERIENCE'

1 *Dialectica*, p. 305.
2 *Sic et Non*, p. 103, lines 338-9; and see ch. 2, n. 25 above.
3 Bacon, *Opus Maius*, part vi, ch. i, ed. J. H. Bridges (1900), p. 168.
4 *Historia Calamitatum*, lines 1-2.
5 *Historia Calamitatum*, lines 4-5.
6 C. Morris, *The Discovery of the Individual 1050-1200* (1972), pp. 79-86, is an introduction to autobiographies.
7 *Chronique des comtes d'Anjou* ed. P. Marchegay and A. Salmon (1856), i, pp. 375-83. For another view, see J. Dunbabin, in *The Perception of the Past in 12th Century Europe* ed. P. Magdalino (1992), pp. 5-6.
8 *Historia Calamitatum*, lines 1608, 1589-90.
9 *Historia Calamitatum*, lines 8-11.
10 See ch. 8, n. 62 below.
11 See ch. 5, nn. 1, 83 above.
12 Heloise i, p. 112, lines 32-3.
13 Dante, *Inferno*, canto 1, line 1.

14   *Historia Calamitatum*, lines 915, 67, 156; and see ch. 4, nn. 29–31 above, and ch. 11, n. 166 below.
15   St Bernard, letter 332, vol. 8, p. 271, lines 9–11; and see ch. 11, nn. 213–14 below.
16   St Bernard, letter 331, vol. 8, p. 269, lines 13–15.
17   *Moralia in Job*, book 9, cited by Heloise ii, p. 121, lines 183–5.
18   For Abelard's love songs, see ch. 7, nn. 28, 29 below. For Abelard's reissue of *Theologia*, see ch. 12, n. 25 and ch. 14, n. 9 below, and Clanchy, in *Journal of Ecclesiastical History* 41 (1990), pp. 2–11.
19   Heloise ii, p. 122, lines 201–2. Heloise i, p. 111, lines 24–5, referring to *Historia Calamitatum*, line 1201.
20   L. T. Topsfield, *Troubadours and Love* (1975), p. 40. J. Martindale, 'Duke William IX and the Historian', in *The Ideals and Practice of Medieval Knighthood II* ed C. Harper-Bill and R. Harvey (1988), p. 105.
21   *De Gestis Regum* ed. W. Stubbs, Rolls Series no. 90, vol. 2 (1889), p. 510.
22   *Historia Calamitatum*, lines 1490–2.
23   *Historia Calamitatum*, lines 530–3; and see ch. 10, nn. 32, 33 below. For Abelard's Poitevin father, see ch. 7, nn. 26, 27 below.
24   Otto of Freising, p. 224, lines 21–4; and see ch. 7, n. 22 below.
25   *Ethics*, p. 28, lines 9–12.
26   *Ethics*, p. 40, lines 7–9.
27   Marcabru, poem xviii, lines 13–18, cited by Topsfield, *Troubadours and Love*, pp. 19, 80. For Marcabru, see R. E. Harvey, *The Troubadour Marcabru and Love* (1989).

CHAPTER 7: KNIGHT

1   For another version of this chapter, see *Medieval Knighthood* vol. 5 (1995), Papers from the Sixth Strawberry Hill Conference, ed. S. Church and R. Harvey, pp. 101–18.
2   Goswin, p. 443a.
3   *Historia Calamitatum*, lines 146–7.
4   See ch. 5, n. 10 above.
5   *Historia Calamitatum*, lines 28–30. Mews (1995), p. 10, n. 8, has a different interpretation of these lines.
6   Suger, *Louis VI*, usually gives Thibaud the title *Comes Palatinus*, e.g. pp. 75, 104, 166.
7   Heloise i, p. 115, lines 190–1.
8   Fulk of Deuil, p. 706.
9   *Historia Calamitatum*, lines 273–5.
10   See ch. 5, nn. 59–63 above.
11   See ch. 9, n. 13 below.
12   See p. 12 above. See also C. J. Mews, 'In Search of a Name and its Significance', *Traditio* 44 (1988), pp. 193ff.
13   Otto of Freising, p. 225, lines 5–6.

14 Otto of Freising, pp. 224–5.
15 *Historia Calamitatum*, lines 186–7.
16 Goswin, p. 442e.
17 *Historia Calamitatum*, line 12.
18 B. Radice's translation in *The Letters of Abelard and Heloise* (1974), p. 57, is: 'volatile temperament'.
19 Trans. H. Waddell, *Medieval Latin Lyrics* 4th edn (1933), p. 183.
20 Waddell, *Medieval Latin Lyrics*, p. 185.
21 *Historia Calamitatum*, lines 11–12.
22 Otto of Freising, p. 224, lines 21–4.
23 Otto of Freising, p. 225, lines 25–6.
24 *Historia Calamitatum*, lines 8–9.
25 See ch. 3, n. 44 above.
26 Migne, *PL* 178, col. 106, no. vi. Mews (1995), p. 1.
27 *Historia Calamitatum*, lines 13–17; and see ch. 3, n. 24 above.
28 Heloise i, p. 115, lines 200–3; and see ch. 3, n. 45 above. For Hilary of Orléans, see ch. 11, n. 117 below.
29 *Historia Calamitatum*, lines 357–9.
30 P. G. Walsh, 'Golias and Goliardic Poetry', *Medium Aevum* 52 (1983), p. 5.
31 See ch. 2, n. 18 above.
32 Heloise i, p. 115, lines 196–7.
33 Heloise i, p. 115, lines 197–8.
34 See ch. 3, n. 52 above.
35 See ch. 3, n. 61 above.
36 St Bernard, 'Liber de Gradibus', vol. 3, p. 14. The steps/degrees are tabulated by B. Pranger, *Bernard of Clairvaux and the Shape of Monastic Thought* (1994), p. 97.
37 'Liber de Gradibus', p. 47, lines 7–8, 17.
38 St Bernard, letter 190, vol. 8, p. 35, line 1; and see ch. 10, n. 47 below.
39 William of Malmesbury, *De Gestis Regum* ed. W. Stubbs, Rolls Series 90 (1889), ii, p. 510; and see ch. 6, n. 21 above.
40 'De Consideratione', vol. 3, p. 429, line 20; p. 430, line 5.
41 L. T. Topsfield, *Troubadours and Love* (1975), p. 40; and see ch. 6, n. 20 above.
42 'Planctus' ed. P. Dronke, *Poetic Individuality in the Middle Ages* (1970), p. 122. Clanchy, in *Journal of Ecclesiastical History* 41 (1990), p. 23.
43 See n. 8 above.
44 *Historia Calamitatum*, lines 14–15.
45 C. K. Scott Moncrieff (1925), p. 3; J. T. Muckle (1964), p. 11; B. Radice (1974), p. 57.
46 D. A. J. D. Boulton, 'Classic Knighthood', *Medieval Knighthood* vol. 5 (1995), Papers from the Sixth Strawberry Hill Conference, ed. S. Church and R. Harvey, p. 78.
47 Psalm 44, verse 4.
48 *Chanson de Roland* (Digby MS), lines 2316–54.

49   *Historia Calamitatum*, lines 156–8.

50   Mews, 'In Search of a Name', *Traditio* 44 (1988), p. 194. P. H. Morice, *Memoires pour servir de preuves à l'histoire ecclésiastique et civile de Bretagne*, vol. 1 (1742), cols. 431, 474.

51   Richard of Poitiers, see n. 26 above.

52   *Historia Calamitatum*, lines 22–3; and see ch. 3, n. 24 above.

53   J. T. Muckle, in *Mediaeval Studies* 12 (1950), p. 175, n. 16.

54   *Dialectica*, p. 146, lines 23, 25; and see p. 142, line 15.

55   J. Dunbabin, 'From Clerk to Knight: Changing Orders', *The Ideals and Practice of Medieval Knighthood* vol. 2 (1988), pp. 26ff.

56   M. T. Clanchy, *From Memory to Written Record* 2nd edn (1993), pp. 226ff.

57   See ch. 10, n. 28 below.

58   Clanchy, *From Memory to Written Record*, p. 312.

59   Byron, *Don Juan*, canto 9, stanza 4.

60   M. Bennett, 'The Medieval Warhorse Reconsidered', *Medieval Knighthood* vol. 5 (1995), Papers from the Sixth Strawberry Hill Conference, ed. S. Church and R. Harvey, pp. 33–4.

61   *Chanson de Roland* (Digby MS), lines 1876–83.

62   F. Stenton ed., *The Bayeux Tapestry* (1957), plate 68.

63   Suger, *Louis VI*, ch. 17, p. 120.

64   Bertran de Born, *Poems* ed. W. D. Paden (1986).

65   Hymns, no. 29.

66   *City of God*, book 22, chapter 22.

67   *Sic et Non*, question 147, pp. 524–6.

68   *Sic et Non*, question 146, p. 522.

69   See ch. 9, nn. 143, 144 below.

70   Heloise ii, p. 120, lines 97–121.

71   Fulk of Deuil, p. 707, lines 22–3.

72   See n. 2 above.

73   *Historia Calamitatum*, lines 135–6.

74   R. W. Southern in *Renaissance and Renewal* ed. R. L. Benson and G. Constable (1982), p. 124, n. 26.

75   Bautier, in 'Nantes conference', pp. 53–71. Mews (1995), pp. 11–12. Marenbon, 'A Life', pp. 11–12.

76   E. Bournazel, *Le Gouvernement capétien* (1975), pp. 35–53.

77   *Historia Calamitatum*, lines 1023–8, 1036–7.

78   St Bernard, letter 78, vol. 7, p. 208, line 14.

79   St Bernard, letter 78, vol. 7, p. 208, line 9.

80   St Bernard, letter 193, vol. 8, pp. 44–5.

81   St Bernard, letter 189, vol. 8, p. 14, lines 1–2.

82   St Bernard, letter 189, vol. 8, p. 14, line 18.

83   I Kings *alias* I Samuel, ch. 17, verse 33.

84   *Theologia Summi Boni*, Mews CCCM, p. 122, lines 222–3.

85   St Bernard, letter 189, vol. 8, p. 14, lines 13–14.

86   Goswin, p. 443b.

87   A. Kingsley Porter, *Romanesque Sculpture of the Pilgrimage Roads* (1923), vol. 2, p. 34 (nave, north side, 4th pier).

88   Ivo of Chartres, especially letter nos. 247 and 280, Migne, *PL* 162, col. 254, 281. R. Bartlett, *Trial by Fire and Water* (1986), p. 118, n. 65.

89   *Historia Calamitatum*, lines 164-5.

90   Migne, *PL* 170, col. 482a. J. H. Van Engen, *Rupert of Deutz* (1983), p. 211.

91   Migne, *PL* 170, col. 483a, 437c.

92   St Bernard, letter 158, vol. 7, p. 366, lines 4-5.

93   See ch. 11, nn. 165-7 below.

94   *Historia Calamitatum*, lines 151-2. Ovid, *Metamorphoses*, book 13, line 89. D. W. Robertson, *Abelard and Heloise* (1972), pp. 112-13.

95   *Historia Calamitatum*, lines 356-8.

96   *Historia Calamitatum*, lines 290-4.

97   *The Wandering Scholars* (1927), p. 108.

98   Luscombe, *School*, p. 9.

99   Heloise i, p. 115, line 196.

100 T. Hunt, 'Abelardian Ethics and Beroul's Tristan', *Romania* 98 (1977), pp. 501-40. H. C. R. Laurie, in *Studi Medievali* 27 (1986), p. 145.

101 *De Nugis Curialium* (1983), p. 211.

102 See n. 13 above.

103 Dronke, *Testimonies*, pp. 17-18, 36. J. R. Clark, in *Mittellateinisches Jahrbuch* 21 (1986), pp. 162, 170. The identification of Heloise with 'Philologia' was denied by Benton, whom R. W. Southern follows, *Scholastic Humanism and the Unification of Europe*, vol. 1, (1995), p. 223. But see Clanchy, in *Medieval Knighthood*, vol. 5, ed. S. Church and R. Harvey (1995), pp. 109-11.

104 Fulk of Deuil, p. 703.

105 Berengar of Poitiers, p. 115; and see ch. 10, n. 44 below.

106 Hymns, no. 29.

107 Baudri of Bourgueil, ed. P. Abrahams (1926), pp. 196-253.

108 *Moralia in Job*, book 31, ed. M. Adriaen, CCCM 143b (1985), p. 1549.

109 Sermon no. 24, Migne, *PL* 178, col. 529d.

110 *Moralia in Job*, pp. 1550-2, 1571-3. Migne, *PL* 178, col. 530-1.

111 *Physiologus Latinus*, 'B text', ed. F. J. Carmody (1939), p. 31.

112 *Physiologus Latinus*, 'Y text', ed. F. J. Carmody (1941), p. 128.

113 Epitaph, p. 65.

CHAPTER 8: LOVER

1   *Historia Calamitatum*, lines 21-2, 24-5; and see ch. 3, nn. 24, 27 above.

2   *Historia Calamitatum*, lines 300-1.

3   *Historia Calamitatum*, lines 1560-1.

4   Letters ed. Muckle, p. 73, line 1. Heloise ii, p. 117, line 1.

5   Heloise iii, p. 241, line 1. This phrase is discussed by L. Georgianna, in *Mediaeval Studies* 49 (1987), pp. 238-40. See also Gilson, *Heloise and Abelard*, p. 73.

6 *Historia Calamitatum*, line 299; and see ch. 3, n. 52 above.

7 *Medieval Humanism*, p. 94; and see ch. 1, n. 40 above.

8 Heloise i, p. 111, line 11; p. 117, line 275. Heloise ii, p. 117, line 1; p. 118, line 33; p. 119, line 54.

9 See n. 5 above.

10 Heloise i, p. 116, line 249; and see ch. 1, n. 16, and ch. 3, n. 54 above.

11 *Historia Calamitatum*, line 30; and see ch. 5, n. 12 above.

12 *Historia Calamitatum*, lines 284–6.

13 *Historia Calamitatum*, lines 305–6.

14 St Bernard, letter 193, vol. 8, p. 45, lines 9–10.

15 Letters ed. Muckle, p. 92, lines 18–19.

16 Heloise i, p. 117, lines 269–70.

17 Dronke, *Women Writers*, pp. 92–7.

18 Heloise ii, p. 121, lines 170–3; and see ch. 1, nn. 43–5 above.

19 See ch. 11, n. 172 below.

20 Letters ed. Smits, no. 10, p. 239.

21 Letters ed. Muckle, p. 94, lines 4–6.

22 Letters ed. Muckle, p. 94, line 8.

23 See ch. 11, pp. 257-8 below.

24 St Bernard, letter 193, vol. 8, p. 44, line 19.

25 Dronke, *Testimonies*, p. 36; and see ch. 7, n. 103 above.

26 Letter ed. McLaughlin, pp. 245–6. I Timothy, ch. 2, verse 11.

27 Dronke, *Testimonies*, p. 36.

28 Heloise ii, p. 122, lines 193–7.

29 Heloise ii, p. 122, lines 212–14, 218–19.

30 Muckle, in *Mediaeval Studies* 15 (1953), pp. 59, 67. Dronke, *Testimonies*, pp. 8–9.

31 Laurie, in *Studi Medievali* 27 (1986), p. 143.

32 Brooke, *The Medieval Idea of Marriage* (1989), pp. 91–2.

33 Dronke, *Testimonies*, pp. 19, 45–6; and see ch. 9, n. 136 below.

34 For the publication of the letters, see ch. 1, n. 55 above.

35 Roscelin, p. 78, line 5. I Kings *alias* I Samuel, ch. 3, verse 20.

36 Heloise i, p. 116, lines 225–7.

37 See ch. 11, nn. 58, 98–107 below.

38 Letters ed. Muckle, p. 88, line 20. Heloise ii, p. 122, lines 203–4. See n. 19 above (Heloise's expulsion from Argenteuil).

39 *Historia Calamitatum*, lines 1341–50.

40 Heloise iii, pp. 242–3. For Ovid's *Art of Love*, see R. J. Hexter, *Ovid and Medieval Schooling* (1986).

41 Heloise ii, p. 122, lines 197–202; and see nn. 28, 29 above.

42 Heloise iii, p. 241.

43 See ch. 3, nn. 49–51 above.

44 Letter ed. McLaughlin, p. 243.

45 Letter ed. McLaughlin, p. 245.

46 Letter ed. McLaughlin, p. 245.

47   See n. 26 above.
48   Letter ed. McLaughlin, p. 246
49   C. Waddell, *The Paraclete Statutes* (1987), p. 13, lines 12, 22; p. 9, lines 4, 6; p. 10, line 21; and see ch. 11, nn. 6, 251 below.
50   Dronke, *Testimonies*, p. 23.
51   Peter the Venerable, letter 115, p. 308, lines 3–5. See the various translations of 'vel ut te alteram' (line 3) by H. Waddell, *The Wandering Scholars* (1927), p. 109; Gilson, *Heloise and Abelard*, p. 121; McLeod, *Heloise*, p. 206; Dronke, *Testimonies*, p. 23; Brooke, *The Medieval Idea of Marriage*, pp. 103, 118.
52   'Sponsa Christi', Letters ed. Muckle, pp. 82, 94; and see n. 22 above. Gilson, *Heloise and Abelard*, pp. 121–2.
53   Heloise i, p. 116, lines 247–8; and see ch. 1, n. 16 above.
54   Heloise ii, p. 124, lines 284–7.
55   Peter the Venerable, letter 115, vol. 1, p. 303.
56   See ch. 13, nn. 167, 168 below.
57   See n. 25 above.
58   Dronke, *Testimonies*, p. 18, 36.
59   Peter the Venerable, letter 115, pp. 303–5.
60   Peter the Venerable, letter 168, p. 401.
61   St Bernard, letter 116. J. Leclercq, *Women and St Bernard* (1989), pp. 45–52.
62   St Bernard, sermon 3 on 'Canticles', para. 1, vol. 1, p. 14, lines 10–12; and see ch. 6, n. 10 above.
63   St Bernard, sermon 83 on 'Canticles', para. 5, vol. 2, p. 301, lines 17–21. É. Gilson, *The Mystical Theology of St Bernard* (1940), p. 138.
64   Peter the Venerable, letter 168, p. 401.
65   Peter the Venerable, letter 167, p. 400.
66   J. Leclercq, *Women and St Bernard* (1989), p. 49.
67   G. Constable, 'The Nun of Watton', in *Medieval Women: Dedicated to R. M. T. Hill* (1978), pp. 208–18.
68   Heloise ii, p. 120, line 122.
69   Heloise ii, p. 121, lines 155–9; and see ch. 9, n. 136 below.
70   Heloise i, p. 116, lines 211–12.
71   Heloise i, p. 116, lines 212–14.
72   Heloise i, p. 116, lines 214–15.
73   Heloise i, p. 116, lines 250–1.
74   Heloise iii, p. 241, lines 5–6.
75   Heloise i, p. 114, lines 141–4.
76   Heloise i, p. 114, lines 139–40.
77   Heloise i, p. 114, lines 143–7. Dronke, *Women Writers*, p. 117.
78   See n. 63 above.
79   Heloise i, p. 114, lines 156–61.
80   Heloise i, p. 114, lines 147–9; and see ch. 5, n. 67 above.
81   Heloise i, p. 114, line 150.

82 *Historia Calamitatum*, lines 569–70, 561–4; and see ch. 9, n. 94 below.
83 Heloise i, p. 117, lines 257, 263–5, 273–4; and see ch. 11, n. 196 below.
84 Heloise i, p. 117, lines 263–5.
85 Heloise i, p. 112, lines 69–70, 73–5.
86 Heloise i, p. 113, lines 110–11.
87 *Historia Calamitatum*, lines 548–9.
88 Sermon 33, Migne, *PL* 178, col. 582d; and see ch. 9, nn. 122–7 below.
89 Heloise i, p. 114, lines 123–5; and see ch. 9, n. 126 below.
90 Heloise i, p. 114, lines 125–6.
91 Heloise i, p. 114, lines 134–6.
92 *Historia Calamitatum*, lines 1385–7.
93 Heloise ii, p. 121, lines 168–71.
94 Heloise ii, p. 123, line 264.
95 Heloise iii, p. 241, lines 10–11; and see St Augustine, *Confessions*, book 8, ch. 21.
96 *Historia Calamitatum*, lines 634–9. Lucan, *Pharsalia*, book 8, lines 94–8.
97 *Historia Calamitatum*, line 639; and see ch. 9, n. 162 below.
98 Lucan, *Pharsalia*, book 9, line 111.
99 Letters ed. Muckle, p. 92. Lucan, *Pharsalia*, book 8, line 85.
100 Heloise i, p. 115, lines 185–6, 192–3; and see ch. 1, n. 1 above.
101 Heloise ii, p. 119, lines 85–9.
102 Letters ed. Muckle, p. 92.
103 Letters ed. Muckle, p. 93; and see ch. 11, n. 262 below.
104 Letters ed. Muckle, p. 93.
105 Heloise ii, p. 119, lines 63–6. Lucan, *Pharsalia*, book 2, lines 14–15. Dronke, *Women Writers*, p. 122. L. Georgianna, in *Mediaeval Studies* 49 (1987), p. 248, argues that Heloise was 'thoroughly Christian'.
106 Heloise ii, p. 122, line 221; and see ch. 1, n. 41 above.
107 See n. 54 above.
108 *Historia Calamitatum*, lines 496–8.
109 *Historia Calamitatum*, lines 509–11.
110 *Historia Calamitatum*, lines 514–26. *De Civitate Dei*, book 8, ch. 2.
111 *Historia Calamitatum*, lines 516, 537, 460, 487.
112 See n. 79 above.
113 St Bernard, letter 190, vol. 8, p. 26, line 6.
114 Dronke, *Women Writers*, pp. 111–12. For Heloise's influence on Abelard's theology, see ch. 12, pp. 275–80 above.
115 *Historia Calamitatum*, lines 244–5; and see ch. 4, n. 122 above.
116 D. W. Robertson, *Abelard and Heloise* (1972), p. xiii.
117 Buytaert CCCM, vol. 12, p. 117, lines 246–8. Translated by R. W. Southern, *St Anselm* (1990), p. 210. See also ch. 12, nn. 135–7 below.
118 *Roman de la Rose*, lines 8781–3.
119 *Leges Henrici Primi* ed. L. J. Downer (1972), pp. 98–9, no. 6, 5.
120 Heloise i, p. 114, lines 119–23.
121 Heloise i, p. 114, line 122; and see ch. 11, nn. 202–5 below.

122 See ch. 11, nn. 249–50 below.
123 Gilson, *Heloise and Abelard*, p. 109.
124 Confession of Faith to Heloise, p. 153.
125 See ch. 3, n. 68 above.

CHAPTER 9: MAN

1 *Historia Calamitatum*, lines 292, 280. Mews (1995), p. 12. In general see E. Sears, *The Ages of Man* (1986). Shakespeare, *As You Like It*, act 2, scene 7.
2 *Historia Calamitatum*, line 46. Mews (1995), p. 11.
3 Heloise i, p. 115, lines 207–8.
4 *Historia Calamitatum*, line 288. Peter the Venerable, letter 115, vol. 1, p. 303; vol. 2, p. 257, for Peter's birthdate. Mews (1995), p. 12, n. 14.
5 *Chansons de Guillaume IX*, ed. A. Jeanroy (1927), no. 1.
6 *Medieval Latin Lyrics* 4th edn (1933), p. 215.
7 *Historia Calamitatum*, lines 349–54.
8 See nn. 1 and 3 above.
9 McLeod, *Heloise*, pp. 34–5, 235.
10 McLeod, *Heloise*, p. 233.
11 *Historia Calamitatum*, lines 284–5.
12 C. J. Mews, 'In Search of a Name and its Significance', *Traditio* 44 (1988), pp. 172–3.
13 *Dialectica*, p. 114, line 30. Mews, 'In Search of a Name', p. 173.
14 *Dialectica*, p. 566, line 23; and see ch. 5, n. 68 above.
15 *Dialectica*, p. 566, line 26. Mews, 'In Search of a Name', p. 173.
16 Luscombe, *School*, p. 225.
17 See ch. 7, n. 84 above.
18 Goswin, p. 443b. J. G. Sikes, *Peter Abailard* (1932), p. 6, n. 3; and see ch. 7, n. 86 above.
19 J. Huizinga, *Men and Ideas* (1959), p. 360, n. 8. P. G. Walsh, 'Golias', *Medium Aevum* 52 (1983), p. 5.
20 See ch. 7, nn. 81, 85 above.
21 Goswin, p. 445b, 445d; and see ch. 7, nn. 108–12 above.
22 Goswin, p. 443c. St Bernard, letter 193, vol. 8, p. 44, line 17.
23 *Vie d'Abélard* (1845), vol. 1, p. 43.
24 Sears, *The Ages of Man*, p. 143.
25 *Historia Calamitatum*, lines 155–8.
26 Fulk of Deuil, p. 706, lines 23–5.
27 Otto of Freising, p. 226, lines 8–9; and see ch. 1, n. 18 above.
28 'Expositio in Hexaemeron', Migne, *PL* 178, cols 771–2.
29 *Theologia Christiana*, book 1, chs 73–5, Buytaert CCCM, pp. 298–302; and Clanchy in *Journal of Ecclesiastical History* 41 (1990), pp. 2–5.
30 'Expositio in Hexaemeron', Migne, *PL* 178, col. 772a.
31 'Liber Divinorum Operum', vision 1, no. 2, Migne, *PL* 197, col. 743d.

32 'Expositio in Hexaemeron', Migne, *PL* 178, col. 761b.
33 *Theologia Christiana*, book 1, ch. 12, Buytaert CCCM, p. 76, lines 149–52; and see 'Expositio in Hexaemeron', col. 761a–b.
34 Heloise ii, p. 120, lines 133–5.
35 See ch. 5, nn. 62, 63 above.
36 *Dialectica*, p. 298, line 33; p. 300, line 32; p. 303, line 15.
37 A. Murray, *Reason and Society in the Middle Ages* (1978), plate vii; M. Camille, *Image on the Edge* (1992), pp. 66–72.
38 *Dialogus* p. 154, line 2992.
39 St Bernard, sermon 'De Canticis', no. 5, vol. 1, p. 22, lines 15–16.
40 St Bernard, letter 192, vol. 8, p. 43, lines 13–14.
41 Heloise ii, p. 120, line 133; and see n. 34 above. G. Zarnecki, *Romanesque Art* (1971), plate 83.
42 *City of God*, book 14, chs 16–26. J. W. Baldwin, *The Language of Sex* (1994), pp. 117–18.
43 *The Body and Society* (1988), p. 422.
44 *Historia Calamitatum*, lines 262–9.
45 Buytaert CCCM, vol. 12, p. 117, lines 246–8; and see ch. 8, n. 117 above.
46 *Historia Calamitatum*, line 1569. John, ch. 15, verse 20; and see ch. 14, nn. 51–2 below.
47 *Historia Calamitatum*, line 270.
48 *Historia Calamitatum*, lines 1347–50; and see ch. 8, n. 39 above.
49 St Bernard, letter 332, vol. 8, p. 271, lines 9–11; and see ch. 11, nn. 213–14 below.
50 Bautier in 'Nantes conference', p. 56, n. 1; p. 76, n. 1.
51 *Historia Calamitatum*, lines 404–6.
52 *Historia Calamitatum*, line 410.
53 *Historia Calamitatum*, lines 410–13.
54 *Historia Calamitatum*, lines 591, 583.
55 *Historia Calamitatum*, lines 390–1. Ovid, *Art of Love*, book 2, lines 574–90.
56 *Historia Calamitatum*, lines 396–7.
57 *Historia Calamitatum*, lines 422, 579–80.
58 Bautier in 'Nantes conference', pp. 76–7.
59 Suger, *Louis VI*, ch. 26, p. 196.
60 Bracton, *De Legibus* ed. S. E. Thorne (1968), p. 417; and see n. 139 below.
61 *Historia Calamitatum*, lines 413–14.
62 *Historia Calamitatum*, lines 416–18.
63 Genesis, ch. 3, verse 12. *Historia Calamitatum*, line 415.
64 McLeod, *Heloise*, pp. 55–7.
65 *Historia Calamitatum*, lines 419–20.
66 *Historia Calamitatum*, lines 418–19.
67 Heloise ii, p. 120, lines 118–20.
68 *Historia Calamitatum*, lines 422–3.
69 *Historia Calamitatum*, line 424.

70 *Historia Calamitatum*, lines 429–30.
71 Fulk of Deuil, p. 707. Bautier in 'Nantes conference', pp. 56, 76. Luscombe (1988), p. 256, n. 54. See also n. 145 below.
72 *Historia Calamitatum*, lines 421–2.
73 *Decretum*, part 8, ch. 141, Migne, *PL* 161, col. 616b. *Panormia* book 6, chs. 5–6, Migne, *PL* 161, col. 1245b.
74 *De Sacramentis* book 2, part 11, ch. 6, Migne, *PL* 161, col. 489c.
75 *Decretum Gratiani* part 2, causa 30, ch. 6, ed. Friedberg, vol. 1, p. 1106.
76 *Historia Calamitatum*, line 331.
77 *Decretum* part 5, ch. 291, Migne, *PL* 161, col. 412b–c. *Panormia* book 4, ch. 66, Migne, *PL* 161, cols 1196–7.
78 *Sic et Non*, questio 131, p. 453.
79 Letter 218, Migne, *PL* 162, cols 221–2.
80 T. P. McLaughlin, in *Mediaeval Studies* 3 (1941), pp. 96–7.
81 Bautier, in 'Nantes conference', p. 60.
82 St Bernard, letters 158, 159, 161.
83 *Historia Calamitatum*, lines 583–4, 590–1.
84 C. N. L. Brooke, *The Medieval Idea of Marriage* (1989), pp. 84–9.
85 *Historia Calamitatum*, lines 559–60.
86 *Historia Calamitatum*, line 561.
87 *Historia Calamitatum*, lines 562–4.
88 J. A. Brundage, *Law, Sex, and Christian Society* (1987), pp. 187 ff.
89 *Historia Calamitatum*, lines 564–6.
90 Summarized by Brundage, *Law, Sex and Christian Society*, p. 162.
91 See n. 79 above.
92 *Historia Calamitatum*, lines 530–4.
93 *Historia Calamitatum*, lines 547–8; and see ch. 8, n. 80 above.
94 *Historia Calamitatum*, lines 566–9.
95 *Historia Calamitatum*, lines 569–70; and see ch. 8, n. 82 above.
96 *Historia Calamitatum*, line 571.
97 *Historia Calamitatum*, lines 573–6.
98 *Historia Calamitatum*, lines 397, 573; and see n. 56 above.
99 Heloise ii, p. 120, lines 112–15.
100 Heloise ii, p. 120, lines 115–16.
101 Letters ed. Muckle, p. 88, lines 16–20; and see ch. 8, n. 38 above.
102 See ch. 8, n. 40 above.
103 Letters ed. Muckle, p. 88, line 17. *Historia Calamitatum*, lines 576–7. Heloise ii, p. 120, line 113.
104 *Historia Calamitatum*, lines 579–81.
105 *Historia Calamitatum*, lines 577–8.
106 See ch. 1, n. 49 above.
107 Cartulary of Buzé, cited by C. J. Mews, in *Traditio* 44 (1988), p. 195, n. 88.
108 J. W. Thompson, *The Literacy of the Laity in the Middle Ages* (1939), pp. 135, 157, n. 102.

109 *Historia Calamitatum*, lines 254–5; and see ch. 1, n. 7 above.
110 Heloise i, p. 115, lines 186–7; and see ch. 1, n. 1 above.
111 *Historia Calamitatum*, lines 437–8.
112 *Historia Calamitatum*, lines 541–5, 476–9; and see ch. 3, n. 11 above.
113 *Historia Calamitatum*, lines 533–5.
114 *Historia Calamitatum*, lines 535–6.
115 *Historia Calamitatum*, lines 557–8.
116 Letters ed. Muckle, p. 90, lines 21–2.
117 Letters ed. Muckle, p. 90, lines 23–5.
118 Heloise i, p. 117, lines 257–74.
119 Ed. P. Dronke, *Poetic Individuality in the Middle Ages* (1970), p. 122, verse II, 2a (my translation).
120 Dronke, *Poetic Individuality*, p. 139.
121 See ch. 11, n. 211 below.
122 Sermon 33, Migne, *PL* 178, col. 582d; and see ch. 3, n. 12 above.
123 *Theologia Christiana* ed. Buytaert CCCM, p. 171.
124 *Historia Calamitatum*, lines 1306–7.
125 *The Medieval Idea of Marriage*, p. 107.
126 See ch. 8, n. 89 above; and Letters ed. Muckle, p. 90.
127 Dronke, *Testimonies*, pp. 19, 45. See also ch. 8, n. 104 above, and ch. 11, nn. 262, 265 below.
128 Confession of Faith to Heloise, p. 152.
129 Letters ed. Muckle, p. 88, lines 14–15. Gilson, *Heloise and Abelard*, p. 48.
130 *Historia Calamitatum*, lines 329, 339–40; and ch. 3, nn. 73, 74 above.
131 *Historia Calamitatum*, lines 578–81; and n. 104 above.
132 *Historia Calamitatum*, lines 584–5.
133 *Historia Calamitatum*, lines 588–9; and ch. 1, n. 13 above.
134 Heloise ii, p. 120, lines 105–9.
135 Dronke, *Testimonies*, pp. 45–6, 19.
136 Dronke, *Testimonies*, pp. 46, 19; and see ch. 8, n. 33 above.
137 See ch. 4, n. 92 above.
138 See ch. 8, n. 70 above.
139 *Leges Henrici Primi* ed. L. J. Downer (1972), ch. 82, pp. 258–9.
140 See n. 55 above.
141 *Historia Calamitatum*, lines 585, 593. Fulk of Deuil, p. 706, lines 12–15.
142 Fulk of Deuil, p. 706, lines 9–11.
143 Fulk of Deuil, p. 707, lines 17–19.
144 Fulk of Deuil, p. 707, lines 19–21.
145 Mews, 'On Dating', p. 97.
146 *Historia Calamitatum*, lines 578–82.
147 Fulk of Deuil, p. 707, lines 16–17. *Historia Calamitatum*, lines 588–9.
148 Brooke, *The Medieval Idea of Marriage*, pp. 22, 107. Luscombe (1979), p. 13.
149 R. Howard Bloch, *Etymologies and Genealogies* (1983), p. 142.
150 Guibert de Nogent, book 3, ch. 11, line 20.

151   *Historia Calamitatum*, lines 1386–7.
152   Linda M. Paterson, *The World of the Troubadours* (1993), pp. 208–14, provides an introduction to surgery.
153   *Historia Calamitatum*, lines 1531–3.
154   *Historia Calamitatum*, lines 597–600.
155   *Historia Calamitatum*, lines 919–24, 1523–33.
156   See n. 132 above.
157   See n. 150 above; and ch. 4, nn. 48–9 above.
158   *Historia Calamitatum*, lines 600–6.
159   *Historia Calamitatum*, lines 607–9.
160   *Historia Calamitatum*, lines 609–10.
161   Fulk of Deuil, p. 706, lines 12–13.
162   See n. 103 above; and ch. 8, n. 97 above.
163   Fulk of Deuil, p. 706, lines 27–31; p. 707, lines 19–21.
164   *Historia Calamitatum*, lines 656–8.
165   Roscelin, p. 79, lines 12–15.
166   See n. 109 above.
167   *Historia Calamitatum*, lines 1489–90, 1492–4.

CHAPTER 10: RELIGIO – 'RELIGION'

1   *La Chronique de Morigny* ed. L. Mirot (1909), p. 54.
2   Ibid.
3   Ibid.
4   See ch. 1, n. 21 above; and Thomas of Morigny, 'Disputatio', book 1, para. 63, ed. N. M. Häring in *Studi Medievali* 22 (1981), p. 337.
5   *Historia Calamitatum*, lines 1540–3; and see ch. 11, n. 162 below.
6   *Historia Calamitatum*, lines 1545–9.
7   *Historia Calamitatum*, lines 1318–20; and C. Lalore, *Collections des Principaux Cartulaires de Troyes* (1875), vol. 2, p. 1.
8   See ch. 11, n. 172 below.
9   I. S. Robinson, *The Papacy 1073–1198* (1990), pp. 69–77.
10   Suger, *Louis VI*, ch. 32, p. 260.
11   Fulk of Deuil, p. 706.
12   See n. 2 above.
13   St Bernard, letter 124, vol. 7, p. 305, lines 9, 13–14.
14   St Bernard, letter 124, vol. 7, p. 307, lines 1–4. Psalm 72, verse 6.
15   Thomas of Morigny, 'Disputatio', book 1, para. 19, ed. Häring in *Studi Medievali* 22 (1981), p. 329, and book 3, para. 4, p. 356.
16   St Bernard, letter 190, vol. 8, p. 24, lines 24–5; and see ch. 1, n. 22 above.
17   Letter ed. Klibansky, p. 6.
18   Roscelin, p. 80, lines 3–4; and cf. p. 79, lines 23–5. St Jerome, *Contra Vigilantium*, ch. 15; and see ch. 11, n. 44 below.
19   *Rule of St Benedict*, prologue.
20   Orderic Vitalis, book 2, ch. 26, ed. M. Chibnall, vol. 4, p. 310.

21 *Historia Calamitatum*, line 655.

22 Sermon 33, Migne, *PL* 178, cols. 598d–599a. The same arguments appear in Abelard's letter 12, ed. Smits, pp. 257–8, and comment at pp. 153–8. For the date of this sermon, see Mews, 'On Dating', p. 124.

23 Sermon 33, Migne, *PL* 178, col. 605b–c; and see ch. 11, n. 95 below.

24 G. Constable, 'Renewal and Reform in Religious Life', in *Renaissance and Renewal in the Twelfth Century* ed. R. L. Benson and G. Constable (1982), p. 53.

25 Constable, 'Renewal and Reform', p. 52.

26 Constable, 'Renewal and Reform', p. 54.

27 *Libellus de Diversis Ordinibus et Professionibus qui sunt in Ecclesia* ed. G. Constable and B. Smith (1972), p. 98.

28 *Historia Calamitatum*, lines 529–32.

29 *Historia Calamitatum*, lines 493–5.

30 *Historia Calamitatum*, lines 506–9.

31 *Historia Calamitatum*, lines 496–500.

32 *Historia Calamitatum*, lines 534–5; and see ch. 6, n. 23 above, and ch. 12, n. 73 below.

33 Ivo of Chartres, letter 218; and see ch. 9, nn. 79, 91, 92 above.

34 *Historia Calamitatum*, lines 71–5.

35 Luscombe, *School*, p. 9, n. 6, citing Richard of Poitiers.

36 Letter 193, line 18; and see ch. 1, n. 25 above.

37 Hymns, no. 44; and see ch. 1, n. 36 above. *Ethics*, p. 54, lines 27–8, 32–3; and see ch. 12, n. 96 below.

38 Mews, 'Lists of Heresies', p. 109, no. 10.

39 *Sic et Non*, p. 89, lines 12–14.

40 *Ethics*, p. 2, line 1.

41 *Sic et Non*, p. 103, lines 338–9; and see ch. 2, n. 25 above.

42 *Historia Calamitatum*, lines 745–6. John, ch. 7, verse 26; and see ch. 14, n. 52 below.

43 Confessio 'Universis', p. 133, line 12.

44 Berengar of Poitiers, p. 115, lines 5–10. John, ch. 11, verses 47–53.

45 Berengar of Poitiers, p. 136. Luscombe, *School*, p. 49, n. 1.

46 See ch. 1, n. 60, and ch. 7, n. 16 above.

47 St Bernard, letter 190, vol. 8, p. 35, line 1; and see ch. 7, n. 38 above.

48 Buytaert CCCM, vol. 11, p. 116, line 214.

49 Buytaert CCCM, vol. 11, p. 116, lines 216–19.

50 Otto of Freising, p. 226, lines 5–6. John of Salisbury, book 3, ch. 1, p. 103, lines 8–9.

51 Otto of Freising, p. 226, line 12.

52 Berengar of Poitiers, p. 117, lines 18–20.

53 *Theologia Summi Boni* Mews CCCM, p. 201, lines 1346–7. *Theologia Scholarium* Mews CCCM, p. 497, lines 2673–4.

54 St Bernard, letter 190, vol. 8, p. 26, line 6.

55 St Bernard, letter 189, vol. 8, p. 14, lines 11–13.

56 Letter of Innocent II, ed. Leclercq, in St Bernard, letter 194, vol. 8, p. 46, lines 9–18.
57 Letter of Innocent II, vol. 8, p. 47, lines 22–3; and see ch. 13, n. 190 below.
58 Peter the Venerable, letter 115, p. 307, lines 7–8.
59 Peter the Venerable, letter 98, pp. 258–9. Mews CCCM, pp. 285–6, 290.
60 St Bernard, letter 192, vol. 8, p. 43, lines 11–13.
61 Luscombe, *School*, p. 22, n. 1. Mews CCCM, p. 268, n. 114, and Mews (1995), p. 16, n. 33.
62 See ch. 13, n. 183 below.
63 *Historia Calamitatum*, lines 151–2; and see ch. 7, n. 94 above.
64 See ch. 13, n. 8 below.
65 St Bernard, letter 189, vol. 8, p. 14, lines 1–5.
66 Peter the Venerable, letter 115, p. 306, lines 22–5.

CHAPTER 11: MONK

1 See ch. 1, n. 14 above.
2 St Bernard, letter 250, vol. 8, p. 147.
3 *Magna Vita St Hugonis* ed. D. L. Douie and D. H. Farmer (1961), vol. 1, pp. 73–4.
4 R. W. Southern, *Western Society and the Church* (1970), p. 227.
5 Heloise iii, p. 242, lines 6–13.
6 C. Waddell, *The Paraclete Statutes: Institutiones Nostrae* (1987), p. 32. Luscombe (1988), p. 273, argues that the rule was not ignored.
7 See nn. 220–30 below.
8 *Historia Calamitatum*, lines 614–22.
9 See ch. 10, nn. 22, 23 above.
10 Sermon 33, Migne, *PL* 178, col. 583b. Isaiah, ch. 56, verse 4. Matthew, ch. 19, verse 12.
11 Migne, *PL* 178, col. 583b.
12 *Magna Vita St Hugonis*, vol. 1, p. 52.
13 *Historians of the Church of York* ed. J. Raine, Rolls Series 71, vol. 1 (1879), pp. 282–4.
14 *Historia Calamitatum*, line 263; and ch. 9, n. 44 above. Letters ed. Muckle, p. 89, lines 33–5.
15 Heloise ii, p. 122, lines 212–14.
16 See n. 12 above.
17 See ch. 9, nn. 149, 151 above.
18 Fulk of Deuil, p. 707, line 21; p. 703, line 1.
19 Fulk of Deuil, p. 705, line 6.
20 Fulk of Deuil, p. 705, lines 7–9.
21 'De Conceptu Virginali', *St Anselmi Opera Omnia* ed. F. S. Schmitt (1946), vol. 2, p. 152, lines 1–4.
22 Prayer of St Anselm cited by J. A. Brundage, *Law, Sex and Christian Society* (1987), p. 186.

23 *Historia Calamitatum*, lines 1381–5.

24 Fulk of Deuil, p. 705, lines 36–8.

25 Fulk of Deuil, p. 705, lines 10–19, 34–5.

26 Dronke, *Testimonies*, p. 27.

27 Luscombe (1988), pp. 255–6.

28 Letters ed. Muckle, p. 89, lines 32, 35; and see n. 14 above.

29 *Ethics*, p. 20, lines 12–14.

30 *Ethics*, p. 20, lines 24–5.

31 See ch. 9, nn. 42, 43 above.

32 See n. 22 above.

33 See n. 15 above.

34 *Magna Vita St Hugonis*, vol. 1, p. 51.

35 H. Waddell, *Medieval Latin Lyrics* Penguin edn (1952), pp. 174–5.

36 *Historia Calamitatum*, lines 651–4.

37 See ch. 10, nn. 29–32 above.

38 Otto of Freising, p. 226, line 8.

39 Luscombe (1979), pp. 14–15.

40 See ch. 4, nn. 64–9 above.

41 *Historia Calamitatum*, lines 942–4.

42 Letter 106; see ch. 2, n. 38 above.

43 Sermon 36 'Super Cantica', vol. 2, p. 4, lines 23–4.

44 See ch. 10, n. 18 above.

45 *Didascalicon*, book 5, ch. 8, ed. C. H. Buttimer (1939), pp. 108–9.

46 See ch. 10, nn. 22, 34 above.

47 *Didascalicon*, book 5, ch. 7, p. 107.

48 *Didascalicon*, book 6, ch. 13, p. 129.

49 See ch. 1, n. 21 above.

50 *Historia Calamitatum*, line 658; and see ch. 9, n. 164 above.

51 *Historia Calamitatum*, line 665.

52 Otto of Freising, p. 226, lines 9–11. Otto conflates Abelard's two releases from obedience to the abbot of St Denis, before and after the council of Soissons in 1121.

53 Luscombe (1979), p. 13. Letters ed. Smits, pp. 201, 211, n. 92.

54 *Historia Calamitatum*, lines 676–9.

55 *Historia Calamitatum*, lines 988–9.

56 *Historia Calamitatum*, lines 992–4.

57 Benton in 'Cluny conference', p. 487, or in his *Culture, Power and Personality in Medieval France* (1991), p. 434.

58 *Historia Calamitatum*, lines 666–7.

59 Roscelin, p. 79, lines 20–5.

60 Roscelin, p. 80, lines 2, 6–7.

61 Roscelin, p. 79, lines 23–9. Letters ed. Smits, pp. 201–2.

62 Roscelin, p. 79, lines 32–5.

63 Roscelin, p. 80, lines 20–4. Letters ed. Smits, p. 200. Benton (n. 57 above), p. 487 or p. 434. Benton in 'Trier conference', pp. 47, 52.

64 G. Constable, 'Suger's Monastic Administration', *Abbot Suger and St Denis* ed. P. L. Gerson (1986), p. 17. J. F. Benton, 'Suger's Life and Personality', ibid. p. 4.

65 *Historia Calamitatum*, lines 910–13. Goswin, p. 445b–c.

66 Goswin, p. 445b–d.

67 *Historia Calamitatum*, lines 934–6.

68 *Historia Calamitatum*, lines 942–5. Bede's commentary on Acts, ch. 17, verse 34, cited by E. Jeauneau in 'Nantes conference', p. 164, n. 2.

69 *Historia Calamitatum*, lines 949–51.

70 *Historia Calamitatum*, lines 952–61.

71 Jeauneau in 'Nantes conference', p. 165. Letters ed. Smits, p. 144.

72 Letters ed. Smits, no. 11, p. 255, lines 153–6.

73 *Sic et Non*, p. 91, lines 54–6.

74 *Sic et Non*, p. 92, lines 84–5.

75 Jeauneau, in 'Nantes conference', p. 168. Letters ed. Smits, pp. 146–9.

76 See ch. 4, n. 112 above.

77 *Historia Calamitatum*, lines 203–21, 243–5.

78 *Historia Calamitatum*, lines 968–70,

79 *Historia Calamitatum*, lines 970–1.

80 *Historia Calamitatum*, lines 976–8.

81 *La Chanson de Roland* ed. F. Whitehead (1942), line 973.

82 *Chanson de Roland*, line 2347.

83 Suger, *Louis VI*, ch. 28, p. 220. See the refs. on the battle standard in R. Cusimano and J. Moorhead, *Suger, The Deeds of Louis the Fat* (1992), pp. 201–2.

84 Suger, *Louis VI*, ch. 28, p. 228.

85 *Historia Calamitatum*, lines 985–7. Bautier in 'Nantes conference', p. 58, analyses Abelard's principal supporters and opponents.

86 *Historia Calamitatum*, lines 1529–31.

87 *Historia Calamitatum*, lines 989–91.

88 *Historia Calamitatum*, lines 996–1016.

89 *Rule of St Benedict*, ch. 44.

90 *Historia Calamitatum*, lines 1018–19.

91 *Historia Calamitatum*, lines 1021–2.

92 *Historia Calamitatum*, lines 1023–8. Bautier in 'Nantes conference', p. 57.

93 *Historia Calamitatum*, lines 1034–7.

94 Cited by H. Leyser, *Hermits and the New Monasticism* (1984), p. 1, n. 2.

95 See ch. 10, n. 23 above.

96 Letters ed. Smits, no. 14, p. 280, line 27.

97 *Libellus de Diversis Ordinibus et Professionibus qui sunt in Ecclesia* ed. G. Constable and B. Smith (1972), pp. 14–17.

98 McLeod, *Heloise*, pp. 121, 270 (citing the cartulary of the Paraclete).

99 C. Charrier, *Heloise dans l'histoire et dans la légende* (1933), map at p. 265.

100   T. Evergates, *Feudal Society in the Baillage of Troyes* (1975), pp. 4–5.
101   *Historia Calamitatum*, lines 1038–44. Psalm 54, verse 8.
102   *Historia Calamitatum*, lines 1053–83.
103   *Historia Calamitatum*, lines 1068–70.
104   For Abelard's citation of St Jerome, see C. J. Mews in *Jérôme entre l'Occident et l'Orient* (Actes du Colloque de Chantilly) ed. Y. M. Duval (1988), pp. 434–5.
105   Heloise i, p. 113, lines 77, 79–84.
106   *Historia Calamitatum*, lines 1115, 1119. The earliest buildings at the Paraclete are discussed by Benton in 'Cluny conference', p. 481, n. 32, and Luscombe (1988), p. 262, n. 85.
107   J. le Goff, *The Medieval Imagination* (1985), p. 54.
108   *Historia Calamitatum*, lines 1112–13.
109   *Historia Calamitatum*, lines 1042, 1044–5.
110   *Historia Calamitatum*, lines 1047–9.
111   *Historia Calamitatum*, lines 1091–3.
112   *Historia Calamitatum*, line 1039.
113   See nn. 55–8 above.
114   *Historia Calamitatum*, lines 1110–11. Luke, ch. 16, verse 3.
115   *Historia Calamitatum*, lines 1109–12.
116   *Historia Calamitatum*, lines 1113–16.
117   Hilarii Aurelianensis, *Versus et Ludi, Epistolae* ed. W. Bulst and M. L. Bulst-Thiele (1989), pp. 30–1. Checklist no. 387. Luscombe, *School*, pp. 52–4.
118   Abelard's 'rivals': *Historia Calamitatum*, lines 1096, 1124–6, 1200ff.
119   *Theologia Christiana*, book 4, pp. 298–301, especially lines 1092–4.
120   *Theologia Christiana*, book 4, lines 1128–46. Clanchy, in *Journal of Ecclesiastical History* 41 (1990), p. 3.
121   Luscombe (1988), p. 261: 'The site was occupied by Abelard in 1123.'
122   Checklist no. 383. The year 1129 is suggested as an alternative to 1128 by J. Verger (acknowledging N. Y. Tonnerre) in 'Nantes conference', p. 113, n. 1.
123   Mews CCCM, p. 21.
124   Clanchy, *From Memory to Written Record* 2nd edn (1993), pp. 116, 119.
125   *Historia Calamitatum*, lines 1121–4.
126   Abelard's only ref. to 'the Paraclete' in *Theologia Christiana* is at book 3, p. 254, line 949.
127   *Historia Calamitatum*, lines 1377–8; and see n. 23 above.
128   *Historia Calamitatum*, line 1139.
129   *Historia Calamitatum*, lines 1193–5.
130   *Historia Calamitatum*, lines 756–9.
131   *Sic et Non*, p. 113.
132   *Historia Calamitatum*, lines 1196–7.
133   *Historia Calamitatum*, line 1041.
134   Benton in 'Cluny conference', p. 489. Hymns, nos. 105, 106.
135   *Historia Calamitatum*, lines 1238, 1304.

136 *Historia Calamitatum*, lines 1201–4.
137 Letters ed. Smits, pp. 123–6, and works there cited. Mews (1995), p. 15.
138 Clanchy, in *Journal of Ecclesiastical History* 41 (1991), pp. 13–14; and see n. 120 above.
139 Heloise i, p. 111, lines 24–5.
140 See ch. 10, nn. 25, 26 above.
141 See ch. 10, n. 23, and ch. 11, n. 95 above.
142 Letters ed. Smits, no. 10, pp. 244–5, lines 158–62. G. Constable, in *Renaissance and Renewal* (1982), p. 64.
143 *Historia Calamitatum*, line 1196, 1209–12.
144 St Bernard, 'Apologia', ch. 1, vol. 5, p. 83.
145 See ch. 13, n. 46 below.
146 *Historia Calamitatum*, lines 1213–15.
147 *Historia Calamitatum*, lines 1221–5.
148 *Historia Calamitatum*, lines 1225–8.
149 *Historia Calamitatum*, lines 1233–4.
150 *Historia Calamitatum*, lines 1239–41.
151 Mews, *Jerome* (see n. 104 above), p. 437.
152 E. G. Bowen, *Saints, Seaways and Settlements in the Celtic Lands* 2nd edn (1977), pp. 170–5. In general see *Gildas: New Approaches* ed. M. Lapidge and D. Dumville (1984).
153 See n. 78 above.
154 Hymns, no. 119.
155 *Historia Calamitatum*, lines 1251, 1243–4; and see ch. 1, n. 2 above.
156 *Historia Calamitatum*, line 1244.
157 *Historia Calamitatum*, lines 8–9; and see ch. 2, nn. 14–15 above.
158 See n. 122 above.
159 *Historia Calamitatum*, lines 1511–12.
160 *Historia Calamitatum*, lines 1530–1.
161 See ch. 10, nn. 1–6 above.
162 *Historia Calamitatum*, lines 1540–2; and see ch. 10, n. 5 above.
163 Suger, *Louis VI*, ch. 29, pp. 232, 236; ch. 28, pp. 224. I have benefited from hearing Dr N. Y. Tonnerre's lecture on 'Celtic Literary Tradition and the Development of a Feudal Principality in Brittany' at Bangor in 1994.
164 McLeod, *Heloise*, p. 283. C. Mews, in *Traditio* 44 (1988), pp. 194–5, n. 88.
165 *Historia Calamitatum*, lines 1501–3.
166 McLaughlin, in *Speculum* 42 (1967), p. 476.
167 *Historia Calamitatum*, lines 1501–23.
168 *Historia Calamitatum*, lines 1541–4.
169 *Historia Calamitatum*, lines 1545–9.
170 *Cartulaire de l'Abbaye de Redon*, pp. 449, 298, cited by F. M. Stenton, *The First Century of English Feudalism* 1st edn (1932), pp. 26–7.
171 *Historia Calamitatum*, lines 1275–7.

172 McLeod, *Heloise*, pp. 93–104. Bautier in 'Nantes conference', pp. 71, 75. T. G. Waldman, 'Abbot Suger and the Nuns of Argenteuil', *Traditio* 41 (1985), pp. 239–72. J. F. Benton and G. Constable, in *Abbot Suger and St Denis* ed. P. L. Gerson (1986), pp. 5, 10, 20–1, 29. See also ch. 8, n. 19 above; ch. 10, n. 8 above.

173 *Historia Calamitatum*, lines 1304–10.

174 See nn. 133–5 above.

175 *Historia Calamitatum*, lines 1311–13.

176 'Cartulaire de l'abbaye du Paraclet', ed. C. Lalore, *Collection des Principaux cartulaires de Troyes* (1875–90), vol. 2, pp. 1–3.

177 *Historia Calamitatum*, lines 1317–20; and see ch. 10, n. 7 above.

178 *Historia Calamitatum*, lines 1344, 1479–80; and see n. 206 below.

179 *Historia Calamitatum*, lines 1482–4.

180 *Historia Calamitatum*, lines 1530–1, 1527–8.

181 *Historia Calamitatum*, lines 1525–6.

182 P. Harbison et al., *Irish Art and Architecture* (1978), p. 67, plate 54.

183 See nn. 158–9 above.

184 *Historia Calamitatum*, lines 1343–4.

185 Sermon no. 30, Migne, *PL* 178, col. 569a. Heloise i, p. 113, lines 93–105. Dronke, *Women Writers*, p. 116.

186 See ch. 10, nn. 2–4 above.

187 Luscombe, *School*, p. 9, n. 4.

188 Letters ed. Muckle, p. 76, lines 48–51.

189 Heloise ii, p. 119, lines 54–5.

190 See n. 162 above.

191 *Historia Calamitatum*, lines 1550–5.

192 *Historia Calamitatum*, lines 1560–1.

193 Luscombe (1988), p. 280.

194 Heloise i, p. 112, lines 62–8. Dronke, *Women Writers*, p. 115.

195 See ch. 8, nn. 83–5 above.

196 Heloise i, p. 116, lines 231, 251; p. 117, lines 257, 266–7, 273.

197 Dronke, *Testimonies*, pp. 33–4, n. 18. Mews (1995), p. 25, n. 72, disagrees.

198 Heloise i, p. 113, line 111; and see ch. 8, n. 86 above.

199 Heloise i, p. 116, lines 235–7.

200 *Historia Calamitatum*, lines 1314–15.

201 Heloise i, p. 117, lines 263–4; and see ch. 8, n. 83 above.

202 Heloise i, p. 116, lines 217–20; and see ch. 8, nn. 120, 121 above. The meaning of this passage is discussed by McLeod, *Heloise*, pp. 250–1, and Luscombe (1988), pp. 263–4.

203 Letters ed. Muckle, p. 73.

204 *Historia Calamitatum*, lines 1483–4; and see n. 179 above.

205 Letters ed. Muckle, p. 73. Heloise i, p. 116, lines 221–4.

206 *Historia Calamitatum*, lines 1479–80; and see n. 178 above.

207 Luscombe (1988), p. 280.

208 *Historia Calamitatum*, lines 1465–72.
209 *Historia Calamitatum*, lines 1475–6. Juvenal, *Satire 6*, line 460.
210 *Historia Calamitatum*, lines 1477–81; and see nn. 178, 206 above.
211 A. Blamires, *Woman Defamed and Woman Defended* (1992), pp. 25–9, 91, 100–3, 228–32, discusses Juvenal, Abelard and Marbod. For Marbod, see also F. J. E. Raby, *History of Secular Latin Poetry* 2nd edn (1957), vol. i, pp. 329–37; and J. Boswell, *Christianity, Social Tolerance and Homosexuality* (1980), pp. 247–9, 370–1.
212 Marbod, letter 6, Migne, *PL* 171, cols 1481d, 1482b. C. H. Lawrence, *Medieval Monasticism* 2nd edn (1989), p. 222.
213 St Bernard, letter 332, vol. 8, p. 271, line 11.
214 J. Leclercq, *Women and St Bernard* (1989), pp. 169–71, discusses the meaning of *muliercula*.
215 See n. 96 above; and *Historia Calamitatum*, lines 1405–8.
216 *Historia Calamitatum*, lines 1368–80.
217 See ch. 9, nn. 119–23 above. Lament for Samson. ed. P. Dronke in *Poetic Individuality* (1970), p. 122, verse II, 2b, and comment at p. 136, n. 1.
218 Juvenal, *Satire 6*, lines 453–4.
219 These critics are discussed by Dronke, *Women Writers*, pp. 128–9.
220 McLaughlin, 'Peter Abelard and the Dignity of Women', in 'Cluny conference', p. 295.
221 McLaughlin, in 'Cluny conference', p. 291.
222 Letters ed. Muckle, p. 268, lines 39–41. Dronke, *Poetic Individuality*, p. 137.
223 *Sic et Non*, ch. 52.
224 Letters ed. Muckle, p. 268, lines 42–3.
225 Letters ed. Muckle, p. 253, lines 12–13. McLaughlin, in 'Cluny conference', p. 295.
226 Letters ed. Muckle, p. 253, line 16.
227 Letters ed. Muckle, p. 254, line 2.
228 Letters ed. Muckle, p. 254, lines 39–41.
229 Letters ed. Muckle, p. 254, line 36; p. 55, lines 14–15.
230 Letters ed. Muckle, p. 258, lines 16–17.
231 Sermon 13, Migne, *PL* 178, col. 485a–b. McLaughlin, in 'Cluny conference', p. 296.
232 Letters ed. Muckle, pp. 264–6. McLaughlin, in 'Cluny conference', pp. 298–301.
233 Heloise iii, p. 245, lines 11–12. L. Georgianna, 'Heloise's Critique of Monasticism', *Mediaeval Studies* 49 (1987), p. 242.
234 Heloise iii, p. 244, line 40.
235 Heloise iii, p. 244, lines 43–4. Gilson, *Heloise and Abelard*, pp. 136–7.
236 See ch. 10, n. 22 above.
237 Letter ed. McLaughlin, p. 259, lines 22–4.
238 *The Book of St Gilbert* ed. R. Foreville and G. Keir (1987), pp. xlii–xlvi.
239 *The Book of St Gilbert*, p. xx.

240 See n. 208 above.

241 Letter ed. McLaughlin, p. 259, lines 24–5.

242 Letter ed. McLaughlin, p. 259, lines 35–8. McLaughlin, in 'Cluny conference', p. 324.

243 Letter ed. McLaughlin, p. 260, lines 19–22.

244 Letter ed. McLaughlin, p. 259, lines 38–9.

245 C. Waddell, 'Peter Abelard as Creator of Liturgical Texts', in 'Trier conference', pp. 267–86.

246 D. E. Luscombe, in *Monastic Studies II* ed. J. Loades (Bangor conference 1991), p. 9.

247 Migne, *PL* 178, cols 677–8. Dronke, *Women Writers*, pp. 135–8; and see nn. 195, 196 above.

248 Migne, *PL* 178, cols 723–30. Dronke, *Women Writers*, p. 137.

249 P. von Moos, 'Le silence d'Héloïse et les idéologues modernes', in 'Cluny conference', pp. 425–68.

250 See n. 201 above.

251 See n. 6 above.

252 Letter ed. McLaughlin, p. 242. Cf. C. Brooke, *The Medieval Idea of Marriage* (1989), pp. 116–17.

253 Heloise iii, p. 242, lines 9–10.

254 See n. 199 above.

255 C. Lalore, *Collections des principaux cartulaires de Troyes* (1875–90), vol. 2, pp. 1–23.

256 See n. 174 above.

257 See n. 208 above.

258 Peter the Venerable, letter 115, p. 305. Brooke, *The Medieval Idea of Marriage*, p. 118.

259 Migne, *PL* 178, col. 379. Luscombe (1988), p. 268, n. 106.

260 Heloise i, p. 113, line 93.

261 Letters ed. Muckle, p. 90, line 14; and see ch. 8, n. 104 above.

262 Letters ed. Muckle, p. 93, line 15; and see ch. 8, n. 103 above.

263 J. Leclercq, *Monks on Marriage* (1982), p. 26. D. Elliott, *Spiritual Marriage* (1993), pp. 137–8.

264 E. Hamilton, *Heloise* (1966), p. 141.

265 McLeod, *Heloise*, p. 187.

266 St Bernard, letter 193, vol. 8, p. 44, line 19.

267 See ch. 8, n. 25 above.

268 Epitaph, p. 65.

269 Jaffé-Loewenfeld, *Regesta Pontificum Romanorum*, no. 8149. Peter the Venerable, letter 98, p. 259.

270 See nn. 65–7 above.

271 Peter the Venerable, letter 115, p. 306, line 27.

272 Peter the Venerable, letter 115, pp. 306–7; and see letter 111, pp. 285–90, defending variety of dress against St Bernard.

273 Peter the Venerable, letter 115, p. 307, line 2.

274 Letter ed. McLaughlin, p. 282, lines 48–9.
275 Letter ed. McLaughlin, p. 263, line 23.
276 Peter the Venerable, letter 115, p. 307, line 18.
277 J. Jeannin, 'La dernière maladie d'Abélard', *Mélanges St Bernard* (1952), pp. 109–15.
278 Peter the Venerable, letter 98, p. 259, line 19.
279 See ch. 8, nn. 59–60 above.
280 'Absolutio Petri Abaelardi' ed. C. J. Mews and C. S. F. Burnett in *Studia Monastica* 27 (1985), p. 62. McLeod, *Heloise*, p. 206.
281 Heloise i, p. 113, lines 76–8.
282 See n. 259 above.
283 Dronke, *Testimonies*, pp. 51, 23. McLeod, *Heloise*, p. 226.
284 Peter the Venerable, letter 115, p. 308; and see ch. 8, n. 51 above.

CHAPTER 12: THEOLOGIAN

1 St Bernard, letter nos 190, 331, 332, 338, vol. 8, pp. 18 (line 16), 270 (line 4), 272 (line 4), 277 (line 10). For a different account of Abelard as a theologian from that in this chapter, see J. Marenbon, 'Abelard's Theological Project', *The Philosophy of Peter Abelard* (1997), pp. 54–81.
2 Letter ed. Klibansky, p. 6.
3 Heloise i, p. 111, line 21; and see ch. 1, n. 21 above.
4 St Bernard, letter 190, vol. 8, p. 24, lines 24–5; and see ch. 1, n. 22 above.
5 *Historia Calamitatum*, lines 159, 161–3; and see ch. 4, n. 39 above. My interpretation differs from that of R. W. Southern, *Scholastic Humanism and the Unification of Europe*, vol. 1: *Foundations* (1995), p. 207, n. 11.
6 *Historia Calamitatum*, lines 189–90.
7 St Bernard, letter 190, vol. 8, p. 18, lines 17–19; and see ch. 5, n. 74 above.
8 V. Flint, *Honorius Augustodunensis of Regensburg* (1995), p. 130 [36].
9 *Didascalicon*, book 2, ch. 2, ed. C. H. Buttimer (1939), p. 25, and see the similar definitions of William of Conches and William of St Thierry cited by G. R. Evans, *Old Arts and New Theology* (1980), p. 34, nn. 35, 36.
10 Mews CCCM, p. 19, n. 10. Mews (1995), p. 33.
11 Mews CCCM, p. 51, n. 35.
12 Augustine, *City of God*, book 6, ch. 5; book 8, ch. 1. Boethius, *Dialogues on Porphyry*, book 1, ch. 3. Isidore, *Etymologies*, book 2, ch. 24, para. 13.
13 See ch. 4, nn. 71 ff. above.
14 John of Salisbury, book 1, ch. 5, p. 21, line 32.
15 *Historia Calamitatum*, lines 692, 695–8.
16 Clanchy, in *Journal of Ecclesiastical History* 41 (1990), p. 17.
17 *Historia Calamitatum*, lines 698–9; and see ch. 2, n. 33 above.
18 *Theologia Scholarium*, Mews CCCM, p. 313, line 1.
19 *Theologia Scholarium*, p. 313, lines 2–3.
20 *Theologia Scholarium*, p. 313, lines 6–8.
21 *Theologia Scholarium*, pp. 313–14, lines 24–6.

22 Mews CCCM, p. 217. *Epistola ad Abaelardum* ed. Ostlender, in *Florilegium Patristicum* 19 (1929), pp. 35–6.

23 *Historia Calamitatum*, lines 704–5.

24 *Historia Calamitatum*, lines 705–8.

25 Mews, in 'Trier conference', p. 184. Mews CCCM, pp. 18–19. Mews (1995), pp. 54, 56.

26 Peter the Venerable, p. 306; and see ch. 10, n. 66 above.

27 *Theologia Scholarium*, p. 314, lines 33–7.

28 Mews, in 'Trier conference', p. 187.

29 *Theologia Scholarium*, pp. 548–9, lines 1580–629.

30 *Theologia Summi Boni*, p. 200, line 1338.

31 M. L. Colish, *Peter Lombard* (1994), p. 48.

32 *Theologia Summi Boni*, p. 194, lines 1143–6.

33 *Scholastic Humanism* (1995), pp. 51 ff.

34 See ch. 4, n. 101 above.

35 Clanchy, in *Journal of Ecclesiastical History* 41 (1990), pp. 15–16. Mews, in *Archives d'Histoire Doctrinale et Littéraire du Moyen Age* 58 (1991), p. 65.

36 'De Incarnatione Verbi' ed. Schmitt, *St Anselmi Opera Omnia* (1946–61), vol. 2, p. 9, lines 20–1; and see ch. 4, n. 62 above.

37 *Theologia Summi Boni*, p. 201, lines 1361–3.

38 *Theologia Summi Boni*, pp. 86–7, lines 4–6, 7–17, 21–4.

39 Otto of Freising, p. 226, lines 14–15. Luscombe, in *Vivarium* 30 (1992), pp. 137–8. Mews, in *Philosophes Médiévaux* 26 (1986), p. 426, concludes: 'In fact Abelard was saying that the three persons of the Trinity were only names to describe properties of a supreme good ultimately beyond definition.'

40 *Theologia Summi Boni*, p. 86n.

41 See ch. 1, n. 24 above.

42 *The Creeds of the Greek and Latin Churches* ed. P. Schaff (1877), p. 67, no. 13.

43 *Historia Calamitatum*, lines 901–2.

44 *Theologia Scholarium*, pp. 338–9, lines 563–5, 567–8.

45 Luscombe, *School*, pp. 117–19. J. G. Sikes, *Peter Abailard* (1932), p. 157.

46 *Theologia Summi Boni*, p. 201, lines 1346–7; and see ch. 10, n. 53 above.

47 *Theologia Summi Boni*, pp. 88–9, lines 63–74.

48 *Theologia Summi Boni*, p. 91, lines 132–4. Isaiah, ch. 6, verse 3.

49 *Theologia Summi Boni*, p. 98, lines 344–5; p. 97, lines 299–301.

50 Abelard's references are brought together by Luscombe, in Dronke, *Philosophy*, pp. 301–2.

51 *Theologia Summi Boni*, pp. 99–106, 198–200. P. Dronke, *Fabula* (1974), pp. 55–68. T. Gregory, 'The Platonic Inheritance', in Dronke, *Philosophy*, p. 68. L. Moonan, 'Abelard's Use of the "Timaeus"', *Archives d'Histoire Doctrinale et Littéraire du Moyen Age* 56 (1989), pp. 7–90.

52 *Theologia Summi Boni*, p. 110, lines 671–5.

53 See ch. 10, nn. 52, 55 above.
54 *Theologia Summi Boni*, p. 201, lines 1346-51.
55 *Theologia Christiana*, book 4, p. 345, lines 2545-8. *Theologia Scholarium*, p. 497, lines 2676-9.
56 *Ethics*, p. 66, lines 16-18.
57 *Ethics*, p. 62, lines 1-4.
58 *Ethics*, p. 62, lines 5, 14-16.
59 *Commentary on Romans*, Buytaert CCCM, p. 121, lines 345-6.
60 *Commentary on Romans*, p. 121, lines 358-63. I have not been able to trace Abelard's Biblical citation; it is not Ezechiel ch. 33, verses 12 and 19, as stated by Buytaert.
61 *Sic et Non*, ch. 158, p. 527.
62 R. I. Moore, *The Birth of Popular Heresy* (1975), pp. 48-9, citing R. Manselli, in *Bulletino dell'Istituto storico italiano per il medio evo* 65 (1953), pp. 47 ff.
63 See nn. 16, 17 above.
64 Moore, *The Birth*, p. 50.
65 *Sic et Non*, p. 103, lines 338-9.
66 See n. 20 above.
67 See ch. 5, n. 58 above.
68 See ch. 5, n. 55 above.
69 See ch. 9, n. 36 above.
70 *Theologia Summi Boni*, p. 111, lines 699-701.
71 *Theologia Summi Boni*, pp. 111-12, lines 702-28. Augustine, *City of God*, book 8, ch. 3.
72 See ch. 8, nn. 109, 110 above.
73 See ch. 9, n. 4 above.
74 'The Repression of Heloise', *Journal of Medieval and Renaissance Studies* 22 (1992), p. 151, and her *From Virile Woman to Woman Christ* (1995), p. 70.
75 See ch. 8, n. 96 above.
76 *Historia Calamitatum*, lines 534-5, 536-7; and see ch. 10, n. 32 above.
77 *Soliloquium*, p. 887.
78 *Theologia Christiana*, p. 149, lines 159-60.
79 Poole, *Illustrations of the History of Medieval Thought and Learning* (1884), 2nd edn (1921), p. 153.
80 A. J. Minnis and A. B. Scott, *Medieval Literary Theory and Criticism: the Commentary Tradition* (1988), pp. 24-5; and see ch. 8, n. 40 above.
81 *Historia Calamitatum*, lines 244-81.
82 O. Lottin, *Psychologie et morale* (1942), vol. 5, pp. 42-3, 48 (no. 50). J. Marenbon, 'Abelard's Concept of Natural Law', *Miscellanea Mediaevalia* 21 (1992), pp. 611-12.
83 See n. 136 below.
84 Confession of Faith to Heloise, p. 152, paras 3, 4, 1.
85 Mews (1995), p. 61. *Ethics*, p. xxx.
86 *Theologia Summi Boni*, p. 117, lines 74-5.

87 Heloise i, p. 116, lines 211–13; and see ch. 8, nn. 70, 71 above.
88 See ch. 4, nn. 93 and 92 above.
89 *Historia Calamitatum*, lines 282–4.
90 Migne, *PL* 178, col. 678c. Dronke, *Women Writers*, p. 136.
91 Migne, *PL* 178, col. 723a.
92 *Ethics*, p. 54, lines 27–8.
93 Migne, *PL* 178, cols. 723–30.
94 See ch. 11, n. 248 above.
95 *Ethics*, p. 52, lines 17–22.
96 *Ethics*, p. 54, line 32 – p. 56, line 4.
97 *Ethics*, p. 56, line 10. Luke, ch. 23, verse 34.
98 *Ethics*, p. 60, lines 1–13; p. 62, lines 5–10.
99 *Ethics*, p. 66, lines 32–5.
100 *Ethics*, p. 66, lines 23–4.
101 See n. 55 above.
102 Mews, 'Lists of Heresies', pp. 109–10, nos 6, 9, 10, 12, 13, 16, 19.
103 Confessio 'Universis', p. 138. *Ethics*, p. 14, lines 14–24.
104 *Ethics*, p. 20, lines 1–6.
105 St Bernard, letter 190, vol. 8, p. 26, line 7.
106 St Bernard, letter 190, vol. 8, p. 20, lines 16–23. 'Bernard had been reading Anselm', G. R. Evans, *The Mind of St Bernard* (1983), p. 156.
107 Letters ed. Smits, no. 14, p. 280, lines 28–9.
108 *Theologia Christiana*, p. 304, line 1230.
109 St Bernard, letter 190, vol. 8, p. 18, line 23; p. 21, lines 10–18; p. 23, lines 1–9; and see ch. 5, n. 51 above.
110 See ch. 11, n. 63 above.
111 *Theologia Scholarium*, pp. 462–3, particularly lines 1663–9.
112 *Theologia Christiana*, p. 306, lines 1310–13.
113 *Theologia Christiana*, p. 307, lines 1317–18.
114 St Bernard, letter 338, vol. 8, p. 278, lines 3–4; and see n. 16 above.
115 See ch. 2, nn. 26–34 above.
116 *Dialogue*, p. 97, lines 1478–81; and see p. 93, line 1385.
117 St Bernard, letter 190, vol. 8, pp. 26–38.
118 *St Anselm* (1990), p. 211. For another view, see D. E. Luscombe, 'St Anselm and Abelard', *Anselm Studies* 1 (1983), pp. 213–18.
119 *De Sacramentis*, book 1, part 8, ch. 3, Migne, *PL* 176, cols. 307–8.
120 Mews, 'Lists of Heresies', p. 108, no. 4.
121 *De Sacramentis*, book 1, part 8, chs 3–4, col. 307.
122 See ch. 4, n. 104 above.
123 E.g. C. M. Kauffmann, *Romanesque Manuscripts 1066–1190* (1975), plate 224, and K. E. Haney, *The Winchester Psalter* (1986), plate 23.
124 Buytaert CCCM, vol. 11, pp. 113–18.
125 See ch. 4, nn. 105–6; and ch. 10, nn. 48–9 above.
126 M. T. Clanchy, 'Law and Love in the Middle Ages', *Disputes and Settlements* ed. J. Bossy (1983), p. 59.

127 *Commentary on Romans*, Buytaert CCCM, vol. 11, p. 117, lines 232–8. R. E. Weingart, *The Logic of Divine Love*, (1970), p. 88.
128 *Theologia Scholarium*, p. 549, lines 1623–6.
129 *Commentary on Romans*, p. 113, lines 124–5.
130 R. Peppermüller, *Abaelards Auslegung des Römerbriefes* (1972), pp. 11–14.
131 *Commentary on Romans*, p. 118, lines 271–4.
132 Sermons, nos 7–12. Weingart, *The Logic of Divine Love*, p. 138.
133 Letters ed. Muckle, p. 92, lines 5–7.
134 Heloise i, p. 114, lines 156–7.
135 *Commentary on Romans*, p. 118, lines 256–61.
136 Letters ed. Muckle, p. 92, lines 24–5; and see ch. 1, n. 44 above.
137 Southern, *St Anselm* (1990), pp. 210–11.
138 Lottin, *Psychologie et morale*, vol. 5, pp. 206–7.
139 St Bernard, sermons on Canticles, no. 20, vol. 1, p. 118, lines 21–6. R. W. Southern, *The Making of the Middle Ages* (1953), p. 233.

CHAPTER 13: HERETIC

1 St Bernard, letter 331, vol. 8, p. 269, lines 16–17.
2 Guibert de Nogent, ch. 17, pp. 428–34.
3 *Historia Calamitatum*, lines 722–6.
4 Ivo of Chartres, letter 7, Migne, *PL* 162, col. 17. Yves de Chartres, *Correspondance* ed. J. Leclercq (1949), pp. 23-7.
5 'De Incarnatione Verbi', ed. Schmitt, *St Anselmi Opera Omnia* (1946–61), vol. 2, p. 5, line 1.
6 Letters ed. Smits, no. 14, p. 280, lines 31–2.
7 'St Bernardi Vita Prima', Migne, *PL* 185, col. 311c. Otto of Freising, p. 228, lines 4–5.
8 St Bernard, letter 189, vol. 8, p. 14, lines 4–5; and see ch. 10, n. 64 above.
9 St Bernard, letter 190, vol. 8, p. 26, lines 25–7; and see ch. 4, n. 147 above.
10 Confessio 'Universis', p. 138.
11 Letter ed. Klibansky.
12 St Bernard, letter 193, vol. 8, p. 45, lines 12–14; letter 331, p. 270, lines 8–10; and see ch. 10, nn. 60–2 above.
13 C. J. Mews, 'St Anselm and Roscelin', *Archives d'Histoire Doctrinale et Littéraire du Moyen Age* 58 (1991), p. 64.
14 William of St Thierry, p. 378, lines 67–8.
15 Peter the Venerable, letter 98, p. 259; and see n. 199 below.
16 Comments by Constable in Peter the Venerable, vol. 2, pp. 164–5; and see P. Zerbi, in 'Cluny conference', p. 220.
17 M. Gibson, 'The Case of Berengar of Tours', in *Councils and Assemblies* ed. G. J. Cumming and D. Baker (1971), pp. 61–8.
18 Roscelin, p. 65, lines 13–17.
19 Letter 136, ed. Schmitt, *St Anselmi Opera Omnia*, vol. 3, p. 280, lines 25–6. Southern, *St Anselm* (1990), pp. 176–80. Mews, 'St Anselm and Roscelin' (n. 13 above), pp. 65–6.

20   Letters ed. Smits, no. 14, p. 280, lines 28–32.

21   Roscelin, p. 63, lines 3–4; p. 65, lines 26–7; and see ch. 4, n. 17 above.

22   Otto of Freising, p. 224, line 229.

23   *Dialectica*, pp. xix, 554–5; and see ch. 5, n. 39 above.

24   Roscelin, p. 65, line 26.

25   See ch. 4, n. 18 above.

26   Mews (1995), p. 10.

27   C. J. Mews, 'In Search of a Name and its Significance', *Traditio* 44 (1988), pp. 172–3.

28   F. Barlow, *The English Church* 1066–1154 (1979), p. 246.

29   Roscelin, p. 65, lines 24–5, 27–8.

30   Migne, *PL* 163, cols. 767–70. Barlow, *The English Church*, p. 246.

31   Roscelin, p. 65, lines 3–4.

32   J. Marenbon, *Early Medieval Philosophy* (1983), pp. 134–5; and see ch. 4, n. 61 above.

33   See n. 27 above.

34   Letters ed. Smits, no. 14, pp. 279–80.

35   Letter ed. Klibansky, p. 7.

36   *Historia Calamitatum*, lines 708–20.

37   See Cono's biography in *Dictionnaire d'histoire et de géographie ecclésias-tique* vol. 13, pp. 461–71; and I. S. Robinson, *The Papacy 1073–1198* (1990), pp. 64, 157, 430.

38   *Historia Calamitatum*, lines 855–6, 717–18.

39   Otto of Freising, p. 226, lines 19–20.

40   Clanchy, in *Journal of Ecclesiastical History* 41 (1990), pp. 15–16.

41   *Historia Calamitatum*, lines 714–15.

42   See ch. 11, nn. 55–8 above.

43   *Historia Calamitatum*, lines 838–9.

44   *Historia Calamitatum*, lines 751–81.

45   S. E. Chodorow, 'Ecclesiastical Politics and the Ending of the Investiture Contest', *Speculum* 46 (1971), pp. 629–37.

46   Benton, in 'Cluny conference', p. 486, n. 41.

47   William of St Thierry, ed. Leclercq, in *Revue Bénédictine* 79 (1969), p. 377, line 16.

48   Robinson, *The Papacy 1073–1198*, p. 156 (abbreviated).

49   Henry archbishop of Sens, Letter to Innocent II, ed. J. Leclercq, in *'Sapientia Doctrina': Mélanges offerts à Hildebrand Bascour* (1980), p. 190, line 96.

50   Chodorow, 'Ecclesiastical Politics', pp. 630–1.

51   Suger, *Louis VI*, ch. 27, p. 204, lines 1–3.

52   Cono's biography, n. 37 above; and Hugh the Chanter, *History of the Church of York* 2nd edn (1990), p. 152.

53   Bautier, in 'Nantes conference', p. 64.

54   *Historia Calamitatum*, lines 723–4; and see n. 3 above.

55   See n. 15 above.

56 Henry archbishop of Sens (see n. 49 above), p. 187, lines 19–23.
57 *Historia Calamitatum*, lines 726–8.
58 *Historia Calamitatum*, lines 731–5.
59 *Historia Calamitatum*, lines 878–80.
60 *Historia Calamitatum*, lines 827–32.
61 Letters ed. Smits, no. 14, p. 279, lines 17–21.
62 *Historia Calamitatum*, lines 844–6.
63 *Historia Calamitatum*, lines 848–51.
64 Otto of Freising, p. 226, lines 23–4.
65 Letters ed. Smits, no. 14, p. 279, line 10. Mews CCCM, pp. 39–44. Luscombe (1988), p. 260.
66 See n. 40 above.
67 'De Incarnatione Verbi', ed. Schmitt, *St Anselmi Opera Omnia*, vol. 2, p. 6, lines 6–7.
68 *Historia Calamitatum*, lines 852–4.
69 *Ethics*, p. 40, lines 3–5.
70 *Contra Petrobrusianos* ed. J. V. Fearns, CCCM vol. 10 (1968), p. 146, lines 2–3 (para. 247).
71 *Theologia Christiana*, p. 204, lines 284–5, 280–2. R. I. Moore, *The Formation of a Persecuting Society* (1987), p. 68.
72 *Theologia Summi Boni*, p. 118, lines 4–12.
73 *Theologia Christiana*, pp. 202–3, lines 229–63.
74 *Theologia Scholarium*, p. 315, lines 77–8.
75 *Theologia Scholarium*, p. 315, lines 74–7.
76 See ch. 12, nn. 20–1 above.
77 *Historia Calamitatum*, lines 254–5, 25–30.
78 *Historia Calamitatum*, lines 262–9.
79 *Ethics*, p. 40, lines 7–8.
80 *Ethics*, p. 40, lines 9–11.
81 Confessio 'Universis', p. 138, lines 12–13. Luke, ch. 6, verse 37.
82 *Theologia Scholarium*, p. 439, lines 985–95.
83 See n. 4 above.
84 See nn. 3, 7 above.
85 See n. 9 above.
86 Mews CCCM, pp. 283–5. Mews (1995), p. 18. Marenbon, 'A Life', pp. 28–9.
87 Confessio 'Universis', pp. 132–8.
88 *Historia Calamitatum*, lines 817–19.
89 St Bernard, letter 189, vol. 8, p. 14, line 17.
90 *Historia Calamitatum*, lines 922–7.
91 *Historia Calamitatum*, lines 863–6.
92 *Historia Calamitatum*, lines 867, 925.
93 *Historia Calamitatum*, lines 869–70.
94 See nn. 2, 3 above.
95 See ch. 12, n. 25 above.

96   *Historia Calamitatum*, lines 851–2.
97   See n. 183 below.
98   *Historia Calamitatum*, lines 896–7.
99   *Historia Calamitatum*, lines 898–900.
100   *Historia Calamitatum*, lines 903–4.
101   *Historia Calamitatum*, lines 905–6.
102   *Historia Calamitatum*, lines 906–9.
103   *Historia Calamitatum*, line 934.
104   *Historia Calamitatum*, line 915.
105   Goswin, p. 445e.
106   The sources for Abelard's trial at Sens are listed by Mews (1995), pp. 45–7, 62–4.
107   *De Nugis Curialium*, i, 24, ed. M. R. James (1983), pp. 78–80.
108   Henry archbishop of Sens (see n. 49 above), p. 189, lines 74–6.
109   Otto of Freising, p. 228, lines 2–4.
110   Henry archbishop of Sens, p. 189, lines 82–3.
111   St Bernard, letter 189, vol. 8, p. 15, lines 5–6.
112   St Bernard, letter 189, vol. 8, p. 15, line 8.
113   Henry archbishop of Sens, pp. 189–90, lines 85–8.
114   St Bernard, letter 189, vol. 8, p. 15, lines 8–9.
115   St Bernard, letter 190, vol. 8, p. 26, lines 8–9.
116   William of St Thierry, ed. Leclercq (see n. 47 above), p. 378, lines 71–2, 74–5.
117   Confessio 'Universis', p. 138.
118   C. J. Mews, 'The *Sententie* of Peter Abelard', *Recherches de théologie ancienne et médiévale* 53 (1986), pp. 132, 169–74.
119   Henry archbishop of Sens, p. 190, lines 99–101.
120   Henry archbishop of Sens, p. 190, lines 101–6.
121   Berengar of Poitiers, pp. 112–14.
122   *Historia Pontificalis* ed. M. Chibnall (1956), p. 19.
123   Mews CCCM, p. 283.
124   Confessio 'Universis', p. 138. 'Apologia Contra Bernardum', Buytaert CCCM, vol. 11, p. 361, line 43.
125   E. Little, in *Bernard of Clairvaux: Studies Presented to Dom J. Leclercq* (1973), pp. 59–61. Luscombe, *School*, pp. 115–42.
126   Mews, 'Lists of Heresies', p. 108.
127   See ch. 12, nn. 38–44 above; and Luscombe, *School*, pp. 115–19.
128   Confessio 'Universis', p. 134.
129   'Apologia Contra Bernardum' (see n. 124 above), p. 361, lines 72–4.
130   'Apologia Contra Bernardum', p. 361, lines 75–7, 70–1.
131   'Apologia Contra Bernardum', p. 362, lines 82–3. Mews CCCM, p. 286, shows that this 'Apologia' was written before Abelard's trial at Sens.
132   'Apologia Contra Bernardum', p. 362, lines 83–4.
133   'Apologia Contra Bernardum', p. 362, lines 84–6.
134   St Bernard, letter 331, vol. 8, p. 269, lines 9–12.

135 St Bernard, letter 190, vol. 8, pp. 17–18; p. 27, line 3; p. 31, lines 18–19; p. 36, lines 9–10.
136 St Bernard, letter 190, vol. 8, p. 27, lines 3, 11, 26.
137 St Bernard, letter 189, vol. 8, p. 15, lines 8–9.
138 Henry archbishop of Sens, p. 189, lines 84–5; p. 190, lines 94–5.
139 Henry archbishop of Sens (see n. 49 above), p. 190, lines 96–7. Samson, archbishop of Reims, in St Bernard, vol. 8, p. 42, line 9.
140 Letter ed. Klibansky, p. 7.
141 St Bernard, letter 187, vol. 8, p. 10, lines 6–7.
142 Letter ed. Klibansky. St Bernard, letter 187.
143 See n. 93 above.
144 Berengar of Poitiers, p. 116, line 10. Henry archbishop of Sens, p. 187, line 90. Geoffrey of Auxerre, 'St Bernardi Vita Prima', Migne, *PL* 185, col. 311c–d.
145 See ch. 11, n. 277 above.
146 See ch. 10, n. 43 above.
147 Migne, *PL* 178, col. 469c, 561c. Book of Daniel, ch. 13, verse 42. C. S. Jaeger, 'Abelard's Silence at the Council of Sens', *Res Publica Litterarum* 3 (1980), pp. 35 ff.
148 J. C. Morison, *The Life and Times of St Bernard* (1863), p. 313.
149 William of St Thierry, ed. Leclercq, p. 377, lines 19–20. St Bernard, letter 193, vol. 8, p. 45, lines 12–15; and see letter 331, p. 270, lines 8–10.
150 Luscombe, *School*, pp. 20–1.
151 See n. 12 above.
152 Luscombe, *School*, pp. 22–3. Mews (1995), p. 17, n. 40.
153 John of Salisbury, *Historia Pontificalis* ed. Chibnall (1956), pp. 63–4. Luscombe, *School*, pp. 27–9.
154 St Bernard, letter 189, vol. 8, p. 16, line 8; letter 338, p. 278, lines 18–19.
155 Otto of Freising, book 2, ch. 28. Mews (1995), p. 17.
156 Mews (1995), p. 17, n. 40 (citing Zerbi). Luscombe, *School*, pp. 23–6.
157 See nn. 140–2 above.
158 St Bernard, letter 182, vol. 8, p. 2, lines 11–12, 15–16.
159 J. Leclercq, 'Literature and Psychology in Bernard of Clairvaux', *The Downside Review* 93 (1975), pp. 15–16.
160 Leclercq, 'Literature and Psychology', p. 16.
161 St Bernard, letter 327, vol. 8, p. 263, lines 9–10.
162 Henry archbishop of Sens, p. 188, lines 41–5. Mews CCCM, p. 283.
163 'St Bernardi Vita Prima', Migne, *PL* 185, col. 311a.
164 Confessio 'Universis', p. 138, line 5. 'Apologia Contra Bernardum' (see n. 124 above), p. 366, lines 230–1.
165 Berengar of Poitiers, p. 117, lines 9–10.
166 St Bernard, letter 158, vol. 7, p. 366, lines 4–5.
167 St Bernard, letter 165, vol. 7, p. 376, line 4; letter 168, p. 380, lines 14–18. In general see G. Constable, 'The Disputed Election at Langres', *Traditio* 13 (1957), pp. 119–52.

168   St Bernard, letter 501, vol. 8, p. 58, lines 15–17.

169   Leclercq, 'Literature and Psychology' (see n. 159 above), p. 16.

170   Peter the Venerable, letter 29 (excerpts), p. 103, lines 29–30; p. 104, lines 1–3; p. 103, lines 38–9; p. 102, lines 24–8; p. 102, lines 38–9; p. 103, lines 1–2. Morison, *The Life and Times of St Bernard*, pp. 222–3.

171   St Bernard, letter 387, vol. 8, pp. 355–6.

172   G. Constable, 'Nicholas of Montiéramey' (alias 'of Clairvaux'), in Peter the Venerable, vol. 2, especially pp. 318–19; and see nn. 197–8 below.

173   St Bernard, letter 189, vol. 8, p. 16, lines 10–11; letter 338, lines 20–1.

174   Constable, 'Nicholas of Montiéramey', pp. 327–30.

175   Constable, 'Nicholas of Montiéramey', p. 320, n. 19.

176   Mews CCCM, p. 285, n. 137; and Mews (1995), p. 19, n. 47. Marenbon, 'A Life', p. 30, n. 100.

177   Berengar of Poitiers, p. 116, line 14. Acts of the Apostles, ch. 25, verse 12.

178   Berengar of Poitiers, p. 116, lines 15–16, 17–18, 26–7.

179   See n. 119 above.

180   See nn. 4–6 above.

181   'St Bernardi Vita Prima', Migne, *PL* 185, col. 311d.

182   John of Salisbury, *Historia Pontificalis* ed. Chibnall, p. 19.

183   Innocent II's public letter is no. 194, in St Bernard, vol. 8, particularly p. 48, lines 9–12. Innocent II's confidential letter is ed. Leclercq, in *Revue Bénédictine* 79 (1969), p. 379. See also Mews CCCM, p. 285, n. 137; Mews (1995), p. 19; Marenbon, 'A Life', pp. 33–4.

184   Migne, *PL* 185, cols. 595–6, para. 14; and see ch. 2, n. 9 above. For Guy of Castello, see nn. 12, 151 above.

185   Innocent II's public letter, p. 48, lines 5–7; p. 46, lines 11–12; and see ch. 10, n. 56 above.

186   Innocent II's public letter, p. 48, line 7. I. S. Robinson, *The Papacy 1073–1198* (1990), p. 108.

187   Innocent II's public letter, p. 48, lines 7–9.

188   Henry archbishop of Sens (see n. 49 above), p. 190, lines 97–106.

189   Innocent II's public letter, p. 48, lines 13–15.

190   Innocent II's public letter, p. 47, lines 21–2.

191   Clanchy, in *Journal of Ecclesiastical History* 41 (1990), pp. 2–3.

192   See ch. 1, n. 4 above.

193   Peter the Venerable, letter 98, p. 258.

194   Peter the Venerable, letter 111, p. 277, lines 6–7. P. Zerbi, in 'Cluny conference', p. 217.

195   Peter the Venerable, vol. 2, pp. 38–9. Cicero, *Ad Herennium*, book 4, ch. 32, para. 43.

196   See n. 109 above.

197   Mews CCCM, pp. 284–5. Constable, 'Nicholas of Montiéramey', pp. 316–17; and see nn. 172–3 above.

198   St Bernard, letter 387, vol. 8, p. 355. Constable, 'Nicholas of Montiéramey', p. 321.

199 Peter the Venerable, letter 98, p. 259, lines 5–6; and see nn. 15, 16 above.
200 Mews CCCM, p. 290, n. 149. Mews (1995), p. 19, n. 50.
201 *Historia Pontificalis*, ed. Chibnall, p. 16 (my translation).
202 See n. 184 above.
203 See n. 181 above.
204 Peter the Venerable, letter 98, p. 259.
205 Mews CCCM, pp. 290, 287–9, 255–6.
206 Confessio 'Universis', p. 133, lines 18–19.
207 See ch. 12, n. 2 above.
208 See ch. 11, nn. 136ff. above.
209 Otto of Freising, pp. 234–7. Mews CCCM, p. 286.
210 Peter the Venerable, letter 115, p. 307, lines 3–4.
211 Innocent II's public letter, p. 48, line 10.
212 Peter the Venerable, letter 115, vol. 1, p. 307, lines 18–19; and see ch. 11, n. 276 above.
213 Peter the Venerable, letter 98, p. 259, lines 6–9.
214 Peter the Venerable, letter 98, p. 259, line 13; letter 115, p. 306, lines 2–3.
215 Peter the Venerable, letter 98, p. 259, lines 17–22.
216 Goswin, p. 445d. St Bernard, letter 189, vol. 8, p. 13, line 16; letter 330, p. 267, line 21. Revelation, ch. 20, verse 2.
217 See ch. 10, n. 1 above.
218 Peter the Venerable, letter 115, p. 307, lines 7–8; and see ch. 10, n. 58 above.
219 Mews CCCM, p. 291.
220 Mews CCCM, p. 290. See also Mews (1995), pp. 19, 20; and L. Grane, *Peter Abelard* (1970), p. 152.
221 Peter the Venerable, letter 167, p. 401, lines 2–4.
222 Absolution, ed. C. J. Mews and C. S. F. Burnett, in *Studia Monastica* 27 (1985), p. 62, and see p. 43.
223 Peter the Venerable, letter 133, p. 338, lines 17–23.
224 Epitaph, p. 65; and see ch. 11, n. 268 above.
225 Noted in 1616 by Duschesne (Andreas Quercetanus), Migne, *PL* 178, col. 176c. I owe this reference to Constant Mews.

CHAPTER 14: HIMSELF

1 *Abélard ou la philosophie dans le langage* (1969), p. 95, trans. J. Marenbon, *The Philosophy of Peter Abelard* (1997), p. 2.
2 Epitaph, p. 65. *Historia Calamitatum*, lines 254–5; and see ch. 1, n. 7, and ch. 9, n. 109 above.
3 M. Haren, *Medieval Thought* 2nd edn (1992), p. 105.
4 See ch. 7, n. 16 above.
5 'Ludam scilicet ut illudar', cited by J. Leclercq, in 'Cluny conference', p. 672.
6 D. Knowles, *The Evolution of Medieval Thought* (1962), p. 122.

7   See ch. 1, n. 28 above.
8   See ch. 2, n. 26 above.
9   See ch. 6, n. 18, and ch. 12, n. 25 above.
10   St Bernard, letter 331, p. 269, lines 15–17.
11   Knowles, *Evolution of Medieval Thought*, p. 124.
12   'Cluny conference', p. 501; or Benton, *Culture, Power and Personality in Medieval France* ed. T. N. Bisson (1991), p. 448. For the forgery question, see ch. 1, n. 55 above.
13   Roscelin, p. 78, lines 16–18.
14   Fulk of Deuil, p. 704, lines 26–7.
15   Fulk of Deuil, p. 704, lines 14–16.
16   Otto of Freising, p. 224, lines 27–8, 31; p. 226, lines 1–3.
17   Clanchy, 'Abelard's Mockery of St Anselm', *Journal of Ecclesiastical History* 41 (1990), pp. 2ff; and see: C. J. Mews, in *Exemplaria* 2 (1990), pp. 476, 493, n. 6; Haren, *Medieval Thought* 2nd edn (1992), pp. 219–21.
18   Dronke, *Testimonies*, p. 14.
19   Dronke, *Testimonies*, pp. 30–1.
20   St Bernard, letter 193, vol. 8, p. 45, lines 7–9.
21   D. W. Robertson Jr, *Abelard and Heloise* (1972), p. 214.
22   See ch. 1, n. 57 above.
23   Robertson, *Abelard and Heloise*, pp. 219–22.
24   *The Cole Porter Songbook*, PolyGram Records Inc., New York, 1956.
25   *The Oxford Illustrated History of Medieval Europe* (1988), p. ix.
26   N. Davies, *A History of Europe* (1996), p. 349.
27   See ch. 12, n. 74 above.
28   *Historia Calamitatum*, line 12.
29   J. T. Muckle, in *Medieval Studies* 12 (1950), p. 165.
30   Confessio 'Universis', p. 132, lines 8–9.
31   Epitaph, p. 65.
32   See ch. 1, n. 26; ch. 2, n. 25; ch. 5, n. 44; ch. 6, n. 2; ch. 10, n. 41 above.
33   John of Salisbury, book 3, ch. 1, p. 103, line 10; and see ch. 4, n. 117 above.
34   John of Salisbury, book 3, ch. 1, p. 103, lines 8–9.
35   See n. 16 above.
36   See ch. 1, n. 59 above.
37   See ch. 11, n. 66; ch. 13, n. 105 above.
38   Gilson, *Heloise and Abelard*, p. 105.
39   See ch. 9, n. 22 above.
40   Epitaph, p. 65.
41   St Bernard, letter 193, vol. 8, p. 44, line 17.
42   See ch. 1, n. 47 above.
43   M. M. McLaughlin, in *Speculum* 42 (1967), p. 488.
44   Hugh of St Victor, *Didascalicon*, ed. C. H. Buttimer (1939), book 1, ch. 1, p. 4, lines 9–11.
45   St Bernard, letter 192, vol. 8, p. 44, lines 2–3.
46   See ch. 5, n. 55 above.

47 See n. 5 above.
48 *Soliloquium*, p. 885.
49 See n. 43 above.
50 *Historia Calamitatum*, lines 1561–2.
51 *Historia Calamitatum*, lines 1569–71. John, ch. 15, verses 20, 18.
52 D. K. Frank, 'Abelard as Imitator of Christ', *Viator* 1 (1970), pp. 107–13.
53 For Ajax, see ch. 7, n. 94, and ch. 10, n. 63 above. For Jerome, see ch. 11, nn. 150, 151 above.
54 Confession of Faith to Heloise, p. 152; and see ch. 5, n. 83 above.
55 Epitaph, p. 65; and see ch. 5, n. 9 above.
56 See ch. 3, n. 68, and ch. 8, n. 124 above.
57 S. Reynolds, *Medieval Reading: Grammar, Rhetoric and the Classical Text* (1996).
58 *Sic et Non*, pp. 89–90, lines 20–30.
59 See nn. 33, 34 above.
60 See ch. 7, n. 38, and ch. 10, n. 47 above.
61 See ch. 10, n. 39 above.
62 *Sic et Non*, pp. 90–1, lines 44–6.
63 Confessio 'Universis', p. 138.
64 St Bernard, letter 193, vol. 8, p. 44, line 18.
65 See ch. 7, n. 112 above.
66 See ch. 8, n. 25, and ch. 7, n. 4 above.
67 Hymns, no. 29.
68 Epitaph, p. 65.
69 Heloise i, p. 117, lines 274–275; and see p. 150 above.

Suggestions for Further Reading

This is not a list of all the works I have consulted, but a selection of writings available in English. C. J. Mews provides a full bibliography in his 'Peter Abelard', *Authors of the Middle Ages* ed. P. J. Geary, vol. 2, no. 5 (1995).

WORKS OF ABELARD IN ENGLISH TRANSLATION

Dialogue of a Philosopher with a Jew and a Christian trans. P. J. Payer (1979).
Ethical Writings trans. P. V. Spade (1995).
Ethics ed. and trans. D. E. Luscombe (1971).
'Exposition of the Epistle to the Romans' (excerpt) ed. E. R. Fairweather, *A Scholastic Miscellany* (1956), pp. 276–87.
'Prologues to the *Sic et Non* and St Paul's Epistle to the Romans' trans. A. J. Minnis and A. B. Scott, *Medieval Literary Theory and Criticism* (1988), pp. 87–105.
'The Glosses on Porphyry' trans. R. McKeon, *Selections from Medieval Philosophers* (1929) i; pp. 208–58. Also trans. P. V. Spade in *Five Texts on the Medieval Problem of Universals* (1994), pp. 26–56.
The Hymns of Abelard in English Verse trans. Sister Jane Patricia (1986).
The Letters of Abelard and Heloise trans. B. Radice (1974).
'The Seventh Letter: Touching the Origin of Nuns' trans. C. K. Scott Moncrieff, *The Letters of Abelard and Heloise* (1925), pp. 131–75.
'Soliloquium' trans. C. Burnett in *Studi Medievali* 25 (1984), pp. 892–4.

SECONDARY WORKS

A. S. Abulafia, *Christians and Jews in the Twelfth-Century Renaissance* (1995).
S. Bagge, 'The Autobiography of Abelard and Medieval Individualism', *Journal of Medieval History* 19 (1993), pp. 327–50.
J. W. Baldwin, *The Scholastic Culture of the Middle Ages, 1000–1300* (1971).
R. L. Benson and G. Constable eds, *Renaissance and Renewal in the Twelfth Century* (1982).

J. F. Benton, *Culture, Power and Personality in Medieval France* [collected papers ed. T. N. Bisson] (1991).

J. F. Benton ed., *Self and Society in Medieval France: The Memoirs of Abbot Guibert of Nogent* (1970).

C. N. L. Brooke, *The Medieval Idea of Marriage* (1989).

M. T. Clanchy, 'Abelard's Mockery of St Anselm', *Journal of Ecclesiastical History* 41 (1990), pp. 1-23.

J. J. Cohen and B. Wheeler, eds., *Becoming Male in the Middle Ages* (1997) (includes 3 articles on Abelard's castration).

M. L. Colish, *Medieval Foundations of the Western Intellectual Tradition, 400–1400* (1997).

P. Dronke, *Abelard and Heloise in Medieval Testimonies* (1976), reprinted in his *Intellectuals and Poets in Medieval Europe*, Storia e Letteratura 183 (Rome, 1992), pp. 247–94.

P. Dronke ed., *A History of Twelfth-Century Western Philosophy* (1988).

P. Dronke, *Women Writers of the Middle Ages* (1984).

G. R. Evans, *Anselm and a New Generation* (1980).

G. R. Evans, *Old Arts and New Theology* (1980).

S. C. Ferruolo, *The Origins of the University: The Schools of Paris and their Critics 1100–1215* (1985).

L. Georgianna, 'Any Corner of Heaven: Heloise's Critique of Monasticism', *Mediaeval Studies* 49 (1987), pp. 221–53.

É. Gilson, *Heloise and Abelard* trans. by L. K. Shook (1953) of Gilson's *Heloise et Abélard* (1938).

L. Grane, *Peter Abelard* trans. by F. and C. Crowley (1970) of Grane's *Pierre Abélard* (1964) in Danish.

L. Grant, *Abbot Suger of St Denis* (1998).

A. Gurevich, *The Origins of European Individualism* (1995).

M. Haren, *Medieval Thought: the Western Intellectual Tradition from Antiquity to the 13th Century* 2nd edn (1992).

Hugh of St Victor, *The Didascalicon* trans. J. Taylor (1961).

C. S. Jaeger, *Ennobling Love: In Search of a Lost Sensibility* (1999).

C. S. Jaeger, *The Envy of Angels: Cathedral Schools and Social Ideals in Medieval Europe 950–1200* (1994).

B. S. James, trans., *The Letters of St Bernard of Clairvaux* (1953).

John of Salisbury, *The Metalogicon* trans. D. D. McGarry (1955).

D. Knowles, *The Evolution of Medieval Thought* (1962).

J. Leclercq, *Monks on Marriage: a Twelfth-Century View* (1982).

J. Le Goff, *Intellectuals in the Middle Ages* (1993).

D. E. Luscombe, 'From Paris to the Paraclete: the Correspondence of Abelard and Heloise', *Proceedings of the British Academy* 74 (1988), pp. 247–83.

D. E. Luscombe, *Peter Abelard*, The Historical Association, London (1979), pamphlet no. G95.

D. E. Luscombe, *The School of Peter Abelard* (1969).

J. Marenbon, *Early Medieval Philosophy: an Introduction* (1983).

J. Marenbon, *The Philosophy of Peter Abelard* (1997) [includes a concise life of Abelard and discussion of the authenticity of the letters of Abelard and Heloise].

M. M. McLaughlin, 'Abelard and the Dignity of Women', in *Pierre Abélard – Pierre le Vénérable* ed. R. Louis, J. Jolivet, J. Châtillon (1975), pp. 287–334.

M. M. McLaughlin, 'Abelard as Autobiographer', *Speculum* 42 (1967), pp. 463–88.

E. McLeod, *Heloise – a Biography* 2nd edn (1971).

C. J. Mews, 'In Search of a Name and its Significance: a Twelfth-Century Anecdote about Thierry and Peter Abelard', *Traditio* 44 (1988), pp. 171–200.

C. J. Mews, 'Orality, Literacy and Authority in the 12th Century Schools', *Exemplaria* 2 (1990), pp. 475–92.

C. J. Mews, *The Lost Love Letters of Heloise and Abelard* (1999).

C. Morris, *The Discovery of the Individual 1050–1200* (1972).

B. Newman, 'Authority, Authenticity and the Repression of Heloise', *Journal of Medieval and Renaissance Studies* 22 (1992), pp. 121–58, reprinted in her *From Virile Woman to Woman Christ* (1995).

J. Pelikan, *The Growth of Medieval Theology 600–1300* (1978).

R. Pernoud, *Heloise and Abelard* (1973).

R. L. Poole, *Illustrations of the History of Medieval Thought and Learning* 2nd edn (1921).

M. B. Pranger, *Bernard of Clairvaux and the Shape of Monastic Thought: Broken Dreams* (1994).

J. G. Sikes, *Peter Abailard* (1932) [survey of his thought].

R. W. Southern, *Medieval Humanism and Other Studies* (1970).

R. W. Southern, *Scholastic Humanism and the Unification of Europe*, vol. 1 *Foundations* (1995).

S. Spence, *Texts and the Self in the Twelfth Century* (1996).

Suger, *The Deeds of Louis the Fat* trans. R. Cusimano and J. Moorhead (1992).

J. H. Van Engen, *Rupert of Deutz* (1983).

E. B. Vitz, 'Abelard's *Historia Calamitatum* and Medieval Autobiography', in her *Medieval Narrative and Modern Narratology* (1989), pp. 11–37.

H. Waddell, *Peter Abelard – a Novel* (1933).

R. E. Weingart, *The Logic of Divine Love: A Critical Analysis of the Soteriology of Peter Abailard* (1970).

B. Wheeler ed., *Listening to Heloise: Essays* (2000).

C. Whitman, *Abelard* (1965) [a poem].

Index